THE IR SOLUTION

STUDENT RESOURCES

- Interactive eBook
- Graded Quizzes
- New Practice Quiz Generator
- New Interactive Exhibits
- Video Quizzes
- Flashcards

- Animated Learning Modules and Simulations
- International Relations NewsWatch
- Glossary
- Review Cards

Students sign in at **www.cengagebrain.com**

INSTRUCTOR RESOURCES

- All Student Resources
- Engagement Tracker
- LMS Integration
- Instructor's Manual
- PowerPoint® Slides
- Test Bank
- Prep Cards
- Discussion Questions

Instructors log in at **www.cengage.com/login**

Print

IR2 delivers all the key terms and all the content for the **International Relations** course through a visually engaging and easy-to-reference print experience.

CourseMate

CourseMate provides access to the full **IR2** narrative, alongside a rich assortment of quizzing, flashcards, and interactive resources for convenient reading and studying.

IR2
James Scott, Ralph Carter, and Cooper Drury

Vice President, General Manager, 4LTR Press
   and the Student Experience: Neil Marquardt

Product Director, 4LTR Press: Steven E. Joos

Content Developer: Victoria Castrucci

Product Assistant: Mandira Jacob

Marketing Manager: Valerie Hartman

Senior Content Project Manager:
   Corinna Dibble

Manufacturing Planner: Ron Montgomery

Production Service: Cenveo® Publisher Services

Sr. Art Director: Stacy Shirley

Cover Designer: cmiller design

Interior Designer: KeDesign/cmiller design

Cover Image: Getty Images,
   © ewg3D/E+/Getty Images

Intellectual Property

   Analyst: Alexandra Ricciardi

   Project Manager: Farah Fard

For product information and technology assistance, contact us at
Cengage Learning Customer & Sales Support, 1-800-354-9706.

For permission to use material from this text or product,
submit all requests online at **www.cengage.com/permissions.**
Further permissions questions can be e-mailed to
permissionrequest@cengage.com.

Library of Congress Control Number: 2014954908

ISBN: 978-1-305-09431-4

Student Edition with CourseMate:
ISBN: 978-1-305-09418-5

Cengage Learning
20 Channel Center Street
Boston, MA 02210
USA

Cengage Learning is a leading provider of customized learning solutions with office locations around the globe, including Singapore, the United Kingdom, Australia, Mexico, Brazil, and Japan. Locate your local office at:
www.cengage.com/global.

Cengage Learning products are represented in Canada by Nelson Education, Ltd.

To learn more about Cengage Learning Solutions, visit **www.cengage.com.**

Purchase any of our products at your local college store or at our preferred online store **www.cengagebrain.com.**

Printed in the United States of America
Print Number: 02   Print Year: 2016

SCOTT / CARTER / DRURY

IR²

BRIEF CONTENTS

© ewg3D/E+/Getty Images

CONTENTS

Part 1
THEORY AND PRACTICE

Part 2
INTERNATIONAL SECURITY

Part 3
ECONOMIC SECURITY

Yannis behrakis/Reuters

Part 4
HUMAN SECURITY

Anadolu Agency/Getty Images

11 Human Rights: Protecting the Most Basic Security 304

12 Managing the Environment: Sharing the World or Dividing the World? 336

© Natalia Klenova/Shutterstock.com

Part 5
LOOKING AHEAD

ABOUT THE AUTHORS

James M. Scott is Herman Brown Chair and Professor of Political Science at Texas Christian University. His areas of specialization include foreign policy analysis and international relations, with particular emphasis on U.S. foreign policymaking and the domestic sources of foreign policy. He is author or editor of seven books (including this one) and more than sixty articles, book chapters, review essays, and other publications. He has been conference organizer and president of both the Foreign Policy Analysis section of the International Studies Association and the Midwest region of the International Studies Association. He is the recipient of the 2012 Quincy Wright Distinguished Scholar Award from the International Studies Association—Midwest. He has also been a two-time winner of the Klingberg Award for Outstanding Faculty Paper at the ISA Midwest Annual Meeting. Since 1996, he has received more than two dozen awards from students and peers for his outstanding teaching and research, including his institution's highest awards for scholarship in 2000 and 2001 and research mentoring in 2002. Form 2005–2014 he was Director of the Democracy Interdependence and World Politics Summer Research Program, a National Science Foundation Research Experience for Undergraduates, and he is currently an associate editor of *Foreign Policy Analysis*.

Ralph G. Carter is Professor and former Chair of the Department of Political Science at Texas Christian University. His areas of specialization include international relations and comparative foreign policy analysis, with particular emphasis on the domestic sources of foreign policy. He is the author or editor of eight books or monographs (including this one), as well as seventy articles, book chapters, review essays, and other publications. In 2006, he became the first person from an undergraduate department to receive the Quincy Wright Distinguished Scholar Award from the International Studies Association—Midwest. He has served the International Studies Association as a member of its Executive Committee and other committees, President of its Foreign Policy Analysis section, President of its Midwest region, Associate Editor of its journal *Foreign Policy Analysis*, and currently is a member of the editorial boards of *Foreign Policy Analysis* and *International Studies Perspectives*. He also has served on the program committee of the American Political Science Association. He has received more than three dozen teaching awards or recognitions, and in 2012 he was named as one of *The Best 300 Professors* by Princeton Review. In 2014 he was named as one of 10 Piper Professors for the state of Texas and received the TCU Chancellor's Award for Distinguished Achievement as a Creative Teacher and Scholar.

A. Cooper Drury is Professor and Chair of Political Science at the University of Missouri. His research and teaching focus broadly on foreign policy and international political economy. More specifically, he focuses on the causes and consequences of economic sanctions. He has published extensively on the use, effect, and consequences of economic statecraft, including two books and more than twenty articles and chapters. He is the recipient of the 2013 Quincy Wright Distinguished Scholar Award from the International Studies Association—Midwest. He has also been a two-time winner of the Klingberg Award for Outstanding Faculty Paper at the ISA Midwest Annual Meeting. Professor Drury has trained over a dozen doctoral students and received his university's Gold Chalk Award for excellence in graduate education and mentoring. He has been the president of the Foreign Policy section of the International Studies Association as well as the president of the association's Midwest region. He is currently the Editor-in-Chief of *Foreign Policy Analysis*.

ACKNOWLEDGMENTS

A special thanks goes to the three talented instructors who created the supplements for *IR*. Their hard work and attention to detail is evident in the quality of these supporting materials. Yasemin Akbaba of Gettysburg College assisted in preparing the *Chapter in Review* and *Instructor Chapter Prep* cards, including the *Guide to Research and Writing in International Relations*. Daniel Fuerstman of the State College of Florida, Manatee-Sarasota authored the Test Bank. Eric Cox of Texas Christian University created the Instructor's Manual. We are grateful for the time and expertise they each brought to this project.

We would also like to thank the following instructors for their and their students' invaluable feedback as we wrote the book:

Olayiwola Abegunrin, *Howard University*

Dilshod Achilov, *Eastern Tennessee State University*

Duane Adamson, *Brigham Young University–Idaho*

Yasemin Akbaba, *Gettysburg College*

Joan Andorfer, *Frostburg State University*

Wayne Ault, *Southwestern Illinois College*

Alex Avila, *Mesa Community College*

Joseph Avitable, *Northwestern Connecticut Community College*

Sangmin Bae, *Northeastern Illinois University*

Kelly Bauer, *George Washington University*

Koop Berry, *Walsh University*

Patricia Bixel, *Maine Maritime Academy*

Patrick Bratton, *Hawaii Pacific University*

Robert Breckinridge, *Mount Aloysius College*

Russell Burgos, *University of California–Los Angeles*

Charity Butcher, *Kennesaw State University*

Jetsabe Caceres, *University of Toledo*

Joseph Chaikel, *Salisbury University/University of Maryland Eastern Shore*

Marijke Breuning, *University of North Texas*

Robert Chisholm, *Columbia Basin College*

Thomas Cioppa, *Brookdale Community College*

May Akabogu Collins, *Miracosta College*

Amanda Cook Fesperman, *Illinois Valley Community College*

Renato Corbetta, *University of Alabama at Birmingham*

Eric Cox, *Texas Christian University*

Bruce Cronin, *City College of New York*

Carrie Currier, *Texas Christian University*

Suheir Daoud, *Coastal Carolina University*

Ursula Daxecker, *Colorado State University*

Michael Deaver, *Sierra College*

Kenric DeLong, *Montcalm Community College*

Brian Dille, *Mesa Community College*

Agber Dimah, *Chicago State University*

Polly Diven, *Grand Valley State University*

John A. Doces, *Bucknell University*

Tom Doleys, *Kennesaw State University*

Pedro G. Dos Santos, *University of Kansas*

Colleen Driscoll, *Quinnipiac University*

Oya Dursun-Ozkanca, *Elizabethtown College*

Toake Endoh, *Hawaii Tokai International College*

Andrew Essig, *DeSales University*

William Felice, *Eckerd College*

Femi Ferreira, *Hutchinson Community College*

Paul Frank, *Sacramento City College*

Brian Frederking, *McKendree Community College*

Daniel Fuerstman, *State College of Florida*

Florencia Gabriele, *Northeastern University*

Caron Gentry, *Abilene Christian University*

Gigi Gokcek, *Dominican University of California*

David Goldberg, *College of DuPage*

SimonPeter Gomez, *Reinhardt University*

Robert Gorman, *Texas State University*

Anna Gregg, *Austin Peay State University*

Vaidyanatha Gundlupet, *University of Texas–San Antonio*

Paul Haber, *University of Montana*

Maia Hallward, *Kennesaw State University*

Tracy Harbin, *Seminole State College*

Natalie Harder, *Patrick Henry Community College*

Brooke Harlowe, *Lock Haven University*

Susan Harris, *Valparaiso University*

Andrea B. Haupt, *Santa Barbara City College*

Paul Hensel, *University of North Texas*

Uk Heo, *University of Wisconsin–Milwaukee*

Eric Hines, *University of Montana–Missoula*

Aaron M. Hoffman, *Purdue University*

Claus Hofhansel, *Rhode Island University*

Aart Holtslag, *University of Massachusetts–Lowell*

Joanne M. Hopkins-Lucia, *Baker College–Clinton Township*

Cale Horne, *Covenant College*

Kasandra Housley, *Ivy Tech Community College–Bloomington*

Michael Huelshoff, *University of New Orleans*

Creed Hyatt, *Lehigh Carbon Community College*

Kate Ivanova, *Ohio State University–Newark*

Viktor Ivezaj, *Oakland University*

Steven F. Jackson, *Indiana University of Pennsylvania*

Mike Jasinski, *University of Wisconsin–Oshkosh*

Thomas Johnson, *Jamestown College*

Harry Joiner, *Athens State University*

Jean Gabriel Jolivet, *Southwestern College*

Michael Kanner, *University of Colorado–Boulder*

Julie Keil, *Saginaw Valley State University*

Phil Kelly, *Emporia State University*

Brian Kessel, *Columbia College*

Richard Kiefer, *Waubonsee Community College*

Moonhawk Kim, *University of Colorado–Boulder*

Richard Krupa, *William Rainey Harper College*

Paul Labedz, *Valencia Community College*

Daniel R. Lake, *State University of New York–Plattsburgh*

Ritu Lauer, *Peninsula College*

James Leaman, *Eastern Mennonite University*

Anika Leithner, *California Polytechnic State University*

Michael Lerma, *Norther Arizona University*

Christopher Leskiw, *University of the Cumberlands*

Yitan Li, *Seattle University*

Timothy Lim, *California State University–Los Angeles*

Timothy Lomperis, *Saint Louis University*

Stephen Long, *University of Richmond*

Anthony Makowski, *Delaware County Community College*

Mary Manjikian, *Regent University*

Khalil Marrar, *DePaul University*

Matthias Matthijs, *American University*

Philip Mayer, *Three Rivers Community Technical College*

Julie Mazzei, *Kent State University*

Mary M. McCarthy, *Drake University*

Paul T. McCartney, *Towson University*

Autumn McGimsey, *Cape Fear Community College*

Daniel McIntosh, *Slippery Rock University*

David J. Meyer, *Regent University*

John Miglietta, *Tennessee State University*

Wesley Milner, *University of Evansville*

Jonathan Miner, *North Georgia College & State University*

Sara Moats, *West Virginia University*

Jason Morrissette, *Marshall University*

Carolyn Myers, *Southwestern Illinois College*

Robert O'Meara, *University of Massachusetts–Amherst/College of Southern Nevada*

Gabriella Paar-Jakli, *Kent State University*

Robert Packer, *Pennsylvania State University–University Park*

James Pasley, *Park University*

Clint Peinhardt, *University of Texas–Dallas*

Dursun Peksen, *East Carolina University*

Jeffrey Pickering, *Kansas State University*

Michael Popovic, *St. Lawrence University*

Dave Price, *Santa Fe College*

William Primosch, *Montgomery College/Northern Virginia Community College*

Steven Redd, *University of Wisconsin–Milwaukee*

Richard Reitano, *Dutchess Community College*

Dan Reiter, *Emory University*

James Rhodes, *Luther College*

Jeff Ringer, *Brigham Young University*

Lia Roberts, *Mount St. Mary's College*

Trevor Rubenzer, *University of South Carolina Upstate*

Joanna Sabo, *Monroe County Community College*

Chris Saladino, *Virginia Commonwealth University*

Selwyn Samaroo, *University of Tennessee–Chattanooga*

Maria Sampanis, *California State University–Sacramento*

Brent Sasley, *University of Texas–Arlington*

Francis Schortgen, *University of Mount Union*

Lou Schubert, *City College of San Francisco*

Susan Sell, *George Washington University*

Michael Shifflett, *Rappahannock Community College*

John Shively, *Metropolitan Community College–Kansas City*

Michael Snarr, *Wilmington College*

M. Scott Solomon, *University of South Florida*

Lori Solomon, *Capital University*

Mark Souva, *Florida State University*

James Sperling, *University of Akron*

Seitu Stephens, *Delaware County Community College*

Robert Sterken, *University of Texas at Tyler*

Feng Sun, *Troy University*

Michael Swinford, *Southern New Hampshire University*

Richard Tanksley, *North Idaho College*

Paul Tesch, *Spokane Community College*

Moses Tesi, *Middle Tennessee State University*

Clayton Thyne, *University of Kentucky*

Jaroslav Tir, *University of Georgia*

Peter Trumbore, *Oakland University*

Krista Tuomi, *American University*

Kimberly Turner, *College of DuPage*

Brian Urlacher, *University of North Dakota*

Brandon Valeriano, *University of Illinois–Chicago*

Adam Van Liere, *University of Wisconsin–LaCrosse*

Alex Von Hagen, *University of Michigan*

Geoff Wallace, *University of Kentucky*

James Walsh, *University of North Carolina at Charlotte*

David Watson, *Sul Ross State University*

Robert Weiner, *University of Massachusetts–Boston*

Robert E. Williams, *Pepperdine University*

Bryungwon Woo, *Oakland University*

Ashley Woodiwiss, *Erskine College*

David Yamanishi, *Cornell College*

Yi Edward Yang, *James Madison University*

Min Ye, *Coastal Carolina University*

Carlos Yordan, *Drew University*

Jeremy Youde, *University of Minnesota–Duluth*

Tina Zappile, *Auburn University*

Dana Zartner, *Tulane University*

1

World Politics:
Seeking Security in a Complicated and Connected World

LEARNING OBJECTIVES

After studying this chapter, you will be able to . . .

1-1 Summarize the complex arena of world politics.

1-2 Identify the nature and challenges of security—international, economic, and human—in international relations.

1-3 Define the levels of analysis in the study of international relations.

1-4 Describe the challenges of cooperation among the actors of international relations.

1-5 Assess the dilemmas of cooperation illustrated by the Prisoner's Dilemma and Stag Hunt scenarios.

After finishing
this chapter go
to **PAGE 17**
for **STUDY TOOLS**

THE MEANING OF SECURITY

Let's begin with a brainstorming exercise. Considering what you know right now about world politics and the interactions that make up international relations, what does it mean to be *secure*? Jot down some ideas, perhaps drawing on current events, previous classes you have taken, and even your own experiences. Now, think about the kinds of things that threaten security as you have just characterized it, and make a list of some of the most important factors, forces, situations, and so on that reduce or diminish security. Finally, consider the kinds of things that improve or enhance security as you have defined it and draw up another list of the most important factors, forces, and situations that make countries and their citizens more secure in world politics.

Members of the United Nations Security Council in March 2014 | What aspect of security could the countries represented here be discussing?

Stan Honda/AFP photo/Getty Images

INTRODUCTION: MAKING SENSE OF WORLD POLITICS

It is likely that your brainstorming produced a relatively complicated collection of ideas. This is no surprise. In fact, it is to be expected. Making sense of world politics can be a daunting task. Although the study of **world politics** once concentrated almost exclusively on the political relationships between the countries of the world, today it involves a much broader range of activities and interactions—political, economic, and social—among these states and a wide variety of non-state actors such as international organizations, non-state national and ethnic groups, transnational corporations, nongovernmental organizations, and individuals. As time has passed, world politics has evolved to include an increasingly diverse set of states from the developed and developing worlds, a rich array of cultural perspectives and values held by states, nations, and individuals, and a great variety of non-state actors. Important resources have changed, as have the nature and characteristics of power, while the traditional issues of world politics have expanded to include a more complex variety of international and transnational matters.

1-1 A COMPLEX WORLD CONNECTED TO YOU

Today there is simply no end to the stream of events and activities that constitute international relations, and, at first blush, there often seems to be no rhyme or reason to them, either. Consider, for example, a few select items from just one 90-day period in 2014.

- Australian security forces foiled a transnational terrorist plot to kidnap and publicly execute Australian citizens in support of the Islamic State in Iraq and Syria (ISIS).

- The U.S. president called on China and the United States to lead the world on global climate change.

world politics political, economic, and social activities and interactions among states and a wide variety of non-state actors such as international organizations, non-state national and ethnic groups, transnational corporations, nongovernmental organizations, and individuals.

- The U.S. and EU tightened economic sanctions on Russia in response to its support for separatist rebels fighting in Ukraine.

- For the second time in 13 years, Argentina defaulted on its debt to holders of government bonds.

- After nearly two months of violence, Egypt brokered a cease-fire between Israel and Hamas to re-establish a truce in Gaza.

- Australia's prime minister announced plans to open Tasmanian forests—a UN World Heritage Site—to commercial logging and to dump soil dredged to create a new commercial port in the Great Barrier Reef.

- UN Human Rights Committee called on Japan to apologize for using slaves in World War II and to compensate the victims.

- The U.S., Jordan, Bahrain, Saudi Arabia, Qatar, and the United Arab Emirates collaborated in a broad campaign of air attacks against Islamic State in Iraq and Syria (ISIS) insurgents in response to escalating ISIS military and terrorist operations across northern Iraq and Syria.

- As the largest Ebola outbreak in Africa ever continued to claim lives—more than 4,000 and counting—the virus spread to the U.S. when several citizens of Dallas contracted the disease after one returned from Liberia with the infection.

- All the while, thousands continued to die from malnutrition and disease around the globe because they do not have access to potable water, food, and basic medicine.

As this brief list suggests, the range of issues and events extends across many areas and in many directions—from conflict to cooperation, and from basic security issues to quality-of-life and survival concerns. Detecting the patterns and forces at work and explaining their causes and consequences appear overwhelming and impossible. What, if any, underlying factors or forces drive such a disparate set of events?

1-1a World Politics and You

At the same time, it can be difficult to connect the dots between events and developments on the world stage and our lives. Students frequently wonder what impact developments such as those we have just introduced have on them personally. World politics can seem like an abstract, far-off realm of movie-like events that appear to have little bearing on our lives. Textbooks such as these frequently go to some lengths to connect students in classrooms to events on the world stage. Frankly, although it can appear distant, world politics affects our daily lives in many

Danny Moloshok/Reuters/Landov

The "New Normal?" Standing in line for airport security | Why do we all have to stand in long lines in our socks or bare feet at the airport now?

ways, from the trivial to the profound. Let's consider a few examples:

- How many of you have been frustrated by long lines and security delays at airports in recent years? What world politics issues and events do you suppose are behind such inconveniences?

- Take a look at the clothing you are wearing today. How many countries do you represent in your wardrobe alone? Which ones are represented? What impact and issues do you think this list indicates?

- Something like 150 million deaths have occurred because of war over the past five centuries, with the vast majority happening in the twentieth and twenty-first centuries.[1] How many of you have, or have had, a family member or friend serve in the armed forces? How many of you live near a military base of some kind? What characteristics and issues of world politics lead countries like the United States to maintain sizable military and security establishments and send their soldiers into harm's way?

The world is increasingly interconnected, and that means events that might appear relatively obscure can have dramatic effects on the lives of individuals on the other side of the world. Just consider the examples of several of the economic crises of the past 15 years or so. In 1997, economic problems in the relatively tiny economy of Thailand exploded into a global financial crisis that seriously affected countries all over the world, including the United States. About a decade later, in 2008 a similar dynamic occurred in the United States, stemming from ballooning real estate prices coupled with risky—and ultimately failed—gambles on complicated debt instruments. Another global financial crisis, the so-called Great Recession of 2008–2010, put over 10% of the U.S. labor force out of work and heavily affected the lives of

Food or fuel? | What are the implications of using crops to replace fossil fuels instead of feeding people?

citizens around the world. Further, in 2010–2011, the excessive borrowing of the Greek government and other countries in Europe triggered yet another financial crisis that ensnared countries all over the world, which continues even today to make the struggle for a global economic recovery and steady growth difficult all across the globe. As these examples suggest, the interconnections between countries often mean that problems in one place can quickly become problems for many places!

Agricultural concerns that connect the people and economies of the world also abound. Food prices are skyrocketing in poor countries. Business decisions by the handful of companies that dominate the global agricultural markets have driven up the cost of seeds to farmers. In the past, farmers could hold back some of their crop production as seed for the following year. However, many new genetically engineered seeds germinate only once and their offspring are sterile, thereby netting the seed companies more sales. Thus farmers are forced to spend a larger share of their income to buy seeds annually just to stay in business. As seeds cost more, farmers are able to plant less. Farmers in poor countries also are more affected by droughts and floods—which may be more likely as climate change occurs—than are their counterparts in wealthier societies.

Some of these agricultural issues have global consequences. Another effect of genetically engineered seeds is the reduction in the number of varieties across and within crops, as it makes more business sense to emphasize production of the highest yield varieties. With less natural variation in the fields, crops face a greater risk from catastrophic blights or infestations; when one variety gets infected, the entire harvest is often threatened because of the increasingly mono-varietal nature of farming. Also, more land globally is being diverted to the cultivation of crops for ethanol-based energy production rather than

for food production. Those fields now produce energy for people rather than food for people. All of these factors result in less food produced in places where it is typically needed most and put more strain on global food stocks.

1-1b Geography and the Small World Phenomenon

It is also helpful to understand how spatially connected states are in the contemporary international system. Consider basic geography for a moment. In the Western Hemisphere, we typically see the world as shown in Map 1-1. Starting from this view, let's take the example of two large countries—Russia and the United States. It is easy to think of these two countries as far apart, but doesn't that really depend on how we look at things? Based on a Pacific-centered perspective, as in Map 1-2, the two states look closer together. They look even closer together from the perspective of the North Pole, as shown in Map 1-3. Now consider that modern technology allows us to travel between New York and Moscow by airplane in less than 11 hours, an intercontinental ballistic missile could reach Russia in 30 minutes, and you can visit the Russian Federation's official website in a matter of seconds. Finally, have a look at Map 1-4, which presents the world from a perspective that is not as familiar to most of us, but more accurately represents the size and location of most countries. How does this alter your view of the relationship between countries?

Increasingly, what happens around the world and in the relations between countries and other important players has real-life and significant consequences for ordinary citizens going on about their lives. So understanding and explaining the patterns and forces at work in world politics is increasingly important. In this textbook, we try to bring some order and focus to the complex arena of world politics and help you develop a better understanding of its dynamics. We blend descriptive content with a conceptual toolbox and practical applications to provide a foundation to understand and explain international interactions.

 1-2

THE SEARCH FOR SECURITY IN A CHALLENGING ENVIRONMENT

Because world politics is such a complex arena, there are many approaches to its study. In this textbook, we emphasize world politics as a search for security.

The Shrinking World

As world politics has evolved, and the technologies of information, communication, and transportation have developed, the geographic landscape of the world has taken on new meaning. One way to begin to understand the changing nature, opportunities, and constraints of geography for world politics is to reflect on the meaning and implications of different perspectives.

Consider Map 1-1, a common image of the world that shows the vast distances between countries such as Russia and the United States, while also illustrating the close proximity of other countries to each other. Now consider Map 1-2: How does this image change your perspective on the possibilities of conflict, cooperation, and interaction between countries?

Map 1-1

Political Map of the World

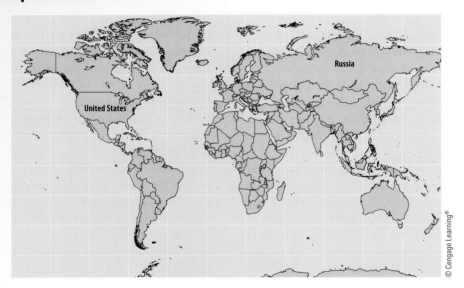

© Cengage Learning®

Map 1-2

An Alternative Perspective of the Political World

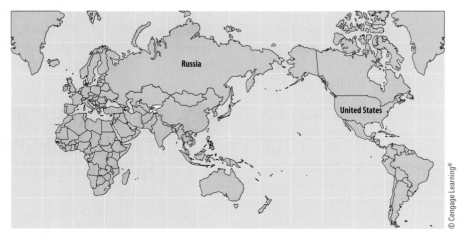

© Cengage Learning®

What if we adopted the perspective shown in Map 1-3? Which countries are neighbors now? What difference, if any, would this perspective make to your sense of which countries are most likely to interact with each other?

Finally, look at Map 1-4, which presents roughly the same perspective as Map 1-1, but with a perspective corrected to more accurately reflect the relative geographic size and location of the continents and countries of the world. What does this image suggest to you about world politics and the relationships between its major players?

Map 1-3

Polar Projection Map

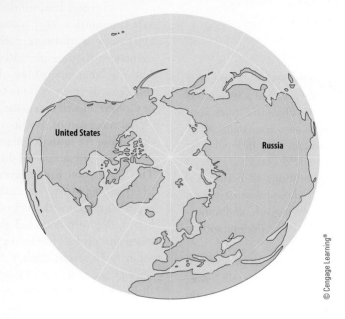

© Cengage Learning®

Map 1-4

The Peters Projection of the World

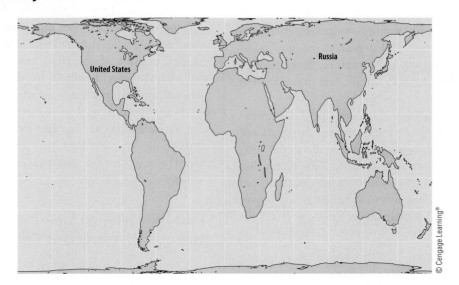

© Cengage Learning®

How do these different perspectives change the way you understand the relationships between countries?

This overarching theme helps deliver focus and coherence to our efforts to make sense of the subject. In our perspective, the key to understanding events, such as those we listed at the start of the chapter, is to consider the broad meaning of security and its pursuit by both states and non-state actors in world politics. We hope that by the time you have worked through this text you will be able to return to those examples—and a wide range of other current events—and be able to provide context and explanation for what drives them.

1-2a The Nature of Security

At its core, **security** is a relatively simple concept: it refers to survival and safety. As one political scientist has characterized it, seeking security involves the "pursuit of freedom from threat."[2] To achieve this, states and other actors in world politics try to maintain their independent identity, functional integrity, and address a substantial range of concerns about the conditions of existence.[3] However, in our perspective, the idea of security has a much broader meaning than it is often given, and understanding its broad scope is critical for understanding world politics.

Traditionally, in world politics, the term *security* has referred principally to the military, intelligence, and law enforcement arenas, with special emphasis on conflict, violence, and war. While these are clearly central issues in world politics, we define security more broadly. In most social interactions, humans seek order and predictability, and that goal cannot be reached without adequate security. One way or another, most of what the players in world politics—states, international institutions, nongovernmental organizations, and other transnational actors—seek in their interactions with one another involves the desire to be safe, and to survive and thrive, broadly speaking.

We prefer to think about security in three arenas or dimensions. The first—*national and international security*—is the most common and what people usually think of when discussing security. This dimension involves issues related to national defense, conflict and war, and arms control and disarmament. So, for example, when countries build up their armed forces, deploy military forces to defend themselves or to disrupt terrorist

security survival and safety, typically referring to the military, intelligence, and law enforcement arenas but also including economic and human dimensions.

networks, install more intrusive screening equipment at airports, and negotiate arms control agreements with other countries, they are seeking national and international security. Recently, we have seen this aspect of security reflected in uses of force in Afghanistan and Iraq, the conflict in Ukraine, the escalation of violence in Israel and the Palestinian Territories, efforts to counter the Islamic State insurgency in Syria and Iraq, and in actions to prevent the spread of nuclear weapons to countries such as Iran.

The second arena or dimension is *economic security*. When countries, corporations, and others seek wealth and prosperity through profitable economic relations and exchanges, they are ultimately seeking economic security. In the current context, we observe this aspect of security reflected in trade competition among countries, cooperation to ensure economic recovery in the wake of the global recession of recent years, and efforts to deal with debt crises for both developed and developing countries.

The third arena or dimension is *human security*. This dimension fundamentally concerns the quality of life that people experience. So when the players of world politics grapple with environmental threats such as pollution, deforestation, and global warming, or try to promote and protect human rights, they are seeking human security. In recent years, this aspect of security has been seen as countries wrestle with appropriate responses to the problem of climate change, as people throughout the world rebel against their governments in pursuit of greater participation and protection for human rights, and as states such as the U.S. and NATO used, or considered using, force to intervene in Libya in support of rebels seeking the overthrow of Muammar Gaddafi, or in Syria in response to alleged uses of chemical weapons by the Assad regime against its citizens. Thus, as we stress the general pursuit of security—freedom from threat—that underlies world politics, we direct our attention to national and international security, economic security, and human security as depicted in Figure 1-1. As you will see, we have organized our text to address these dimensions of security into Part Two (international security), Part Three (economic security), and Part Four (human security).

1-2b Fundamental Challenges: Anarchy, Diversity, and Complexity

In world politics, the search for security is quite complicated. As we devote our attention to the players of world politics and their interactions in pursuit of this multifaceted objective, we focus on three fundamental challenges that influence the behavior,

FIGURE 1-1   THE PURSUIT OF SECURITY IN THREE ARENAS

interactions, and processes of world politics: anarchy, diversity, and complexity. As we will see throughout our text, these challenges are linked together, as well (Figure 1-2).

1. **The *anarchy* of the international system.** There is no central, authoritative government over the players of world politics, both states and non-states. This absence of authority has pervasive effects on the nature of world politics across almost every issue, from international conflict to the prospects and forms of international cooperation. Formal anarchy does not mean chaos or disorder, or that there are no **norms**, that is, regular patterns of behavior in world politics. Neither does it necessarily mean that there is always conflict and war.

   It means, simply, that *there is no central government.* Unlike established countries, world politics does not have authoritative central bodies to make, enforce, and adjudicate laws; the international institutions that do exist—such as the United Nations and the World Court—are dependent on the states that form them and have only the very limited authority states are willing to give them. Formally, there is no authority above the nation-state, and this structural fact has enormous implications for conflict, economic relations, and efforts to meet transnational problems and challenges, such as human rights and the environment.

2. **The *diversity* in the international system.** World politics is characterized by a myriad of players. About 200 states

FIGURE 1-2   THE FUNDAMENTAL CHALLENGES OF WORLD POLITICS

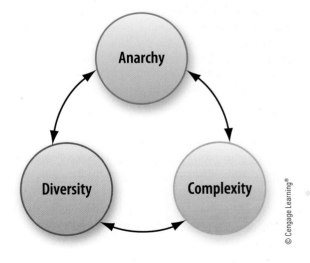

anarchy   the absence of central government in world politics.

norms   commonly held standards of acceptable and unacceptable behavior.

diversity   variation in values, norms, identities, goals, and other political, economic, and cultural factors in world politics.

Seeking Security

As the Cold War came to an end, U.S. leaders began to consider how to position the United States to be secure in the post–Cold War world. Led by then–defense secretary Dick Cheney, in 1991–1992, U.S. Department of Defense officials Paul Wolfowitz, I. Lewis Libby, Zalmay Khalilzad, and others drafted a strategy document stressing the importance of maintaining and extending U.S. dominance in world politics. A key excerpt of that planning document advanced the following assertions:

Our first objective is to prevent the reemergence of a new rival. This is a dominant consideration underlying the new regional defense strategy and requires that we endeavor to prevent any hostile power from dominating a region whose resources would, under consolidated control, be sufficient to generate global power. These regions include Western Europe, East Asia, the territory of the former Soviet Union, and Southwest Asia. There are three additional aspects to this objective: First, the United States must show the leadership necessary to establish and protect a new order that holds the promise of convincing potential competitors that they need not aspire to a greater role or pursue a more aggressive posture to protect their legitimate interests. Second, in the non-defense areas, we must account sufficiently for the interests of the advanced industrial nations to discourage them from challenging our leadership or seeking to overturn the established political and economic order. Finally, we must maintain the mechanisms for deterring potential competitors from even aspiring to a larger regional or global role.[4]

This approach to security reflected a particular set of assumptions about the nature of security and how a powerful state such as the United States should seek it, but it also has some very significant implications for the foreign policy behavior of other states too! Consider the following questions about the conception of security that underlies this argument.

1. What assumptions and arguments about security inform this policy paper?

2. What aspects of security would this approach best advance, and what aspects might it complicate for the United States, and for other countries?

3. What are the implications of this approach for U.S. foreign policy and the foreign policies of other members of the international community?

---

and many thousands of nationalities are involved, as are hundreds of international organizations and thousands of non-governmental organizations. Businesses of various shapes and sizes, including those transnational corporations whose production facilities and reach extend across borders and regions, interact with each other, with the governments of countries, with international organizations, and with groups and individuals all over the world. The diversity of these players is staggering. States come in different shapes and sizes and are differentiated by size (geographic and population), wealth (from the very rich to the very poor), type of economy, and regime type (from the many flavors of both democratic and nondemocratic systems). But there are widely differing ideas, religions, cultures, and subcultures that divide the players in world politics as well. Such diversity has important consequences for international interactions.

3. **The *complexity* of international interactions.** In part due to the many different players and values just described,

world politics is an extraordinarily complex arena. The players of world politics are increasingly connected and interdependent, with many linkages stretching across and between them. World politics involve multidimensional issues, state and non-state actors, national, international, and transnational processes, and many other factors, all connected in ways that can confound the players as they seek international, economic, and human security. Imagine playing a game of chess, but on a system of boards arranged in multiple levels so that moves and players operate in multiple channels with multiple linkages.[5] In effect, this is what the "game board" of world politics approaches, which generates both challenges and opportunities for all the players as they pursue their preferred outcomes. Indeed, these connections and linkages may create problems and complications, but they also often reduce the impact of anarchy by enabling—and sometime forcing—the players of world politics to work together.

These three challenges permeate our examination of world politics in the chapters that follow. For example, the anarchic structure of the international system is a foundational element for understanding

complexity the multidimensional issues, actors, and connections that characterize international relations.

and managing conflict and war, and it affects global economic interactions, the pursuit of wealth, the prospects for protecting human rights, and environmental cooperation. Diversity of identity, values, and culture is a critical issue for human rights and human security, while also having a great impact on conflict and economic relations. The complexity of the global political system often forces the players of world politics together, sometimes leading to cooperation on problems that transcend borders, and sometimes leading to conflict. Complexity can facilitate global economic interactions and coordination to address such problems as the recent economic and financial crises of the past 15 years or so, but it can also make it difficult to pursue international security, economic security, and human security at the same time.

1-3 THE LEVELS OF ANALYSIS AND INTERNATIONAL RELATIONS

By now you have almost certainly gained some appreciation for how complicated it is to make sense of world politics. The search for security across international, economic, and human dimensions, and the three central challenges (anarchy, diversity, and complexity) of world politics, involve a dizzying array of actors and events, but they can still be understood if we have the right tools. For analytical purposes, these things can be organized into **levels of analysis** that help us comprehend the interactions, causes, and consequences of world politics.

The broadest of these levels is the **systemic or international level**, where attention is directed to the broad patterns and interactions among the players of world politics, and emphasis is placed on the impact of the structural characteristics of the international system itself—including anarchy, the distribution of power, interdependence, globalization, and others—on those interactions.

At the **state or national level**, attention is directed to the states—or units—themselves, and emphasis is placed on the attributes of countries and nations, such as the type and processes of government or the economy, culture, or other national attributes, and how these factors shape policy goals and behavior and the interactions among the players.

At the **individual level**, attention is directed to people—policymakers, business CEOs, and other influential persons. This level of analysis emphasizes the personalities, perceptions, and preferences of individual decision makers and their effects on policy and interactions. This includes leaders such as Barack Obama (United States), Vladimir Putin (Russia), Hassan Rouhani (Iran), Xi Jinping (China), and others from the non-state actor arena, such as investors and philanthropists George Soros and Warren Buffett, U2 singer and African aid activist Bono, actress and Goodwill Ambassador for the UN High Commissioner for Refugees Angelina Jolie, Nobel Peace Prize winner and founder of the International Campaign to Ban Landmines Jody Williams, Microsoft founder and foundation head Bill Gates, and Aga Khan of the Aga Khan Development Network.

Thinking in terms of levels of analysis points us to certain kinds of issues and events but also prompts different kinds of questions and explanations. Table 1-1 summarizes these levels of analysis and identifies some explanations at those levels that you will find in upcoming chapters. As you review the table, note the last column, which includes some very simple explanations at each level of analysis to the case of the 2003 Iraq War. At the system level, the emphasis for explanation might be on the challenge posed by Iraq to gain power and influence in the region. The state level might stress the impact of the regime types of the two principal protagonists, while the individual level might emphasize the personalities and worldviews of President George W. Bush and his closest advisors, and their dislike and resentment of Saddam Hussein. One thing of which to make special note is that each of these explanations may help to explain the war, even if they differ in their focus.

Specifying these levels of analysis serves at least two important purposes in the study of world politics. First, they offer very useful guides for organizing information, events, and the factors that shape them so that we can make distinctions between them.

levels of analysis different perspectives from which international relations may be examined.

systemic or international level locating the causes of behavior and outcomes in the nature and characteristics of the international system.

state or national level locating the causes of behavior and outcome in the nature and characteristics of states/nations.

individual level locating the causes of behavior and outcomes in the nature and characteristics of people.

TABLE 1-1 LEVELS OF ANALYSIS AND WORLD POLITICS

LEVEL	FOCUS	KEY VARIABLES	SAMPLE EXPLANATIONS FOUND IN UPCOMING CHAPTERS	EXAMPLE: 2003 IRAQ WAR
System	Structural characteristics of the international system are central to explaining patterns of behavior in world politics.	Anarchy Distribution of power Interdependence Globalization	Balance of power	Iraq seeks greater power and influence in the region and challenges the dominant power; United States uses force to defeat the challenge.
State	Characteristics of countries (national attributes) are central to explaining patterns of and variations in behavior in world politics.	Regime type Economic system Culture	Democratic peace Capitalist peace	Authoritarian Iraq behaves aggressively and threatens its neighbors; democratic United States leads a coalition of other (mostly democratic) states to respond and try to transform the Iraqi regime to a democracy to prevent future threats.
Individual	Characteristics of individuals are central to explaining the foreign policy behavior of states and other players in world politics.	Personality Psychology Individual worldviews and preferences Perceptions and misperceptions	Aggressive vs. non-aggressive leaders Leadership style and worldviews Cognitive processes	President George W. Bush and key advisors view Saddam Hussein as an aggressive and threatening leader and choose to use force to overthrow him.

© Cengage Learning®

Second, they guide explanation, helping us to organize cause-and-effect relationships, ask different kinds of questions, and be aware of interactions and explanations that link up across the levels of analysis.

One simple and recognizable illustration may help clarify these contributions. Consider a serious traffic jam in a heavily populated area. Observing and explaining its causes and effects might take place from the perspective of the helicopter that sees the jam from above and can describe and explain its broad pattern and consequences. This is similar to the system level of analysis focusing on the broad structure that affects behavior (in this case, road networks and traffic patterns). But one might also focus on the two cars that collided and examine their unique characteristics, actions, and role in the traffic jam, which would be similar to focusing on state-level factors in world politics. Finally, one can consider the individual drivers and their decisions, such as the person texting a friend instead of paying attention to driving, and explain things at that level, which is similar to the individual level of analysis. One thing to note right away is that the kinds of questions that can be asked and the kinds of explanations that can be offered from each perspective are different, but all of them shed light on the phenomenon to be explained (the traffic jam).

theories tools for explaining cause-and-effect relationships among often complex phenomena.

Look again at Table 1-1 and examine it carefully to be sure you are comfortable with the level of analysis concept before you move on.

 1-4

EXPLAINING THE PATTERNS OF WORLD POLITICS

As we work together to build a better understanding of the dynamics of world politics, focusing on the pursuit of security in the face of the three fundamental challenges described previously, we want to improve our ability to explain the patterns of world politics that we encounter and identify. In such a complex arena, this requires the use of theoretical and conceptual shortcuts that focus attention on critical cause-and-effect relationships. **Theories** are essential tools for the explanation of complex realities, and they help us to strategically simplify the world to bring important features into clearer relief. One way to understand theories of world politics is to think of them as lenses, such as those you might find in a good pair of sunglasses. Such lenses might come in a variety of colors, and each shade filters out some portion of the light in order to improve vision. Theory is like that: a good theory simplifies reality to reduce the white noise and sharpen the clarity of key factors, which aids in the explanation of patterns and the prediction of likely developments.

As we discuss in Chapters 3 and 4, the pursuit of security in world politics can be interpreted in a variety of sometimes complementary and sometime contradictory ways. In these chapters, we present a number of theoretical paradigms or frameworks with which to examine world politics to make sense of how the world works:

- *Realism*, which revolves around the issue of conflict and power and stresses the role of states pursuing their self-interests
- *Liberalism*, which tends to emphasize cooperative approaches and addresses the role and influence of non-state actors
- *Constructivism*, which builds on the social construction of reality and stresses the role of the identity, ideas, culture, norms and interactions of people
- *Foreign policy analysis*, which emphasizes the individuals and groups who make decisions, and the processes and policies that they produce
- *Marxism*, which stresses class-based economic interests and the role of wealth and who controls it as the key to behavior
- *Feminism*, which focuses on gender issues and approaches, and asks what the world would be like if it were not historically dominated by men

Realism and liberalism have long dominated the study of world politics, especially in the United States, but each of these broad paradigms grapples with the meaning and consequences of anarchy, diversity, and complexity differently, and therefore present different versions of the nature and dynamics of world politics. After we present these theories and concepts clearly and thoroughly in Chapters 3 and 4, we then (1) apply the theoretical lenses throughout the remainder of the book and (2) explicitly include in each chapter discussions of theories and Theory in Action boxes considering how theories and concepts influence real-world behavior and policy.

1-5 DILEMMAS OF COOPERATION IN INTERNATIONAL RELATIONS: THE PRISONER'S DILEMMA AND THE STAG HUNT

Let's bring this first chapter to a conclusion by considering two ideal-type situations often introduced to highlight some of the patterns and challenges of world politics.

1-5a The Prisoner's Dilemma

The first situation is known as the **prisoner's dilemma**. Imagine two individuals who are suspected (for good reason) of being involved in a crime, say a major theft. The authorities isolate the two suspects in separate rooms so they cannot communicate. Both suspects know that if they remain silent, they will be charged for lesser violations and receive minor punishment and very short jail time due to lack of evidence for their more serious offense. However, in their separate rooms, each is informed that if they confess and betray the other suspect, the one who confesses will receive immunity for cooperating with law enforcement and go free, while their partner will be prosecuted and punished for the crime. If both confess, they both go to jail (with somewhat reduced terms for cooperating with the authorities). Realize that even if both thieves do not want to rat out their partner and are willing to split the loot evenly, they must think defensively. It's not just what one suspect might gain from confessing, but what they would lose if they keep quiet and their accomplice confesses. What do you think will happen? What would you do? This situation is represented in Table 1-2.

1-5b The Stag Hunt

The second situation is known as the **stag hunt** and was described by the political philosopher Jean Jacques Rousseau in the eighteenth century. Imagine a village, a hunting society, organizing a hunt to bring down a great stag that will feed the whole village and provide other benefits, such as its hide. To bring down this stag, the hunters plan an approach that depends on each hunter collaborating with the rest by covering a specific area so that the stag will be trapped and killed. However, while the hunt is proceeding, one of the hunters flushes a rabbit. He immediately recognizes that if he pursues and kills the rabbit, he will be fed, although the rest of the hunters will end up losing the stag because it will escape through the area vacated by the hunter who is abandoning the hunt and chasing the rabbit for himself. What do you suppose happens? Put yourself in the place of the hunter who sees the rabbit. What would you think? What would you do?

> **prisoner's dilemma** a situation in which two prisoners must decide whether to collaborate with each other or not.
>
> **stag hunt** a situation in which hunters must decide whether to collaborate with each other or act on their own.

TABLE 1-2   THE PRISONER'S DILEMMA

		SUSPECT B	
		CONFESS	**REMAIN SILENT**
SUSPECT A	**CONFESS**	Suspect A—10 years Suspect B—10 years	Suspect A—Free Suspect B—20 years
	REMAIN SILENT	Suspect A—20 years Suspect B—Free	Suspect A—1 year Suspect B—1 year

© Cengage Learning®

1-5c Considering the Implications of the Prisoner's Dilemma and the Stag Hunt

Together these two stories highlight several key issues about the nature of world politics. Both of them suggest there are important structural obstacles for cooperation between states, and other players, in world politics. In particular, these scenarios illustrate the tension between pursuing self-interest and broader collective interests. They also suggest that the conditions of the game provide powerful incentives for the players to see things through the lens of self-interest rather than more broadly. In the prisoner's dilemma, for example, it is logical for the suspects to confess, even though they each could derive greater mutual benefits through cooperation. By confessing, they give up the best mutual outcome, but they avoid the worst outcome—being held solely responsible and serving a long jail term. The opposite is true in the stag hunt, where it is easier to cooperate and bring down the stag rather than grab the rabbit.

In world politics, a similar result can be seen in arms races, where two countries give up the best outcome (mutual cooperation to avoid them and control armament), instead choosing to build up their weaponry so they are not victimized if the other country cheats and builds up its own while the first does not. Perhaps neither really wants to continue to arm itself (best outcome), but both choose to do so (less desired) to avoid being vulnerable if the other one does (worst outcome). Even if we all want our leaders to be honest and not break the promises they make in international treaties, the prisoners' dilemma suggests otherwise. Imagine if all the states with nuclear weapons agreed to eliminate all of those weapons. The world might be considered a safer place. Let's say that the United States went along with this agreement, but the Russians did not. Instead, they kept a secret stockpile of

nuclear weapons, but only for defensive purposes. Would that make you feel safe? What if other countries cheated on the agreement? Do you think that, just in case, it would be a good idea for the United States to cheat, as well—just for defensive purposes? Do you think the United States would be irresponsible if it didn't cheat? Notice how something as simple and good as maintaining a good defense of one's country can make cooperation so difficult.

The prisoner's dilemma isn't just about conflict, however. For example, few people would dispute that pollution is a bad thing and that cars significantly contribute to the world's pollution. If everyone agreed to cut back driving by simply riding a bike for any trip within two miles of their home (that's 40% of all trips), pollution would be significantly reduced. If everyone did this, we would all enjoy cleaner air, but if everyone did this *except* you, you would still get clean air—and the convenience of driving a car (particularly when it's raining, snowing, extremely hot, etc.). Thus, by cheating on the agreement, you would get all the benefits and none of the costs. The problem, of course, is that few people would ride a bike and give up the convenience with only the hope that the rest of the world will eventually do the same.

Similarly, the two scenarios suggest that part of the underlying issue is trust. In the study of world politics, this is often referred to as a **commitment problem**—countries have a hard time committing to cooperative courses of action that assure their partners that they will keep their end of the deal for mutual benefit and forego the possibility of their own short-term gains. In the stag hunt, for example, the individual hunter must choose between cooperating for the good of all or defecting for selfish gain. But each hunter must also consider the possibility that another member of the hunting party might be faced with a similar choice and must consider the consequences of cooperating with the group if another member does chase the rabbit.

In this case, the game between the players isn't a competition like it is for the prisoners. Instead, this is a coordination and reassurance game. The hunter who flushes the rabbit will also get her dinner from the stag. Further, by going after the rabbit, the hunter will betray

commitment problem countries have a hard time committing to cooperative courses of action that assure their partners that they will keep their end of the deal for mutual benefit and forego the possibility of their own short-term gains.

Defeating the Prisoner's Dilemma, and Getting a Stag and Not a Rabbit?

The paradox of the prisoner's dilemma (PD) is that what is mutually best for the two people or states involved is not best for the individual person or state. If more than two people or states are involved in a PD-type situation, it is referred to as a **collective action problem**. Whether 2 or 20 actors are involved, individually reasonable choices lead to bad outcomes for all. But not all PD situations end in the default outcome; sometimes the involved states cooperate with each other so that they attain the mutually beneficial outcome (in the PD story, cooperation means that neither prisoner confesses). For example, the Americans and Soviets came to several nuclear arms control agreements that limited the number of nuclear weapons in the world, and as discussed in Chapter 8, states have not engaged in trade wars after World War II. So how can the prisoner's dilemma be overcome?

The first solution is an actor that has the strength and wealth to force other countries to follow the rules. In the PD story, this would be the case if both suspects worked for an organized crime syndicate, such as that headed by the fictional Vito Corleone of the *Godfather* film trilogy. If the prisoners ratted each other out, they would face serious consequences from the mob boss, such as sleeping with the fishes. In the international arena, this solution is difficult because only a few times in history has one nation been powerful enough to enforce cooperation. That is one of the keys to anarchy—there is no world government or police to keep states from misbehaving.

The second solution is referred to as a "tit-for-tat" strategy. The idea behind this strategy is to begin by trusting the other actor, but if the other actor betrays you, then punish him by not cooperating. Of course, this strategy only works if the PD situation is one that repeats over and over. In that situation, you can switch between cooperating and not cooperating depending on what the other actor does. If the other actor does the same thing, then both actors will cooperate with each other over time. For the PD story, imagine two criminals who worked together for most of their lives and trust each other implicitly—they would not rat on each other.

This cooperative situation does not spring up out of nowhere, however. During the Cold War, the United States and Soviet Union initially developed great distrust for one another as they found themselves competing and conflicting over issue after issue in Europe and around the world. With time and repeated interactions in settings such as the UN, the two states began to trust each other enough to attempt an arms reduction treaty. Forums such as the UN provide an important place for states to interact on a public stage so that they can build cooperative or hostile reputations. As the United States came to realize that the Soviets were not as aggressive after Premier Joseph Stalin's death as they had been under Stalin's rule and the Soviets realized that the United States could also be trusted, they negotiated ways to "trust but verify," the phrase used by President Ronald Reagan during the arms negotiations with Soviet President Mikhail Gorbachev.

The solution to the stag hunt (SH) is both easier to attain but also less clear than the PD situation. In SH situations, the hunter who sees the rabbit must decide between sure individual gain and likely collective gain. If she trusts her fellow hunters, it is an easy decision: hunt the stag because there is more meat and everyone will benefit. However, if she does not completely trust her fellow hunters, then she must decide how likely it is that the other hunters will go after the stag or after a rabbit if they see one. So how can she be sure the other hunters won't go after a rabbit?

First, if the hunters, or states, are all part of a cohesive group, then trust has already been developed. For example, the Canadians and British are close allies with the United States. These states are very unlikely to betray each other; so cooperating is easy. The less positive, cooperative history a pair of states shares, the less able they will be to cooperate.

Second, if there is a way that the actions of all the hunters can be seen by each other, then no one can chase the rabbit without the others knowing. Since all hunters prefer the stag and can see each other, they know no other hunter will go for the rabbit. Imagine hunting on a grassy plain where each hunter can see the other. In the international context, this means the actions of all states must be transparent. For example, the best way to compel North Korea to curtail its nuclear program is for the powerful states in the region (China, Japan, Russia,

---

collective action problem a condition in which the uncoordinated actions of individuals lead to less than optimal outcomes because, although many individuals would benefit from some cooperative action or actions, few incentives lead any particular individuals to assume the costs of such actions.

South Korea, and the United States) to place unified pressure on North Korea. Together these states would have more influence than if they acted alone (which is why North Korea continues to object to multistate talks). Since for any one of these states to back away from the unified talks would be a public act, they can trust that each of the other states will not back down from the unified position. Solving the SH situation is both as easy as trusting each of the other actors and as hard as developing that trust.

1. Summarize the factors discussed previously that could enable the participants in a prisoners' dilemma to cooperate. What other factors might also contribute?

2. What factors best enable the participants in a stag hunt situation to trust each other and cooperate?

3. What are the short- and long-term implications of the actions associated with the stag hunt scenario?

the society and make it very likely that she will be kicked out of the village. Thus, there are plenty of reasons for the hunter to stay the course and go after the stag. However, all the hunters need to know that they are equally committed to the stag hunt so that a rabbit will tempt none of them. What would ensure that the hunter continued the stag hunt?

CONCLUSION: SEEKING SECURITY AND CONTENDING WITH CHALLENGES

The tensions revealed in the prisoner's dilemma and stag hunt scenarios are rooted in the very same challenges we have introduced in this chapter: anarchy, diversity, and complexity. Contending with them forms a major part of world politics and the interactions among the various players. Furthermore, these are not merely academic questions: There are potentially enormous consequences for countries and other players as they grapple with the dilemmas of self-interest and mutual interest, between doing what is best for oneself and what is best for the group, and between short-term and long-term perspectives. As we bring this introductory chapter to a close, let us return once more to our initial question about security. Consider again the ideas you brainstormed at the outset. Given some of the ideas discussed in the interim, how would you revise your thinking about the meaning of security in light of the challenges of anarchy, diversity, and complexity?

THINK ABOUT THIS THE COOPERATION PUZZLE IN WORLD POLITICS

At first glance, the benefits of cooperation seem obvious and compelling. They can be observed at almost any level of interaction. In fact, we all engage in cooperation when we obey traffic laws when driving—if we didn't there would be traffic accidents all over the place, many of them lethal. Yet, in world politics, cooperation appears less often and is more difficult to attain than we might expect. It would make sense for countries to cooperate in order to control the costly acquisition or dangerous spread of weapons, but often they do not, even when cooperating would be in their mutual best interest. Attempts at mutually beneficial collaboration to promote economic growth and development and to protect the environment are frequent, but these attempts also frequently fail. The players of world politics work together to establish institutions, norms, and rules to shape behavior in mutually beneficial and predictable ways, but those efforts are often incomplete and episodic or fleeting. And, while most states are at peace with most other states most of the time, many observers would argue that conflict and war happen regularly enough to be the rule and not the exception in world politics. All countries are not necessarily "engaged in, recovering from, or preparing for war," as Professor Hans Morgenthau, a famous international relations scholar, once argued, but certainly war happens persistently enough to make us wonder why countries do not cooperate to prevent it more often.

Hans Morgenthau

Why is cooperation so hard in world politics and what conditions make it most likely?

STUDY TOOLS 1

LOCATED AT BACK OF THE BOOK:
☐ Rip out Chapter in Review card

LOCATED ON COURSEMATE:
Use the CourseMate access card that came with this book or visit CengageBrain.com for more review materials:

☐ Review Key Terms Flash Cards (Print or Online)
☐ Download Chapter Summaries for on-the-go review

☐ Complete Practice Quizzes to prepare for the test
☐ Walk through a Simulation, Animated Learning Module, and Interactive Maps and Timelines to master concepts
☐ Complete Crossword Puzzle to review key terms
☐ Visit IR NewsWatch to learn about the latest current events as you prepare for class discussions and papers

REVIEW QUESTIONS

1. What does it mean to be secure in international relations?

2. How might anarchy, diversity, and complexity pose challenges for the pursuit of security in international relations?

3. What are levels of analysis through which we can attempt to understand and explain international relations?

4. What are the key challenges for cooperation in international relations?

FOR MORE INFORMATION . . .

For more on security and the dynamics of world politics:

Booth, Ken, and Nicholas Wheeler. *The Security Dilemma: Fear, Cooperation and Trust in World Politics*. New York: Palgrave-MacMillan, 2007.

Buzan, Barry, and Lene Hansen. *The Evolution of International Security Studies*. Cambridge: Cambridge University Press, 2010.

Ferguson, Yale, and Richard Mansbach. *Globalization: The Return of Borders to a Borderless World?* New York: Routledge, 2012.

Flint, Colin. *Introduction to Geopolitics*. New York: Routledge, 2012.

Lauren, Paul Gordon, Gordon A. Craig, and Alexander George. *Force and Statecraft: Diplomatic Challenges of Our Time*. New York: Oxford University Press, 2006.

Nye, Joseph S., Jr. *The Future of Power*. New York: Public Affairs Press, 2011.

Reveron, Derek, and Kathleen Mahoney-Norris. *Human Security in a Borderless World*. Boulder: Westview, 2011.

2 | The Players and the Playing Field:
Anarchy, States, and Non-State Actors

LEARNING OBJECTIVES

After studying this chapter, you will be able to…

2-1 Summarize how the search for security has evolved in a changing international system.

2-2 List the major types of actors and relationships of the pre-Westphalian international system.

2-3 Differentiate the major types of actors and relationships of the Westphalian international system.

2-4 Recognize the major types of actors and relationships of the neo-Westphalian international system.

After finishing this chapter go to **PAGE 52** for **STUDY TOOLS**

A LOOK AT THE PLAYERS: THE SYRIAN CIVIL WAR

The Arab Spring of 2011 was a watershed event. Uprisings ousted long-standing authoritarian regimes in Tunisia and Egypt and threatened others. In Libya, a populist uprising developed into a civil war. NATO intervened militarily on behalf of Libyan civilians targeted by their own country's military forces, and another long-standing authoritarian regime was forced from power. Similar violence in Syria did not produce an international response. Why not?

The Syrian violence began when the military-backed regime of Bashar al-Assad refused to undertake reforms in the face of large-scale demonstrations. Instead, the military was unleashed upon the people. In May 2011, the European Union imposed economic sanctions on the Syrian regime, as did the United States, and the United States and numerous other Western governments called for Assad to step down. In October 2011, a UN Security Council resolution condemning Syria was vetoed by both Russia and China. For its part, the Arab League suspended Syria's membership and imposed sweeping sanctions on the regime, as did neighboring Turkey. These were unprecedented moves. Yet the violence continued. Groups such as the al-Nusra Front (an al-Qaeda affiliated group), the Islamic State of Iraq and Syria, and the Free Syrian Army rallied to the defense of the rebels, and France, Kuwait, Qatar, Saudi Arabia, Turkey, the United Kingdom, and the United States provided direct or indirect military support to some rebel groups. The Assad regime was backed by Hezbollah, the Popular Front for the Liberation of Palestine General Command, and volunteers from Iran's Revolutionary Guards, Quds Force, and Basij militia. Direct military support for the regime came from both Russia and North Korea. By 2014, millions of refugees had been displaced—with over a million in Lebanon alone—and the estimated death toll ranged from 150,000 to 220,000.[1]

Even the use of chemical weapons by the regime against its challengers did not trigger a military response from the international community. Instead, a Russian proposal to have the regime turn over its chemical weapons to be destroyed was the strongest alternative on which international agreement could be reached.

This episode raises interesting questions:

1. What types of international actors were involved?

2. Which were the most significant actors?

3. Who had power and on what was it based?

Protest against Assad of Syria in front of the White House in Washington D.C. on September 24, 2011 | Why didn't the world act to stop the repression in Syria as it did in Libya in 2011?

2-1 THE SEARCH FOR SECURITY IN A CHANGING WORLD

You are probably familiar with different types of international actors. You're a citizen of a country (or a *state* as we say in international politics), you may be a member of the local Amnesty International chapter on your campus, and someone you know may work for a multinational corporation. These examples represent different types of international actors in world politics. The playing field for such actors is the **international system**, which consists of the players and the relationships between them. Both the players and the relationships matter. In the modern era, the players, or **international actors**, are of several broad types. **States**—such as France or Japan—are typically easy to identify, as they occupy defined spaces on maps. There are about 200 such states; the newest one is South Sudan, which became a recognized state in 2011. There are also **non-state actors**. Some non-state actors are transnational actors composed of states such as the United Nations (UN), the European Union (EU), or the African Union (AU). These are typically termed **international governmental organizations (IOs)**. Other non-state actors are organizations that allow individuals to join, such as Amnesty International, Greenpeace, or the Red Cross. These are usually called **nongovernmental organizations (NGOs)**. Some are commercial business entities such as General Motors, British Petroleum (BP), or Bayer, which are commonly referred to as **multinational** or **transnational corporations (MNCs or TNCs)**—when their production facilities and

international system the constellation of international actors and the relationships between them.

international actors those who act in the international system; these actors can include states or non-state actors.

state a political-legal unit that: (1) has an identifiable population, (2) is located within defined borders recognized by others, and (3) has a government with sovereignty.

non-state actors international actors that are not states. They may include IOs, NGOs, multinational corporations, and individuals.

international governmental organizations (IOs) international organizations whose membership is restricted to states.

nongovernmental organizations (NGOs) organizations whose membership is not restricted solely to states.

multinational corporations (MNCs) companies that have subsidiaries (other companies) in multiple countries. Also known as **transnational corporations (TNCs)**.

Greenpeace's "Aurora" the Polar Bear marches in both London and Moscow to protest actions taken in the Arctic | What types of international actors are in play here?

transactions cross the boundaries of several countries. Others are **transnational advocacy networks (TANs)** such as al-Qaeda. Local or **subnational actors** can be identified, too. These might include *individuals* who change the world around them, like the Dalai Lama or Bono. Other subnational actors may be *governmental units* within a state that influence world politics with their actions, such as when the Spanish city of Barcelona sends a trade mission to China. As you can see, the numbers and types of international actors appear almost endless, and we take a closer look at them later in this chapter.

The international system includes the ongoing relationships among these actors as well. International actors do not just bump up against each other randomly. There are expectations about what actors should do in certain situations. There are both written rules and unwritten norms that condition how these actors behave. For example, the United States may be the only superpower in the international system at this point, but that does not mean it can do anything it wants.

transnational advocacy networks (TANs) networks defined by reciprocal, voluntary actions across national borders that (1) must include non-state actors (like individuals acting alone, social movements, or NGOs), (2) may include states or IOs as well, (3) represent a recurring, cooperative partnership with (4) differentiated roles among the component parts.

subnational actors those international actors normally seen as subparts of a state, such as individuals or local governmental entities.

interdependence mutual connections and reliance between international actors.

Other international actors prefer order, and thus they want to be able to anticipate what actors like the United States will do whenever possible. The presence of expectations, rules, and norms makes anticipating such actions somewhat easier. As you'll see, both the actors and their relationships matter.

2-1a Anarchy and Interdependence

One of the defining structural characteristics of the international system is anarchy. As we said in Chapter 1, formal anarchy does not mean chaos. Anarchy simply means the lack of a central, overarching authority that governs world politics and the actors involved in it. There is no equivalent of the cop on the corner to make sure that rules and norms are followed or that expectations are met. International actors, particularly states, will often pursue their own interests with seemingly little concern about how their actions affect others, in part because no one has the responsibility, authority, and power to make them behave. In such circumstances, some international actors behave as if the only law is the law of the jungle—the survival of the fittest.

However, anarchy is not the only significant structural characteristic. The fact that most international actors do not behave in a purely self-interested fashion suggests that anarchy is not absolute. There are other features of the international system that help to create order. One of these important structural characteristics is **interdependence**, which refers to the mutual connections that tie states and other players to each other. No state is fully independent and able to provide for all its needs and manage all its problems, and the mutual dependencies that exist and continue to grow link players together. While not all of these dependencies are equal, and interdependence between different actors varies, the bottom line is that what one state does often affects other states. In other words, power differences exist and such asymmetries can be important elements of how states interact. China has more options regarding what it does than do states like Moldova or Haiti. However, the interdependence that exists—in varying levels and degrees—creates significant connections between the players that force them to interact with each other and often result in greater cooperation than would otherwise be expected. Therefore, while formal anarchy is an essential feature, it does not mean that states or other players are not connected.

Similarly, while there are no authoritative central bodies—those that can enforce laws—to govern the international political system, formal anarchy does not mean there is no order, organization, or meaningful institutions in world politics. In part due to interdependence, but also due to common goals and common problems, the international system has many international organizations whose members are the sovereign states of the anarchic system. These organizations, such as the United Nations, the World Bank, the International Monetary Fund, and many others provide forums for members to coordinate efforts to solve common problems. Moreover, while these organizations' authority is severely constrained by its members, they often exercise limited authority, help to develop norms and rules, and frequently have resources (provided by their members) to address problems. The international system is anarchic, but a level of structure exists within it to some degree.

Furthermore, even for major powers such as the United States, China, or Germany, there are costs to be paid for not meeting others' expectations or not following well-established rules and norms. International actors are often concerned with reciprocity—the practice of behaving toward others as they behave toward you—and therefore follow these rules and norms to help ensure that others do, as well. Violating rules and norms can result in costs ranging from international scorn to economic or military punishment. Despite the formal anarchy of the system, the international system is like a society in some ways. Those who repeatedly choose to act outside its rules, norms, and expectations are typically seen as outlaws. So when North Korea is called out for failing to follow the rules of the system, spokespersons for the regime react to such labels because those words sting. In the anarchic international system, diplomatic communications can lessen or inflame tensions between actors as well as clarify or obscure an actor's intentions;

Why is it okay for some states to have nuclear weapons but not others?

sometimes words are substitutes for actions and at other times they trigger the very reactions they are trying to prevent![2] So, how do we protect ourselves?

2-1b The Security Dilemma

The most tempting response to the question of how we protect ourselves is the simplest one. In the words of *The Sopranos* theme: "Get yourself a gun." In an anarchical system, self-help is the norm, as states must depend on themselves to provide for their own security and protect their own interests. The consequence of self-help is a **security dilemma**. How does one society increase its own security without seeming to jeopardize the security of others? Often, the things that states do to make themselves secure threaten—or at least appear to do so—the security of other states.

When we think of rivals such as India and Pakistan or Israel and Iran, the dangers involved in the security dilemma become self-evident. India and Pakistan share a border, they have fought three major wars since 1947, of which India has won all three, and they have had minor border clashes virtually each year. In 1998, India detonated a series of atomic devices, and Pakistan did the same just a few weeks later. There seems no doubt that rivals like these two adjoining states would benefit from more cooperation. Yet as the prisoner's dilemma in Chapter 1 showed, cooperation is hard to achieve. The gains that come from both sides' cooperation are

> **security dilemma** the steps that states take to make themselves secure often result in threats to other states, whose reactions to those threats make the first state less secure; thus, what a state does to gain security can often make it less secure.

Women in India's military serve as guards along their country's border with Pakistan | What goes through the minds of Pakistani border guards when they see such very serious-looking female counterparts on the Indian side?

attractive, but the risks to one side if it cooperates and the other doesn't are profound—literally life-and-death in this case! Prudence suggests that each country should continue to arm itself and watch the other closely. So the next war could be fundamentally more deadly.

For their part, Israel and Iran have not fought each other directly, but Iran's former President Mahmoud Ahmadinejad called for the destruction of Israel. More to the point, Iran has been a primary financier of the Hezbollah militia in Lebanon, which Israeli forces were unable to defeat following a series of border clashes in 2006. Now Israel's government is troubled by Iran's apparent effort to develop nuclear weapons, but Israel is reputed to have 100 to 200 nuclear weapons itself. Each of these rivals is watching the other's actions closely. A strike by Israel against Iran, or by Iran against Israel, could happen, and the state that launched the attack would probably claim it acted in self-defense.

The security dilemma captures the idea of seeking security while trying not to create the very war one hopes to avoid. This is nothing new; history has repeated itself for centuries. For understanding international politics,

Treaties of Westphalia two treaties in 1648 that ended the Thirty Years' War and created the modern international system.

feudalism a socio-economic-political system in which rulers would grant land to the local aristocracy in return for their loyalty and support, and others work the land in return for food, shelter, and protection from the local aristocracy.

Thirty Years' War (1618–1648) a series of wars that created many modern European states.

the key turning point in history came in 1648 with the **Treaties of Westphalia** that ended the Thirty Years' War. Given the importance of these agreements, we can divide the international system's history into three periods: the pre-Westphalian system, the Westphalian system, and the neo-Westphalian system.

2-2 THE PRE-WESTPHALIAN SYSTEM (PRE-1648)

For most of human history, geography limited people's contact. Oceans, rivers, mountain ranges, dense forests, and deserts divided peoples and limited their interaction. Individuals might live their whole lives within just a few miles of their place of birth. Over time, innovations like domesticating plants and animals led to larger communities and thus larger political organizations. Year-round agriculture and constantly occupied communities began approximately 7,000 years ago with the Sumerian culture in ancient Mesopotamia.[3] Around the globe, monarchies and empires thereafter rose and fell, but *modern international politics arose out of European history*. The combination of Europe's advantages—temperate climate, adequate rainfall, arable land, natural resources, navigable rivers, and multiple maritime linkages—allowed its inhabitants to expand and dominate others.[4] Thus, we can say the international system is Eurocentric.

While the Romans used both military force and technological innovations such as a superior system of roads to knit much of Europe together, after the fall of the Roman Empire a weak monarchy system evolved. That system was dominated by **feudalism**, a socio-economic-political system in which rulers would grant land to the local aristocracy in return for their loyalty and support. In return for the landowners meeting their material needs, peasants would work the land. As monarchs became stronger, the territories they could control grew larger and better integrated, becoming the bases of modern states—and modern state rivalries.

The **Thirty Years' War** (1618–1648) was the watershed event in modern international politics. It began as a religious conflict between Protestants and Catholics in the Holy Roman Empire when the pope tried to force rulers who had converted to Protestantism to return to Catholicism. Because the Holy Roman Empire stretched across all of Central Europe, over time virtually every European power became involved. The Danes, Dutch, Swedes, Spanish, French, and others sequentially entered conflicts that became more about power—and who would rule where—than just about religion alone. When the wars finally ended with the Treaties of Westphalia, many of Europe's modern states had broken free from the Holy Roman Empire, and a new international system was created based on sovereign states and the principle of nonintervention into their domestic affairs. In short, within a state's borders, the religion of both the people and their ruler was their business, not the business of outsiders, and the modern state system was born.

2-3 THE WESTPHALIAN SYSTEM (1648–1989)

The idea of borders as barriers to political interference from outside was very important in the Westphalian system, and, as we'll see, within those borders different types of governing regimes developed.

2-3a States and Their Characteristics

States were the primary actors in the Westphalian international system. A state is a political-legal unit that meets three conditions: (1) it has an identifiable population, (2) it is located within defined territorial borders recognized by others, and (3) its government possesses sovereignty. To be sovereign means to be self-governing. Regardless of the form of government a state uses, governments will have someone in charge on a day-by-day basis—that person is the **head of government**. States will also have someone who symbolically represents the entire state and its people—that person is the **head of state**. In **parliamentary systems**, the heads of government are called prime ministers, but the titles of the heads of state may vary. For example, parliamentary heads of state may be monarchs (like in the United Kingdom or Thailand) or presidents with relatively weak powers (as in Greece or Italy). In **presidential systems**, strong presidents are both the head of state and the head of government (as in Brazil or the United States). Just to confuse us, a few states have **semi-presidential systems**, in that prime ministers are responsible for most day-to-day governing but presidents also have some significant policy-making roles. Good examples of these are France and Russia. In nondemocratic, **authoritarian systems**, the head of government and head of state may be the same person, who could be a monarch (as in Saudi Arabia), a dictator (as in Democratic Republic of the Congo—and isn't that name ironic?), a son of a military officer who rose to power through force (as in Syria), the leader of the only political party that is allowed to function (as in China), and so on.

In addition to a sovereign government, states have a capital city that is the seat of government. In the capital city, foreign embassies can be found representing those other states that extend diplomatic recognition to the state in question. **Embassies** are properties that house the permanent diplomatic missions of other countries. They can range from modest office suites to entire buildings to complexes of multiple buildings. They are noteworthy in that they have the benefit of **extraterritoriality**. For example, that means when one steps into the Peruvian Embassy in Washington, D.C., that person has left the jurisdiction of the United States and entered the jurisdiction of Peru. As such, those in the Peruvian Embassy are exempt from U.S. laws as long as they remain within the embassy. Thus extraterritoriality explains why some people accused of wrongdoing will seek asylum in the embassies of other states. Working in these missions are professional **diplomats**—those individuals occupying positions in the foreign policy establishments of states or the management of other organizations who represent and negotiate on behalf of their country or employer. Accredited diplomats who may work in the embassy or

head of government the person who is in charge of a state's government on a day-by-day basis and ensures that basic state functions and services are met.

head of state the person who symbolically represents a state and its people.

parliamentary systems governments with a prime minister as the head of government and either a monarch or president as head of state.

presidential systems governments with strong presidents as both the head of state and the head of government.

semi-presidential systems governments with prime ministers who are responsible for most day-to-day governing but also have presidents who have some significant policy-making roles.

authoritarian systems nondemocratic governments with leaders who rule via force, whose basis of power is the ability to coerce others or a submissive citizenry.

embassies properties that house the permanent diplomatic missions of other countries, typically located in the capital city of a state.

extraterritoriality the principle that one is exempt from prosecution of the laws of the state; typically applied in the case of an embassy.

diplomats individuals occupying positions in the foreign policy establishments of states or the management of other organizations who represent and negotiate on behalf of their country or employer.

Diplomatic Immunities

Diplomats are normally exempted from prosecution for violating local laws in the host state, because laws vary considerably across states and—since diplomats represent another sovereign state—how they are treated can be seen as sending a message about that state. But what happens when diplomats or their family members do bad things? The offenses could be minor; during the Cold War, Soviet diplomats had a reputation for shoplifting underwear at fine department stores! Those crimes were typically ignored. On the other hand, in the 1990s, a Georgian diplomat drove drunk and killed a 16-year-old girl in Washington, D.C. With the permission of the Georgian government, that diplomat was prosecuted, convicted of manslaughter, and served time in both U.S. and Georgian prisons.

In December 2013, India's deputy consul general in New York City—Devyani Khobragade—was arrested and indicted for visa fraud and making false statements to law enforcement officials. The visa fraud involved Khobragade's claim that she was paying her Indian housekeeper $4,500 a month, but the housekeeper said she was actually paid less than the U.S. minimum wage. Upon her arrest, Khobragade was treated like any other criminal suspect, which included being strip-searched before being escorted to her jail cell. Incensed at her treatment, Indian officials upgraded her diplomatic assignment to the Indian Embassy where she had full diplomatic immunity. At that point, the State Department ordered her to leave the country, she did, and subsequently a U.S. diplomat was ordered to leave India. Lost in this exchange were any concerns about the housekeeper or her allegation that she was not allowed by her employer to return home to India.[5]

So was this a case of India being insulted by the United States or a human trafficking case going unpunished? How could this matter have been handled better?

---

any associated **consulates**—offices where other diplomatic officials work to facilitate commerce, travel, and cultural exchanges—enjoy **diplomatic immunity**. Even when they leave the grounds of the embassy, accredited diplomats are still largely exempt from the laws of the state in which they work. Thus, if an accredited diplomat (or even an immediate family member of one) is accused of a crime, typically the most a state can do is to expel the diplomat or person from the country. Of course, the other state involved may expel one of the first state's diplomats in retaliation, as indicated in the box Spotlight On: Diplomatic Immunities.

This practice is really a very pragmatic idea based on reciprocity: If countries are to be able to sustain communication—even in times of violent conflict—and try to resolve disagreements, they must have confidence that their official representatives and negotiators will be able to engage in diplomacy safely. Yet, embassies and embassy officials are increasingly the targets of state and non-state actors. During 2012 and 2013, terrorist attacks resulting in deaths have occurred at a U.S. consulate in Libya, the U.S. embassy in Turkey, Indian and U.S. consulates in Afghanistan, the Russian embassy in Libya, and the Iranian embassy in Lebanon. If diplomats of states are targets of violence, what implications do you think this holds for the conduct and future of diplomacy—especially since these attackers are principally non-state actors? Would you want to be a career diplomat? Consider the box Spotlight On: Who Represents the United States Abroad?

2-3b States, Diplomacy, and Negotiation in World Politics

Any consideration of Westphalian state sovereignty would be incomplete without also discussing what the diplomats who represent states do, which we turn to next.

THE NATURE AND ROLE OF DIPLOMACY Have you ever had a disagreement with a friend or acquaintance you had to work out? Maybe it took the intervention of another person to help. In either case, you were engaged in **diplomacy**. In international relations, diplomacy is the art and practice of conducting negotiations between nations. Sometimes the results are surprising.

consulates offices other than embassies where diplomatic officials facilitate commerce, travel, and cultural exchanges.

diplomatic immunity the principle that accredited diplomats are exempt in almost all cases from prosecution under the laws of the state where they are assigned.

diplomacy the art and practice of conducting negotiations between nations.

Who Represents the United States Abroad?

The professional diplomats in the United States are generally Foreign Service Officers found in the Department of State. FSOs, as they are known, are selected through a challenging process of examination (the Foreign Service Officers Exam), which consists of a written test, a personal narrative and interview for those who pass the written test, an intensive on-site oral examination involving a variety of problem-solving and applied activities, and a final review. Those who clear all these hurdles are then placed on a rank-ordered list and offered assignments as positions become available. It is no wonder that, like most professional diplomatic corps, the U.S. Foreign Service is often considered elitist! After all, the demand to join is high, job openings are generally limited, and the selection process is very difficult. Even applicants who do well in each part of the process are not guaranteed a position.

FSOs serve abroad in embassies in the capital cities of foreign countries, in consulates in major cities of foreign countries, in other missions abroad, in international governmental organizations such as the United Nations, and in the United States, as well. In their duties, they generally engage in five major activities:

1. They represent the U.S. government overseas.
2. They present the views of foreigners to the U.S. government.
3. They engage in diplomacy and negotiations on behalf of the United States.
4. They analyze and report on events abroad.
5. They provide policy advice to their superiors.

In recent years, those FSOs have conducted their duties in dangerous workplaces, as diplomats have increasingly been targeted for attacks based upon the regime they represent. Coinciding with this greater risk is the fact that FSOs are becoming increasingly diverse. In the past, most FSOs were white, male Protestants who typically attended Ivy League schools. This pattern tended to make the Foreign Service an exclusive "old boy network" in which family, background, education, and connections mattered a great deal. Over time, much has changed for the professional diplomatic corps of the United States and other countries. In the United States, women, minorities, and individuals who are not from the Northeast, not Protestant, and are not upper or upper-middle class, have become an increasingly large part of the U.S. Foreign Service. A significant step in this process occurred when Madeleine Albright was named the first woman to serve as U.S. secretary of state in 1996 by President Bill Clinton. Secretary Albright was followed by Condoleezza Rice in George W. Bush's presidency, and Hillary Clinton in Barack Obama's presidency. Nonetheless, the process of change has been slow for the United States and other countries, and the professional diplomatic corps of most states continues to be overrepresented by men.

This pattern extends to the top of the diplomatic pyramid as well. According to the Worldwide Guide to Women in Leadership, as of January 2014, only the European Union and 23 countries—about 11 percent of the world's total—had female foreign ministers (see http://www.guide2womenleaders.com/). How would international relations be different if more diplomats were women?

In 2013, economic sanctions on Iran by the European Union and the United States—based on Iran's refusal to allow international inspections of its nuclear program—began to significantly impact the Iranian economy. Meeting in Geneva, the foreign ministers of China, the European Union, France, Germany, Iran, Russia, United Kingdom, and United States reached an interim six-month agreement to limit Iran's enrichment of uranium and to allow international inspections of Iran's nuclear facilities. In return, Iran got some limited relief from the sanctions while leaving the vast bulk of sanctions in place. Sometimes the actions are less newsworthy but still significant. In 2012, **UN Secretary-General** Ban Ki-moon urged UN members to work together to forge more sustainable development strategies for everyone—rich and poor! These examples demonstrate the heart of diplomacy: communication and negotiation in pursuit of cooperation and conflict resolution.

THE ART OF DIPLOMACY Let's now consider some general features and key characteristics of what many regard as the heart of diplomacy: bargaining and negotiation. Diplomacy often involves a complicated mix of bargaining (a term usually meaning more competitive

UN Secretary-General the head of the UN Secretariat, the UN's administrative leader elected by the UNGA at the recommendation of the UNSC.

A U.S. Marine and FBI investigator at the U.S. Embassy in Tanzania after the terrorist bombing attack in 1998 | Why was the U.S. embassy targeted here in Africa rather than a more populated country in Europe, and how might this affect the conduct of diplomacy?

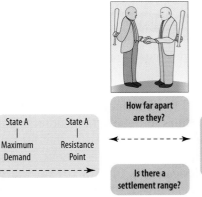

U.S. Secretary of State Hillary Clinton and other U.S. diplomats meet with Pakistan's Prime Minister Yousef Raza Gilani in October 2009 | What issues might the United States and Pakistan be discussing?

and conflictual diplomacy) and negotiation (a term usually meaning more collaborative problem solving). In fact, diplomacy generally occurs when there are "both common interests and issues of conflict. Without common interests there is nothing to negotiate for; without conflict there is nothing to negotiate about."[6]

We can imagine a hypothetical conflict between two states as depicted in Figure 2-1. As the figure suggests, each state has its maximum demand, or ideal preference for an outcome, and diplomacy is involved in communicating those preferences. Each state also has its bottom line, or initial resistance point, which is the minimum it will accept, from the outset of the diplomatic interaction. Part of diplomacy is trying to learn what that resistance or reservation point for the other side is, while protecting one's own. Between the two resistance points is what we could call a **settlement gap**, the distance between the minimum demands of each side. It is also very important to consider how pressures from the domestic context— public opinion, key interests, or elites—affect the positions and flexibility of the other side. How far apart the two sides are greatly affects the possibility of a successful diplomatic resolution to the conflict.

Closing the settlement gap is the art of diplomacy. Obviously, persuasion might be involved, as might threats (see Chapter 6 and its discussion of compellance/

coercive diplomacy). Either or both sides might introduce a wide variety of "carrots" (rewards such as foreign aid) and "sticks" (punishments such as sanctions) to stress common interests and/or potential costs of failing to resolve the matter. Diplomats might also try to use a **linkage strategy** to connect other issues to the resolution of the current one. State A, for example, might agree to State B's preference on another issue of concern between them if State B moves closer to State A's position on the first one. The parties to this conflict might even invite in a third party or parties to try to help them close the gap.

For diplomats on both sides of a dispute, the key is to find a "yesable" solution.[7] Simply put, the other side should have something to say yes to—a benefit that appears desirable and enables them to avoid appearing as if they just gave in. In effect, diplomats have to try to

settlement gap the difference between the minimal preferences of two parties to a negotiation.

linkage strategy in diplomacy, the strategy of connecting solutions on one issue to proposals on another to facilitate agreement.

FIGURE 2-1   THE STRUCTURE OF NEGOTIATION

State A	State A	How far apart are they?	State B	State B
Maximum Demand	Resistance Point	← - - - - →	Resistance Point	Maximum Demand

Is there a settlement range?

© Cengage Learning®

fashion proposals that encourage their counterparts to see that they have interests in and benefits from their adoption. The trick is finding how to do so, and that leads us to the forms diplomacy may take.

THE FORMS OF DIPLOMACY Now that we have a basic sense of what diplomacy involves, let's consider some of the styles and types of diplomacy and how they have evolved over time. Modern structures and practices of diplomacy owe their shape and form to the development of the state system after the Treaties of Westphalia (1648) and, especially, since the early nineteenth century and the European Congress of Vienna (1814–1815).

Early diplomacy in the state system was very much an elite activity. First controlled by royalty, nobility, and other elites, by the early twentieth century diplomacy became the arena of professional diplomats. As time passed, however, the arena for diplomacy expanded considerably. This was partly a function of advances in communication and transportation technologies, which made state leaders able to communicate directly with much greater ease. As modern transportation made the world shrink, meetings became more possible, and communications technologies (telephones, computers, and the like) allowed governments to link directly to each other and bypass their embassies. The expansion of global news networks, satellites, television, and the Internet also make leaders much less dependent on their embassies for news and information about a foreign country.

As these technological changes took place, an interesting "back to the future" kind of development occurred. Just as the early dominance of elites as the principal diplomats (e.g., royalty and nobility) gave way to more professional diplomatic corps by the mid-nineteenth century,

since then there has been a return to the very high-level, personal diplomacy among leaders and their closest advisors and foreign policy personnel. State leaders can fly almost anywhere in the world in a day or two, so physically getting together for face-to-face **summit meetings** is much easier now than it was a hundred years ago.

However, other forms of diplomacy have also thrived and expanded. While much diplomacy continues to be carried out on a bilateral basis between two countries, increasingly **multilateral diplomacy** is common. As we discuss in Chapter 6, the United States and Soviet Union engaged in bilateral diplomacy to work out cooperative arrangements to try to control their nuclear arms competition all throughout the Cold War, and the United States and Russia recently concluded a new installment of those agreements in 2010. However, most of the major arms control negotiations of the past two decades have involved a large number of countries in multilateral talks (see Chapter 6 for more on such treaties). Multilateral diplomacy has also been the norm in addressing a great variety of other issues in world politics, many of which we address in other chapters. Complicated talks among hundreds of participants are the norm for issues related to trade and finance (see Chapter 8), international development (see Chapter 10), human rights (see Chapter 11), and the global environment (see Chapter 12). Globalization, the growth in the number and types of international actors, and the increasingly complicated and interconnected issue agenda all contribute to this shift, but it raises a question: in what ways does this development— the trend to multilateral diplomacy—help and hinder successful diplomatic outcomes?

Another form of diplomacy occurs when parties to a conflict seek the help of others to resolve their disagreements. In 1906, U.S. President Theodore Roosevelt won the Nobel Peace Prize for mediating the 1905 war between Russia and Japan. More recently, both Brazilian President Luiz Inacio Lula da Silva and Turkish Foreign Minister Ahmet Davutoglu tried to bridge the differences in a variety of Middle East conflicts.

We can identify four main types of such **third-party diplomacy**, and Table 2-1 provides a very simple

World leaders can take their issue stances directly to another country's public, as Russian Prime Minister Vladimir Putin did in 2010 through an interview with CNN's Larry King | What effect might this have on U.S.–Russian relations?

Alexei Nikolsky/RIA Novosti/Pool/Reuters/Landov

summit meetings diplomatic meetings involving the top officials of their respective states (hence "the summit").

multilateral diplomacy diplomacy involving three or more states at a time; typically many states are involved.

third-party diplomacy the engagement of an outside party in the negotiations between the actual parties to a dispute to facilitate a resolution of the disagreement.

TABLE 2-1	TYPES OF THIRD-PARTY DIPLOMACY
1. Good offices	The least intrusive form of third-party involvement. The third party provides a place for the two sides to negotiate.
2. Mediation	The third party organizes the talks and proposes possible options to settle the dispute, but no settlement is forced on the participants by the third party.
3. Arbitration	The participants present information and views and agree in advance to accept an option developed by and determined by the third party to be in the best interest of all concerned.
4. Adjudication	In a court-like proceeding, the participants present their positions to the third party, who acts like a judge and decides which of the positions is "correct." The participants agree in advance to abide by the third party's decision.

© Cengage Learning®

introduction of each of them. Let's think about these approaches to third-party diplomacy for a moment. First, notice that as we move from good offices to adjudication, the parties of the dispute relinquish more and more control over the outcome. What do you think that suggests about the kinds of disputes that are submitted for these types of diplomacy? Second, consider what makes a good third party in these situations.

AP Images/Ron Edmonds

Mediating peace in the Middle East | Why do parties to a dispute sometimes need the help of a third party?

track II diplomacy the activities and involvement of private individuals, nongovernmental organizations such as civil society organizations, and religious and business leaders in dialogue and negotiation to facilitate conflict resolution.

conference diplomacy large diplomatic meetings of many officials from states, international organizations, nongovernmental organizations, academia, and other non-state actors.

epistemic communities networks of experts who bring their knowledge and expertise to the political arena to help policymakers understand problems, generate possible solutions, and evaluate policy success or failure.

Should the third party be strictly neutral, or should the third-party participant have important interests at stake, as well?

Like so many other aspects of world politics, the arena of diplomacy has broadened to include a great many non-state actors, as well. This development includes the expanding role of international organizations such as the United Nations. However, it also includes a growing role for other non-state actors, including nongovernmental organizations (NGOs) and private individuals. A common way to refer to this type of diplomacy is **track II diplomacy**. Track II diplomacy may involve private citizens (including celebrities such as U2's Bono and former leaders such as Jimmy Carter or Tony Blair), nongovernmental organizations, academic experts or specialists, and so on. Track II diplomacy offers ways to explore solutions to particular issues, conflicts, and disagreements without the burdens of formal state-to-state negotiations.

An interesting consequence of this much more complex diplomatic environment is the rise of **conference diplomacy**. While large meetings of officials focusing on a restricted set of issues are nothing new, the term has taken on special meaning in recent decades. Often under the sponsorship of international organizations such as the UN, large, issue-based conferences have been held to bring together representatives of states, international organizations, academia and **epistemic communities**, nongovernmental organizations, individuals, and non-state national groups.

Major global conferences on land mines, women, population, human rights, the environment, and other issues have been held over the past several decades, some of which have now been regularized into annual or periodic meetings. Examples include the 1992 Earth Summit on environmental issues held in Rio de Janeiro—the Rio +20 conference on sustainable development was held in 2012—and the World Conference on Women—the fourth of which was held in 1995; currently, efforts are underway to organize a fifth such conference in 2015 (see Table 2-2).

TABLE 2-2 CONFERENCE DIPLOMACY AND THE WORLD CONFERENCE ON WOMEN

CONFERENCE	LOCATION	PARTICIPANTS	KEY RESULTS
First World Conference on Women	Mexico City, Mexico June 1975	133 UN member states; about 4,000 NGO attendees and participants in parallel meeting	Established a World Plan of Action and the UN Development Fund for Women
Second World Conference on Women	Copenhagen, Denmark July 1980	145 UN member states; about 4,000 NGO attendees and participants in parallel meeting	Copenhagen Program for Action, stressing need for attention to equal access to education, employment, and health care services; declared UN Decade for Women
Third World Conference on Women	Nairobi, Kenya July 1985	157 UN member states; 15,000 NGO representatives in parallel meeting	Adoption of Nairobi Forward-Looking Strategies, stressing the eradication of violence against women and the promotion of peace and development
Fourth World Conference on Women	Beijing, China September 1995	189 UN member states; 30,000 representatives from 2,500 NGOs in parallel meeting	Adoption of the Beijing Platform and the Beijing Declaration, identifying 12 areas of concern, including poverty, education, health care, violence, inequality of economic and political opportunity
Fifth World Conference on Women	Targeted for 2015	To be determined	To be determined

© Cengage Learning®

Among other things, these multilateral conferences on women helped to establish UN Women, a section of the United Nations focused on gender equality and the empowerment of women. UN Women was established in July 2010, combining several existing, but separate areas of UN work including the UN Development Fund for Women (UNIFEM) and the Office of the Special Adviser on Gender Issues and Advancement of Women (OSAGI).

By bringing together this mix of actors and stakeholders, conferences help to create and sustain the regimes for specific issue areas and generate momentum toward solutions to multilateral problems. As we discuss in Chapter 13, transnational advocacy networks help to create and disseminate the principles and norms that contribute to the structures and institutions of cooperation. Such networks provide particularly good opportunities for non-state actors to affect diplomacy and world politics because they are so public and high profile, gain so much media attention, and constitute situations in which states are probably more open to the input of non-state actors than most situations.[8]

2-3c Nations and Other Players

As noted earlier, states are the most important actors and their borders are very important in the Westphalian system, but not all territories identified on maps are independent states. In some cases, they are not truly sovereign. For example, Hong Kong is a part of China that used to be governed by the British. Now governed by the Chinese, Hong Kong is allowed considerable local autonomy to make its own policies within some broad parameters set by the government in Beijing, and the Chinese government reports economic statistics for Hong Kong

AP Images/Ron Edmonds

U2 lead singer Bono with U.S. President George W. Bush after they attended a meeting of Inter-American Development Bank to discuss poverty relief in 2002 | How can celebrities such as Bono contribute to diplomatic efforts to solve international problems?

separately from the rest of China. Similarly, Puerto Rico and the U.S. Virgin Islands are U.S. territories that have considerable local autonomy within broad parameters set by the government in Washington, D.C.

In other cases, territories may be self-governing and may be relatively sovereign within their own borders, but they lack diplomatic recognition by other states. Taiwan fits this description. China claims this island off its coast, but Taiwan largely acts as an independent state and many other states treat it as one—except for the fact that they do not establish an embassy in the capital city of Taipei nor send or receive ambassadors there. Abkhazia and South Ossetia also illustrate this pattern. These are breakaway provinces inside the Republic of Georgia that are recognized only by Russia and a few other states like Nicaragua, Venezuela, and Nauru. (Can you find the latter on a map?)

Another clarification is appropriate at this point. Typically, one will hear the terms *country* and *state* used interchangeably. *State* is the more legal term in international politics, but there is no real harm in using these as synonyms. However, the terms *nation* and *state* are often used interchangeably in casual conversation, and that usage is inaccurate. The word **nation** is a sociocultural term for a group of people who possess a collective identity that is a product of multiple factors: shared ethnicity, religion, language, culture, history, and the like. In a few states like the United States and Canada, the most important factor producing that sense of collective or national identity may be a sense of shared values that lead people to identify with each other, but in most states collective or national identity is generally based on more visible factors like ethnicity, race, or religion. In any event, the nation concept is fundamentally about distinguishing us from them. When a state's population is largely comprised of members of one nation, the term **nation-state** is appropriate. So Armenia, Cuba, and Japan are nation-states, because nearly all their population shares a common ethnicity. On the other hand, Kuwaitis and Qataris do not constitute even a bare majority of the populations of Kuwait and Qatar,

nation an identifiable group of people who share a collective identity typically formed around bonds based on factors like shared language, culture, etc.

nation-state a state in which nearly all of the population are members of the same nation.

Map 2-1

Kurdistan

How many states would lose territory and people if Kurdistan became independent?

respectively, so the term *nation-state* does not apply in such cases.

More challenging cases come in the Middle East and Southwest Asia. A vexing issue of competing nationalisms involves the Israelis and Palestinians. They essentially claim the same territory known as Palestine, but both cannot have it. Since 1948, the Israelis have controlled most of the territory, and thus the Palestinians have been a nation without a state, an issue whose importance was emphasized again in the escalating violence during the summer of 2014. Here we have one territory with two nations. A different example is represented by the Kurds. Kurds share a common language and history and see themselves as a single nation. However, as Map 2-1 shows, the area in which they would constitute the majority of the population—a potential Kurdistan—overlaps the boundaries of Iran, Iraq, Syria, Turkey, and to a small extent, Armenia. Thus, we have one nation that spans multiple states but still does not have a state of its own. An even more complicated case can be found in Revenge of Geography: Who Are the Afghans?

An even more compelling illustration of the differences between nations and states can be found in Africa. During the age of imperialism, colonial

Who Are the Afghans?

Afghanistan has long been difficult to govern. Part of that difficulty is physical. Someone once described Afghanistan as a pile of rocks! Mountain ranges crisscross the country, separating its inhabitants from each other. Much of the landscape is harsh and rugged, and no national system of roads links the country together. Outside of the major cities, it is commonplace for Afghans to be suspicious of strangers, as they tend to live fairly isolated lives, with many not venturing more than a few miles from their homes during their entire lifetimes. If physical geography isn't enough to make Afghanistan difficult to govern,

cultural geography is. As shown by Map 2-2, Afghanistan is a land of many nations.

The largest group of Afghans is the Pashtuns. They comprise approximately 42 percent of the population and follow a way of life called Pashtunwali—a set of cultural rules and traditions that govern ethical behavior, good manners, and the like. The next largest group is the Tajiks at 27 percent of the population. The next largest groups after the Tajiks are the Hazaras and Uzbeks at approximately 9 percent of the population each, followed by Aimaks at 4 percent, Turkmen at 3 percent, and Balochs at 2 percent. About half of the Afghan population speaks Dari—an Afghan form of Persian—while the Pashtuns

Map 2-2

Afghanistan's Tribal Areas

Afghanistan Ethnic Groups

Uzbekistan · Kyrgyzstan · China · Tajikistan · Turkmenistan · Mazār-e Sharif · Herāt · Kābul · India · Kandahar · Iran · Pakistan

Ethnic Group Concentration (approx.)

Pashtun · Balochi · Tajik · Kyrgyz · Ismaili
Hazara · Nuristani · Turkmen · Uzbek

© Cengage Learning®

With these different nationalities included, is it any wonder that Afghanistan is hard to unite, much less govern?

Maps of World, www.mapsofworld.com.

Map 2-3

Pashtunistan

Afghanistan - Pakistan
"Pashtunistan"

Mazar-i-Sharif

Herat

Afghanistan

Kabul Jalalabad
                  Peshawar
                        Islamabad

North Waziristan

Tarin Kowt
              South Waziristan

Lashkar Gah

Kandahar

Quetta   **Pakistan**

Karachi

Legend
◾ Pashtunistan
— Afghanistan Pakistan Border
◯ Main Cities

© Cengage Learning®

If Pashtunistan were an independent state, what would that mean for Afghanistan and Pakistan?

speak Pashto. Both Dari and Pashto are considered the official languages of Afghanistan.

So who speaks for Afghanistan? The leaders have traditionally been Pashtuns, since they are the largest single group, but there are more combined non-Pashtuns in Afghanistan than Pashtuns. Complicating this is the fact that there are many more Pashtuns; they just happen to live across the border in Pakistan! As Map 2-3 shows, if Pashtunistan was a nation-state, it would encompass much of both Afghanistan and Pakistan. Plus, we cannot ignore the fact that the Afghan Tajiks may have emotional bonds to Tajikistan next door, that Afghan Uzbeks may have similar ties to Uzbekistan, that Afghan Turkmen may look to Turkmenistan, and that even Afghan Balochs may look with yearning eyes toward the Balochistan provinces in southeastern Iran and southwestern Pakistan.

So the example of Afghanistan is confounding and raises multiple questions.

1. Who are the Afghans? Are they the Pashtun minority or the non-Pashtun majority?

2. Who speaks for Afghanistan?

3. Does Afghanistan really exist, other than as lines on a map that don't mean much once you are there?

4. Is Afghanistan a multinational state simply lacking a strong central government?

5. If it lacks sovereignty, is it a failed state?

Source: "Afghanistan," *The CIA World Factbook*, https://www.cia.gov/library/publications/the-world-factbook/geos/af.html.

Map 2-4

Murdock Ethnic Map (1959)

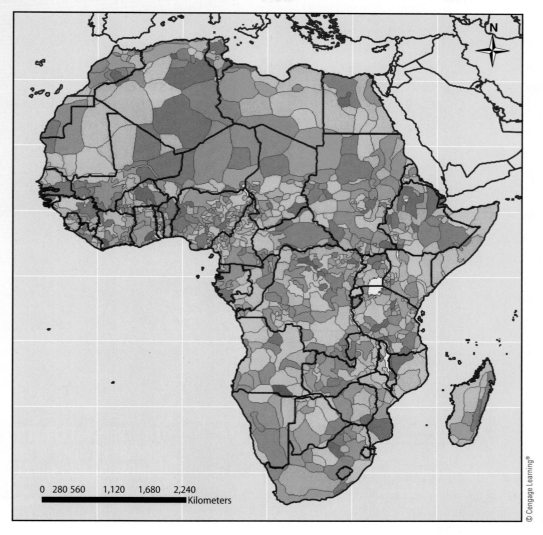

Given the divergence between state borders and the borders of human communities, is it any wonder that internal violence plagues much of the African continent?

Source: George P. Murdock, *Africa: Its Peoples and their Culture* (New York: McGraw-Hill, 1959).

powers established borders based on convenience or the amount of territory they could control. Those borders rarely corresponded with the national groupings of the indigenous people. Since African states maintained their former colonial borders when they became independent, it is little wonder that many of those states continue to suffer from a lack of a collective identity on the part of their citizenry.

Map 2-4 shows how little correspondence there is between state borders and groups based on national ties.

The roughly 200 states in the international system vary widely across a number of dimensions. As shown in Table 2-3, they can be large or small, rich or poor. They vary widely as well in the degrees of freedom their citizens experience. As the map of freedom shows

TABLE 2-3 THE RANGE OF STATES IN THE INTERNATIONAL SYSTEM

FIVE LARGEST STATES (in square miles)[a]	FIVE SMALLEST STATES (in square miles)[b]
1. Russia (6.6 million)	1. Vatican City (0.2)
2. Canada (3.9 million)	2. Monaco (0.7)
3. United States (3.71 million)	3. Nauru (8.5)
4. China (3.70 million)	4. Tuvalu (9)
5. Brazil (3.3 million)	5. San Marino (24)
FIVE LARGEST STATES (est. population 2013)[c]	**FIVE SMALLEST STATES (est. population 2013)[c]**
1. China (1,349,585,838)	1. Vatican City (839)
2. India (1,220,800,359)	2. Nauru (9,434)
3. United States (316,438,601)	3. Tuvalu (10,698)
4. Indonesia (251,160,124)	4. Palau (21,108)
5. Brazil (201,009,622)	5. Monaco (30,539)
FIVE WEALTHIEST STATES (IMF 2012 GDP in millions)[d]	**FIVE POOREST STATES (IMF 2012 GDP in millions)[d]**
1. United States ($16,244,575)	1. Tuvalu ($40)
2. China ($8,221,015)	2. Kiribati ($175)
3. Japan ($5,960,269)	3. Marshall Islands ($182)
4. Germany ($3,429,519)	4. Palau ($234)
5. France ($2,613,936)	5. Sao Tome & Principe ($263)

Sources:
[a] Geography About.com, http://geography.about.com/od/countryinformation/a/bigcountries.htm
[b] Geography About.com, http://geography.about.com/cs/countries/a/smallcountries.htm
[c] CIA World Factbook, https://www.cia.gov/library/publications/the-world-factbook/rankorder/2119rank.html
[d] "Report for Selected Countries and Subjects." World Economic Outlook Database, October 2013. International Monetary Fund.

(Map 2-5), they can also be politically free, partly free, or not free based on their regime type and protection of political rights and civil liberties.

As Table 2-4 shows, some of the states with the strongest non-nuclear militaries may surprise you. Did you expect to find South Korea and Italy on the list? What about Brazil? Was that a surprise? Almost certainly the presence of the United States as the number one conventional military power did not come as a surprise, but what does this number one ranking mean? How strong is the U.S. military, and how do others react to it? Those questions are addressed in Foreign Policy in Perspective: The U.S. Military and Its Impact on Global Armaments.

Regardless of its degree of military power, to be a state these actors must be sovereign, and borders

TABLE 2-4 TEN STRONGEST CONVENTIONAL MILITARY POWERS IN THE WORLD (COMPARING NON-NUCLEAR FORCES ONLY, 2013)

1. United States	6. France
2. Russia	7. Germany
3. China	8. South Korea
4. India	9. Italy
5. United Kingdom	10. Brazil

Source: http://www.globalfirepower.com/countries-listing.asp.

© Cengage Learning®

are the key to **Westphalian sovereignty**. According to this notion of sovereignty, *within a state's borders there is no higher authority* than the government of the state itself. Thus, sovereign states do not allow others to intervene in their internal, domestic affairs, a principle which was included in Article 2 of the United Nations Charter in 1945. Westphalian sovereignty also has an external component. Sovereign states are free to choose their own

Westphalian sovereignty the idea that within a state's borders there is no higher authority than the government of the state itself.

Map 2-5
Map of Freedom

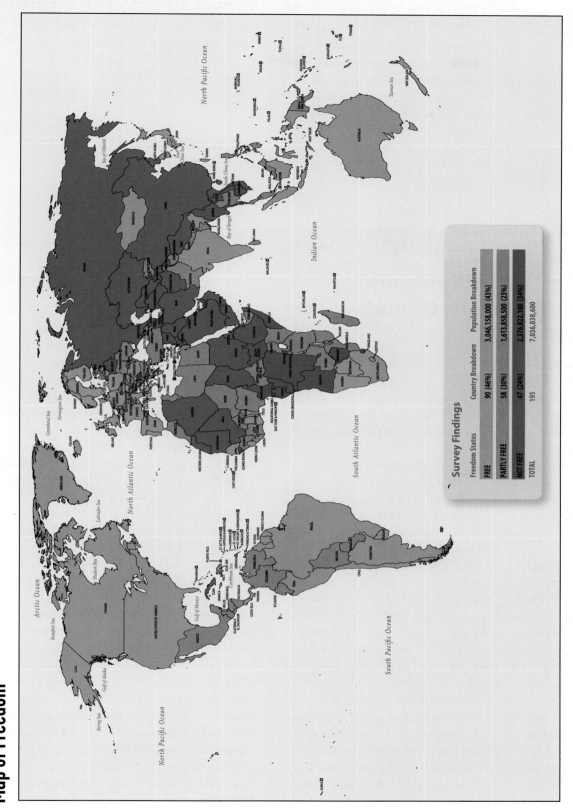

Do any of these classifications of free, partly free, or not free states surprise you?
© Cengage Learning®

courses of action in the world beyond their borders, and with that freedom comes the opportunity to succeed or to fail.

States were not the only actors in the Westphalian system; non-state actors developed as well and existed alongside states. However, our focus at this point is on state actors, because they were clearly the preeminent actors in the state-centric Westphalian international system. However, those non-state actors became more important and influential in the neo-Westphalian system, which we discuss in section 2-4.

2-3d The Evolution of the System

Over the 341-year sweep of the Westphalian era, states developed and gained strength. Some got so strong that by the latter half of the twentieth century, the Cold War risked the threat of global annihilation. The ending of the Cold War brought this system to a close.

THE EMPOWERMENT OF STATES From a European-based system in the seventeenth century, the Westphalian system expanded globally along with the growth of

---

FOREIGN POLICY IN PERSPECTIVE

The U.S. Military and Its Impact on Global Armaments

In the Westphalian system, states were clearly the most powerful international actors. Since power was measured in military terms, it was rational for states to seek to increase their military power. The more power, the better, right? From that perspective, what does the case of the United States demonstrate?

As Table 2-4 shows, the United States has the most powerful conventional military in the world, but that does not convey the degree of dominance of the United States in the military arena. The United States leads the world in not only conventional but also in nuclear weapons. During the Cold War, the United States had more than 12,000 strategic nuclear warheads (those with the range to be launched from one continent and hit targets on another). By 2011, the New START Treaty had restricted the United States and Russia to no more than 1,550 deployed strategic nuclear warheads per side. However, only strategic nuclear warheads were restricted. The United States also has tactical nuclear weapons with shorter ranges. Estimates of the number of these that have been deployed vary from 1,670 to 3,300. While Russia may have more tactical nuclear warheads than the United States (perhaps 3,000 to 4,000), Russia's ability to deliver either strategic or tactical nuclear weapons pales in comparison to the U.S. ability to use long-range missiles, shorter-range missiles, submarine-launched missiles, and bombers to do so. No other state can rival the United States when it comes to the combination and numbers of nuclear weapons and the multiple ways to deliver them. The fact that the United States has not used nuclear weapons since 1945 does not

change the fact that it is the only state in the world that has done so.

However, the United States has also amply demonstrated its willingness to use conventional military force. From 1945 to 2000, the United States used military force 383 times, thereby averaging about seven uses of force per year. The fact that U.S. military spending comprises over 40 percent of all global military spending further indicates that the United States is committed to maintaining its dominance over others. Does this pursuit of military power make the United States more secure? The security dilemma suggests that other states must consider how to protect themselves from the military might possessed by the United States. How do they do that?

For those once labeled by U.S. leaders as rogue states, like Iran and North Korea, development of nuclear weaponry is of paramount importance. In their view, possessing nuclear weapons will deter the United States from attacking them in the future. Iranian leaders have publicly noted how the United States is less confrontational in its treatment of North Korea (which has already tested nuclear weapons) than it is with Iran (which has not). Besides trying to develop nuclear weapons, Iran has also sought to protect itself by buying Russian-made diesel-electric submarines, which could pose a very real threat to U.S. naval forces based in the Persian Gulf. Also, Venezuela's late President Hugo Chavez routinely cited U.S. military threats as the reason for buying sophisticated conventional weapons from Russia. Rising powers in the international system such as China and India are modernizing their militaries and beginning to develop the foundations for blue water navies—those that can project force far from their shores. Oil and natural gas revenues provide the funds necessary for the Russians to modernize their military, as well.

Thus, in the Westphalian system, states face pressures to defend themselves and their borders, as illustrated by the security dilemma. Some questions arise:

1. How powerful does a state need to be to defend itself in the Westphalian system?

2. Do higher levels of U.S. military spending at some point become counterproductive, in that they encourage potential rivals to increase their military spending, as well?

3. How much military spending can the United States afford while recovering from a global recession, or do high levels of military spending address other U.S. goals or needs?

Sources: William G. Howell and Jon C. Pevehouse. *While Dangers Gather: Congressional Checks on Presidential War Powers* (Princeton, NJ: Princeton University Press, 2007); Nikolai Sokov. "Issue Brief: Tactical Nuclear Weapons (TNW)." *Nuclear Threat Initiative*, May 2002, http://www.nti.org/e_research/e3_10a.html; Amy F. Woolf. "U.S. Strategic Nuclear Forces: Background, Developments, and Issues," CRS Report for Congress, Congressional Research Service, July 14, 2009, http://fpc.state.gov/documents/organization/128350.pdf.

European **imperialism**—the colonization of other territories by European states, which is why a European-based regional system is now the basis of world politics. The American and French Revolutions introduced the initial development of a **democracy** norm to the system. Over time, more and more states gave their citizens a meaningful role in choosing their leaders, or, if not, they at least tried to call themselves democracies. For example, North Korea's official name may be the Democratic People's Republic of Korea, but that regime is unlikely to be confused with a real democracy anytime soon. In fact, no country with the word *democratic* in its name is actually a real democracy.

A norm that developed most significantly in the French Revolution and spread through the Westphalian system is **nationalism**—the emotional connection of the mass public with the state. By the early twentieth century, most citizens were emotionally invested in their state, identifying themselves as members of that collectivity, taking pride in its accomplishments and being offended by any perceived slights by others. Nationalistic rivalries played an important role in the origins of World War I. A series of small wars early in the twentieth century liberated much of the Balkan area of southeastern Europe from the control of the Ottoman Empire (i.e., modern Turkey), leaving Serbia as an emerging power in the region. Serbia turned its sights on the neighboring territory of Bosnia and Herzegovina, which was part of Austria-Hungary at the time. When a Serb assassinated Austria-Hungary's Archduke Franz Ferdinand and his wife Sophie in 1914, the result was a war that spread rapidly. The war initially pitted Austria-Hungary and its ally Germany (known as the Central Powers) against Serbia and its ally Russia, which was part of an alliance with France and Great Britain called the Triple Entente. As the Great War went on, Bulgaria and the Ottoman Empire joined on the side of the Central Powers, and Italy, Romania, Greece, and later the United States joined the Allied Powers. Nationalism helped fuel World War I, but its massive cost in lives and treasure led to an armistice in 1918 and the subsequent **Treaty of Versailles** in 1919, a peace treaty with lasting consequences.

Nationalism did not diminish following the war's end. In February 1917, a revolution swept the Russian royal family from power, and in October 1917 a second revolution brought a communist regime led by Vladimir Lenin to power. Although **communism** rejected capitalism and saw nationalism as a tool to oppress the working class, once Lenin became the leader of this new state called the Soviet Union, he found nationalism to be a useful tool in mobilizing the public. This was particularly the case in 1918 when, following the Soviet Union's withdrawal from World War I, the Allied Powers of Britain, France, the United States, Japan, and others invaded Soviet territory. While the official Allied goal was to prevent arms and supplies from falling into German hands, the Allies also wanted to prevent the new communist regime from consolidating its power. Lenin found appeals to traditional Russian nationalism very helpful in repelling the invaders, most of whom had left by 1920.

Lenin called on other Europeans to join the Soviets in revolutions against their capitalist regimes. After the physical and human carnage of World War I, which Lenin attributed to the excesses of capitalism, some Europeans

imperialism control and exploitation by one state of the economy, culture, and/or territory of others, usually called colonies.

democracy a form of governance in which the people have a meaningful choice in selecting their rulers.

nationalism the emotional connection of the mass public to their state.

Treaty of Versailles the treaty in 1919 that ended World War I, imposed heavy penalties on Germany, and created the League of Nations.

communism the anti-capitalist economic philosophy created by Karl Marx that promoted centralized control of a country and its economy for the equal redistribution of resources to the country's citizens.

found his message appealing. Ardent nationalists found communism frightening, however, as it called for the demise of the state. Opposition to communism helped lead to the most extreme application of nationalism: the rise of **fascism** in Italy and Germany. Italy's Benito Mussolini and later Germany's Adolf Hitler both rose to power in part based on their violent opposition to local communists, but their fascist ideology glorified violence and viewed successes on the battlefield as proof of the superiority of their respective nations.[9]

The nationalist ambitions of Japan and Germany led to World War II, which in some ways started as early as 1931 when Japan began its war with China by invading the Chinese province of Manchuria. In 1939, war began in Europe with the German invasion of western Poland and the later Soviet invasion of eastern Poland and Finland. In 1940, Germany defeated Belgium, Denmark, France, Luxembourg, the Netherlands, and Norway, and launched an air war against Britain; the Soviets invaded Latvia, Lithuania, and Estonia; and Germany's ally Italy invaded the British colony of Somaliland and then Egypt and Greece. Seeing one-sided progress, both Romania and Japan joined in a military alliance with Germany and Italy (known as the Axis Powers), and then the Japanese invaded the French colony of Indochina and the Dutch East Indies.

In 1941, the war had widened further. In violation of a nonaggression pact signed just two years earlier, the Germans invaded the Soviet Union, and so the Soviets entered the anti-German alliance with the British. Soviet leader Joseph Stalin took the manipulation of nationalism to new heights. In what the Russians still call the Great Patriotic War, he ignored communism's rejection of nationalism by calling on Russians to defend the Russian Rodina (or Motherland) against the Germans. The United States entered the war in December when the Japanese attacked the U.S. naval base at Pearl Harbor,

British Prime Minister Churchill, U.S. President Roosevelt, and Soviet Communist Party Chairman Stalin meet at Yalta in 1945 | How might history be different if the United States had not used atomic bombs against Japan?

Hawaii, in an attempt to knock out the U.S. Pacific Fleet so the Japanese Empire could expand without serious resistance. Then based on their alliance with Japan, Germans declared war on the United States.

The Germans were unable to defeat the Soviets (or the Russian winter—talk about the revenge of geography!) and were gradually forced back after failing to capture Stalingrad in 1943. When U.S. and British forces invaded France in 1944, it was only a matter of time before the Germans wore down in what had become a two-front war in Europe. The Germans surrendered in May 1945, and following the U.S. detonation of atomic bombs over the Japanese cities of Hiroshima and Nagasaki, the Japanese surrendered in August 1945.

THE COLD WAR The last major phase of the Westphalian system was the **Cold War**, a period of intense rivalry and competition between two large blocs of states—an anticommunist bloc led by the United States and a procommunist bloc led by the Soviet Union—which lasted from 1947 until 1989. Each bloc had its own primary military alliance: the U.S.-led **North Atlantic Treaty Organization (NATO)**, which bound together the United States, Canada, and most Western European states, and the Soviet-led **Warsaw Pact**, which bound together the Soviet Union and its Eastern European allies. Although the two superpowers never directly engaged each other, confrontations involving the superpowers or their client states erupted around the world.

In 1947, communist involvement in the Greek civil war led the U.S. to proclaim the **Truman Doctrine**—the

fascism a political ideology that glorifies the state over the individuals who comprise it and relies on nationalism and violence to bond the citizenry to the state.

Cold War a period of intense rivalry and competition from 1947–1989 between the United States and its allies on the one hand, and the Soviet Union and its allies on the other.

Truman Doctrine the policy that the United States would help states resisting communist expansion.

NATO the **North Atlantic Treaty Organization**, a military alliance structure created following the outbreak of the Korean War in 1950 and led by the United States.

Warsaw Pact the military alliance created by the Soviet Union as a response to the 1955 addition of West Germany into NATO.

policy that the U.S. would help states resisting communist expansion. In 1948, Soviet leaders tried to shut off Western access to the jointly occupied city of Berlin, the former German capital. The U.S. and Western powers responded with the Berlin Airlift, which resupplied West Berliners with food and supplies and the crisis abated in 1949. Also in 1949, the Soviets detonated their first nuclear bomb and the Chinese Communist Party took control of the Chinese mainland. In 1950, the communist regime in North Korea launched a surprise invasion of South Korea. The Korean War ended in a tie in 1953, but it also led to the establishment of NATO and the rearmament of the U.S. to a war-footing. In 1961, Berlin was the focus again as the Soviets built a wall separating the two halves of the city to prevent East Europeans from using defection to West Berlin as a way to escape communist control. The United States responded by sending more troops to West Berlin and with a presidential visit to West Berlin by President John Kennedy.

In 1962, the Soviets challenged the United States by putting short and medium range missiles in Cuba, which was a new communist ally after the revolution led by Fidel Castro. These missiles posed the threat of a nuclear attack on the southeastern portion of the United States with only a few minutes' notice. By placing U.S. military forces on global alert and imposing a naval embargo against Cuba, the U.S. was able to pressure the Soviets to remove their missiles. Six months later, the U.S. removed similar missiles facing the Soviet Union from bases in Turkey. This nuclear brinksmanship led the two superpowers, along with the British, to agree to a treaty limiting nuclear testing which served as a building block for the later nuclear nonproliferation regime.

Still, proxy wars between superpower clients continued in Vietnam in the 1960s and early 1970s, in Angola in the 1970s, and in Nicaragua and El Salvador in the 1980s. By the late 1980s the Soviet Union's economy began to fail as it reached the limits of what a command economy could order people to produce. Furthermore, the Soviet Union could not keep up with the U.S. defense rearmament program under President Ronald Reagan, and it was shaken by the challenge to Soviet supremacy by the Polish people and Pope John Paul II and the costs of fighting a decade-long war in Afghanistan. In 1989, Soviet President Mikhail Gorbachev announced that Soviet client states in Eastern Europe would be allowed to determine their own policies, and East Germans quickly knocked holes in the Berlin Wall. At that point, the Cold War was over, and a new international system—the neo-Westphalian system—emerged. We turn to it next.

David Brauchli/Reuters/Landov

In 1989, Berliners knocked down the Berlin Wall that had separated that city since 1961 | What is the significance of the peaceful destruction of the Berlin Wall after almost 40 years?

2-4 THE NEO-WESTPHALIAN SYSTEM (1990–PRESENT)

After the Cold War ended and the Soviet Union collapsed into 15 relatively weak states, new pressures emerged in the international arena. The result is an international system in which the states remain the central actors, but are now buffeted from within and without by other actors, networks, and problems that readily span national borders. While sovereign states are still the most powerful international actors, in the neo-Westphalian system some non-state actors possess a considerable amount of power and influence in world politics. Wars between states (interstate wars) are less commonplace, but internal conflicts within states (intrastate wars) are more frequent and far more destructive. Thus, we can say we have moved into a neo-Westphalian system, a new, modified version of the previous Westphalian system that is marked by a comparative rise in importance of non-state actors, the phenomenon of globalization, some subsequent relative weakening of states, and a new principle of responsible sovereignty. However, before we address these characteristics of the new system, we need to discuss the development of these non-state actors over time.

2-4a The Development of Non-State Actors

While states were the dominant actors in the Westphalian system, they were not the only actors. Non-state actors were plentiful but played secondary roles. Significant nongovernmental organizations (or NGOs) early in this period were as diverse as the Catholic Church and the Dutch and British East India Companies. The leaders of the Catholic Church tried to influence what states did and how they did it. For their part, large commercial organizations such as the two East India Companies often acted as agents for their respective states in the economic realm, and state leaders normally prevailed if the interests of these companies and their home governments diverged.

By the twentieth century, improvements in global transportation and communication enabled the number and importance of non-state actors to rise. One significant type of non-state actor rising in numbers and influence was the multinational corporation (MNC). Multinational corporations with names ranging from Apple to Zurich Financial Services became notable players in the international system. NGOs were another significant type of non-state actor, and they were often devoted to particular issues. Indeed, for almost any problem you can think of in international relations—poverty, injustice, women's rights, the environment, and any other—NGOs arose to address it. Some NGOs were so successful at humanitarian

work they won the Nobel Peace Prize. These NGOs included, among others, the American Friends Service Committee and the Friends Service Council, the International Committee of the Red Cross and the League of Red Cross Societies, Amnesty International, and International Physicians for the Prevention of Nuclear War.

As transportation linkages improved and international interactions became more routine, other international governmental organizations (IOs) arose. Many of these IOs focused on a narrow range of international cooperation. For example, the Universal Postal Union began in 1874 to handle international mail. In 1930, the Bank for International Settlements was created to coordinate routine transactions between the central banks of sovereign states. The **League of Nations** was formed in 1920 with a broader mission: try to keep the peace and institutionalize cooperation following World War I.

However, since 1945 the most prominent IO has been the **United Nations (UN)**. Like its predecessor the League of Nations, the UN was created in 1945 to keep the peace and institutionalize international cooperation. Its principal organs are the **General Assembly**, **Security Council**, **Economic and Social Council**, **Secretariat**, and the **International Court of Justice** (or **World Court**). We discuss the UN and its principal organs in Chapter 7, where you will also find an organizational chart that shows its many agencies and offices. There are also transnational advocacy networks, which may include individuals, social movements, NGOs, and at times state actors, and these are discussed in detail in Chapter 13. They may also include other subnational actors, like individuals or other political entities, as discussed in Chapters 11 and 12. Just in case this discussion of types of non-state actors has been confusing, see Table 2-5.

As we said earlier in the chapter, non-state actors existed in the Westphalian system, but their enhanced roles are really at the heart of the shift to the neo-Westphalian system. This shift has been marked by the rising importance of such non-state actors, globalization, a subsequent relative weakening of states as actors, and a new principle of responsible sovereignty. Let's address each of these in turn.

2-4b The Rise of Non-State Actors

In the neo-Westphalian system, states are still the most powerful actors, but non-state actors have increasingly become important players in international politics, at times even rivaling some states for influence. One example is the rise of multinational corporations.

League of Nations an international institution created after World War I for collective security and the resolution of disputes between states.

United Nations (UN) an international institution established after World War II to promote peace and security, the development of friendly relations and harmony among nations, and cooperation on international problems.

(UN) General Assembly the plenary body of the UN in which all UN members have a seat. Functioning on a majority rule decision process, it is the central forum for discussion of global issues.

(UN) Security Council (UNSC) a 15-member council that carries the primary UN responsibilities for peace, security, and collective security operations.

Economic and Social Council the component of the UN handling matters considered economic or social, broadly defined.

UN Secretariat the bureaucracy and administrative arm of the UN.

International Court of Justice also known as the **World Court**, this international institution was created in 1946 as part of the United Nations systems to apply international law to resolve conflicts brought voluntarily to it by states.

TABLE 2-5 TYPES OF NON-STATE ACTORS

TYPE OF NON-STATE ACTORS	IDENTIFYING ELEMENT	EXAMPLES
International Governmental Organizations (IOs)	Only states may be members	United Nations; European Union; World Trade Organization
Nongovernmental Organizations (NGOs)	Members include at least some non-state actors	Amnesty International; Aga Khan Development Network; International Red Cross and Red Crescent Societies
Multinational Corporations (MNCs)	Commercial entities dedicated to making a profit whose subsidiaries span multiple states	Bayer; General Motors; Unilever
Transnational Advocacy Networks (TANs)	Networks of groups that press on behalf of their agendas; cannot be comprised solely of state actors	Refugee Research Network; International Campaign to Ban Landmines; al-Qaeda
Subnational Actors	Those that normally fall within a state	Angelina Jolie; City of Barcelona, Spain; State of California

© Cengage Learning®

TABLE 2-6 THE TOP TEN MULTINATIONAL CORPORATIONS IN 2013 AND THEIR CLOSEST STATE COMPARISONS (BY REVENUES AND GDP, IN BILLIONS OF DOLLARS, RESPECTIVELY)

MNCS	STATES
1. Royal Dutch/Shell ($481.7)	25. Belgium ($483.9)
2. Walmart ($469.2)	27. Taiwan ($474.1)
3. ExxonMobil ($449.9)	27. Taiwan ($474.1)
4. Sinopec ($428.2)	28. Austria ($394.9)
5. China National Petroleum ($408.6)	28. Austria ($394.9)
6. BP ($388.3)	29. South Africa ($384.3)
7. State Grid Corporation of China ($298.4)	35. Malaysia ($303.7)
8. Toyota ($265.7)	38. Hong Kong ($263.3)
9. Volkswagen ($247.6)	43. Finland ($247.6)
10. Total ($234.3)	44. Pakistan ($225.6)

Sources: State data: "Report for Selected Countries and Subjects," *World Economic Outlook Database*, October 2013, International Monetary Fund, retrieved October 8, 2013; MNC data: "Global 500," *Fortune*, retrieved July 8, 2013.

© Cengage Learning®

As Table 2-6 shows, if one compares the largest MNCs by their annual sales revenues to states by their **gross domestic product (GDP)** (their annual output of goods and services), the top multinational corporation in 2013—Royal Dutch/Shell—produced more revenue (almost $482 billion) than all but 24 of the 189 states ranked by the International Monetary Fund. It is thus no exaggeration to say that large multinational corporations now rival many states in terms of their *economic* clout.

While it might not seem surprising that seven of the ten largest corporations in the world are energy companies (oil companies Royal Dutch Shell, Exxon-Mobil, Sinopec, China National Petroleum, BP, Total, and the Chinese electric company State Grid), note that only two of the top ten are U.S. corporations (Walmart and ExxonMobil). So the rise of MNCs is a truly global phenomenon. Not only do these firms have considerable financial clout, at times they face a growing set of global rivals that have the power of states behind them: **sovereign wealth funds**. Such funds that invest money provided by the government of their state are not new, but they have grown rapidly in the neo-Westphalian era. As Table 2-7 indicates, each of the top ten sovereign wealth funds has assets in excess of $150 billion; three of these are from China, four are from the Middle East, one is from Europe, and two are from Singapore. When you compare Tables 2-6 and 2-7, it is clear that in a globalized economy wealth is spreading far beyond North America and Europe.

Besides the commercial roles played by MNCs and sovereign wealth funds, other NGOs provide a variety of

gross domestic product (GDP) the total amount of goods and services produced in a state.

sovereign wealth funds investment funds owned by states.

TABLE 2-7	TOP TEN SOVEREIGN WEALTH FUNDS (BY BILLIONS OF DOLLARS IN ASSETS UNDER MANAGEMENT, 2013)		
SOVEREIGN WEALTH FUND		**STATE**	**ASSETS**
1. Government Pension Fund—Global		Norway	$818
2. SAMA Foreign Holdings		Saudi Arabia	$676
3. Abu Dhabi Investment Authority		United Arab Emirates	$627
4. China Investment Corporation		China	$575
5. SAFE Investment Company		China	$568
6. Kuwait Investment Authority		Kuwait	$386
7. Hong Kong Monetary Authority Investment Portfolio		China–Hong Kong	$327
8. Government of Singapore Investment Corporation		Singapore	$285
9. Temasek Holdings		Singapore	$173
10. Qatar Investment Authority		Qatar	$170

Source: Sovereign Wealth Fund Rankings, 2013. Copyright © Sovereign Wealth Fund Institute. Reproduced by permission.

services in the global community. These include many types, among which are:

- Humanitarian relief programs (such as the France-based Doctors Without Borders or British-based Oxfam)

- Economic development programs (such as the U.S.-based Bill and Melinda Gates Foundation or the Switzerland-based Aga Khan Development Network)

- Educational programs (such as Belgium-based Education International or the Switzerland-based Foundation for Education and Development)

- Civil society development programs (such as U.S.-based groups like the Global Fund for Women or the National Endowment for Democracy)

- Human rights empowerment and protection programs (like UK-based Amnesty International or U.S.-based Human Rights Watch)

- Environmental protection programs (like Friends of the Earth International or Greenpeace)

Many of these NGOs are able to accomplish things states cannot do well, or sometimes cannot do at all. For example, the use of the Internet has expanded so rapidly that state bureaucracies would have difficulty keeping up with the technological changes required to manage domains and route messages. Thus a series of NGOs has arisen to handle these matters, including the Internet Society, the Internet Architecture Board, and the Internet Engineering Task Force. Sometimes states that need help are reluctant to accept help from or be indebted to other states for political or status reasons. However, there seems to be far less stigma from accepting assistance from a nongovernmental organization. Aid from NGOs may be seen as having fewer strings or

conditions attached. For example, communist North Korea has faced famine multiple times in the neo-Westphalian period. It will not readily accept food aid from capitalist states, so food aid must be funneled through NGOs or the UN in order to be acceptable to the North Korean regime.

Individuals can be influential non-state actors as well, particularly when they work with international organizations. Celebrities can carry a lot of media attention to an issue, such as when Bono raises money for African economic development, George Clooney raises money for victims of the violence in Darfur, or Richard Gere presses for better treatment of Buddhists by the Chinese regime. Angelina Jolie brings media attention

Angelina Jolie serves as a goodwill ambassador for the UN's High Commissioner for Refugees | What can a global celebrity do for refugees like these?

Pope (now Saint) John Paul II meeting with the Communist leader of Poland as the Cold War neared its end | How did a pope help bring down a communist regime?

to the plight of many living in camps through her role as a goodwill ambassador of the United Nations High Commissioner for Refugees, much like Audrey Hepburn did before her as a goodwill ambassador for UNICEF. Religious leaders also get involved as key individuals, such as the Dalai Lama pressing the case for Tibetan independence from China or Pope John Paul II supporting Polish independence from Soviet control in the waning days of the Cold War.

Yet one does not have to be a celebrity to help change the world. Jody Williams was a teacher and an aid worker before she joined the International Campaign to Ban Landmines, and both she and the group won the Nobel Peace Prize. Norman Borlaug was an agronomist working in Mexico who pioneered new types of high-yield, disease-resistant wheat to help feed the world; he also won the Nobel Peace Prize.

Finally, some individuals become famous, or even infamous, for their impact on others. Osama bin Laden was just another wealthy young Saudi until he heard the call to go to Afghanistan and join the **mujahideen** to fight the Soviet invaders of that country in the 1980s. The mujahideen's victory over the Soviets led him to believe that, if Allah willed it, even superpowers could be defeated by the devout. Thus when the United States failed to heed his calls to leave Saudi Arabia and end its support for Israel, his group **al-Qaeda** initiated a series of terrorist attacks on the United States that ultimately left nearly 3,000 dead on September 11, 2001. Bin Laden subsequently became the "most wanted" man in the world, and many around the world were relieved (and some were joyful) when he was killed in Pakistan in 2011.

2-4c Globalization and Its Effects

Along with the relative rise of these non-state actors, a second characteristic of the neo-Westphalian system is the phenomenon called **globalization**. Globalization refers to the increasing integration of global society through economic, technological, political, and cultural means. While trade has long tied states together, these ties have become stronger in recent years, making states and peoples more interdependent on each other than ever before. Multinational corporations long ago realized that setting up subsidiaries in other states where they did business made considerable sense, so now U.S. autoworkers no longer just work for Chrysler, Ford, or General Motors. They might be making vehicles for BMW, Honda, Hyundai, Mazda, Mercedes-Benz, Mitsubishi, Nissan, Subaru, or Toyota.

Restaurant chains are another good example of global economic connections. Just stroll Paris's Avenue des Champs-Elysees from the Arc de Triomphe to the Place de la Concorde. On arguably the most famous street in France, one finds Pizza Hut and Kentucky Fried Chicken franchises. Then there's the tale of the little Japanese girl getting off the airplane from Tokyo, walking into Los Angeles International Airport, and saying, "Look, Mommy, they have McDonald's here, too!" While that story might be apocryphal, consider the facts. In 2011, McDonald's had more foreign franchises (13,053) than U.S. franchises (12,484).[10] In 2010, Yum! Brands made more money from its 3,700 KFC and Pizza Hut franchises in China than it did from the 19,000 KFC, Pizza Hut, Taco Bell, Long John Silver's, and A&W franchises it owned in the United States.[11] Globally, Subway has more than 28,000 restaurants in 86 countries.[12]

Relatively recent technological innovations spurred the rate of such global interconnections. For over 100 years, transportation technologies were essentially limited to how fast trains could run or ships could sail. Then came the airplane. With the development of

mujahideen those who fight to liberate Muslims or traditionally Muslim lands from control by nonbelievers; the insurgency resisting the Soviet invasion of Afghanistan is the most widely known example.

al-Qaeda translated as "the base," this is an fundamentalist Islamic transnational terrorist organization. It is responsible for many attacks on Western countries and moderate Islamic countries. Most infamously, it organized, funded, and perpetrated the September 11, 2001, attacks in the United States.

globalization the increasing integration of global society through the spread of technology, foreign trade, transportation, cultural exchange, political institutions, and social connections.

"Fulla," a Barbie-like doll designed to capture the attention of Muslim girls | Why does the Muslim world need an alternative to Barbie dolls?

A woman in rural India with her mobile phone | Is there anywhere mobile phones aren't found?

modern jet air travel, now one can go from one side of the world to the other in about a day. Even when flying to and from non-hub airports, travel time is still considerably faster than ever before. For example, flying from Lincoln, Nebraska, to Kinshasa, Democratic Congo, can be done in as few as 22.5 hours—with the right flight connections—or it can take as long as 42 hours. Still, getting from the middle of the United States to the middle of Africa in less than two days would shock nineteenth-century travelers.

Arguably, even more important than air travel is the lower cost of moving freight on a global basis. This was first noticeable with the development of larger and larger oil tanker ships, as they became so large that they could not transit important passages like the Suez Canal. These vessels carrying larger liquid cargoes at a lower unit cost were followed by the development of modern container ships. Carrying pre-loaded containers of a standard size lowered the cost of shipping by making it easier and faster to load and unload such cargo vessels, and the less time ships are in port the more time they are at sea making money. As transoceanic transport ships increased in size and speed, the cost of doing business around the world dropped significantly, and firms found it increasingly cost-effective to locate their operations and sell their products in many different countries.

Communication technologies have also been transformed. Improvements in mobile phone technologies in the last few decades lowered the cost to communicate over wide distances so that most people on the planet can now afford to own mobile phones. The global population is now over 7 billion, and the number of mobile phones expected to be in use by the end of 2014 is 7.3 billion.[13] Thus it is nearly as common to see mobile phone usage in urban areas of developing states as it is in the richest societies on the planet.

Information technologies have also evolved. Two generations ago, typical television viewers were limited to local over-the-air broadcasts; rarely did such signals travel more than seventy-five miles. With the advent of cable and satellite television, viewers can watch channels from all over their country, the region, or the world. For example, a family in Beirut with a satellite dish might watch daily news programming from the Qatar-based al Jazeera network, family programming on French channel Cinépop, and American movies on HBO or Showtime, while the teens might slip into another room to watch videos on MTV, VH-1, or YouTube!

Then there are the movies. With only a few exceptions (like India's "Bollywood" or China's film industry), moviemakers now go after the global market. For example, in 2013 *Iron Man 3* led the world in box office gross receipts at $1.2 billion; of that total, $409 million was made in the United States and $791 million was made outside the United States. All of the top sixteen grossing films of 2013 (in descending order, *Iron Man 3, Despicable Me 2, The Hunger Games: Catching Fire, Fast & Furious 6, The Hobbit: The Desolation of Smaug, Monsters University, Gravity, Man of Steel, Frozen, Thor: The Dark World, The Croods, World War Z, Oz the Great and Powerful, Star Trek Into Darkness, The Wolverine,* and *Pacific Rim*) sold more tickets outside the United States than inside.[14] All-time worldwide box office grosses are even more indicative of the power of the global movie market. The top five highest-grossing movies of all time (as of early 2014) are, in order: *Avatar* (2009), *Titanic* (1997), *Marvel's The Avengers* (2012), *Harry Potter and the Deathly Hallows—Part 2* (2011), *Iron Man 3* (2013), and *Transformers: Dark of the Moon* (2011). All of these films sold more tickets abroad than in the United States.[15] Thus when conservatives in non-Western societies complain about foreign ideas and values undermining their culture, the impact of movies and television are often cited as examples.

The Internet clearly plays into this argument, as well. The ability to access all that is on the information superhighway is also now a global phenomenon. In 1990, there were only 2 million Internet users worldwide. By 2012, it had more than quintupled to over 2.4 billion users worldwide, with Asia leading the world with one billion users, Europe second at over 500 million, North America third at 274 million, and Latin America and the Caribbean fourth at 255 million.[16] A consequence of this openness is that regimes have less control over information than before. China and Google have repeatedly struggled over the Chinese regime's desire to put parts of the Internet off-limits to Chinese users, and in 2011 Egypt's military-dominated regime learned that populist revolutions can be organized via online social media.

The combination of satellite television and the Internet has revolutionized global information sharing. Now very few places can be considered remote. International news channels, whether using broadband or satellite transmissions, can show riots in Greece or Thailand in real-time streaming video. English-language newspapers are available online for all regions of the world and most individual states. The Westphalian emphasis on borders and preventing interventions into one's own domestic affairs has been rendered far less relevant by these technological innovations.

In short, globalization means international interactions are easier and far more commonplace. As a result, international interdependence is clearer than ever to see. What happens in one state or region of the world influences others in ways that are hard to ignore, and vice versa. The Westphalian distinction between foreign and domestic becomes harder to discern. Yet evaluating globalization from a normative perspective is difficult, as it produces effects that are both positive and negative. As a think tank report points out:

> The globalized world sweeps away regulation and undermines local and national politics, just as the consolidation of the nation state swept away local economies, dialects, cultures and political forms. Globalization creates new markets and wealth, even as it causes widespread suffering, disorder, and unrest. It is both a source of repression and a catalyst for global movements of social justice and emancipation. The great financial crisis of 2008–2009 has revealed the dangers of an unstable, deregulated, global economy but it has also given rise to important global initiatives for change.[17]

2-4d New Stresses on States

The third major characteristic of the neo-Westphalian system is an increase in the numbers and types of stresses on states. Borders drawn on maps become less meaningful, as groups within states identify more with others based on geography, tribe, clan, or religion. In Norway, domestic terrorists rely on violence to press their political agenda against what they see as the "Muslimization of Europe." In France, Corsicans press for autonomy for their island and citizens of Algerian descent agitate for greater acceptance within French society. In Russia, Chechen and Dagestani suicide bombers attack subways and train stations, seeking independence or revenge for loved ones lost in Russian counterterrorist operations. In Ukraine, Russian-speaking people in the eastern provinces seek greater autonomy, and even integrations into Russia. In the eastern fringes of the Democratic Republic of the Congo (DRC), Tutsi militias attack non-Tutsi communities, killing or enslaving the innocent, which prompts elements of the Rwandan army to intervene in the DRC in search of the Tutsi militants. Muslim militias target Christians in both Nigeria and Central African Republic, prompting Christian militias to respond in kind. In Iraq, Sunni groups rebel against the Shiite-dominated regime, and target Kurdish populations in the north, while in Israel and the Palestinian Territories, violent struggle continues between Israelis and Arabs. Finally across the board, Islamist groups inspired by or networked with al-Qaeda launch attacks in the United States, United Kingdom, Spain, Saudi Arabia, Yemen, Iraq, Syria, Pakistan, Afghanistan, the Philippines, and Indonesia.

Beyond such violence, internal economic threats arise as non-state actors pursue their own agendas. In 2005, the government of the Iraqi province of Kurdistan signed a contract with Norwegian oil company DNO to develop oil fields there, despite the fact that no laws had yet been passed determining who had the legal rights to develop Iraq's oil reserves. That multimillion-dollar deal would have been advantageous to DNO and Kurdistan, but it was clearly contrary to the national interests of Iraq. The contract was subsequently cancelled by the national government in Baghdad, and DNO was forced to pay damages to Iraq.[18] In 2011, ExxonMobil began investigating oil deals in Iraq's Kurdistan region, again without the blessing of Iraq's central government! In the United States, investment firms seeking to maximize their profits in real estate and real estate derivative securities minimized or hid the risks from investors. While a number of these firms made impressive profits, the resulting housing collapse of 2008 undermined the national and global credit markets, created the Great Recession of 2008–2010, and put both the national and global economy in danger.

In the neo-Westphalian system, external pressures buffet states, as well. Economic crises often force states to turn to the International Monetary Fund (IMF) to stop runs on their currency, as did several Asian states in 1997. The IMF ultimately put together aid packages totaling over $100 billion to bail out the currencies of Indonesia, South Korea, and Thailand, which were rapidly becoming worthless. In 1998, the IMF lent $22 billion to Russia to stop a similar run on its currency. Not only are these loans that must be repaid, they come with conditions on what the recipients must do to put their economies on a sounder footing—steps that often generate widespread opposition at home. Since 1999, seventeen European Union members have formed a Eurozone, in which they share the euro as their common currency. However, the Great Recession of 2008–2010 exposed fundamental weaknesses in the economies of Greece, Spain, Portugal, Italy, Ireland, and more recently, in France. With some states facing bankruptcy, the EU, the European Central Bank, and the IMF forced painful budget cuts on regimes in return for financial bailouts. The resulting domestic protests over the social impact of slashing government budgets contributed to changes to the parties in power in eight states (Greece, Ireland, Italy, Portugal, Spain, Slovenia, Slovakia, and the Netherlands).

External pressures on states may be political as well as economic. For example, Amnesty International is often successful precisely because it focuses unwanted attention on states that incarcerate political prisoners. In recent years, the following have been targeted for pressure by Amnesty International: Belarus for violating Europe's rejection of capital punishment, China for its imprisonment of dissidents, Honduras for human rights abuses, Israel for its use of lethal force against Palestinian civilians in the Gaza Strip, Saudi Arabia for its disproportionate execution of foreign nationals, and the United States for the widespread use by police of chemical sprays and stun guns. At some point, regimes will often change their behavior to get the media spotlight to move on to another target.

Even well-intentioned acts can pressure states. For example, most in the West would assume that free and fair elections and the creation of **civil society organizations** represent positive advancements in a society. However, the Russian regime takes a different view. Most observers questioned the legitimacy of Russia's presidential election returns in both 2008 and 2012. Local protests of those elections were broken up by Russian security forces, and the rights of protesters were restricted by new, tougher laws. Russian civil society groups were also targeted with new restrictions, including being classified as "foreign agents" if they accepted funding from foreign entities. In 2013, hundreds of Russian civil

©Kojoku/Shutterstock.com

Police detain participants of the demonstration against newly elected president Vladimir Putin on May 6, 2012, in Moscow, Russia | Why did President Vladimir Putin's 2012 election spark violent demonstrations?

civil society organizations NGOs that voluntarily work together to serve the greater social and political good within a society; they build the voluntary relationships that bind society and its members together.

society groups were subjected to surprise inspections by Russian prosecutors looking for any type of violations of laws or regulations, a move seen by most as an effort to make it harder for those groups to operate at all. Also, the U.S. Agency for International Development was prohibited from funding any projects in Russia and UNICEF was ordered to cease its operations there as well. In short, Vladimir Putin's regime resorted to extreme measures to keep its domestic and foreign critics in check.

2-4e The Changing Meaning of Sovereignty

A fourth and final hallmark of the neo-Westphalian system is a fundamental change in what sovereignty means. Westphalian sovereignty was clear. Inside one's borders, there was no higher authority than the state. States had no right to intervene in other states' internal affairs. However, the results of World War II opened the door to seeing sovereignty differently. How Germany treated Jews, Roma peoples (also known as Gypsies), homosexuals, and others was sufficiently horrible to lead others to say that such actions were wrong, regardless of whether they occurred within a state's borders or not. Later events at the dawn of the neo-Westphalian period would reinforce this idea.

For example, in 1990, Iraq invaded and occupied Kuwait. When Iraqi forces were expelled from Kuwait, Iraqi Shi'ites and Kurds tried to break free from Saddam Hussein's Sunni-based Iraqi regime. The returning Iraqi military forces turned on those Iraqi citizens, as Iraqi forces had previously done in the 1988 Anfal campaign in which conventional and chemical warfare attacks killed at least 50,000 Kurds and possibly as many as 180,000.[19] Even though this Iraqi use of force was inside its own borders, the international community acted. In 1991, the UN passed **UN Security Council Resolution 688**, which authorized the UN and its members to intervene in Iraq to protect Iraq's citizens from their own government. Similarly, that same year the government of Somalia was overthrown, a civil war resulted, and no group was able to govern the country. Civilian refugees needed international aid to survive, and in 1992 the UN Security Council passed a number of resolutions authorizing a military intervention into Somalia to ensure that humanitarian supplies got to those refugees. In 1992, war broke out in the former Yugoslavian territory of Bosnia-Herzegovina, and **ethnic cleansing** ensued, whereby one ethnic group (be it the Bosnian Serbs, the Bosnian Croatians, or the Bosnian Muslims) would purge or "cleanse" an area of its rivals by forced expulsion, violence, or death. Again, the UN declared this practice to be illegal under international law, thereby justifying intervention by outsiders. The **genocide** in Rwanda in 1994, which resulted in at least 800,000 dead and possibly hundreds of thousands more, just contributed to this momentum.[20] In short, in the early 1990s it became increasingly clear that populations at times needed protection their government could not provide or even protection from their own government. These operations were termed **humanitarian interventions**.

In 1995, the UN Secretary-General's Special Representative for Internally Displaced Persons, Sudanese diplomat Francis Deng, first coined the idea of **responsible sovereignty**.[21] He argued that the Westphalian idea of sovereignty as a state's responsibility to control its borders and protect its territory had to give way to the idea of sovereignty as the responsibility of a state to protect its citizens (**neo-Westphalian sovereignty**). At the 2005 UN General Assembly meeting, world leaders agreed that if a state did not meet its responsibility "to protect its populations from genocide, war crimes, ethnic cleansing, and crimes against humanity," it was up to others to step in and do it themselves.[22] Increasingly, the idea of protecting one's citizens evolved past physical protection from violence in the form of international security; to some it also implied protecting one's citizens from other common threats—like economic deprivation, environmental threats, and so on—or economic and human security as we call them in this text.[23] While some states did not give up the narrower view of Westphalian sovereignty, the broader concept of responsible sovereignty became more firmly entrenched as a norm of the

UN Security Council Resolution 688 a 1991 resolution authorizing UN members to intervene in the domestic affairs of Iraq.

ethnic cleansing a form of violence in which an ethnic group purges or cleans a territory of its rival ethnic groups, by forced expulsion, violence, or death.

genocide the act of killing an entire group of people (such as a nation, an ethic group, a religion, a cultural group, etc.) because of who they are and not because of something they have done.

humanitarian interventions military or non-military interventions into a state by outside groups for the purpose of protecting endangered people and meeting the needs of the state's residents.

responsible sovereignty the idea of sovereignty as a state's responsibility to protect its citizens.

neo-Westphalian sovereignty the idea of sovereignty as a state's responsibility to protect its citizens.

neo-Westphalian system. In short, states could no longer do whatever they wanted within their own borders without eliciting potential interventions from others in the international system.

The bottom line is some issues are clearly transnational now. International security, economic security, and human security matters now often transcend national boundaries. As we will see later in Part Four of our text, issues in the global commons—those areas not controlled by any one state and shared by all—confound the ability of single actors to deal with them. Issues like international terrorism, crime, pollution, and humanitarian protection present complex challenges to the global community.

In essence, the neo-Westphalian system has been transformed, and is still being transformed, by significant changes in the norms or rules by which international politics is conducted. For example, views on the use of force have changed. In the early 20th century, U.S. President Theodore Roosevelt could champion speaking softly but carrying a big stick. Those who possessed sufficient force routinely threatened its use or actually used it; it seemed as natural at the time as the evolutionary phrase "survival of the fittest" and was captured by the notion of **Social Darwinism**. Today, force is viewed as a legitimate state action only if used in self-defense or as a last resort when stakes are high. Otherwise, those who violate these norms risk being viewed as aggressors, who might then face punishment from others in the international system. Deciding how to respond to situations in which people are at risk often depends on the theoretical approaches decision makers employ, as the box on Theory in Action: Responsible Sovereignty and Humanitarian Interventions suggests.

Other norms that arose during the late Westphalian era have taken on new importance in the neo-Westphalian system. For example, **supranational regimes** (IOs whose rules can override those of their member states in limited circumstances) are becoming somewhat more commonplace. For example, the **Nuclear Non-Proliferation Regime** is a set of rules for how states develop, maintain, and regulate nuclear power and nuclear materials. Those who have signed and ratified the **Nuclear Non-Proliferation Treaty** agree not to develop nuclear weapons if they have not previously done so and also agree to spread nuclear technology only under rules specified by the International Atomic Energy Agency.[24] Another example of a supranational regime is the **World Trade Organization**, which supports and develops the free-trade regime in world politics.[25] To promote and support free trade and more open economies, the WTO makes the rules of trade for its 159 state members, administers those rules, and authorizes penalties against those states that violate its rules. While supranational regimes like these deal with a limited set of issues, others deal with an array of issues across a specified geographic jurisdiction. A good example is the **European Union (EU)**, an IO that can make decisions on a variety of issues that constrain its twenty-seven member states.[26]

CONCLUSION: SAME PLAYERS BUT A CHANGING FIELD?

By and large, the same types of actors found in prior periods are found in the current neo-Westphalian international system: states and non-state actors like IOs, NGOs, multinational corporations, transnational networks, and individuals (Figure 2-2). However, their numbers and political significance have changed. States are still the most significant actors in the system, but in relative terms their ability to dominate the international system has decreased somewhat as the power of non-state actors has increased. IOs, NGOs, multinational corporations, transnational networks, and notable individuals are rapidly rising in both numbers and influence, and at times they rival the power of some states. Under certain circumstances, non-state actors can do things that states cannot or will not do, and thus they supersede states in influence at times.

Social Darwinism the idea of the "survival of the fittest" applied to international politics.

supranational regimes international organizations or sets of rules that can bind states even against their will.

Nuclear Non-Proliferation Regime a formal treaty and its related rules set by the International Atomic Energy Agency regulating how states may develop, maintain, and use nuclear power and nuclear materials.

Nuclear Non-Proliferation Treaty a treaty prohibiting those with nuclear weapons from providing them to others and those without nuclear weapons from seeking them.

World Trade Organization a supranational organization that promotes free trade between member countries, sets the rules for international trade, administers them, and authorizes penalties for states that violate them. The WTO replaced the GATT in 1995.

European Union (EU) a supranational organization with 27 member states.

Responsible Sovereignty and Humanitarian Interventions

The theory of responsible sovereignty is a radical departure from prior notions of sovereignty. Under Westphalian sovereignty, state borders were to be clear demarcations separating the domestic and international arenas. As noted earlier, Article 2 of the UN Charter reaffirms that states are not to intervene in the domestic affairs of any other states. However, the end of the Cold War coincided with a number of instances in which state regimes preyed on their own people or could not protect their people from becoming victims of violence within their borders. While a limited multinational effort helped protect some Iraqi Kurds from the Iraqi military from 1991–1997, the international community had little response to genocidal violence in the Bosnian civil war from 1992–1995 or the Rwandan genocide in 1994. As a result, in 1995, Francis Deng proposed that states should intervene when regimes will not or cannot protect their citizens.

Yet the number of successful humanitarian interventions since 1995 arguably seems quite small. The United States and NATO intervened in Yugoslavia in 1999, Australia intervened in East Timor in 1999, the United Kingdom intervened in Sierra Leone in 2000, the African Union intervened briefly in the Darfur and Burundi conflicts in 2003 and again in Darfur in 2008 as part of a joint AU/UN force, the United States intervened briefly in Haiti in 2004, NATO intervened in Libya in 2011, and one might consider the U.S.-led effort to change regimes in Iraq in 2003 a successful humanitarian intervention in the sense that some saw it as a way to protect the Iraqi people from a brutal regime.

By contrast, the number of instances where citizens go unprotected and either no one intervenes or the intervention is unsuccessful seems quite large. Cases could be made for the need for humanitarian interventions in a variety of places since 1995. A partial list would include the Democratic Republic of the Congo, Central African Republic, Burundi, Sudan, Uganda, Zimbabwe, and Somalia in Africa. It could also include Afghanistan, Pakistan, Syria, and North Korea in Asia, and Haiti again in Latin America. The list could also include specific troubled regions of otherwise stable states—like the northern Caucasus region of Russia (in Chechnya and Dagestan, for example) or northern Mexico, where the government has lost control of some areas to violent drug cartels.

So what is stopping such interventions? IOs cannot intervene unless their members provide the military personnel and are willing to pay the costs of the operation. Few such instances can be found. States with the wealth and military power to do so often do not define these situations as vital to their national interests, and, as such, they are largely unwilling to act. Simply put, these situations are not deemed to be worthy of their cost in lives and treasure. In select instances, the state that would be the target of the intervention rejects what it sees as external interference, as would be the case in Russia, for example.

1. So what do you think? How do you see the world and world politics? Should nationalism (and national interests) trump our humanitarian impulses?

2. What is our responsibility to others?

3. What are human lives worth? Does it depend on who and where they are?

4. Is responsible sovereignty a concept whose time has not yet come?

We'll see in the next two chapters that your answers may depend on which international relations theories make the most sense to you.

Source: James Kurth. "Humanitarian Intervention after Iraq: Legal Ideals vs. Military Realities." *Orbis* 50 (2006): 87–101.

Perhaps more noticeable are the changes in the relationships that also comprise the international system. Norms have changed, with new restrictions on the actions of states. It is no longer acceptable for the strong to push around the weak. Genocide or crimes against noncombatants are not acceptable just because they happen inside a state's borders. States are increasingly being held responsible to protect their populations and to meet their minimum human needs, and thus the concept of responsible sovereignty now exists alongside Westphalian notions of sovereignty. States see benefits in joining supranational organizations that may, at times, tell them that they cannot do what they want. The end of the Westphalian international system opened the door to numerous changes in

FIGURE 2-2   INTERNATIONAL SYSTEMS TIMELINE

International Systems Timeline

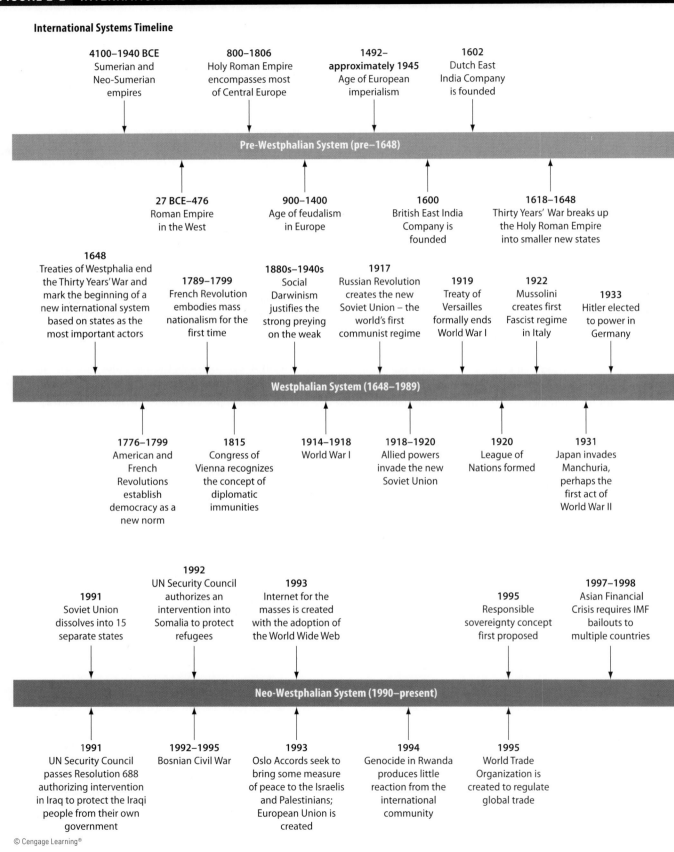

© Cengage Learning®

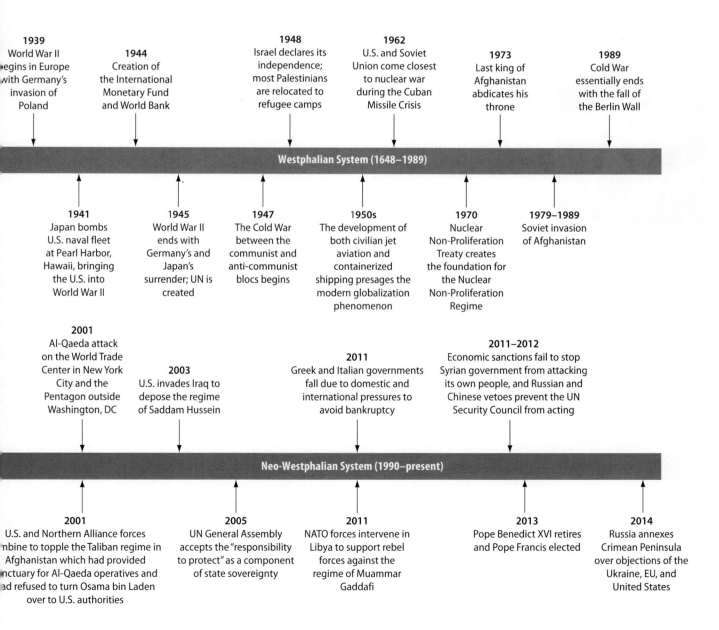

1939
World War II begins in Europe with Germany's invasion of Poland

1944
Creation of the International Monetary Fund and World Bank

1948
Israel declares its independence; most Palestinians are relocated to refugee camps

1962
U.S. and Soviet Union come closest to nuclear war during the Cuban Missile Crisis

1973
Last king of Afghanistan abdicates his throne

1989
Cold War essentially ends with the fall of the Berlin Wall

Westphalian System (1648–1989)

1941
Japan bombs U.S. naval fleet at Pearl Harbor, Hawaii, bringing the U.S. into World War II

1945
World War II ends with Germany's and Japan's surrender; UN is created

1947
The Cold War between the communist and anti-communist blocs begins

1950s
The development of both civilian jet aviation and containerized shipping presages the modern globalization phenomenon

1970
Nuclear Non-Proliferation Treaty creates the foundation for the Nuclear Non-Proliferation Regime

1979–1989
Soviet invasion of Afghanistan

2001
Al-Qaeda attack on the World Trade Center in New York City and the Pentagon outside Washington, DC

2003
U.S. invades Iraq to depose the regime of Saddam Hussein

2011
Greek and Italian governments fall due to domestic and international pressures to avoid bankruptcy

2011–2012
Economic sanctions fail to stop Syrian government from attacking its own people, and Russian and Chinese vetoes prevent the UN Security Council from acting

Neo-Westphalian System (1990–present)

2001
U.S. and Northern Alliance forces combine to topple the Taliban regime in Afghanistan which had provided sanctuary for Al-Qaeda operatives and had refused to turn Osama bin Laden over to U.S. authorities

2005
UN General Assembly accepts the "responsibility to protect" as a component of state sovereignty

2011
NATO forces intervene in Libya to support rebel forces against the regime of Muammar Gaddafi

2013
Pope Benedict XVI retires and Pope Francis elected

2014
Russia annexes Crimean Peninsula over objections of the Ukraine, EU, and United States

how international politics is routinely conducted and in how security is defined and protected. So what do such changes suggest regarding the roles played by anarchy, diversity, and complexity in the current international system? How you make sense of these changes—and their meanings—may depend on the degree to which you see these events through realist, liberal, constructivist, feminist, or other lenses, and we turn to those next.

John Mearsheimer

THINK ABOUT THIS ARE STATES STILL THE MOST IMPORTANT PLAYERS IN WORLD POLITICS?

Scholars studying world politics have long focused on the sovereign state as the main, even only, important actor in the international system. Well-known modern realist theorists such as Hans Morgenthau, Kenneth Waltz, and John Mearsheimer place the state at the center of all that really matters in world politics. However, in the last several decades, other scholars have seen things differently. People such as Richard Rosecrance questioned the basis of state power, and others such as Robert Keohane and Joseph Nye, Margaret Keck and Kathryn Sikkink, and Alexander Wendt have increasingly focused on the role and influence of non-state actors.

Kathryn Sikkink

Now that you have read and thought about our discussion of the playing field and actors in world politics, as well as the trends and evolution that have occurred, what do you think?

In what ways are states still the most important players in world politics, and in what ways are they limited and challenged by non-state actors?

STUDY TOOLS 2

LOCATED AT BACK OF THE BOOK:
☐ Rip out Chapter in Review card

LOCATED ON COURSEMATE:
Use the CourseMate access card that came with this book or visit CengageBrain.com for more review materials:
☐ Review Key Terms Flash Cards (Print or Online)
☐ Download Chapter Summaries for on-the-go review

☐ Complete Practice Quizzes and Crossword Puzzles to prepare for the test
☐ Walk through a Simulation, Animated Learning Module, and Interactive Maps and Timelines to master concepts
☐ Watch the videos for real-world application of this chapter's content
☐ Visit IR NewsWatch to learn about the latest current events as you prepare for class discussions and papers

1. What are the major types of actors in the international system?

2. What do key terms like *anarchy, interdependence*, the *security dilemma*, and *globalization* mean?

3. What made the Westphalian system different from the pre-Westphalian system and the neo-Westphalian system?

4. What are the major features of diplomacy and how have they evolved from the pre-Westphalian to neo-Westphalian systems?

5. Why have states managed to be the most significant international actors for hundreds of years, and how might that be changing?

6. What major events or developments mark each of these three international systems over time?

FOR MORE INFORMATION . . .

For more on:

States, try the CIA's *The World Factbook*, which includes basic information on all states and a number of other specific territorial units (like Hong Kong, for example), available at https://www.cia.gov/library /publications/the-world-factbook/index.html.

IOs, see the list provided by the staff at the Northwestern University library, available at http://libguides.northwestern.edu/IGO.

NGOs associated with the UN, see the listings and links available at http://www.ngo.org/index2.htm.

Multinational corporations, see at least a partial listing of MNCs at http://en.wikipedia.org/wiki /List_of_multinational_corporations.

Nobel Peace Prize recipients, see the listing at: http://nobelprizes.com/nobel/peace/.

3 | Powerful Ideas:
Realism, Liberalism, and Constructivism

LEARNING OBJECTIVES
After studying this chapter, you will be able to . . .

3-1 Identify the nature and use of theory and describe the components of theory.

3-2 Explain the foundations of the realist approach in terms of its conception of (a) the nature of the international system, (b) its relevant actors, (c) important resources, and (d) central dynamics.

3-3 Explain the foundations of the liberal approach in terms of its conceptions of (a) the nature of the international system, (b) its relevant actors, (c) important resources, and (d) central dynamics.

3-4 Explain the foundations of the constructivist approach in terms of its conception of (a) the nature of the international system, (b) its relevant actors, (c) important resources, and (d) central dynamics.

3-5 Assess the uses and applications of each approach as contending and complementary lenses for understanding international relations.

After finishing this chapter go to **PAGE 82** for **STUDY TOOLS**

EXPLAINING A "DEMOCRATIC PEACE"

Since 1945, a significant and growing body of empirical evidence presents some intriguing findings regarding regime types, the outbreak of war, and the resulting casualty counts. First, democracies have been involved in, and have even started, wars with nondemocratic countries. For example, the United States has been engaged in militarized disputes over 500 times since the late nineteenth century and has used military force 383 times between 1945 and 2000.[1] The United Kingdom and France have been involved in militarized conflicts with other nations more than any other state, and they are two of the three oldest democracies in the world.

Second, wars in which one country is a democracy tend to incur many more battle deaths than wars between two nondemocracies. That is, a war between two autocracies is usually much less bloody than a war between an autocracy and a democracy.

Third, nondemocratic countries have warred with each other regularly. Yet *two stable democracies do not appear to have ever gone to war with each other*.[2] Thus, there seems to be something to the idea of a **democratic peace**. In addition to not fighting with each other, democracies also seem less likely even to threaten each other with the use of force or sanction each other, and their diplomatic disputes tend to be settled more peacefully and quickly.

1. What factors might explain these patterns?

2. If democracies are more peaceful, then why are their wars with autocracies so bloody?

3. Are democracies really *more* peaceful?

democratic peace state-level theory of war stating that institutional and normative characteristics of democratic regimes lead them to peaceful relations with each other.

©iStock.com/amck

What best explains the role and consequences of weapons such as nuclear missiles?

INTRODUCTION: POWERFUL IDEAS

The playing field of world politics is terribly complicated, as we explained in the preceding chapter. It combines a number of structural characteristics, a wide variety of actors, and a broad range of activities into a complex mix that is often hard to comprehend. How is one to make sense of the complex international system, international actors, and interactions—doing more than merely describing events that occur? The short answer is through the use of theory—an analytical tool essential for the explanation of complex realities.

3-1 THEORY AND INTERNATIONAL RELATIONS

The idea of theory may seem daunting or perhaps even boring, but it is simply a way to explain the world around us. Theorizing is something we all do every day, whether

we know it or not. Truly, facts—or, in the case of international relations, the behavior of international actors—have little meaning without an explanation (theory) to connect them. For example, Russia's actions to annex Crimea, part of Ukraine, in 2014 are simply fact. However, those facts mean something more if one understood that states compete with each other in the international arena, or that Russia has long sought to maintain friendly regimes and control over countries around its periphery, or that eastern Ukraine and the Crimea region are heavily populated by people of Russian descent. In short, explaining Russia's actions—and even predicting its next steps—demands that we think about cause-and-effect relationships.

This is theory—an explanation of how events and actions fit together. Theorizing is essential to any effort to understand why international actors behave the way they do; why the events and actions that make up world politics occur; and what they mean. In the next two chapters, we consider a number of theoretical perspectives that offer explanations for the complicated dynamics of world politics. In this chapter, we compare three central approaches—realism, liberalism and constructivism; in the next, we examine several additional alternatives—feminist theory, Marxist-based theories, and foreign policy decision-making approaches. These perspectives highlight different aspects of world politics and provide sometimes complementary but more often contending explanations for the behavior, patterns, and outcomes we observe in the international system.

3-1a Thinking Theoretically

To begin, let's first consider the meaning of theory and theorizing. As we have suggested, theory is an explanation for connecting events, actions, behaviors, and outcomes. More specifically, it is a set of analytical tools for understanding the cause-and-effect relationships between phenomena. For example, as you worked your way through the democratic peace exercise at the top of this chapter, you engaged in theorizing about world politics. Indeed, people theorize every day, sometimes explicitly, more often implicitly, sometimes naively, and sometimes with great sophistication. In some respects, virtually every decision humans make involves theorizing at some level, from diagnosing why the car failed to start in the morning (a cause-and-effect model: is it the battery, the starter, or is the car out of gas?) to determining why you did not do as well on an exam as you anticipated (did you fail to study or get sufficient sleep the night before, did you misunderstand the instructions on how to prepare for the exam, or were the instructions confusing?).

Policymakers also rely on and are influenced by theories of various kinds. For example, world leaders must understand some economic theory so they can construct policies that help their economies grow. The 2008–2010 stimulus packages adopted by the United States and many other countries to counter flagging economic growth were enacted because leaders in many countries believed that putting money into a recessionary economy would help spur its growth, not unlike shocking a patient whose heart has stopped or priming an old-fashioned water pump. Similarly, when the UN authorizes economic sanctions against Iran, or NATO implements sanctions against Russia, they do so hoping that the economic pressure from the sanctions will lead those countries to change their behavior. Each of these policy actions is based on a theory.

3-1b The Analytical Uses of Theory

As analysts, we depend on theory to explain the choices of policymakers and the consequences of policies they enact. Why did the Soviet Union seek a nonaggression pact with Nazi Germany before World War II when the two countries appeared to be rivals—maybe even

David Silverman/Getty Images

Israel breaks ground for new section of West Bank Barrier | What are the consequences of Israeli decisions to build settlements on territory claimed by Palestinians?

outright enemies—up to that point? What led American leaders to believe the United States, Canada, and Mexico would all benefit from a free-trade agreement linking their economies? Why do Israeli leaders keep building residential settlements in areas claimed by Palestinians, knowing that such construction will alarm not only the Palestinian people but also many others in the world? What led President Obama to send more troops to Afghanistan in 2009–2010? Why did the Russians deploy troops into Ukraine and annex Crimea in 2014? We cannot answer these questions without relying on theory.

As we discussed briefly in Chapter 1, theory is a way to explain the patterns of world politics—or any other subject area for that matter—and theories help us to make strategic simplifications of the world to bring important features into clearer focus. In fact, one useful way to understand theories of world politics is to think of them as lenses, such as those you might find in a good pair of sunglasses. If it is too bright, you can't see very well, but with good sunglasses, you can see and understand the world around you. Moreover, the lenses in sunglasses come in a variety of colors, and each shade filters out a different portion of the light in order to sharpen and improve vision, so each pair lets you see the same world around you in a different way. In effect, theory simplifies reality to reduce the "glare of the sun" and to sharpen the clarity of key factors. This aids in the explanation of the most important behaviors and even the prediction of likely developments.

A similar metaphor is sitting in a very loud restaurant. Perhaps there is loud music, crying babies, or worse, both. The noise is so loud that you cannot hear your friends talk. The white noise in the restaurant is like a bunch of irrelevant facts. To understand the strong relationship between the United States and Canada, does it help to know that both flags have white and red or that the Canadian flag has a maple leaf on it while the American flag has stars? Of course not—that information is simply white noise. Theory simplifies reality by cutting out all of that unneeded information so that we can better understand the important forces at work in the world, just like turning down the music and quieting the unhappy babies in the restaurant would let you hear your friends better.

As a simplifying device intended to improve understanding of complex reality, theory has particular meaning for the study of the empirical—or real—world. Contrary to popular usage (e.g., "oh, that is just a theory . . ."), which often casts theory as something fictional or unrelated to "reality," empirical theory is really just a cause-and-effect explanation of real or observable phenomena in the world that addresses "why" questions, not "what happened" questions. For example, let's go back to our opening puzzle about peace between democracies. Theory is the explanation we offer to the question of *why* democratic countries apparently do not go to war with each other. **Empirical theory** links important aspects of the world to outcomes and specifies the mechanisms that link the two. As important, empirical theory allows us to test those explanations against the events that happen in the real world to gauge the theory's utility or value. Thus, empirical theory differs from **normative theory**, which seeks to advocate how the political world *should be* and is often referred to as political philosophy.

3-1c Theory and Causation: The Components of Theory

Empirical theory aims at explaining *causal* relationships and patterns among the phenomena being studied. This is a difficult task because of the complexity of the world and, unlike theory in other sciences, it is difficult, even impossible, to create and manage laboratory experiments that allow us to isolate cause and effect as one might do in a study of disease or nuclear physics. And one can almost never repeat an experiment to retest empirical findings in world politics—imagine the absurdity of attempting to rerun the 1982 Falkland Islands war between Argentina and the United Kingdom!

With these difficulties in mind, social scientists stress three fundamental requirements that increase our confidence when we claim causality in the social world.

Cause and Effect | Sometimes a causal chain is simple, and other times it is very complex.

Think in terms of two factors, A (cause) and B (effect), which you think are related:

- A and B must change together, or you cannot claim that one causes change in another—this is called *covariance*.

- A must come before B in time because causes must come before effects or they cannot be causes.

- Other plausible or likely causes of B (say, C, D, E, and F) must be eliminated or accounted for as best as possible in order to isolate the true impact of A on B—this is called *nonspuriousness*.

There are other considerations that affect the quality and utility of a theory, but these three requirements are essential.

With these essentials for causal argument in mind, theory identifies a set of concepts (e.g., democratic governments, war), specifies their interrelationships (peaceful relations), and, most importantly, *explains the reasons* for those relationships. A theory links these concepts, relationships, and explanations with hypotheses: if–then statements about particular relationships and outcomes that should be observable in reality if the explanation, or theory, is useful. For example, "if two countries are democratic, then they will choose not to fight each other." As such, theory involves three central

empirical theory theory based on real-world observations and explanations.

normative theory theory based on prescription and advocacy of preferred outcomes.

elements: description, explanation, and prediction. Theory also usually offers a basis for prescription as well, but we regard that as a secondary by-product of these three main components. Let us briefly consider each of these elements.

DESCRIPTION Theory directs attention to particular aspects of the world that are most important to the phenomenon in question. It tells us which facts are important. As such, it offers a descriptive element, but it is not mere description. Indeed, as one of our former professors used to emphasize to us, "facts without theory are trivia." They are dots without any connections. For example, if you see a man wearing a hockey goalie's mask, carrying an ax, and running down the street, you might conclude that either he is insane or it is Halloween. Both conclusions require a theory to connect the person with your conclusion. To theorize is to move up the ladder of abstraction from simple description to *selective* description of those aspects of reality that are most important. In part, this requires observers to see individual events as part of classes or types of events in order to gain perspective on the enormously complicated world around us.

EXPLANATION Theory provides cause-and-effect explanations of the linkages between those aspects of the world on which it focuses. As such, theory provides answers to why those descriptive concepts are linked. For example, the mere statement that democracies do not go to war with each other is not a theory. A theory is constructed if you said: (1) in democracies leaders are constrained by and answerable to the people who elect them, and (2) consequently, when two democratic countries are in a dispute, both leaders are constrained by their electorates and less able to go to war. Note that in the first case, we simply offered a description of an empirical observation: democracies don't fight each other. In the second case, we are provided with a potential explanation for why democracies do not fight one another. Explanation is fundamental to theorizing. The most important role theories play is to explain what happens in the real world.

PREDICTION Theory provides a basis for anticipating future events and developments. This aspect of theory is really a derivative of the first two—knowing what to observe, and understanding how things are connected. By observing and understanding the peaceful relations between democracies since World War II, we can also forecast that democracies will not fight each other. If, for example, you theorize that key characteristics of democratic government, such as an informed electorate, lead countries with such regimes to settle their disputes peacefully, you should be able to predict what will

happen in the future if: (1) two democratic governments with informed electorates have a dispute (then they are unlikely to fight); (2) democratic governments with informed electorates spread throughout the world (then there should be fewer wars worldwide). Conversely, if you theorize that the peace between democracies since World War II is a function of other factors, such as the existence of a common major enemy or high levels of trade between democratic states or the presence of a free press in democratic countries, then you would base your predictions on those things.

A BASIS FOR PRESCRIPTION Theory may also provide a basis for prescribing behavior or policy—that is, it may lead to normative conclusions about what *should* be. Because theory tells us what to observe, why things are connected, and what will happen in the future, then if we are able to alter certain things, we might be able to alter the future. For example, medical researchers have shown that moderate exercise helps lower blood pressure, cholesterol, and excess body fat and increase heart and lung function—all things that increase health and life expectancy. From that we can predict that people who engage in moderate exercise will generally be healthier and live longer. Knowing those facts, causal relationships, and predictions, a government might prescribe a policy that all school-age children should be taught physical education in school in the hope that it would lead to more people moderately exercising. Businesses may find ways to encourage their employees to exercise more often in order to lessen their health care costs or reduce absences. Thus, understanding and predicting what will happen may allow us to change what will happen.

The evidence and theory that link democratic governance and peaceful relations between countries provide a good example of international relations theory. If democracies do not fight each other, then a policy prescription for making progress toward a peaceful world might be promoting democratization in other countries. If more countries are democratic, then there should be more peaceful relations in the world. In fact, many U.S. presidents have argued exactly this idea in recent decades. Many other examples abound, and you can probably generate some interesting policy prescriptions from some of your insights from the opening exercise of this chapter.

Let's wrap up this overview with a few concluding thoughts. First, theory should be tested against empirical evidence to gauge its accuracy and utility. For example, we might theorize that countries with McDonald's restaurants never fight each other (the "Golden Arches" theory described by the author Thomas Friedman), but

St. Petersburg, Russia, May 29, 2011: A McDonalds Restaurant at Nevsky Avenue | What are the implications of the spread of McDonalds to countries around the world?

more complicated ones, all other things being equal. Detail and complexity for their own sake are of no advantage to explanation unless they really offer better explanations.

Third, theorizing can take place in a given level of analysis (e.g., explanations that stress system-level, state-level, or individual-level factors), or it can link explanations across levels of analysis. But good theory is clear about which approach is being utilized.

Finally, try to remember that theories are tools to be used to better understand and explain events and situations. They are simply an explanation of the facts. It may be that one or another theoretical approach is preferable to some situations, but not others. You do not necessarily have to choose one theoretical approach and ignore others. Instead, you might treat theory like tools in a toolbox: which ones are most helpful for given situations? After all, hammers are great for pounding nails but lousy for cutting boards neatly!

<table>
<tr><td>3-2</td><td></td></tr>
</table>

3-2   THE REALIST PERSPECTIVE ON WORLD POLITICS

Almost 2,500 years ago, the Greek historian Thucydides wrote about the conflict and competition among Greek city-states led by Athens and Sparta. According to Thucydides, at the heart of the conflict was "the growth in Athenian power and the fear which this caused in Sparta." In a memorable episode of this contest between Athens and Sparta, the Athenians demanded surrender from the tiny island of Melos and threatened invasion and devastation if they were refused. Thucydides' account records that as the Melians pleaded for justice and fairness, the Athenian commander told them they were wasting their time. In matters of such import, he asserted, "The strong do as they will, and the weak suffer what they must."

From this episode, Thucydides tied the conflict between Athens and Sparta to the core of what we now know as realist theory: their competition for power and influence, and the security dilemma it prompted between them. In the Melian tale, Thucydides reasoned that ideals such as justice and fairness had little relevance for the relations between states. Instead, leaders must focus on security and survival, the accumulation of power needed to protect their interests. Thus, the Melians should have joined the Athenians to ensure their future security.

parsimony   the principle that simple explanations are preferable to complex explanations when other things are equal.

until we test this theory with evidence, we won't know if there is any value to it. In fact, this particular argument does not stand up well to empirical scrutiny, as there are a number of examples since 1989 in which militarized disputes between countries with McDonald's restaurants occurred, and since there are almost certainly other factors at work determining both the presence of McDonald's and peaceful relations between countries. Can you think of some?

Second, many scholars and scientists embrace the principle of **parsimony** in their efforts. Parsimony holds that the simplest explanations should be preferred over

The Democratic Peace and Democracy Promotion

The belief that democracies are more peaceful in their relations with one another has long motivated democratic leaders to advocate the spread of democratic institutions to other countries. In the United States, for example, President Woodrow Wilson, in his influential "Fourteen Points" speech of 1918, advocated the spread of democracy and self-determination for all nations to make the world safer, more peaceful. More recently, every U.S. president since Jimmy Carter in the 1970s has made a similar appeal. President Carter advocated protecting and promoting human rights and democratic governance, and President Ronald Reagan called for a "crusade for freedom" on behalf of democracy.

As the Cold War ended, subsequent administrations placed even greater emphasis on promoting democracy. President George H. W. Bush expanded U.S. democracy promotion with such actions as the use of U.S. military force in Panama in 1989, and with special aid to the countries of Eastern Europe (the 1990 Support for Eastern European Democracy—or SEED—Act) and the former Soviet Union (the 1992 Freedom Support Act). When Bill Clinton assumed office, the United States expanded its efforts even further. According to President Clinton, in his 1995 State of the Union address, "ultimately, the best strategy to ensure our security and to build a durable peace is to support the advance of democracy elsewhere."

Twenty-first-century presidents have continued the commitment. As George W. Bush stated in his 2005 inaugural address, "The best hope for peace in our world is the expansion of freedom in all the world. . . . So it is the policy of the United States to seek and support the growth of democratic movements and institutions in every nation and culture." More recently, at a major speech in Cairo in June 2009, Barack Obama expressed his "unyielding belief that all people yearn for certain things: the ability to speak your mind and have a say in how you are governed; confidence in the rule of law and the equal administration of justice; government that is transparent and doesn't steal from the people; the freedom to live as you choose. These are not just American ideas; they are human rights. And that is why we will support them everywhere."

Nor are these sentiments exclusive to the United States. A relatively recent study examined the foreign policies of 40 countries between 1992 and 2002 and concluded that they engaged in substantial and widely varying commitments and efforts to promote democracy in other countries.[3] Overall, these efforts by the United States and others included such things as diplomatic approaches, economic efforts such as the provision of foreign aid, and even military intervention to protect or establish democratic regimes.

1. What theoretical foundations are policymakers drawing on when they prescribe such policies?

2. What cause-and-effect assumptions do they make?

Instead, they did not join Athens, and as a result, the Athenian military destroyed Melos to demonstrate its power and prevent the Melians from aligning with Athens' key rival, Sparta.

Thucydides was one of the first realist writers, and although **realism** is the oldest theory of international relations, it is still widely accepted and used today. Realism is not only accepted as a way to understand the world but also as a policy guide. That is, the theory offers explanation for how states act in the international system, and like the story of Athens and Melos, it also offers guidance

on how states *should* act. Thucydides tells the story of Melos to explain what happened and, just as important, to teach leaders how to avoid the fate that befell Melos. He points out that they should have sided with Athens (or called on Athenian enemy Sparta for an alliance), regardless of whether it was the just or fair thing to do; it was the choice that would have saved their lives.

Thus, realism acts as both an explanation and a guide or prescription for policy. Particularly since World War II, realism has been the predominant approach to international relations around the world. According to many observers, states such as China, Russia, and the United States all tend to act as realists. We say "tend" to act as realists because complexity is everywhere in international relations. As you will see when we discuss liberalism, no state follows a strictly realist-type foreign policy.

realism a major theoretical approach to international relations emphasizing the competitive, conflict-ridden pursuit of power and security among states in world politics.

The realist perspective traces back to thinkers and scholars such as Thucydides, Sun Tzu, Shang Yang, Niccolò Machiavelli, and Thomas Hobbes. The theory is rooted in a very pessimistic view of human nature. Hobbes famously characterized the **state of nature**—a hypothetical situation where there was no government—as "solitary, poor, nasty, brutish, and short." That is, he argued that if there were no government to constrain people from acting, then there would be no functioning society. There would be a perpetual fear and a war of all against all. Perhaps the best way to imagine Hobbes' state of nature is to think of apocalyptic-style movies/television shows and books such as *The Road, 28 Days Later, The Walking Dead,* and *Mad Max.* In these stories, humans almost universally turn on each other in horribly violent ways and only cooperate out of fear. That is the world that Hobbes claims would exist if it were not for governments to constrain people and force them to behave. He notes that because of the fear that their fellow humans will kill them, people want the government to maintain order. The overriding point is that people are violent and cooperate only out of fear.

Building on these foundations, the more modern-day roots of realism include E. H. Carr, whose *Twenty Years Crisis: 1919–1939* describes how the realities of power politics destroyed what he characterized as idealistic hopes and plans for peace and cooperation after World War I and led to World War II. It also includes Hans J. Morgenthau, whose *Politics Among Nations* stresses "the national interest defined in terms of power" as the main factor motivating states in international politics.

Realism is the simplest of theories of world politics, which contributes to its power and pervasiveness. It rests on a parsimonious leveraging of a very few key things about the international system and its parts to explain very broad patterns of behavior and interaction. Although there are many variants and flavors of realist theory, they tend to be unified around a common core of ideas and assumptions. While many thousands of pages have been devoted to developing and articulating realist theories of international relations, we can focus on a number of core elements to gain a working familiarity with the perspective and its descriptive, explanatory, predictive, and prescriptive applications.

At the risk of simplifying the nuances and subtleties, let us consider what realism offers for (1) the nature of the international system, (2) its relevant actors, (3) important resources, and (4) central dynamics. We will adopt this scheme in our discussion of liberalism and constructivism as well to make it easier to compare and contrast these three major approaches. Since we will further discuss and apply these theories in our subsequent

book sections on international security, economic security, and human security, our purpose here is to provide initial summaries as starting points for our efforts to explain and understand the patterns and interactions of world politics.

3-2a Realism and the Nature of the International System

According to realists, one central characteristic of the international system overshadows all others and forms the foundation of the explanations the perspective offers. That characteristic is anarchy—which quite simply means the absence of central authority, not chaos, as we discussed in Chapter 2. While the international system is more complicated than this simple portrayal, realists tend to argue that other aspects of the system are less significant and can be ignored as secondary factors, for the most part. For realists, the absence of a central government to establish order and wield power and authority establishes a fundamentally Hobbesian world in which the main players of world politics must rely on themselves and themselves alone to protect their interests and accomplish their goals. In this **self-help** world, power is both a central instrument and a primary objective to ensure survival and security. Indeed, according to realists, the anarchy of the international system makes it the domain of power, not law, morality, society, or institutions. And, according to realists, this main structural aspect of the international system ensures that conflict is always possible . . . and is the central problem of world politics.

Anarchy as the central feature of the international system has several other consequences for the system. First, anarchy means there is no higher governing authority above the main political units—states. Hence, states are **sovereign**—possessing the sole authority to govern within their borders. In combination with self-help, sovereignty also means that states are responsible for securing their own interests and, at least in principle, that they are not obligated to follow rules or decisions made by others unless they so choose or are coerced into doing so by a more powerful state.

Second, the international system is stratified, with different levels of resources, wealth, and power possessed

state of nature a hypothetical condition before the advent of government.

self-help individual actors are responsible for making themselves secure and protecting their own interests.

sovereign having supreme authority over territory and people.

by different states. Realists tend to differentiate between great or major powers and other powers, with some also identifying middle powers. This **stratification** is important for realists for at least two reasons: (1) realists argue that states with different levels of power act differently from each other because of their position in the anarchic system, with great powers having the greatest freedom of choice and action, as well as the most influence; and (2) realists argue that states seek to preserve or gain power—to move up this hierarchy—as a way of securing their interests and influence. And the central ingredient of these differing levels of power and state efforts to be powerful is military might, which we discuss later in the chapter.

Finally, as we discussed in Chapter 2, the anarchic international system and its self-help characteristic establishes persistent security dilemmas. Simply put, since states are responsible for their security and survival, they must take action to protect themselves. However, the actions states take to secure themselves frequently appear potentially threatening to other states, who naturally take steps to protect their own security. The results often produce situations of greater potential danger, so the dilemma is clear: the actions a state takes to secure itself often wind up making it even less secure because of the action–reaction cycles they produce. Realists express a variety of views on this feature of international politics, from those who argue that some states have good, essentially defensive, intentions to those who assert that most states prefer dominance and actively seek it. In either case, security dilemmas arise and spur conflict and competition (see Spotlight On: Variants of Realism).

3-2b Realism and the Relevant Actors of International Relations

Within the anarchic system of world politics, not surprisingly, realists concentrate on the state as the central, and usually only, actor of consequence in the international system. It is not that realists fail to recognize that other players—many of whom we discussed in the preceding chapter—exist. Instead, realists assert that nonstate actors are either of secondary importance or are derivative of states. Yes, a realist would say, there are international organizations such as the UN, but such organizations are creations of states, they serve the

interests of states, and they reflect the preferences of the most powerful states. But to realists, it is the states that are the primary players.

As we previously suggested, in the realist simplification of world politics, these states are sovereign and self-help-oriented, which means they are basically self-interested and self-regarding. As in the stag hunt example from Chapter 1, realists portray states as fundamentally selfish actors seeking their own security. That does not necessarily mean that cooperation among them is impossible. It suggests, however, that such cooperation will be highly dependent on calculations of self-interest and benefits, and so will be temporary and highly constrained by suspicion and mistrust since no state can really count on another to forego opportunities for advantages. For realists, states may join together to counter a common enemy or prevent another state from becoming too powerful, but they are unlikely to sustain that cooperation once the common threat has been addressed, as the British and Americans were unable to sustain their cooperation with the Soviets after the defeat of Germany in World War II.

Moreover, it is common for realists to simplify even further about states. Rather than consider how societal forces, complex governments and processes, different regime types, or different political parties and individual leaders affect states, many realists prefer to treat the state as a **unitary actor** (i.e., like a billiard ball, a single moving part) that responds to the structures and dynamics of the international system rationally. Treating states as unitary actors lets us see them as if they are single rational entities. In effect, states such as North Korea and the United States think and act as single actors: North Korea "decides," the United States "negotiates," the two countries "threaten." That way we don't need to know about the particular leaders or groups and their preferences inside the countries. These rational actors calculate their national interests and goals and take action accordingly.

Thus, in this realist simplification, states are also fundamentally undifferentiated except for power and capabilities. That is, realists filter away much of the descriptive detail of states (type of government, culture, leader characteristics, and the like) and assume that all states want the same things and are affected by the international system in similar ways, with the only significant difference being how much power and capability they have to act. Those states with greater power and capabilities have more opportunity to act than those without such resources. As Thucydides suggested, strong states pursue their interests and weaker states have little choice but to go along, one way or another. To return to our example of North Korea and the United States, for

stratification unequal distribution of power, influence, and/or other resources.

unitary actor the simplified conception of a state as a single entity or actor.

Variants of Realism

As a theoretical perspective, realism comes in many flavors:

- *Classical realism.* This variant of realism finds its roots in the political philosophy of Thomas Hobbes and emphasizes the aggressive, power-seeking, and selfish nature of human beings as the ultimate source of state behavior. As well-known classical realist Hans Morgenthau wrote, the first principle of classical realism is that "politics, like society in general, is governed by objective laws that have their roots in human nature."[4] In world politics, the state is the collective reflection of individual human nature carrying out the pursuit of power.

- *Neo-realism.* This variant, by contrast, focuses on the nature of the international system rather than human nature. According to leading neo-realist theorists such as Kenneth Waltz, the anarchic structure of the international system causes the units in the system (states) to seek their own security through the accumulation of power, thus leading to balance-of-power politics. Thus, it is not greed or a selfish nature that pushed states to do what they do; the system made them do it!

- *Neo-classical realism.* This variant has been advocated by theorists such as Gideon Rose and Randall Schweller, and attempts to bridge the divide between the first two variants by starting with the structure of the international system to explain broader international outcomes and patterns, but then adding in state- and individual-level factors to help to explain the differing foreign policies of particular states.

We can also distinguish between defensive and offensive orientations of realism.

- *Defensive realism* stresses that states are interested in being secure from threats but are faced with security dilemmas that generate fear and uncertainty. As key advocates such as Robert Jervis and Stephen Walt suggest, defensive realists do not argue that states always seek to maximize their power or seek dominance, and that there are conditions in which states can be more or less secure.

- *Offensive realism,* advocated by such theorists as John Mearsheimer, by contrast, stresses that states (especially great or aspiring-to-be-great powers) always seek power and dominance. As Mearsheimer put it, "States pay close attention to how power is distributed among them, and they make a special effort to maximize their share of world power. . . . Given the difficulty of determining how much power is enough for today and tomorrow, great powers recognize that the best way to ensure their security is to achieve hegemony now, thus eliminating any possibility of a challenge from another great power."[5] In the course of these efforts, great powers naturally come into conflict with each other.

Think about how each of these variants reflects the central core of realism, and how they differ from each other. What are the strengths and weaknesses of each variant? How might each one capture and explain important parts of world politics?

---

realists, what distinguishes these states from each other is their power and resources as well as the national interests that arise from their respective capabilities and positions in the international system. What is not relevant are differences in type of government, the personalities of a single leader, and other such details.

As we described in the box Spotlight On: Variants of Realism, different schools of thought within realism exist, of course. Neo-classical realists place greater emphasis on the individual leaders and states and their interests and the ways their choices and actions then shape the resulting international system, while neo-realists stress the structure of the system and its central role in shaping the general behavior and interactions of states. However, all variants tend to treat the state as a rational, self-interested actor seeking power and influence in the pursuit of security.

3-2c Realism and the Important Resources of International Relations

In the anarchic system of sovereign states seeking their own interests, realists stress the importance of power and capabilities. As Hans Morgenthau, an early and influential realist theorist in the twentieth century, put it, states pursue "the national interest defined in terms of power." As we just noted, realists contend that the anarchy of the international system makes it the domain of power and capabilities. To put it simply, according to realists, power rules in world politics. States seek it and wield it. Its distribution affects how states act and the likelihood of conflict. But what is power?

There are many definitions, but a very simple starting point captures the realist concept of power very

Military Power and World Politics

Both realists and liberals argue that military power is important to world politics. However, for most realists, military power is the *sine qua non* of world politics—the essential ingredient for any state's power and security. The website GlobalFirepower.com collects data on the military power of countries of the world (45 categories of information) and then ranks countries from most to least powerful. Here is their ranking of the top six military powers in the world, with their figures on military personnel and defense spending drawn from their ranking system for 2014 (Table 3-1).

After looking over this information, think about the measure of power represented, but also think about the ranking of these countries as the top six most powerful countries. If realists are right, that means these should be the most powerful countries in the world. How well does this list represent power and influence in world politics? Who is not on this list that you think should be?

TABLE 3-1	THE MOST POWERFUL COUNTRIES IN THE WORLD?	
COUNTRY	**ACTIVE MILITARY PERSONNEL**	**DEFENSE BUDGET**
United States	1.43 million	$611 billion
Russia	766,000	$77 billion
China	2.29 million	$126 billion
India	1.33 million	$46 billion
United Kingdom	205,500	$53.6 billion
France	228,656	$43 billion

© Cengage Learning®

well: **power** *is the ability to get what you want.* For realists, power in world politics is both an instrument and a goal (i.e., states seek it as both means and an end), and its acquisition and use is part of the basic fabric of state behavior and interactions. As the Morgenthau statement in the previous paragraph indicates, the realist concept of power is that states *must* seek it to secure themselves and their interests in an anarchic world.

At least three key features of power dominate the realist perspective. First, power is *relative* and *relational*. For a realist, it makes little sense to discuss power except in terms of relationship. Power compared to what? At its heart, the realist notion of power turns on the view that what matters most is how power is distributed and how gains in power by one state compare to those of another. In effect, a realist determines power not by assessing what a state has (e.g., 100 nuclear missiles or 5 aircraft carrier battle groups) so much as what a state has compared to another (100 *more* nuclear missiles, 5 *more* carrier battle groups) and how the advantage (or disadvantage) is changing (growing, shrinking, remaining stable). This leads to what realist theorists discuss as the **relative gains** problem: states are more (or, at least, as much) concerned with the growth of their own power

Yang Lei C/Xinhua/Landov

Chinese Military Parade, October 2009 | Why do countries put their militaries on parade and celebrate their military strength?

power   the ability to get what you want.

relative gains   the comparative effect of a decision or situation on an actor relative to those of another actor.

Geography and Power

Map 3-1

Islands of Security? The Geographic Location of the United States, United Kingdom, and Japan

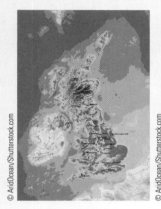  

Does the world seem safer for countries mostly surrounded by water?

The geographic location and characteristics of a country can be a significant source of power, and of perceptions of safety or vulnerability. Look at Map 3-1 and the location of the United Kingdom, the United States, and Japan. These three states share one feature in common: all three are effectively island states bounded by water from most or all of their neighbors. Although not an island, for the United States the presence of two large bodies of water like the Atlantic and Pacific Oceans separating it from other major powers in Europe and Asia has long offered a degree of protection and security, as well as freedom of movement and easy access to trade routes via the oceans. Behind these two vast moats and easy transportation avenues, the geographic size and relatively abundant natural resources of the United States have also contributed to its potential power and ability to be secure. The United Kingdom and Japan both enjoy the protection of water separating them from others, as well as offering avenues for trade and economic activity. But note in the case of both countries, that separation—especially from potentially major rivals in Europe and Asia—is more limited and, in combination with their smaller size and natural resource endowments, can contribute to isolation and feelings of vulnerability, as well.

Contrast the geographic locations and implications of these virtual island states with the geography of other countries. Germany, for example, is surrounded by other countries and must consider what power is needed to defend its borders on all sides. Israel also has concerns stemming from the geography of its borders and its neighboring states. What other states have geographic locations with significant implications for their power and security? What about states with mountainous borders or large deserts separating them from their neighbors? How about countries such as Egypt and Panama, whose geography and location provide transportation links between bodies of water (i.e., in the Suez and Panama Canals)? What consequences derive from these features? What about those without any obvious geographic features marking their territory?

1. How do geographic features add to and detract from power and security?

2. What power advantages have countries like the United States enjoyed because of their location and ocean borders?

3. How have changing technology and globalization affected the significance of geography for power and security?

TABLE 3-2 RESOURCES OF POWER IN WORLD POLITICS

RESOURCE	EXAMPLES
Geographic resources	Size of territory; defensible borders
Natural resources	Arable land; raw materials
Economic resources	Wealth; industrial capacity; technological leadership and development
Military resources	Quantity and quality of armed forces; advanced military technology; military leadership
Human resources	Population; education and skills; leadership; national image and morale

© Cengage Learning®

resources as they compare with another's than they are with **absolute gains**, or how much of the resource they have or gain on its own. Think of it this way: a concern for relative gains suggests that a state would rather increase its power by five points per year if their rival only gains three points a year instead of gaining 10 points if their rival gains 12 points. To a realist, the first scenario means a relative gain of two, and the second means a relative loss of two!

Second, realists view power in a hierarchical fashion, with military power the most important and essential for the ability to get what one wants in world politics. Realists acknowledge that power has many sources and that many resources are necessary for a state to be powerful. As Table 3-2 shows, these sources and resources include underlying factors such as geographic and territorial characteristics and attributes, natural resources, and other factors that realists often characterize as *potential*

absolute gains the total effect of a decision or situation on an actor.

sources of power. Factors such as wealth, industrial or technological capacity, and the like are also important. But, a realist would say, they are important ultimately as a means by which a state can develop and deploy military power in pursuit of security and influence. As Robert Art, a realist scholar, has stated, force is, ultimately, the final judge of world politics. As realists would quickly point out, there is a good reason why virtually all states—and all major powers—devote considerable resources to develop their military forces.

Furthermore, realists tend to treat power as *fungible*, meaning that power resources can be converted into influence easily, just as a dollar can be quickly and easily turned into many things: food, soft drinks, iTunes downloads, and so on. Realists see power similarly: states with it—especially military might—can turn it into positive outcomes across many issue areas, including diplomatic negotiations, trade relations, and many more. The more (military) power a state has, the more likely it is to get its way on a whole host of issues.

One way to understand this power equation is shown in Figure 3-1. In this depiction, the application of power begins with resources like those we have already discussed.

FIGURE 3-1 THE APPLICATION OF POWER

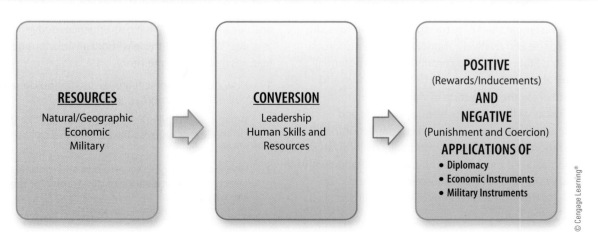

RESOURCES
Natural/Geographic
Economic
Military

CONVERSION
Leadership
Human Skills and
Resources

POSITIVE
(Rewards/Inducements)
AND
NEGATIVE
(Punishment and Coercion)
APPLICATIONS OF
• Diplomacy
• Economic Instruments
• Military Instruments

© Cengage Learning®

These resources are harnessed and converted into actual capabilities, which depends heavily on the abilities of society and the leaders making the decisions. Once converted, these capabilities are applied as foreign policy instruments. We can broadly classify such instruments into three categories: (1) diplomacy (which involves bargaining and negotiation, as we discuss in Chapter 7); (2) economic instruments (which involve aid, trade, and sanctions, as we discuss in Chapter 9); and (3) military instruments (e.g., the use of force, as we discuss in Chapter 5). For realists, while each of these instruments is important, ultimately military power trumps all.

3-2d Realism and the Central Dynamics of International Relations

From these foundations, the last element of the realist approach is easy to understand: in an anarchic world characterized by insecurity, self-help, and security dilemmas, states seek power to protect their interests and ensure their survival. Since power is relative and ultimately based on military strength, states cannot ever really have enough or trust others to be satisfied in an environment where *conflict is the norm*. As realist theorist Hans Morgenthau once famously argued "all states are either preparing for, recovering from, or engaged in war." Viewed through this lens, world politics is essentially states vying with one another for power and influence, with powerful states asserting themselves and seeking advantage over one another, while weaker states cope with the consequences. In this competitive world, states are much like billiard balls colliding with each other on a regular basis as they pursue and protect their national interests and seek and wield power. As the philosopher Thomas Hobbes wrote in *Leviathan*, in the absence of "a common power to keep them all in awe, they are in that condition which is called war; and such a war is of every man [or state] against every man [or state]."

Moreover, in this world, realists generally view international politics as **zero-sum** situations. Building on their emphasis on relative gains, realists tend to argue that in any given scenario there must be a winner and a loser, so that gain by one state necessarily means a loss by another. In the example on the difference between absolute and relative gains, for instance, the two-point gain by the first state by definition means a two-point loss (in relative terms) by the other, not a gain (one greater, one lesser) by each. This tendency to see power and other interactions in zero-sum terms reflects the realist presumption of conflictual or competitive

relations in world politics. As realist theorist John Mearsheimer argues, in this context the central aim of powerful states is to dominate at least their region and potentially more.

According to realists, which states, and particularly how many, have power greatly shapes the general patterns of world politics, with some **distributions of power** contributing to more conflict and war, some to less, while all distributions are subject to change as those out of power seek more of it and those in power seek to preserve it. As we discuss in more detail in Chapter 5, when we discuss conflict and causes of war, realists often categorize particular periods of international relations by identifying the number of great powers. The international system can be **unipolar**, with one great power, **bipolar**, with two, or **multipolar**, with more than two. Some realists discuss **tripolar** systems as an intermediate state between bipolar and multipolar systems. According to realists, each of these distributions creates different patterns, constraints, and opportunities for states seeking power and security. For example, in *The Tragedy of Great Power Politics*, John Mearsheimer explains the frequency and likelihood of war as a function of the distribution of power. According to Mearsheimer, unipolar or hegemonic systems experience the fewest wars. Rigid bipolar systems, where most states are tightly aligned with one or the other of the two major powers, are more violent, while loose bipolar systems are even more prone to war. Multipolar systems, with many major powers, are the most war-prone. At the heart of explanations such as this is the central dynamic stressed by realists—the competition for power and security among self-interested states.

zero-sum a condition in which one party's benefit or gains requires comparable losses by another party.

distribution of power a characteristic of the international system emphasized by realists based on the number of great or major powers and how power is distributed among them in a given period of time.

unipolar a distribution of power in the international system in which there is one great power.

bipolar a distribution of power in the international system in which there are two great powers.

multipolar a distribution of power in the international system in which there are more than two great powers.

tripolar a distribution of power in the international system in which there are three great powers.

TABLE 3-3 SUMMARY OF REALISM AND WORLD POLITICS

KEY FEATURES	REALIST INTERPRETATION
Nature of the international system	Anarchic; self-help
Relevant actors	States
Important resources	Power, especially military
Central dynamics	Conflict; zero-sum calculations
Anarchy	Fundamental structural condition generating fear, uncertainty, and conflict
Diversity	States have different levels of power and competing interests
Complexity	Generated from stratification of power and competing self-interests of states

© Cengage Learning®

This quite naturally leads to a central dynamic of world politics that realist theorists typically emphasize: **balance-of-power politics**. We discuss this dynamic in more detail in Chapter 6, but let's note here that this term generally refers to the pattern of activity that occurs as states take action to make themselves secure by seeking power, countering the efforts of real or potential rivals to gain power advantages, and using power to counter security threats from others. According to realists, states monitor their security environment and take actions to meet perceived threats from others by seeking power. According to many realists, since all states make these kinds of calculations and take these kinds of steps, the balance of power is much like the magic of the market in capitalism: as each state pursues its self-interests in this way, balances tend to emerge.

In sum, realism directs our attention to the pursuit of power and security in an anarchic and conflict-ridden world, highlighting the role of states and their national interests (see Table 3-3 for a summary). Yet realism is not the only theoretical approach to consider. Let's now take up its primary competitor.

balance of power politics patterns of shifting alliances, force, and counterforce among states as they seek power, counter the efforts of rivals, and confront security threats.

liberalism a major theoretical approach to international relations emphasizing the role of individuals, norms, and institutions to explain patterns of cooperation and conflict in world politics.

3-3 THE LIBERAL PERSPECTIVE ON WORLD POLITICS

Like realism, **liberalism** has a lengthy intellectual history, from thinkers such as Hugo Grotius, Baron de Montesquieu, and Immanuel Kant to the present day. To be sure, the term *liberal* means a lot of different things in different contexts, but in international relations theory, it is used quite differently than in domestic politics, so it is important not to confuse them. In contrast to realism, liberalism rests on a much more optimistic view of human nature and progress. Rather than the Hobbesian view of a violent state of nature, liberal theorists are more likely to embrace John Locke's view. For Locke the state of nature (i.e., the world without central government) depicted an uncertain and often insecure world in which conflict was possible, but in which reason and reciprocity led mostly to harmonious relationships. As E.H. Carr described it in *The Twenty Years' Crisis*, liberalism builds on the conception of mutual interests among states that can suffer from suspicion, misunderstanding, or ineffective institutions, but can be overcome by reason, education, communication, institutions, and law.

Just as Thucydides illustrates realist thinking, Immanuel Kant provides a good depiction of liberal thinking. According to Kant in *Perpetual Peace*, states could overcome conflict and establish lasting cooperative relationships by embracing a series of norms to guide behavior. Most important, the combination of "republican" or democratic government in states, international institutions to help coordinate and guide them, and a cosmopolitan law ensuring "hospitality" and commercial relations among the states and their citizens would overcome the threat of war and establish the "state of peace."[6]

As Kant's prescriptions suggest, liberal theory takes a more complicated approach to world politics that directs attention to more concerns than does realism. In fact, many liberals object that realism is not very "realistic" because it oversimplifies world politics too severely and overlooks key factors and broad patterns of behavior. Some liberal theorists point out that war is, in fact, a relatively rare occurrence when one considers the number of states, their many interactions, and the potential conflicts among them. Liberal theorists also argue that *cooperation is much more common* than realism suggests. While early liberalism was heavily committed to prescriptions for peace, more recent liberal theory has emphasized explanations for the patterns of cooperation and conflict in world politics. To do so, liberal theory relaxes each of the central assumptions of realism and

© Gl0ck/Shutterstock.com

A monument to German philosopher Immanuel Kant | What leads liberal theorists like Kant to believe in the possibility of "perpetual peace?"

central government in world politics. However, unlike realists, liberal theorists usually point to one or more of several additional features of the international system that also play important roles in world politics and reduce the impact of formal anarchy.

First, liberal theorists point to the presence of **international norms** and mutual interests among states that mitigate the effects of anarchy. As Hedley Bull stressed in *The Anarchical Society*, these shared norms and common interests create opportunities and expectations for cooperation and understanding. They also condition and temper the self-help impulses that realists ascribe to the anarchic structure. Thus states may have the right to meet their energy needs by developing nuclear power, but a relatively sophisticated set of norms exists—called the nonproliferation regime—regarding how states should do so and how they should allay the fears of others as they develop nuclear power resources. When states violate such norms, virtually the entire international system reacts negatively toward their actions—just ask Iran or North Korea.

Second, liberal theorists point to interdependence among states as an important characteristic. As Robert Keohane and Joseph Nye describe in *Power and Interdependence*, states are connected by mutual dependencies to one degree or another so that no state is truly self-sufficient or able to go it alone. The deeper these connections are—in terms of economic interactions like trade and investment, political connections, and societal and cultural linkages—the more consequences there are for state behavior and interactions. According to liberal theorists, interdependent states are less likely to engage in violent conflict, more likely to collaborate to resolve problems, and more likely to behave as partners because they have a greater stake in getting along with others. States that are less connected with others—like North Korea or Myanmar—have less to lose if they challenge norms of cooperation; there is less stopping them from becoming violent. Hence, interdependence reduces the impact of the anarchic structure of world politics.

Third, liberal theorists point to **institutions** as important characteristics—as well as players (see our next section on relevant actors) of the international system. While liberal theorists agree that international institutions are constrained and incomplete, they typically

offers a less parsimonious set of explanations. However, liberal theory tends also to be more fragmented because it directs our attention to many more factors in world politics than does realism. To better understand this, let's consider the four elements of our comparative framework where liberalism is concerned.

3-3a Liberalism and the Nature of the International System

Most liberal theorists accept that the international system is basically anarchic, and that this structural characteristic has important consequences for international relations. However, they typically object to the realists' emphasis and definition. To liberal theorists, it makes more sense to discuss the *formal* anarchy of the system, acknowledging the absence of a formal, authoritative,

international norms unwritten rules or expectations of behavior.

institutions structures, patterns, and mechanisms for establishing norms, rules, order, and cooperation in world politics.

argue that such institutions still matter and thus place greater emphasis on them than realists. According to liberal theorists, international institutions dampen and moderate the effects of anarchy by providing arenas for cooperation and communication, norm building, coordination, and problem solving. While few liberal theorists would characterize international institutions as more powerful, more authoritative, or more important than the governments of states (especially the most powerful and influential ones), they typically see institutions playing a more significant and independent role in world politics than do realist theorists and seek to incorporate their influence into explanations of world politics.

In Chapter 6, for example, we discuss **collective security**, which has its foundations in liberal theory as an institutional mechanism for states to manage and prevent conflicts. As we discuss in detail in that chapter, the basis of collective security is that states form an organization like the League of Nations or the United Nations and commit themselves to joining together to respond to any attack by one member on any other member. This approach is a method for managing power and responding to threat by pooling resources to bring a preponderance of power to bear on an aggressor. As such, it places great emphasis on the role that the collective security organization can play in shaping the behavior of states and reducing the effects of formal anarchy by promoting communication and cooperation and offering something other than stark self-help scenarios to states.

As a consequence of this general liberal view of the international system, which adds a number of potentially important characteristics to the formal anarchy emphasized by realists, liberal theorists see more opportunities for cooperation and peace in world politics. In particular, system-level dynamics such as the security dilemma tend to be viewed more as trust and communication problems than as fundamental and unalterable consequences of anarchy. Norms, interdependence, and institutions can all reduce, or even eliminate, security dilemmas.

3-3b Liberalism and the Relevant Actors of International Relations

Liberal theorists also depart from their realist counterparts on the question of which players are important. As Keohane and Nye suggested, liberals relax the two

main assumptions of realist theorists when it comes to players.[7] First, many liberal theorists relax the assumption of the state as unitary and undifferentiated actors. Instead, liberal theorists often see the importance of the individuals, governmental institutions and agencies, and societal forces in shaping state behavior and interactions. Liberal theorists are far more likely to study the impact of personality and decision-making factors and processes, different types of regimes and governments, cultural variations, interest groups and corporations, and other subnational players and factors on world politics.

Second, liberal theorists tend to relax the assumption of the state as the only important actor, as well. Non-state actors such as those reviewed in Chapter 2—international governmental organizations (IOs) such as the United Nations and the World Trade Organization; nongovernmental organizations (NGOs) such as Amnesty International, Greenpeace, and the International Red Cross; multinational or transnational corporations (MNCs/TNCs) such as Nike, Toyota, IBM, and Siemens; and transnational advocacy networks (TANs) like the Red Crescent Societies or al-Qaeda—are also considered significant. Many liberal theorists argue that such players are potentially important actors on a wide range of issues and frequently influence states and affect behavior and outcomes in ways that go far beyond the realist treatment of them as secondary, derivative, and mostly unimportant players. For liberal theorists, leaving them out of explanations frequently produces incomplete and/or misleading conclusions. The question for liberal theorists is when and how do these players play important roles. Hence, for liberal theorists, a much greater concern for the diversity of the actors of world politics both complicates and enriches explanations of the patterns of world politics.

3-3c Liberalism and the Important Resources of International Relations

Liberal theorists are also concerned with power as a critical resource in world politics. However, liberal theorists depart from realists on the nature and characteristics of power and influence. At least three key differences have great importance in liberal explanations of world politics.

First, the liberal lens stresses the *multidimensional* nature of power. Much more than realists, who acknowledge the great range of power resources but stress military power as the essential and central component, liberal theorists recognize the importance of military power but argue that there are many sources of power and influence in world politics. Military might is one,

Variants of Liberalism in World Politics

Like realism, as a theoretical approach liberalism has a number of flavors. Because liberal theorists see a more complex international system and a broader variety of actors who matter in world politics, they also point to a variety of moving parts that drive the patterns of behavior—cooperation and conflict—in which states and non-state actors engage. Let's consider four variants.

- *Political liberalism*. This variant stresses the importance of regime type, especially democracy, on relations between states. A good representation is the democratic peace theory, which attributes peaceful relations between democracies to the democratic characteristics of the governments and societies. Advocates point to the absence of war between democracies over time and often stress the fact that countries that have fought with each other in the past have stopped doing so once they shared democratic regime types.

- *Economic/commercial liberalism*. This variant stresses the importance of trade and economic exchange on relations between states. This tradition goes back a long way, to Adam Smith in the nineteenth century, and Norman Angell in the early twentieth century, who argued (ironically, just before the outbreak of World War I) that trade had grown so important to European countries that war was unthinkable. More recently, scholars such as Erik Gartzke have advanced a capitalist peace argument. U.S. presidents such as Bill Clinton and George W. Bush have reflected this variant of liberalism when advocating for extending and deepening trade with China to help maintain peaceful relations between the two countries.

- *Institutional liberalism*. This variant stresses the importance of international institutions and organizations such as the United Nations for cooperative relations between states and other actors in world politics. Advocates of this variant emphasize the role of institutions in promoting communication, building norms, and facilitating cooperation and predictability in world politics. Scholars such as Bruce Russett and John Oneal have argued that more significant institutional linkages between countries is a good predictor of peaceful relations. A good example is the role of international financial institutions such as the International Monetary Fund and the World Trade Organization in promoting cooperation and coordination on economic policy to help avoid the escalation of economic conflict into violence between states as occurred during the 1920s and 1930s when such institutions did not exist. The development and role of the European Union in integrating the conflict-ridden states of Europe into a peaceful community is often pointed to as a good example, as well.

- *Societal/ideational liberalism*. This variant of liberal theory stresses the role of shared identity, culture, norms, and societal connections on relations between societies. For example, many observers interpret the European Union as an international organization created on the basis of post–World War II cooperation that was forced upon Europeans by the United States in return for Marshall Plan aid. Yet the degree of cooperation that now marks this union of states willing to cede some of their sovereignty to the larger entity seems unlikely had there not already been some shared bonds based on similar religious, cultural, and linguistic ties.

and it is important in many situations. However, other sources and types of power can also be critical, and, since many of the players in world politics do not possess military power at all (e.g., NGOs, IOs, MNCs/TNCs) but still exert influence, the sources of their power are also important. Even some states have greater influence than their military power would suggest. For example, liberal theorist Richard Rosecrance has stressed the rising importance of "trading states" (e.g., Germany, Japan) and "virtual states" (e.g., Japan, South Korea, Singapore) since the mid-1980s, whose power and influence is important but fundamentally unrelated to military might. Thus, for liberal theorists, economic resources, natural resources, human resources (such as skills and education), and ideas can all be important elements of power in their own right, and not merely as contributors to a state's military capabilities.

Reflecting this liberal emphasis on the multidimensional nature of power, Joseph Nye has differentiated between **hard power** and **soft power** in world politics.[8] Where hard power includes the realist conceptions of the "the ability to get what you want" through coercive

hard power power based on coercive means such as military force.

soft power power based on attraction and persuasion rather than coercion.

The essence of power? | How do these two images illustrate competing conceptions of power?

means such as military force, soft power involves "the ability to get what you want through attraction rather than coercion." It depends more on ideas, appeal, cooperative relations with allies, and productive connections between countries. In particular, image and credibility and the appeal of ideas enable a state or other actor to exercise power over preferences, not just power over actions. Effective soft power results in "the ability to get another to want what you want." According to Nye, military power (hard), economic power (hard and soft), and soft power are all important.

Building on the multidimensional nature of power, liberal theorists tend to reject the realist emphasis on its hierarchical nature, as well. Instead, the liberal lens tends to view power as *situation specific* or *context dependent*. No single power resource is paramount in every situation. Instead, as Keohane and Nye argued in *Power and Interdependence*, there are multiple hierarchies of power determined by the issue at hand and other contextual factors. Having the world's largest and most powerful military may have been the most significant source of power in the conflict between the United States and Saddam Hussein's Iraq in 2003. It may not be the only or even the most important factor in countering the threat from al-Qaeda, and it may be completely irrelevant in a trade dispute between the United States and Japan. Similarly, the economic power and influence of Germany or Japan may be central to shaping decisions about how to deal with the recent global economic crisis, but largely unrelated to confronting Iran over nuclear weaponry. Even military power itself is context dependent, according to liberal theorists. How else can one explain the failures of the United States in Vietnam and the Soviet Union in Afghanistan, both situations in which the world's superpowers confronted

substantially weaker, poor, developing countries but were unable to translate their clear advantages in military power into success? Similarly, despite more than a decade of effort and all the military and economic resources deployed and expended by the U.S. over that time, violence and rebellion continued in Iraq, escalating in 2014 as insurgents challenged the U.S.-backed regime and seized territory. Or, as liberal theorists would argue, military power is largely irrelevant to resolve issues of economic competition and trade relations between the United States and Japan, prevent certain countries from unsustainable whaling practices, or convince Brazil to protect its rain forest from further destruction. Hence, liberal theorists are much more skeptical about the fungibility of power, preferring to treat issue areas separately.

3-3d Liberalism and the Central Dynamics of International Relations

From these foundations, the general orientation of liberal theorists emerges: In a formally anarchic world in which states and other actors share some common interests and goals and are interdependent to various degrees and connected through institutions and other channels, cooperation, competition, and conflict are all possible, but conflict is not the norm. Some situations and issues promote cooperation and reduce the likelihood of conflict, especially violent conflict. States are important actors, but their behavior and interactions are shaped by the individuals, groups, organizations, and institutions that make up their country and government, and by non-state actors in the international system. Power is multifaceted and wielded in a variety of ways. Unlike realists, who tend to see the dynamics of world politics as the unfolding of similar behavior in cycles, liberals see the dynamics of world politics more in terms of progress and change that unfolds over time in a more linear fashion.

A relatively recent example that illustrates this point is the debate over the future of Europe and NATO after the end of the Cold War in 1989. Realists such as John Mearsheimer predicted that the end of the Cold War would trigger a return of conflict and competition in Europe and the likely end to the NATO alliance, since the common threat posed by the Soviet Union was the reason for the cooperation (both between countries such as France and Germany, and between European states and the United States, in general). With the disappearance of that common threat, Mearsheimer expected the return of former patterns of conflict as the enduring forces of world politics asserted themselves. As Mearsheimer colorfully put it, "we will soon miss the Cold War."

By contrast, liberal theorists such as Stanley Hoffman, Robert Keohane, Bruce Russett, and Thomas Risse countered that many things have changed since World War II. The spread of democracy, the development of norms against war among European countries, influential and cooperative institutions such as the European Union, and shared interests and benefits from cooperative practices have all fundamentally changed relations among European states such as France and Germany, and relations between Europe and the United States, as well. With such changing dynamics and progress, these theorists argued, a return to violent conflict is highly improbable. Two decades later, which perspective has been more accurate? By comparison, how would realists explain the EU decisions to continue bailing out Greece with financial assistance?

For liberal theorists, when conflict occurs, it can be traced to factors such as misunderstanding, miscommunication, cultural differences, bad regimes, and other such causes. Leaders, decisions, processes, regimes, and institutions shape the general patterns of world politics. So, liberal theorists are especially interested in explaining the patterns of cooperation that characterize much of world politics, while also accounting for the exceptions of violent conflict.

However, and in large part as a consequence of the liberal conception of power (i.e., its multidimensionality and situation-specific nature) and the international system, liberal theorists tend to see world politics as a **positive-sum** game rather than a zero-sum game. Because of mutual interests and goals, the possibilities of trade-offs across issue areas, and the multidimensional nature of power and influence, liberal theorists see many more possibilities for win-win scenarios and often argue that absolute gains rather than relative gains is the relevant perspective for most actors most of the time. This perspective contributes to the liberal view of the possibility of cooperative relations among states. For example, the North American Free Trade Agreement (NAFTA) created a special trade zone with Canada, the United States, and Mexico. Each country gained significantly from the increased flow of goods and services, but Mexico benefited more than the United States and Canada, relatively speaking. As a smaller, less-developed economy, Mexico had more to gain by selling goods in the huge U.S. and Canadian markets. This did not stop the United States and Canada from entering into the agreement because they were concerned with the absolute gains to be made from trade rather than the relative gains that would be made (Table 3-4).

positive-sum a condition in which all parties to an issue can benefit or "win."

TABLE 3-4	SUMMARY OF LIBERALISM AND WORLD POLITICS
KEY FEATURES	**LIBERAL INTERPRETATION**
Nature of the international system	Formal anarchy; with interdependence, shared norms, international institutions linking the players
Relevant actors	States and non-state actors (e.g., international institutions, multinational or transnational corporations, international nongovernmental organizations, transnational advocacy networks)
Important resources	Multidimensional and situation-specific power; hard and soft power
Central dynamics	Cooperation, competition, and conflict; positive-sum calculations
Anarchy	Meaningful characteristic of the international system generating security dilemmas and complicating cooperation and coordination
Diversity	A wide array of players, from states to non-state actors, with different perspectives, values, institutions, and preferences struggle to cooperate and communicate
Complexity	Webs of connections between states and societies create both opportunity and challenges for world politics

© Cengage Learning®

3-4 THE CONSTRUCTIVIST PERSPECTIVE ON WORLD POLITICS

The third perspective on world politics for our discussion in this chapter is **constructivism**. Constructivist theories of international relations find their foundations in the field of sociology and thinkers such as Emile Durkheim and Max Weber. While Nicholas Onuf may have been the first international relations scholar to use the term "constructivism," arguing that we live in "a world of our making," Alexander Wendt is probably best known for this approach, which sees "facts" as "socially constructed." In other words, ideas and facts mean what we as members of a social group agree they mean. This perspective challenges the basic assumptions of realism and liberalism by asking fundamental questions about such concepts as anarchy or the nature and meaning of power. For example, is the international arena like the Wild West, the school playground without teachers, or a large family just trying to get along?

Both realism and liberalism make several assertions about the international arena. They both claim, for example, that anarchy—the absence of central government—is the prevailing condition in the world. Realism asserts that states are the primary actors; while liberalism also emphasizes states, it expands the list of actors to include non-state actors (e.g., IOs and MNCs), as well. What do these assumptions mean? Does the anarchy that defines the international system necessarily mean a violent, fearful environment like Hobbes described or an environment more like a troop of chimpanzees where there is real structure, cooperation, and altruism? In contrast to realism and liberalism, constructivism directs our attention to the meanings behind ideas and actions and the ways that interactions shape expectations and behavior.

3-4a Constructivism and the Nature of the International System

As we have said, anarchy does not mean chaos, but simply the absence of central government. Even in anarchy, we see both order and structure in world politics,

and the existence of institutions such as the UN, WTO, and others make that clear. But what about the world Hobbes described? Think about the way that Hollywood depicts the American West during U.S. territorial expansion. Almost universally, everyone either carries a gun in these movies or lives in fear of subjugation by those with guns. The Old West is depicted as a true **Hobbesian world** in which everyone lives in fear of others and life is "nasty, brutish, and short," at least until the hero saves everyone by killing the villain. The moral is quite simply that one must provide for one's own security (self-help). This depiction is generally how realists see the world. States must defend themselves or be subjugated by more powerful states. Certainly, during the era of colonial expansion, imperial wars, and gunboat diplomacy, this description appeared accurate. Powerful countries like the United Kingdom took over weaker countries like India, and the powerful countries fought with one another (e.g., United Kingdom and France). Is this how the world works today?

According to prevailing international norms, military conquest is no longer acceptable, at least for the purposes of owning another country. The 2001 U.S. invasion of Afghanistan (authorized by the UN for collective security) and the 2003 U.S. invasion of Iraq both officially aimed at removing an international threat. However, without engaging in a debate over the relative merits of these two operations or what goals the United States may truly have had in these two cases, it has not colonized the two countries the way it would have before the middle of the twentieth century. In both cases, the governments in Afghanistan and Iraq regularly criticize the United States and its operations. Colonial governments never did such things, in part because officials from the imperial power ran the colonial governments.

So what has changed? The international system is still formally anarchic. There is no world government with a true enforcement mechanism, and the UN does not have any authority that is not first granted to it by the individual member states. Yet, there is definitely a difference in what is considered acceptable behavior by states between now and just 60 years ago. Instead of the Wild West, the international system seems to be more like a somewhat unruly family. Some members of the family get along very well (e.g., the United States and Canada), others misbehave (e.g., North Korea, Iran), but generally, most of the family members cooperate with each other at least to some degree. States do not, as suggested by realism, constantly engage in conflict or preparation for conflict. In fact, as John Mueller (1989) argued in *Retreat from Doomsday: The Obsolescence of*

---

constructivism a major theoretical approach to international relations emphasizing the importance of ideas, collective identities, and the social construction of reality.

Hobbesian world a brutal, dangerous, self-help world without central authority described by the philosopher Thomas Hobbes.

Russia and the Eurasian Union

Alexsey Druginyn/AFP/Getty Images

In January 2015, Russia led some of its partner states of the former Soviet Union, Belarus and Kazakhstan, to establish the "Eurasian Union," building on and extending existing trade agreements to further integrate the countries of the region along a variety of dimensions, including labor, investment and energy. Motivated by Russian President Vladimir Putin's vision of a trade and political bloc capable of challenging the United States, China, and the European Union, the Eurasian Union is characterized by some observers as "a new geopolitical force capable of standing up to Russia's competitors on the world stage."[9] According to Putin (then Prime Minister) in 2011, when the foreign policy initiative was first announced, "We suggest a powerful supranational association capable of becoming one of the poles in the modern world."[10] The implications of this foreign policy initiative were not lost on Western leaders. Then U.S. Secretary of State Hillary Clinton characterized it as the possible "resovietization" of the region in December 2012. Western concerns increased after the Russian annexation of Crimea from Ukraine in 2014. Would Ukraine be coerced to join this union?

In light of the theoretical perspectives discussed in this chapter, how should the Eurasian Union foreign policy initiative be interpreted and explained?

1. Why would Vladimir Putin seek to establish a new Eurasian Union?

2. What would realists, liberals, and constructivists offer to explain the initiative and its likely consequences?

3. What foreign policy responses from the U.S., China and the states of the European Union are most likely, according to these three theoretical perspectives?

Major War, as a practice, large-scale war is a social institution that has become steadily less acceptable and more abhorrent to more and more states as they have learned of its true costs over time.

This change in perspective and behavior is at the heart of what constructivists emphasize in their explanations of the patterns of world politics. Thus, rather than treat anarchy as a given condition, political scientist Alexander Wendt provided the constructivist view, arguing that "Anarchy is what states make of it."[11] That is, anarchy is socially constructed, not determined by the environment. **Social construction** simply means that a concept is created by the interactions within a society. For example, fashion is a social construction. The clothes worn in the 1970s were considered very good-looking then, but jokes were made about them in the 1980s (and today, for that matter). There is nothing about the clothes that are or are not inherently fashionable. Instead, society's opinion changed and redefined what was fashionable. Something that is not a social construction is rain. The environment, specifically the

> **social construction** a concept is created by the interactions and ideas within a society.

level of moisture in the sky, determines whether or not it will rain. Society's opinion has no influence over the rain. Realists and liberals see anarchy like rain—something that is determined by the environment. Social constructivists like Wendt see anarchy like fashion—something that the actions and opinions of a society create.

According to Wendt, we can identify three ideal types of anarchy, each with very different implications for action. In *Hobbesian anarchy*, the system is much like realists depict, where states are adversaries and conflict is a normal part of their competition for power and survival. In *Lockean anarchy*, the system is more like liberals describe it, with states viewing each other as rivals, but in which cooperation, competition and conflict all occur. In *Kantian anarchy*, states see each other as friend and no longer fear each other or consider using force against each other. Instead, they find peaceful ways to settle their disputes and support each against other threats. Thus, "anarchy" itself is what states make of it and it does not determine state behavior.

If a central characteristic like anarchy is something that is constructed by the actions and opinions of states and non-state actors in the international system, then the meaning and characteristics of anarchy can change over time. During the colonial era, it was acceptable to conquer small states and thus make war for profit. In the current, post-colonial era, war for profit is not considered acceptable. This change is the result of a different social construction of what anarchy means. Just as fashions have changed over the years, so have the rules that states generally follow. Thus, the patterns of behavior that stem from "anarchy" in world politics will evolve and change, and will be different for different groups. For example, "anarchy" means something very different for the states of the NATO alliance than it does for the states of Africa, the Middle East, or South Asia. In the first group, "anarchy" does not mean self-help, security dilemmas and competition at all, but in the other groups, it often does!

3-4b Constructivism and the Relevant Actors in International Relations

Like liberalism, the constructivist perspective sees a more complicated array of players in world politics. Of course, constructivists pay attention to the state as a major player—some, like Wendt, treat world politics as an essentially state-centric system. But constructivists tend to see states more like liberals than realists: complicated and multifaceted entities rather than unitary, rational actors. Moreover, because constructivists emphasize the role of norms and ideas, they tend to stress the importance of people, groups, and cultural factors within states as very important. These are where the ideas come from and are held!

Like liberals, constructivists also see significance in a variety non-state actors and organizations, including international institutions, nongovernmental organizations, and transnational networks. Moreover, constructivists pay close attention to cultural groups in world politics—nations or ethnic groups and their experiences, ideas, and values. Finally, constructivists emphasize the importance of the identities and interests of the players as central to understanding their behavior. As we have just described, though, these aspects of the relevant actors are also socially constructed. Hence, what "Russia" means to the United States is shaped by U.S. culture and experience, but also by the patterns of interactions and shared experiences between the two countries. "Russia" meant something particular during the Cold War between the two countries (rival, enemy), something else in the post-Cold War environment (vanquished? partner?), and, perhaps, something else again in the wake of the aggressive actions taken against neighboring states such as Georgia (2008) and Ukraine (2014).

For example, constructivist scholars such as Michael Barnett and Martha Finnemore stress the importance of state identities and interests and the way the norms of the international society shape them. In particular, Finnemore argues that these norms are shaped, supported and spread by international organizations that help guide states toward particular behavior and understandings of their interests. Constructivist scholars like Peter Katzenstein emphasize how domestic culture and groups within states shape their identities and interests, and the norms and behavior they embrace. Finally, constructivist scholars such as Margaret Keck and Kathryn Sikkink point to the role of transnational actors and in shaping state interests about a variety of things, often serving as "norm entrepreneurs" who advance particular values and expectations and influence state behavior (see our discussion of transnational advocacy networks in Chapter 13).

3-4c Constructivism and the Important Resources of International Relations

Like liberal theorists, constructivists take a more complex and multidimensional view of power. Constructivists accept some of the material or tangible aspects of power that both realists and liberals stress, but push further than both of those perspectives to stress the **ideational** aspects of power and influence. In effect, they push the conception of "soft power" even further than liberals. In this conception, ideas, norms, identities—ways of thinking about yourself and others—and statements are an important part of what constitutes power and influence. Constructivists call this discursive power and stress that the meaning of things is an important element of power as well as the empirical nature of things. According to constructivists, discursive power works by producing and reproducing shared meanings, which shape how people understand the material world, their own and others' identities, and their relations with others. Thus, the nature of power and the relevant resources of power are also understood through social construction. To constructivists, the basis of power is not in the material power of states or institutions, but the ideas that people believe in and the shared understandings they develop. It is not that the material world and tangible resources of power do not matter, but that their meaning depends on shared ideas, norms and interpretations.

Consider, for example, the picture of the nuclear missile in its silo at the outset of this chapter. To a realist, this missile is a tangible example of the most important aspect of power—military strength. To a liberal, this missile may represent power and influence, but is not likely to be relevant in the relations between the United States and Canada, or between the U.S. and Japan. To a constructivist, social construction does not mean that there is some question about whether this is a missile or not, but that the meaning of the missile depends on the combination of identity, interests, and interactions of the players. So, this missile, possessed and deployed by the United Kingdom, is not a threat to the U.S., nor is it particularly relevant to the relationship between the U.S. and the U.K. However, this same missile deployed by North Korea takes on an entirely different meaning for power and security for countries such as South Korea and Japan, and results in a very different pattern of actions and interactions.

Indeed, most Americans probably think that it's okay that the United States, United Kingdom, and France have nuclear weapons. During the Cold War, nuclear weapons in the hands of the British and French were not viewed in anything like the same way as those controlled by Soviet leaders, but instead were interpreted as contributing to American power. Now, since the end of the Cold War, some people may also be comfortable with Russia and China having such weapons, too. Further, most people outside of North Korea probably think it's not okay that North Korea has a nuclear weapon. What about the nuclear arsenals of India, Pakistan, and Israel?

David Lomax/Hulton Archive/Getty Images

Paramilitary members of the Protestant "Ulster Defense Association" barricade a street | If the title didn't tell you who the combatants were, would you know if they were Catholic or Protestant?

If you live in a Muslim state in the Middle East such as Syria, you probably think it's really bad that the Israelis have nuclear weapons. If you are Israeli, you probably think it is not only a good thing but also necessary for your survival, and that the real negative scenario would be the possession of nuclear weapons by Syria! Why else would the Israelis conduct military strikes on countries such as Iraq (1981) and Syria (2007)? On the surface, one can understand why these two different views can exist. Syria and Israel are historic enemies (although not currently fighting) and each side would see the other as threatening. That is exactly the point of constructivism! Security is defined or constructed by each country. Thus, Syria sees itself as a good state that has a bellicose and nuclear-armed neighbor, while Israel sees itself as a good state whose neighbors—although militarily weaker—are threatening its survival and can't be allowed to possess such weapons.

3-4d Constructivism and the Central Dynamics of World Politics

Since a central idea behind constructivism is that all social relationships are constructed by people and therefore are subject to change, it follows that the central dynamics of world politics are subject to great variation

ideational emphasizing the centrality of ideas and norms in shaping behavior and interactions.

over time and among different pairs or groups of states. The historically intense hatred between the Protestants and Catholics in Northern Ireland provides a useful example. Northern Ireland has been a part of the United Kingdom since 1921, and in 1971, civil violence broke out between the Protestant-controlled government and the Catholic **Irish Republican Army (IRA)**. For decades, the violence raged between these two groups and the division between Protestants and Catholics widened. Like all conflicts, the causes are complex and multiple. Economic disparities between the two groups and a lack of political representation by the Catholics contributed to the divisiveness. However, it is also important to realize that the hatred between the two groups was fostered by a social construction. There was nothing identifiable between these two groups that one could see visibly. They spoke the same language. They lived in the same country. Within the Irish Catholic community, however, there was the belief—created by the Irish Catholic community—that the Protestants were not really Irish and should not be governing Northern Ireland; further, they thought Northern Ireland should be reunited with the Republic of Ireland. Conversely, the Irish Protestants believed that the Catholics were trying to drive them from their homes and would stop at nothing to rid Northern Ireland of their presence. To be sure, there was some truth to both of these beliefs— the IRA and Northern Ireland government (and British armed forces) were fighting. However, if there had been a reason for the hatred beyond their partially misinformed beliefs such as the enslavement of one group by the other, then compromise would not be possible. The two sides would prefer to continue fighting until one side lost.

Irish Republican Army (IRA) the militant terrorist organization in Northern Ireland that fought to remove the Protestant leaders from power and the British military from Northern Ireland.

consociational democracy a form of government that guarantees representation to the different ethnic or religious groups within the country.

negative peace a lack of conflict between two countries or groups.

positive peace a situation between two countries that is not simply a lack of conflict, but a mutual affinity for each other.

Hutu a socially constructed race in central Africa that was supposed to be poorer and physically shorter than its rival group, the Tutsis.

Tutsi a socially constructed race in central Africa that was supposed to be more elite, wealthier, and taller than their rival group, the Hutus.

Instead, a peace process slowly began in 1994 and ended with an agreement that provided for a governing body based on **consociational democracy**—that is, guaranteed representation for both Protestants and Catholics. While problems continue, there has been a shift in the social construction of the two sides. They are no longer bitter enemies, but perhaps cordial opponents. The shift involved years of diplomatic debate but also a shift in how the two communities perceived or socially constructed their view of each other.

You might ask if the peace in Northern Ireland is simply the result of the two sides getting tired of fighting. If that were the case, you might expect only a **negative peace**, the mere absence of fighting. Instead, there is real cooperation in Northern Ireland, suggesting that there is a **positive peace** between the two groups. Also, if groups that defined themselves as enemies simply grew tired of fighting, then how could we explain the continual fighting in the Middle East between the Israelis and their Arab neighbors? To end a conflict and build peace, the two sides must no longer define each other as enemies.

Another perhaps more stark and sad example that highlights the constructivist view on the central dynamics of world politics is Rwanda, home to two main ethnic groups: the **Hutus** and **Tutsis**. The two groups date back approximately 2,000 years and were perceived by colonial powers to have slightly different physical features. Supposedly, Hutus were shorter and Tutsis had a narrower nose. After a long history as a German colony, Belgium took control of the country after World War I. In 1935, the Belgians issued identity cards identifying each Rwandan as either Hutu or Tutsi—considered by the Belgians to be different races. After almost 2,000 years, however, lineage was difficult to determine (can you trace your relatives back that far?). So the Belgians based the identity of the two races on the physical differences, and when that was not apparent, then the number of cattle owned by the family would determine their race (families with more cattle were determined to be Tutsi).[12]

Unfortunately, the ridiculous idea of determining a person's ethnicity based on his or her economic status had fatal consequences. The 1935 identity cards artificially constructed two groups that competed for political and economic power and left the smaller group, the Tutsis, in control of the country. Over the years, the competition intensified to the point of open conflict and revolt. In 1994, the Hutu-controlled government and militias began murdering both Tutsis and politically moderate Hutus on a massive scale. In the end, the Rwandan

A pair of friends in Rwanda, one Hutu and the other Tutsi | These two men are friends, but a few years before this picture was taken, they would have been bitter enemies willing to murder each other with a machete. How can such "enemies" be friends?

genocide claimed approximately 800,000 people, many of them hacked to death by their neighbors using machetes.

The root of the genocide was the socially constructed race division put in place by the Belgians. To be sure, the genocide was preceded by a conflict that took years to develop and in which both sides played a part. For the Belgians' part, they did not anticipate such a horrendous outcome. However, the actual division was socially constructed, and it killed almost a million people. For a chilling representation of the Rwandan genocide, watch the film *Hotel Rwanda (2004)* or alternatively, the documentary *The Ghosts of Rwanda* (2004). Both films will leave you horrified.

Another example of the importance of changing social constructions and their impact on the central dynamics of world politics came in 2010 when ten people were arrested by U.S. authorities who suspected them of spying for Russia. During the worst days of the Cold War (say in the 1950s or early 1960s), such a spy scandal would have had serious repercussions. Tensions would likely have increased over already high levels and military readiness would likely have been set to a higher level, both possibly leading to a political crisis of some sort.

Yet consider what happened in 2010. Russian Prime Minister Vladimir Putin (a former career Soviet intelligence officer with the KGB) denounced the arrests as "unfounded" on the day they were announced in the press, but beyond that statement, nothing much was said by the Russians. Less than two weeks later, Russian and American airplanes met on the tarmac of a Vienna airport where the ten individuals arrested in the United States were swapped for four Russians previously imprisoned on charges of spying for the United States or United Kingdom.

Why were both the U.S. and Russian governments so eager to resolve this matter in a low-key way? The answer lies in their mutual effort to reset their relationship in a more positive manner following the elections of Barack Obama and Dmitry Medvedev as their respective presidents. Because these two presidents met frequently, discovered that they got along well with each other, and made the explicit decision to find ways for their states to cooperate and to put past rivalries behind them as best they could, we can say they created a new social construction of friendship and cooperation. Thus, "friends" minimize their reactions to such negative situations like spy scandals, but "rivals" or "enemies" or opponents do not. Neither Medvedev nor Obama was willing to let a minor espionage case sabotage an emerging positive relationship. Part of that social construction was the fact that both leaders were newly elected. Without any past political fights between them, both Medvedev and Obama desired a friendly relationship, so their identities as newly elected leaders influenced their preferences and the policies they chose. Thus, the definition of friendship was a social construct determined by the parties themselves. But, in the wake of the aggressive Russian actions against Ukraine in 2014, including the use of military power and the annexation of Crimea, a part of Ukraine, into Russia, what might have happened if the same spying crisis had occurred later in 2014?

Yet another good example of the power of social construction came in 1967. During the **Six-Day War** pitting Israel against Egypt, Jordan, and Syria, a U.S. naval vessel was attacked. The USS *Liberty* was in international waters north of the Sinai Peninsula where Israeli and Egyptian forces were fighting when it was attacked by Israeli aircraft and torpedo boats. The ship was heavily damaged, 34 on board were killed, and 170 were injured. Had this involved an attack by the Soviet Union or one of its allies during this Cold War era, severe military reprisals would have resulted, perhaps leading to

genocide the deliberate killing of a religious, ethnic or racial group.

Six-Day War the 1967 war between Israel, Egypt, Jordan, and Syria. Israel won the war and took control of the occupied territories (the Gaza Strip, West Bank, and Golan Heights).

U.S. President Obama and Russian President Medvedev meet during a U.S.-Russian Summit | Just a few years before this picture was taken, the Russian and U.S. governments were very angry with each other. How can two countries completely "reset" their relationship?

TABLE 3-5	SUMMARY OF CONSTRUCTIVISM AND WORLD POLITICS
KEY FEATURES	**CONSTRUCTIVISM**
Nature of the international system	Socially constructed, dynamic anarchy
Relevant actors	States, organizations, people, ideas
Important resources	Determined by the social construction
Central dynamics	Often conflict; but changes from state to state
Anarchy	Structure of the international system that is determined by state's actions and statements
Diversity	Different social definitions of the world and other actors
Complexity	Fashioned by the changing social constructions of the world

© Cengage Learning®

World War III. Yet in this case, the Israelis said it was an honest mistake in wartime, President Lyndon Johnson did not question that explanation, and the Israelis ultimately paid $14.5 million in compensation to the families of the dead and injured and for damages to the ship itself.

While it may have been an honest mistake on Israel's part, it may also have been intentional. The *Liberty* was a spy ship operated by the U.S. National Security Agency (NSA) and was engaged in eavesdropping on battlefield communications during the war. The Israelis may have simply wanted to prevent others from having access to that intelligence information. Had the Israelis not been seen as "friends" by President Johnson, their explanation might not have been accepted and the more sinister motive might have been attributed to them. In hindsight, it seems highly likely that the social construction of the U.S.–Israeli relationship as one of "friends" rather than of "rivals," "competitors," or even "enemies" made a considerable difference in the U.S. response.

These examples show the power of the social construction of ideas as a way to explain the dynamics of world politics (Table 3-5). Political realism would be unable to explain these episodes, due to its emphasis on states as unitary actors rationally pursuing their national interests denned largely in terms of military power. Liberalism recognizes that **substate actors** exist and can matter but would be unequipped to explain the intrastate violence in Northern Ireland or Rwanda or the lack of interstate violence between the United States and Israel. Liberalism would understand the 2010 spy episode as a chance for former rivals to cooperate, but it would not explain why the two states chose to cooperate. It would be less sensitive to the importance each president placed on consciously choosing in early 2009 to be friends, and thus how their newly nurtured friendship constrained and shaped their reactions to these arrests. Social constructivism provides a different lens through which all these real-world situations can be explained.

CONCLUSION: DUELING THEORIES?

The three major approaches to understanding and explaining international relations each simplify international reality, although they do so in different ways, highlighting different features and elements of the international system, its relevant actors and their resources, and the major patterns and dynamics that emerge (Table 3-6). Recent events since the turn of the century appear to pit the three perspectives against each other once again. Realism, liberalism, and constructivism have been cast as contenders and as complementary

substate actors groups within a state such as political parties, insurgents, or ethnic groups.

TABLE 3-6   COMPARING THE THEORIES

FEATURE	REALISM	LIBERALISM	CONSTRUCTIVISM
Nature of the international system	Anarchic; self-help	Formal anarchy, plus interdependence, shared norms, international institutions	Socially constructed, dynamic anarchy
Relevant actors	States	States and non-state actors	States, organizations, people, ideas
Important resources	Power, especially military	Multidimensional and situation-specific power; hard and soft power	Determined by social construction
Central dynamics	Conflict; zero-sum calculations	Cooperation, competition, and conflict; positive-sum calculations	Conflict, cooperation, but changing patterns from state to state
Anarchy	Fundamental structural condition generating fear, uncertainty, and conflict	A characteristic of the international system generating security dilemmas and complicating cooperation and coordination	Structure of the international system that is determined by ideas, interactions, and statements
Diversity	States have different levels of power and competing interests	State and non-state actors, with different perspectives, values, institutions, and preferences struggle to cooperate and communicate	Different social definitions of the world and other actors
Complexity	Generated from stratification of power and competing self-interests of states	Webs of connections between states and societies create both opportunity and challenges for world politics	Fashioned by the changing social constructions of the world

© Cengage Learning®

explanations for different situations. Consider what you now know about theory in general, and these three major theoretical approaches in particular: Is the current context an example of the consequences of **hegemony** (the dominance of one state), with rivals and challenges to the dominant power (the United States) emerging? Or is it an example of the dynamics of liberalism, with zones of peace and zones of turmoil in the world? Could it be the

> **hegemony** domination of the international system by one country.

THINK ABOUT THIS PEACE IN EUROPE AFTER 1945

For centuries Europe was among the most violent places in the world. In the early twentieth century, this pattern of persistent warfare culminated in the two largest wars of world history, World Wars I and II. However, since World War II's end, this region has enjoyed persistent peace. Large-scale warfare appears as a thing of the past, and most of Europe is now united and cooperating in the European Union. The 2012 symbol of the Nobel Peace Prize, shown below, represents this peace through its dove carrying an olive branch. In 2012, the EU was awarded the Nobel Peace Prize, an act that would likely have been unimaginable less than a century before. Consider this dramatic change in fortune for Europe before and after 1945 in light of the main elements of the three theoretical perspectives we have discussed in this chapter.

How would realists, liberals, and constructivists explain peace in Europe after World War II, and which explanations do you find most/least helpful?

PEACE PRIZE 2012

enpi-info.eu

© Julien Hautcoeur/Shutterstock.com

ideas, interests and interactions that shape the behavior of states have developed to establish new norms and patterns of behavior? Or are elements of all three perspectives at work at the same time? At the end of the day, we must theorize to arrive at answers. But hold on: if you find these theoretical approaches to be a bit inadequate, there are others to consider, and they are the focus of our next chapter.

STUDY TOOLS 3

LOCATED AT BACK OF THE BOOK:
☐ Rip out Chapter in Review card

LOCATED ON COURSEMATE:
Use the CourseMate access card that came with this book or visit CengageBrain.com for more review materials:

☐ Review Key Terms Flash Cards (Print or Online)
☐ Download Chapter Summaries for on-the-go review

☐ Complete Practice Quizzes to prepare for the test
☐ Walk through a Simulation, Animated Learning Module, and Interactive Maps and Timelines to master concepts
☐ Complete Crossword Puzzle to review key terms
☐ Watch the videos for real-world application of this chapter's content
☐ Visit IR NewsWatch to learn about the latest current events as you prepare for class discussions and papers

REVIEW QUESTIONS

1. What is theory, and what are its central purposes?

2. What are the main areas of agreement and disagreement between realists, liberals, and constructivists in their conception of the international system?

3. What are the main areas of agreement and disagreement between realists, liberals, and constructivists in their conception of the relevant actors in international relations?

4. What are the main areas of agreement and disagreement between realists, liberals, and constructivists in their conception of power and influence in international relations?

5. What are the main areas of agreement and disagreement between realists, liberals, and constructivists in their conception of the major patterns of behavior and interaction in international relations?

FOR MORE INFORMATION . . .

For more on realism, liberalism, constructivism, and the explanation of world politics, see:

Burchill, Scott, Andrew Linklater, Richard Devetak, Jack Donnelly, Terry Nardin, Mathew Paterson, Christian Reus-Smit, and Jacqui True. *Theories of International Relations*, 4th ed. New York: Palgrave-MacMillan, 2009.

Doyle, Michael W. *Ways of War and Peace: Realism, Liberalism and Socialism*. New York: W.W. Norton, 1997.

Drezner, Daniel. *Theories of International Politics and Zombies*. Princeton, NJ: Princeton University Press, 2011.

Dunne, Tim, Milja Kurki, and Steve Smith. *International Relations Theories: Discipline and Diversity*, 2nd ed. Lond on: Oxford University Press, 2010.

Sterling-Folker, Jennifer, ed. *Making Sense of International Relations Theory*. Boulder, CO: Lynne Rienner, 2005.

Viotti, Paul R., and Mark V. Kauppi. *International Relations Theory*, 5th ed. New York: Longman, 2011.

4 | Alternative Perspectives on International Relations

LEARNING OBJECTIVES

After studying this chapter, you will be able to . . .

4-1 Understand how the foreign policy perspective provides a foundation for international relations.

4-2 Explain how economic class as explained by Marxist theory can be the driving force for how nations interact with each other.

4-3 Describe the different aspects of world systems theory and how they explain international relations.

4-4 Outline the ways in which gender affects and is affected by international relations.

After finishing this chapter go to **PAGE 111** for **STUDY TOOLS**

ALTERNATIVES TO REALISM AND LIBERALISM?

As we noted in the prior chapter, one of the very first realists was Thucydides who wrote during the war between Athens and Sparta in ancient Greece. Thucydides wrote, "the strong do what they can and the weak suffer what they must." This simple statement emphasizes the role of power in international relations, and although it is over 2,000 years old, it is still used and taught today.

However, if Thucydides was right, then why hasn't the United States forcefully annexed Mexico's oil fields and the Baja? The oil fields contain a valuable resource, and Baja, California, is prime oceanfront real estate with tremendous value (imagine miles of beach just south of San Diego). To conquer these territories from the Mexican government is well within the power of the U.S. military. To be sure, Mexico would attempt to resist, but the capabilities of the U.S. military far surpass the Mexican military. And why stop with Mexico? Canada's oil and gas fields to the north would also make a valuable addition for the United States. Again, the United States is dramatically more powerful and could sweep aside the Canadian resistance to the limited invasion needed to take those properties.

If Thucydides was right about how states act—that they are only concerned with direct threats to their security—then there is little reason to believe that other countries would come to the aid of Mexico and Canada. Any states that could challenge the U.S. military and aid Mexico and Canada are far away. By taking those territories, the United States wouldn't directly encroach on China, Russia, or Europe, so why would other nations care if the United States gained some nice property and some additional energy resources?

Before you dismiss this scenario as implausible, realize that historically countries in North America did conquer territories from each other. Large parts of California, Arizona, New Mexico, and Texas used to be part of Mexico, and Canada was concerned that the United States might invade it immediately after the American Civil War because it had such a large army.

This episode raises some interesting questions:

1. Why is this scenario so unthinkable?

2. Are the realists like Thucydides wrong? Is security no longer the main concern of states?

3. Has something changed over the years so that taking land from another country is not acceptable? If so, how do you explain this change?

German Chancellor Angela Merkel and U.S. President Barack Obama review troops | In what ways does gender matter most in world politics?

INTRODUCTION: ALTERNATIVES TO REALISM, LIBERALISM, AND CONSTRUCTIVISM

In the previous chapter, we discussed the three most commonly used theories of how the world works. Each theory has a different view of how states interact and what is required for them to cooperate. This chapter presents three different challenges to those three dominant theories. First, **foreign policy analysis** switches the focus of understanding how states behave in the international arena to the people and groups that make the foreign policy decisions within each country. Instead of simply saying a state seeks security in the international system, foreign policy analysis examines how a dictator might try to increase her security or how a legislature might constrain a leader's attempt to strengthen the state's military power. Second, critical economic theories like **Marxism** and **world systems theory** suggest that realist, liberal, and constructivist assumptions are somewhat misguided and that the key factor to understanding interstate behavior is wealth and who controls it. These theories will argue that states act the way they do because

of the system of wealth production and extraction and not for any other reason. Finally, **feminist international relations theory** suggests that we should look through a different lens to see what the world would look like if it were not historically dominated by men. What are the consequences of a historically male-dominated political world, and what would be different if women had played

foreign policy analysis a theoretical approach that focuses on the process and outcomes of foreign policy decisions made by the people and groups that determine a state's actions in international relations.

Marxism an argument developed by Marx and Engels that asserted all politics was determined by social class and that the world would progress through historical economic epochs.

world systems theory a theory inspired by Marxism that argues the world is divided into three economic zones (by their level of development) and that these zones determine how states interact, with wealthier countries exploiting poorer countries.

feminist international relations theory a feminist approach to understanding international relations that focuses on the role of women and gender and how historically the world has been male dominated.

an equal role in politics during the Peace of Westphalia? Would the international system be different from what it is today?

Throughout the chapter, we present each of these theories as an alternative perspective on international relations. We also discuss their shortcomings and why they have not become as widely used as realism, liberalism, and constructivism. It is important to understand, however, that we do not have to either accept or reject these perspectives categorically. Instead, we can learn from each of them and adapt our views of international relations so that we better understand the world around us. The goal of this chapter is not to suggest that the theories discussed in Chapter 3 are wrong, but to provide a range of ways to look at states and their behavior. By understanding the many different lenses available, we are able to select and adapt the ones that make the most sense to us and apply them to the issues and circumstances in which they are most useful.

4-1 FOREIGN POLICY ANALYSIS

The first theory to deviate from realism, liberalism, and constructivism is foreign policy analysis, though scholars of international relations use different terms for this approach. The study of foreign policy is best understood by its **agent-centered approach**. What that means is to understand how states interact, we must focus on agents—the individuals and groups who make decisions within the state.

For realism, states are assumed to be unitary, rational actors. In Chapter 3, we discussed the idea of a *unitary actor*. The notion of the state as a rational actor underlies realist and some of liberal theorizing as well. This **rational actor model** simplifies our understanding and explanation of the behavior of states by assuming a common, unified approach to decisions, as summarized in Figure 4-1. Though there are many versions of this approach, they commonly simplify the decision process to assume that actors respond to problems by

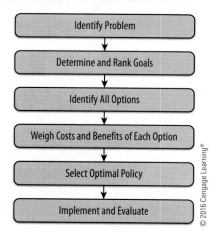

FIGURE 4-1 THE RATIONAL ACTOR MODEL

Identify Problem

↓

Determine and Rank Goals

↓

Identify All Options

↓

Weigh Costs and Benefits of Each Option

↓

Select Optimal Policy

↓

Implement and Evaluate

© 2016 Cengage Learning®

ranking-ordering their goals, identifying available options, and weighing the costs and benefits of each. Then, once that is done, the actor selects the option to provide the greatest benefits at the lowest costs, in light of the rank-ordered goals that were specified, and carries out the decision, watching to see whether the course works or not so that adjustments can be made if needed.

For example, a realist would describe the 2014 Russian incorporation/annexation (invasion?) of Crimea simply as that—Russia decided to take Crimea from Ukraine in order to increase its security. For explanatory purposes, the rational actor model therefore presumes purposive and goal-oriented behavior consistent with the idea of maximizing benefits and minimizing costs. It also assumes that all actors behave the same, simplifying away differences in individuals, groups, decision processes, societal factors, and regime characteristics.

These are precisely the characteristics that foreign policy analysis pays attention to. Returning to the Russian annexation of Crimea, foreign policy analysis would explain it differently, focusing on the agents involved. For example, a foreign policy analysis approach might focus on Russian President Vladimir Putin. Thus, the invasion might be explained as driven by Putin's aggressive beliefs about international relations and his desire to expand his power.

Both of these explanations could be correct—or useful—depending on the situation, but there are cases in which looking at the agents making foreign policy is a necessary part of the explanation. For example, when President Obama declared a "red line" in Syria after evidence appeared that the Assad regime had used chemical weapons, he indicated that the United States would intervene with military force. It therefore seemed clear that the U.S. would attack the Syrian government.

agent-centered approach understanding and explaining international relations by focusing on the individuals and groups who make decisions within the state.

rational actor model as unitary actors, all states make decisions according to a rational process in which goals are ranked, options identified and evaluated, and selections made to maximize benefits according to the goals of the actor.

However, perhaps in attempt to back down from his threat, President Obama asked the U.S. Congress to authorize a military strike. The U.S. House of Representatives was strongly opposed to the idea of military intervention. As a result, the United States did nothing. To understand this episode, we need to look at the agents involved—in this case, the president and members of Congress. While constructivists might say Congress socially constructed the reality involved, a realist or liberal would not be able to explain these events except to say that the U.S. did not intervene in Syria after the discovery that chemical weapons were used.

Agents can be a variety of people or groups. In the examples above, we discussed individuals, Putin and Obama, and a group or governmental institution, Congress. There is no correct answer to what a state's agent or agents are. In some cases, individual characteristics are important to consider. Putin's aggressive, expansionist personality, Ronald Reagan's mistrust of the Soviets, Saddam Hussein's narcissistic personality, and Hugo Chavez's anti-American focus are all examples of specific individual characteristics that might affect a state's foreign policy.

Most of the time, however, it makes more sense to think of groups of leaders. President Obama has a cabinet of advisors who help him make decisions. Similarly, President Xi Jinping of the People's Republic of China works with the Politburo Standing Committee of the Chinese Communist Party to make decisions. Thus, whether in a democracy or authoritarian regime, the agent of the state—the key decision maker—is usually a group of individuals.

Other groups that can be considered agents are interest groups, the media, and even public opinion. We can also consider the regime or government itself an agent. Unlike realists, however, we understand that a state's government is not the entire state, and unlike liberals we realize that there may be multiple leaders within a society. Thus, for example, we can think of the U.S. government, but any decisions it makes are made in the context of American public opinion, interest groups, the media, and so on. Thus, foreign policy analysis might focus on individuals, small groups, bureaucratic organizations, legislatures, domestic/societal forces such as interest groups and public opinion, and different regime types.

4-1a Individual Explanations of Foreign Policy

When we focus on individuals as the key agent in foreign policy decision making, there are many different possible approaches. The common characteristic is that they all show how individual preferences or human characteristics affect how leaders make decisions. Political scientist Herbert Simon wrote about how humans make decisions. He suggested that there are those who are rational decision makers, making decisions like a computer, perfectly logical and with no emotion (much like a Vulcan from Star Trek). On the other end of this spectrum are the emotional decision makers, those who make decisions without any consideration for reality. Most leaders—and most people—fall in between these two opposites in what Simon called **bounded rationality**. This concept means that leaders try to be rational or logical when making decisions, but there are limits or bounds on our ability to be rational.

For example, have you ever taken an immediate dislike to someone after meeting him or her? Even without interacting with someone, we can have a negative reaction to that person. Why? It's not logical or rational to have a "gut feeling" and distrust someone without getting to know them, but most people have had this experience. Now imagine that you are the leader of a country. What if you have that reaction to another leader? Will that affect how you negotiate with them? What if it's the other way around—for some reason, you just trust the other leader for no other reason than a "gut feeling." Would you be more willing to make a trade deal or sign a treaty with that leader? Thus, our emotions, personality, and preferences limit our ability to be perfectly rational.

To put this idea of bounded rationality to work, scholars developed different theories for how leaders make decisions. One theory, **operational code analysis**, argues that leaders have a tendency to (1) prefer either conflict or cooperation and (2) believe they are either very effective or limited in their ability to control others. This does not mean that leaders who prefer conflict are immoral warmongers; it just means they believe that the world is a conflictual place and often one must use force to protect oneself. Similarly, a leader preferring cooperation will still go to war; that leader's preference only means a cooperative strategy might be tried first, if possible.

Stephen Walker developed a way to measure a leader's conflict/cooperation and effective/limited beliefs

bounded rationality the idea that leaders want to make rational or logical decisions but are limited by their lack of knowledge or other human factors.

operational code analysis the idea that leaders have a tendency to (1) prefer either conflict or cooperation and (2) believe they are either very effective or limited in their ability to control others.

from a distance. Since leaders such as Putin, Merkel, and Obama aren't likely to take personality tests for researchers, Walker created a way to measure their beliefs from their speeches. By coding what and how leaders say things in scores of their speeches, scholars are able to see how much they prefer conflict or cooperation, how much control they believe they have, and how they learn over time. For example, President Carter started his time in the White House preferring cooperation and believing he had considerable ability to affect other leaders. After the Soviet invasion of Afghanistan and the Iranian Hostage Crisis, his beliefs were nearly identical to those of Ronald Reagan—he believed that the world was conflictual and chaotic, and that leaders must use force to protect their countries.

Another individual explanation of foreign policy is **prospect theory**. According to scholars such as Rose McDermott and Jack Levy, this theory argues that humans are rational, but that changes depending on the situation. The best way to describe this is through a simple exercise:

- In Scenario 1, you are presented with two choices: Option 1—80 percent chance of winning $1,000 or Option 2—40 percent of winning $2,500. Most people choose Option 1. It's almost a "sure thing," and even though Option 2 has a greater utility (the payoff multiplied by the probability), people prefer to be risk averse in these conditions.

- In Scenario 2, you are also presented with two choices: Option 1—80 percent chance of losing $1,000 or Option 2—40 percent change of losing $2,500. In this case, most people go with Option 2. They are willing to risk more money with the hope that they won't lose anything.

In the first scenario, you are in the **domain of gains**, that is, you're ahead and less willing to take risks. In the second scenario, you are in the **domain of losses**, and much more willing to accept risky options. Another way to think of this is: would you work harder to get a

The White House/Getty Images News/Getty Images

President Obama considering options for the raid that killed Osama bin Laden | What difference does an individual leader make?

promotion or keep your job if it was threatened? The promotion is in the domain of gains while getting fired is clearly in the domain of losses. Most people would fight hardest to keep their job.

So how does this relate to foreign policy analysis? Leaders will find themselves in these domains and act accordingly. For example, in 1960, an American U-2 spy plane was shot down over the Soviet Union. President Eisenhower found himself in the domain of losses because the United States had been caught violating Soviet airspace and illegally gathering photos. Instead of admitting the spying, Eisenhower took the far riskier option and denied it. Once the Soviets showed the world the incontrovertible evidence, Eisenhower was caught not only spying but also lying to the public. The fallout included the Soviets cancelling an important summit meeting with Eisenhower, an event that was meant to top off his legacy as president.

Another view of individuals as the agents of foreign policy is **poliheuristic theory**. Alex Mintz argues that important foreign policy decisions are broken into two different stages. In the first stage, the leader rules out all of the unacceptable options. During that part of the decision process, the leader usually focuses on domestic political issues. For example, German Chancellor Angela Merkel may want to use the military to remove Russian forces from Ukraine, but she knows that the German public would not support such a move at this time. Therefore, it is an unacceptable option and should not be considered further. This stage is not necessarily rational. Instead of evaluating each option against the others, some options are simply removed from consideration. In the second stage, the leader rank orders the

prospect theory the idea that humans are rational but their rationality is situationally biased; that is, they are more risk-averse when things work in their favor and more risk-taking when things aren't going well.

domain of gains situations in which decision makers seek to preserve their advantages.

domain of losses negative situations in which decision makers will engage in more risk-taking to change the status quo.

poliheuristic theory the idea of decision making as a two step process: first, options found unacceptable or impossible are discarded, and then, the remaining options are rationally considered.

Are We Genetically Coded for Violence? A Neurobiological Theory of Violence and International Relations

What makes a person strap on a bomb, walk into crowd, and detonate it? What makes a soldier jump on a grenade to save her comrades? While these two instances are different, there is a strong similarity. In both cases, these persons know their lives will end, they are taking action for something in which they devoutly believe, and only a small portion of the population would take either of these actions. There is another possible similarity—both may carry a gene that, when activated, makes them prone to violence. Professors Rose McDermott and Peter Hatemi are leading the study of this phenomenon and its consequences for international relations. As you probably are already thinking, defense ministries such as the U.S. Department of Defense are very interested in this gene and how it is activated—wouldn't you want to know who would bomb your troops' barracks?

These analyses show that a small portion of all populations carry this gene, but it is only activated when the person experiences extreme violence or hardship during the early stages of their life. This experience could be a famine, being a refugee, living in a warzone, or even experiencing a military intervention. In these cases, the gene is likely to be activated. As a result, in countries suffering from severe economic hardship and violence, there are more people willing to commit extreme violent acts. As the number of violent events increases, such as suicide bombings, the environment continues to activate the gene in children and young adults, creating a vicious cycle.

While the connection to international relations should be clear—violent states are likely to continue to produce violent individuals—there is also a perverse impact. Imagine that a country is experiencing a moderate level of famine and civil unrest, and the UN authorizes a humanitarian military presence to keep the peace and help secure food deliveries. That military intervention, though intended to be humanitarian, may spark increased tensions that activate the gene in the younger generation. Thus, the humanitarian intervention may actually lead to more violence in the future. The increased future violence activates more of these genes, creating a downward spiral.

This research is very much on the frontier of what we know about genetics and violence, and could promise to expand our understanding of conflict around the globe in the future. Still, it is still in its early stages and should be viewed with a careful eye. This research could have both good and bad implications. For example, if we could identify the gene carriers, we might be able to provide counseling that reduces their penchant for violence, but governments could also simply jail them or even kill them. It seems that the implications for this research are even more interesting than the idea of genetically predisposed violence.

1. What are the implications of such a human gene for the patterns of world politics and the possibilities for conflict and cooperation?

2. What might the implications for world politics be if we could *identify* a human gene that makes some people prone to violence? How might different countries around the world respond to this kind of information?

3. Should states reconsider intervention, even if it is for humanitarian purposes, and increase development aid in an attempt to alleviate economic hardship?

remaining options and selects the best one, effectively rationally maximizing the choice but only on the "acceptable" options.

A good example is the attempted hostage rescue during the Iranian Hostage Crisis. After the Islamic revolution in Iran, college students stormed the U.S. Embassy on November 4, 1979, and held 52 Americans hostage for 444 days. After several months, President Carter launched a risky rescue mission. Scholars show that Carter had ruled out the "do nothing" option early in cabinet deliberations. Once that option was considered unacceptable, the president selected the best remaining option. Unfortunately, the rescue mission failed, and the hostages were not released until January 20, 1981.

Poliheuristic theory provides two important perspectives on how foreign policy decisions are made. First is the two-stage decision-making process, and second is the idea of unacceptable options. While we may not realize it, we all follow a similar process when making big decisions. We all rule out those options that are simply not possible before we consider which option might be best. For example, the United States may not like the fact that the Japanese government plans to begin whaling again, but military strikes and nuclear weapons are not acceptable options to convince the Japanese to cease whaling. Once those options and others are ruled out, the Obama administration could determine which of the remaining policies is the best choice.

4-1b Group Explanations of Foreign Policy

In a famous study of the Cuban Missile Crisis, Graham Allison showed that leaders in the U.S. government held different opinions on how to deal with the Soviet missiles in Cuba based on the organization in which they worked. The Army commanders recommended that President Kennedy order an invasion, the Air Force recommended bombing to destroy the missiles, and the Navy suggested a blockade. In a classic example of "where you stand is determined by where you sit," each commander's solution was a reflection of the job they held. This is a classic example of the **organizational/bureaucratic politics model** of foreign policy.

The bureaucratic politics approach rests on three characteristics of bureaucratic organizations (every state has them) that affect the process of decision making: hierarchical structure, specialization, and routinization. Bureaucratic organizations are hierarchically structured with divisions of authority from top (most authority) to bottom (least authority). Specialization means that organizations are established to attend to particular tasks and, within organizations, offices exist for increasingly specific responsibilities as you move down the hierarchy. At the same time, the further down the hierarchy you go, the more routine behavior becomes, as bureaucratic personnel are increasingly likely to follow "standard operating procedures" to do their jobs.

Because of these basic characteristics, foreign policy decision making is affected by bureaucratic politics. At the top of the bureaucratic organizations, agency leaders tend to approach foreign policy problems with information, perspectives, and policy preferences that reflect their organizational viewpoints and specialization.

Often, competition over policy options among agencies and their personnel occurs, and the result is frequently "political bargaining, coalition building, and compromise."

Further down in the organizations, agencies and personnel tend to follow their own routines and stress their own responsibilities and perspectives as well. Each bureaucracy develops its own organizational missions and standard operating procedures. As a consequence, organizational behavior tends to be "incremental" in nature, where members of organizations act very similarly from one day to the next. Bureaucratic policymaking also tends to reflect established bureaucratic repertoires and routines, with standard operating procedures for addressing a set of issues. Another aspect of organizations and their influence on how we think is budgets. In addition to influencing how we see the world and what policy options we develop, we associate our future with the organization. As a consequence, people want their organization to succeed. For example, when President Carter authorized Operation Eagle Claw to rescue the hostages in Iran, each of the armed services wanted to be involved. There was infighting between the Navy, Army, and Marines about the roles each would play the mission. That infighting, driven by a desire to be part of the action and justify future budgets, contributed to the failure of the operation. Finally, bureaucratic agencies can pursue contradictory policies as each organization pursues its own course within its jurisdiction. All of these characteristics of bureaucratic culture and processes affect the foreign policy behavior of the state in significant ways, and this approach focuses on them to understand why a certain state engages in particular foreign policy behavior on a specific issue or problem, rather than assuming a coherent, unitary, and rational process.

Foreign policy decisions are affected not only by which organizations are involved in a leader's decision but also how the leader structures her **advisory group**. Studies show that the more restricted the flow of information within an advisory group, the more extreme the state's foreign policy will be. Thus, leaders who allow only the most senior advisors to directly speak to them tend to be more likely to use military force compared to an open or collegial advisory system. In the more open group, senior and junior advisors openly share ideas and often arrive at more inventive policies short of using military force.

Another way in which group politics can affect foreign policy in a democracy is how much of a majority the leader has. In the United States, the president appoints top executive branch officials. Thus, the secretary of state and the secretary of defense work directly for the president.

organizational/bureaucratic politics model foreign policy decisions are the products of large bureaucratic organizations doing what they know to do or see as in their organizational interest.

advisory group the set of individuals from whom leaders seek decision-making assistance.

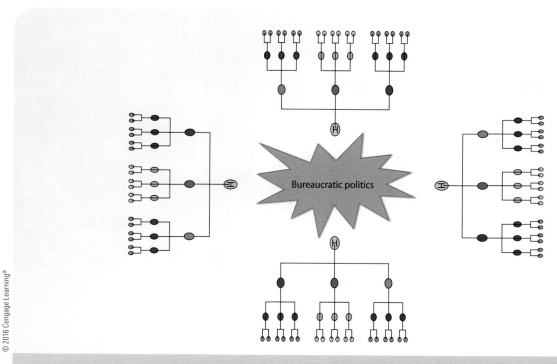

Bureaucratic politics

How can cooperation between large or rival organizations be achieved?

In a parliamentary democracy with **proportional representation**, most governments are coalitions. That is, they are a coalition of cooperative political parties. So, for example, a government could be composed of a pro-union party, a socialist party, and an environmental party. Research by Juliet Kaarbo and Ryan Beasley shows that these coalition governments engage in more extreme foreign policies compared to single-party

President Barack Obama and his advisers meet in the White House Situation Room to discuss U.S. plans to capture Osama bin Laden | How do you think the relationship between a leader and his or her advisers affects foreign policy decisions?

governments, like those in the United States and United Kingdom. The reason is twofold. First, coalitions often include more extreme parties, and these political parties can demand more extreme policies, effectively hijacking a state's foreign policy. Second, because there are multiple parties in the government, it is hard for the public to determine who is to blame for a policy. In the U.S., this is impossible since only one party—the party of the president—is held responsible for foreign policy. In other democracies, however, it is not uncommon to have more than three parties in the government. If that were the case, who would you blame for a problem?

4-1c Societal Explanations of Foreign Policy

Another approach to understanding international relations from a foreign policy perspective is to look at the interest groups within a country. The most famous of these interest groups within the United States are typically tied to a specific country and so they lobby the government for more favorable policies toward their

proportional representation a democratic system in which parties or factions get approximately the same percentage of legislative seats as votes they received in the most recent election.

preferred country. For example, for years the Cuban American National Foundation was a well-organized Cuba interest group that focused pressure on the Castro regime in Havana; it virtually dominated U.S. policy toward Cuba in the 1980s and 1990s. Another well-organized group is the **American Israel Public Affairs Committee (AIPAC)**, a pro-Israel interest group. AIPAC lobbies the U.S. for favorable policies toward Israel such as the selling of military weapons technology and sanctions on Iran. Its influence is so significant that other groups try to counter it (like the group J Street for those who think Israel should compromise more in the hope of peace) or mimic it (like the America India Public Affairs Committee).

These groups certainly have an influence on U.S. foreign policy, but their focus is limited to one country (Cuba/Israel/India) or region (the Middle East). As you will see in Chapters 8 and 13, there are other international groups that can have an impact on a country's foreign policy that is not limited to a single country. Groups focused on human rights and multinational corporations focused on profits can affect how a state makes its foreign policy. Groups like Amnesty International can push even the most powerful countries to levy economic sanctions on states that violate human rights, and multinational corporations spend countless dollars on influencing policies about interstate trade and finance.

While all of these groups can have a big impact on a country's foreign policy, perhaps the most powerful is simply public opinion. In a democracy, leaders must satisfy their public's demands or be voted out of office. As a result, leaders try to either figure out what their public wants or lead the public to what the leader wants. For example, following the Battle of Mogadishu in 1993, when 18 American soldiers were killed, President Clinton feared that there would be a public backlash against him, partly because of media coverage of the event. Consequently, he announced the withdrawal of U.S. forces from Somalia. Though such a backlash did not occur, Clinton's belief that it would led him to shift U.S. foreign policy. In this case, Clinton followed his perception of what the public wanted.

The importance of public opinion is so strong that scholars argue leaders will engage in conflicts just to divert the public's attention away from other problems. Called **diversionary theory** (see Chapter 5 for more

Former Yugoslav leader Slobodan Milosevic whips up public opinion against Bosnians in 1989 | What motivates leaders to direct their people's attention to enemies abroad?

discussion on this idea), there is some evidence that leaders are more likely to use the military when they face domestic economic crises, domestic criticism, or worse, a scandal. The classic example is President Clinton's bombing of sites in Sudan and Afghanistan after the intern with whom he had an affair—Monica Lewinski—testified before Congress. Perhaps the most outrageous illustration is the movie *Wag the Dog*, in which the president's "fixer" hires a Hollywood producer to create a fictitious war with Albania after the president was caught in a sex scandal. Whether or not leaders consciously use the military when they are facing political attacks at home is not clear, and fiction like *Wag the Dog* is clearly just that, fiction. There is, however, a slight preference for leaders to be more active during these periods.

4-1d Regime Explanations of Foreign Policy

Thus far, we have examined individual and societal theories of foreign policy. Most of these theories suggested that human nature was not purely rational or logical. Instead, it was argued that personality characteristics or preferences bounded rational decision making. Thus, leaders are mostly rational, but their human nature can get in the way. There is a group of foreign policy scholars who assume that leaders are purely rational, but they still take an agent center approach to understanding foreign policy.

The most powerful of these theories was developed by Bruce Bueno de Mesquita and his colleagues in a book titled *Political Survival*. The theory is quite simple and applies to all types of regimes—from democratic to autocratic. The theory argues that leaders want to stay in power and to do so they must satisfy at least half of

American Israel Public Affairs Committee (AIPAC) a pro-Israel interest group, thought to be the most influential interest group impacting U.S. foreign policy.

diversionary theory the idea that leaders under domestic pressures will use military force more readily to distract their opponents or rally the public behind their leadership.

the people who are in the **selectorate**, the group that selects the leader. In a democracy, the selectorate are the people who are eligible to vote. To become a leader in a democracy, then, you must get half of the voters to choose you. That half is called the **winning coalition**.

In an authoritarian country, clearly the selectorate is not the voters. Instead, it is the powerful elites that the leader needs to support him or her. These elites are usually military generals, the wealthiest business people, and perhaps political party leaders. Even in a state like North Korea, Kim Jong-un must have the support of generals and those who control the state-owned industries. This does not mean it is democratic, it just means that a leader cannot rule by sheer force of will. They must have the support of some people.

Thus, the key different between a democracy and an autocracy is the size of the selectorate, and that has a dramatic effect on how the leader makes her foreign policy. In a democracy, the leader must satisfy most of the public, and therefore must provide "peace and prosperity." That means a healthy economy and either no war or at least a successful war. Democratic leaders who have a bad economy or lose a war are very unlikely to be reelected.

In an autocracy, however, the leader only needs to satisfy a few people. Therefore, the economy can be in poor condition as long as the leader pays off his supporters. Further, he can engage in wars and even lose, as long as the generals are satisfied, which can be as simple as launching occasional attacks and using or testing their newest weapons.

What does this mean for our understanding of international relations? Democratic leaders will tend not to engage in conflict, because they fear becoming entangled in a war that leads to their electoral defeat. If they do go to war, however, they will go "all in," so to speak, because they must win the war to stay in office. Authoritarians will engage in limited wars and prefer not to go "all in" because that would hurt their military, which could lead to a coup d'état by one of their dissatisfied generals. While the political survival theory of foreign policy does not give us details about the individuals and human nature, it does provide a clear and concise way of understanding how the agents who make foreign policy balance their domestic political constraints and international pressures.

4-1e FPA as the Foundation for International Relations

If we do not consider these different perspectives, foreign policy theorists would argue, we are missing out on important details that realists, liberals, and constructivists ignore. Further, foreign policy theories

provide answers to why states are not always rational, why they do not always follow what a realist or liberal theorist might expect. An invasion of Cuba during the Missile Crisis would almost surely have resulted in the release of the operational nuclear missiles in Cuba. Nuclear war would have followed. While this was not the goal of the Army, an invasion made the most sense from their perspective. What if President Kennedy had chosen the invasion and nuclear war had followed? How would a realist, liberal, or constructivist explain this outcome?

The other important benefit that foreign policy theories provide is the foundation for understanding international relations. Realists assume that states are unitary, that their actions are the actions of a single decision maker. Liberals and constructivists may focus on leaders and society, respectively. Foreign policy analysis looks deeper and explains how those decisions are made within the state, often down to the group and individual level.

4-2 MARXIST THEORY

We turn now from the foreign policy analysis focus on agents to an economic approach to understanding world politics. Marxist theory is very different from realism, liberalism, and constructivism because it starts from a very different view of the world, one in which economic class is the driving force rather than power.

"The history of all hitherto existing society is the history of class struggles."[1] This quote from *The Communist Manifesto* sums up the Marxist theory approach to international relations. In its most basic form, the approach asserts that all actions by people and states are driven by economic desires rather than desires for power, security, and so on. The radical departure from realism, liberalism, and constructivism comes from the idea that states do not seek security, they seek to make their capitalist class—that is, the wealthiest individuals in the country—wealthier.

The theory laid down by Karl Marx and Friedrich Engels was part theory, part historical interpretation, and part policy prescription. Before turning to what they said, it is worth discussing the two men a little. Both men were born in Prussia (modern-day Germany) to relatively wealthy parents. Marx married and had seven

---

selectorate those in a state who provide the power base for a leader.

winning coalition the half of the voters you must get to win an election.

children (and an eighth with the family maid), but only three lived to become adults. Marx never held a regular job and for much of his adult life he lived mostly hand-to-mouth from the support of Engels, various inheritances, and payments for his writings.

Marx was more than just a poor philosopher, he was an activist who worked to form labor unions and communist parties in several countries. He devoted himself to helping workers in Prussia, France, and the United Kingdom at different times in his life. In his era, workers were treated horribly, and Marx believed that they should have an equal share of the fruits from their long hours of labor. His activities placed him in dangerous situations, as the owners of the factories he tried to organize did not take kindly to his goal of helping their workers. He was kicked out of several countries for "subversive" activity, which was often the same activity that we see labor unions engage in today—peacefully.

Engels had a lifelong partner, Mary Burns, but he never married because he did not believe in the institution. Though Marx never wrote about the status of women, Engels stated that, through economic equality, men and women could reach an equal status and be respectful of each other's gender. Like Marx, he was both philosopher and activist, but unlike his lifelong friend, he worked for his father's textile firm. Without his financial support, Marx and his family would have starved. Together, they composed an effective team. Only eleven people attended Marx's funeral. That did not mark the end of Marx, however; it was the beginning of what has become one of the biggest changes in thinking about politics and economics.

Now let's turn to what these two philosophers wrote. We will focus on the theory and later discuss a spin-off of Marxism. The theory actually focuses on the individual and class rather than on the state, but what it says about individuals very much involves states. Marxist theory sees the state of nature not at all like the realists and liberals; it asserts that humans like to be productive, and if unconstrained by society and government, they will live peacefully and happily with each other working, building, and creating.

DAVID GANNON/AFP/Getty Images

Statue of Karl Marx and Friedrich Engels in Berlin, Germany | When they were alive, many considered these two men to be radicals and trouble-makers. How are they viewed today, and how have their ideas affected the way we understand politics and economics?

The obstacle to this utopia is the misguided pursuit of wealth that develops through human history.

The theory suggests that after leaving the most primitive tribes, humans developed a society with two economic classes: workers and the wealthy. Those classes exchanged labor for money, but at no point in history has that exchange been equal. Instead, the wealthy class takes wealth from the workers by paying them less than their labor is worth. This process of exploitation began with feudalism during medieval times. The wealthy class (royalty or lords) owned all land and resources, while peasants (serfs) owned nothing and worked on the lord's land in exchange for the right to live there, the right to eat some of the food produced on the land, and protection. The serfs were not free to leave, but they were not slaves. In return for working his land, the lord provided law and order for the peasants.

With the development of specialized skills (e.g., a blacksmith, a weaver), the economy and society industrialized. This change in the economy led to the end of feudalism and the birth of **capitalism**. In capitalist societies, workers (also called the **proletariat**) were free and could sell their labor to the capitalist class (also called the bourgeoisie) who were typically not willing to pay what their labor was worth. The **capitalist class** thus profited off of the laborers' effort and actually did no work themselves.

Marx and Engels theorized that eventually, the proletariat would rise up and revolt against the capitalists, overthrow them, and take control of the government. The new government would take complete ownership of the economy for the proletariat, and it would begin to break

capitalism an economic system in which workers sell their labor for wages, there is no central authority over the economy, and market forces determine what is purchased and what is sold.

proletariat the working class that sold its labor for less than its value to the capitalists.

capitalist class or bourgeoisie the owners of businesses, factories, etc., that make profits from the work of laborers but do not work themselves.

down the old capitalist institutions. Part of this process would be to reeducate everyone so that they understood humans are happier as workers, not as wealthy individuals living off the work of others. This government would be considered socialist. After reeducating everyone and destroying the old capitalist institutions, over time the government itself would wither away and society would become truly communist, a utopia where everyone cooperated and the human vices inspired by capitalist greed and envy had been eradicated. As a well-known quote from Marx (who borrowed it from others) states, this utopia would thrive as wealth/production was cooperatively and collectively gained "from each according to his ability, to each according to his need."

4-2a Marxist Theory and International Relations

You may be asking yourself what this has to do with international relations! Where are the states, the diplomats, the armies, the non-state actors? There are two connections that make Marxist theory more than an economic explanation of society and relate it directly to international relations.

First, unless a state was socialist, its motives were to promote the wealth of the capitalist class. According to the theory, the capitalist class controlled the government, and thus all policies, foreign and domestic, were made to benefit the capitalists. Marxist theory asserts that wars are not fought for territory or security, but for the profit they will bring the wealthy class. For example, a communist interpretation of World War II would assert that a newly wealthy class within Germany was attempting to gain access to markets, resources, and more labor. By attempting to conquer other colonies and annex territory in Europe, the Nazi Party was acting on behalf of German capitalists who wanted to expand their wealth beyond Germany's borders. The German economy had been suffering very badly prior to the military buildup and war preparations. Once Adolf Hitler took control of the country, he began building up the economy. Marxist theory would cite this as evidence that Hitler was trying to rebuild and expand the wealth of the capitalists rather than creating a master race that would last thousands of years.

It is worthwhile to stop for a moment and think about this interpretation and what it means. Marxist theory would argue that Hitler really didn't care about the Jews or his Aryan master race. Instead, he was simply rebuilding the economy and eliminating a portion of the wealthy capitalist class. Thus, it was simply a fight over wealth. This same argument would be applied to

other genocides, such as Rwanda. Instead of race being the motivating factor, it was the competition for money that was simply disguised as a racial issue. What do you think of this argument? Is there some truth to the Marxist interpretation? Does it seem one-sided to you?

Another example comes from the first leader of the first communist state, the Soviet Union. Vladimir Lenin argued that relatively rich and powerful countries such as Britain and France needed colonies to continue expanding the wealth of their capitalist class and to delay the inevitable socialist revolution. In *Imperialism: the Highest Stage of Capitalism*, Lenin argued that these wealthy states might be nearing the brink of a revolution, but by conquering new colonies, they could extract more wealth from the colony and pay off the workers within the home state. For example, to keep British workers from revolting, Great Britain needed to acquire more and more colonies to extract wealth for the capitalists and pay the British proletariat more so that they would not overthrow the government. According to Lenin, capitalist states would compete for such colonial acquisitions (empires) and would engage in war with each other as a consequence. In fact, Lenin predicted that once the entire world had been colonized, the big imperial powers would turn on each other and the final conflict would end in their destruction and a series of successful socialist revolutions. Lenin explained World War I as a function of this imperialism pattern.

The second connection between Marxist theory and international relations concerns the process of societies shifting from capitalism to **socialism**. The theory asserted that socialism would spread worldwide. Marx and Engels saw the spread of communism to be an inevitable, evolutionary process, but other communist leaders such as Stalin interpreted Marx and Engels to mean that a socialist state was obligated to compel **regime change** in other states. That is, it was the responsibility of socialist countries to violate other states' sovereignty and promote socialist revolutions in those countries. Not all socialist countries followed this philosophy, nor did many have the ability to actively promote social revolts. The Soviet Union, however, very actively promoted social revolution around the world. In the years between World Wars I and II, some limited support was given

socialism an economic-political system in which the government controls the economy and redistributes wealth to create economic equality in the country.

regime change the change of a country's government or type of government.

to the **Chinese Communist Party** led by Mao Zedong, and in 1949 the Chinese Communists prevailed in their civil war and came to power in Beijing. After World War II, beginning with the division of Germany into East and West components and continuing through Eastern Europe, the Soviet Union provided significant support, mostly in the form of military aid, to communist insurgents and politicians. It also put significant pressure on the United States, United Kingdom, and France to withdraw any objections to the Soviet influence in Eastern Europe.

In many cases, the Soviets were successful, and in others they were not. In Hungary, Czechoslovakia, Bulgaria, Romania, and Poland, the Soviet Union was successfully able to install socialist governments under their control. Although the Soviets had to intervene in Hungary and Czechoslovakia at different points during the Cold War, these countries remained socialist until the fall of the Soviet Union.

The Soviets also failed in many cases. They supported the communists in Greece during its brief civil war following World War II, but the British and Americans threw their support behind the anti-communist elements. In Italy, the Soviets gave support to communist candidates, but the United States successfully deployed its newly formed Central Intelligence Agency to fund heavily the anti-communist candidates in the national elections. The anti-communist parties generally prevailed as a result. In Yugoslavia, the Soviets were unable to control the socialist government led by Josip Tito. Yugoslavia was socialist, but Tito did not want to follow the edicts from Moscow. When Stalin demanded Tito visit, Tito declined, realizing that it would be a one-way trip to Moscow. He continued to build a socialist economy, but he developed closer ties with Western Europe and the United States to counter the pressure from the Soviets.

As the Cold War went on, the Soviets continued to support communist insurgents in countries around the globe. They supported Fidel Castro in Cuba, Ho Chi Minh in Vietnam, Mengistu Haile Mariam in Ethiopia, the Popular Movement for the Liberation of Angola in (you guessed it) that country, and Daniel Ortega in Nicaragua, to name just a few. This pressure by the Soviets was often countered by U.S. support of anti-communist factions in these countries and others.

Chinese Communist Party the only legal political party in the People's Republic of China. It controls all aspects of the government.

colonies territories that are legally owned and controlled by another country, typically called the imperial power.

Cuban leaders Fidel and Raul Castro speak to a crowd | Fidel Castro was in power for longer than ten U.S. presidents. What will happen to Cuba once he and his brother Raul are gone?

The point to draw from these historical examples is that Marxist theory is directly tied to international relations. The theory was often interpreted to prescribe an activist foreign policy, and thus it had a profound impact on world politics. While there are realist, liberal, and constructivist interpretations of the Cold War, the communist perspective is that socialism was supposed to spread, by force if need be, across the globe. Understanding this goal certainly provides one explanation of why the Soviets and Americans fought the Cold War.

4-2b Marxist Theory as an Alternative Lens

While very often wrong in its final predictions, Marxist theory and its adaptations do provide an alternative and non-mainstream perspective on international relations. **Colonies** were certainly an economic gain for the country that controlled them; states like the United Kingdom profited handsomely from colonies such as India. It is also true that the imperial powers often fought for the control of colonies. To this day, states often act to secure greater resources such as oil. While one can argue that oil is a strategic resource needed for security, one cannot deny it also fuels the economy. While the global socialist revolution never occurred, the perspective offered by Marxist theory gives us a different and often helpful perspective on international relations. While the search for security is key to understanding international relations, wealth is still a powerful motive and economic security may at times trump international security.

Thus, for Marxist theory, the capitalist drive for wealth determines behavior—often in a very crude way. For example, rich states might colonize poor societies. A variant of the idea that the drive for wealth determines

Combating Communism in Afghanistan

After a series of civil wars, foreign interventions, and coups, the communist party in Afghanistan took power and initiated a series of reforms in the late 1970s. The Afghan people did not welcome the reforms because they contradicted local traditions and Islamic practices. Insurgents, namely the mujahideen, began attacking the government around the country, and the weak, corrupt leadership turned to the Soviet Union for military support. Beginning in October 1979, the Soviets engineered an invasion and rolled troops into Afghanistan in December. For the next ten years, the Soviets fought the Afghan mujahideen. The Soviets failed to attain their goal of maintaining Afghanistan as a communist state and left with a weakened and demoralized military.

The mujahideen did not fight without support, of course. The U.S. government provided significant covert military support in excess of $600 million a year, mostly in weapons. One of the most important parts of this effort was the Stinger anti-aircraft missile. This shoulder-fired infrared missile proved critical in fighting the Soviets' biggest military advantage, their helicopter gunships.

So why would the United States give any funds to a group of fundamental Islamic rebels in a country almost 7,000 miles away with no strategic value and no valuable resources? One word—communism. Throughout the Cold War, the United States maintained a policy of containment toward the Soviet Union. Up until the 1970s, most Americans and U.S. officials generally believed that all communist countries were working together. To be sure, many communist states were under the influence of Moscow, but communism did not quite reach the sinister conspiracy as portrayed in Cold War movies such as *The Manchurian Candidate* and *Big Jim McLain*. The idea was to contain the Soviets from expanding their empire. What the policy effectively did was to combat the growth of communism around the globe.

It is important to realize that the United States wasn't trying to open new capitalist markets in Afghanistan. By funding the mujahideen, the United States was fighting its primary rival in the world—the Soviet Union. So from one perspective, this wasn't a war about capitalism and communism; it was about power. However, the United States dedicated itself, especially early in the Cold War and under President Reagan in the 1980s, to containing the Soviet Union, and much of the rhetoric was about containing communism. There was no difference between the struggle against the Soviets for power and the struggle against communism. They were effectively the same thing.

That is why at every opportunity the United States tried to thwart the Soviets or communists assumed to be tied to the Soviets. The Central Intelligence Agency and the U.S. military engaged in operations in Italy, Vietnam, Cuba, Guatemala, Korea, Honduras, Iran, and Chile, to name just a few. Sometimes the operations were effective, but often they were not. In a simple but poignant line from the miniseries *The Company*, a senior CIA officer explains why their job is so important: "The Goths are at the gate." The line refers to the idea that communists are barbarians and the United States is the only line of defense for the free world. In an interview, a former CIA officer explained that, during initial training in the 1950s, the CIA talked about "the only good communist is a dead communist."

One consequence of this overpowering belief that communism was like a cancer was the support of some radical groups, such as the Afghan mujahideen. After the Soviets withdrew from Afghanistan, the country fell back into a civil war, largely between powerful warlords, but by 1996, Afghanistan was ruled by the Taliban, an outgrowth of the mujahideen and conservative Islamic schools (madrassas) in Pakistan. Five years later, Osama bin Laden, whose work had been aided by the United States during the Soviet occupation, orchestrated the September 11, 2001, attacks on the United States.

1. Do you think there was any way to avoid this outcome?

2. Is it a bad idea to support radicals even if they are the enemy of your enemy?

3. Is the U.S. war on terrorism extreme enough to have consequences like those caused during the Cold War?

behavior is **dependency theory**, which offers a somewhat more sophisticated look at the way the search for wealth influences behavior. With dependency theory, which divided the world into a "core" of wealthy capitalist states and a "periphery" of less developed countries,

dependency theory a theory of development that argues that the dominance and exploitation of poor countries by rich countries prevents progress and development in the poor countries and makes them dependent on the wealthy countries.

First Arabian-American oil company well in Saudi Arabia | For more than 70 years, the United States has been involved in the Middle East because of its valuable oil. How fair was this relationship in the 1950s and what about now?

the rich core does not have to take over the poorer or weaker societies of the periphery by force. Instead, they simply have to control the wealth or resources found in the poorer or weaker societies and shape or control the governments of those countries. That can be accomplished via one-sided economic relationships.

In the **Middle East**, that relationship might be centered on oil. So for years, states such as the United Kingdom, France, and the United States used their oil corporations to try to control certain Mideast regimes. By finding the oil, producing it, and paying royalty fees to the local elites in charge of those Mideast states, Western corporations enriched local elites beyond their prior expectations. As a result, the local power structure had financial incentives to remain loyal to the needs of the states enriching them. For their part, the wealthy states now had reasonably certain access to a needed resource at an attractive price. Yet since initially the local elites rarely had the engineering, technical, or managerial expertise to run their own oil industries without outside help, they often were constrained to take whatever offer the wealthy outsiders made them because their other alternative was to do without that new source

Middle East the region of the world that encompasses countries in Northeast Africa and Southwest Asia.

United Fruit Company a U.S. company that owned and controlled vast plantations in Latin America.

of wealth. Thus, local elites became dependent on wealthy states, and the wealthy states could often manipulate this dependency to get what they wanted from the poorer state.

While oil was the focus of such dependency relationships in the Mideast, in other states it might be other vital natural resources—like bauxite ore (for making aluminum) or copper ore in Chile, gold in the Democratic Congo, diamonds in Sierra Leone, and so on. Oftentimes, multinational corporations were the agent that accomplished the wealthy state's goal of creating dependency relationships. In fact, one of the main tenets of the dependency perspective is that such corporations were key instruments of the core.

A good example came from one company in Guatemala. In the 1950s, the **United Fruit Company** practically owned Guatemala. It was the largest single landowner in the state, the largest single employer, and it owned the only railroad line and only telephone company in Guatemala. At some point, whatever the U.S.-owned United Fruit Company wanted in Guatemala, it tended to get from the Guatemalan government. When the Guatemalan regime led by President Jacobo Arbenz chose to stand up to United Fruit in 1953–1954, the company appealed to the U.S. government for help. Given that U.S. Secretary of State John Foster Dulles and his brother Allen Dulles, the Director of Central Intelligence at the time, had previously worked for the Wall Street law firm of Sullivan and Cromwell that represented United Fruit and that John Foster Dulles was a member of United Fruit's board of directors, the company had sympathetic ears at high levels of the U.S. government. Thus, it seems unsurprising that the CIA organized a military coup that toppled the offending Arbenz regime and replaced it with one more friendly to United Fruit's corporate interests. As a reward, the new Guatemalan government led by Carlos Castillo was showered with increased levels of U.S. foreign aid, so long as it continued to do what the United States and United Fruit wanted it to do. The regime consequently became increasingly dependent on the economic goodwill of the United States to remain in power.

In addition to the dependence of the local ruling elites in the poor countries on the wealthy corporations, the theory argued that poor states were dependent on the wealthy to develop, modernize, and grow their economies. Because corporations like United Fruit (now Chiquita Brands International) could extract all of the profits from Guatemala's fruit plantations, the Guatemalans themselves were left only with enough money to survive—not enough to develop and grow. The theory argued that such foreign investment and ownership of

Workers in Guatemala harvest bananas for Del Monte | While your bananas may only cost a few dollars for a bunch, fruit is big business in Latin America. How much do you think these workers benefit from the wealth they help produce?

property and resources in the poor countries made it impossible for them to develop into modern economies. So Guatemala continued to produce low-cost bananas but not higher-cost manufactured items like automobiles or computers. However, empirical evidence showed that foreign direct investment did help grow the economies of these poor countries, suggesting that the theory, while intuitive, was factually inaccurate. Considerable debate continues to surround the idea of poor states' dependence on wealthy states. In countries where the foreign investment is well managed and regulated by the local government, considerable economic advancements have been made. However, there were still many cases similar to Guatemala in the 1950s.

4-3 WORLD SYSTEMS THEORY

Using the foundations created by Marx and Engels and the innovations of the dependency argument from the 1960s, scholars in the 1970s developed an alternative economic theory of international relations. World systems theory (WST) took the idea of unequal exchange between the classes that was the basis for Marxist theory and applied it to the international system. The theory asserts that instead of a universal capitalist class ruling the world, each state acts according to its position in the economic system. Like structural realism, state behavior according to WST is very much determined by the state's economic characteristics relative to other states in the world.

It is easy to understand this theorizing—which can become rather dense if one is not careful—by looking

at the way that WST describes the world. WST asserts there are three zones or types of states. The first zone is the **core**. Core states are the wealthiest, most powerful, and most industrialized, and they basically call the shots in the world economy. These countries make the most profitable and advanced products of the particular time, they have the strongest and most efficient governments, they are often at the forefront of technological innovation, and they have the greatest influence in world politics. A good example of a core state is the United States. It produces goods and services such as military weapons, computers, pharmaceuticals, software, and financial and legal services. Like other core states, its economy is diversified, and so it also sells a great deal of agricultural products and heavy equipment. The U.S. government is large and—while you may often have trouble with your student loans—very efficient compared to other countries. Other examples of core states are Germany, France, Japan, Australia, the United Kingdom, Norway, and Sweden, among others.

The second economic zone is the **semi-periphery**. Semi-peripheral states tend to produce goods and services and do not rely on the export of raw materials (e.g., lumber, food, oil) for their economy. However, those goods and services are not as profitable as the core country's products. For example, semi-peripheral states will tend to export textiles, household items, some types of industrial equipment, and so on. The economy will be industrializing and developing toward that of the core, but it will be at least one generation behind core country products. The government will be stable and relatively efficient, but still developing toward the core zone level of efficiency. These states will have a strong voice in the world, but not compared to the core states.

A good example of a semi-periphery country is India. It has a strong, stable democracy, although the government does have efficiency issues. It exports textiles, rugs, jewelry, and drilling equipment, as well as (refined) fuel oil, steel, chemicals, vehicles, and both information technology services and information technology software engineers. India has significant influence in the world, but not when compared to the United States, Japan, Germany, or the United Kingdom. Other semi-peripheral states include Mexico, China, South Africa, Chile, Brazil, and Russia.

core the economic zone composed of wealthy countries producing high-end products.

semi-periphery the economic zone composed of middle-income countries that produce secondary products.

The last zone is the **periphery**. These states have weak governments, tend to sell only raw materials or cheap labor, and have almost no influence in world politics. Examples of these states are unfortunately plentiful. Bangladesh, Vietnam, Indonesia, most of sub-Saharan Africa, and most of Central America and the Caribbean are all peripheral states. They make very small profits off of their raw materials and cheap labor; their governments tend to be the most unstable and corrupt in the world; they have almost no voice on the world stage.

Before you read any further, think of a few states we haven't discussed thus far and see if you can identify which zone they occupy. Is a wealthy state like Saudi Arabia in the core, semi-periphery, or periphery? What about Spain or Singapore? It isn't always wealth that determines what zone a state is classified as, but what its economy produces and consumes, as well as how wealthy and educated its residents are. In Map 4-1, you find a depiction of countries that fall into each zone. Do you find any surprises?

periphery the economic zone composed of poor countries that primarily export raw materials.

These three zones operate in a hierarchical fashion. Like Marx's view of the capitalist class, the core dominates and extracts profits from the semi-periphery and periphery, the semi-periphery dominates and extracts profits from the periphery, and the periphery is simply left in relative poverty. Like Marxist theory, WST argues that wars are fought between the different zones to enforce the world order. For example, WST explains the U.S.-led invasion of Iraq in 2003 as the leading core state attacking a periphery state because the core state (the United States) believed that the periphery state (Iraq) was attempting to gain considerable power with weapons of mass destruction. The Cold War is explained as a war between two rival economic systems—capitalism and communism. WST asserts that it is not security that the United States and Soviet Union sought, but dominance over the economic system.

Like Marxist theory, WST fails in many of its predictions. Part of the reason for this failure is that the theory, again like Marxism, also advocates social change. Part of that advocacy characterizing both theories is the prediction of future events. Realism, liberalism, and constructivism make no such sweeping predictions as the fall of capitalism. As such, they are not subject to the same critique. Marxist theory and WST both take that risk, so to speak, though it does not pay off. If one removes

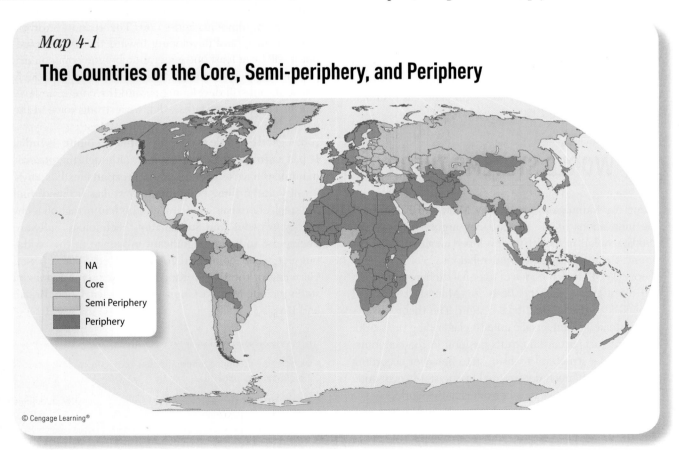

Map 4-1

The Countries of the Core, Semi-periphery, and Periphery

NA
Core
Semi Periphery
Periphery

© Cengage Learning®

the politicized aspect of both theories, one can see the explanatory benefits: the importance of economic conditions, wealth as a motive, and so on. When applying these theories to the world, however, it is important to realize that both WST and especially Marxist theory are ideologies in addition to theories.

Critics also note that WST tends to consider the zones—and the class structure that underlies them—as more important than the actual states that compose them. Like Marxist theory, the state is not emphasized relative to the three zones. While some—realists and liberals, for instance—may consider this problematic, it is valuable to consider how some characteristics may transcend state boundaries. Economic connections across zones or classes may be one of those characteristics. Wealthy states, corporations, and individuals very often have similar preferences and work together to attain their mutual goals. A good example of these is the **World Economic Forum** held in Davos, Switzerland, every year, which brings together wealthy individuals, corporate leaders, industry leaders, and heads of government of selected core states to coordinate economic policies and initiatives. However, those same states, corporations, and individuals often have competing goals, and conflict arises from that competition.

So does the World Economic Forum provide evidence that WST is right or wrong? What does it say about Marxist theory? What about the other examples? Which one of these theories (and don't forget about realism, liberalism, and constructivism) is right or at least most right? Like the rest of international relations, the answer is not simple. WST and Marxist theory have a point that economic interests cross state borders, but governments are typically not simply an illusion covering up economic struggle. Instead, we should consider the power of economic interests when we also consider the politics of international relations. Ultimately, as students of international relations, we should consider all possibilities and not limit ourselves to one perspective or theory.

(4-4) # FEMINISM

Like the constructivist and Marxist approaches to international relations, the feminist approach offers a different perspective from liberalism and realism. In fact, feminism often uses a constructivist approach to explain the role of women in world politics and the consequences world politics has specifically for women. Like Marxist theory, it suggests not just an explanation of international relations but also a goal to seek: equality for women.

The similarities with Marxist theory, however, end with the alternative nature of the approach and the desire for social change. Marxist theory, as we discussed, focuses solely on class and economic conflict. It does not leave room for the idea that men and women are different, act differently, and that there are consequences specific to men and women. It does suggest that if economic disparities are eliminated, then men and women will be equal, but gender inequality is only a side effect of economic equality. The idea that fundamental differences exist in the behavior and outlook of men and women is one of the assumptions that some feminists use in their approach to international relations.

The feminist approach can be broken into three themes. The first theme tends to be the most speculative. It raises the question of whether world politics would be different if women held more or most leadership positions in states. This first theme addresses how women may behave differently from men in a political environment and how that different behavior would shape world politics. For example, would war be less common if women represented half (or more) of the world's leaders?

The second theme is related to the first, but worth considering as a separate idea. Instead of asking whether the world would be different if there were more women in leadership roles, this form of feminism asks whether our entire view, our entire way of thinking about international relations, is masculinized. That is, all of the realist and liberal thinkers—at least at first—were men. Perhaps the development of our theories themselves is gender biased and should be reexamined. As you probably notice, these first two themes have commonalities, but it is important to realize the difference. The first suggests we are thinking about international relations correctly, we just need more women involved. The second suggests that our thinking about international relations is biased. The two can be compatible, but they are distinct from each other.

The third theme is more empirical and reverses the focus of the first theme. Instead of looking at what impact women may or could have had on world politics, this branch of feminist international relations focuses on the impact world politics has on women. For example, do women suffer economically more than men during a war?

World Economic Forum a forum held in Switzerland every year that brings together wealthy individuals, corporate leaders, industry leaders, and heads of government to coordinate economic policies and initiatives.

4-4a The Impact of Women on International Relations

Although women make up 49.8 percent of the world's population, only about 12 percent of the world's leaders are women; only 24 states have a chief executive who is a woman. To be sure, there are many other women in leadership positions, such as three of the last four U.S. Secretaries of State: Madeleine Albright, Condoleezza Rice, and Hillary Clinton. It is also important to highlight the role of women such as Aung San Suu Kyi, the leader of the pro-democracy opposition party in Burma who spent more than two decades under "house arrest" by the autocratic government, during which time she received many awards, including the Nobel Peace Prize. Another example is Princess Diana, often thought of for her private life and death, who tirelessly campaigned against land mines and pushed the British royal family into more philanthropic roles before her death. Even considering these women, there are still currently only 24 in the top leadership position of their countries out of 196 countries in the world; Table 4-1 identifies them. Further, the number of women in any political leadership role is still well below half. This gender imbalance in world leaders begs the question: if women comprised half of the world's leaders, would there be a difference in international relations?

Some theories argued that there would in fact be differences. Following the basic stereotypes of men and women, some feminist scholars argued that women would be more peaceful and cooperative leaders than men. Instead of being realists, women would tend to be more liberal in their approach to international relations. They would be less concerned with national and international security, for example, and more concerned with economic and human security—and economic security would be defined partly as economic equality. Instead of being coercive, women leaders would engage other countries with aid and diplomacy. More importantly, they would interact with countries not to gain power but to develop a better relationship that would focus on peace, equal development, and,

TABLE 4-1 FEMALE COUNTRY LEADERS, 2014

COUNTRY	LEADER	TOOK OFFICE IN
Germany	Chancellor Angela Merkel	Nov. 22, 2005
Liberia	President Ellen Johnson-Sirleaf	Jan. 16, 2006
India	President Pratibha Patil	Jul. 25, 2007
Argentina	President Cristina Fernandez de Kirchner	Dec. 10, 2007
Bangladesh	Prime Minister Sheikh Hasina Wajed	Jan. 6, 2009
Lithuania	President Dalia Grybauskaite	Jul. 12, 2009
Costa Rica	President Laura Chinchilla	May 8, 2010
Trinidad and Tobago	Prime Minister Kamla Persad-Bissessar	May 26, 2010
Brazil	President Dilma Rousseff	Jan. 1, 2011
Kosovo	President Atifete Jahjaga	Apr. 7, 2011
Thailand	Prime Minister Yingluck Shinawatra (deposed by Thai military coup, May 2014)	Aug. 8, 2011
Denmark	Prime Minister Helle Thorning-Schmidt	Oct. 3, 2011
Jamaica	Prime Minister Portia Simpson Miller	Jan. 5, 2012
Malawi	President Joyce Banda	April 7, 2012
South Korea	President Park Geun-hye	Feb. 25, 2013
Slovenia	Prime Minister Alenka Bratusek	March 20, 2013
Cyprus (North)	Prime Minister Sibel Siber	June 13, 2013
Senegal	Prime Minister Aminata Touré	Sept. 3, 2013
Norway	Prime Minister Erna Solberg	Oct. 16, 2013
Latvia	Prime Minister Laimdota Straujuma	Jan. 22, 2014
Central African Rep.	President Catherine Samba-Panza	Jan. 23, 2014
Chile	President Michelle Bachelet	March 11, 2014
Malta	President Marie-Louise Coleiro Preca	April 7, 2014
Peru	Prime Minister Ana Rosario Jara Velásquez	July 22, 2014

Don Emmert/AFP/Getty Images

Heads of the wealthiest states meet at the G-8 Summit | German Chancellor Angela Merkel stands out as the only woman in this group of the world's most powerful leaders. Would the world be different if half of the leaders were women?

perhaps, the environment. The result would be a more peaceful planet.

This perspective is often ascribed to **difference feminists**. This feminist perspective sees men and women as different in their basic nature. These differences can be attributed to genetic/hormonal differences (e.g., estrogen versus testosterone) and/or socially constructed differences (e.g., more boys play competitive contact sports than girls). These basic differences mean that women would be better at negotiating a peace treaty while men would be better at fighting a war. Both can be considered as important and needed, but both must also be considered equal. That is, difference feminists argue that only male traits are values in international relations, so there is more conflict in the world. If more women were in leadership roles, then there would be greater balance and peace in the international system.

The problem with this perspective was that as women ascended to lead different countries, they tended to act just like their male counterparts. That is, women were no less coercive and tough than men when leading a country. For example, Margaret Thatcher, the prime minister of the United Kingdom from 1979–1990, was referred to as the "Iron Lady," not because she was engaging, nurturing, and peaceful, but because she talked and acted very tough. Thatcher engaged the

Soviets with very harsh diplomacy but then convinced her close ally, President Ronald Reagan, that the new Soviet leader, Mikhail Gorbachev, was someone with whom they could negotiate. Up to that point, Thatcher had no intention of negotiating with the Soviets! In 1982, early in her tenure, Argentina invaded the **Falkland Islands**, British owned and populated islands approximately 300 miles off the coast of Argentina. Thatcher led a successful and short (72-day) war to reclaim the islands. She made it clear from the start of the invasion that she would not negotiate with the Argentinians at all. It was also widely reported at the time that Thatcher urged George H. W. Bush to take a hardline, aggressive approach to Iraq's invasion of Kuwait in 1991.

While Thatcher may be the archetypal female leader, she was by no means different from other women in leadership positions like Indira Gandhi of India or Golda Meir of Israel. As more and more (although it is

difference feminists the feminist perspective that argues that men and women are fundamentally different in their abilities, particularly their approach to conflict.

Falkland Islands a group of islands approximately 300 miles off the coast of Argentina owned by the United Kingdom and populated by UK citizens.

Zones of Wealth and Peace?

Looking at Map 4-2, do you notice any particular patterns? The wealthiest states tend to be north of the equator with the most notable exceptions being Australia, Brazil, and Chile. Notice also how the poor and rich states are clustered around each other (see Chapters 8 and 10 for a discussion of this pattern).

Now also note how violence tends to occur in the same groups of countries that are also poor. Clearly, just being born in a country like Somalia means your life would be completely different than if you were born in Germany. The average German lives to be 80.4 years old, but the average Somalian lives to only 51.6. Perhaps this is the first revenge geography has on humans—quite simply, the country in which you were born.

Looking at these two conditions—poverty/violence and wealth/peace—how does Marxist theory explain these patterns? If all conflict is based on economic classes, are there fewer classes in wealthy countries? Shouldn't there be conflict, according to Marxist theory, in all non-socialist countries? What about world systems theory?

Map 4-2

World Map Showing GDP Per Capita and Internal Violence

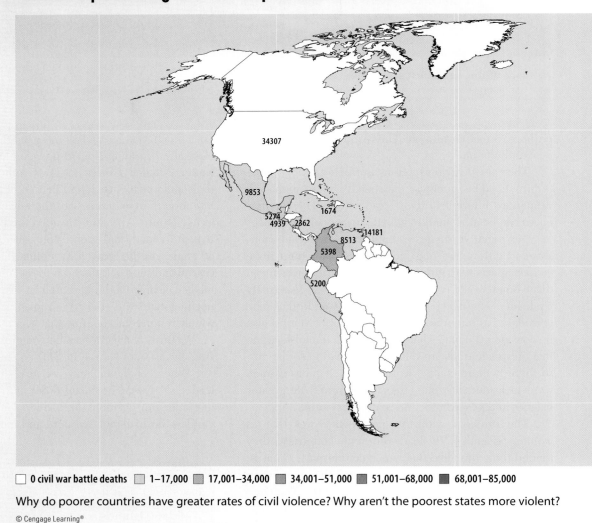

☐ 0 civil war battle deaths ☐ 1–17,000 ☐ 17,001–34,000 ☐ 34,001–51,000 ☐ 51,001–68,000 ☐ 68,001–85,000

Why do poorer countries have greater rates of civil violence? Why aren't the poorest states more violent?

© Cengage Learning®

Using WST terms, why is the periphery so much more violent than the core?

These theories would likely point out the unequal relationship between the wealthy states and the poor states. Both theories might assert that the wealthy states extract surplus from the poor countries to pay off the middle and lower classes in their own countries. In order to extract the surplus, the wealthy states instigate conflict in the poor states to keep them from fighting back. That is why, according to these theories, there is little conflict in wealthy states but considerable violence in poor states.

Constructivists might suggest that in poor countries, the difference between rich and poor people is so extreme, that many of the poor feel deprived and believe that violence is the only rational option to improve their condition. In wealthier countries, the poor are better off and the difference between them and the wealthy is not usually so extreme. Thus, the violence could be the result of a socially constructed view emphasizing deprivation.

1. Does one of these explanations make more sense to you? Why?

2. What might be done to help solve this poverty–conflict nexus?

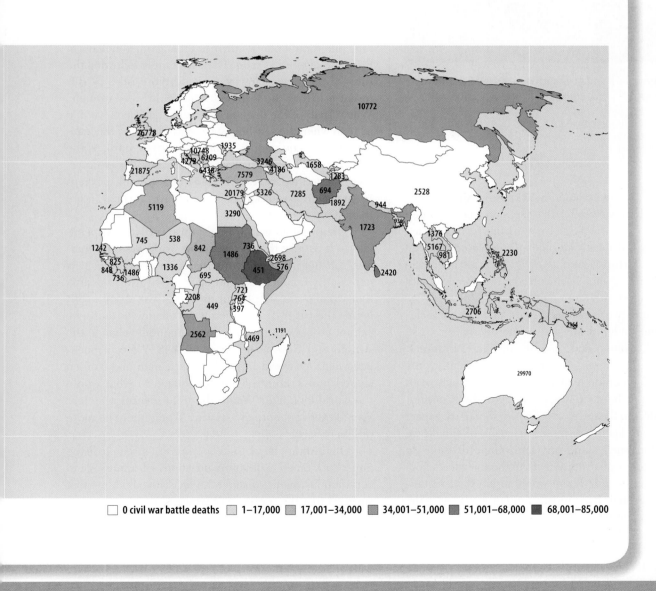

☐ 0 civil war battle deaths ☐ 1–17,000 ☐ 17,001–34,000 ☐ 34,001–51,000 ■ 51,001–68,000 ■ 68,001–85,000

Prime Minister Kamla Persad-Bissessar of Trinidad and Tobago | Not all women leaders are from powerful countries. Prime Minister Persad-Bissessar is the chief executive in a traditionally male-dominated country. What would it be like to be the first woman leader of a male-dominated country?

to use the military when appropriate, that leader would either be replaced by another leader or the country would eventually be taken over by more aggressive states. Thus, to stay in power and maintain the integrity of the state, the leader—man or woman—would have to forego his or her own pacifism and act assertively, even coercively, like other leaders.

This response is based on the self-help characteristic of the international system. If one leader tried to be engaging rather than coercive, passive rather than assertive, other states would quickly take advantage of that state. No one was going to help Margaret Thatcher retake the Falkland Islands, and the Argentinians were not responsive to engagement. She had to take the islands back by force.

The second response to the idea that female leaders are no different from their male counterparts is based on the tiny number of state leaders who are women. The idea is that in the current self-help, anarchic system, one should not be surprised that women behave in the same manner as men. They are simply following the rules of the game. However, would those rules be different if half of the leaders in the world were women? What if half of the leaders of Europe had been women in 1648 when the self-help system was born? If the leadership had been gender-balanced in 1648, perhaps the system would have evolved into a more cooperative, less competitive system. Instead of self-help, perhaps "responsible sovereignty" would have formed more than 360 years ago.

The problem with this response is that it is speculative. It asserts that because the world system (anarchy, self-help) is male constructed or conceived, it is necessarily competitive and aggressive. It also asserts that women are simply not as aggressive as men. But is this the case? There is no way to know because we cannot go back in time and fundamentally change the structure of European society in 1648. We can speculate what the world would be like if men and women shared power hundreds of years ago. So what would the world look like? Would there be sovereign states? Would there be more or less war? Would there be more or less poverty?

On the other hand, there is empirical research on the impact of women in other organizations—businesses and corporations, agencies, and even legislative bodies—that suggests that the presence of women in those organizations has an impact, and that those with significant numbers of women exhibit a different decision-making style and pursue different agendas.[2] For example, legislatures with more women tend to consider and debate social policy (e.g., medical coverage and regulation) more than

clearly still very few) women held those positions, they proved to behave very much like the men who preceded them. They were tough, did not shrink from conflict, and certainly did not fit an older stereotype of women as peaceful, nurturing mothers who feared conflict. So perhaps women—when leading a country—really do not behave any differently from men.

There are two potential responses to the conclusion that the gender of the leader does not matter. First, even though women and men are obviously different, the leadership position—whether it is president, prime minister, or autocratic leader—requires that both men and women act the same way to be successful. Consider female leaders in the developing world: should we expect their gender to lead to different behavior, or should we expect factors such as poverty and ethnic divisions to cause them to act no differently than the male leaders of the developing world? Some would argue that, regardless of the personal characteristics and preferences of the leader, they must act pretty much like all other leaders or cease to be effective and thus cease being the leader. For example, imagine a pacifist was elected to a country's presidency. If that leader did not stand up to the pressures of other leaders, including showing a willingness

economic policy (e.g., tax rates). In other words, men and women may prioritize issues differently and thus pursue different agendas when given the opportunity.

When do such opportunities arise for women? One interesting hallmark of this research suggests that there is a sort of critical mass or threshold (about 30 percent) that must be reached. In organizations in which women constitute less than 30 percent of the personnel (or leaders), little difference can be identified. In those with more than 30 percent, some research finds that this critical mass empowers a kind of solidarity in which women's different style, approach, and preferences are evident. In effect, where there are few women, those in power or leadership tend to conform to the male-dominated context, but where there is a critical number, they do not.[3]

This perspective is promoted by **liberal feminists**. This feminist view does not require that there is a fundamental difference between the politics of men and women. Instead of suggesting that both men and women should be in equal leadership roles because they bring different abilities to the table, liberal feminists suggest that simply having more women in leadership roles is important and will make a difference. The women will lead in the same way that men do, but if there is an equal number of men and women, there will be different issues discussed (might human security issues matter more and international security issues matter less?) and most importantly, gender equality for women.

It is important to note the difference between these two perspectives. Liberal feminists see an equal number of women and men in leadership roles being important because it promotes overall gender equality, which is a good thing. Difference feminists go further and suggest that women are more peaceful and less aggressive than men, and thus more women leaders will create an environment in which there will be more peace.

There is some fascinating research in this area that actually begins to tell us what effects gender equality might have on international relations. For example, whether or not women are in leadership positions, do countries that have higher levels of respect for women act differently from those that discriminate against them? The answer is yes—when a country has greater gender equality it is less likely to initiate a war, although it may still be attacked by other countries. Further, countries with greater gender equality tend to be less likely to have civil wars.[4] Thus, whether women directly influence international politics or whether countries that treat women equally and thus indirectly influence international affairs, the status of women matters when one is trying to understand international relations!

4-4b The Impact of Women on International Relations Theory

In addition to the practical idea that more women leaders could change the world, an even more fundamental argument about gender and international relations exists. We have discussed IR theorists such as Thucydides, Machiavelli, Hobbes, Morgenthau, and others. Each of these thinkers has a very common characteristic—with the exception of Rose McDermott, they are all men. What if all of our theories about international relations are gender biased? Those theories are read and studied by all world leaders even before they rise to power. That means that those theories guide how leaders—men and women—act in the international arena. But what if they're wrong or at least biased toward masculine traits such as competitiveness and aggression?

Many feminist scholars ask this question. The problem that we face may be that the international system is not as competitive and dangerous as we think, or perhaps it is but doesn't have to be. What if we instead thought of other nations as friends or partners? What if instead of coercion, diplomacy and negotiations were given longer to work? It certainly seems reasonable to think that war would be less likely and that the international system would be more peaceful.

Another problem with defining the world as hostile and women as peaceful is that doing so helps exclude women from the study and practice of international relations. J. Ann Tickner argues that by defining world politics in masculine terms—dangerous, hostile, competitive, and so on—women have to be considered irrelevant. That is, if women are good at peace but international relations is about conflict, then what do women have to offer? Tickner points out that we must consider alternative definitions of the international system that include feminine viewpoints. Only then can we both include more women in the study and practice of foreign affairs and better understand the world in which we live.

You may be thinking that much of this discussion sounds similar to constructivist ideas about anarchy, and you would be right! The idea that our understanding of the international system is gender biased is based on the idea that it is socially constructed. In the male-dominated world—particularly in centuries past—women rarely helped construct the international system. If they

liberal feminists the feminist perspective that argues men and women can approach issues such as conflict the same way, but that it is important to have equal representation of the two genders.

had, concepts such as security, anarchy, and sovereignty might have very different meanings today.

While we cannot go back in time to change our theories and practices, we can be aware of them as we try to figure out how the world works. As students of international relations, we should take time to question the assumptions that create the foundation for realism and liberalism. For example, is the idea of self-help purely masculine? If it is, how would the international system function if we had a gender-balanced view of anarchy? Note, we are not suggesting a feminine view, but one that includes the perspectives of both sexes. Perhaps anarchy would mean less self-help and more collective action that rooted out aggressive states and reformed them.

Although not directly related to gender, studies of baboons by Robert Sapolsky show that troops in which there are no aggressive males tend to be more peaceful and when outside aggressive males join the troop, they are quickly taught the non-aggressive norms of the troop. Perhaps a gender-balanced international system would work the same way: conflict would be rare and aggressive states would be ostracized until they became less bellicose. States are not like baboons, but we should be proactive in that kind of questioning and thinking when we examine the world.

4-4c The Impact of International Relations on Women

Now that we have discussed the theoretical and speculative question of how women might affect international relations and whether our theories of international relations are gender biased, we must turn to how world politics affects women. Generally speaking, women do not hold an equal status in countries around the world. If they did, in 2010 the UN would not have felt the need to create the United Nations Entity for Gender Equality and the Empowerment of Women (or UN Women). Some examples may be useful to illustrate the situation. Holding a job means a greater level of independence and worth, but instead of making up an equal half of the workforce, women only comprise 46 percent in the United States, 44 percent in the United Kingdom, 45 percent in France, and 42 percent in Germany. While Germany has a female chancellor, Angela Merkel, only 32 percent of the parliament (the Bundestag) is made up of women.[5] That percentage is actually quite high when one considers that in the U.S. House of Representatives and Senate, women comprise only 18 percent of the members.

These examples pale in comparison to the status of women in developing countries. In some fundamentalist theocracies such as Iran, women have few rights and protections relative to men. Severe religious restrictions

require women to cover their bodies and hair while in public, and when they do not, the punishment can include death. In Iran, only 27 percent of the workforce is made up of women. That does not allow for much independence or worth for women.

When the Taliban controlled Afghanistan, women older than 11 years of age could not leave their home without their husband or a close male relative. If a woman was widowed and did not have any male relatives in the area, she could literally starve to death in her own home.

In China, boy babies are considered to be more valuable than girls. As ultrasound examinations have become available, more and more abortions are being performed when the baby is a girl. The sex-selection abortions have become so rampant that for every 100 girls born, there are 120 boys born. Even more horrific, newborn girls are regularly found in dumpsters, abandoned and left for dead by their parents.[6]

Because women are often at a disadvantage in a country, particularly in poor and developing countries, they tend to be hurt more than men when there is upheaval in a society, and few events cause more upheaval than international war and civil war. When a country slips into conflict, whether it is with another state or a civil war, there is normally potential violence within the society, higher levels of stress and anxiety, and severe economic disruption.

Normally, war causes a great deal of turmoil within a country. In the United Kingdom during World War II, there was food and fuel rationing and curfews. In non-democratic countries, the restrictions are usually

Jalil Rezayee/EPA/Landov

Body of an Afghan woman who was murdered for allegedly having an illicit relationship in 2011 | This woman could have been a world leader if she had been born in another country. Might she have been the next Margaret Thatcher or Mother Teresa? How can a country develop if it represses half of its population like this?

more severe. In addition to rationing and curfews, there is often forced relocation, forced labor, and severe punishment for any dissent of the government. In this climate, violence against women is more common. The stresses of the war and the new restrictions initiated by the government make domestic violence against women more likely. The likelihood of rape increases when a civil war is being fought in the country, as soldiers and insurgents often use rape as a way to punish their enemy indirectly.

Wars often mean that men are drafted to fight, leaving women to work to support the war effort. The new employment for women can create new independence for them, but wars normally cause economic recession, as well. The economic downturn creates pressure within the society, and higher levels of unemployment can lead to domestic violence as families try to cope with less money.

Unlike war, globalization has differing effects on the status of women. Globalization in the form of foreign trade and investment often means more employment opportunities, especially for women who have traditionally had less access to education and training in developing countries. These jobs give both greater worth and more autonomy to the women. On the negative side, many of these jobs are criticized for being sweatshops where the employees work long hours for little pay and have no security. However, considerable evidence indicates that the more empowered and successful women are in a society, the better that society performs in the global economy.

While the jury is still out, so to speak, on the effects of globalization on women, recent studies show that economic sanctions—often considered a peaceful, humane method of coercing a state—have harmful effects on women. Economic sanctions cause a country's economy to shrink. As a consequence, unemployment goes up, and in developing countries, women lose their jobs first. Even though women usually earn less than men in these countries, they are still fired from their positions before men. The stress from the shrinking economy also causes more domestic violence and a lower respect for women in poorer countries. Although this effect is smaller compared to the violence against women during wars, it highlights how vulnerable women can be to world events—events that are completely outside of their control.

4-4d Half of the Population but Not Half of the Input

What can be concluded about the feminist perspective on international relations? First, feminism takes a very constructivist approach to the world. Since the primary argument is that the social system tends to place men in positions of power and those positions shape international relations, then the construction of the social system has had a huge if not sole defining impact on world politics. There is no biological reason that men would hold most of the positions of political leadership, so constructivism provides the best way to explain the current situation.

Second, because men dominate the positions of leadership, it is hard to know if women would act any differently. As the opening photo of Angela Merkel and Barack Obama asks: How does gender really matter? While many of the arguments about women being different leaders are hypothetical, we do know that legislatures like the German Bundestag, which has 30 percent women as legislators, tend to prioritize some issues differently. Only the future will tell us how different women may act when they hold more leadership positions; in the near-term we may look at leaders like Argentina's Cristina Fernandez, Brazil's Dilma Rousseff, or Germany's Angela Merkel as well as Trinidad and Tobago's Kamla Persad-Bissessar. Last and certainly not least, we know that women, particularly in less-developed countries, are subject to far worse conditions and treatment than men. Wars, sanctions, economic decline—all of these factors hurt women more than men. Even worse, in many countries women do not have basic rights such as freedom to choose their spouse, where they live, how many children they have; the list goes on.

What we should take way from this discussion is the importance of considering the feminist viewpoint. We cannot forget that when a war starts, it is bad for everyone, but particularly bad for women. We must also ask ourselves, must international relations work "this way" or could it change if the leaders of the world were more evenly balanced between men and women?

CONCLUSION

So when are these alternatives most useful? Or, are realism, liberalism, or constructivism more helpful approaches to understanding international relations? The answer to this question is threefold.

First, we must evaluate each of the perspectives. To do this, we want the same qualities found in a good answer to an exam question: completeness and succinctness. The best perspective is the one that offers the most complete explanation of the question we want to answer and does not contain useless information. For example, the predictions of Marxist theory are not helpful for understanding international relations, but the singular focus on economic relationships does provide a lot of information. Foreign policy analysis provides details about how individual agents behave, but is that too much

TABLE 4-2 SUMMARY OF HOW FOREIGN POLICY ANALYSIS, MARXIST THEORY, AND FEMINISM

KEY FEATURES	FOREIGN POLICY ANALYSIS	MARXIST THEORY	FEMINISM
Nature of the international system	Anarchy	Hierarchical	Anarchy, historically male dominated
Relevant actors	Agents (individuals, groups, societal groups)	Economic classes	States, organizations, people
Important resources	Decision-making power/influence	Wealth, military to gain wealth	Power
Central dynamics	Small group decision making	Class conflict	Conflict as defined by male-dominated history
Anarchy	Exists in the lack of central supranational organizations	Exists in the competition between the wealthy classes in different states	Lack of central authority, historically defined as conflictual by male leaders
Diversity	Differences in leadership structures/paths to legitimacy	Differences in economic classes is the only meaningful diversity	Historically low because of a lack of female leaders, now changing
Complexity	Created by the need to satisfy multiple constituency or elite groups	Created by the single driving force of economic class	Shaped by the differences that female leaders bring to the world

© Cengage Learning®

information? Table 4-2 summarizes each of the theories we discussed in this chapter. For each theory you should ask yourself if it tells "the whole truth and nothing but the truth." Do you think the theory tells you what you need to know to understand the main cause-and-effect relationships, without telling you more than you need to know?

Second, we must answer the question: when is each theory most compelling? These theories each make compelling arguments as to how the world operates. While Marxist theory often made incorrect predictions, there is certainly truth in some of its characterizations of how people and states relate to each other. Money matters! Foreign policy analysis shows us how leaders can make irrational or illogical decisions, but aren't many of their decisions rational and logical? While feminism shows us that anarchy is socially constructed and does not have to mean competition and conflict, does that mean that there isn't a lot of competition and conflict in the world today? To answer that question, simply look at the conflicts in Iraq, Afghanistan, Somalia, Syria, and so on. So perhaps the feminists are right but so are the realists? What we must do at the end of the day is decide how we as citizens of the world think the world works. Armed with the knowledge of these different perspectives, we can better see the patterns that exist and persist in international relations.

The third answer to the question "which is best?" is simply, why pick just one? There are definitely aspects of these theories that do not fit together. Marxist theory invalidates the ideas of feminism. Foreign policy analysis calls the idea of a unitary state into question. However, the idea that economic class is a powerful driving force seems pretty intuitive. So does the evidence that states will follow less aggressive foreign policies if they have greater gender equality. Perhaps the best way to understand international relations is to consider all of these approaches. When carpenters build a house, they use more than just a hammer. For us, each theoretical lens we have considered in this chapter, and in the previous one, may help us gain insights on particular problems and situations. Like the carpenter, perhaps we should use all of the tools at our disposal to understand the complex world around us.

THINK ABOUT THIS THE VALUE OF ADDITIONAL LENSES

For centuries, scholars and other careful observers relied on realism to make sense of international relations. Later, liberalism— and then constructivism—arose as ways to interpret world events and make sense of them. For most of the modern era, explanations swung between those these theories like a pendulum. Yet obviously, those were insufficient tools in some instances or others would not have developed the more recent approaches we now refer to as foreign policy analysis, Marxist theory, or feminism.

In light of Chapter 3 and our discussion in this chapter, what "corrections" to realism, liberalism, and constructivism presented by foreign policy analysis, Marxist theory, and feminism are most helpful to explaining world politics? Least helpful?

STUDY TOOLS 4

LOCATED AT BACK OF THE BOOK:
☐ Rip out Chapter in Review card

LOCATED ON COURSEMATE:
Use the CourseMate access card that came with this book or visit CengageBrain.com for more review materials.

☐ Review Key Terms Flash Cards (Print or Online)

☐ Download Chapter Summaries for on-the-go review
☐ Complete Practice Quizzes to prepare for the test
☐ Walk through a Simulation, Animated Learning Module, and Interactive Maps and Timelines to master concepts
☐ Complete Crossword Puzzle to review key terms
☐ Visit IR NewsWatch to learn about the latest current events as you prepare for class discussions and papers

REVIEW QUESTIONS

1. What alternatives to realism, liberalism, and constructivism exist, and which of them are the most compelling?

2. What does studying individuals, groups, and institutions and their role in decision making add to our understanding of world politics?

3. How important is economic class? Can the struggle between the classes explain all international relations?

4. What does Marxist theory do to explain how nations interact?

5. How are women treated in the world? Do world events have a different impact on them compared to men?

6. What does anarchy really mean? How has that meaning changed over time?

FOR MORE INFORMATION . . .

For more on:

Foreign policy analysis, see Beasley, Ryan, Juliet Kaarbo, Jeff Lantis, and Michael Snarr, *Foreign Policy In Comparative Perspective: Domestic and International Influences On State Behavior*, 2nd ed. Washington DC: CQ Press, 2012.

Marxism, see Marx, Karl, and Friedrich Engels. *Das Kapital*. Various printings.

World systems theory, see Wallerstein, Immanuel Maurice. *World-systems analysis: an introduction*. Durham, NC: Duke University Press, 2004.

Feminism, see Tickner, J. Ann. "Why Women Can't Run the World: International Politics According to Francis Fukuyama." *International Studies Review* 1 (2002): 3–11. See also Tickner, J. Ann. *Gender in International Relations: Feminist Perspectives on Achieving Global Security*. New York: Columbia University Press, 1992.

5 | Understanding Conflict:
The Nature and Causes of Conflict and War

LEARNING OBJECTIVES
After studying this chapter, you will be able to . . .

 5-1 Identify the nature and forms of armed conflict.

 5-2 Describe the evolution of and trends in armed conflict.

 5-3 Assess the causes of interstate and intrastate war at the (a) system, (b) state, and (c) individual levels of analysis.

After finishing this chapter go to **PAGE 141** for **STUDY TOOLS**

A PACT TO END WAR

On August 27, 1928, jubilant diplomats and leaders celebrated their amazing achievement. That day, the leaders of the United States, France, Britain, Germany, Italy, and Japan signed what they believed to be a breakthrough agreement that would change the world: The General Treaty for the Renunciation of War, also known as the Kellogg–Briand Pact for its two central authors—American Secretary of State Frank Kellogg and French Foreign Minister Aristide Briand. The agreement outlawed aggressive war, prohibiting the use of war as "an instrument of national policy" except in matters of self-defense. Less than a year later, 31 additional countries—including the Soviet Union, Spain, and China—had joined the pact. It took force shortly thereafter and was registered with the League of Nations in September 1929, after which another eight countries joined the agreement. The treaty remains in force today.

The jubilation was premature, of course. In 1931 Japan invaded Manchuria, in 1935 Italy invaded Ethiopia, and in 1939 the world was plunged into World War II as Germany and the Soviet Union attacked Poland and then extended their aggression to other countries. Japan also extended its military efforts in Asia and the Pacific, culminating in the 1941 attack on the United States. Clearly, aggressive uses of force by one state against another continued after World War II and continue as well today.

This case raises some fundamental questions:

1. Why did this international agreement fail to achieve its purpose and promise?

2. What forces in world politics worked against the pact's aims to eliminate war?

3. Has the window of opportunity closed for such an international agreement?

Olga Maltseva/AFP/Getty Images

Russian tanks deploy in Crimea against Ukrainian forces as Russia annexes the territory in 2014 | Why do wars persist as a problem in world politics?

INTRODUCTION: INTERNATIONAL CONFLICT

Conflict and war have long been regarded as *the* central problems of international relations. It is no wonder these issues have occupied center stage. In Chapter 3, we quoted a well-known statement by the realist international relations theorist Hans Morgenthau, whose words are especially relevant here: "All states are either preparing for, recovering from, or engaged in war." The traditional approach to security in world politics has long emphasized the survival and safety issues connected to conflict and war as the most important matters of world politics. In this approach, security typically means power and survival, territorial integrity, and political independence, with the state as the primary focus and other non-state actors such as terrorists, freedom fighters, and international organizations as secondary. This is the traditional arena of interests and military power, emphasizing the problem of conflict and war between and within states and often involving other non-state actors.

War of various kinds is a persistent feature of world politics over the centuries. Its implications for the survival of states and its enormous costs in lives and treasure have combined to keep it at the center of attention for policymakers and for international relations scholars seeking to explain it, predict it, prepare for it, and prevent it. Conflict and war have exacted monumental costs—lives, material, wealth, and power—from those states, groups, and individuals it has involved. For the United States, for example, participation in war has cost some $7 trillion (and counting) and over 2.5 million in dead and wounded over its history as an independent country. Some estimates place global casualties from war at close to 4 billion when both direct and indirect casualties are included.

In Part Two of our text, we examine the arena of international security. This chapter focuses on understanding conflict and war—especially the nature and causes of these security issues—which are central challenges in the international security arena. We begin with an overview of conflict and war and its various forms and then discuss the changing patterns of armed conflict over time. We then turn to the causes and consequences of war. In Chapter 6, we focus our attention to the strategies states and other actors have used to manage conflict and achieve security. Finally, in Chapter 7 we consider efforts to gain security and manage conflict through structures and institutions of cooperation.

Kevin Dietsch/UPI/Landov

Popperfoto/Getty Images

The costs of war | With the human toll of war so high, why does it continue?

5-1 THE NATURE OF ARMED CONFLICT

Even the most optimistic observer of world politics would have to concede that conflict and war are persistent patterns of world politics. It is (happily) true that most conflicts among the players of world politics are resolved without resort to violence. However, even though war is relatively rare (thank goodness) given the number of states and national groups in world politics that could be fighting with each other at any given time, armed clashes of varying scope and size have been a regular feature in international relations and armed conflict continues to occur around the world. According to John Keegan, in the *History of Warfare*, while the particular features and practices of war have varied according to the particular historical and societal contexts in which it occurred, it is a universal phenomenon crossing space and time. By some accounts, close to 15,000 violent clashes between different groups have occurred over recorded history, with about six hundred significant wars taking place since the year 1500. As Map 5-1 and Figure 5-1 show, since World War II, and at present, armed conflicts involved countries and peoples from all over the globe.

5-1a War and Its Types

In the simplest account of this persistent and important phenomenon of world politics, the self-interests of players clash and violence sometimes erupts. **War**—organized, violent (i.e., military) conflict between two or more political parties—occurs when the participants engage in armed struggles to gain or defend territory, resources, influence, authority, and other things of high value. The participants can involve two or more states (**interstate war**), two or more groups within a territory (intrastate, or **civil war**), or a combination of states and non-state groups (**extra-systemic** or **extra-state war**). Such armed struggles obviously range from small-scale, localized disputes to large-scale, even global conflicts.

To better understand war, we can distinguish between a variety of types, which leads us to consider the evolution of war over time, as well.

CONVENTIONAL WAR Conventional war is typically characterized as armed conflict between two or more states in which military forces of each side are used against each other and in which weapons of mass destruction such as nuclear, biological, or chemical weapons are generally not used. However, conventional wars may be **general wars**, involving multiple participants

war organized, violent (i.e. military) conflict between two or more parties.

interstate war armed conflict between two or more states.

civil war armed conflict between competing factions within a country, or between a government and a competing group within that country over control of territory and/or the government.

extra-systemic or extra-state war armed conflict between a state and a non-state entity, such as colonial wars and wars with non-state national or terrorist groups.

conventional war armed conflict between two or more states in which military forces of each side are used against each other, and in which weapons of mass destruction such as nuclear, biological, or chemical weapons are not used.

general war armed conflict in which the participants seek to conquer and control territory of their opponents and use the full available arsenals against military targets and against the infrastructure of a country.

Map 5-1
Armed Conflicts, 2012

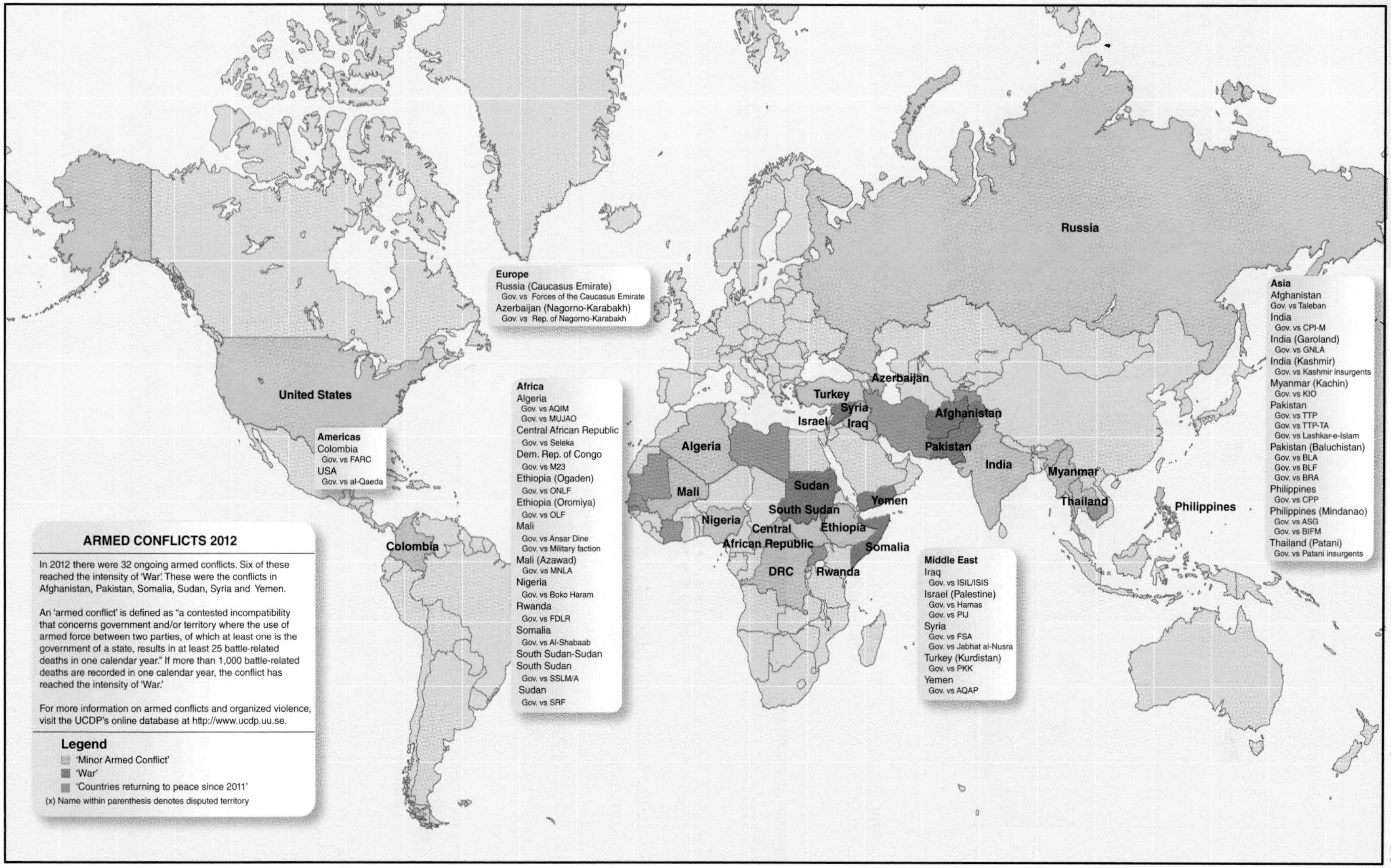

Asia
Afghanistan
Gov. vs Taleban
India
India (Garoland)
Gov. vs CPI-M
Gov. vs GNLA
India (Kashmir)
Gov. vs Kashmir insurgents
Myanmar (Kachin)
Gov. vs KIO
Pakistan
Gov. vs TTP
Gov. vs TTP-TA
Gov. vs Lashkar-e-Islam
Pakistan (Baluchistan)
Gov. vs BLA
Gov. vs BLF
Gov. vs BRA
Philippines
Gov. vs CPP
Philippines (Mindanao)
Gov. vs ASG
Gov. vs BIFM
Thailand (Patani)
Gov. vs Patani insurgents

Middle East
Iraq
Gov. vs ISIL/ISIS
Israel (Palestine)
Gov. vs Hamas
Gov. vs PIJ
Syria
Gov. vs FSA
Gov. vs Jabhat al-Nusra
Turkey (Kurdistan)
Gov. vs PKK
Yemen
Gov. vs AQAP

Europe
Russia (Caucasus Emirate)
Gov. vs Forces of the Caucasus Emirate
Azerbaijan (Nagorno-Karabakh)
Gov. vs Rep. of Nagorno-Karabakh

Africa
Algeria
Gov. vs AQIM
Gov. vs MUJAO
Central African Republic
Gov. vs Seleka
Dem. Rep. of Congo
Gov. vs M23
Ethiopia (Ogaden)
Gov. vs ONLF
Ethiopia (Oromiya)
Gov. vs OLF
Mali
Gov. vs Ansar Dine
Gov. vs Military faction
Mali (Azawad)
Gov. vs MNLA
Nigeria
Gov. vs Boko Haram
Rwanda
Gov. vs FDLR
Somalia
Gov. vs Al-Shabaab
South Sudan-Sudan
South Sudan
Gov. vs SSLM/A
Sudan
Gov. vs SRF

Americas
Colombia
Gov. vs FARC
USA
Gov. vs al-Qaeda

ARMED CONFLICTS 2012

In 2012 there were 32 ongoing armed conflicts. Six of these reached the intensity of 'War.' These were the conflicts in Afghanistan, Pakistan, Somalia, Sudan, Syria and Yemen.

An 'armed conflict' is defined as "a contested incompatibility that concerns government and/or territory where the use of armed force between two parties, of which at least one is the government of a state, results in at least 25 battle-related deaths in one calendar year." If more than 1,000 battle-related deaths are recorded in one calendar year, the conflict has reached the intensity of 'War.'

For more information on armed conflicts and organized violence, visit the UCDP's online database at http://www.ucdp.uu.se.

Legend

Minor Armed Conflict
'War'
'Countries returning to peace since 2011'
(x) Name within parenthesis denotes disputed territory

What do the locations and occurrences of conflict around most of the world indicate?

Source: Data from Uppsala University Research, *Uppsala Conflict Data Program UCDP Conflict Encyclopedia*, www.ucdp.uu.se/database (accessed June 28, 2012).

© Cengage Learning®

FIGURE 5-1   ARMED CONFLICT BY REGION, 1946–2012

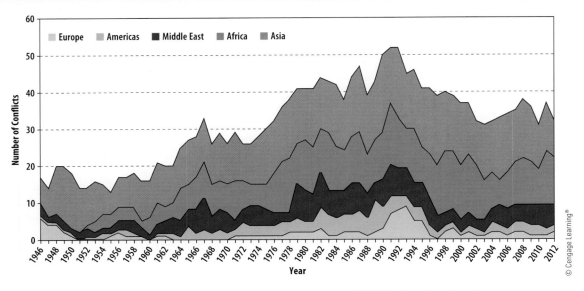

Source: Data from Uppsala University Research, *Uppsala Conflict Data Program UCDP Conflict Encyclopedia*, www.pcr.uu.se /digitalAssets/66/66314_1armed-conflict-by-region.pdf.

SPOTLIGHT ON

Defining War Empirically

War may fall into the category of "I know it when I see it" for many, but concepts like this must be carefully defined in empirical terms. Political scientists have employed several standards in their efforts.

Correlates of War

In the well-established Correlates of War data project, an empirical threshold of 1,000 battle deaths distinguishes *war* from other, smaller armed disputes. The Correlates of War data define a militarized interstate dispute—or MID—as the threat, display, or use of military force short of war (less than 1,000 battle deaths) by one member state explicitly directed toward the government, official representatives, official forces, property, or territory of another state. Note that this is a relatively restrictive definition that excludes some military engagements including the U.S. military operations in Iraq since 2003.

Uppsala Conflict Data Program

The Peace Research Institute of Oslo (PRIO) defines war empirically in the same way (an armed conflict reaching a cumulative total of 1,000 battle deaths, and then an annual total of 1,000 battle deaths each subsequent calendar year) in its Uppsala Conflict Data Program. PRIO also defines a major armed conflict as one in which a cumulative total of 1,000 battle deaths has been reached, with at least 25 battle-related deaths occurring each subsequent calendar year. A minor armed conflict involves 25 battle-related deaths prior to reaching the one thousand battle-death total.

1. Given these definitions, was the U.S. invasion of Iraq a war? What about the subsequent occupation and "state-building" in Iraq?

2. Is the current conflict in Afghanistan a war by these definitions? What about the U.S. use of force in Libya? The recent armed conflict in Ukraine?

Source: http://COW:www.correlatesofwar.org; http://UCDP:www.pcr.uu.se /research/ucdp/program_overview.

seeking to conquer and control the territory of their opponents and in which the full range of the available arsenal of conventional weapons is used against military targets and against the infrastructure of a country.

Such large-scale warfare is exemplified by World War I and II in the twentieth century. From the early seventeenth century, major powers increasingly resorted to general war until the incredible devastation of the two world wars in the twentieth century ushered in changes. **Limited wars** involve the use of conventional weapons (i.e., not weapons of mass destruction), but also do not involve the full military might of the participants nor do they seek the complete victory over the opponent but instead a smaller, more limited goal. In the 1991 Gulf War, for example, the United States and its allies deployed a portion of their military capabilities for limited goals (expelling Iraqi forces from Kuwait) and did not conquer and occupy Iraq once its forces were defeated. In short, such wars may be limited in terms of their geographic scope or the amount of military force brought to bear.

UNCONVENTIONAL WAR In contrast to conventional war, **unconventional war** involves armed conflict in which traditional battles between the organized militaries of the participants are less prominent (or avoided altogether). According to the U.S. Department of Defense, instead of these traditional approaches, unconventional war is a broad category involving

> A broad spectrum of military and paramilitary operations, normally of long duration, predominantly conducted through, with, or by indigenous or surrogate forces who are organized, trained, equipped, supported, and directed in varying degrees by an external source. It includes, but is not limited to, guerrilla warfare, subversion, sabotage, intelligence activities, and unconventional assisted recovery.[1]

Typically, unconventional warfare not only involves targeting civilian populations much more directly, as well as other non-military targets, but it means that the forces involved are not traditional organized military forces. Two examples of this type of warfare may be helpful here. First is the war in Vietnam where the guerrilla Vietcong forces—considered insurgents by today's definition—first engaged in military conflict with the French until 1954 and then with American troops after the United States began its intervention. Second, when the Soviets occupied Afghanistan in the 1980s, they battled the mujahideen, a guerrilla or insurgent force that did not fight the Soviets head-on but instead launched harassing attacks against Soviet troops in outlying areas.

Since the introduction of **weapons of mass destruction** in World War I and II, the use of such weaponry has been characterized as unconventional warfare, as well. This complicates the definition of war because both world wars are usually considered conventional, and yet, unconventional weapons were used in both. It is still correct to consider both of those conflicts

The changing face of war | What is the effect of such unconventional soldiers on warfare? Could you shoot a child-soldier like this if you were a soldier?

AP Images/Karel Prinsloo

conventional, but today, if weapons of mass destruction were widely used in a conflict, it would certainly be considered unconventional.

CIVIL WAR While conventional war means armed conflict between two or more states, civil war involves armed conflict between competing factions within a country or between an existing government and a competing group within that country over control of territory and/or the government. Civil wars come in various sizes and shapes, from expansive general wars like the American Civil War of the 1860s to more limited or unconventional conflicts like those in Syria after 2011. Table 5-1 lists most of the civil wars since the end of World War II. Civil wars may initially pit factions within a country against each other, but they frequently become internationalized. As we discuss later in this chapter, this may occur as the conflict or its consequences spill over the country's borders or if external parties become involved in the conflict. A good example is the 2011 conflict in Libya, in which resistance to the dictatorship of Colonel Muammar Gaddafi and his 40-plus years of rule soon resulted in intervention by U.S. and NATO forces, along with limited support from

limited war armed conflict with conventional weapons for limited goals and without use of full available arsenals.

unconventional war armed conflict in which civilian and non-military targets are emphasized, forces used include nontraditional forces outside organized militaries, and in which a wide array of weaponry including weapons of mass destruction may be employed.

weapons of mass destruction (WMD) nuclear, chemical, and biological weapons.

TABLE 5-1　SELECT CIVIL WARS SINCE 1945

Greek Civil War, 1946–1949	Georgian Civil War, 1991–1993
Paraguayan Civil War, 1947	Tajikistan Civil War, 1992–1997
Palestinian Civil War, 1947–1948	Yemen Civil War, 1994
Costa Rican Civil War, 1948	First Chechen War, 1994–1996
Vietnamese Civil War, 1954–1975	Iraqi Kurdish Civil War, 1994–1997
Guatemalan Civil War, 1960–1996	First Congo War, 1996–1997
Congo Civil War, 1960–1966	Nepalese Civil War, 1996–2006
North Yemen Civil War, 1962–1970	Republic of Congo Civil War, 1997–1999
Dominican Civil War, 1963	Albanian Rebellion, 1997
Rhodesian Bush War, 1965–1980	Cambodian Civil War, 1997–1998
Cypriot Civil War, 1967–1974	Guinea-Bissau Civil War, 1998–1999
Nigerian Civil War, 1967–1970	Second Congo War, 1998–2003
Cambodian Civil War I, 1970–1975	Kosovo War, 1998–1999
Pakistani Civil War, 1971	Second Chechen War, 1999–2009
Angolan Civil War, 1975–2002	Second Liberian Civil War, 1999–2003
Lebanese Civil War, 1975–1990	Cote d'Ivoirian Civil War, 2002–2007
Mozambican Civil War, 1975–1992	Darfur (Sudan) Civil War, 2003–2009
Cambodian Civil War II, 1978–1993	Haitian rebellion, 2004
Nicaraguan Civil War, 1979–1990	Civil war in Libya, 2011
Salvadoran Civil War, 1979–1991	Colombian Civil War, ongoing (1964)
Peruvian Civil War, 1980–2000	Afghan Civil War, ongoing (1978)
Sri Lankan Civil War, 1983–2009	Ugandan Civil War, ongoing (1987)
Sudanese Civil War, 1983–2005	Somali Civil War, ongoing (1991)
First Liberian Civil War, 1989–1996	Civil war in Chad, ongoing (2005)
Sierra Leonean Civil War, 1991–2002	Civil war in Iraq, ongoing (2003)
Algerian Civil War, 1991–2002	Civil war in Syria, ongoing (2012)
Burundi Civil War, 1993–2005	Civil war in Ukraine, ongoing (2014)
Rwandan Civil War, 1990–1993	

© Cengage Learning®

other states in the region, to establish a no-fly zone and attack government forces and targets, in part to try to prevent wide-scale attacks on civilians.

ASYMMETRIC WAR Directly related to unconventional war, **asymmetric war** pits two or more groups of very different military size or power against each other. To overcome the disadvantages stemming from this imbalance of power and technological superiority, the smaller or weaker participant often resorts to

asymmetric war　armed conflict between two or more groups of very different military size or power.

IEDs (improvised explosive devices)　a homemade bomb, often placed on roadsides and other sites, fashioned from an explosive device and a detonator, usually triggered by remote device or "booby-trap" mechanism.

unconventional tactics rather than engage in an almost certainly futile attempt to fight a traditional battlefield war. These may include those described by the U.S. Department of Defense earlier, such as guerrilla warfare, subversion, and sabotage, including the use of **IEDs (improvised explosive devices)** to use against the more powerful adversary. These tactics may also involve attacks that turn the technology of the adversary on itself in improvisational approaches. Take, for example, some of the al-Qaeda terrorist network attacks on the United States. In 1998, trucks loaded with explosives were used to bomb U.S. embassies in Kenya and Tanzania. In 2000, a small boat filled with explosives was directed into the USS *Cole*, a U.S. Navy destroyer docked in Aden, Yemen, where it was refueling. The attack damaged the vessel and killed 17 sailors. And, of course, al-Qaeda operatives seized control of four U.S. airliners and flew them into the World Trade Center towers in New York and

Terrorist attacks on the World Trade Center, September 11, 2001 | How can a country defend against the use of such "weapons"?

the Pentagon in Washington, DC, in 2001. (The fourth plane crashed in Pennsylvania after passengers struggled with the hijackers to regain control of the plane.) In these latter dramatic and devastating attacks, which resulted in the deaths of nearly 3,000 people, no explosives were even used—the "bombs" were the hi-tech airliners themselves. In such warfare, traditional measures of "success" and "victory" like capturing enemy territory or their national capitals are obviously much less important, if not completely irrelevant.

5-1b Terrorism

No up-to-date discussion of conflict and war can ignore the problem of **terrorism**. Clearly, terrorism is a form of unconventional and asymmetric war. Definitions of terrorism are more difficult than might be expected (yet another example of "I know it when I see it"). As a label, it has often been attached to violence perpetrated by groups the observer does not like. This calls to mind the old cliché that "one man's terrorist is another man's freedom fighter." As noted terrorism expert Bruce Hoffman has argued,

> terrorism is a pejorative term. It is a word with intrinsically negative connotations that is generally applied to one's enemies and opponents,

or to those with whom one disagrees and would otherwise prefer to ignore. . . . If one identifies with the victim of the violence, for example, then the act is terrorism. If, however, one identifies with the perpetrator, the violent act is regarded in a more sympathetic, if not positive (or, at the worst, an ambivalent) light; and it is not terrorism.[2]

How then can we understand this form of violence? There is no single, universally accepted international definition of terrorism to guide us. There are, however, plenty of definitions to consider. According to Walter Laqueur, there are over a hundred major definitions that emphasize a wide variety of things.[3] For example, consider the following:

- The League of Nations (1937): all criminal acts directed against a State and intended or calculated to create a state of terror in the minds of particular persons or a group of persons or the general public.

- U.S. Department of State: premeditated, politically motivated violence perpetrated against non-combatants by subnational groups or clandestine agents, usually intended to influence an audience.

- U.S. Federal Bureau of Investigation: unlawful use of force or violence against persons or property to intimidate or coerce a government, the civilian population, or any segment thereof, in furtherance of political or social objectives.

- U.S. Department of Defense: unlawful use of—or threatened use of—force or violence against individuals or property to coerce or intimidate governments or societies, often to achieve political, religious, or ideological objectives.

- The Council of Arab Ministers (1998 Arab Convention for the Suppression of Terrorism): any act or threat of violence, whatever its motives or purposes, that occurs in the advancement of an individual or collective criminal agenda and seeking to sow panic among people; causing fear by harming them; or placing their lives, liberty, or security in danger; or seeking to cause damage to the environment or to public or private installations or property or to occupying or seizing them; or seeking to jeopardize a national resource.

Or these from noted experts on the problem:

- Walter Laqueur: Terrorism constitutes the illegitimate use of force to achieve a political objective when innocent people are targeted.

terrorism indiscriminate violence aimed at noncombatants to influence a wider audience.

FIGURE 5-2 DEFINING TERRORISM BY MEANS AND TARGETS

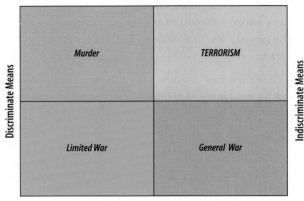

© Cengage Learning®

- Bruce Hoffman: The deliberate creation and exploitation of fear through violence or the threat of violence in the pursuit of political change.

- Brian Jenkins: Terrorism is the use or threatened use of force designed to bring about political change.

What shall we make of these various efforts? Some are narrowly focused on non-state actors attacking governments and populations, while others are broadly construed and could involve a wide range of perpetrators and actions.

Perhaps political scientist Peter Sederberg provides a useful approach. In *Terrorist Myths: Illusions, Rhetoric and Reality*, he urges us to focus on the act first, and then consider who might be engaged in it. In his view, this might help us salvage the concept—in effect, anyone engaging in the act is engaging in terrorism. So what defines the act of terrorism according to Sederberg? As Figure 5-2 shows, if we distinguish between targets (combatants or noncombatants on the vertical axis) and means (discriminate or indiscriminate on the horizontal axis), we can place terrorism in one of the four resulting cells and identify it as the combination of *indiscriminate* violence (e.g., a suitcase bomb left on a subway platform, which does not discriminate among its victims—anyone who happens to be there is hurt or killed) directed at *noncombatants* (civilians not part of the armed forces or national command/leadership).[4] The remaining cells in the figure help us to differentiate other forms of violence such as murder, limited war, and general war. Supplementing

state-sponsored terrorism includes covert and overt repression of and violence against civilian populations, and more extreme acts such as genocide, supported or perpetrated by the state.

this, we might draw on elements of the preceding definitions to also draw a distinction between the victims of the violence (those injured by the bomb blast) and the audience of the violence (the society or government the act is intended to influence). This approach allows us to refrain from labeling terrorists based on their goals or purposes.

Who then engages in terrorism? Many definitions from the political and academic world exclude governments, focusing on non-state actors. However, it is quite possible for states to be engaged in terrorism if they employ violence in certain ways. Such **state-sponsored terrorism** includes covert and overt repression of civilian populations, and more extreme acts such as genocide (which we discuss in more detail in Chapter 11).[5] State-sponsored terrorism also includes states that fund, arm, or aid terrorist groups such as Libya's support of the planning of the airline bombing over Lockerbie, Scotland (1988), or Iran's arming of Hezbollah in Lebanon and Hamas in the Palestinian Gaza Strip over the past several decades. Such state-sponsored terrorism would also include those times when the terrorist attack is conducted by agents of the state itself, such as North Korea's bombing of a diplomatic meeting in Burma that killed a number of South Korean government representatives.

For non-state terrorism, which is of particular importance in our discussion of types of conflict and war, there are several ways to classify those who resort to such tactics. According to Cindy Combs, one simple distinction is between "crazies" (emotionally disturbed individuals who resort to terrorism), "criminals" (individuals using terrorism for personal gain), and "crusaders" (individuals using terrorism in pursuit of a collective cause).[6]

According to Sederberg, a useful classification scheme has four categories:[7]

1. *Criminal terrorists.* Individuals and groups using terrorism for financial gain. Examples would include the narco-terrorism of drug cartels or, perhaps, the violence employed by various organized crime groups.

2. *Nihilist terrorists.* Individuals and groups using terrorism for the destruction of order without an agenda for its replacement. Examples would include the Red Army Faction or Baader-Meinhof gang in Germany, the Red Brigades in Italy, and, perhaps, the Weather Underground in the United States.

3. *Nationalist terrorists.* Individuals and groups of particular ethnic/cultural identity who engage in terrorism in pursuit of the interests of their ethno-nationalist groups. Such groups typically target the governments ruling them and seek autonomy and independence. Examples include the Irish Republican Army, the Palestinian Liberation Organization, the Basque separatists (Spain), Chechen separatists (Russia), and others, including, perhaps, Hamas.

Al-Qaeda and Modern Revolutionary Terrorism

The most prominent revolutionary terrorist organization of the last decade has been al-Qaeda, a radical Islamist movement seeking an end to foreign influence in the Middle East and the institution of Islamist regimes throughout the region.

Founded in the late 1980s out of the network of individuals who joined in the struggle to defeat the Soviet Union in Afghanistan, al-Qaeda (which means "The Base" in Arabic) quickly shifted its focus from resisting Soviet aggression in Afghanistan to its current aims. Among the events central to its resurgence were the 1991 Gulf War, which put Western troops in Saudi Arabia and elsewhere in the Persian Gulf region, and the ongoing Israeli–Palestinian conflict, which al-Qaeda associated with U.S. and Western support for Israel.

Al-Qaeda became an expansive network that made use of modern communication and information technology, as well as more traditional modes of operation. The center—al-Qaeda itself—was led by Osama bin Laden and a *shura* (or council) of about two dozen people from Afghanistan and northwest Pakistan after the September 11, 2001, attacks on the United States. It had a military committee to train and plan attacks, a finance committee to raise and distribute funds to its operatives and cells, and other committees for reviewing the purposes and plans it pursued to ensure that they were consistent with their interpretation of Islamic law and for publicizing its cause. Some reports indicated that, at one time, al-Qaeda might have fielded thousands of trained recruits across 40 or 50 different countries. According to the U.S. Department of State, al-Qaeda has at least two guerilla forces operating in Iraq and in Pakistan.

Al-Qaeda is more than its central core, however. Its essence is as much defined by its extensive network of alliance and collaboration with other indigenous movements from around the world as from its own central forces. This is especially true since the September 11, 2001, attacks, as the central headquarters has been increasingly isolated and its ability to plan and execute significant attacks has been substantially degraded by the efforts of the United States and its allies in the war on terrorism. These subsidiaries, many of which existed independently of al-Qaeda prior to making common cause, are often driven by local, nationalist, or subnationalist motives. Such affiliates can be found throughout Southeast Asia, Africa, and the Middle East. The U.S. Department of State also identifies at least three affiliated al-Qaeda organizations connected to the core organization: al-Qaeda in the Arabian Peninsula (primarily based in Yemen), al-Qaeda in Iraq, and al-Qaeda in the Islamic Maghreb (North Africa from Morocco to Libya).

Al-Qaeda–led and al-Qaeda–sponsored terrorism has targeted noncombatants in many countries. The most well known were the major attacks on the United States on September 11, 2001, but their use of suicide attacks and coordinated bombings also occurred in Indonesia (2002), Turkey (2003), the United Kingdom (2009), Yemen (2009), and many others. Other plots, such as the December 25, 2009, attempt to blow up Northwest Airlines Flight 253 as it approached its destination in the United States, failed or were averted.

Al-Qaeda and its network of affiliates remains a central security concern for the world. Although it is widely believed that the central organization has been weakened and isolated, the broader network remains active. According to the U.S. Department of State, by 2010, the al-Qaeda of the September 11, 2001, attacks has changed considerably and may no longer really exist. In its place is a "diffuse global network and philosophical movement composed of dispersed nodes with varying degrees of independence."[8] Just before the May 2011 raid in which U.S. special forces located and killed Osama bin Laden, a former official in Australian counterterrorism argued:

Despite nearly a decade of war, al Qaeda is stronger today than when it carried out the 9/11 attacks. Before 2001, its history was checkered with mostly failed attempts to fulfill its most enduring goal: the unification of other militant Islamist groups under its strategic leadership. However, since fleeing Afghanistan to Pakistan's tribal areas in late 2001, al Qaeda has founded a regional branch in the Arabian Peninsula and acquired franchises in Iraq and the Maghreb. Today, it has more members, greater geographic reach, and a level of ideological sophistication and influence it lacked ten years ago.[9]

The impact of the deaths of bin Laden and other top al-Qaeda leaders over the past several years may be seen in the decline in attacks and casualties. However, as a source of threat to global security, this modern revolutionary terrorist network remains significant and challenging.

---

4. *Revolutionary terrorists.* Individuals and groups who engage in terrorism in pursuit of broader regional or global transformations of the social and political order.

Examples would include some revolutionary Marxist organizations during the Cold War, and, more recently, groups such as Hezbollah and al-Qaeda.

Terrorism in 2012

In 2012, a total of 6,771 terrorist attacks occurred worldwide in 85 different countries, resulting in more than 11,000 deaths and more than 21,600 injuries. In addition, more than 1,280 people were kidnapped or taken hostage. The total number of attacks worldwide dropped significantly, however, as did the number of deaths.

- Although terrorist attacks occurred in 85 different countries in 2012, they were heavily concentrated geographically. Over half of all attacks (55%), fatalities (62%), and injuries (65%) occurred in just three countries: Pakistan, Iraq, and Afghanistan.

- The highest number of fatalities occurred in Afghanistan (2,632); however, the country with the most injuries due to terrorist attacks was Iraq (6,641).

- The average lethality of terrorist attacks in Nigeria (2.54 deaths per attack) is more than 50 percent higher than the global average of 1.64. The average lethality of terrorist attacks in Syria (4.94 deaths per attack) is more than 200 percent higher than the global average. The average number of people wounded per terrorist attack was especially high in Syria, where 1,787 people were reportedly wounded in 133 attacks, including four attacks that caused 670 injuries.

- In contrast, the rates of lethality for India (0.42 deaths per attack), the Philippines (0.77 deaths per attack), and Thailand (0.78 deaths per attack) were relatively low among the countries with the most attacks.

Source: U.S. State Department, *Annex of Statistical Information: Country Reports on Terrorism 2012, May 2013*, http://www.state.gov/documents/organization/210288.pdf.

As a form of violence—even warfare—and as a problem for world politics, terrorism is not new. It has always been a tactic of weaker and disadvantaged groups in conflict with others. However, experts on the matter generally date the modern era of terrorism at about 1968 when members of the Popular Front for the Liberation of Palestine hijacked a passenger jet from Israel's El Al Airlines and held its passengers hostage, seeking the release of Arab terrorists jailed in Israel (the prisoners were released in order to get the hostages back). Since then, it has become more salient as an international issue. Of course, the dramatic attacks on the United States on September 11, 2001, served to increase attention to the importance of the problem, as well. As a form of violence and war in the modern world, the empirical evidence suggests that while incidents of terrorism have been declining since the early 1980s (see Table 5-2 and Figure 5-3), if one looks only at major or significant terrorist attacks, they have increased more than eight times since the early 1980s.

Terrorism involves a wide variety of tactics, including bombing, hijacking, kidnapping, and many others. Suicide attacks have been employed with greater frequency in recent decades, as well. Responding to these attacks is challenging, of course. Like other unconventional fighters, terrorists are more difficult to locate and target. They don't wear uniforms or identification badges. In general, addressing this challenge has some combination of the following efforts: reducing vulnerability through national and international security measures like strengthening airport security; increasing information and intelligence on potential threats so that they can be countered; enhancing cooperation across national and international jurisdictions; dissuading enemies from attempting attacks; disarming and eliminating attackers through coercion; and reducing recruits and terrorist havens and harbors.

TABLE 5-2 INCIDENTS OF TERRORISM WORLDWIDE

	2005	2006	2007	2008	2009	2010	2011	2012
Attacks worldwide	11,023	14,443	14,435	11,725	10,969	11,641	10,283	6,771
People killed, injured, or kidnapped as a result of terrorism	74,327	74,616	71,856	54,653	58,711	49,928	43,990	34,033
People worldwide killed as a result of terrorism	14,482	20,515	22,736	15,727	15,310	13,193	12,533	11,098
People worldwide kidnapped as a result of terrorism	35,050	15,787	4,981	4,869	10,750	6,051	5,554	1,283

© Cengage Learning®

FIGURE 5-3 TERRORIST ATTACKS SINCE 1971

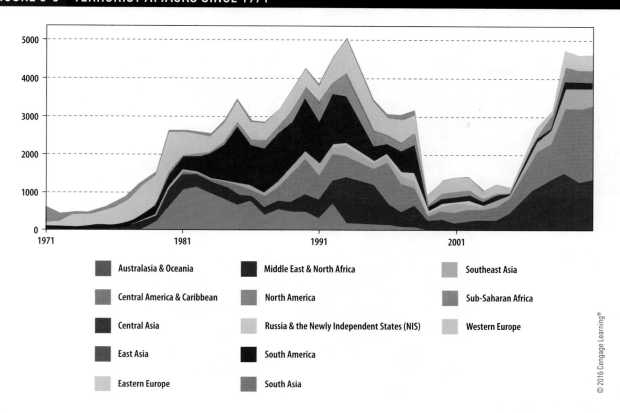

Australasia & Oceania

Central America & Caribbean

Central Asia

East Asia

Eastern Europe

Middle East & North Africa

North America

Russia & the Newly Independent States (NIS)

South America

South Asia

Southeast Asia

Sub-Saharan Africa

Western Europe

© 2016 Cengage Learning®

5-2 THE NATURE AND EVOLUTION OF WAR IN WORLD POLITICS

It is probably not surprising that the nature of war has evolved over time. A simple way of illustrating some of the changes is to think about the depiction of warfare in the well-known imagery of film. Consider the battle scenes of *Braveheart* (1995), which depicts the armed struggles between Scotland and England in the thirteenth century, in which axes, swords, pikes, and archery were deployed in largely hand-to-hand battles. Fast-forward to the battle scenes shown in the movie *The Patriot* (2000), depicting the American Revolution of the late eighteenth century, where muskets and cannon dominated, or those of *Glory* (1989), set in the American Civil War, in which artillery, longer range (though still inaccurate) rifles, and other weaponry appear. Now, fast-forward to the battle scenes of *All Quiet on the Western Front* (1930) or *Gallipoli* (1981) (World War I) or *Saving Private Ryan* (1998) (World War II), which show the impact of technological advances in weaponry such as automatic weapons, air power, and armored vehicles. *Platoon* (1986), set in

the Vietnam conflict of 1960s, shows the complications of military clashes between less developed indigenous forces and modern armies. Recent depictions of war in *Black Hawk Down* (2001), *Jarhead* (2005), and the documentary *Restropo* (2010) depict modern conflicts on the battlefields of the late twentieth and early twenty-first century, highlighting the contrasts and complications of technologically advanced militaries in conflict with unconventional forces. This string of films also nicely illustrates the shifts from the traditional battlefields of the past to the often highly ambiguous contexts of current armed struggles.

5-2a Increasing Deadliness

The images of war depicted in these films highlight a number of trends in war. At least five of these are especially interesting and provide a good context for our focus on the causes of war in this chapter. First, war has become increasingly destructive and deadly over time. Consider that from the time of Rome to 1899, the average period of time necessary for 1 million people to die in war was about 50 years. Since 1900, that period is one year. According to political scientist Jack Levy, from 1500 to 1975, there were 589 wars exacting some 142 million deaths. Four times as many

Evolution of warfare | What happens when warfare evolves from picks and spears to high-tech weaponry?

of those deaths (80 percent of the total) occurred in the twentieth century than in the four centuries leading up to it.[10] The imagery in the films illustrates the technological advances in weapons and changes in the war-fighting organizations that have combined to help drive this trend. In one sense, human beings have been extremely efficient in developing ever-expanding abilities to kill each other in great numbers. What other factors help to explain the increasing deadliness of war over this time period?

5-2b More Limited Wars

A second trend appears counterintuitive to the first in some ways: since 1945, wars have become more limited. While the size and scope of warfare steadily increased through 1945, since that time, military conflict has been considerably more limited. This is especially true for the major powers of the post-1945 era, which have largely refrained from the large-scale conflict of the first half of the twentieth century. The advent of the nuclear age and the incredible destructive power of nuclear weapons have contributed to this trend, as major powers

have refrained from the use of the most destructive of modern weapons available to them, and from wars that might result in their use. The development of increasingly precise smart weapons and smart technology has also played a role. It also appears to be the case that war has become less deadly, in the sense that there has been a decline in battle deaths since 1945, as shown in Figure 5-4. What other factors help to explain these shifts? As we discuss later, some observers have argued that, for the developed world at least, major war has become obsolete.[11]

5-2c War in the Developing World

A third trend is that wars have increasingly been located in the second tier or the developing world since 1945 (see Map 5-2). It is a very interesting empirical fact that *all wars* since 1945 have occurred in the less-developed parts of the world and have either pitted a developed country (or countries) against forces from the less-developed world (e.g., the U.S.–Vietnam conflict, 1954–1973; the USSR–Afghanistan conflict, 1979–1989; or the first and second U.S.–Iraq conflicts of 1991

FIGURE 5-4 DEATHS FROM WAR AFTER WORLD WAR II

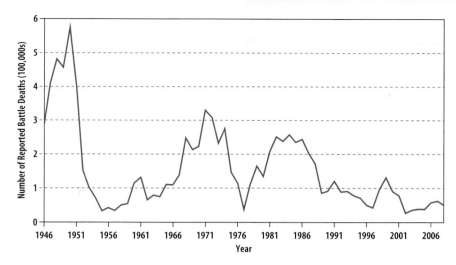

Source: Based on data from: Human Security Report Project. Human Security Report 2012: Sexual Violence, Education, and War: Beyond the Mainstream Narrative. Vancouver. Human Security Press, 2012. Found here: http://hsrgroup.org/docs/Publications /HSR2012/Figures/2012Report_Fig_5_2_GlobalSBBDs46-08.pdf AND HERE: http://hsrgroup.org/docs/Publications/HSR2012 /Figures/2012Report_Fig_7_1_GlobalNSConflictsBDs.pdf.

Map 5-2

Map of Major Conflicts since World War II

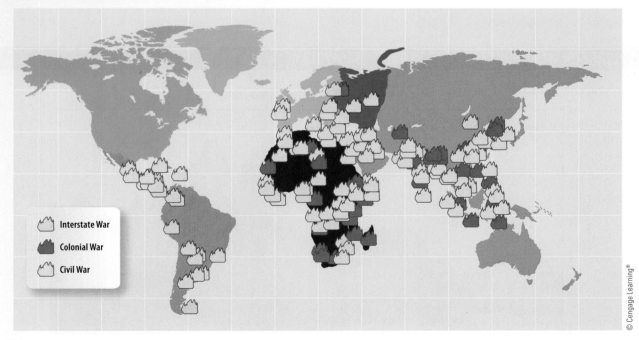

What parts of the world has conflict most affected since World War II?

Source: Data from "Conflict Map," *Nobelprize.org*, http://www.nobelprize.org/educational/peace/conflictmap (accessed May 22, 2012).

TABLE 5-3	MOST FRAGILE AND MOST STABLE STATES IN THE WORLD, 2014

MOST FRAGILE STATES	MOST STABLE STATES
South Sudan	Finland
Somalia	Sweden
Central African Republic	Denmark
Democratic Republic of Congo	Norway
Sudan	Switzerland
Chad	New Zealand
Afghanistan	Luxembourg
Yemen	Iceland
Haiti	Ireland
Pakistan	Australia

Source: The Fund For Peace, Fragile States Index (http://ffp.statesindex.org)
© Cengage Learning®

and 2003), or they have involved two or more forces from the developing world (e.g., the Cambodia–Vietnam War, 1975–1989; the Iran–Iraq War, 1980–1988; and the Second Congo War, 1998–2003). Unless one counts the fighting between Serbia, Croatia, Bosnia, and other parts of the former Yugoslavia—which is really a civil war—no conflicts since 1945 have been between two developed countries. Another way to look at this is to compare the most fragile and most stable states in the world, as we show in Table 5-3. Again, what

do you make of this comparison and what it might mean for conflict? Also, consider what factors might help to explain the more general and very interesting empirical trend.

5-2d More Civil War

Fourth, over time, and especially since 1989, war has become increasingly internal, as civil war has become the most common form of warfare. Figure 5-5 graphically shows this phenomenon, highlighting the growth of civil and internationalized civil wars, and the decline— almost disappearance—of interstate and extra-systemic (e.g., colonial) wars. For example, according to the Uppsala Conflict Data Project, of the 116 armed conflicts from 1989 to 2003, 109 were intrastate conflicts and only seven were interstate. In no period of history since the emergence of the state system in the seventeenth century has the difference between these two types of conflict been so dramatic. What causes might help to explain this post-1989 shift?

5-2e More Unconventional War

The last fundamental trend that is worth noting is the shift from conventional to unconventional war over the last half of the twentieth century and early twenty-first century. While unconventional war is

FIGURE 5-5   MILITARY CONFLICTS BY TYPE, 1946–2012

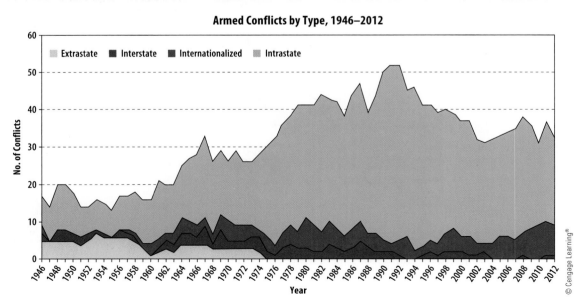

Source: Uppsala Conflict Data Program, http://www.pcr.uu.se/digitalAssets/196/196107_conflict_types_2012jpg.jpg

"Non-Trinitarian" War

According to Martin van Creveld in *The Transformation of War*, modern war has undergone a dramatic shift from conventional, state-centered conflict over political interests to more complicated conflicts with little distinctions between military forces and populations. Van Creveld suggests that five questions must now be asked in order to understand and address modern conflicts:

1. By whom is war fought (state and/or non-state participants)?

2. What is war all about (relationships between participants and noncombatants)?

3. How is war fought (strategies and tactics)?

4. For what is war fought (e.g., political wars, religious wars, and struggles for national or ethnic existence)?

5. Why is war fought (motives of individual soldiers)?

Van Creveld's argument focuses on the decline of the nation-state as the dominant force in war, and his perspective has implications for how countries and other actors organize for and address conflicts. *The Transformation of War* has been required reading for officers in the U.S. Army since its publication.

Source: Martin van Creveld, *The Transformation of War* (New York: Free Press, 1991).

---

related to civil and extra-state war, its distinguishing characteristics involve participants, tactics, and weaponry. Perhaps most dramatically illustrated in the rise of terrorism and the images of modern commercial airliners used as weapons that crashed into buildings in New York and Washington, DC, on September 11, 2001, the 2004 train bombings in Madrid, Spain, and the sequence of attacks against tourists and civilians in Mumbai, India, in 2008, this shift has been marked by dramatic changes in participants and strategies/tactics and weapons. According to the famous nineteenth-century study *On War* by Carl von Clausewitz, war was depicted as a state-centered, **trinitarian** concept with specific distinctions between governments, military forces, and populations.[12] In this conception, as von Clausewitz wrote, war was "the continuation of politics by other means" and fundamentally tied to the policies and interests of states. Increasingly since 1945, however, armed struggle has involved non-state actors and has blurred, ignored, or rendered irrelevant the distinctions between government, military forces, and population. Weaponry increasingly involves more than typical military arsenals. The civil wars, insurgencies, and terrorism of the post-1945 period are characterized by Martin van Creveld as **non-trinitarian**, or unconventional, war and pose significant challenges because of their nature. What force and factors underlie this shift, and what implications does it have for explaining and managing conflict in world politics?

Taken together, these five trends suggest that we can distinguish between three, or perhaps four, general eras

of warfare since the emergence of the state system in the seventeenth century.

- The Era of Great Power War, 1648–1945
- The Era of Limited War, 1946–1989
- The Era of Civil War, 1989–2001
- The Era of Unconventional War, 2001–present

Let us now turn to explanations of conflict to better understand what causes war.

5-3 WHY WARS BEGIN

Now that we have a sense of the evolution of conflict in world politics and the aspects of both continuity and change that are apparent, we turn to explanations for the causes of war in world politics. To do so, we need to think both practically and theoretically to build a better understanding of the problem of conflict. Indeed, comprehending broad explanations is essential for making sense of particular cases and a critical aspect of understanding patterns.

Even a moment's reflection on the overarching patterns just discussed might lead you to conclude that the

trinitarian war armed conflict in which the roles and participation of government, militaries, and populations are distinct.

non-trinitarian war armed conflict in which the roles and participation of government, militaries, and populations are blurred.

problem of conflict in world politics is what we might call *overdetermined*. That is, there would seem to be a great variety of possibilities for explaining conflicts, any one of which appears convincing as an explanation. And yet, it is certain that conflict is multicausal and that no one explanation is sufficient, either for explaining one particular war or for understanding a pattern of conflict. To consider the question of what causes war, let us reflect on two dimensions: (1) the factors over which conflict occurs and (2) the explanations of why war occurs.

5-3a The Causes of War: Factors Leading to Conflict

Take a moment and reflect on the examples of wars that we have considered to this point. What would you identify as the main purposes over which these wars were fought? What key issues generate international conflict?

Chances are that *territory* is at the top of most lists and for good reason. A great many studies of war identify territory as the most significant source of conflict among all the actors of world politics. For example, according to political scientists John Vasquez and Marie Henehan, of all the issues that spark conflict, territorial disputes have the highest probability of escalating to war.[13] A study by K. J. Holsti concluded that more than half of the wars over the past three centuries involved conflict over territory.[14] States and others fight over territory for a variety of reasons, including access to and control of important resources, strategic features or locations such as defensible borders (e.g., mountains, rivers, and other bodies of water), transportation routes and chokepoints, and others, or cultural features related to the race/ethnicity of a population, history or traditions, and other similar

Military forces staff a defensive position against potential invaders | Why is territory such a central part of warfare?

considerations. It is also the case that geography and territory matter in another way: states and others that are in closer proximity to one another are more likely to engage in armed conflict. Simply put, if two countries are next to each other, it is easier for them to fight than if they are on opposite sides of the world.

Holsti's study of conflict from the Westphalian to the neo-Westphalian period provides a good guide to other key factors, as well. As you consider this list, remember that conflicts and wars can arise from multiple issues and rarely have just one source. According to Holsti, while territory is the most frequent issue involved in conflict, other issues have also led to conflict and war:

- *Nation-state creation.* The "search for statehood" and independence has been a powerful motivator for conflict and war and has become increasingly important over the past 300 years.

- *Ideology.* According to Holsti, ideas have been increasingly important to world politics and international conflict. Good examples include the twentieth-century wars over fascism and communism (World War II; the Cold War) and, perhaps, the impact of democratic governance on peaceful relations among regimes sharing that type of government.

- *Economics.* Many conflicts and wars in the earlier parts of the Westphalian era involved competition for economic resources, markets, and/or transportation. According to Holsti, such issues have become much less central to war over the last 100 years or so as interdependence, international norms, and international regimes have worked against outright warfare over them. Still, key economic resources have been identified as issues underlying a number of recent conflicts, including the 1991 Gulf War and, perhaps, the 2003 U.S. intervention in Iraq.

- *Human sympathy: Ethnicity, religion, and war.* According to Holsti, acting on behalf of others out of sympathy—particularly to protect perceived religious and ethnic kin abroad, or for humanitarian purposes, has often been an important factor behind international conflict. India's intervention in East Pakistan (now Bangladesh) in 1971, and the more recent U.S.–led multilateral operations in Kosovo (1999) and Libya (2011) are good examples of such instances.

- *Predation and survival.* This issue involves effort to eliminate another state (usually for territorial or identity reasons). According to Holsti, this issue has been behind conflict and war most commonly in the twentieth century.

- *Other factors.* States have (occasionally) gone to war to defend allies and to defend or restore the balance of power. However, these factors are more important to understanding why states join ongoing wars rather than why the wars began in the first place.

Holsti's study is certainly not exhaustive or definitive, but it does help to identify key issues that often motivate war. Overall, he concludes that "relatively abstract issues—self-determination, principles of political philosophy and ideology, and sympathy for kin—have become increasingly important as sources of war while concrete issues such as territory and wealth have declined."[15] If Holsti is correct, there is at least one potentially very important implication to this pattern: issues related to territory and wealth are more open to compromise and much more easily resolved through nonviolent approaches than issues involving statehood, ideology, and identity.

What other issues can you think of that lead to war between and among the players in world politics? In particular, given our earlier discussion of key trends in the evolution of war, have the conflicts since Holsti concluded his study (1989) reinforced these findings, or do you see important differences?

5-3b The Causes of War: Explaining the Patterns

Let us now turn to efforts to explain the causes of war more theoretically. A good way to organize thinking about the causes of war is to rely on the levels of analysis we introduced earlier in the textbook: system, state, and individual. As we will see, theorists from the realist, liberal, and alternative perspectives offer explanations at each of these levels to help make sense of why conflict and war are persistent and recurring patterns in world politics. Contending, and sometimes complementary, explanations at each level of analysis highlight particular cause-and-effect relationships and focus on particular mechanisms to shed light on the problem of war. As we consider each level of analysis, you might think back on the opening account of the failed Kellogg-Briand pact and consider how explanations at each level help us to understand the failure of this effort to bring war between states to an end.

SYSTEM-LEVEL EXPLANATIONS The broadest category of explanations focuses on attributes of the international system to explain recurring patterns of conflict and war. As we discussed in Chapter 1, at this level realists, liberals, and others direct our attention to broad patterns in the interactions among the players of world politics, and emphasis is placed on the impact of the structural characteristics of the international system itself on such matters as the frequency and likelihood of conflict. Such characteristics include anarchy, the distribution of power, interdependence, and others.

In Chapter 3, our discussion of realist theory described that perspective's emphasis on international anarchy and its consequences for world politics. This is a good entry point to system-level explanations of conflict and war. Remember that the core of this argument stressed how anarchy—the absence of central government in world politics—creates a variety of consequences, including self-help and self-interested behavior, power seeking, and security dilemmas. For realists then, this essential structural characteristic is at the root of international conflict because it establishes conditions in which competition, mistrust, and clashing interests are common—the normal state of affairs in world politics. In effect, the anarchic system creates conditions of insecurity and competition in which conflict is all too common. This is at the heart of what Hans Morgenthau meant when he asserted that "all states are either preparing for, recovering from, or engaged in war." Realist theorist John Mearsheimer goes even further, arguing that the structural conditions stemming from anarchy "create powerful incentives for great powers to think and act offensively with regard to each other."[16]

An alternative perspective here would suggest that the violence-producing nature of anarchy is simply a social construction. Why can't anarchy be peaceful? A lack of governance does not have to equate violence. Would you commit murder if you were certain you could get away with it? Other reasons to act violently must exist, and many social constructivists point to the fact that most leaders and scholars believe in the *idea* that anarchy is violent. Violence becomes self-fulfilling: we believe that anarchy is violent, and so we act in a way that makes anarchy violent.

As an entry point, this system-level argument is helpful, but as you can see from the constructivist perspective (and the question about committing murder), it is limited. The main problem is that international anarchy is a constant condition, while conflict and war vary considerably. War happens more or less frequently over time and involves some states but not others. General, mostly unchanging conditions like anarchy, self-help, and the security dilemma provide little explanation of this variance. Moreover, conflict and war occurred long before the modern international system emerged in the sixteenth and seventeenth centuries, so other factors must be involved.

System-level explanations address the first issue, while explanations at other levels are more helpful in the second. Let us consider some further system-level explanations that stress attributes of the international system that vary and may help to shed light on the patterns of conflict and war. One of these is that particular

TABLE 5-4 BIPOLARITY, MULTIPOLARITY, AND WAR

BIPOLARITY	MULTIPOLARITY
More Stable	**More Stable**
Two major powers create a solid balance.	More actors increase opportunities for peaceful interactions.
War anywhere could become war everywhere.	More actors increase the number of states who could oppose an aggressor.
Certainty and calculation are easier.	More actors mean more mediators to moderate conflicts.
Control over allies is easier.	More actors may slow the rate of arms races.
Conflict is only likely between the two major powers.	States cannot focus on only one adversary.
Balance of power is easier to identify and achieve.	Hostility is diffused.
Shifts in the power of most states does not matter.	Ambiguity, uncertainty, and unpredictability increase with more actors and complexity.
Less Stable	**Less Stable**
Levels of hostility are very high.	Opportunities for conflict increase.
There are no mediators to moderate conflict between the major powers.	Diversity of interests increases.
Conflict anywhere can draw in the major powers.	Misperception and miscalculation increase in situations of greater complexity and uncertainty.
Stalemate between major powers may enable conflicts in peripheral areas.	More states mean that unequal distributions of resources are more likely.
Clarity and certainty might lead to war.	

© Cengage Learning®

distributions of power are more or less conflict prone. The distribution of power refers to the number of major powers that exist at a given moment and how power is distributed among them. According to many realist theorists, the frequency of war is largely determined by this structural factor. In fact, a lively debate over whether bipolar (systems with two major powers) or multipolar (systems with more than two major powers) distributions are more or less war prone has long existed among theorists. Table 5-4 summarizes some of the arguments on either side of this debate. What do you think it means for this kind of theorizing that a good case can be made for both sides of the argument?

A recent example of a systemic argument based on the distribution of power comes from John Mearsheimer. He argues that bipolar distributions—situations with two dominant powers—are the least conflict prone, in large measure because there is less fear among major powers over the prospect of attack. Multipolar systems—more than two great powers—are more conflict prone than bipolar systems because there are more axes of potential conflict and the great powers are less sure of who their allies are. However, Mearsheimer distinguishes between two types of multipolar systems: *balanced multipolar systems* (those without a potential dominant hegemonic state) are less warlike than *unbalanced multipolar systems* in which a potential hegemon exists and generates considerable fear among the other major powers.[17] Other realists argue that unipolar "moments," periods when there is only one dominant power, tend to be the most stable distributions of power, but they tend also to be brief because other states prefer not to be dominated. Such unipolar moments are likely to prompt challengers and balancing efforts by others who seek to avoid or curtail domination.

Other theorists point to structural characteristics related to power to advance additional arguments. For example, some argue for what is known as **power transition theory**, which asserts that wars are most likely when *changes* in power distributions occur—when some states are relatively rising in power (and thus want to demonstrate their power or others want to stop them) or when others are falling in power (and thus want to prove that they are still powerful or become targets of opportunity for other more powerful states). The outbreak of World War II fits this theory—the United Kingdom was falling in power while Germany was rising.[18] Still others argue for **cyclical theories of war** based on the rise and relative decline of leading powers in the international system (**hegemons**, or unipolar power distributions). In these

power transition theory systemic theory holding that wars are most likely when changes in power distributions occur.

cyclical theories of war conflict based on the rise and relative decline of leading powers in the international system in which stability occurs as the victors in major wars assert themselves, and war occurs as a function of the subsequent and inevitable rise of challengers to those dominant powers.

hegemon a country that is an undisputed leader within its region or the world. After World War II, the United States was considered the world hegemon.

arguments, stability occurs as the victors in major wars assert themselves, and war occurs as a function of the inevitable rise of challengers to those dominant powers over time.[19] Both of these categories rest on the premises of realist approaches to world politics, especially the idea that states seek power and security for themselves first and foremost.

These arguments share a common emphasis on realist structural factors—the competition for power and security in an anarchic world. However, other system-level explanations are offered by liberal theorists and radical theorists. For liberal theorists, a key systemic characteristic central to the causes of war (or, more accurately, the reduction of its frequency) is interdependence. As we discussed in earlier chapters, interdependence is the mutually dependent linkages between the players of world politics. Some liberal theorists argue that conditions of greater interdependence among players in the international system result in significantly reduced instances of war among them. Such interdependence may be economic (increased trade or investment, for example) or political (increased ties through international institutions). These factors, according to liberal theorists, reduce the effects of formal anarchy and create greater cooperation and peaceful relations.[20] By contrast, theorists such as those advocating the world systems approach we discussed in Chapter 4, argue that the capitalist structures of the international system generate competition for resources and markets between developed states and also generate conflict between the developed and developing states that often leads to war and subsequent subjugation of the developing state.[21]

Feminist theory provides another alternative theoretical approach that operates at the level of the international system. Although this may also be interpreted as an individual-level explanation, some view this as systemic, so we can consider it here, as well. For many feminist theorists, wars occur primarily because most states are male-dominated entities. From this perspective, wars are likely because men are more inclined (biologically and culturally) to rely on violence to resolve disputes than are women, who are more inclined to rely on verbal tools to resolve differences.[22] As female leaders become more numerous in the international system, will wars become less commonplace? Time will tell.

System-level explanations are potentially powerful and attractive because they are relatively simple. However, they are often very general and more successful explaining broader patterns such as systemic conditions under which war is more or less frequent (or more or

less intense). They are generally less helpful in explaining the participants of wars or particular wars. For help in these areas, we turn to state-level and individual-level explanations.

STATE-LEVEL EXPLANATIONS While explanations at the system level emphasize attributes of the international system, as the name implies, state-level explanations direct attention to the states—or units—themselves. Emphasis is generally placed on various attributes of countries and nations, such as the type and processes of government, economy, or culture, and how these factors affect the behavior and interactions of the participants in conflict. The main point of explanation at this level is that particular qualities of some states lead them to be more (or less) conflict prone or warlike. While a central point of realist arguments at the systemic level is that war is normal and always possible in an anarchic international system, state-level arguments are quick to point out that states and other actors are not equally violent. In fact, as the data from the Correlates of War project indicated, between 1816 and 1980, over 50 percent of the members of the international system never participated in any international war![23] State-level arguments thus grapple directly with the question of which states are the most likely participants in war.

Among the **national attributes** that arguments at the state level point to in order to explain why some states are more warlike than others, five attributes are most commonly identified.[24]

- *Type of government.* Some arguments stress that certain regime types are more warlike, while others are less so. Democracies are often believed to be more peaceful than authoritarian regimes, at least in the sense of initiating war. Since democratic governments are accountable to the populace and to legal/institutional constraints, while authoritarian regimes are not, or less so, in any event, democracies should be less war prone. In fact, while democracies do not seem less likely to be involved in war in general, they are much less likely to threaten or resort to force with other democracies. Thus, a democratic peace based on a joint democracy effect appears to exist.[25]

- *Type of economy.* Some theorists argue that the type of economy or other economic characteristics are connected to the war-proneness of states. Some liberal theorists have argued that capitalist economies are more peaceful than others because of their emphasis on trade,

national attributes features of states or nations such as regime type, type of economy, culture, geography, resources, and the like.

It's Lonely (and Temporary?) at the Top

By virtually any indicator, after the fall of the Soviet Union and the end of the Cold War, the United States was alone at the top of the power structure of the international system. According to some observers, its preeminence at the end of the Cold War was unprecedented in history. As G. John Ikenberry characterized it about a decade after the Cold War's end, "No other great power has enjoyed such formidable advantages in military, economic, technological, cultural or political capabilities. We live in a one-superpower world, and there is no serious competitor in sight."[26] The end of the Cold War in 1989 and the subsequent collapse of the Soviet Union spurred this situation, but the United States widened the gap between itself and other major powers in years immediately after these events. Even today, with rising competitors such as China, Europe, and India, among others, the U.S. economy remains at the center of the globalized world (still almost twice the size of its nearest competitor), its military is without peer, and it spends nearly as much on defense as the rest of the world combined. It has managed costly military operations in Bosnia (1994), Kosovo (1999), Afghanistan (2001–2015?), and Iraq (2003–2011) without losing its power advantages over the rest of the world.

But it is lonely at the top as the "king of the hill" in world politics. The economic challenges of recent years, including the so-called Great Recession of 2008 to 2010 and its aftermath, as well as increasingly formidable challenges from China, India, Russia, and others, have combined to call the U.S. position and role into question. Realist international relations theorists tell us that, historically, while such "top dogs," or hegemons, occasionally emerge (usually from a major war), their reigns rarely last. As John Mearsheimer wrote,

Great powers are rarely content with the current distribution of power; on the contrary, they face a constant incentive to change it in their favor.... Since no state is likely to achieve [or keep] global hegemony, however, the world is condemned to perpetual great-power competition.... This unrelenting pursuit of power means the great powers are inclined to look for opportunities to alter the distribution of world power in their

favor.... But not only does a great power seek to gain power at the expense of other states, it also tries to thwart rivals bent on gaining power at its expense. Thus a great power will defend the balance of power when looming change favors another state, and it will try to undermine the balance when the direction of change is in its favor.[27]

As proponents of cycle theories of war conclude, hegemons will face rivals and challengers.

So, what, if anything, is the king of the hill to do to stay on top? One does not have to look far to see signs of concern, whether from anti-American sentiment in other countries or from increasingly assertive rising powers such as China. Old allies in Europe appear uncomfortable with American leadership and dominance and less willing to follow the U.S. lead on an increasingly wide variety of issues. Globalization and the increasing complexity of world politics also combine to limit and constrain *any* state's ability to exert power and leadership. Ikenberry has recently amended his earlier assessment to express concerns over the ability of the United States to shape world politics as wealth and power become less concentrated in the United States and states in general.[28] Others have concluded that the United States has already declined relative to other states so much that the world is already multipolar. What, if anything, can the United States do to preserve its leadership and preeminence in world politics and avert conflicts and wars with other major powers?

Consider the various theoretical perspectives in Chapters 3 and 4 and, especially, the explanations for war in this chapter.

1. What factors indicate that the United States is or is not likely to face increasingly serious rivals and challengers for power?

2. What can the United States do to arrest its decline, preserve its leadership, and prevent a rising challenger from becoming a new king of the hill?

3. What can the United States do to avert conflict and war with other major powers?

4. In what ways is seeking and maintaining top-dog status in the interests of the United States, and in what ways is it not? Would it be better not to be the king of the hill?

wealth, and profit.[29] One does not shoot one's customers; as the saying goes, it's bad for business. By contrast, alternative theorists such as John Hobson and Vladimir Lenin argued precisely the opposite, holding that

capitalism motivated states to compete with each other for resources and markets and resulted in wars between them, especially as imperialism drove them to try to control other parts of the world. Socialist states, on the other

Rational Actors and Bargaining Theories of War

The connection between politics and war goes back a long time, with Carl von Clausewitz's connection of war to the policies and interests of states acting as a good example. In recent decades, some scholars have extended this general approach to develop a "bargaining model of war" that treats war as part of the range of behavior—from diplomacy to military force—in which states (and other actors such as ethnic groups) engage as they compete and struggle over scarce resources. In the bargaining model of war, war itself is just a continuation of bargaining as states try to gain favorable outcomes for themselves. As Dan Reiter has characterized it:

Fighting breaks out when two sides cannot reach a bargain that both prefer to war. Each side fights to improve its chances of getting a desirable settlement of the disputed issue. The war ends when the two sides strike a bargain that both prefer to continuing the war, and the outcome is literally the bargain struck. Finally, the duration of peace following the war reflects the willingness of both sides not to break the war-ending bargain.

Many scholars have applied this theory to the explanation of decisions to go to war, how, and how long wars are fought (as states gain information about costs, benefits, and bargaining positions), when they end, and what consequences they produce. At the heart of this model is the conception of states as rational actors calculating preferences, costs, and benefits on the basis of the information they have and gain (about themselves and their opponents) through their actions.

This approach to explaining war does not consider the role that state-level factors such as regime type, culture, or the psychological trauma a war can visit on the people of a country play in the causes of war. Nor does it consider the role of individual leaders and their personalities and psychological characteristics emphasized by the individual-level explanations we discuss in this chapter. It only considers war as a policy option available to a rational, unitary state. Thus, your openness to this approach to understanding war may depend on the degree to which you think war is a rational act, or states are rational actors!

Source: Dan Reiter, "Exploring the Bargaining Model of War," *Perspectives on Politics* 1, no. 1 (2003): 27–43.

---

hand, would be more peaceful because they were not motivated by this need.[30]

- *Demographic, cultural, physical, or geographic attributes.* This rather broad cluster of explanations is more of a grab bag than a unified argument. Realists, for example, have long argued that larger, more powerful states are more likely to engage in war than other states.[31] Others have argued that population pressures such as growth, overcrowding, and lateral pressure generated by rising demands for resources lead some states to engage in war.[32] Many studies conclude that borders create points of friction that often result in war, so states with more borders, or contested borders, engage in war more frequently than those without such contiguity issues.[33]

- *Level of political instability.* Another common state-level condition often associated with war is the *scapegoat* or **diversionary theory**. Popularized by movies such as *Wag the Dog* and *Canadian Bacon*, this explanation holds that states suffering from poor economic conditions (like high inflation, unemployment, or economic recession/depression) or other internal strife (generated by ethnic or other divisions) are more likely to resort to force outside their borders in efforts to divert attention from those internal problems and generate unity in the face of some external enemy. In the flipside of this argument, states with

such conditions may well be attractive *targets* for attack by others, as well![34]

- *Previous war involvement.* Additional explanations based on national attributes stress prior experiences with war. A **war weariness** argument explains that states that have most recently experienced a significant, costly war are more peaceful in the aftermath because of the impact of those costs and experiences on the population, public opinion, and leaders. For example, after the costly and protracted Vietnam conflict, the United States was often said to be reluctant to commit American troops to another conflict. This "Vietnam syndrome" continues to receive attention and may have been reinforced by subsequent experiences in Somalia (1993) and Iraq (2003–2011). In particular, American leaders appear to be significantly more constrained in their decisions to introduce ground forces into potentially long-term

diversionary theory states suffering from poor economic conditions or internal strife are more likely to resort to force outside their borders in efforts to divert attention from those internal problems.

war weariness states that have most recently experienced a significant, costly war are more peaceful in the aftermath because of the impact of those costs and experiences.

operations.[35] In *The Retreat from Doomsday: The Obsolescence of War*, John Mueller introduces another variant of this argument, pointing to a learning function for developed states that have participated in the major wars of the twentieth century. According to Mueller, by the middle of the twentieth century, virtually all of Europe, North America, and the developed world elsewhere had recognized this through the experiences of World Wars I and II, and by 1990 this recognition had spread even further. Thus, just like social conventions such as slavery and dueling, societies learned through experiences that practices like these, and war, were costly, unacceptable, and just plain wrong.[36]

While the empirical evidence in support of these various explanations is mixed, the theories provide insights into state-level attributes that may contribute to our understanding of why some states participate in war more often (or less often) than others. Yet explanations of war at the state level are less helpful in explaining why particular wars occur. It is to the individual level that we turn for help in that type of explanation.

INDIVIDUAL-LEVEL EXPLANATIONS In many ways, the third level of analysis is the least abstract set of explanations since this level directs our attention to people and their attributes. In some individual-level explanations, emphasis is on general aspects of **human nature**. Other individual-level explanations focus on the specific characteristics of individual leaders, including their personalities, perceptions, psychology, and policy preferences. In effect then, explanations at this level focus either on the nature of humans in general or on the nature of some humans in particular.

Explanations emphasizing human nature generally focus on arguments that humans are inherently aggressive. From philosophers such as St. Augustine, Thomas Hobbes, and Reinhold Niebuhr to psychologists and sociobiologists such as Sigmund Freud, Konrad Lorenz, and Edward O. Wilson, scholars have often attributed national violence in the form of war to innate characteristics of human beings. For example, there are a variety of explanations that trace the causes of war to biological factors. In ethology—the study of animal behavior—researchers attribute war to human aggressive and territorial instincts that developed through biological evolution.[37] In effect, war occurs as a function of human instincts and satisfies some basic human needs. Sociobiologists such as Edward O. Wilson combine ethological studies with other biological factors as well as psychology, anthropology, and sociology to explain war—and its variations—as a consequence of the interaction between genes and the cultural environment, emphasizing the centrality of aggression in this complex mix. However, such arguments suffer from the same limits as the system level argument about anarchy: if human nature is aggressive, why is war not constant? Why are some people and some societies peaceful? How, in short, do we explain peace?

One answer to this is the feminist approach that suggests the rules and patterns of the international system were established by men. We introduced this argument at the system level, but it can also be considered as an individual-level argument in some forms. Because males are often considered to be more aggressive, the rules are very competitive (e.g., self-help) rather than cooperative. Because the rules are set in place, it doesn't matter if a leader is a man or a woman, but the ultimate cause of conflict is the male-created/dominated rules. If instead of a competitive game, what if the rules inspired cooperation? This explanation, however, suffers from the same issue as war being innate to human beings.

Perhaps then the individual-level explanations stressing the particular characteristics of *some* individuals—national leaders—and their individual makeup provide helpful insights into what causes war. In particular, perhaps explanations at this level shed light on specific wars and the decisions to engage in them. There are dozens of approaches to this level of explanation, from "differences in willingness to take risks, different perceptions (and misperceptions) of the environment and of one's opponents, different images of the world and operational codes, difference in ability to change or adjust present images, different psychological needs, different personality traits, and differences in ability to deal with stress."[38] One line of explanation has stressed **psychological needs** and the possibility that some individuals are more power oriented or compensate for low self-esteem by acting more aggressively. Other studies emphasize **personality traits** such as dogmatic, domineering, or authoritarian personalities that might lead individuals with such traits to be more likely to advocate the use of force in particular situations. Similarly, studies suggest that extroverts seek more cooperative outcomes than introverts, while narcissism is usually associated with hostility, aggression, and power-seeking behavior. Finally, another line of explanation focuses on cognition and the propensity for misperception and miscalculation.

human nature innate characteristics of human beings, said to be a cause of war by some.

psychological needs essential emotional and psychological requirements of humans, said to be hierarchical by theorists such as Maslow.

personality traits varying characteristics of individuals, some of which may lead to more aggressive behavior and preferences.

Constructing the Democratic Peace

The joint democracy effect, or "democratic peace thesis," is a theory that contends that institutional and normative characteristics of democratic regimes lead them to peaceful relations with each other. As we noted at the outset of Chapter 3, a significant and growing body of empirical evidence supports this theory: while democracies have engaged in war with non-democracies and non-democracies have warred with each other, *two stable democracies have never gone to war with each other* and are also much less likely to threaten or use force short of war with each other. Thus, there seems to be something to the idea of a democratic peace.

Policymakers in democratic countries have embraced the main outlines of this international relations theory. Motivated by the idea that democracies are more peaceful in their relations with each other, many countries have implemented policies of democracy promotion to spread democracy more widely throughout the international system. According to one study of the foreign policies of forty countries between 1992 and 2002, there were substantial, although widely varying, commitments and efforts toward this end through individual and multilateral approaches.[39] For the United States, as Allison and Beschel suggested shortly after the end of the Cold War, "the democratic revolutions of 1989, coupled with the retreat of authoritarian regimes in Latin America and parts of Asia and Africa, have prompted a resurgence of interest throughout the U.S. government and society at large in promoting democracy."[40]

Recent evidence of U.S. interest in the promotion of democracy and better human rights practices may be found in policy statements of post–Cold War American presidents. For example, in its 1994 *National Security Strategy of Engagement and Enlargement*, the Clinton administration argued:

Our national security strategy is based on enlarging the community of market democracies. . . . The more that democracy and political and economic liberalization take hold in the world, particularly in countries of strategic importance to us, the safer our nation is likely to be and the more our people are likely to prosper.

George W. Bush used his 2005 inaugural address to declare that "the best hope for peace in our world is the expansion of freedom in all the world. . . . So it is the policy of the United States to seek and support the growth of democratic movements and institutions in every nation and culture." Even more recently, Barack Obama echoed these views in a major speech in Cairo in June 2009. President Obama stated:

I do have an unyielding belief that all people yearn for certain things: the ability to speak your mind and have a say in how you are governed; confidence in the rule of law and the equal administration of justice; government that is transparent and doesn't steal from the people; the freedom to live as you choose. These are not just American ideas; they are human rights. And that is why we will support them everywhere.

It is interesting to note that military operations in Afghanistan beginning in 2001 and in Iraq beginning in 2003 involved relatively extensive efforts to establish more democratic regimes in each country, not just win wars and vanquish foes. More recently, U.S. initial responses to the so-called Arab Spring in 2011 and 2012 also involved support for democratization in places such as Egypt and Libya. The United States has also supported multilateral efforts to promote and sustain democracy and better human rights practices through international organizations such as the UN.

Consider the nature and evolution of conflict and war and the connection between the international relations theory and the policies of the United States and others who have embraced democracy promotion.

1. What are the strengths and weaknesses of translating this theory on the causes of war and peace into foreign policy?

2. What policy actions might be adopted, and what are their potential positive and negative consequences?

3. What are the likely consequences for putting theory into action like this for conflict and war?

In truth, factors such as these are almost certainly interconnected, and almost certainly play out in varying ways in the small-group contexts of most foreign policy decisions. For example, a **groupthink** argument suggests that the characteristics of some decision groups

> **groupthink** characteristics of some decision groups that result in a shared viewpoint or preference that leads the group to ignore relevant information and exclude dissenters from that viewpoint in order to protect it.

turn the particular mix of personalities and group structure into a situation in which the participants get locked into a single way of thinking and ignore relevant information. In certain situations, this phenomenon can lead to decisions to use force. A good example of this is U.S. decision making on Vietnam under President Lyndon Johnson and his advisors, and it may characterize U.S. decisions to go to war in Iraq in 2003 under George W. Bush, as well. In both cases, scholars argue that the presidents and their advisors were convinced that war was the only logical choice and refused to consider seriously other options.[41] Moreover, different regime types probably connect to these factors as well, with individual characteristics of leaders probably more important to understanding war in regimes in which such individuals are more powerful and less constrained by structures and processes of accountability.

EXPLAINING CIVIL WARS Before we leave this section, we should take some time to address the causes of civil wars that, as we have seen, are an increasingly important aspect of international conflict. In his classic work *Why Men Rebel*, political scientist Ted Robert Gurr offers a **frustration-aggression theory** for rebellion and civil war. According to Gurr, while frustration over lack of fairness, repression, inequality, and other matters does not necessarily lead to violence, it can do so if it is persistent and intense. **Relative deprivation** is critical to understanding when that threshold is crossed. Relative deprivation is the discrepancy between what people think they deserve and what they actually think they

can get. According to Gurr, "The potential for collective violence varies strongly with the intensity and scope of relative deprivation among members of a collectivity."[42] It is therefore a very subjective phenomenon (even rich people can feel relative deprivation!), and frequently the sense of relative deprivation depends on the awareness of the opportunities and conditions of others.

More specifically, civil wars can arise from issues related to population, from the pressures on scarce resources (such as land) generated by population growth to issues related to diversity and identity (as ethnic groups motivated by nationalist sentiment within a state seek greater autonomy). Repression and other government policies may be at the heart of civil war, prompting disaffected groups to rebel. In recent years, identity issues related to what some characterize as "ancient ethnic hatreds" have been offered as explanations for intrastate conflict and war as multiethnic states have struggled to sustain themselves.[43] Legacies of colonialism may also be related to civil war. One prime example we introduced in Chapter 2 is the legacy of state boundaries in Africa drawn largely by European colonizers that fit poorly with the **ethnic geography** of the continent, resulting in a wide array of pressures on regimes and borders including **irredentist claims** to territory with people of similar ethnic identity, kinship rallying, minority group status, and a variety of others. Issues related to resources are also behind civil wars, with groups seeking to gain control of key areas, resources, and the government to ensure benefits. A recent example from another region is the conflict in Ukraine in 2013–2014, which not only pitted the Russian-speaking people from the eastern and southern regions of the country against the regime and the Ukrainian-speaking regions, but also involved intervention by Russia (see Map 5-3). Some recent arguments even link environmental issues such as deforestation to pressure for civil war.[44] Regime behavior, including repression, corruption, illegitimacy, and poor economic performance can also contribute to civil war.

As our earlier discussion of empirical and historical trends in conflict and war indicated, ethnic conflict has become increasingly violent and all too common since World War II and, especially, since the end of the Cold War. In general, the origins of ethnic conflict have been linked to three general categories of explanation.[45] **Primordialism** stresses the fundamental, psychological bonds of kinship and identity that establish ethnic differences that divide people and often generate "ancient ethnic hatreds." Essentially, historical feuds between groups continue and ferment into active civil violence today. **Instrumentalism** stresses the role of leaders who

---

frustration-aggression theory resort to violence under conditions of persistent denial of expected treatment, for example, fairness and equality.

relative deprivation discrepancy between what people actually have and what they think they deserve based on what others actually have.

ethnic geography the spatial and ecological aspects of ethnicity (e.g., where groups live in relation to one another), which affect the culture, politics, and social practices of states, nations, groups, and individuals.

irredentist claims (or irredentism) claims to territory in another state based on historical control or the presence of people with common ethnic identity.

primordialism stresses the fundamental bonds of kinship and identity that establish ethnic differences that divide people and often generate ancient ethnic hatreds.

instrumentalism stresses the role of leaders who emphasize and exacerbate ethnic differences (and commonalities) as a means to their own ends.

Map 5-3
Ethno-linguistic Map of Ukraine

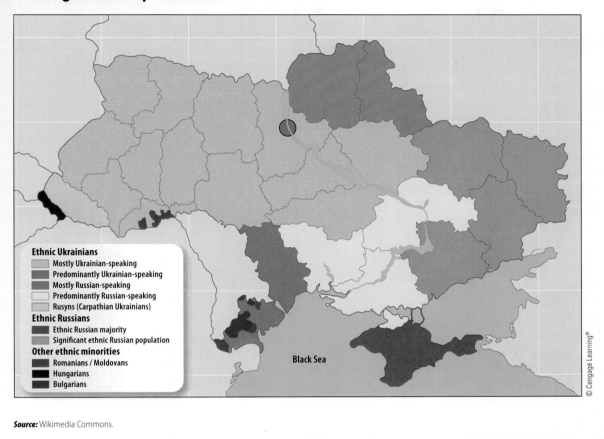

Ethnic Ukrainians
- Mostly Ukrainian-speaking
- Predominantly Ukrainian-speaking
- Mostly Russian-speaking
- Predominantly Russian-speaking
- Rusyns (Carpathian Ukrainians)

Ethnic Russians
- Ethnic Russian majority
- Significant ethnic Russian population

Other ethnic minorities
- Romanians / Moldovans
- Hungarians
- Bulgarians

Black Sea

© Cengage Learning®

Source: Wikimedia Commons.

emphasize and exacerbate ethnic differences (and commonalities) as a means to their own ends. For example, Slobodan Milosevic rose to power partly on his campaign against the ethnic Albanians in Kosovo—using the historical divide between the Muslims and Orthodox Christians as a means to gain support and power. Some research even suggests that leaders order campaigns of rape and violence against women of other ethnic identities to dehumanize them and increase the sense of identity and cohesion among the soldiers committing the crimes.[46]

Constructivism emphasizes the social construction of identity and the ways that social interactions define ethnicity for groups of people. When an ethnic identity is defined as being in opposition to another ethnic group, then conflict is more likely. For example, being an Irish Catholic might mean you don't like Irish Protestants, or being an Arab might mean you don't like Jews. These identities can be historical or recently constructed, making the conflict between them difficult to manage.

In short, there are "greed-based" (mostly in the instrumentalism and primordialism categories) and "grievance-based" (mostly in the primordialism and constructivism categories) explanations of civil war that point to internal factors or causes of civil conflict. In addition, there are external factors that influence the onset and nature of civil wars. Such external factors include the presence of conflict in neighboring countries (which may spill over or drag in a neighbor) and intervention in the form of military support for armed groups by major regional or global powers (which may hasten or prolong the violence). These external connections help to make civil war a significant issue in world politics.

constructivism (and ethnicity) emphasizes the social construction of identity and the ways that social interactions define ethnicity for groups of people.

Ethnic Geography and Civil War in the Former Yugoslavia

During most of the Cold War, the multinational state of Yugoslavia was a relatively stable place in which appeals to the unifying idea of "the new Yugoslav man" appeared to outweigh the more diverse ethnic identities of the country. Serbs, Croats, Slovenes, Albanians, Montenegrins, Bosnian Muslims, and others lived together in relative peace. Images from the Bosnian capital of Sarajevo during the 1984 Winter Olympics drove home the impressions of a stable country in which diverse people lived and worked together peacefully. Yugoslavia's efforts to keep both East and West at arm's length during the Cold War further reinforced this sense of unity.

Map 5-4

Ethnic Map of Yugoslavia circa 1991

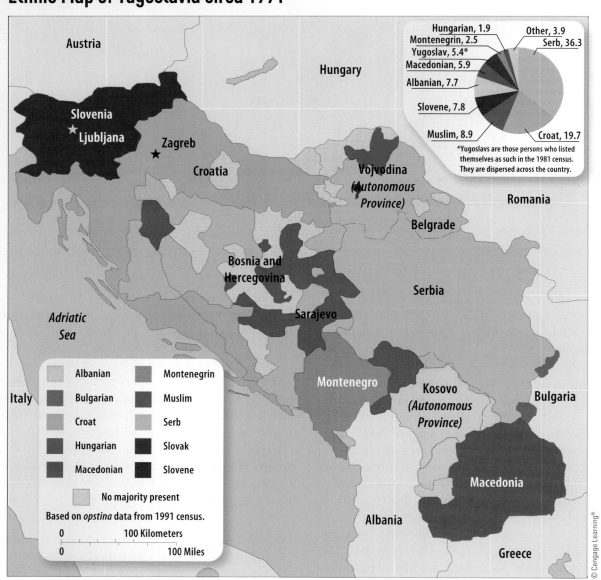

*Yugoslavs are those persons who listed themselves as such in the 1981 census. They are dispersed across the country.

Based on *opstina* data from 1991 census.

Source: Data courtesy of the University Libraries, The University of Texas at Austin.

Fast-forward less than a decade. As the Cold War ended, Serbs led by Slobodan Milosevic asserted themselves and advanced their dominance of Yugoslav political institutions, provoking nationalist backlash from other ethnic groups seeking to preserve and extend their autonomy. In Slovenia, Croatia, Bosnia, and Macedonia, parties dominated by members of those ethno-national groups rose to power (usually via elections). Led by Milosevic, Serbia began to support and encourage Serbian groups to exercise self-determination and resist the other groups. Conflict flared, first in Slovenia which was able to break away, and then in Croatia as ethnic Croatians faced off with ethnic Serbs. Other conflicts erupted elsewhere. United Nations peacekeeping actions supported a cease-fire in Croatia, but a full-scale war soon broke out in Bosnia, the most ethnically fragmented of the former Yugoslav republics. This conflict soon spread to include Croatia and Serbia and led to horrendous atrocities, ethnic cleansing and attempted genocide, chiefly (though not solely) by Serbs against the Bosnian Muslims. This conflict raged until 1995, when a succession of Bosnian Croat victories over Bosnian Serbs, an intervention by NATO and UN-backed forces, and direct diplomacy by the United States produced the Dayton Peace Accords, which divided Bosnia-Herzegovina between its ethnic groups. Efforts to punish the most egregious violators of human rights led to the creation of the UN Security Council's International Criminal Tribunal for the former Yugoslavia (ICTY), a special tribunal to prosecute military and political leaders of the Bosnia Serbs such as Duško Tadić (convicted in 1997 of war crimes and crimes against humanity) and Ratko Mladić (finally captured on May 26, 2011) and even Slobodan Milosevic himself (arrested in 2001 and who died in prison during his trial in 2006), among others.

Map 5-5

Political Map of Yugoslavia circa 1996

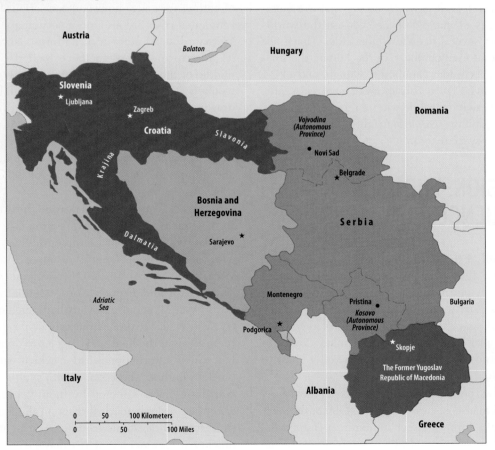

What do the changing boundaries and borders of the former Yugoslavia suggest about the importance of ethnic geography?

Source: Data courtesy of the University Libraries, The University of Texas at Austin.

Involving competing goals of territorial integrity and national self-determination, as well as an "ethnic security dilemma," the disintegration of the once-stable and peaceful Yugoslavia into vicious civil war was heralded by many as a sign of the rising importance of ethnic geography after the end of the Cold War.

1. What factors explain the relative peace of Cold War Yugoslavia and its dramatic descent into civil war and genocidal violence after 1989?

2. What are the central causes of this civil conflict?

3. What role did geography—and ethnic geography—play?

4. What are the implications of this episode for our understanding of conflict and war, especially in the post–Cold War context?

5. What do the changing boundaries and borders of the former Yugoslavia suggest about the importance of ethnic geography?

In the end, the issues underlying civil war parallel those for interstate war: territory, resources, identity, and others. And the underlying causes mirror those for interstate war as well, with multiple levels at work. For world politics, understanding civil war is critical for at least three reasons. First, it is the most common form of conflict in the contemporary global context. Second, it has exacted enormous costs from the societies it has affected. For example, it is worth noting that the most heinous instances of mass violence seen on the world stage in the last several decades—genocides—have all stemmed from internal conflicts: in the Sudan, the former Yugoslavia, Rwanda, Cambodia, Congo, and elsewhere. Finally, as Figure 5-5 showed, civil wars are increasingly internationalized, whether by drawing in external parties, spilling over into neighboring countries, or through proxy warfare.

CONCLUSION: THE CONSEQUENCES OF WARS

As we suggested at the outset of this chapter, war is a costly enterprise. It is, most certainly, a social and political phenomenon, one perpetrated by humans against each other. It is persistent and resilient, affecting people across time and space from the beginning of recorded history to the present. Springing from many sources, whatever its issues and causes, it has exacted a ghastly toll on the world.

Indeed, the political, economic, social, environmental, and human costs are extensive. Obviously, war exacts costs in the form of direct and indirect casualties. By some estimates, close to 4 billion people have been casualties of war over time—nearly two-thirds of the earth's current population. Enormous amounts of money have been spent preparing for, engaging in, and recovering from war. Beyond these direct costs there are other less direct ones. Economically, for example, the consequences of war include the hardships of hunger, refugees and forced migration, and degradation of essential public services (such as potable water). In fact, as some have argued, the public health consequences of war are extensive. Casualties from hunger and disease and other indirect consequences of war usually exceed the immediate casualties.[47] War also disrupts the economies of both victor and vanquished in a serious fashion. Environmental costs are also often very steep. For instance, Vietnam lost 20 percent of its forests and one-third of its mangrove swamps to the extended conflict in the middle of the twentieth century. In 1991, the Gulf War resulted in one of history's largest oil spills when withdrawing Iraqi troops destroyed and set fire to Kuwaiti oil wells. War-torn societies also suffer from significant degradation of human rights and gender equality as well. In short, armed conflict has affected human well-being and diminished the quality of life of billions of people over time.

The costs of war extend beyond these areas, as well. Both winners and losers of wars often face serious political consequences. For example, the cost of winning a war may deplete a society's resources. Look at World War II winners like Britain, France, and Soviet Union. The British and French were essentially broke after World War II, and the Soviets had much of their country destroyed. Further, winners of major wars often find themselves at the heart of struggles to define and maintain a new international order, which can place great burdens on both those states with such responsibilities and those states affected by them.[48] Losing wars can also exact serious political costs on the leaders responsible for the decisions to engage in fighting. Elected officials in democratic states may face punishment at the ballot box on election day, and authoritarian rulers may face efforts to overthrow or assassinate them.[49] Not surprisingly, these political consequences often have important effects on the decisions of a leader on

Casualties of war | How does war affect societies? We know entire generations can be profoundly affected by a war; what will the impact be on these children's generation?

whether to go to war, how hard and how long to fight, and when to quit.[50] Finally, losing wars can cast long shadows over countries and their subsequent decisions and behavior in world politics. Think about the consequences of World War II for German and Japanese politics, for instance. Or, consider the long shadow the Vietnam War cast over American politics and military strategy.[51]

These and other costs and consequences help to explain the jubilation that diplomats must have felt in 1928 when they celebrated the Kellogg-Briand Pact. Yet, as we have seen, that episode was not the hoped-for turning point. War has changed over time, but it

persists. It is fought for many purposes and has many causes. Indeed, conflict is endemic to a world characterized by anarchy, diversity, and complexity, and states and non-state actors grapple with persistent conflicts in the pursuit of security. In the next two chapters, we examine efforts to manage conflict and provide security. Before we move on, we might consider again the forces that work against efforts to manage and reduce conflict and war, as well as those areas of potential. Reflect on the causes of war we have reviewed here and consider what avenues they suggest for the successful management of conflict and achievement of security in world politics.

THINK ABOUT THIS THE FUTURE OF WAR

Consider the changing nature of armed conflict over the past few centuries, and the major explanations of its causes. Some perspectives and explanations, such as those of major realist thinkers such as John Mearsheimer or individual-level analyses stressing human nature, seem to suggest that war is likely to persist as a major problem for world politics. Others, such as those of major liberal thinkers such as Michael Doyle and advocates of the democratic peace theory, seem to offer more optimistic assessments. One—John Mueller—even argued that major war was now obsolete! Given what you have learned about the trends in and explanations for war, reflect on the problem of war and its nature and impact in future world politics, focusing particularly on the possibility that major wars can

AP Images/Kevin Fitzsimons/Ohio State University

John Mueller, seen here on "The Daily Show with Jon Stewart"

be controlled, reduced, and, indeed, even eliminated as a problem in world politics.

Can major wars be made a thing of the past?

REVIEW QUESTIONS

1. What is war, and what are its major forms?

2. What is terrorism, and why is it a challenging form of warfare?

3. How has war evolved over time? What are the main elements of change and continuity? What factors best explain the changes?

4. What are the main explanations for the causes of war at the international level of analysis? In what ways are these explanations most useful?

5. What are the main explanations for the causes of war at the state level of analysis? In what ways are these explanations most useful?

6. What are the main explanations for the causes of war at the individual level of analysis? In what ways are these explanations most useful?

FOR MORE INFORMATION . . .

For more on the causes of war and international conflict, see:

Cashman, Greg. *What Causes War? An Introduction to Theories of International Conflict*. Lanham, MD: Lexington Books, 1993.

Combs, Cindy. *Terrorism in the 21st Century*, 6th ed. Englewood Cliffs, NJ: Prentice Hall, 2010.

Jesse, Neal, and Kristen Williams. *Ethnic Conflict: A Systematic Approach to Cases of Conflict*. Washington, DC: CQ Press, 2011.

Lake, David, and Donald Rothschild. *The International Spread of Ethnic Conflict*. Princeton: Princeton University Press, 1998.

Levy, Jack, and William Thompson. *The Causes of War*. New York: Wiley-Blackwell, 2010.

Waltz, Kenneth. *Man the State and War*. New York: Columbia University Press, 2001.

6 | Seeking Security:
Managing Conflict and War

LEARNING OBJECTIVES

After studying this chapter, you will be able to . . .

6-1 Identify the challenges of seeking international security in world politics.

6-2 Describe and evaluate power-based approaches to international security embraced by realists, including military might, alliances, and the uses of force.

6-3 Describe and assess cooperation-based approaches to international security embraced by liberals, including arms control and disarmament, collective security, and security communities.

After finishing
this chapter go
to **PAGE 174**
for **STUDY TOOLS**

CHINA'S GROWTH IN MILITARY POWER

China is the largest country in the world by population, second largest by size of economy, and fourth largest by territory. In recent years, many observers have been alarmed at China's rapid growth in military power. According to the U.S. Department of Defense, which publishes an annual report specifically on China's military might (and that alone should tell you something about the importance of the issue!), China increased its military spending between 1996 and 2013 by more than seven times, as Figure 6-1 shows. China's official figures show another 12 percent increase in 2014, and, as military experts are quick to point out, the official expenditures (now exceeding $130 billion per year) grossly underestimate actual expenditures, which probably now exceed $250 billion. At least as interesting as these overall figures are the priorities China is emphasizing in its efforts to increase its military power. These include ballistic and cruise missiles, submarines, electronic warfare (including so-called cyberwar) capabilities,

and high-tech weapons such as stealth aircraft. China also commissioned its first aircraft carrier in 2012, much sooner than was previously estimated.

China is not involved in any wars, nor does it have an extended system of global alliances and military bases to fund. It does face continued tension over the future of Taiwan, confrontations with Japan, the Philippines, and Vietnam over maritime claims in the South and East China Seas, and internal security concerns. However, China's borders are mostly unthreatened.

1. Why would China devote so much of its resources to such a dramatic increase in military might?

2. What concerns might this dramatic growth in military power address, and what benefits might it provide?

3. What consequences might this steady expansion of military capabilities have in the region and in the world?

4. How might this affect other countries?

U.S. soldiers being readied for deployment | How do you gain security in world politics?

Vitaly V. Kuzmin/Getty Images

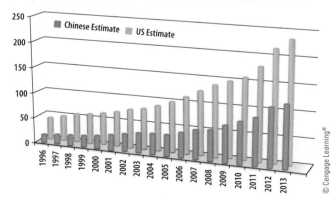

FIGURE 6-1 CHINA'S DEFENSE SPENDING 1996–2013

Legend: Chinese Estimate, US Estimate

© Cengage Learning®

Source: *Pentagon Report on China's Military, 2010–2014.*

6-1 THE CHALLENGE OF INTERNATIONAL SECURITY

In the pursuit of international security, states and other players in the arena of world politics frequently come into conflict with each other. The combination of the anarchy of the international system, the diversity of the players and their perspectives and interests, and the complexity of issues and interactions these players face almost ensure that clashes will occur. As we have seen in the last chapter, all too frequently those clashes can become violent and result in armed conflict, large or small. Managing this challenge—seeking security and dealing with conflict—is therefore one of the most critical concerns the players of world politics face.

States and other players have a variety of ways to seek international security in world politics. In this chapter we consider the particular challenges of attempting to manage conflict while also providing security. We begin by reviewing the essential context of the challenge the players in world politics face, highlighting the main features of the security dilemma, the pursuit of power, and the potential for conflict. We then turn to fundamentally realist-based approaches to conflict and security, involving weapons, alliances, and the use of force. Then, we discuss liberal alternatives, involving arms control and disarmament, collective security, and the development and maintenance of a democratic and capitalist peace. We conclude with some enduring challenges before moving on to discuss the structures and institutions of cooperation in Chapter 7.

The players in world politics—both states and non-state actors—seek security. They want to protect themselves from threats to either their survival or essential interests, and they want to be physically safe from

CHAPTER 6: Seeking Security: Managing Conflict and War 145

attack from other actors. For states, the protection of **political sovereignty** and **territorial integrity** is especially important in a world without central government. Traditional views of international security emphasize the ability of a state to protect itself from threats against its welfare and survival, usually through the accumulation of military power. International security can also be viewed more cooperatively to emphasize areas of common interest that link states as they try to address shared concerns for safety and well-being. As we will see in Parts Three and Four, challenges to economic security and human security also motivate the players of world politics.

However, the enduring problem of war, discussed in the preceding chapter, and the persistent efforts of states to seek power and acquire military arsenals suggest that the pursuit of security often results in insecurity, arms races, conflict spirals, and, sometimes, war. The interests and objectives of states and other players are often different—leading to disagreement, fear, uncertainty, and conflict. The absence of authoritative central institutions in world politics often makes coordination and cooperation difficult, prompting fear from the players that their interests will not be protected unless they take action themselves. Hence, the core elements of the security challenge stem from the combination of anarchy, diversity, and complexity of world politics. At the foundation of this fundamental challenge are the security dilemma and the challenge of power.

6-1a The Security Dilemma

As we explained in Chapters 2 and 3, security dilemmas stem from the paradoxical situation in which the things one does to be secure often end up creating even greater insecurities. This dilemma rests in large part on the anarchic structure of world politics. As we described in Chapter 2, any society, even an international one, without a central coercive authority will pose dangers as the members try to figure out how to protect themselves from real and potential threats. In such systems, self-help is the norm, as states must depend on themselves to provide for their own security and protect their own interests. They cannot turn to a cop on the corner for protection. Unfortunately, as states engage in self-help, the consequence is a security dilemma. How does one society increase its own security without seeming to

jeopardize the security of others? This dilemma is made even more serious by the diversity of the players in world politics. Differences in size and influence, culture, and perspective often lead to very different interpretations on the nature and meaning of actions and events. Add in the problem of complexity, in which multidimensional issues, state and non-state actors, national, international, and transnational processes, and many other factors are linked together, and it is easy to see how choosing actions to gain security and manage conflict might wind up producing the opposite result!

Whatever approach to world politics one takes—realist, liberal, constructivist, Marxist, or feminist—conditions can generate action-reaction cycles. Whether one thinks all states seek power and domination (realists), some states behave aggressively (liberals), states misunderstand and miscommunicate (liberals and constructivists), core states dominate peripheral states (Marxists or world systems theorists), states are driven by constructed identities and interactions (constructivists), or state behavior is masculinized by the dominance of men in leadership positions (feminists), conflict, and sometimes war, are often the logical result of the security dilemma. Each state may take actions it sees as defensive and nonthreatening, but such actions often alarm others and could cause exactly what each is trying to avoid. This then is a central challenge facing the players of world politics as they seek security and try to manage the conflict that appears inevitable because of anarchy, diversity, and complexity.

6-1b The Challenge of Power

Think back to our discussion in Chapter 3, where we noted that power is often considered the currency of world politics: those players who have power generally are more able to get what they want than those who do not. Of course, this simple conception hides a great deal of complexity. We have already reviewed how power is seen differently through different lenses and how a great variety of resources—from raw military might to the appeal of ideas—are involved. In terms of security and conflict, the focus of this chapter, the context of the security dilemma involves a corresponding power dilemma: how do states and other players accumulate and apply power in pursuit of international security?

Several challenges are at the heart of this dilemma. First, whether power is viewed as zero-sum or positive-sum is a major issue. We introduced these concepts in Chapter 3, where we also described them in terms of relative and absolute gains. In terms of the pursuit of power and security, the zero-sum approach—in which there must be a winner and a loser, so that advantages for one

---

political sovereignty the principle that a state has authority and independence to rule without interference within its own borders.

territorial integrity the principle that other actors should not violate the territory or boundaries of a state.

generally mean disadvantages for another—presumes conflictual or competitive relations in world politics and efforts by states to accumulate power for themselves to ensure their safety and survival. In contrast, the positive-sum approach—in which mutual interests provide opportunities for win-win situations—sees possibilities for collaborative efforts to establish mutual security and cooperative efforts to manage conflict.

A second challenge of power stems from the significant disparities among states and other actors in world politics. As even the most casual observer can easily see, and realists are quick to point out, power is not evenly distributed throughout the international system, and probably can never be. These disparities between the haves and have-nots of power create challenges for all concerned because they generate uncertainty, fear, threats, and competition. Moreover, larger, more powerful states are often forced to view security more broadly than simply their own narrow welfare and survival, taking interest in the problems and conflicts of others, while less powerful states are often forced to contend with the actions and concerns of the more powerful. For example, a recurring tension of the post–Cold War era has been Russia's desire to dominate a sphere of influence around its borders and the resulting efforts by affected countries such as Georgia, Poland, Latvia, Lithuania, Estonia, and Ukraine to resist those Russian pressures.

Overall, managing the challenges of anarchy, diversity, and complexity in the pursuit of security leads to a number of typical strategies. Virtually every state seeks to build military power of some kind for security reasons, and many states actively use that military might to gain security and resolve conflict. States also form alliances to expand their power and protect themselves against common threats or enemies. Throughout history, states have also engaged in a variety of efforts to control the accumulation, spread, and use of military might, and they have attempted to work together and pool power to gain security and manage or reduce the likelihood of conflict. Communities of states with similar interests, identities, and other common linkages have sought to harmonize relations with each other in security communities, as well. Throughout these approaches, a range of non-state actors have also been engaged in activities and interactions that both enhance and complicate the management of conflict and the pursuit of international security. Let's consider these efforts to gain security, categorizing them in terms of realist approaches (military power, alliances, and use of force) and liberal approaches (arms control and disarmament, collective security, and security communities).

6-2 REALIST APPROACHES TO SECURITY AND CONFLICT

An ancient Roman scribe once wrote, "If you want peace, prepare for war" (*si vis pacem, para bellum*). For centuries, this saying has summarized realist approaches to security and conflict. In a dangerous world, the argument goes, states must accumulate military capabilities to deter potential attackers, defend against attacks, and extend power and influence. States generally have two basic options: building their own military might and forging alliances to increase military capabilities.

6-2a Weapons

Most states expend considerable resources on military and security forces. With the exception of very small microstates, such as many of those in the Pacific Ocean, virtually every country in the world maintains military forces. Exceptions are Costa Rica, which abolished its armed forces in 1948, and Grenada, which has not maintained its own armed forces since 1983. Both of these countries still maintain small internal security forces. To understand this approach to international security, let's consider the expenditures states make and key characteristics of military might. We will consider the uses of military force later in this section.

BUYING SECURITY? As realists are quick to point out, most countries devote considerable sums of money to build their military forces, and this has been a relative constant in world politics. Over time, states—especially major powers—have engaged in the accumulation

U.S. naval aircraft deployed on the USS George Washington in the East China Sea in July 2014 | How do you think other states in the region view U.S. military power?

U.S. Navy Seaman Everett Allen

of military might and the development of ever more capable weaponry. In the last chapter we noted how the evolution of warfare could be nicely illustrated through the imagery of popular films. The same is true of military technology, from the swords and spears of films like *Braveheart* and *Gladiator* to the high-tech weaponry depicted in *Body of Lies* or *The Hurt Locker*. The development and accumulation of such increasingly capable weaponry has been a central story in world politics, and the major arms race of the Cold War period between the United States and the Soviet Union was merely a more modern version—albeit increasingly deadly with the development of nuclear weapons—of an age-old dynamic.

States continue to acquire weapons. Although global military spending declined between 1988 and 2000 in the wake of the Cold War, it rose steadily after that, soon exceeding even 1988's levels, before leveling off and then declining in 2012 and 2013. Table 6-1 shows the top ten countries by their military expenditures. Not surprisingly, the list contains what most observers would regard as the most powerful countries in the world, and the United States is at the very top as it has been for decades. Indeed, as Figure 6-2 shows, the United States by itself spends almost as much on the military as the rest of the world combined: nearly 50 percent of global military expenditures (about $600 billion in 2013). Since 2000, the United

TABLE 6-1	TOP TEN COUNTRIES IN MILITARY SPENDING, 2013
COUNTRY	**U.S. DOLLARS (BILLIONS)**
United States	600.4
China	122.2
Russia	68.2
Saudi Arabia	59.6
United Kingdom	57.0
France	52.4
Japan	51.0
Germany	44.2
India	36.3
Brazil	34.7

Source: International Institute of Strategic Studies, *Military Balance*, 2014.

States has nearly doubled its annual military spending. In the same time frame, both China and Russia have also dramatically increased their military spending. However, even with these changes, the United States still spends about 5 times more on the military than China, 9 times more than Russia, and over 60 times more than Iran!

Of course, large states have more resources to allocate to military spending. Table 6-2 shows the countries that spend the most of their available resources on the military.

FIGURE 6-2   U.S. AND GLOBAL MILITARY SPENDING

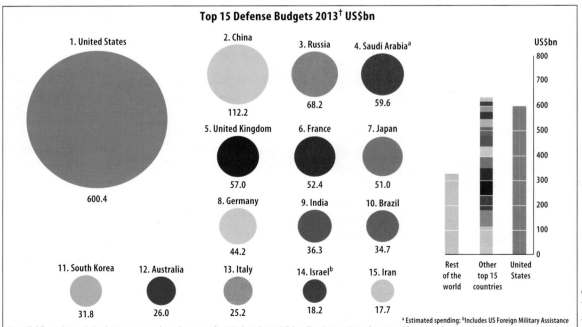

Source: The International Institute for Strategic Studies, *The Military Balance*, 2014.

TABLE 6-2	TOP 25 COUNTRIES IN MILITARY SPENDING AS A PERCENTAGE OF GDP, 2013
Eritrea	20.9%
Saudi Arabia	8.9%
Oman	8.4%
United Arab Emirates	6.9%
Israel	6.2%
Chad	6.2%
Azerbaijan	4.6%
Jordan	4.6%
Algeria	4.5%
United States	4.4%
Russia	4.4%
Angola	4.2%
Armenia	4.2%
Lebanon	4.1%
Syria	4.0%
Yemen	4.0%
Mauritania	3.8%
Burundi	3.8%
Bahrain	3.7%
Namibia	3.7%
Djibouti	3.7%
Singapore	3.6%
Kyrgyzstan	3.6%
Morocco	3.5%
Sudan	3.4%

Source: Data are from Stockholm International Peace Research Institute's Military Expenditure Database, 2014, http://www.sipri.org/research/armaments/milex/milex_database.

TABLE 6-3	ESTIMATED SIZE OF CURRENT MILITARY FORCES	
COUNTRY	APPROXIMATE ACTIVE MILITARY FORCES	MILITARY FORCES AS A PERCENT OF POPULATION
China	2.3 million	0.17%
United States	1.5 million	0.50%
India	1.3 million	0.11%
N. Korea	1.1 million	4.76%
Russia	766,000	0.52%
S. Korea	690,000	1.34%
Pakistan	660,000	0.35%
Iran	525,000	0.67%
Turkey	510,000	0.69%
Egypt	470,000	0.57%
Vietnam	455,000	0.52%
Myanmar	406,000	0.75%
Brazil	318,000	0.16%
Thailand	305,000	0.44%
Indonesia	302,000	0.13%
Syria	295,000	1.28%
Colombia	283,000	0.60%
Mexico	280,000	0.24%
Germany	250,000	0.31%
Japan	248,000	0.19%
Iraq	246,000	0.75%
France	239,000	0.38%
Saudi Arabia	234,000	0.84%
Eritrea	202,000	0.23%
United Kingdom	178,000	0.28%
Congo	159,000	0.23%

Source: Data are from International Institute of Strategic Studies, *The Military Balance*; population data from World Bank World Development Indicators.

Ranking military spending as a percentage of gross domestic product—or as **defense burden**—presents a very different view: poorer, often conflict-ridden countries are high on this list. Indeed, it is hard to avoid the conclusion that the countries least able to afford to spend their resources on the military still do so, at quite high rates.

According to realists, states devote these resources to their militaries to counter threats and to gain or maintain power. However, given their rather bleak view on the prospects for peace and security, it is NOT surprising that realists do not contend that amassing military might means that conflict will be avoided. In fact, they are much more likely to argue that the military power is necessary to deal with the inevitable conflicts that arise in the dangerous, anarchic world they see. In their view, failing to accumulate power leaves a state vulnerable, severely limiting its ability to preserve its national, economic, and human

security. Before moving on, stop and reflect for a moment: how do you think this affects the security dilemma?

MILITARY FORCES Traditionally, much of the money spent on defense has gone to building larger and larger armed forces. Indeed, the number of military personnel in a given state has long been an important measure of military might, and over the centuries states have assembled ground, naval, and (more recently) air forces to wield the weaponry they have accumulated. Table 6-3 shows the overall size of the military forces for a number

defense burden the ratio of military spending to overall gross domestic product of a country.

of countries, as well as the size of the military relative to population. Major powers such as the United States and China maintain the largest forces in sheer numbers, while mid-sized powers such as the European states of France, Germany, and the United Kingdom field smaller, but still sizable, forces. Other key countries such as India and Pakistan field sizable militaries, as well. In terms of the size of the military relative to overall population, Table 6-3 shows that some mid-sized and smaller countries devote considerably greater human resources to their military might than major powers like the United States. Indeed, the numbers in Table 6-3 illustrate the realist perspective that security concerns lead most countries, both major powers and smaller states, to desire and seek militaries of significant size. That major powers would do so is not terribly surprising, but why do smaller states devote such substantial shares of their obviously limited resources to this purpose?

Increasingly, however, sheer numbers are misleading because they do not account for such factors as military technology or even less tangible factors such as troop quality and training, leadership, and morale. For example, at the time of the 1991 Gulf War, Iraq had the world's fourth largest army . . . but that did it little good as the technologically superior forces led by the United States quickly overwhelmed the poorly trained and unenthusiastic Iraqi forces. Images of Iraqi troops surging from their fortified positions with their hands up to surrender in the early moments of the 1991 military operations are among the most striking of the war. Some Iraqi troops even surrendered to Western journalists! In the second war in Iraq in 2003, although the Iraqi army of about 375,000 troops significantly outnumbered U.S. forces, those numbers again did it little good in the face of U.S. military technology and tactics. However, the vast technological superiority of U.S. military forces in the Vietnam War was insufficient to overcome the will and commitment of the Vietnamese forces fighting against them. So military force is the combination of numbers of troops, their quality of training and leadership, quality and quantity of armaments, the ability to project that military power elsewhere, and the troops' willingness to fight.

HIGH-TECH: THE REVOLUTION IN MILITARY AFFAIRS The most advanced militaries are less distinguished by the sheer size of their forces, and more defined by the technology they deploy. Over the past several decades in particular, significant advantages have accrued to those countries able to harness advances in weaponry and information technology. Major powers

THE REVENGE OF GEOGRAPHY

Security and Geography

Since 1815, Switzerland has managed to sit out Europe's wars, including the two World Wars and the Cold War of the twentieth century. The country has done so without amassing a sizable military and without forging alliances with powerful states. As of 2013, the Swiss military totaled only about 178,000 troops. At the same time, Switzerland has also largely been able to avoid being a battleground, a target for invasion, or a candidate for conquest, and has firmly established itself as a neutral player in world politics, even while hosting a significant range of international organizations and institutions and being heavily engaged in the international economy.

Contrast the Swiss experience with that of Poland, which has spent a great deal of the Westphalian era trying to avoid invasion or attempting to cope with conquest and occupation. Situated on the great northern plain of Europe, the territory of what is now Poland has long been a route for and location of invasion and battles. During both World War I and World War II, this territory was a target for invasion and battleground for surrounding great powers like Germany and the Soviet Union. Polish

history is replete with occupation, conquest, and efforts to find security through alliances with countries like France and Britain to help overcome its vulnerability. It has been attacked, dominated, occupied, and dismembered by Prussia, Germany, Russia, the Soviet Union, and the Austro-Hungarian Empire.

Why was Switzerland so much more successful than Poland at avoiding attack and maintaining its independence and security? Part of the answer lies in simple geography. Poland's experiences in world politics are driven in large measure by its location between other powerful states, along with its relatively indefensible borders along the northern plains of Europe. There are few physical barriers between Poland and its neighbors to the east, west, or south, and being located directly between competing great powers is not an ideal spot! Switzerland, by contrast, not only has the advantage of being out of the vortex of great powers, but it has the incredible advantage of having its borders secured by some of the most rugged mountain ranges in Europe. The simple physical location and attributes of these two countries dramatically colors their sense of and experiences with security and the security dilemma.

Map 6-1

Borders in Europe

How do defensible borders change a country's security?

Think about the examples of Switzerland and Poland and consider how similar factors affect other states and their perspectives on security, as well.

1. How does the geography and location of the United States, separated from Europe and Asia by two vast oceans, affect its sense of security?

2. How does the geography and location of Israel affect its sense of security and its relations with its neighbors?

3. How might geography affect the strategies a state adopts to ensure its security?

The revolution in military affairs: high-tech weapons | How has the advance of military technology affected conflict and security?

have always sought advances in weaponry to provide advantages on the battlefield, and history and evolution of warfare is full of situations in which revolutionary equipment and tactics delivered advantages that often resulted in very one-sided victories. Examples include the incredibly devastating effects of the English longbow on the heavily armored French cavalry in the battles of Crécy (1346) and Agincourt (1415), the success of the German Panzer armies and blitzkrieg tactics in the early years of World War II, and, as noted, the U.S. successes in 1991 and 2003 in Iraq. Consequently, as realists would predict, major powers regularly seek to develop and obtain the most advanced and powerful weaponry to gain advantage over real and potential rivals.

A major revolution in the technology of war occurred with the beginning of the nuclear age in August 1945. After the United States used two atomic bombs against Japan at Hiroshima and Nagasaki, developing and deploying nuclear weapons became a significant aspect of military power with dramatic consequences. States deploying nuclear arsenals are automatically more likely to be regarded as military powers. However, the existence of nuclear weapons transformed the ways strategists thought about war. As U.S. strategist Bernard Brodie stated shortly after World War II, "Thus far the chief purpose of our military establishment has been to win wars. From now on its chief purpose must be to avert them. It can have almost no other useful purpose."[1]

The prospect of nuclear annihilation changed the nature of military power in important ways, especially for countries such as the United States and the Soviet Union, whose vast nuclear arsenals made any direct conflict between the two countries dangerous because of the possibility of escalation. The nuclear age thus transformed great power war by making it much more risky (a state, in particular its civilian population, can be destroyed without being defeated on the battlefield), so direct military confrontations between countries deploying nuclear arsenals diminished considerably. In spite of the high-stakes tensions of the Cold War, for example, the United States and Soviet Union never directly confronted one another militarily, and the fear of a nuclear war during the 1962 Cuban Missile Crisis drove home the potential consequences of this technological revolution.

Thus a series of new concerns arose with respect to nuclear might. First, states with nuclear arsenals felt the need to possess weapons in quantities and with capabilities (explosive power, accuracy) sufficient to ensure the ability to retaliate. Ensuring a second-strike capability became critical, and the action-reaction cycle of arms competition between the major nuclear powers ensued. Second, acquiring nuclear capabilities became important to other countries. Britain, France, and China followed the United States and the Soviet Union to each develop their own nuclear arsenals, in part to ensure that they could deter nuclear strikes themselves with the threat of retaliation, and in part to ensure that they had a seat at the table with the major powers. These five states are the official nuclear weapons states, but they have been joined by India (1974) and Pakistan (1998), which publicly tested nuclear devices, and Israel, which has not publicly acknowledged possession of nuclear weapons but is widely believed to have an arsenal of between 100 and 200 weapons. North Korea tested nuclear weapons in 2006, 2009, and 2013 and is suspected of possessing sufficient material for about a dozen nuclear weapons. Finally, preventing the spread of nuclear weapons and

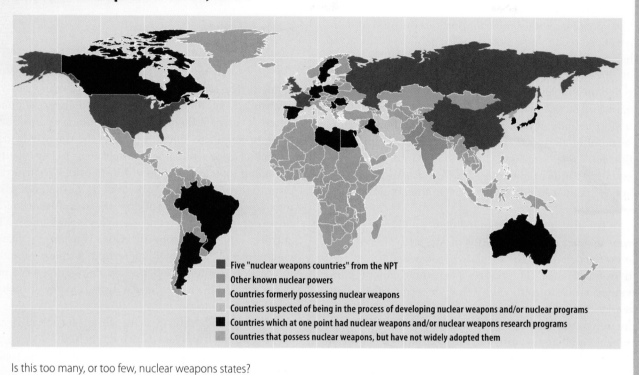

Map 6-2

Nuclear Weapons States, 2011

- ■ Five "nuclear weapons countries" from the NPT
- ■ Other known nuclear powers
- ■ Countries formerly possessing nuclear weapons
- ■ Countries suspected of being in the process of developing nuclear weapons and/or nuclear programs
- ■ Countries which at one point had nuclear weapons and/or nuclear weapons research programs
- ■ Countries that possess nuclear weapons, but have not widely adopted them

Is this too many, or too few, nuclear weapons states?

© Cengage Learning®

weapons materials to other states has become a major issue, as well (see Map 6-2). In addition to efforts to construct international agreements and institutions such as the Nuclear Non-Proliferation Treaty (1968), the Comprehensive Test-Ban Treaty (1996), and the International Atomic Energy Agency (1957), a variety of efforts, from the offering of benefits and rewards to more coercive measures including military operations, have been undertaken to prevent other states from gaining nuclear capabilities.

In the current context, the technological revolutions affecting military power have also involved efforts to build better, more capable, and more efficient weapons (e.g., faster, more heavily armored tanks, or more lethal bombers and fighter jets) as usual, but also through new advances in battlefield technology and tactics. The so-called **revolution in military affairs** stresses the "evolution of weapons, military organizations, and operational concepts among advanced powers [and] focuses on the changes made possible by advancing technology."[2] Embraced by major powers (such as the United States and China), many other more developed countries (like

Canada, the United Kingdom, France, Germany, the Netherlands, and Australia), and other countries (such as Russia and India), the recent transformation emphasizes the combination of intelligence; surveillance and reconnaissance capabilities (driven by technologies such as satellite imagery and unmanned remote-operated vehicles in the air and on the ground); command, control, and communications capabilities (driven by advances in information technology, including battlefield computers); and precision weaponry and forces (including highly accurate missiles and artillery, highly efficient firepower, and stealth technology that hides military assets more effectively). Because of the high cost of developing and deploying such weaponry, wealthier states have a significant advantage in the acquisition and use of these weapons.

revolution in military affairs the transformation of weapons, military organizations, and operational concepts for military force that leverages the information and communications revolutions of the latter twentieth and early twenty-first centuries.

The United States, in particular, has a significant edge over both its friends and potential rivals. However, other countries have not stood still while the U.S. has developed its capabilities. As we described at the outset of the chapter, China has drastically expanded its military spending, with significant portions devoted to more advanced technology, tactics, and capabilities. Russia too has paid attention to these matters. In 2014, as it used its force to pressure Ukraine and annex Crimea, Russia relied on a much more modern and nuanced set of strategies and tactics that indicated its progress in the revolution in military affairs. Its operations relied on a skillful blend of modern, well-equipped and trained rapid reaction forces, special forces, technology, information and communications technology, and cyber warfare to isolate Ukrainian forces from their command and control centers.[3]

These examples help to highlight another important consequence of the acquisition of weaponry in pursuit of power and security: the regular appearance of **arms races** between states. These are peacetime competitions among rivals to outdo the other in terms of weapons acquisition or capabilities; they can be driven by fear or by design.[4] Whether it is competition to field the most capable and largest army of heavily armored knights on horseback during medieval times, the naval arms races before and after World War I, or the nuclear arms race between the United States and the Soviet Union during the Cold War, as states have sought weapons to provide for power and security, they have engaged in competition to field the biggest and the best weaponry. Such races tend to be interdependent: the efforts and decisions of each state to develop and deploy specific types of weapons are dependent on the parallel decisions of the rival state(s). Military spending tends to be reciprocal and driven by action–reaction or stimulus–response processes.[5] Empirical evidence to date suggests that many arms races escalate to war, although most wars are not preceded by arms races and, indeed, a great many arms races do not end up in war, either.[6] In the current context, the competition among states such as the United States, China, and Russia in hi-tech weaponry and strategies/tactics is a good example of these arms racing tendencies. What are the implications of arms races, and the underlying effort to acquire weaponry, for security itself?

6-2b Alliances

Realists also emphasize the efforts of states to forge **alliances** with other states to counter threats and increase strength. The logic of this approach to international security is relatively straightforward: When there are common interests between them, such as a common enemy, states agree to cooperate militarily to meet the threat. Alliances in general involve offensive commitments to join together in military operations (think of the Soviet–German pact prior to the outbreak of World War II), or the more common defensive commitments to come to each other's aid in the event of an attack (good examples include the NATO alliance, especially during the Cold War). Such alliance commitments first have a deterrent purpose intended to ward off a potential attack, and then a defensive purpose intended to enable the allied states to defeat such an attack if it were to occur.

We can identify at least three essentially realist approaches to alliances. First, such alliances might be driven by **protection** dynamics. In this approach, a small state might engage in an alliance with a larger, more powerful state to gain its help and protection from a dangerous neighbor or adversary. Because the small state does not have the resources to provide security through its own military might, it may seek out a powerful state instead, as Poland sought an alliance with both Britain and France before the outset of World War II. Even countries like Costa Rica and Grenada, which have eliminated their militaries, engage in alliances to help secure themselves. In fact, it is largely because of its relationship to the United States that Grenada was able to dismantle its military forces.

Second, **bandwagoning** might drive such alliances. In this approach, a state allies with a powerful state after deciding that the benefits of siding with the more powerful state are greater than the costs of doing so.[7] Bandwagoning may result from the calculation that opposition to the more powerful state (by itself or by others) is unlikely to succeed, or from the calculation that the opportunity to share in the benefits of the stronger state's pursuit of power is compelling, whether those benefits involve payoffs from the stronger state or a share of any spoils of war that might ensue. A good example is the behavior of central European states, such as Hungary and Romania, in the years around the start of World War II, when they joined with Nazi Germany. Another more

arms race peacetime competition in armaments by two or more states driven by conflict interests, fear, and suspicion.

alliance formal commitments between states to cooperate for specific purposes such as mutual defense.

protection (in alliances) an arrangement by a small state to gain help from a larger state.

bandwagoning (in alliances) siding with a rising power to gain benefits.

Map 6-3

U.S. Alliances

- ■ NATO member states, including their colonies and overseas possessions, Compacts of Free Association
- ■ Major non-NATO allies, plus Taiwan
- ■ Signatories of Partnership for Peace with NATO

Why does the United States have so many alliances?

© Cengage Learning®

recent example was the several smaller European states that sided with the U.S.-led invasion of Iraq in 2003 in direct opposition to Germany and France. Bandwagoning involves *unequal exchange* because the smaller and more vulnerable state makes concessions to the larger power and accepts a subordinate role.[8]

Finally, such alliances might be driven by **balancing** dynamics. In this approach, a state allies with other states to counter the power or threat of another.[9] In this dynamic, alliances are most likely to form when power imbalances emerge. In essence, as one state's power grows, it presents a potential threat to others, which may join together to counter the first and more (or potentially more) powerful state. Shared concerns over the possible threat posed by the growing power of the first state lead the others to *balance* against it by making an alliance. The alliance between France and Russia in the years before World War I reflects their concern with the rising power of Germany, as does the British decision in the same period to abandon its historical role as offshore balancer to join France and Russia to counter the rising

challenge of Germany. Similarly, one interpretation of the NATO alliance uniting the United States, Canada, and most western European states emphasizes the need to counter the Soviet threat in Europe.

We should also note that realists are not the only ones who turn to alliances. Liberals also embrace this approach, although with a very different perspective. Because of their perspective on the nature of security and the international system in which it is pursued, realists tend to view alliances as temporary arrangements that states should be willing to quickly make and break in order to meet threats. Liberals tend to see them as more enduring and based on cooperation, common values and identities, and mutual interests. The NATO alliance provides a nice illustration. For realists, NATO was fundamentally an alliance made necessary by the need to counter the Soviet Union during the Cold War. Liberals, on the other hand, point to

balancing (in alliances) forming coalitions to counter the rising power and threat of a state.

TABLE 6-4 BALANCE OF POWER

BALANCE OF POWER AS:	MEANING
Description	A snapshot of the distribution of power in the world at any given moment.
Equilibrium	A condition in which power is roughly balanced among the world's major powers so that no one has a significant edge.
Dynamic	A pattern of behavior by states seeking to compete in anarchy and manage security through internal (arms) or external (allies) efforts to counter real or potential rivals and gain power advantages.

© Cengage Learning®

NATO's continued existence and expansion after the Cold War's end (when the threat against which it formed had disappeared) and stress the cooperative links and shared values and interests that have helped it persist and evolve. Not very long ago, Robert Gates, the former U.S. secretary of defense, publicly called into question the usefulness and effectiveness of NATO, a position that might appear questionable with the conflict between Russia and Ukraine and the corresponding heightened tension between NATO and Russia in 2014. What do you think? Will NATO continue or fade away and dissolve?

The effect of alliances is unclear. Some historical evidence suggests that most alliances are followed by war, and that wars involving alliances are larger and involve more states (which might appear to be self-evident and fall into the "duh" category of empirical research), but the same evidence shows that most wars are not preceded by alliances. Furthermore, the impact of alliances on conflict (and, thus, in providing security) depends heavily on the nature and credibility of the alliance commitments themselves. In principle, the more credible the commitment, the more likely the alliance is to deter the potential attack. Firm alliance commitments are more credible, but also serve to encourage more risky and confrontational behavior by alliance partners, which may trigger armed conflict rather than prevent it. Given this mixed record, what types or characteristics of alliances do you think are likely to be most successful in the pursuit of security?

6-2c Balance of Power

Together, these two approaches to security—arms and alliances—form the core of **balance of power politics**. Although this term is used in a variety of ways in world politics (see Table 6-4), the broadest meaning refers to the pattern of activity that occurs as states take action to make themselves secure by seeking power, countering the efforts of real or potential rivals to gain power advantages, and using power to counter security threats from others. According to realists, states monitor their security environment and take actions to meet perceived threats from others by seeking power. **Internal balancing** occurs when states independently build up their military might, as we discussed earlier. **External balancing** occurs when states join with others in alliances to combine their might to meet a common rival or threat. Such arrangements are likely to be temporary and short lived: according to realists, as the conditions that give rise to the alliances change, we should expect alliances to appear and disappear relatively fluidly. To paraphrase the words of Lord Palmerston, a nineteenth-century British statesman, countries have no permanent friends or enemies, only permanent interests. According to many realists, since all states make these kinds of calculations and take these kinds of steps, the balance of power is much like the magic of the market in capitalism: as each state pursues its self-interests in this way, balances tend to lend themselves to periods of stability, however brief.

Balance of power dynamics may occur at the level of the whole international system, as the Cold War contest between the United States and the Soviet Union after World War II illustrates, or at the regional level. In the latter, we might observe the patterns of balance of power dynamics in Asia, Africa, the Middle East, Latin America, and so on. Realists emphasize that states are likely to prefer internal balancing because they have more control in that approach, especially since alliances among self-interested states (as realists would characterize them) are likely to be rather unreliable and subject to change.

6-2d Using Force

Of course, realists are quick to point out that in a dangerous and anarchic world force will be used, and relatively frequently. States wishing to be secure must have power to secure themselves, and power, to realists, depends on the ability to use military force. Two leading theorists put it

balance of power politics patterns of shifting alliances, force, and counterforce among states as they seek power, counter the efforts of rivals, and confront security threats.

internal balancing countering the power of a rival by increasing one's own power and military might.

external balancing countering the power of a rival by forming coalitions with other states.

well: to one, military force "is the most important material factor making for the political power of a nation,"[10] and to the other, "force serves, not only as the *ultima ratio* [or, final argument], but indeed as the first and constant one."[11]

APPLYING MILITARY FORCE In pursuit of security, states may use force in a variety of ways. According to the Militarized Interstate Dispute data often used by political scientists who study war and the use of force, these uses include:

- *Threats of force*, which include threats to blockade, to forcibly occupy territory, to declare war, and to use force, including nuclear weapons or other weapons of mass destruction.

- *Displays of force*, which include placing forces (including nuclear forces) on alert, mobilizing armed forces, public displays or operations of land, air, or naval forces in or outside a state's territory; and purposeful border violations with military forces (without combat).

- *Uses of force*, which include blockades, occupation of territory or seizure of material or personnel, small-scale military clashes or raids (with less than 1,000 total battle-deaths), and declarations of war.

- *Interstate war*, which involves sustained military combat resulting in more than 1,000 total battle-deaths.[12]

STRATEGIES LINKING FORCE TO SECURITY How can states apply their military power through these means to obtain security? In general, we can identify at least four main uses that may translate military power into security.

Deterrence Over the centuries, states have long sought to amass military might to keep adversaries from attacking them. This is really the essence of **deterrence**, the possession of sufficient military might so that would-be adversaries understand any potential gain from attacking would involve costs so high that the attack is just not worth it. Deterrence is, in effect, the threat, "Don't attack, or else." While this use of force has a long history, its role and significance increased considerably after World War II with the advent of the nuclear age.

Led by strategists such as Bernard Brodie and Thomas Schelling, among others, deterrence is commonly understood to rest on three components. First, in order for a state to be able to deter a potential aggressor, it must have the necessary military capability to retaliate in a very damaging way. Second, a state must make a commitment in order to deter. That is, a state must issue a threat that a certain action will result in retaliation. Third, a state must somehow demonstrate its will—to convince the target that such a retaliation would be carried out if necessary. Hence, both capability and credibility are central to successful deterrence.

A nuclear missile in its silo | What is the effect of such devastating destructive power on the use of force?

Michael Dunning/Photographer's Choice/Getty Images

Military strategists often distinguish between direct and extended deterrence and between immediate and general deterrence. **Direct deterrence** involves the use of retaliatory threats to discourage attacks against the state making the deterrent threat, while **extended deterrence** involves retaliatory threats to discourage attacks against allies and friends of the state making the deterrent threat. **Immediate deterrence** involves the threat to retaliate against attackers who are believed to be actively considering specific military operations against the target, which is readying itself to respond. **General deterrence**, by contrast, involves threats to retaliate in a context of underlying politico-military competition, but when there is no active military conflict generating the need to respond.

After World War II, nuclear deterrence was a central part of the defense strategies of both the United States and Soviet Union. Not only did each of these countries build increasingly large and powerful arsenals for direct

deterrence persuading a potential adversary to refrain from attacking through the threat of costly retaliation.

direct deterrence the use of retaliatory threats to discourage attacks against the state making the deterrent threat.

extended deterrence retaliatory threats to discourage attacks against allies and friends of the state making the deterrent threat.

immediate deterrence the threat to retaliate against attackers who are believed to be actively considering specific military operations against the target.

general deterrence threats to retaliate in a context of underlying politico-military competition, but when there is no active military conflict generating the need to respond.

deterrence of each other, but they also made commitments to extend their nuclear umbrellas to important allies. For the United States, for example, Europe, Japan, and others were included in the extended deterrence commitment, while the Soviet Union included its allies in Eastern Europe and elsewhere.

Immediately after World War II, when the United States was the sole nuclear power, and even after the Soviet Union had acquired nuclear weapons but could not use them against U.S. territory, the United States could make nuclear threats more freely. During the Eisenhower administration in the 1950s, for example, the United States relied on a **massive retaliation** strategy based on the threat to "respond in places and with means of our own choosing," as then–Secretary of State John Foster Dulles famously said. Indeed, part of the U.S. approach in this time period was known as **brinkmanship**, or the strategy of escalating conflicts or crises to nuclear threats in order to force the other side to back down. This risky approach to deterrence was employed in conflicts over Berlin, the Taiwan Straits, and other places.[13]

As the nuclear arms race accelerated and the Soviet Union expanded its nuclear arsenal to match and, in some ways, to exceed that of the United States, brinkmanship and the underlying strategy became far too risky to maintain. From the early 1960s to the end of the Cold War, the basis of deterrence for both sides became what was known as **mutually assured destruction (MAD)**. This approach was pretty simple: It amounted to a "you shoot, I shoot, and we are both dead" threat that established a basic nuclear stalemate and made conflicts very dangerous. In terms of deterrence, MAD rested on the ability of both sides to field a secure, second-strike capability of sufficient size to destroy a significant portion of the other side's society, usually in what was known as **counter-value** targeting (or targeting cities and industrial centers), no matter what kind of attack was directed against them. That is, even if one side unleashed a

A B2 Spirit bomber—part of the U.S. nuclear deterrence triad that includes ballistic missile submarines, intercontinental ballistic missiles, and heavy bombers—at Hickam Air Force Base in Hawaii | How do such deterrent forces contribute to security?

Tech. Sgt. Shane A. Cuomo

counter-force strike designed to destroy nuclear arsenals and other war-fighting abilities, the other side would still be able to retaliate with a devastating second strike in return. Clearly, therefore, MAD depended on an arsenal and the ability to fire the weapons (command and control) even in the face of a nuclear strike.

At its heart, the nuclear arms race that dominated the Cold War was an action–reaction cycle of competition to ensure that no weapons gains of the other side could eliminate this fundamental second-strike, or MAD, capability. Both the United States and Soviet Union developed increasingly powerful and accurate nuclear weapons, deploying them on land (intercontinental ballistic missiles, or ICBMs, as well as medium- and short-range, or so-called tactical nukes—in part to extend deterrence to allies and in part to enhance the retaliatory threat), through the air (as gravity bombs and, later, cruise missiles), and across the sea (as submarine-launched ballistic missiles, or SLBMs). The Anti-Ballistic Missile Treaty (ABM) of 1972 was even concluded to limit the ability to defend against missiles in order to help ensure the stability of a second strike.

Deterrence actually represents a so-called peaceful use of force because it rests on the threat, not the actual use of force. Indeed, if the retaliatory act is necessary, deterrence has failed! It is far easier to succeed, in one sense, because successful deterrence requires an adversary to refrain from doing something; that is, behavior change is not really necessary. At the same time, it is much more difficult to know if deterrence is succeeding because it is hard to know whether the potential attack was ever really going to happen and because it can fail at the margins if adversaries figure out ways to carry out their intentions short of the attack, or

massive retaliation the threat to respond to provocations with disproportionate and devastating nuclear attacks.

brinkmanship the strategy of escalating conflicts or crises to nuclear threats in order to force the other side to back down.

mutually assured destruction (MAD) the ability of both sides to field a secure, second-strike capability of sufficient size to destroy a significant portion of the other side's society.

counter-value targeting an adversary's cities and industrial centers for nuclear strikes

counter-force targeting an adversary's nuclear arsenals and other war-fighting abilities for nuclear strikes.

potential attack, that prompted the deterrent threat. For example, did U.S. deterrence policy prevent the Soviet Union from attacking the United States (or vice versa) during the Cold War? There were no direct attacks, so it must have, right? But did the United States or the Soviet Union ever really intend to attack the other? And what about all the other ways short of a direct attack the two countries found to take action against the other? Finally, if the possession of nuclear weapons meant that the United States and the Soviet Union could not fight with each other out of fear of mutual annihilation, doesn't that logic suggest that many, most, or even all states should have nuclear arsenals?

Defense Just like it sounds, the defensive use of force means having the ability to fight off an attack, to deny an attacker a victory. **Defense** involves deploying and using military force to protect oneself, ward off an attack, and minimize damage from the attack to the greatest extent possible (e.g., by defending territory in a way that keeps an attacker from gaining control of it).[14] The key to gaining security in this strategy is to build sufficient, usable military capabilities to fight off an attack. Defensive force can also contribute to deterrence, as the more substantial, clearer, and more obvious the defensive capabilities are, the greater the likelihood that a potential attacker will refrain from attacking in the first place. And yet, in the event of an imminent or actual attack, defensive force improves a state's ability to be secure by fighting it off.

Prevention and Preemption The preventive and preemptive uses of force are related to defense in many ways. The central idea behind both is that there is a threat facing the state, against which it is best to strike first before an attack can be unleashed. Rather than waiting to repel an attack (defense), the state strikes first to head off the attack. In effect, preventive and preemptive uses of force are based on the view that, in some situations, the best defense is a good offense. What is the difference between preemption and prevention? The strategies are not very precisely defined and are highly controversial and subject to political argument, as well. In general, **preemption** occurs when the threat of attack is *imminent*, that is, expected within a matter of weeks, days, or even hours, while **prevention** occurs when the threat is seen as *inevitable*, that is, expected sometime in the more distant future.[15] Preemption steals the advantage of striking first. By getting in the first blow, it is hoped that the force of the impending attack can be blunted. Prevention, on the other hand, is a matter of striking while the balance of forces is more favorable to the so-called defender rather than awaiting attacks when adversaries have more of an advantage.[16] Needless to say, both preemptive and, especially, preventive uses of force are highly controversial because they involve using force first, which is sometimes hard to distinguish from outright aggression.

For example, in June 1967, Israel watched while its neighbors (Egypt, Syria, and Jordan) mobilized their forces in preparation for military operations against it. Rather than wait for the imminent attacks, Israel struck first in what came to be called the Six-Day War, with a series of devastating preemptive strikes that savaged its adversaries' military forces. In a matter of days, Israel effectively destroyed the forces arrayed against it and gained control of large pieces of territory in and around its borders (see Map 6-4), including the Sinai Peninsula (from Egypt), the Gaza Strip (essentially from the UN), the West Bank and East Jerusalem (from Jordan), and the Golan Heights (from Syria). Did Israel engage in a justifiable preemptive strike in the face of imminent attacks by its foes as its defenders assert, or did it engage in aggression against its neighbors as its critics claim? Does it matter?

Fast-forward to 1981, when Israel sent fighter jets into Iraq to bomb the Osirak nuclear reactor (purchased from France) under construction near Baghdad. Both Iraq and France maintained the reactor was part of a 20-year-old Iraqi program intended for scientific research and the peaceful production of nuclear energy, but Israel was convinced it was intended to manufacture nuclear weapons. Rather than wait for Iraq to acquire such capabilities and any benefits that might accrue from their possession, Israel dispatched a squadron of American-made F-15 and F-16 fighters, which passed through both Jordanian and Saudi airspace (without permission) during the raid and destroyed the reactor. Was this attack a preemptive strike and thus defensive or was Israel striking first to maintain its dominance in the region?

More recently, remember that part of the rationale for the 2003 U.S. invasion of Iraq was that Iraq was engaged in the production and stockpiling of weapons of mass destruction that, Bush administration officials argued, were likely to be shared with and used by al-Qaeda terrorists in future attacks. As then–Vice President Dick Cheney argued, administration officials apparently believed that, whether or not Iraq was involved in the September 11, 2001, terrorist attacks on the United States (it was not), it would most likely be involved in the *next* set of attacks and thus had to be stopped before such capabilities were developed. And, in September 2007, Israel conducted another airstrike,

defense deploying and using military force to fight off an attack.

preemption the use of military force to strike first when an attack is imminent to blunt the effectiveness of the impending attack.

prevention the use of military force to strike first when an attack is inevitable to take advantage of more favorable balance of forces rather than wait for an adversary to gain the advantage from which to strike.

Deterrence after the Cold War?

Many scholars and policymakers give credit to the nuclear standoff between the United States and Soviet Union during the Cold War for what diplomatic historian John Lewis Gaddis called the "long postwar peace" between the two superpowers and their primary allies. Indeed, deterrence received a tremendous amount of attention during the Cold War. Once the Cold War ended, a whole series of questions about nuclear deterrence and its role in the new context emerged.

One major question involved the issue of nuclear proliferation, or the spread of nuclear weapons to more states. With the Soviet Union dissolving into 15 individual republics—some of which possessed parts of the Soviet nuclear arsenal—control over the Soviet arsenal and the elaborate research and production facilities (and scientists!) emerged as a major concern, while the tension between India and Pakistan fueled their efforts to acquire nuclear capabilities, as well. The efforts of states such as Iraq, Libya, North Korea, and Iran raised further concerns. How to respond to such pressures generated debates related to deterrence.

Some scholars and practitioners pointed to the logic of deterrence and the relative stability of the Cold War to advocate the spread of nuclear weapons to new states. Realist theorists John Mearsheimer and Kenneth Waltz, among others, essentially argued that the logic of deterrence would prevail and more countries with nuclear weapons would result in more stability among them, as they would find themselves in the same kind of stalemate as the United States and Soviet Union did during the Cold War. Others such as Scott Sagan argued that proliferation would greatly increase the possibility of nuclear accidents, theft of nuclear weapons, or other purposeful uses of the weapons. Most states and the United Nations adopted policies designed to prevent the spread of nuclear weapons. Hence, while a lively debate over theories of deterrence continued, in world politics existing nuclear weapons states took action to deter and prevent the spread of such capabilities.

Second, another shift in deterrence after the Cold War is the increasing concern for ways to deter smaller-scale attacks. In many ways, countries no longer prepare for a large-scale nuclear attack as the NATO and Warsaw Pact countries did during the Cold War. Instead, states seek ways to deter or protect themselves from smaller attacks such as a single bomb or missile. This has led some countries—principally the United States—to continue to develop the capability to shoot down incoming missiles. This capability is referred to as either **national missile defense** or **theater missile defense**, depending on whether the system protects the entire country or surrounds a specific theater or area, such as the East Asian region containing the Koreas. The effectiveness of these systems is not particularly good, and, in fact, it is not clear how well they might perform. However, all the powerful states in the world watch carefully when the United States performs tests of the system.

The post–Cold War world also prompted renewed attention to the fact that deterrence is not just nuclear deterrence. It applies to conventional weapons, as well. Taiwan maintains a strong military with powerful defensive capability to deter the Chinese from invading the island state. The United States and South Korea maintain a large military presence on the border with North Korea along with a large minefield designed to deter the North Koreans from launching an attack on the South. In fact, any country that has an opponent or enemy or even potential enemy must deter those threats. Can you think of any country that doesn't face some threat from the international system (hint: there are a few . . . sort of)?

By far, the most significant area of concern about deterrence stemmed from the dramatic rise in salience of civil war, unconventional war, and asymmetric war—and the related increase in the importance of non-state actors in conflict (see Chapter 5)—which called into question the continued relevance—and even possibility—of meaningful deterrence. Perhaps the most dramatic aspect of this issue is terrorism. The basic idea behind deterrence is that if attacked, the state can counterattack and hurt badly the original attacker. Of course, this fundamental equation depends on the attacker having what amounts to an identifiable return address! Immediately after September 11, 2001, Saddam Hussein made a statement that he was not involved in

national missile defense the capability to protect a country from nuclear attack by shooting down incoming missiles.

theater missile defense the capability to protect a specific or limited geographic area from nuclear attack by shooting down incoming missiles.

the attack and that he felt bad for the American people (though he also said the government deserved it). Why would he make such a statement? Because if he had been involved, the United States would have known where to direct its military to counterattack. Instead, the U.S. government had to chase down al-Qaeda and its leader bin Laden for more than ten years. While the U.S. military has been successful in many regards, the terrorist threat still remains.

That is the key difficulty when deterring terrorism: terrorist organizations hide and are often not directly connected to a single country. Therefore, it's hard to deter a group that you can't counterattack. North Korea isn't likely to attack South Korea because if it does the South Korean and U.S. militaries will retaliate. North Korea can't really hide; everyone knows where it is and it cannot be moved! The same cannot be said for terrorist groups. If they attack, where does the victim counterstrike? If states can't legitimately threaten a counterstrike, deterrence is difficult, if not outright impossible.

Changes in the international context since the end of the Cold War thus raise a number of interesting questions.

1. Would the spread of nuclear weapons into the hands of more states extend the logic of deterrence and promote stability, or would it create a more dangerous world?

2. How can states deter terrorists and other non-state actors? Is it even possible?

3. Now that the big threat of a large nuclear war is gone, are smaller nuclear exchanges more likely between such places as Pakistan and India or Israel and Iran?

4. Consider countries without opponents—Costa Rica and Grenada don't have militaries and Switzerland has a very limited capability. How do these states fit into the system where all other countries need to deter their opponents?

Map 6-4

Israel/Palestine in 1967 and Today

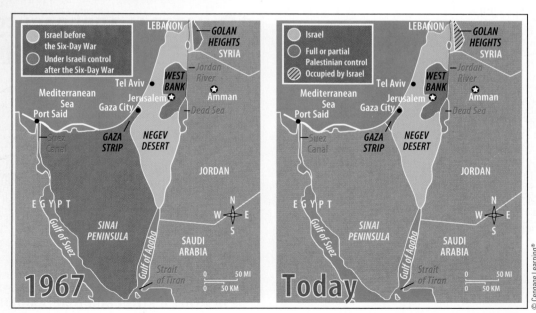

What are the costs and benefits to Israel's preemptive/preventive strikes?

this time against Syria, targeting a suspected nuclear site believed to be in development with the help of the North Koreans. Although the Israeli government refrained from public comment, this attack was apparently to prevent the development of a nuclear reactor the Israelis feared would lead to the ability to produce fissile material for making nuclear bombs. Twice in 2013 Israel bombed other Syrian targets, destroying missiles the Israelis said were bound for Lebanon to be used against Israel by Hezbollah. In each of these cases, these are preventive force justifications, however controversial they may be.

Compellence The final strategy for using force to gain security that we want to discuss is **compellence**. The first to use this designation was strategist Thomas Schelling, who characterized compellence as the use of military force to stop a foe from doing something it was already doing or force it to start doing something it was not yet doing.[17] To do so, the state engaging in compellence undertakes military actions that will stop only when its adversary engages in the desired response. For example, in March 1999, the Clinton administration led NATO to initiate military strikes against Serbia to force it to cease its military operations in Kosovo, withdraw its forces, and end its atrocities against Kosovar civilians. For more than two months, NATO engaged in a large-scale bombing campaign involving about 1,000 NATO aircraft against targets in both Kosovo and Serbia. In early June, President Slobodan Milosevic gave in to NATO demands and withdrew Serbian forces, making way for a NATO force (KFOR) and Russian peacekeepers to enter Kosovo to enforce the agreement. This use of force is a good example of compellence.

A classic example of compellence is the U.S. use of force in the 1962 Cuban Missile Crisis. In October 1962, faced with the discovery that the Soviet Union was placing nuclear missiles in Cuba, the United States mobilized forces and employed a naval blockade, while preparing for further military action, to persuade the Soviet Union to dismantle and withdraw its missiles. After 13 very tense days, nicely dramatized by the 2000 film *Thirteen Days*, the Soviet Union backed down and the crisis passed. As then–Secretary of State Dean Rusk characterized it, the United States and Soviets were "eyeball to eyeball" with military action, even nuclear war in the balance, but averted the crisis by blending force and diplomacy. It is for this reason that compellence is often labeled **coercive diplomacy**.

> **compellence** the use of military force to stop a foe from doing something it was already doing, or force it to start doing something it was not yet doing.
>
> **coercive diplomacy** a strategy that combines threats and the selective use of force with negotiation in a bargaining strategy to persuade an adversary to comply with one's demand.

Compellence may be the easiest strategy to evaluate in terms of success, but the hardest strategy to use. It is successful when the adversary (target) stops (or starts) doing what was demanded by the state deploying the force. However, because compellence requires the target to act, usually very publicly, in response to a combination of threat and punitive action, it also tends to trigger concerns about prestige, reputation, and losing face. Consequently, it may trigger resistance and escalation or even strategic withdrawal followed by future challenges that threaten a state's security in new, even more serious, ways.

For realists, pursuing security consistently involves some combination of these approaches: acquiring military might, forging alliances, and using force to protect oneself, one's friends, and one's interests. As Robert J. Art aptly summarized:

> The efficacy of force endures. For in anarchy, force and politics are connected. By itself, military power guarantees neither survival nor prosperity. But it is almost always the essential ingredient for both. Because resort to force is the ultimate card of all states, the seriousness of a state's intentions is conveyed fundamentally by its having a credible military posture. Without it, a state's diplomacy generally lacks effectiveness.[18]

To return to the words of that Roman scribe we mentioned earlier, "If you want peace, prepare for war." But what happens if everyone behaves this way?

6-3 LIBERAL APPROACHES TO SECURITY AND CONFLICT

If realists are fond of the saying that those who want peace should prepare for war, liberal theorists might well embrace the view of early twentieth century peace advocates that "those who want peace should agree to keep it" (*si vis pacem para pactum*). As you might expect, the more liberal approaches to security and conflict management emphasize cooperation and coordination. Let's be clear: it is not that liberal theorists do not see a dangerous world, or that they see no role or use for military power. Rather, they tend to see greater opportunities for cooperation based on mutual interests.

6-3a Arms Control and Disarmament

Liberal approaches tend to view the security dilemma as driven by uncertainty and, ultimately, problems with trust and understanding. Consequently, it is no surprise that a central approach to international security from a liberal perspective is the construction of agreements to control or eliminate weapons. Such agreements help to resolve the security dilemma, reduce uncertainty, and avoid arms races and the threats that arise from the accumulation of military might. In contrast to realists, who look to power and capabilities to ensure security, liberals see such dynamics as one of the main reasons for insecurity and the escalation of conflict into violence. Controlling those dynamics has thus always been a priority for liberal approaches to security. In effect, if your rival doesn't have a gun, he can't shoot you, and if *both* of you aren't engaged in efforts to accumulate weapons, you are less likely to feel threatened or be threatening. In such a context, your mutual interests might be more obvious, and your ability to manage conflicts and disagreements peacefully when they occur might be improved.

Arms control and disarmament are related but distinct approaches to security and conflict. **Disarmament** stresses the elimination (or, at least, the drastic reduction) of weapons, while **arms control** generally stresses restraint or regulation of the amount, type, positioning, or use of weapons. The two overlap when such efforts target specific types of weapons for elimination, which could be characterized as either targeted disarmament or qualitative arms control (see the following). However, most advocates of arms control believe that general disarmament is an unrealistic (and, perhaps, undesirable) outcome. At the same time, many advocates of disarmament argue that arms control is a half-measure at best that fails to address the moral imperatives of disarmament. Let's consider arms control first, and then turn to disarmament.

In part, both arms control and disarmament rest on the premise that controlling weaponry and the competition to acquire it will make states more secure and better able to manage conflict. Arms control, in particular, is committed to establishing limits and stability in the military competition between countries, to reduce uncertainty and promote trust and cooperation.[19] Controlling the escalatory spiral of weaponry in this fashion should thereby lead to better management of the security dilemma.

ARMS CONTROL Table 6-5 provides a list of major arms control agreements since World War I, while Table 6-6 shows the basic aspects of arms control, identifying the key features of participants, purposes, and types. In terms of participants, arms control can be unilateral, although instances in which a single state voluntary refrained from acquiring weapons are highly unusual and often only temporary. Bilateral agreements between rivals and competitors are much more common but are frequently limited in their impact because they only involve two main parties. Unless the world is essentially bipolar, as during the Cold War between the United States and the Soviet Union, the broader effect of bilateral agreements can be limited. Multilateral agreements, which range from just a few participants to arrangements involving most states, are potentially more far-reaching (depending on the number of participants) but are also much more difficult to achieve because of the multiple perspectives and interests involved, as well as the difficulty in monitoring and verifying compliance.

Let's focus on the types of agreements and consider a few examples:

1. *Rules of war.* Societies have long had concerns with trying to find limits on the occurrence and acceptable practices of war. In Chapter 5, we introduced the example of the Kellogg-Briand Pact to outlaw war, which is an example of the first. As noted in our following discussion of collective security, the treaty establishing the League of Nations also banned aggression among its members. The Geneva Conventions of 1864, 1906, 1929, and 1949 are an example of the latter, establishing rules for the treatment of wounded and captured soldiers, as well as civilians, during times of war. The Hague Conventions of 1899 and 1907 established a variety of limits on the use of weapons and war crimes (see also our discussion of this topic in Chapter 7).

2. *Communication and administration.* Arms control agreements of this type focus on measures to improve cooperation and communication to reduce tension between participants. A central example is the conclusion of the 1962 Hotline Agreement to establish a direct and dedicated communication link between the United States and the Soviet Union—often seen as a bright red phone in the White House in movies and television—in the aftermath of the Cuban Missile Crisis, which was updated in the 1980s to include more modern communications and the establishment of nuclear crisis centers in both countries. This agreement is a good example of efforts to improve direct communications between adversaries so that violent conflict might be better controlled or avoided altogether. The tenuous links between leaders during the incredible tension of the missile crisis in 1962 was the prime motivator in this accord.

3. *Confidence-building measures.* While virtually any agreement might be considered a confidence-building measure, because in principle they should all contribute to trust

> **disarmament** the elimination of arsenals or classes or types of weapons.
>
> **arms control** regulation of the amount, type, positioning, or use of weapons.

TABLE 6-5 MAJOR ARMS CONTROL TREATIES SINCE WORLD WAR I

TREATY	YEAR ENTERED INTO FORCE	FOCUS	MEMBERS
Washington Naval Treaty	1922	Limited major naval vessels	Multilateral
Geneva Protocol on Chemical and Biological Weapons	1925	Bans use of chemical and biological weapons	Multilateral
Antarctic Treaty	1959	Bans military activity in Antarctica	Multilateral
Limited Test Ban Treaty	1963	Bans nuclear tests except underground	U.S., UK, USSR; others joined later
Outer Space Treaty	1967	Bans nuclear weapons in space	U.S., UK, USSR; others joined later
Treaty of Tlatelolco	1967	Nuclear weapons free zone in Latin America and the Caribbean	Multilateral
Nuclear Non-Proliferation Treaty	1970	Bans acquisition of nuclear weapons by non-nuclear states	Multilateral
Strategic Arms Limitation Treaty I	1972	Limited nuclear weapons arsenals	U.S., USSR
Anti-Ballistic Missile Treaty	1972	Limited strategic missile defense systems	U.S., USSR
Seabed Arms Control Treaty	1972	Bans nuclear weapons on ocean floor	U.S., UK, USSR; others joined later
Biological Weapons Convention	1975	Bans all biological weapons	Multilateral
Threshold Test Ban Treaty	1990 (1974)	Limits size of nuclear tests	U.S., USSR
Strategic Arms Limitation Treaty II	(1977) never ratified	Limited nuclear weapons arsenals	U.S., USSR
Treaty of Rarotonga	1986	Nuclear weapons free zone in South Pacific	Multilateral
Intermediate-Range Nuclear Forces Treaty	1988	Banned intermediate-range nuclear forces from Europe	U.S., USSR
Conventional Forces In Europe Treaty	1992	Limited key categories of conventional weapons for NATO and Warsaw Pact forces	NATO; Warsaw Pact
Strategic Arms Reduction Treaty I	1994	Reduced nuclear arsenals	U.S., Russia
Comprehensive Nuclear Test Ban Treaty	(1996) not in force	Bans all nuclear explosions	Multilateral
Treaty of Bangkok	1997	Nuclear weapons free zone in Southeast Asia	Multilateral
Ottawa Treaty on Anti-Personnel Mines	1999	Banned land mines	Multilateral
Open Skies Treaty	2002	Protects unarmed aerial surveillance	Multilateral
Treaty of Moscow	2003	Limits number of deployed nuclear warheads	U.S., Russia
Treaty of Semipalatinsk	2008	Nuclear weapons free zone in Central Asia	Multilateral
Treaty of Pelindaba	2009	Nuclear weapons free zone in Africa	Multilateral
Convention on Cluster Munitions	2010	Bans cluster bombs	Multilateral
New Start (Strategic Arms Reduction Treaty)	2011	Reduces existing active nuclear arsenals by 50%	U.S., Russia
Arms Trade Treaty	2013 (pending)	Regulates international trade in conventional weapons	Adopted by UN General Assembly, April 2013; 118 signatories, 32 ratifications (enters into force with 50 ratifications)

TABLE 6-6 PARTICIPANTS, PURPOSES, AND TYPES OF ARMS CONTROL

PARTICIPANTS OF ARMS CONTROL	PURPOSES OF ARMS CONTROL	TYPES OF ARMS CONTROL
Unilateral	Reduce likelihood of conflict and war	Rules of war
Bilateral	Reduce likelihood of uncontrollable war	Communication and administration
Multilateral	Reduce resources devoted to armaments	Confidence-building measures
	Control proliferation of weapons of mass destruction	Geographic agreements
	Establish and reinforce restraints on violent behavior	Quantitative limitations
	Contribute to progress toward disarmament	Qualitative limitations
		Horizontal proliferation control

Source: Adapted and summarized from Chapters 2 and 3 in Christopher Lamb, *How to Think About Arms Control, Disarmament and Defense* (Englewood Cliffs, NJ: Prentice Hall, 1988).

and cooperation, this type of arms control agreement usually refers to much more specific arrangements for transparency and information sharing on military matters to reduce the fear and uncertainty that often occur. Agreements to share information on military exercises and troop movements, allowing inspections and observers, and a wide variety of other restraints that promote openness, transparency, and predictability are at the core of this type of agreement. In the 1970s and 1980s, for example, the Conference on Security and Cooperation in Europe and its successor, the Organization for Security and Cooperation in Europe, established agreements to provide for advance warning of military exercises by rival NATO and Warsaw Pact forces and to allow observers from the other side, all in order to lessen the tension between the two blocs.

4. *Geographic agreements*. This type of agreement limits or bans military activities and arms competitions in specific locations. Generally, these agreements are very straightforward. For example, in 1959 the United States, the Soviet Union, and others agreed to the complete demilitarization of Antarctica to avoid competition and conflict over military bases and activities there. Similarly, the 1967 Tlatelolco and Outer Space treaties banned the placement of nuclear weapons in Latin America and in outer space, respectively, while the 1971 Seabed Arms Control Treaty did the same for the ocean floor. At present, there are five agreements establishing nuclear-weapons-free zones throughout the world: Latin America, as noted, the South Pacific (the Treaty of Rarotonga), Southeast Asia (the Treaty of Bangkok), Africa (the Treaty of Pelindaba), and Central Asia (the Treaty of Semipalatinsk). However, only the Latin America treaty has the full compliance of all the official nuclear powers: the United States has not agreed to the South Pacific or Africa agreements, and none of the nuclear powers has agreed to the Southeast Asia or Central Asia accords.

5. *Quantitative limitations*. Just like it sounds, this category of agreement establishes some numerical limitation on some or all arsenals. For example, the Washington Naval

Agreement of 1922 and the London Naval Treaty of the next decade set limits for Britain, France, Italy, Japan, and the United States on the number of battleships and cruisers allowed to each party, based on tonnage limitations. The Strategic Arms Limitation Talks (producing SALT I in 1972 and SALT II in 1979) set limits on the number of nuclear weapons delivery vehicles that the United States and Soviet Union could develop (although SALT II was never ratified by the United States). The Strategic Arms Reduction Talks (START) initiated in the 1980s by U.S. President Ronald Reagan and Soviet President Mikhail Gorbachev resulted in a 1991 agreement (START I) that limited the two sides to 6,000 total nuclear warheads and 1,600 total delivery vehicles (e.g., intercontinental ballistic missiles, submarine-launched ballistic missiles, and bombers). In 2010, the United States and Russia concluded and ratified the so-called New START treaty, which reduced nuclear delivery vehicles by half, to 800, and limited deployed nuclear warheads to 1,550.

6. *Qualitative limitations*. This type of agreement controls types of weapons, not just numbers. The 1987 Intermediate Nuclear Forces (INF) treaty between the United States and Soviet Union eliminated an entire class of nuclear weapons from the two sides' arsenals. Similarly, the 1997 Chemical Weapons Convention prohibited the development, production, acquisition, stockpiling, retention, transfer, or use of chemical weapons by its 190 members (only Angola, Burma, Egypt, Israel, and North Korea, although both Burma and Israel have signed—but not ratified—the accord).

7. *Horizontal proliferation control*. Agreements of this type seek to limit the spread of weapons and weapons technology beyond states that currently possess them. The best-known example of this type of agreement is the 1968 Nuclear Non-Proliferation Treaty (NPT), which was extended indefinitely in 1995. This agreement, which currently has 190 members, limits nuclear weapons to the five official nuclear weapons states (United States, Russia, Britain, France, and China), and establishes procedures for the peaceful use of nuclear energy by the non-nuclear

Arms, Arms Control, and War

Seeking security through the acquisition of arms or through arms control and disarmament depends in part on whether one views weapons as a cause of war. Spiral theorists believe that the anarchic environment of world politics leads otherwise peaceful actors to arm themselves out of fear and uncertainty.[20] As the security dilemma suggests, others react by arming themselves, leading to increased tension and an action-reaction cycle in which arms are acquired in greater amounts. Eventually, this cycle "spirals out of control and some incident touches off a war no one really wanted."[21] Aggressor theorists, by contrast, believe that some states are naturally warlike, requiring other states to be prepared to fight to protect themselves and punish the aggressor.[22]

Spiral theorists thus argue that arms cause war by contributing to misperception, fear, and insecurity. Arms control and disarmament are therefore vital as they promote communication and cooperation and help to prevent or break the spirals that lead to war. The most extreme spiral theorists will advocate unilateral disarmament measures as signals of peaceful intentions. For aggressor theorists, such actions are foolish. Instead, they argue for military strength as a necessary deterrent to aggressors. Arms control is undesirable, even dangerous, because it may create vulnerability or a false sense of security. Spiral theorists view shows of strength by aggressors as escalatory steps in the conflict spiral, while aggressor theorists view conciliatory actions like disarmament as dangerous acts of appeasement likely only to encourage aggressors.[23] In some ways, this argument is not that different from the debate over allowing guns to be carried on college campuses; some see that as inherently dangerous, and others see it as necessary to protect oneself from evildoers.

The arms control policies of various countries are heavily influenced by the particular theories their leaders embrace, whether they recognize it or not. British Prime Minister Neville Chamberlain was driven by a simple spiral theory in his efforts to head off war in Europe before World War II, while other European leaders tended to be influenced by aggressor theories in the run-up to World War II, competing with each other to demonstrate resolve and deploy military force. One or the other of these approaches guided American presidents (and probably their Soviet counterparts) for the last 50 years. And, often, disputes among leading diplomats and foreign policy advisors based on these competing perspectives have resulted in challenges, delays, and even failures in efforts to negotiate. What do you think?

1. Do arms cause war or ensure peace?

2. What is the role of arms control and disarmament in providing security?

3. What kinds of arms control and disarmament are most likely to satisfy both spiral and aggressor theorists?

4. How can a country best be safe without appearing to threaten another?

weapon states. Four non-members of the NPT are known or believed to have nuclear weapons: India, Pakistan, North Korea, and Israel. North Korea, which was initially a member of the NPT, withdrew in 2003. Efforts to complete a Comprehensive Nuclear-Test-Ban Treaty (adopted by the UN in 1996) are also geared toward preventing the spread of nuclear weapons. More than 160 states have ratified the treaty, and another 34 have signed, but not ratified, it (including the United States, Iran, China, Israel, and Egypt).

DISARMAMENT Although some advocates of arms control see it as an opportunity to make progress toward more general disarmament, historically disarmament movements have tended to involve the public, social movements, and nongovernmental organizations more often and more extensively than states themselves. There are instances of involuntary disarmament, in which a state is forced to relinquish its arsenals by those who have defeated it in war. For example, after military victories Rome famously forced disarmament on Carthage in a third-century agreement, while Napoleon forced Prussia to disarm in an 1806 treaty. Following both World War I and World War II, the victorious Allies forced disarmament on their defeated foes, as well. However, in all these cases, these forced outcomes were short lived, and the defeated states soon found ways to re-arm (and, in fact, often to retaliate against those who forced the disarmament on them).

In the late nineteenth and early twentieth centuries, efforts in The Hague conferences (1899 and 1907) and the world disarmament conference of the 1930s embraced disarmament goals but produced few results. The Hague conferences mostly restricted the use of certain kinds of weapons, while the 1930s endeavor collapsed under the tensions of that period and the rise of German power. Indeed, German withdrawal from the conference in 1933 effectively destroyed any prospect of success.

The advent of the nuclear era gave some new impetus to disarmament efforts specifically focused on nuclear weapons. The devastating power and destructiveness of these weapons led many to advocate for their elimination. In fact, right after World War II, the United States proposed a nuclear disarmament pact known as the **Baruch Plan** for its principal author Bernard Baruch (an influential American financier and statesman). The Baruch Plan proposed to establish a UN Atomic Development Authority (ADA) to take control of all nuclear energy activities. The ADA would supervise and control the peaceful use of nuclear power and monitor member states for compliance. As the only state with nuclear weapons at the time, the United States reserved the right to maintain its arsenal until all other countries relinquished control over their nuclear energy activities to the ADA. The Soviet Union insisted that the United States disarm first before the ADA was established. Both sides refused to accept the other's proposal, and the plan failed. Subsequent official efforts toward nuclear disarmament generally followed suit.

However, since World War II, there have been a wide variety of nuclear disarmament efforts led by the publics of various states and social movements and nongovernmental organizations within and across national boundaries. For example, it was significant public pressure in the United States and Europe, in part by mothers concerned about contaminated milk, that led the Soviet Union, United States, and Britain to conclude the 1963 Partial Test Ban Treaty, which eliminated testing in the atmosphere and seas. Peace movements made up of citizens, scientists, and others in Japan, Britain, the United States, and elsewhere in Europe and the rest of the world regularly pressed for progress toward nuclear disarmament in the decades following World War II. Their efforts contributed to agreements limiting testing, proliferation, disposal of nuclear material, and, eventually, nuclear arms control.

A good example is the anti-nuclear movement that spread in the early 1980s. Prompted by increased tension between the United States and Soviet Union and plans to expand nuclear arsenals and the deployment of missiles in Europe, as well as the collapse of arms control talks, anti-nuclear demonstrations erupted in the United States and across Europe. Citizens, scientists, and religious organizations (including the Catholic Church) advocated for control, reduction, and eventual elimination of nuclear weapons. In the United States, the nuclear freeze and nuclear disarmament movements conducted large-scale demonstrations

and lobbied American policymakers to take steps to curtail the nuclear arms race. In Germany, anti-nuclear groups pressured the government to oppose the expanded deployment of American nuclear missiles. Although unsuccessful in achieving their central goals, the pressure these and other groups brought to bear contributed to the resumption of arms control talks between the United States and the Soviet Union and the conclusion of the INF treaty in 1987.

Even more recently, the sixtieth anniversary of the U.S. use of atomic bombs against Japan in 1945 prompted public demonstrations calling for nuclear disarmament. In 2008, Norway convened an International Conference on Nuclear Disarmament, and, in the wake of the 2011 Fukushima nuclear disaster in Japan (see Chapter 12), some renewed efforts for nuclear disarmament occurred, as well. However, while these efforts on the part of non-state actors are significant, states thus far have resisted nuclear—or any other type of—disarmament. Arms control remains the more productive result.

6-3b Collective Security

A second major liberal approach to security and conflict is **collective security**. In many ways, this approach is the liberal answer to the balance of power politics discussed previously. Indeed, it was frustration with the results of balance of power politics—which many blamed for the start of World War I—that led to efforts to construct a collective security system in the period between the two World Wars. This highlights a significant point: while balance of power politics happen on their own, collective security has to be constructed.[24] Collective security requires a concerted effort at cooperation and coordination and the establishment of institutions.

The premise is not complicated. It can be summarized in the simple phrase "an attack on one is an attack on all," or, as in the famous motto from Alexandre Dumas's *Three Musketeers*, "all for one, one for all." As these ideas suggest, the basis of collective security is that states form a community to maintain peace among its members. All members of the community agree to respond together to an attack by one or more member states on any other members. This approach is a method for managing power and responding to threat by

---

Baruch Plan a nuclear disarmament proposal authored by U.S. statesman Bernard Baruch after World War II to place nuclear weapons and energy activities under the control and authority of the United Nations.

collective security states join together into an organization, ban the use of force by its members, and commt themselves to joining together to respond to any attack by one member on any other member.

pooling resources to bring a preponderance of power to bear on an aggressor. Improved security is thus gained in three ways. First, the collective security institution provides a forum for multilateral diplomacy and negotiation to promote understanding and communication and to resolve conflicts and disagreements before they escalate to more serious levels. It establishes norms, rules, and procedures that stress peaceful conflict resolution. Second, the threat of collective action should deter most potential aggressors, who should calculate that the promise of an overwhelming response by the community would negate the potential benefits of any attack. Third, in those instances in which the collective security regime fails to resolve the issue or deter the potential attacker, the pooling of might in response (often, but not necessarily always, military) should be sufficient to defeat and punish the attacker and defend the victim. This demonstration should, in itself, provide important signals and lessons to future potential attackers.

A collective security system thus depends on several key components.

1. *Universal membership.* Collective security is meant to keep peace among the members of the arrangement, unlike alliances which typically involve an agreement to defend each other in the event of an attack from another state outside the alliance. It is important for collective security that all major states are members.

2. *Agreement to renounce the use of force.* The members of a collective security system must agree that they will not use force against each other to resolve their disagreements.

3. *Commitment to respond to the use of force.* The members of a collective security system must agree that they will respond to the use of force by any member of the system against any other member of the system by joining together to punish the attacker and defend the victim.

Note that these basic requirements are more complicated than they initially appear. They require that aggression be definable and identifiable so that an attacker can be punished. They also require that the pooled might of the community exceeds the might of any individual member so that a collective response can be successful. Furthermore, they require that all members be prepared and *willing* to commit their resources in defense of any other state, no matter which state or how small, and no matter which state the attacker might be. Finally, a collective security system probably requires a central organization that can coordinate discussion and decisions for the community.

Three attempts at some form of collective security have occurred in the modern state system. In the nineteenth century, the major powers in Europe (Britain, Russia, Austria, Prussia, and eventually France) joined in the Concert of Europe, which operated from 1815 to 1854. The concert rested on a shared commitment to the peace settlement of 1815 (the Congress of Vienna) and to the principle that any change to the territorial status quo embodied in that agreement would be arranged through negotiation among the members of the concert or face punitive action by one or more members of the concert. Although the Concert of Europe helped to preserve peace in Europe for 40 years, it eventually failed for at least three reasons: (1) the commitment to the status quo among the members of the concert deteriorated, leading to increasing conflict and pressure for change to the 1815 agreement; (2) changes in power among member states and rising states outside the concert, combined with the exclusion of minor states from the concert, led to the inability of the concert to manage conflict; (3) the lack of a central organization made it difficult to manage the complex discussions and negotiations necessary to preserve the peace, as well as to facilitate coordinated responses to states challenging the 1815 agreement.

After World War I, the victorious states established the League of Nations explicitly to construct a collective security system for multilateral and collective efforts to provide security and keep peace and to avoid a repeat of the devastating war that had just ended. The members of the league committed themselves to refrain from aggression against other members and to the principle that any act of aggression against any member was an act of war against all members. Unlike the Concert of Europe, the league included a wide variety of members, both large and small. In the event of aggression, the members agreed to impose diplomatic and economic sanctions against the aggressor and, with the unanimous recommendation of the league's executive council, to contribute military resources to a military action in response.

However, the League of Nations proved ineffective in the face of the increasingly severe conflict of the 1920s and 1930s. One problem was that key states were not included in the league, including the United States (which refrained from joining) and the Soviet Union (which was excluded until the 1930s). Moreover, the league's effectiveness suffered because some states—such as Italy, Japan, and Germany—were considerably less committed to the status quo than others. Perhaps most important, the league failed when its members proved unwilling or unable to punish countries such as Japan and Italy when they engaged in military actions in Manchuria and Ethiopia, respectively. Key members of the league proved reluctant to expend their resources in defense of smaller states, and other calculations of interest (e.g., the concern that Italy might be needed to help resist Germany) increased their unwillingness to confront the aggression.

After World War II, the victorious powers again sought to construct a collective security system to manage conflict and keep peace, establishing the United Nations and, in particular, the UN Security Council, in 1945, for that purpose. The members of the UN pledge to refrain from the use of force against each other and to use the UN for help in resolving conflict that might arise between them. The UN charter empowers the UN Security Council—made up of five permanent members (the U.S., Russia, China, France, and Britain), each of which holds veto power over any resolution, and ten rotating members—to identify threats to peace and acts of aggression and to take action in the form of diplomatic or economic sanctions or the use of force to restore international peace and security.

Like its predecessor, the UN has proven less effective as a collective security organization than its creators hoped. During the Cold War, the veto power possessed by the United States and the Soviet Union effectively paralyzed the Security Council and prevented collective security actions. The only exception occurred in the case of the Korean War in 1950, when the UN Security Council authorized military action by members to help South Korea repel the invasion by North Korea. This authorization was possible only because the Soviet Union was boycotting UN Security Council meetings in protest over the refusal of the United States and other members to seat the new communist regime in mainland China as the official representative of that country. The United States and its allies preferred to continue to recognize the nationalist (and pro-U.S.) regime that had been overthrown in 1949 and had fled to Taiwan, rather than turn over China's seat (and UN Security Council veto) to the new communist regime. The communist Chinese regime (People's Republic of China) did not get the China seat in the UN until 1971!

While its formal collective security operations languished during the Cold War, the UN was able to engage in extensive **peacekeeping** operations in support of its collective security mission. During the paralysis of the UN Security Council caused by the Cold War conflict between the United States and Soviet Union, the UN developed a peacekeeping role as an extension to its collective security purpose. In these first-generation peacekeeping operations, the UN typically provided a small multinational force—occasionally called blue helmets for the UN-provided headgear they wear—to help keep peace by providing a buffer between parties in conflict, often along a border or an agreed-upon cease-fire line. Usually very lightly armed, and never intended to engage in combat, these peacekeeping forces were drawn from the military forces of neutral states or smaller powers that were not aligned with any of the major parties to

Howard Davies/CORBIS

United Nations armored vehicles on patrol | Why hasn't collective security been more effective in preventing and resolving conflict?

the conflict. These forces monitored the peace and helped the parties to the conflict refrain from the temptation to restart hostilities. In this sense, they served as a basic deterrent to continued fighting.

In general, first-generation peacekeeping required three levels of agreement:

1. Agreement among the parties of the conflict to accept the peacekeeping (that is, there should be a peace to *keep*; these forces did not *make* peace).

2. Agreement among the major powers to fund the peacekeeping operation (UN authorization usually through the UN Security Council).

3. Agreement from other states to provide the peacekeeping forces.

The first UN peacekeeping operation was the UN Truce Supervision Organization in 1948 sent to Israel to help sustain a cease-fire between that newly established state and its Arab neighbors. In total, 69 UN peacekeeping missions have been authorized all over the globe, at a total cost of about $69 billion.

After the Cold War's end, there was optimism that the UN could take up its collective security role, and the initial authorization of military action to repel Iraq from Kuwait after its 1990 invasion fueled that hope. However, in the conflicts of the post–Cold War period, the 1991 Gulf War proved the exception rather than the rule.

peacekeeping the provision of third-party forces from the UN or other regional organizations to help keep peace by providing a buffer between parties in conflict, often along a border or an agreed-upon cease-fire line to monitor and maintain the peace.

In part due to the changing nature of conflict and war during this period (especially the rise of intrastate conflict), which we discussed in Chapter 5, and in part because member states found that they continued to have competing interests in the new environment, the post–Cold War world did not provide any greater incentives for successful collective security actions. Additionally, if the states did not have an interest in the conflict, they were often unwilling to put any of their troops in harm's way. The unwillingness or inability to act in the face of such conflicts as Somalia, Bosnia, Rwanda, Darfur, Kosovo, and others showed that the will to engage in collective security was still lacking. Hence, traditional collective security peace operations continued to languish.

In contrast to traditional collective security operations, the UN made much more significant contributions in its peacekeeping operations. The vast majority of these operations have occurred since 1990 and the end of the Cold War. After the end of the Cold War, second-generation peacekeeping developed, in which the peacekeeping forces were much more substantial and much more complex. As of 2014, there were 28 active UN missions (see Maps 6-5 and 6-6) involving more than 100,000 troops and another 20,000 civilians from 115 different countries. These second-generation peace operations differed from their first-generation predecessors in some significant ways.

As we noted, first-generation peacekeepers, who generally relied on a preexisting cease-fire and the consent of the parties involved in the conflict, were lightly armed and very rarely authorized to use force in anything other than direct self-defense. Second-generation peacekeeping forces such as those deployed in Somalia, the former Yugoslavia, and elsewhere around the world are typically larger, more complex (involving both military and civilian personnel), and more capable. They are also engaged in a broader range of military, security, political, and humanitarian activities, and they are frequently authorized to use force to make or enforce peace. In fact, their operations are often authorized under the UN Charter's Chapter VII authority, which allows the UN Security Council to take military and nonmilitary action to "restore international peace and security." Indeed, while the evolution did not start there, in many ways the failure of the more traditional peacekeepers initially deployed to help defuse

Map 6-5

Ongoing UN Peacekeeping and Political/Peacebuilding Operations, 2014

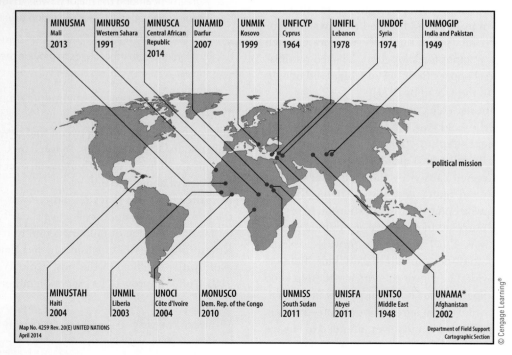

MINUSMA Mali 2013 | MINURSO Western Sahara 1991 | MINUSCA Central African Republic 2014 | UNAMID Darfur 2007 | UNMIK Kosovo 1999 | UNFICYP Cyprus 1964 | UNIFIL Lebanon 1978 | UNDOF Syria 1974 | UNMOGIP India and Pakistan 1949

* political mission

MINUSTAH Haiti 2004 | UNMIL Liberia 2003 | UNOCI Côte d'Ivoire 2004 | MONUSCO Dem. Rep. of the Congo 2010 | UNMISS South Sudan 2011 | UNISFA Abyei 2011 | UNTSO Middle East 1948 | UNAMA* Afghanistan 2002

Map No. 4259 Rev. 20(E) UNITED NATIONS
April 2014

Department of Field Support
Cartographic Section

© Cengage Learning®

Source: United Nations, http://www.un.org/Depts/Cartographic/map/dpko/PKO_BN.pdf

Map 6-6

Ongoing Political and Peacebuilding Missions, 2014

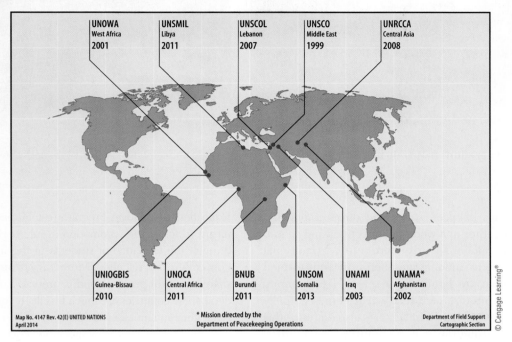

UNOWA West Africa 2001
UNSMIL Libya 2011
UNSCOL Lebanon 2007
UNSCO Middle East 1999
UNRCCA Central Asia 2008

UNIOGBIS Guinea-Bissau 2010
UNOCA Central Africa 2011
BNUB Burundi 2011
UNSOM Somalia 2013
UNAMI Iraq 2003
UNAMA* Afghanistan 2002

Map No. 4147 Rev. 42(E) UNITED NATIONS
April 2014

* Mission directed by the
Department of Peacekeeping Operations

Department of Field Support
Cartographic Section

© Cengage Learning®

What do the number and locations of UN peacekeeping operations indicate about their role and effect?

Source: United Nations, http://www.un.org/Depts/Cartographic/map/dpko/DPA_BN.pdf.

the violent conflict in the former Yugoslavia as Serbs, Croats, Bosnians, and others fought over control and the future of their territories helped to spur the shift to more muscular and capable peace operations and forces. Finally, because these second-generation peace operations often occur in complicated civil war situations, the consent of the parties involved is not always a prerequisite—which also means the peacekeepers are more likely to face hostility and have to engage in more dynamic peacemaking, peacekeeping, and peace-enforcing activities.

These characteristics of second-generation peace operations helped to increase their capabilities and their impact. Indeed, many evaluations of these operations agree that they make important contributions to peace and security, especially in civil wars. However, these same characteristics also ensure that their tasks are more difficult, since they often involve ongoing conflicts and tenuous cease-fires. Moreover, as you might expect, the kinds of conflicts that gain UN attention and subsequent peace-keeping forces are often the most difficult and intractable conflicts, which makes success even more challenging.

Collective security faces formidable challenges. In addition to the need to establish a central organization to facilitate decision making and coordination, the three cases introduced here suggest that major powers must also share common interests and a general commitment to peace, and probably the status quo, for collective security to work effectively. Moreover, major powers must be willing to expend resources on behalf of others in pursuit of common interests. Aggression must be identifiable, and the collective action problem must be overcome so that members of the organization cannot stand aside and hope that some other state will take up the burden. In the end, a realist might ask, if these conditions existed, would a collective security system be necessary?

6-3c Security Communities and the Democratic and Capitalist Peace

The final liberal approach to security is probably the most indirect but perhaps the most effective, as well. Inspired in part by the ideas of the philosopher Immanuel Kant, its emphasis is on developing a

UN peace operations in Bosnia and Somalia | Why did the shift from first- to second-generation peace operations occur, and what has been its impact?

network of ties between states and other actors that link states together in a web of connections and shared interests.[25] In such a **security community**, traditional security concerns among members are transformed because people are bound by a sense of community and common interest such that war becomes virtually unthinkable.[26] Constructivist scholars also embrace this argument, stressing the shared identities and interests and complex interactions that transform the relationships between societies.[27]

What strategies help to establish security communities? Liberal approaches generally look to a cluster of interlinked approaches to build security communities and manage conflict. First, many advocates of this approach stress building common identity and understanding among states. Efforts to foster societal contact and exchanges and to promote democracy are good examples of such approaches. Fostering **cultural exchange** reduces the distance between peoples and builds understanding. Programs such as the U.S. Fulbright

Educational Exchange Program (established in 1946) are meant to foster the "promotion of international good will through the exchange of students in the fields of education, culture and science." **Democracy promotion** leads to shared political practices and is premised on the fact that democratic countries are much less likely to go to war with each other and much more likely to resolve conflicts peacefully (see discussions of democratic peace in Chapters 3 and 5 and of democracy promotion in Chapter 9).

Second, advocates of this approach have attempted to "build peace in pieces" by promoting transnational cooperation on economic and social problems that grow to link societies together.[28] Based on theories of **functionalism** and **neo-functionalism**, this approach stresses specific technical cooperation on economic and social issues that build linkages and shared interests among societies. As these linkages deepen and become more routine, they expand to more areas, leading to even greater cooperation and institutional connections.[29] A good example of this can be seen in the development of the European Union. Beginning as the European Coal and Steel Community in the 1950s, the integrative approach inspired by functionalism and neo-functionalism and embraced by leaders such as Jean Monnet (a founding father of the EU) led to stronger and more extensive linkages as the early organization grew into the European Union of today, with its extensive institutions and single common currency for many of its members. Along the way, it helped transform European relations from the highly conflict-ridden patterns that led to the two devastating World Wars in the twentieth century to the peaceful security community we see today. Could this success be duplicated in other regions of the world?

Third, and related to the previous point, advocates of this strategy emphasize the cultivation of

security community a group of states bound by shared identities and interests and complex interactions among which security threats are virtually nonexistent.

cultural exchange programs involving the exchange of citizens—students, teachers, scientists, artists, and others—between countries to foster cultural understanding and cooperation.

democracy promotion a cluster of activities ranging from diplomacy to aid to intervention designed to foster and support democratization in other countries.

functionalism and neo-functionalism technical cooperation on economic and social issues that build linkages and shared interests among societies and expand to more areas, leading to even greater cooperation and institutional connections.

China's Pursuit of Security

China is generally regarded as a rising power whose role and influence in world politics is swiftly expanding. Its purposes and foreign policy actions therefore garner a great deal of attention from its neighbors in the regions, especially Taiwan and Japan, and leading powers such as the United States. According to the U.S. Defense Department, which annually reports on Chinese military capabilities and strategies, China

> continues to pursue a long-term, comprehensive military modernization program designed to improve the capacity of its armed forces to fight and win short-duration, high-intensity regional military conflict. Preparing for potential conflict in the Taiwan Strait appears to remain the principal focus and primary driver of China's military investment. However, as China's interests have grown and as it has gained greater influence in the international system, its military modernization has also become increasingly focused on investments in military capabilities to conduct a wider range of missions beyond its immediate territorial concerns.

China's pursuit of its security and interests has led it to adopt more muscular approaches in a variety of areas. Again, the U.S. Defense Department describes Chinese initiatives with some apparent concern:

> Beijing is investing in military programs and weapons designed to improve extended-range power projection and operations in emerging domains such as cyber, space, and electronic warfare. Current trends in China's weapons production will enable the [People's Liberation Army, or PLA] to conduct a range of military operations in Asia well beyond Taiwan, in the South China Sea, western Pacific, and Indian Ocean. Key systems that have been either deployed or are in development include ballistic missiles (including anti-ship variants), anti-ship and land attack cruise missiles, nuclear submarines, modern surface ships, and an aircraft carrier. The need to ensure trade, particularly oil supplies from the Middle East, has prompted China's navy to conduct counter-piracy operations in the Gulf of Aden. Disputes with Japan over maritime claims in the East China Sea and with several Southeast Asian claimants to all or parts of the Spratly and Paracel Islands in the South China Sea have led to renewed tensions in these areas. Instability on the Korean Peninsula could also produce a regional crisis involving China's military. The desire to protect energy investments in Central Asia, along with potential security implications from cross-border support to ethnic separatists, could also provide an incentive for military investment or intervention in this region if instability surfaces.

What does China's foreign policy behavior mean? Consider the perspectives on the pursuit of security discussed in this chapter, as well as the relevant ideas from previous chapters.

1. What best explains Chinese actions?

2. In what ways do these actions contribute to and challenge China's security?

3. What might other countries think about China's foreign policy behavior and how might they react?

Source: Office of the Secretary of Defense, *Annual Report to Congress: Military and Security Developments Involving the People's Republic of China 2013.*

---

interdependence and institutions that help states coordinate their actions as they develop mutual interests. One aspect of this involves economic ties, with the argument that developing and deepening economic relationships such as trade and financial networks contributes to a "capitalist peace" that dramatically reduces the potential for violent conflict.[30] Another, which motivated a large portion of post–World War II institution building, stresses the development of international institutions to help coordinate and govern economic policy and interactions (see our discussion in Chapter 8). Part of the logic of the post–World War II international institutions such as the International Monetary Fund and the World Bank, as well as less formal institutions—such as the G7, G8, and now, G20—is that the norms, rules, and decision procedures that promote economic coordination within these

institutions help to reduce conflict and foster a sense of community. International institutions of other kinds to address social problems such as the environment, health, and a variety of other issues produce similar effects.

In the end, advocates argue, strategies such as these build community and transform the security calculations of states and societies. According to their advocates, they transform and redefine the security dilemma and reduce the situations in which conflict erupts into violence. By trying to create and spread zones of peace, these strategies contend with the challenges posed by anarchy, diversity, and complexity by reducing uncertainty and fear and building common interests and cooperation. What do you think of the long-term prospects of such efforts to transform relations among states and societies?

CONCLUSION: SEEKING SECURITY

National and international security remains an elusive, central issue in world politics. While power-based and cooperation-based approaches have been advocated and embraced over time, security challenges remain, conflict persists, and violence still erupts far too often. But, as we have seen in the previous chapter, there has been an evolution to the nature of conflict, and to the nature of security, as well. Few observers would argue that security is not a challenge in the current world, nor would many argue that conflict and war have disappeared. And yet, security issues have changed. The French no longer harbor fears of war with Britain or Germany, or vice versa. The United States and Russia no longer compete in a high-stakes arms race to develop and accumulate stockpiles of the most deadly weapons ever known, in arsenals capable of destroying the world many times over. Optimists might argue that even the rapid military growth of China should not unduly alarm the EU or United States, as China's sizable trade interactions with both these entities make any future war with them look less appealing. But military spending continues at significant levels, and force continues to be used to resolve conflicts. Are people and states more secure today or less? And what strategies have contributed to that condition?

Finally, now that you have considered major arguments on the causes of war (Chapter 5) and approaches to security (this chapter), think back to our initial discussion of the prisoners' dilemma in our very first chapter. Remember that the essence of the prisoners' dilemma is that each prisoner ends up choosing a course of action that provides less benefit in order to avoid suffering a greater cost. Which of the approaches to security we have discussed here do you think is most likely to produce the optimal outcomes, and under what conditions? And which ones are most likely to produce less beneficial outcomes?

THINK ABOUT THIS WEAPONS, FORCE, AND SECURITY

Immanuel Kant

© iStock.com/Steven Wynn

Realists from Thomas Hobbes to John Mearsheimer have long argued that military power and the use of force are the essential ingredients for survival and prosperity. Liberal theorists from Immanuel Kant to Robert Keohane and Joseph Nye have argued that military power and the use of force involve consequences that often outweigh their advantages, and so contribute to insecurity as often as not. Consider the role of military power in the approaches to security discussed in this chapter, and their relative strengths and weaknesses.

Thomas Hobbes

© Georgios Kollidas/Shutterstock.com

Do weapons/military arsenals contribute to security or insecurity in world politics?

REVIEW QUESTIONS

1. Why is security such a challenge in world politics?

2. According to realists, how do arms and alliances contribute to security?

3. How can military force be used to produce security?

4. According to liberals, how can arms control and disarmament contribute to security?

5. How does collective security address the problem of security and conflict, and what are its strengths and weaknesses?

6. What is a security community, and how is it developed?

FOR MORE INFORMATION . . .

For more on ways to manage conflict and seek international security, see:

Art, Robert J., and Kenneth Waltz. *The Use of Force: Military Power and International Politics*, 7th ed. New York: Rowman and Littlefield, 2009.

Claude, Inis L. *Power and International Relations*. New York: Random House, 1962.

Kay, Sean. *Global Security in the 21st Century: The Quest for Power and the Search for Peace*, 2nd ed. New York: Rowman and Littlefield, 2011.

Larsen, Jeffrey, and James Wirtz, eds. *Arms Control and Cooperative Security*. Boulder, CO: Lynne Rienner Press, 2009.

Morgan, Patrick. *International Security: Problems and Solutions*. Washington, DC: CQ Press, 2006.

7 | Building Peace:
Structures and Institutions of Cooperation

LEARNING OBJECTIVES

After studying this chapter, you will be able to . . .

7-1 Identify the underlying challenges to cooperation in pursuit of security.

7-2 Describe the nature and functions of international law.

7-3 Evaluate the nature and functions of international organizations.

After finishing
this chapter go
to **PAGE 209**
for **STUDY TOOLS**

A NEW WORLD ORDER?

In 1990, Iraq invaded the neighboring state of Kuwait. Would opportunities for cooperation be strengthened by efforts to meet this challenge, or would such hopes collapse? American President George H. W. Bush addressed a joint session of the U.S. Congress and, in his speech, he argued that:

> Out of these troubled times . . . a new world order . . . can emerge: a new era—freer from the threat of terror, stronger in the pursuit of justice, and more secure in the quest for peace. An era in which the nations of the world, East and West, North and South, can prosper and live in harmony. A hundred generations have searched for this elusive path to peace, while a thousand wars raged across the span of human endeavor. Today that new world is struggling to be born, a world quite different from the one we've known. A world where the rule of law supplants the rule of the jungle. A world in which nations recognize the shared responsibility for freedom and justice. A world where the strong respect the rights of the weak.

After months of preparation, a UN-sanctioned, American-led military coalition drove Iraqi forces from Kuwait. President Bush again appeared before a joint session of the U.S. Congress on March 6, 1991, less than a week after the successful conclusion to the first Gulf War. President Bush stated:

> Twice before in this century, an entire world was convulsed by war. Twice this century, out of the horrors of war hope emerged for enduring peace. Twice before, those hopes proved to be a distant dream, beyond the grasp of man. . . .
>
> Now, we can see a new world coming into view. A world in which there is the very real prospect of a new world order. In the words of Winston Churchill, a "world order" in which "the principles of justice and fair play . . . protect the weak against the strong." A world where the United Nations, freed from cold war stalemate, is poised to fulfill the historic vision of its founders.

Two decades later, one would be hard-pressed to find similar optimism for this "new world order" or the role of the United Nations. Conflict and violence continue, and perhaps the most poignant evidence for this failure is the brutal deaths of 800,000 Rwandans in 1994 while the UN and the world failed to act. The elusive quest for a world of cooperation in which international law and international institutions establish justice and peace continues. We haven't "passed that test" yet.

1. Why are the structures of peace and cooperation so hard to achieve in world politics?

2. Why isn't the rule of law the norm in relations between countries?

3. What might contribute to progress in these areas?

UN Secretary-General Ban Ki-Moon addresses the 67th UN General Assembly at the United Nations headquarters in New York | What gives the leader of the UN influence?

INTRODUCTION: ACHIEVING COOPERATION

Cooperation to achieve peace and security is often challenging in world politics. While the benefits of cooperation seem pretty obvious, achieving it is almost always harder than it initially appears. States and non-state actors cooperate extensively across a wide variety of matters—from the mundane to the life threatening—to achieve common goals and to manage conflicts and disagreements without resort to violence. And yet, in many situations, countries simply fail to cooperate at all, despite their best efforts and the high stakes involved. Cooperation is both commonplace and yet hard, as contradictory as that seems.

For example, since 1994 the United States and most of its friends and allies have basically agreed on a set of rules for how the high seas and its resources will be governed; these rules are contained in the **Law of the Sea Convention**. The United States has signed the convention and chooses to follow its rules, but the U.S. Senate has never formally ratified it. To its critics in the Senate, approving the convention would undermine U.S. sovereignty by denying the United States the ability to do what

it wants regarding the seas and their resources either now or at some point in the future. So despite endorsements by Democratic and Republican presidents (Bill Clinton and George W. Bush, respectively), the ratification of the treaty by 165 other countries and the EU, and the fact that the United States already follows the convention, critics are not persuaded. In addition to helping to ensure freedom of operation by the U.S. Navy in and around the world's oceans and key transit points, the convention also includes rules about handling piracy on the high seas, protecting commercial fishery stocks, and regulating deep-sea mining of rare minerals—just to cite three examples. All of these issues are clearly in the international and economic security interests of the United States, but as long as some leaders and elites see cooperation as "giving something up," it will be hard to accomplish.[1] So while cooperation is smooth for some issues, the road to gaining cooperation and institutionalizing it can be long and bumpy, and not all concerned will want to come along for the ride.

> **Law of the Sea Convention** a treaty that first went into force in 1982 and then was revised in 1994; 165 states are parties to this treaty, as is the EU, which sets rules for the use and protection of the high seas and its resources.

Somali pirates attack the cargo ship _Maersk Alabama_ in a scene from the 2013 movie _Captain Phillips_ | How does the threat of piracy encourage countries to cooperate?

In the last two chapters, we have focused our attention on understanding the nature and causes of conflict and war and on the strategies state and non-state actors have used to manage conflict and achieve international security. In this chapter, we turn to efforts to gain security and manage conflict through structures and institutions of cooperation. We begin by considering the challenges of cooperation faced by the players in world politics. We then turn to a discussion of international law and international organization as cooperative approaches to international security. We conclude by considering the prospects and problems for states and non-state actors as they try to cooperate in their quest for mutual security.

7-1 COOPERATION AND ITS CHALLENGES

At first glance, the benefits of cooperation seem obvious and compelling: peace, prosperity, justice, resources, and expertise shared to solve difficult problems that cross borders. Yet, in world politics, cooperation is often more difficult to attain than we might expect. Countries clearly benefit from working together on a wide array of common problems. Cooperation to control the costly acquisition or dangerous spread of weapons occurs, as does collaboration to promote economic growth and development or protect the environment. However, in all of these areas, the players in world politics often struggle to establish and sustain cooperation. Those observing the world through the realist lens might argue that cooperation appears as the exception rather than the rule. While cooperation can benefit everyone, actually establishing

the institutions, norms, and rules for cooperation is incomplete and episodic.

Let's take a recent example. There's no question that violence and death come as a result of the ready availability of conventional arms in the international system. These weapons, from assault rifles and machine guns to high explosives, are needed for the legitimate defense of states. But such weapons also find their way into the hands of rebel groups, terrorists, and criminal networks, thereby fueling more death and destruction. In 2013 the UN concluded an Arms Trade Treaty to create international rules to prevent conventional weapons from getting into the wrong hands. To date, 121 countries have signed the treaty, and 53 have ratified it, meaning it will go into effect on December 24, 2014. The U.S., Russia, and China have not ratified the agreement, although the U.S. did sign the treaty. While major weapons manufacturers in the international system have a vested interest in ensuring that their sales to legitimate buyers are not constrained, each passing day without more regulation of such weapons means more deaths globally that might have been avoided. So cooperation is needed, but achieving it is hard.

Throughout this text, we have stressed three underlying challenges affecting world politics, and these challenges are just as important for efforts to cooperate in the pursuit of international security as they are for other issues. First, the anarchic nature of world politics complicates cooperation. The absence of a central enforcer to prevent and punish wrongdoing creates incentives for the major political players—states—to take care of themselves and their own interests instead of cooperating. As our discussion of the prisoner's dilemma and stag hunt scenarios in Chapter 1 suggested, cheating is relatively easy and both cheaters and those they cheat against know it, which really affects their willingness to trust and cooperate.

Just as important, the diversity of world politics also complicates cooperation. Even if anarchy could be managed, the fact that states and societies are so different—in size, regime type, economic capabilities, culture, interests, and many other factors—makes achieving harmony very hard. Add in the variety of non-state actors with their own identities, interests, and purposes, and this diversity just gets more difficult to manage. Is there any wonder that cooperation often seems so hard to produce and sustain?

Finally, the complexity of world politics also complicates cooperation. Over time more and more players—states and non-state actors—are engaged across more and more issues that are linked together and affect them. At times, these linkages provide opportunities for

Confiscated conventional weapons in the Gaza Strip | Why is it so hard to control the possession of such weapons, and how do they affect conflict and security?

cooperation, since they can enable players to give and take across several issues to arrive at mutual benefits. In effect, giving on one matter can be linked to getting on another. However, these complex links among actors and issues can also make finding and maintaining common ground on any given issue just that much harder.

As we have pointed out in previous chapters, these challenges are at the heart of conflict and international security issues in world politics. Yet, states and other actors in world politics rely extensively on cooperative approaches to many problems and disagreements. Let's take up two key means by which states and other players in world politics seek international security through the structures and institutions of cooperation: international law and international organization. As we do so, keep in mind the challenges that anarchy, diversity, and complexity pose for each area.

7-2 INTERNATIONAL LAW: NORMS AND RULES WITHOUT CENTRAL AUTHORITY

The first structure of cooperation that we want to consider is international law. According to one popular definition, **international law** is "a body of rules which binds states and other agents in world politics in their relations with one another."[2] Liberals and constructivists have long stressed the development, application, and prospects of international law as a way to manage conflict and

enhance security and trust among states. Realists, on the other hand, tend to be very skeptical of the prospects—and even the desirability—of international law. Alternative theories often see international law as a means that the rich and powerful use to structure the rules of the system for their own benefit. Understanding the role, promise, and problems of international law depends on understanding its nature, sources, and application.

7-2a The Nature of International Law

Beginning with the Dutch jurist Hugo Grotius, whose *On the Law of War and Peace* (1625) is widely regarded as the first book on international law, and particularly following the Treaties of Westphalia (1648), international law was thought to hold great promise for the establishment of peace and justice in world politics. Yet one question we must take up right away is whether international law is really law at all. Some analysts, especially realists, like to place the term in quotes (i.e., "international law") to indicate that it is not really *law* as we understand the term. While *anarchy* does not mean chaos, the anarchic nature of world politics means that there are no central, authoritative institutions to make, enforce, and interpret laws that govern the members of the international system, unless the members themselves act. There is no international legislature to pass laws, and there is no international executive branch full of enforcement agencies to see that laws are obeyed. Furthermore, while there are a variety of courts that have been established for the international system, none of them can compel compliance.

In short, international law is law in the absence of central authority, and that makes it different from domestic law. While liberal theorists acknowledge the impact of decentralization, they stress international law's importance for order and its impact on state behavior, often arguing that the vast majority of states choose to follow international norms and rules most of the time—just like most drivers slow down in school zones even when they can see that there are no police in sight. For realists, these characteristics make international law highly suspect and limited. In such a decentralized environment, they argue, adherence to norms and rules is driven by calculations of self-interest and capability, not legal obligation, so "international law" is really just a set of convenient practices that states have concluded serve their interests . . . and which may be changed or ignored.

> **international law** a body of rules that binds states and other agents in world politics in their relations with one another.

The Just War Tradition and International Law

Hugo Grotius is often credited with being the father of international law, and one area to which he devoted a great deal of attention was the idea of rules for "just wars." Building on the philosophical and theological traditions and work of Augustine and Aquinas, Grotius set the just war tradition in international legal terms. Clearly tied to Western traditions and thought, including the moral arguments of philosophers and the Catholic Church, the development of international laws of war has long emphasized two questions: (1) *jus ad bellum*, or when the use of force is justified; and (2) *jus in bello*, or how wars should be fought once they have started.

The principles of *jus ad bellum*—which were and are the principal concern of international organizations such as the League of Nations and the United Nations in their efforts to keep the peace—emphasize such elements as just cause (*causa justa*, i.e., a case of aggression), competent authority (*auctoritas principis*, i.e., only duly constituted public authorities can decide to use force), right intention (*intentio recta*, i.e., the war must be waged for the purpose identified), last resort (i.e., other alternatives must be exhausted before the resort to war), and proportionality (i.e., the benefits expected from the war must equal or exceed the harm or evil to which it is a response). In recent years, the idea that the use of force should be authorized by the UN or another international organization to be legitimate has also gained significance.

The principles of *jus in bello*—which were the focus of efforts such as the Geneva and Hague conventions (and treaties banning the use of chemical and biological

Hugo Grotius

weapons) to limit specific kinds of warfare and practices—stress the lawful ways that combatants must behave during war. This aspect of the laws of war emphasizes such elements as distinguishing between combatants and noncombatants (i.e., force and violence should be directed only against combatants), proportionality/necessity (the level of force used should not be excessive and should be directed to the defeat of the military forces of the enemy, to limit unnecessary death and destruction), and fair treatment of enemy prisoners of war.

The development of the just war tradition in international law has also included attention to *jus post bellum*, or justice after war, which addresses post–conflict issues such as peace agreements and war crimes tribunals.

Recommended reading: Brian Orend, *War and International Justice* (Waterloo, Canada: Wilfrid Laurier Press, 2001); and Michael Walzer, *Just and Unjust Wars* (New York: Basic Books, 1977).

International law is also law in the absence of another factor that we commonly consider as part of law: shared values and principles. The great diversity in the perspectives, experiences, governments, characteristics, and cultures of the world's societies makes common values and principles hard to come by in world politics. Since a lot of international law has roots in European political thought, it is not surprising that those from different cultures have occasionally questioned why such law should apply to them. What, then, are the sources of international law?

7-2b The Sources of International Law

So where does international law come from then? Since there is no central legislature in world politics that makes law, it obviously comes from other places. Most scholars look to Article 38(1) of the modern-day World Court, or International Court of Justice, as the starting point on the sources of international law. According to this 1946 statute, international law comes from international conventions (treaties) agreed to by states, international custom, "general principles of law recognized by civilized nations," and judicial decisions and the writings of eminent jurists. Of these, the first two are understood as primary sources and the last two as secondary ones. Since 1946, the practices and decisions of international organizations such as the United Nations are also considered a fifth source of international law. Let's take each of these up briefly to explore their nature and implications for world politics. As we briefly review these sources, think carefully about how they influence the nature and application of international law—especially in terms of the consequences of anarchy, diversity, and complexity.

TREATIES The source of international law most comparable to legislation is treaties. A **treaty** is a formal, written agreement among states and is regarded as binding on the signatories. Indeed, a key principle of international law is *pacta sunt servanda*—or "the treaty must be served"—which holds that a formal agreement between states establishes legal obligations that should be upheld once made. Thousands and thousands of treaties and conventions exist, touching on practically every aspect of world politics, from ending wars (the Treaty of Versailles) to regulating fossil fuel emissions (the Kyoto Protocol). However, states are not obligated to sign treaties, and the 1969 **Vienna Convention on the Law of Treaties** (yes, there is a treaty on treaties!) makes it clear that states that are forced to sign treaties are not obligated to uphold them. So what does that mean for treaties as law? International anarchy and its corollaries—sovereignty and self-help—are seen in the voluntary nature of treaties, and the fact that only members of treaties and conventions are bound by them limits their scope. What are the implications for international law?

CUSTOM Although treaties are probably the most significant source of international law in the contemporary context, historically most law derives from **custom**, which the World Court defined as "general practice [of states] accepted as law." Note that two things are present here: a general behavior *and* the idea that it is required (known as *opinio juris*). In effect, this source of international law indicates that law is what many states choose to do repeatedly over a period of time! For example, over time most states sharing a river as their boundary chose to mark their border at the midpoint of the river—or the midpoint of the deepest channel in the river where ships could navigate—as that location worked best for all concerned. What are the consequences of a reliance on custom for the development and application of international law, especially given principles such as state sovereignty?

GENERAL PRINCIPLES The first auxiliary source of international law rests on the idea that evidence of a

Hilippe Wojazer/AFP/Getty Images

France's President Nicolas Sarkozy (R) and Afghanistan's President Hamid Karzai (L) sign a Friendship and Cooperation Treaty in Paris on January 27, 2012 | Why do states such as France and Afghanistan commit themselves to the obligations in treaties?

general practice among states might be seen by identifying laws and practices that many states have adopted and enacted in their own societies. To the extent that many states have laws that look the same, such generally accepted and adopted laws suggest a custom and may form the basis for a treaty codifying the practices. For example, virtually all societies have national laws against assault, murder, or damaging the property of others, so international law recognizes these as general principles that should be respected internationally, as well.

COURT DECISIONS AND WRITINGS OF JURISTS The second auxiliary source of international law points us to what other courts (both domestic and international) and legal experts (lawyers, judges, etc.) have identified as law in previous decisions and legal writing. For the most part, the court decisions involve those of international courts like the World Court or more recently the European Court of Justice. However, in recent decades court decisions at the national or even local levels have also been referenced. Indeed, the emerging principle of

treaty formal, written agreements among states.

Vienna Convention on the Law of Treaties a 1969 agreement among states defining the nature and obligations regarding treaties under international law.

custom the general practice of states accepted as law; a source of international law.

The World Court in The Hague | What are the possibilities and limitations for international law as a means to solve international problems?

Protestors in London rally in support of prosecution of former Chilean leader Augusto Pinochet | What are the implications of Pinochet's indictment and arrest in Europe?

universal jurisdiction—most powerfully and extensively developed in Europe—asserts that states themselves can prosecute violators of certain international laws even if the alleged violator is from another country.

A good example of this principle came in 1998 when former Chilean dictator Augusto Pinochet was indicted by a judge *in Spain* for human rights violations *in Chile* during his rule in the 1970s and 1980s. Pinochet was then arrested *in London* and was held for almost a year and a half as the British government engaged in legal proceedings and considered sending Pinochet to Spain for trial. Ultimately, the British government decided not to extradite Pinochet to Spain for trial (due to his poor health) and sent him home to Chile where he was eventually indicted for human rights crimes in 2001. Pinochet died in 2006 before legal proceedings could be completed, but this instance shows how a jurist's interpretation of international law can help shape it.

DECISIONS OF INTERNATIONAL ORGANIZATIONS

Although not mentioned in the World Court's statute, increasingly since 1946 the decisions of the most authoritative international organizations have also been considered sources of international law. For the most part, those decisions stem from the norms and principles

embodied in the charters that establish such organizations, and which member states sign when they join. In some ways then, ensuing decisions—such as when the United Nations Security Council pronounces a judgment on state behavior or the World Trade Organization rules against a member state's trade practices—are more like interpretation and application of "treaty law," with the organization's charter as the treaty. However, such organizations also contribute to international law in at least three other ways. First, they interpret customary law and help to shape what is regarded as custom and the legal obligations on states that stem from them. Second, they help develop norms and laws with their decisions and recommendations on what should be considered international law. Finally, there is considerable opportunity for international organizations to enter into poorly defined areas of international law to assert legal principles. Many of the more authoritative organizations—the UN Security Council again comes to mind—issue decisions that are partly applications and interpretations and partly assertions of principles.

Together, these sources provide the international community with the emerging and evolving norms and rules of international law. But how are these norms and rules enforced in a world without a central enforcer?

7-2c Compliance and Enforcement

Many observers quickly (and rightly) point out that most states uphold their obligations to most international laws most of the time, and that such norms are important guides to and constraints on their behavior. Given that so much of international law emerges from custom

universal jurisdiction the idea that states have a right and a duty to enforce international law when it comes to the most serious human rights abuses such as genocide, crimes against humanity, torture, war crimes, extrajudicial killings, and forced disappearances, regardless of where these offenses may occur or whether or not the alleged violator is from another country.

and treaty, which states enter into voluntarily, this is not surprising. And to the extent that these norms and rules help states either manage or avoid disagreements and conflicts, international law is an important factor in cooperation. As liberals would assert, in an increasingly interdependent world in which states and other actors must interact regularly and extensively across many issues, international law contributes to orderly and predictable patterns that help to guide behavior. Moreover, the principle of **reciprocity** leads most states to follow laws and conventions so others will be more likely to do so as well. Indeed, it is easy to point to a whole host of matters—from mundane things like international postal agreements and air traffic control to wealth and prosperity-related issues involving trade, finance, and investment to international security matters involving border disputes, war, and violence—in which international norms, rules, and laws are central to successful (and peaceful!) resolution of problems between states and societies. Too often, we take these things for granted and, liberal theorists would say, the regular observance of international law in these matters is the norm for most states, most of the time.

However, realists might counter that it is not the "most of the time" that matters most, but what happens when significant violations occur. As we have seen, most states do not attack other states most of the time (thankfully). But what happens when one does? Most states may engage in fair trade practices most of the time. But what happens when a trade dispute does arise or a state is found to have violated a trade rule? And what about human rights issues? When violations of human rights standards occur in a given country, what enforcement occurs?

In general, the enforcement dilemma for international law follows closely on the challenges posed by anarchy, diversity, and complexity. Since central institutions are weak, the actors in world politics cannot rely on them for strong enforcement. That leaves three main avenues.

NATIONAL ENFORCEMENT States enforce some international law through their own national legal systems. In many such issues of **national enforcement**, national and local governments consider, and even integrate, international law into their rules and practices. Some states have integrated international law into their own national constitutions either by revision or when they were initially drafted. For example, the Constitution of the United States declares that properly ratified treaties and conventions *are* the law of the land and therefore have the same status as any other law.

South African police beat African women with clubs in Durban in 1959 | In the face of the violence of apartheid, why did the United States wait until 1985 to apply sanctions?

And, as we have seen, some states are aggressively advancing the principle of universal jurisdiction to use their national legal systems to apply key international legal principles.

HORIZONTAL ENFORCEMENT The most common approach is **horizontal enforcement**—those measures that states can take when a state violates an international law and other states can attempt to punish the violator themselves. This enforcement approach is a direct function of the anarchic international system in which states are sovereign actors. States can protest diplomatically, even severing diplomatic ties. They can threaten and enact economic sanctions (see Chapter 9 for a thorough discussion of this form of economic statecraft) by boycotting or embargoing trade with the violator. They can even threaten or use force in a wide range of ways to punish the violator.

The problems with these horizontal mechanisms are pretty obvious, and a good reason why international law is not very evenly applied. If states themselves determine when a violation occurs, and what to

reciprocity in international law, the principle that a state follows international law so that others will do so in return.

national enforcement states enforce some international law through their own national legal systems.

horizontal enforcement those measures that states themselves can take when a state violates an international law and other states can attempt to punish the violator themselves.

The Marshall Islands, International Law, and the World Court

In April 2014, the Marshall Islands, a small state in the Pacific Ocean (population 68,000, about the same size as Sheboygan, Wisconsin), sued nine other states in the World Court for violating the non-proliferation regime and Non-Proliferation Treaty (see Chapter 6). This island state was the site of almost six dozen nuclear tests in the 12 years after World War II, the results of which caused long-term harm to its citizens and territory. According to the foreign minister of the Marshall Islands, "Our people have suffered the catastrophic and irreparable damage of these weapons, and we vow to fight so that no one else on earth will ever again experience these atrocities."

According to the Marshall Islands, as signatories of the NPT, the U.S., U.K., France, Russia, and China—the official nuclear weapons states of the treaty—were obligated to work toward nuclear disarmament by Article VI of the treaty. The Marshall Islands also brought the case against India, Pakistan, North Korea, and Israel for violating what the Marshall Islands characterized as customary international law against acquiring nuclear weapons. The court documents filed in the cases assert that "the long delay in fulfilling the obligations enshrined in article VI of the NPT constitutes a flagrant denial of human justice."

India, Pakistan, Israel, and North Korea are not signatories of the NPT. Moreover, only the U.K., India, and

Photo courtesy of National Nuclear Security Administration/Nevada Field Office

Nuclear test at the Bikini Atoll, Marshall Islands, 1954 | What chance does tiny Marshall Islands have to win a case in the World Court against countries like the United States, United Kingdom, France, Russia, China, India, Pakistan, Israel, and North Korea?

Pakistan have accepted the compulsory jurisdiction of the World Court.[3]

1. Why do you think the Marshall Islands would choose to go to the World Court to achieve its goals on this matter?

2. What do you think of the chances of the Marshall Islands of getting the accused states to court, much less winning the case against them? Why?

3. What does this example suggest about the nature of international law and its enforcement?

---

do in response, that opens the door for very selective application of law. Friends, allies, trading partners, and states with cultural ties might be protected by some states. For example, the United States proved reluctant to apply sanctions to South Africa in the 1970s and early 1980s, in large part because of that country's strategic importance and economic ties, in spite of the brutally repressive white minority apartheid regime that systematically violated the core human rights of the majority black population.

Even the measures available to states in this horizontal approach are problematic. Diplomatic protests might be significant for small issues, but for major issues involving security, they are likely to be too weak. For example, diplomatic protests did not stop the Russian

annexation of Crimea or further incursions into eastern Ukraine in 2014. As we detail in Chapter 9, economic sanctions are problematic and available research suggests they rarely work, while imposing costs on the sanctioning state itself, as well as ordinary citizens in the target state. Using military force to enforce international law is very costly, and most states do not have the capacity for doing so. That means the world depends on the most powerful countries for such actions, and those countries may have other interests at stake. Finally, to the extent that horizontal enforcement is likely to work, it is most effective when the measures are broadly enacted by a relatively large multilateral coalition. Given the great diversity of interests, linkages, and capabilities, assembling such a coalition is difficult to achieve.

The United States and the World Court

When are international institutions most likely and least likely to matter? Realists, liberals, constructivists, Marxists, feminists, and foreign policy theorists are all likely to have different answers to this question. Let's take a look at three examples of the World Court and cases involving the United States and consider what insights they offer on the role and influence of the World Court in practice. Remember, the U.S. has regularly been a champion of the establishment of international courts and other organizations, but its relationship to them has been complex and highlights several key issues about the role and application of international law in world politics.

The United States and Iran, 1980

In the aftermath of the Iranian revolution, conflict between the United States and Iran escalated, and in late 1979, Iranian militants seized the U.S. Embassy in Tehran, taking 66 Americans hostage. Although some were released, 52 Americans were held for 444 days by the Iranian government, which took control of the hostages from the militants soon after their capture. The United States protested and tried to gain the release of the Americans, including bringing the case to the World Court. In 1980, the World Court ruled that the hostage taking was a violation of international law and ordered the release of the hostages. Iran simply refused. The United States condemned Iran's decision and ratcheted up pressure, eventually attempting a military rescue mission that failed. The hostages were finally released in January, 1981, on the same day that President Ronald Reagan took office, replacing Jimmy Carter.

The United States and Nicaragua, 1984

In the 1980s, the United States and Nicaragua were embroiled in a conflict stemming from the 1979 revolution in that country that overthrew longtime dictator and U.S. ally Anastasio Somoza and replaced his regime with a leftist government led by the Sandinistas, a revolutionary movement that had spearheaded the rebellion against the Somoza regime. Concerned that a leftist regime with ties to Cuba and the Soviet Union would pose a threat to the Central American region, the United States soon took steps against the Sandinista regime, including organizing, equipping, and supporting the Contras, a counterrevolutionary movement composed largely of former Somoza

supporters and disaffected Nicaraguan peasants, to fight against the new regime. In the course of this conflict, the United States engaged in the mining of Nicaragua harbors to inflict damage on shipping. Nicaragua charged the United States with violating international law in the harbor mining and what it characterized as aggression against Nicaragua and brought the complaint to the World Court. The United States first argued that the World Court did not have jurisdiction and then argued that the United States was exercising its rights to self-defense. The World Court found in favor of Nicaragua and concluded that the United States had engaged in unlawful use of force in the mining and support for the Contras. It called on the United States to "cease and refrain" its unlawful use of force and to pay reparations to Nicaragua. The United States refused to comply, rejected the ruling, and promptly withdrew its acceptance of the World Court's compulsory jurisdiction. Subsequent efforts by Nicaragua to bring the World Court's judgment to the United Nations for support failed: The United States vetoed UN Security Council resolutions supporting Nicaragua several times in 1985 and 1986, and when the UN General Assembly voted 94 to 3 that the United States should comply with the court's ruling (only El Salvador and Israel joined the United States in opposing the resolution; on a subsequent resolution of the same nature, only Israel joined the United States), the United States ignored the resolution.

The United States and Iran, 1988

In 1988, the USS *Vincennes* fired on and downed Iran Air Flight 655 in the Persian Gulf during the U.S. naval operation to protect Kuwaiti oil transport and other shipping. All 290 people onboard were killed. Iran charged the United States with violations of international air traffic laws and took the case to the World Court. In 1989, the United States agreed to take part in the proceedings, in part to avoid appearing hypocritical at a time that it was arguing for broader international cooperation and reliance on international law and organization for international conflict resolution. Seven years later, in 1996, the United States and Iran reached an agreement with the World Court's help to settle the dispute and end the case without the World Court's ruling. The United States agreed to pay $61.8 million to compensate the Iranian victims' families, but the settlement did not involve any admission or acceptance of legal guilt or responsibility.

Even more recent situations help to illustrate the dilemmas underlying these cases. For example, the United

States is a member (since ratification in 1990) of the international Convention Against Torture and Other Cruel, Inhuman or Degrading Treatment or Punishment. What do you think would happen if the World Court concluded that the United States had violated international law through the aggressive interrogation procedures implemented in the post–September 11 war on terrorism?

1. How might realists, liberals, constructivists, Marxists, feminists, and foreign policy theorists explain these cases and their outcomes?

2. What do these cases suggest about the enforcement of international law?

VERTICAL ENFORCEMENT There are international institutions that enforce international law, as well. However, because of the anarchic character of the international system, few international institutions have the authority to enforce international law outright. **Vertical enforcement** is rare and, instead, most international institutions are limited to identifying and condemning violations and recommending or authorizing the member states of the organizations to take actions to enforce a rule or punish a violator. For example, members of the United Nations sign a charter to gain membership, and when they violate principles of the charter, their actions can be discussed in the UN General Assembly, which can call for actions by other members in response. The UN Security Council can also consider alleged violations and authorize punitive actions such as sanctions and even the application of military force. In both cases, however, member states themselves must agree to take up the measures and are not bound to do so.

International courts also play a role, although generally not much like the courts with which we are familiar. The International Court of Justice—or World Court—which we discussed earlier, is a 15-judge panel located in The Hague in the Netherlands and can hear cases on disputes between states (but only between states, and only states can bring cases). The judgments of the World Court are supposed to be binding. However, the World Court does not have **compulsory jurisdiction**; both parties to a dispute must voluntarily submit the case to the court before it can act. When the court does render a judgment, it relies on the members themselves to agree to implement it, as well. Since its establishment right after World War II, the World Court has been involved in less than 150 cases. Think about that for a moment—over 60 years of operation in

world politics, with all the issues and disputes that have occurred among all the many states…and less than 150 of them have gone to the court! That should tell you something about its role.

There are other international courts that play a role, but most of them are limited by the same issues already highlighted. Regional organizations such as the Organization of American States (in the Western Hemisphere) and the African Union have courts whose operations are much like the World Court. The European Court of Justice, by contrast, which is the highest court of the European Union and interprets EU laws for all member states, is much more authoritative. Another example is the relatively new International Criminal Court (ICC), which we discuss in detail in Chapter 11. The ICC exists to try individuals (not states!) accused of committing aggression, genocide, war crimes, and crimes against humanity. Specialized international courts also exist to help interpret and apply international law. Examples include the World Trade Organization Dispute Settlement Body, the International Tribunal on the Law of the Sea, and special tribunals established for conflicts in the former Yugoslavia, Rwanda, Cambodia, Lebanon, and Sierra Leone.

CONTINENTAL/AFP/Getty Images

The World Court meets in 2004 to hear a dispute between Palestinians and Israel | What kinds of issues are most likely to come before the World Court?

vertical enforcement the enforcement of international law by international institutions.

compulsory jurisdiction in international law, the condition in which parties to a dispute must submit the case to a court.

INTERNATIONAL ORGANIZATIONS: THE EUROPEAN UNION, THE UNITED NATIONS, AND MANY OTHERS

Our second structure of cooperation is international organizations. Let's consider the nature and role of international organizations (IOs) and reflect on why sovereign states—which tend to guard their sovereignty and independence so jealously—would establish international institutions in the first place. Then, we will review the types of IOs that exist, with some brief description of a few examples. We will then conclude this section with a short evaluation of the United Nations and its role and functions in fostering cooperation.

7-3a Why Do International Organizations Exist?

It is at least a bit puzzling that independent states in an anarchic world establish international institutions that constrain their independence and freedom in various degrees. And yet, according to the *Yearbook of International Organizations*, there are well over 6,000 IOs (not including non-governmental organizations), which include conventional institutions like the United Nations, the World Trade Organization, and many other more specialized bodies like the International Labor Organization and the World Health Organization. This is a large number in a world that is supposedly dominated by just under 200 independent states! Understanding why they exist is contentious, and multiple perspectives and arguments have been offered. For analytical purposes, we can organize the arguments into two categories: power-based explanations and problem-based explanations.

POWER-BASED EXPLANATIONS One set of arguments stresses that IOs reflect state interests and, in particular, the interests of the most powerful states. For example, both realist and Marxist-based approaches to world politics like world systems theory argue that powerful states create IOs to support norms and practices that advance their interests and channel other states into behavior that the powerful prefer. Realists stress self-interested states, while Marxist-based approaches stress economic elites and the interests of powerful capitalist states, but the common core of the argument is that such states sponsor organizations such as the United Nations or the World Trade Organization to control and constrain the behavior of others. Liberal approaches also offer power-based arguments—often contending that powerful states establish IOs to serve very broad interests in order and stability, while sacrificing narrower and more specific outcomes and bearing the costs of providing some "public goods" for the overall benefit of all (and themselves, of course).[4] Some also argue that less-powerful states also attempt to establish or steer IOs toward protecting and asserting their interests, relying on their ability to outnumber powerful states in voting procedures within existing IOs to redirect and create new IOs.[5] The example of the United States and the World Court nicely illustrates this dynamic: the United States supported the World Court when its interests were served in the case of the Iranian Hostage Crisis but ignored it in the Nicaraguan case when its interests were not served.

PROBLEM-BASED EXPLANATIONS Another perspective focuses on the linkages among and common problems faced by states and other actors in world politics. These arguments—usually offered by liberal and constructivist theorists—emphasize the need and desire among states and others to cooperate to address problems together in order to expand benefits and reduce conflict. A good example of this argument is the one we discussed in the last chapter (Chapter 6) when we described theories of functionalism and neo-functionalism and the promotion of transnational cooperation on economic and social problems that grow to link societies together.[6] In the context of this chapter, IOs are established to enable specific technical cooperation on economic and social issues that build linkages and shared interests among societies. The benefits from these linkages and the cooperation they promote often expand to more areas, leading to even greater cooperation and institutional connections.[7] As we said in Chapter 6, a good example of this can be seen in the development of the European Union and the various institutions it now involves.

Another example of this explanation focuses on the presence of transnational problems that transcend state boundaries and cannot be addressed by actions by any one state. The need to address such issues—like those of the environment, disease, and others—leads states to establish IOs to help coordinate their efforts more effectively and efficiently. We might also include arguments that center on the need to cooperate to provide and sustain collective goods. In Chapter 12, we discuss the concept of "the tragedy of the commons," in which common resources (like the oceans) are susceptible to abuse or overuse, in which case IOs may help states share and preserve such resources or refrain from short-sighted exploitation in favor of longer-term calculations. In any of these cases, the bottom line is that states have reasons to cooperate and manage conflicts, and that, once established, the IOs that are created take on lives of their own and influence and channel state behavior.

THE ROLES AND FUNCTIONS OF IOs There are strengths and weaknesses to both power-based and problem-based explanations by themselves. Together, however, these arguments suggest a range of roles and functions for IOs as structures and institutions for cooperation and conflict management. Thus, IOs:

- Serve as instruments for states to advance their interests and influence other states to play the game of world politics according to the rules and interests of the powerful.

- Serve as forums for states to communicate, negotiate, and advance their interests, and may even provide support for bargaining and negotiation in third-party diplomacy.

- Generate and disseminate information and technical expertise.

- Regularize interactions and habits of behavior on issues, and facilitate national and transnational linkages and networks that contribute even further to norms of procedure and behavior.

- Coordinate and pool resources to address common problems.

- Contribute to the generation of and institutionalization of norms and rules.

- Reduce uncertainty, enhance communication and interactions, and reduce the incentives for cheating in world politics.

- Constrain state behavior and expand avenues for punishment.

In short, IOs perform many different roles and functions in the contemporary system. Of course, different perspectives tend to stress some over others. Realists, for example, tend to see IOs as instruments of states seeking to advance their interests, used by the most powerful states when it suits them, and ignored by them when they do not. Liberals and constructivists tend to see IOs as more important in their own right, and they emphasize their roles in generating and disseminating norms and rules, coordinating behavior, and constraining states. Marxists are actually quite similar to realists, tending to see IOs as instruments of the wealthy, dominant states of the core, or, when established by the developing world, as instruments of poorer states seeking to break the exploitative and dependent relationships with the core by using the power of their numbers (especially in IOs run by majority-rule decision-making, which we discuss in the next section).

7-3b Types of International Organizations

With as many as 6,000 IOs in the world today, we cannot identify and discuss them all. However, we can think about types of organizations and provide examples of each. Once we do that, we can think about some of the most prominent examples of IOs. Then, we will devote attention to two of the most important IOs in world politics: the European Union, the most powerful regional IO, and the United Nations, the most expansive global, multi-purpose IO.

TYPE I: SCOPE AND MEMBERSHIP One good way to develop a sense of the IOs is to categorize them according to scope (or the range of issues they address) and membership (or who is eligible to join them). For scope, a simple distinction we can make is between IOs that address multiple issues across the political, economic, and social spheres or just a single issue. In terms of membership, we can simply distinguish between IOs that allow any state to join (global) and those who restrict membership on the basis of geographic region (regional). If we combine these two dimensions, we get the categories shown in Table 7-1. Let's take up each with some examples.

TABLE 7-1	A TYPOLOGY OF INTERNATIONAL ORGANIZATIONS	
MEMBERSHIP	**SCOPE**	
	SINGLE ISSUE	**MULTIPLE ISSUE**
GLOBAL	International Monetary Fund World Bank World Trade Organization	United Nations
REGIONAL	Andean Common Market European Environment Agency Inter-American Institute for Cooperation on Agriculture Asia-Pacific Economic Cooperation	European Union Organization of American States African Union Association of Southeast Asian Nations

© Cengage Learning®

Map 7-1

The European Union

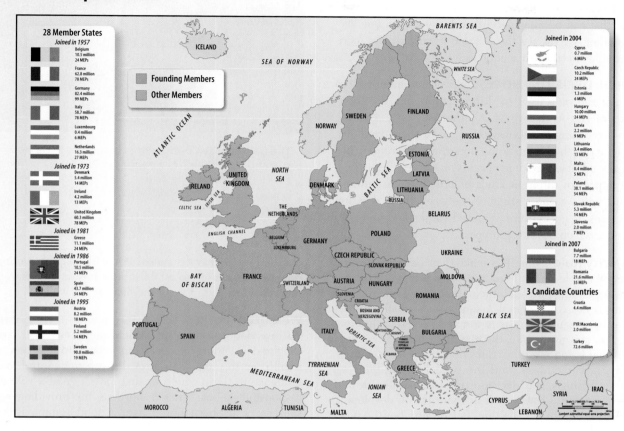

28 Member States

Joined in 1957

Belgium
10.5 million
24 MEPs

France
62.8 million
78 MEPs

Germany
82.4 million
99 MEPs

Italy
58.7 million
78 MEPs

Luxembourg
0.4 million
6 MEPs

Netherlands
16.3 million
27 MEPs

Joined in 1973

Denmark
5.4 million
14 MEPs

Ireland
4.2 million
13 MEPs

United Kingdom
60.3 million
78 MEPs

Joined in 1981

Greece
11.1 million
24 MEPs

Joined in 1986

Portugal
10.5 million
24 MEPs

Spain
43.7 million
54 MEPs

Joined in 1995

Austria
8.2 million
18 MEPs

Finland
5.2 million
14 MEPs

Sweden
90.0 million
19 MEPs

Founding Members
Other Members

Joined in 2004

Cyprus
0.7 million
6 MEPs

Czech Republic
10.2 million
24 MEPs

Estonia
1.3 million
6 MEPs

Hungary
10.00 million
24 MEPs

Latvia
2.2 million
9 MEPs

Lithuania
3.4 million
13 MEPs

Malta
0.4 million
5 MEPs

Poland
38.1 million
54 MEPs

Slovak Republic
5.3 million
14 MEPs

Slovenia
2.0 million
7 MEPs

Joined in 2007

Bulgaria
7.7 million
18 MEPs

Romania
21.6 million
35 MEPs

3 Candidate Countries

Croatia
4.4 million

FYR Macedonia
2.0 million

Turkey
72.6 million

What benefits does membership in the EU provide to the countries of Europe?

© Cengage Learning®

First, there are a wide variety of *global, single-issue IOs* that include members from all over the world but concentrate on a single issue. Examples of these include the International Monetary Fund, which emphasizes balance of payments and financial matters, and the World Trade Organization, which addresses the trade relations and trade practices among its members. Many other such IOs exist for issues related to the environment, global health, human rights, nuclear energy, and a great variety of other things.

Second, there are many *regional, single-issue IOs*. One very common issue on which such IOs focus is economic cooperation, and APEC, or Asia Pacific Economic Cooperation, is a good example of this type of IO. In fact, a very large number of the regions and even subregions of the world (the Andean Common Market illustrates a subregional IO of this type) have some kind of economic organization to promote trade and economic integration.

The example mentioned—the Andean Common Market—is a customs union for Bolivia, Ecuador, Colombia, and Peru. Just as for global IOs of this type, regional, single-issue IOs exist for the environment, global health, human rights, nuclear energy, and a great variety of other things.

Third, *regional, multiple-issue organizations* are also on the rise. Perhaps the best and most powerful example of these is the European Union (see Map 7-1 and our more detailed discussion in the next section). The EU unites 28 European countries in an economic, social, and political organization characterized by a common market and currency (for 18 of its members), with central political and economic institutions such as the European Parliament, the Council of the European Union, the European Council, the European Commission, the European Court of Justice, and the European Central Bank. Other regional, multi-issue IOs include the Association of Southeast Asian Nations (ASEAN) and the Economic Community of

Western African States (ECOWAS). Like the EU, many of this type of IO began as a regional, single-issue IO (economic) and have expanded into other issue areas.

Fourth, the most obvious *global, multi-issue IO* is the United Nations, which addresses virtually every issue that can be imagined in world politics in one way or another. We discuss the UN and its subsidiaries more thoroughly in the next section as well.

TYPE II: DECISION PROCESS Scope and membership are not the only ways to distinguish among the thousands of IOs in the world. Another way is to separate them according to the ways they make their decisions. This not only highlights some important differences, but it also lends itself to some insights on the role, influence, and impact of different kinds of IOs. For the purpose of analysis, we can distinguish between three decision processes: majority rule, weighted voting, and unit veto systems, which has two subtypes.

Majority Rule Some IOs make their decisions on the basis of simple or modified **majority rule**, with the results depending purely on the numbers. A good example of this is the UN General Assembly, where all member states have equal representation and each state has one vote. On any given issue, the majority rules (a two-thirds threshold is required for issues related to peace and security, new members, and the peacekeeping budget). Not surprisingly, this decision rule is generally favored by less-powerful states such as those of the developing world, for the simple fact that they outnumber the powerful and wealthy. So, for example, in 1974, developing states (known as the Group of 77, or G-77 then) used the UN General Assembly to pass the Declaration on the Establishment of a New International Economic Order designed to give greater control and advantage to developing states in economic relationships like trade, finance, aid, and investment. Not surprisingly, this resolution was

The UN Security Council votes to require Syria to surrender its chemical weapons in 2013 | How do you think the possession of the veto by the United States, France, Russia, United Kingdom, and China affects the UN Security Council?

opposed by developed states. IOs with majority voting rules are often used to establish new IOs or subsidiaries that reflect the interests of the majority, as well.

Weighted Voting Other IOs adopt a **weighted voting** decision rule in which member votes are weighted according to some factor related to size, power, wealth, or the like. This provides greater control and influence to those countries that have a greater role or responsibility, bear greater burdens for providing resources, or just have more power. A good example is the **International Monetary Fund (IMF)**. All members of the IMF are represented but are assigned a share of the vote based on the size of their contribution—or quota—to the IMF's lending capital (which is, in turn, based on the size of the country's economy). France and the United Kingdom, for example, each have about 4.5 percent of the votes, while Japan and Germany have just over and just under 6 percent, respectively. China has less than 4 percent, but the United States has almost 17 percent of the vote, the largest share. Contrast this with, say, Sierra Leone, which has 0.07 percent of the vote, Chile, which has about 0.4 percent, or Brazil, which has about 1.75 percent. It is also worth noting that IMF decisions for aid and financing usually require a 70 percent majority or 85 percent majority for major decisions (so the United States can block any major decision all on its own). At its creation, the United States had over 30 percent of the vote, with obvious implications.

Unit Veto In IOs with a **unit veto** decision rule, some or all members can block decisions with their votes. As U.S. President Abraham Lincoln is reported to have once said, "Gentleman, the vote is 15-1 . . . the 1 prevails." A pure unit veto decision rule requires unanimity, so every member effectively exercises a veto. In the League

majority rule in international organizations, a decision process that relies on voting with one vote per member, in which gaining a majority of the votes prevails.

weighted voting in international organizations, a decision rule in which member votes are weighted according to some factor related to size, power, or wealth.

International Monetary Fund (IMF) one of the Bretton Woods organizations created in 1946 to help maintain a cooperative international financial system. The IMF helps countries facing balance-of-payment problems with short-term loans and also helps countries reschedule their debt.

unit veto in international organizations, a decision rule in which some or all members can block decisions with their votes: in a pure unit veto decision rule every member exercises a veto; in a modified unit veto, only some members have the veto power.

TABLE 7-2

TABLE 7-2 UN SECURITY COUNCIL VETOES BY P-5 MEMBERS, 1946–2014

Country	1946–1959	1960–1969	1970–1979	1980–1989	1990–2000	2001–2014
U.S.	0	0	21	42	5	11
U.K.	2	1	12	14	0	0
France	2	0	7	7	0	0
Russia	66	14	6	4	2	8
China*	0	0	1	0	2	5

NOTE: China's seat on the UNSC was held by Taiwan from 1949–1971 before the UNGA voted to recognize the People's Republic of China (mainland) as the lawful representative of China.

Source: data compiled from Security Council Veto List, http://www.un.org/depts/dhl/resguide/scact_veto_en.shtml.

of Nations, the forerunner to the United Nations, every member of the League Council could exercise veto power on any substantive issue before the league. A modified unit veto assigns the veto power to some members of the IO. The best example of this decision rule is the UN Security Council, which is made up of 15 members. Ten of those members are elected by the UN General Assembly (with regional allocations for Africa, Latin America, Asia, Europe, Eastern Europe, and "other areas") for two-year terms, and each of these members has one vote in the UNSC. The other five members are permanent—the United States, Russia, China, France, and the United Kingdom. These **P-5** (or "perm-5," as they are often known) are the main founders of the UN, the world's first official nuclear weapons states, and each possesses a veto so that if any one votes against a substantive UNSC measure, it is defeated (see Table 7-2 on the use of the UNSC veto power). Passage of UNSC substantive measures also requires at least nine affirmative votes, so in effect, the ten elected members together have a collective veto to block the perm-5 in the unlikely event they are unified.

How do these categorizations help us understand IOs? Although there are exceptions, in general the more narrowly drawn the IO is (e.g., scope and membership) the more likely it is to exercise more authoritative influence over its members. Why do you think this might often be the case? What might realists, liberals, constructivists, and Marxist-based approaches say about this? Also, weaker states tend to prefer majoritarian IOs, while more powerful states tend to prefer IOs with weighted or unit veto systems. Finally, in general the most authoritative IOs in the world today—the ones whose decisions are the most binding on their members—tend to be less representative and less egalitarian in their decision schemes. The UNGA, for example, is the most representative IO in the world and makes its decisions on majority voting, but its measures are very rarely binding. The UNSC, which includes less than 10 percent of the world's member states and is dominated by the P-5, is among the most powerful and authoritative. Again, consider why you think this is the case and what realists, liberals, constructivists, and Marxist-based approaches might offer as explanations.

7-3c Key International Organizations in World Politics

With these ways of distinguishing between IOs in mind, let's briefly summarize some of the major international organizations.

The International Monetary Fund The IMF was established at the end of World War II as part of the Bretton Woods system of international financial organizations to improve cooperation and coordination of the world's economy. With 29 original members led by the U.S., the IMF steadily increased global membership to its current status with 188 members. A global, single-issue organization with weighted voting, the IMF originally served two purposes: (1) a source of emergency lending for countries with balance of payments crises, with loans drawn from the pooled resources of IMF member states; (2) an exchange rate regime in which member currencies were pegged within a small range of fluctuation to the value of the U.S. dollar, which itself was fixed at the value of $35 per ounce of gold. To achieve the first purpose, the IMF has granted short-term loans to aid countries with financial crises—a good example is the IMF lending in the late 1990s to the countries disrupted by the Asian currency crisis—with conditions typically attached to guide liberal reforms in recipient states. The IMF's exchange rate regime ended in 1971 when the U.S. unilaterally suspended the fixed exchange rate of the dollar, starting a floating exchange rate system that continues today. Since its existence, the IMF has also served as a kind of global economy watchdog, collecting and disseminating economic information about member states and the world economy to facilitate planning and coordination. IMF activity in this arena became more public beginning in the 1990s.

P-5 (Perm-5) the five permanent members of the UN Security Council—the United States, Britain, France, China, and Russia—each of which holds veto power.

FIGURE 7-1   THE WORLD BANK GROUP

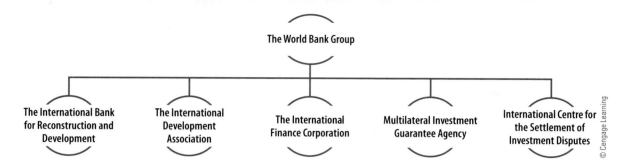

The World Bank Group

The International Bank for Reconstruction and Development · The International Development Association · The International Finance Corporation · Multilateral Investment Guarantee Agency · International Centre for the Settlement of Investment Disputes

© Cengage Learning

The World Bank Also created as part of the Bretton Woods system, the **World Bank** is actually a group of five institutions (see Figure 7-1) created to provide long-term developmental loans to members. Also a global, single issue institution with weighted voting procedures, the World Bank began with the same original members as the IMF, and expanded to its current membership of 188 states over the years after World War II. The World Bank's voting power is weighted by member contributions, which are based on member states' economies. Since 2010, the most powerful members (in terms of their voting weight) are the U.S. (15.85%), Japan (6.84%), China (4.42%), Germany (4.00%), the U.K. (3.75%), France (3.75%), India (2.91%), Russia (2.77%), Saudi Arabia (2.77%), and Italy (2.64%). The main emphasis of the World Bank's lending activities is poverty reduction. Since the end of the Cold War, in the neo-Westphalian era the World Bank has increasingly emphasized sustainable development in its activities.

The General Agreement on Tariffs and Trade/ World Trade Organization During the Bretton Woods conference, the diplomats involved tried to create an organization that would govern international trade as well, but the negotiations for an "International Trade Organization" to stand along the IMF and World Bank failed, largely because of disagreements over agriculture. Instead, the General Agreement on Tariffs and Trade (GATT) was created by 23 founding members led by the U.S., U.K., and France with a more limited goal: to promote free trade in the world. Over time,

membership grew to its current 159 member states (2013) in the GATT successor, the World Trade Organization. Unlike the IMF and World Bank, GATT/WTO does not operate with a weighted voting system, but in a consensus-oriented fashion with each member state having an equal voice.

The organization promoted trade liberalization through **Most-Favored Nation (MFN)** status (in the United States, MFN is now referred to as NTR, or Normal Trade Relations). Each GATT member was required to give all other members the lowest tariff rate available—this rate was considered the MFN rate. Progress toward trade liberalization took place over a series of negotiating rounds targeted at reducing tariffs and other barriers to trade. During these rounds, GATT encouraged states to reciprocate toward each other when making trade deals. Thus, if Canada offered Japan a lower tariff rate on imported sake, Japan should offer Canada a lower rate on its imports of maple syrup. In 1995, GATT was finally replaced by the World Trade Organization (WTO), which created a central body with enforcement powers over free trade rules and practices. Basically, if one state blocks another state from selling its products, the two states can go to the Dispute Settlement Body—effectively a "trade court"—and the WTO will determine if a rule is being broken. If the trade barrier is illegal under WTO rules, then the plaintiff state is permitted to sanction the other state to regain the revenue lost by not being able to sell its goods and services. In short, the WTO has the ability to write rules, administer them, adjudicate disputes, and penalize those who break the rules—effectively enforcing the agreements GATT could only hope were accepted voluntarily.

Examples of Regional Single-Issue Organizations

In the last several decades of the twentieth century, many regional organizations focused on particular issues were established. As noted, one area for the growth of such organizations is economic cooperation, with the Andean Common Market, which we discussed earlier, as an example. Another good example in the category of

World Bank a Bretton Woods organization created in 1945 that provides loans and grants to countries for long-term development. The World Bank started by helping fund the reconstruction of Europe after World War II and later focused on helping countries in the developing world grow their economies.

Most-Favored Nation (MFN) the trade status that members of the GATT gave to each other, ensuring that each received the best trade terms available. MFN could also be granted to non-members if a country chose to do so.

economic cooperation is Asia-Pacific Economic Cooperation (APEC), established in 1989 to foster economic growth, strengthen the Asia-Pacific community, and reduce tariffs and other trade barriers across the Asia-Pacific region. APEC currently has 21 members, including the major Asian states plus Pacific states like the U.S., Canada, Australia, New Zealand, Chile, Mexico, Peru, and Russia. There are many, many other regional organizations focused on different issues as well, far too many to summarize here. Two illustrations identified in Table 7-1 highlight this area, however. The Inter-American Institute for Cooperation on Agriculture was originally established in 1942 to promote the development, coordination, and expansion of regional agricultural production and trade in the Western Hemisphere. In the last decades of the twentieth century, it expanded to 33 states in the region, and increasingly concentrated on sustainable agricultural development. The European Environment Agency serves as another example, but in a different way, since this agency was created within the European Union, a much larger, regional, multi-issue organization (see our discussion in the following pages). Established in 1990, the European Environment Agency began its activities in 1993–1994, providing information and coordinating the efforts of EU members to pursue environmental safety and environmentally sustainable economic development.

Examples of General Regional Organizations

Our last category includes broad, regionally based organizations that address a wide scope of issues. Regionalism, typically defined by geographic proximity (although some "regional" organizations expand out of their geographic area) and interdependence among a specific group of states (as well as non-state actors), is based on the idea of building and fostering cooperation among such players for their mutual benefit. In the latter twentieth and early twenty-first centuries, regional organizations became increasingly important in world politics. There are a variety of such IOs, with different degrees of development, scope, influence, and authority.

In the Middle East, regional organizations are the least developed, despite the unifying ties of language, ethnicity, and religion. In 1945, the League of Arab States was established by Egypt, Jordan, Syria, Iraq, Lebanon, and Saudi Arabia to promote and foster Arab unity, but its role has been very limited. Its main body is a council formed of the foreign ministers of its member states, which now includes 22 countries. It also has a defense council, an economic council, and other agencies, but its role continues to be limited. The Gulf Cooperation Council (GCC) was established in 1981 and includes the six Arab states of the Persian Gulf region: Bahrain, Kuwait, Qatar, Saudi Arabia, Oman, and the United Arab Emirates. The GCC was created to promote economic cooperation among its members, but also as a response to threat posed by Iran after the Iranian revolution. While the GCC has free trade among its members, its main institutions—a Supreme Council (whose decisions must be unanimous and therefore operates according to a pure unit veto system) and Ministerial Council—do most of the GCC's work, and its role and influence have been limited to serving as a forum for its members to discuss and coordinate their activities.

In Asia, in addition to APEC (which we discussed above), there is the Association of Southeast Asian Nations (ASEAN), originally established in 1967 by Indonesia, Singapore, Malaysia, Thailand, and the Philippines. Very de-centralized and more informal than other organizations in regions, ASEAN stresses consultation, coordination, and consensus-building, and has expanded to ten members with the addition of Vietnam, Cambodia, Laos, Brunei, and Myanmar (Burma). ASEAN focuses on economic growth and development and regional security and cooperation. In 1994, ASEAN established the ASEAN Regional Forum (ARF) to promote cooperative security in Asia, which now includes 28 members (including the EU, U.S., Russia, India, China, Canada, and others).

In Africa, the great diversity of the continent's peoples and states has worked against strong regional organizations. In 1964, 31 states of Africa established the Organization of African Unity (OAU), a loosely structured association emphasizing voluntary cooperation. In its early years, it functioned mainly as a forum, but also made contributions to conflict resolution in a variety of African disputes, offering mediation in some and peace keeping in others. In 2002, the OAU was replaced with the African Union (AU), with 54 current members. The AU strengthened the regional institutions and added some additional agencies to improve cooperation and coordination in the region. These include an Assembly of Heads of State and Government, the supreme body of the organization, and a commission that serves as the administrative arm for day-to-day activities. A new Peace and Security Council (with 15 rotating members) promotes collective security, engages in conflict resolution, and authorizes interventions for peace and humanitarian purposes. The AU also established a Pan-African Parliament in 2004, mostly as a consultative body, to which each member sends five legislators (one of which must be a woman). The AU also created the Economic, Social and Cultural Council, the African Court of Justice, the African Central Bank, the African Monetary Fund, and the African Investment Bank. Since Africa is such vast continent, it is not surprising to find that subregional organizations have also been established, including the Economic Community of West African States (ECOWAS) and the Southern African Development Community (SADC) as well.

The Western Hemisphere has a long history of regional initiatives going back to the nineteenth century that led to the 1948 establishment of the Organization of American States (OAS) by 21 countries of the region. It now includes 35 countries from North, Central, and South America and the Caribbean. Located in Washington, DC, the OAS includes a General Assembly, Permanent Council, Inter-American Council for Integral Development (all of which are one state, one vote, majority institutions), a secretariat to handle day-to-day activities, and an Inter-American Court of Human Rights and an Inter-American Development Bank. The OAS also has a number of specialized agencies that address health, gender, and cultural matters, among other things. The role of the OAS has expanded since the end of the Cold War, moving from U.S.-dominated efforts to resist communism to a greater variety of roles in conflict resolution, support for democracy and human rights, and other activities. The Western Hemisphere also has a number of subregional organizations, mostly geared toward economic cooperation. These include the North American Free Trade Agreement (NAFTA), the Common Market of the South (MERCOSUR), the Andean Community (discussed above), the Central American Common Market (CACM), and the Caribbean Community (CARICOM).

7-3d The European Union: The Most Powerful Regional Organization

The European Union is the largest, most developed and most authoritative multi-issue regional organization in the world. No other regional organization even comes close, and many observers and advocates of European integration have often discussed the possibilities of a "United States of Europe" as the logical and likely endpoint of the efforts toward European integration that began after World War II. Why do you think Europe has had so much more success than other regions in building a regional organization? After all, this was the location of regular and bloody wars among its major states for hundreds of years!

Political Science scholars Margaret Karns and Karen Mingst suggest that regionalism fundamentally requires deliberate policy choices by leaders, but is also heavily influenced by a cluster of additional factors. The most important of these are: basic power dynamics among the states of the region; common identities, based on such things as culture, religion, historical experiences, common ideology, and even common external threats; regime types, with similar governments more likely to be able cooperate; economic connections and interdependence; and perhaps even similar economic systems and levels of development.[8] Let's keep these factors in mind as we consider the origins, development, structures, and roles of the European Union.

Origins and Foundations of the European Union

After centuries of war, culminating in the devastation of World War II that left much of the continent of Europe in ruin, European leaders began after the war to try to build regional institutions that would unite their countries in cooperative structures that would help them work together and avoid such costly wars in the future. Driven by the ideas of functionalism, developed by people like David Mitrany and Jean Monnet, who argued that relatively small, practical steps toward integration could "build peace in pieces," as Mitrany put it in his 1946 book *A Working Peace System*, European leaders took steps to build the habits and practices of cooperation. Jean Monnet, often regarded as "the father of Europe" for his contributions to European integration, helped to develop the first serious step toward a united Europe, the 1950 Schuman Plan, named for French foreign minister Robert Schuman, to create the European Coal and Steel Community. In 1951, in the Treaty of Paris, the ECSC came into being, establishing a common market centered on the trade of French coal and German steel, with an international institution to coordinate and manage the market. Joined by France, West Germany, Italy, Netherlands, Belgium, and Luxemburg, the ECSC linked the economies of all six states, especially West Germany and France. Its creators hoped that it

© James M. Scott

Robert Schuman, one of the founders of the European Union | How has the development of the EU changed relationships among the countries of Europe?

would not only foster economic growth and cooperation, but also "make war not only unthinkable but materially impossible," as Schuman put it. In this way, what is now the European Union was born.

The Development of the European Union The European Union of today grew slowly from the ECSC, as its founders intended. In 1957, the Treaty of Rome established the European Economic Community (EEC), which began in 1958, for the six members of the ECSC to deepen economic integration and create a broader common market for goods and services beyond coal and steel. Fifteen years later, in 1973, the EEC expanded, with long-time holdout Britain joining with Ireland and Denmark to become members of the community. Norway, which was also to join at that time, did not when its citizens rejected the agreement. At this time, a European Monetary Union (EMU) was also established to deepen economic and political integration by harmonizing the currencies of all nine member states by tying their values to the German Deutschmark, but fiscal and monetary crises among member states caused its collapse just a short time later.

In the 1980s, the European Monetary System (EMS) was established to replace the EMU, and the first common European currency—the ecu—was created, although only for use as a reserve currency and not circulated like British pounds, French francs, and German deutschmarks. Further political development ensued. In the mid-1980s, Greece (1985), Spain, and Portugal (1986) joined the European Community, and the member states also pushed their integration forward with the Single European Act, which finished the creation of the common market and laid the foundations for the broadening and deepening of European integration after the Cold War's end.

What we know now as the European Union (EU) emerged in 1992 with the conclusion of the Maastricht Treaty, which not only strengthened European political and legal structures (broad areas of economic and social policy, labor, and citizenship), but also laid the groundwork for the single European currency—the euro—to be used by member states, replacing their own national currencies. The Maastricht Treaty also established the Common Foreign and Security Policy (CFSP), to foster more cooperation and coordination of the foreign and defense policies of the members. Austria, Finland, and Sweden joined the EU in 1995, bringing membership to 15.

The EU continued to broaden and deepen after Maastricht. The treaties of Amsterdam (1997), Nice (2003), and Lisbon (2007) all strengthened EU institutions and regional democratic practices. The EU also continued to expand, this time to the east to include members of eastern Europe for the first time. In 2004, ten new states, Cyprus, Czech Republic, Estonia, Hungary,

Latvia, Lithuania, Malta, Poland, Slovak Republic, and Slovenia, all joined the EU. Romania and Bulgaria followed in 2008, and Croatia joined in 2013. The EU now has 28 members spanning western and eastern Europe. Furthermore, the euro was successfully introduced on January 1, 1999, replacing the national currencies of 18 of the 28 EU members—the so-called Eurozone, consisting of Austria, Belgium, Cyprus, Estonia, Finland, France, German, Greece, Ireland, Italy, Latvia, Luxemburg, Malta, the Netherlands, Portugal, Slovakia, Slovenia, and Spain. The U.K. remains a notable holdout.

Structure and Operations While the EU has many agencies and sub-agencies that attend to a broad array of matters (see Figure 7-2) today, the EU structure revolves around five main institutions with executive, legislative, and judicial functions. The most powerful institution is the **European Commission (EC)**, which is basically the executive branch of the EU. The Commission is a supranational institution, meaning that it has powers above and beyond the member states. It has its own budgetary powers, which gives it substantial independence from member state pressures, and its purpose is to represent the interests of the European Union as a whole, not any individual member states. Its head is the President of the Commission (in 2014, Portugal's Jose Manuel Barroso) and it includes a 28-member cabinet that oversees policy development in agriculture, trade, social policy, the environment, and many other areas. Each member state of the EU is represented: as each cabinet office is led by an individual from a different EU member country. However, the President of the Commission (not the member states themselves) appoints these individuals.

The **European Council** is made up of the heads of government of the EU member states who come together collectively at EU Summits twice every six months (more frequently if needed) to represent the interests of their member states within the EU. As you might expect, these meeting are very publicized and the European Council is perhaps the most publicly visible of the EU institutions. However, in reality, it has little executive or legislative power over EU policy, mostly serving as an advisory and agenda-setting body.

The legislative institutions of the EU include the Council of Ministers (CoM) and the European

European Commission (EC) the executive branch of the EU. The Commission is led by a president, has budgetary powers, and includes a 28-member cabinet that oversees policy development in agriculture, trade, social policy, the environment, and many other areas.

European Council made up of the heads of government of the EU member states, the European Council represents the interests of their member states within the EU.

FIGURE 7-2 MAJOR PARTS AND FUNCTIONS OF THE EU

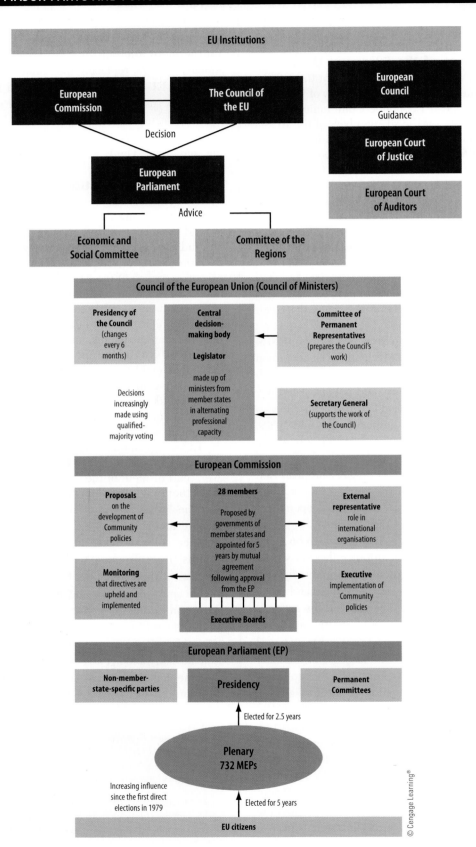

© Cengage Learning®

FIGURE 7-3 EUROPEAN PARLIAMENT SEATS PER COUNTRY, MAY 2014

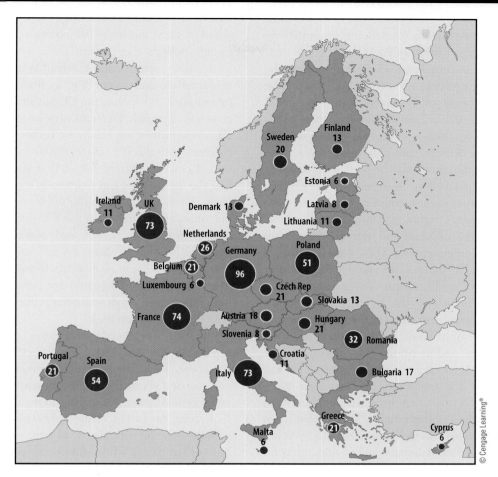

Source: European Parliament, http://www.bbc.com/news/world-europe-11721707.

Parliament (EP). The **Council of Ministers**, more formally the Council of the European Union, is the more powerful of the two and can be seen as an "upper house" like the U.S. Senate. Council membership varies depending on the issue at hand: When defense and security matters are on the agenda, member states send their defense ministers; when foreign affairs are at hand, foreign ministers attend; if the issue is economic, finance ministers show up. But no matter who attends, when the council meets its members represent their member states and are themselves members of their national governments. Any and all EU legislation must be approved by the Council of Ministers. Most of the time, the European Parliament (see Figure 7-2) must also approve legislation (see Figure 7-2), but in some instances the council has exclusive legislative authority and the parliament can only serve in an advisory function. Thus, the council is widely regarded as the more powerful of the two legislative institutions, though attempts to democratize the EU by extending

the powers of the parliament have increasingly been made.

The **European Parliament (EP)** is the second of the two legislative institutions and is often seen as the "lower house," like the House of Representatives in the United States (see Figure 7-3). The 2007 Lisbon Treaty fixes EP seats at 751 from 2014 forward, and those seats are allocated proportionally according to population. Germany has the most seats (96), while Estonia, Cyprus, Malta, and Luxemburg have the minimum (6). All of these representatives to the European Parliament are directly elected, so the EP is regarded as the most democratic of

Council of Ministers made up of sitting ministers of their national governments, the Council of Ministers represents member states and approves all EU legislation.

European Parliament (EP) the EU legislative body made up of directly elected representatives, the EU Parliament amends, approves or rejects EU laws, together with the Council of Ministers.

the EU institutions. No other regional IO—or any IO for that matter!—has such a body with real authority. Elections are held every five years (since 1979), and citizens in each member state directly elect their representatives, who serve only in the European Parliament (not in their member state parliaments) and are elected to serve the interests of European citizens and the EU as a whole, not the specific interests of their home states. In the EP, representatives sit with fellow members of their political parties (e.g., Conservative, Social Democrat, Greens, etc.) from all over Europe, not with other representatives from their home countries. The parliament amends, approves, or rejects EU laws, together with the Council of Ministers, in areas such as consumer protection, the single market, workers' rights, asylum and immigration, agriculture, the environment, and animal welfare, but not in foreign and defense policy. The EP also has shared authority over the EU budget (with the Council of Ministers) and oversees the European Commission.

The judicial branch of the EU is the **European Court of Justice**, widely regarded as the most successful international court of its kind. The ECJ is truly a supranational institution, and its rulings take precedent over even national law. It is charged with interpreting EU law and ensuring that it is applied equally across all member states. There is one judge for each member state. The power of the ECJ is illustrated by the fact that when national law is seen to be in violation of EU law, member states must change their national laws to come into compliance with EU law.

Contributions and Challenges The role of the EU in European politics is constantly evolving. As the founders of European integration hoped and intended, the EU has broadened and deepened over the decades since World War II, and peace and cooperation among its members is a reality, not a dream. Even former enemies such as France and Germany now see themselves as partners in a zone of peace. Furthermore, member states have come to see their interests collectively, not just as those of individual states. While European citizens still see themselves as British, French, German, etc., they also have developed a common identity as Europeans. Today, the EU controls the monetary policy of most of its members, and no member state in the Eurozone has monetary policy autonomy. Politically, integration is not as deep, and member states still enjoy substantial policy autonomy.

European Court of Justice the EU's judicial branch whose rulings take precedent over even national law. It is charged with interpreting EU law and ensuring that it is applied equally across all member states.

Challenges remain though. While the EU has tried to enhance common foreign and defense policy, and has had some success harmonizing policy among members, member states enjoy the full power to pursue whatever foreign policies they prefer. Thus, in the face of challenges such as terrorism, the Iraq War, Iranian nuclear proliferation, and responding to Russian pressure and intervention in Ukraine, the EU has struggled to follow a common approach. Disputes over whether to widen the EU even further, especially to Turkey or Ukraine, and relations with the U.S. also continue to plague its members. Economically, the Great Recession of 2008–2010 and the 2009 European debt crisis rocked the EU and led to disenchantment in the public over the costs and outcomes of integration as the EU responded to severe budget deficits in Greece and other member states' financial bailouts to shore up and revive their economies. This led some economists to warn that the monetary union of the EU could not survive without fiscal integration, as a single currency without a single fiscal policy cannot sustain itself.

In fact, so-called "Eurosceptics" question the EU future. In the May 2014 European elections to the European Parliament, many observers were shocked and worried about the significant gains made by right-wing, generally anti-EU parties in many member states. In France, for instance, the right-wing National Front won the election with almost 25 percent of the vote (the most of any party), while other right-wing parties gained seats in the U.K., Denmark, and Austria. Left and center parties still hold the majority in the EU Parliament, but these results caused many EU supporters to worry about a possible change in public opinion and political power.

On the other hand, many now advocate for further integration—to the culmination of a fully integrated Europe. Recently, for example, Viviane Reding, vice president of the European Commission, argued that pushing the European Union to become a "United States of Europe" is the "best weapon against the Eurosceptics," and called for "a true political union" to be put on the agenda for future EU elections. According to Reding, "We need to build a United States of Europe with the Commission as government and two chambers—the European Parliament and a 'senate' of Member States."[9] In May 2014, the Italian prime minister, Matteo Renzi, echoed this call, saying "For my children's future I dream, think and work for the United States of Europe . . . a stronger and more cohesive Europe is the only solution to the solve the problems of our time."[10] What do you think of the possibility of a "United States of Europe?" What would it mean for world politics?

7-3e The United Nations

Let's conclude our discussion of IOs by focusing on the United Nations, which offers a good example of the nature, roles, influence, and challenges facing the structures and institutions of cooperation and conflict management. We'll consider its background, purposes, structure, and roles in peace/security and other areas of world politics.

HISTORICAL FOUNDATIONS OF THE UNITED NATIONS Although the UN was established in 1945, its roots extend back to two international institutions from the nineteenth and early twentieth centuries. The first is the **Concert of Europe** (1815–1854), which we introduced in the last chapter. Composed of Great Britain, Russia, Austria, Prussia, and in 1818, France, the concert was a multilateral organization established in the Congress of Vienna to promote stability and cooperation, multilateral diplomacy (mostly informal), and to help sustain the balance of power after the Napoleonic Wars. It did not include minor powers and was fundamentally committed to preserving the status quo.

The Crimean War of 1854 resulted in the collapse of the Concert of Europe, and the next historical precursor to the UN did not appear until the end of World War I (1914–1918). In the wake of that war's devastation, the Treaty of Versailles produced the League of Nations, an IO dedicated to collective security (see Chapter 6) and the resolution of disputes between states. The League of Nations began with 32 members (ironically, not the United States, which had been the prime instigator of the idea in the first place) and grew to include 57 members by 1938, on the eve of World War II. A general Assembly included all members, while a League Council consisted of great powers as permanent members,

The League of Nations meets to consider German rearmament in 1935 | Why did the League of Nations fail to check aggression before World War II? Could a different organization have stopped it?

with a few smaller powers regularly rotating membership. As we discussed in Chapter 6, the central focus of the League of Nations was collective security, but it proved unable to meet the challenges of that task. Its members had difficulty defining aggression and enlisting the support of great powers to counter it when it did not directly involve them. Further, the League Council's requirement for unanimous decisions prevented it from responding to the aggression by Germany, Italy, and Japan that caused World War II.

7-3f Enter the United Nations

Thus the **United Nations** did not emerge from scratch after World War II. Many of its features have their origins in the Concert of Europe and League of Nations. World War II was still underway when diplomats from many countries, led by the United States and Britain, began work on the new organization. Its name derives from U.S. President Franklin Roosevelt's 1942 description of the 26 states cooperating to fight the Axis powers as the "united nations." Fifty-one countries joined and drafted the UN Charter in San Francisco in 1945.

Concert of Europe a nineteenth century multilateral organization composed of Great Britain, Russia, Austria, Prussia, and France to promote stability, cooperation, and multilateral diplomacy.

United Nations an international institution established after World War II to promote peace and security, the development of friendly relations and harmony among nations, and cooperation on international problems.

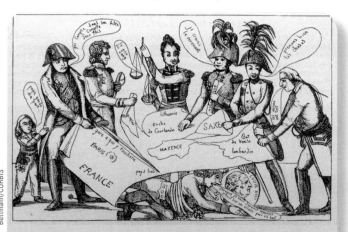

Members of the Concert of Europe argue over a map of Europe | How do you think the exclusion of minor powers affected the Concert of Europe?

The Basic Purposes of the UN

According to Chapter I of the United Nations Charter, the new IO formed after World War II had four main purposes:

Article I

The Purposes of the United Nations are:

1. **To maintain international peace and security,** *and to that end: to take effective collective measures for the prevention and removal of threats to the peace, and for the suppression of acts of aggression or other breaches of the peace, and to bring about by peaceful means, and in conformity with the principles of justice and international law, adjustment or settlement of international disputes or situations which might lead to a breach of the peace;*

2. **To develop friendly relations among nations** *based on respect for the principle of equal rights and self-determination of peoples, and to take other appropriate measures to strengthen universal peace;*

3. **To achieve international co-operation in solving international problems of an economic, social, cultural, or humanitarian character,** *and in promoting and encouraging respect for human rights and for fundamental freedoms for all without distinction as to race, sex, language, or religion; and*

4. **To be a centre for harmonizing the actions of nations** *in the attainment of these common ends.*

Article II

The Organization and its Members, in pursuit of the Purposes stated in Article I, shall act in accordance with the following Principles.

1. *The Organization is based on the principle of the* **sovereign equality of all its Members.**

2. *All Members, in order to ensure to all of them the rights and benefits resulting from membership,* **shall fulfill in good faith the obligations** *assumed by them in accordance with the present Charter.*

3. **All Members shall settle their international disputes by peaceful means** *in such a manner that international peace and security, and justice, are not endangered.*

4. *All Members shall* **refrain in their international relations from the threat or use of force against the territorial integrity or political independence of any state,** *or in any other manner inconsistent with the Purposes of the United Nations.*

5. *All Members shall give the United Nations every assistance in any action it takes in accordance with the present Charter, and shall refrain from giving assistance to any state against which the United Nations is taking preventive or enforcement action.*

6. *The* **Organization shall ensure that states which are not Members of the United Nations act in accordance with these Principles** *so far as may be necessary for the maintenance of international peace and security.*

7. **Nothing contained in the present Charter shall authorize the United Nations to intervene in matters which are essentially within the domestic jurisdiction of any state** *or shall require the Members to submit such matters to settlement under the present Charter; but this principle shall not prejudice the application of enforcement measures under Chapter VII.*

It is interesting to see the broad scope envisioned for the United Nations. Please have a look at the full UN Charter at http://www.un.org/en/documents/charter/index.shtml.

When the countries that would be the Permanent 5 of the UN Security Council and a majority of the remaining signatories ratified the charter, the UN was born in October 1945. Shortly after that, the League of Nations officially disbanded.

Although the UN shared its predecessor's emphasis on peace and security, it was designed to be a broader IO from the start. The UN Charter identifies its main purposes as peace and security, the development of friendly relations and harmony among nations, and cooperation on international problems (see Spotlight On: The Basic Purposes of the UN). It also embraces the sovereign equality of all states and restricts the UN from interfering in the domestic jurisdiction of its members.

The UN is a universal IO, with all states entitled to membership once they sign and ratify the UN Charter. From the original 51 members, the UN grew to its current membership of 193 countries, driven by the decolonization of Africa, Asia, and the Middle East during its first three decades, and then the post–Cold War emergence of independent states primarily from the former Soviet Union and eastern/central Europe. Once they join, member states participate in an extensive IO, which has its headquarters in New York and major offices in Geneva (Switzerland), Vienna (Austria), and

The United Nations in New York | What do you think are the UN's primary contributions in world politics?

The UN General Assembly meets in 2012 | The UNGA is the most representative body in the world, but it is also very limited in its authority. Why do you think that is the case?

Nairobi (Kenya). The UN also has regional commissions and specialized agencies located throughout the world.

THE STRUCTURE OF THE UNITED NATIONS As Figure 7-4 shows, there are six principal organs of the UN, each of which has its distinctive nature and role to meet the UN's basic purposes. Let's briefly summarize each of them, although even a brief look at Figure 7-4 indicates that we will not be able to describe every piece and subpiece. (You can explore the myriad of agencies, commissions, councils, and committees at http://www .un.org/en/aboutun/structure/index.shtml.)

The UN General Assembly (UNGA) As we described earlier, the **United Nations General Assembly** is the plenary body of the UN, so all UN members have a seat in the assembly. It functions on a "one state–one vote," majority-rule principle (with two-thirds majority required for some issues), and it is the central forum for discussion of global issues. As less-developed countries gained numerical dominance, the UNGA began to reflect the perspectives and priorities of those countries, as it offered the smallest countries in the world their most important diplomatic opportunities. The UNGA may debate any issue that arises under the UN Charter, and its work is achieved mostly through its wide range of committees that operate year-round. The UNGA meets formally each year in September, where it typically takes up 300 or so resolutions for discussion and voting and when member states make presentations and speeches.

The UN Security Council (UNSC) As we described earlier, the **United Nations Security Council** is a 15-member council that carries the primary UN responsibilities for peace, security, and collective security operations. It can meet at any time it is deemed necessary and hold meetings each year in conjunction with

the UNGA meetings, as well. Operating via the P-5 veto system we already discussed, the UNSC is entitled to investigate any dispute it considers important for international peace and security, and UN members can bring issues to the UNSC, as well. The Cold War largely froze the UNSC, with the United States and Soviet Union taking turns blocking most of its potential operations. Since the Cold War ended, it has been more active, and it engages in a range of efforts from resolutions condemning specific behavior, efforts to mediate conflicts before they erupt, authorizing sanctions against states deemed to violate the peace, dispatching peacekeeping forces and establishing cease-fires to provide opportunities for conflict resolution, and authorizing military action against aggressors (see Chapter 6 for more on the UN, collective security, and peacekeeping).

The Secretariat The **UN Secretariat** is basically the UN's bureaucracy—its major administrative arm. Employing some forty-five thousand staff in New York and around the world, the Secretariat manages and administers the activities authorized by the UNGA and the UNSC. As suggested by the entries on Figure 7-4, the Secretariat's offices and functions run a wide range, from peacekeeping operations and humanitarian issues to public information and facilities safety.

United Nations General Assembly (UNGA) the plenary body of the UN in which all UN members have a seat. Functioning on a majority rule decision process, it is the central forum for discussion of global issues.

United Nations Security Council a 15-member council that carries the primary UN responsibilities for peace, security, and collective security operations.

UN Secretariat the bureaucracy and administrative arm of the UN.

FIGURE 7-4 THE STRUCTURE AND INSTITUTIONS OF THE UNITED NATIONS

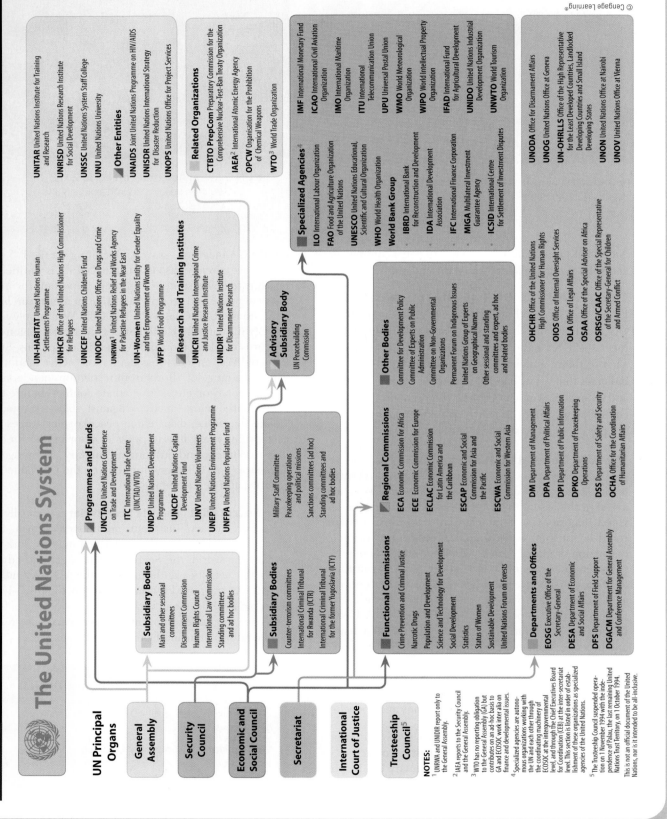

The United Nations System

UN Principal Organs

General Assembly

Security Council

Economic and Social Council

Secretariat

International Court of Justice

Trusteeship Council[5]

Programmes and Funds

UNCTAD United Nations Conference on Trade and Development
- ITC International Trade Centre (UNCTAD/WTO)
UNDP United Nations Development Programme
- UNCDF United Nations Capital Development Fund
- UNV United Nations Volunteers
UNEP United Nations Environment Programme
UNFPA United Nations Population Fund

UN-HABITAT United Nations Human Settlements Programme
UNHCR Office of the United Nations High Commissioner for Refugees
UNICEF United Nations Children's Fund
UNODC United Nations Office on Drugs and Crime
UNRWA[1] United Nations Relief and Works Agency for Palestine Refugees in the Near East
UN-Women United Nations Entity for Gender Equality and the Empowerment of Women
WFP World Food Programme

Research and Training Institutes

UNICRI United Nations Interregional Crime and Justice Research Institute
UNIDIR[1] United Nations Institute for Disarmament Research

UNITAR United Nations Institute for Training and Research
UNRISD United Nations Research Institute for Social Development
UNSSC United Nations System Staff College
UNU United Nations University

Other Entities

UNAIDS Joint United Nations Programme on HIV/AIDS
UNISDR United Nations International Strategy for Disaster Reduction
UNOPS United Nations Office for Project Services

Related Organizations

CTBTO PrepCom Preparatory Commission for the Comprehensive Nuclear-Test-Ban Treaty Organization
IAEA[2] International Atomic Energy Agency
OPCW Organisation for the Prohibition of Chemical Weapons
WTO[3] World Trade Organization

Specialized Agencies[4]

ILO International Labour Organization
FAO Food and Agriculture Organization of the United Nations
UNESCO United Nations Educational, Scientific and Cultural Organization
WHO World Health Organization

World Bank Group
- IBRD International Bank for Reconstruction and Development
- IDA International Development Association
- IFC International Finance Corporation
- MIGA Multilateral Investment Guarantee Agency
- ICSID International Centre for Settlement of Investment Disputes

IMF International Monetary Fund
ICAO International Civil Aviation Organization
IMO International Maritime Organization
ITU International Telecommunication Union
UPU Universal Postal Union
WMO World Meteorological Organization
WIPO World Intellectual Property Organization
IFAD International Fund for Agricultural Development
UNIDO United Nations Industrial Development Organization
UNWTO World Tourism Organization

Subsidiary Bodies

Main and other sessional committees
Disarmament Commission
Human Rights Council
International Law Commission
Standing committees and ad hoc bodies

Subsidiary Bodies

Military Staff Committee
Peacekeeping operations and political missions
Sanctions committees (ad hoc)
Standing committees and ad hoc bodies
Counter-terrorism committees
International Criminal Tribunal for Rwanda (ICTR)
International Criminal Tribunal for the former Yugoslavia (ICTY)

Advisory Subsidiary Body

UN Peacebuilding Commission

Functional Commissions

Crime Prevention and Criminal Justice
Narcotic Drugs
Population and Development
Science and Technology for Development
Social Development
Statistics
Status of Women
Sustainable Development
United Nations Forum on Forests

Regional Commissions

ECA Economic Commission for Africa
ECE Economic Commission for Europe
ECLAC Economic Commission for Latin America and the Caribbean
ESCAP Economic and Social Commission for Asia and the Pacific
ESCWA Economic and Social Commission for Western Asia

Other Bodies

Committee for Development Policy
Committee of Experts on Public Administration
Committee on Non-Governmental Organizations
Permanent Forum on Indigenous Issues
United Nations Group of Experts on Geographical Names
Other sessional and standing committees and expert, ad hoc and related bodies

Departments and Offices

EOSG Executive Office of the Secretary-General
DESA Department of Economic and Social Affairs
DFS Department of Field Support
DGACM Department for General Assembly and Conference Management

DM Department of Management
DPA Department of Political Affairs
DPI Department of Public Information
DPKO Department of Peacekeeping Operations
DSS Department of Safety and Security
OCHA Office for the Coordination of Humanitarian Affairs

OHCHR Office of the United Nations High Commissioner for Human Rights
OIOS Office of Internal Oversight Services
OLA Office of Legal Affairs
OSAA Office of the Special Adviser on Africa
OSRSG/CAAC Office of the Special Representative of the Secretary-General for Children and Armed Conflict

UNODA Office for Disarmament Affairs
UNOG United Nations Office at Geneva
UN-OHRLLS Office of the High Representative for the Least Developed Countries, Landlocked Developing Countries and Small Island Developing States
UNON United Nations Office at Nairobi
UNOV United Nations Office at Vienna

NOTES:

[1] UNRWA and UNIDIR report only to the General Assembly.

[2] IAEA reports to the Security Council and the General Assembly.

[3] WTO has no reporting obligation to the General Assembly (GA) but contributes on an ad-hoc basis to GA and ECOSOC work inter alia on finance and developmental issues.

[4] Specialized agencies are autonomous organizations working with the UN and each other through the coordinating machinery of ECOSOC at the intergovernmental level, and through the Chief Executives Board for Coordination (CEB) at the inter-secretariat level. This section is listed in order of establishment of these organizations as specialized agencies of the United Nations.

[5] The Trusteeship Council suspended operation on 1 November 1994 with the independence of Palau, the last remaining United Nations Trust Territory, on 1 October 1994.

This is not an official document of the United Nations, nor is it intended to be all-inclusive.

© Cengage Learning®

Where Does the UN Call Home?

In 1945, the United Nations was established and its main headquarters was located in New York City. This geographic location was not an accident and has significant consequences. In many respects, the location of the UN reflected the realities of power of the time. The United States was by far the most powerful country in the world at the end of World War II, and it was also the one major power that had not been devastated by the incredible destruction of that global conflict. The United States was also the main force behind the creation of the UN, joining with Britain and others to advocate for its establishment. It also did not hurt that an American billionaire (John D. Rockefeller, Jr.) was willing to donate the land in New York City for the new organization!

However, locating the UN in New York has not been uncontroversial. For one, Americans have had a complicated love-hate relationship with the UN over time, sometimes celebrating its presence and activities, and other times attacking it as an anti-American organization encroaching on U.S. sovereignty. One former State Department official once went so far as to suggest that the land on which the UN sits be chopped off and allowed to float out to sea! For other countries, the location of the UN in New York has regularly raised concerns that its geographic home signals an American, North American, or Western bias. And concerns about the advantages its location affords to the United States have also been raised. In the late 1980s, for example, the UN General Assembly invited Palestinian Liberation Organization head Yasser Arafat to speak to the UN in New York, but the United States refused to allow him to enter the country (despite a UN vote in which only the United States and Israel opposed the visit—the United Kingdom abstained—and a broad international consensus that the U.S. act was a violation of international law). The UN General Assembly moved the meeting to Geneva, Switzerland, in response so Arafat could address the General Assembly. In 2014, the U.S. refused to issue a visa for Iran's UN Ambassador Hamid Aboutalebi to enter the country, as he had participated in taking U.S. diplomats hostage in Iran in 1979. Iran's leadership was seriously annoyed!

Map 7-2

UN Headquarters in New York and Sites for the Other Offices and Programs

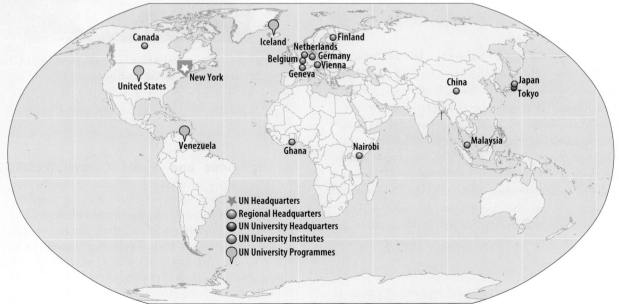

Does it matter where the UN locates its offices and headquarters?

© Cengage Learning®

Seeing New York as the UN's home has generated a lot of debate.

The UN has tried to address this concern by addressing geography, as well. As a consequence, the UN has set up regional headquarters in Geneva, Vienna, and Nairobi (although the fact that two of these are in Europe is not lost on observers). As shown in Map 7-2, the UN has also established important regional commissions throughout the world and has taken other steps to make its home reflect its nature. For example, the UN University is headquartered in Tokyo and has institutes in Belgium, Canada, China, Finland, Germany, Ghana, Japan, Malaysia, and the Netherlands, and programs in Iceland, United States, and Venezuela.

1. What is the significance of the UN's physical location?

2. What benefits does the United States derive from hosting the UN headquarters in New York City?

3. How might realists, liberals, constructivists, Marxists, and feminists interpret and explain this issue?

Bettmann/CORBIS

The U.S. and Soviet ambassadors to the UN face off in the UN Security Council over the Soviet placement of missiles in Cuba in 1962 | How might major-power agreement and disagreement affect the role and impact of the UN Security Council?

The Secretariat is directed by the **UN Secretary—General**, a very high-profile figure elected by the UNGA at the recommendation of the UNSC who serves a five-year term. There have been eight UN Secretaries-General since 1946, each of whom has brought a distinctive style and agenda (see Figure 7-5 for the names and dates of these leaders). The UN Secretary-General enjoys some discretion in administering the UN budget and can call special sessions of the UNGA. The occupant of the position can also bring issues to the UNSC for consideration, as well. According to the UN Charter, the UN Secretary-General must be impartial when serving this role.

UN Secretary-General the head of the UN Secretariat, the UN's administrative leader elected by the UNGA at the recommendation of the UNSC.

AP Images/Heribert Proepper

UN Secretary-General Ban Ki-moon speaking at the UN Climate Summit in Copenhagen, 2009 | How can the leader of an international organization affect the decisions of the leaders of states?

The Economic and Social Council (ECOSOC)

The UN's goals involving problems of an economic, social, and cultural nature are primarily the responsibility of ECOSOC, and it is by far the broadest and largest of the UN's organs. It has 54 members elected by UNGA for three-year terms and meets one month of each year. As Table 7-3 shows, ECOSOC at least nominally supervises a wide array of commissions, committees, and specialized agencies, the most well-known of which include the World Trade Organization and IMF (see Chapter 8), the Commission on Human Rights (see Chapter 11), the UN Children's Fund (UNICEF), the World Health Organization, the International Atomic

TABLE 7-3   UN SPECIALIZED AGENCIES, FUNDS, AND PROGRAMS

ECOSOC FUNCTIONAL COMMISSIONS	ECOSOC AD HOC BODIES
• Statistical Commission	• Ad Hoc Open-ended Working Group on Informatics
• Commission on Population and Development	**EXPERT BODIES COMPOSED OF GOVERNMENTAL EXPERTS**
• Commission for Social Development	• Committee of Experts on the Transport of Dangerous Goods and on the Globally Harmonized System of Classification and Labelling of Chemicals
• Commission on the Status of Women	
• Commission on Narcotic Drugs	
• Commission on Crime Prevention and Criminal Justice	• Intergovernmental Working Group of Experts on International Standards of Accounting and Reporting
• Commission on Science and Technology for Development	• United Nations Group of Experts on Geographical Names
• Commission on Sustainable Development	**EXPERT BODIES COMPOSED OF MEMBERS SERVING IN THEIR PERSONAL CAPACITY**
• United Nations Forum on Forests	
ECOSOC REGIONAL COMMISSIONS	• Committee for Development Policy
• Economic Commission for Africa (ECA)	• Committee of Experts on Public Administration
• Economic and Social Commission for Asia and the Pacific (ESCAP)	• Committee of Experts on International Cooperation in Tax Matters
• Economic Commission for Europe (ECE)	• Committee on Economic, Social, and Cultural Rights
• Economic Commission for Latin America and the Caribbean (ECLAC)	• Permanent Forum on Indigenous Issues
• Economic and Social Commission for Western Asia (ESCWA)	**OTHER RELATED BODIES**
ECOSOC STANDING COMMITTEES	• Committee for the United Nations Population Award
• Committee for Program and Coordination	• Executive Board of the International Research and Training Institute for the Advancement of Women
• Committee on Non-Governmental Organizations	• International Narcotics Control Board
• Committee on Negotiations with Intergovernmental Agencies	• Program Coordinating Board of the Joint United Nations Program on HIV/AIDS

© Cengage Learning®

Energy Agency, the UN Educational, Scientific and Cultural Organization (UNESCO), and a whole host of others on such things as the status of women, population, and refugees. Seventy percent of the human and financial resources of the UN fall under ECOSOC's purview. The UN officially describes ECOSOC as

> the central forum for discussing international economic and social issues, and for formulating policy recommendations addressed to Member States and the United Nations system. It is responsible for:
>
> 1. promoting higher standards of living, full employment, and economic and social progress;
>
> 2. identifying solutions to international economic, social and health problems;
>
> 3. facilitating international cultural and educational cooperation; and encouraging universal respect for human rights and fundamental freedoms.[11]

While it is often highly controversial—the United States has regularly tussled with ECOSOC and its subsidiaries, including UNESCO (which the United States boycotted from 1984–2003 on the grounds that it was not only bloated and inefficient, but also anti-American

in its words and deeds; in 2011 the United States stopped funding UNESCO for its admission of Palestine as a member)—the sheer magnitude of the agencies, commissions, and programs under its auspices, resource constraints, and the substantial independence of a great many of its specialized agencies have all combined to reduce ECOSOC's influence, even while its component parts play increasingly important roles.

The Trusteeship Council Originally established to supervise territories emerging from colonial rule after World War II, the Trusteeship Council contributed to the process of decolonization in the first three decades of the UN. It discharged its last responsibility in 1994 with the independence of Palau and has suspended its operations.

The International Court of Justice (World Court) We discussed the World Court in the section on international law in this chapter. This organ is the principal judicial body of the UN. The UNGA and UNSC elect its 15 judges to nine-year terms, and they must come from different countries. Their decisions are rendered by majority vote.

Let's take up two last points before we move on. First, we want to emphasize the range and extent of the

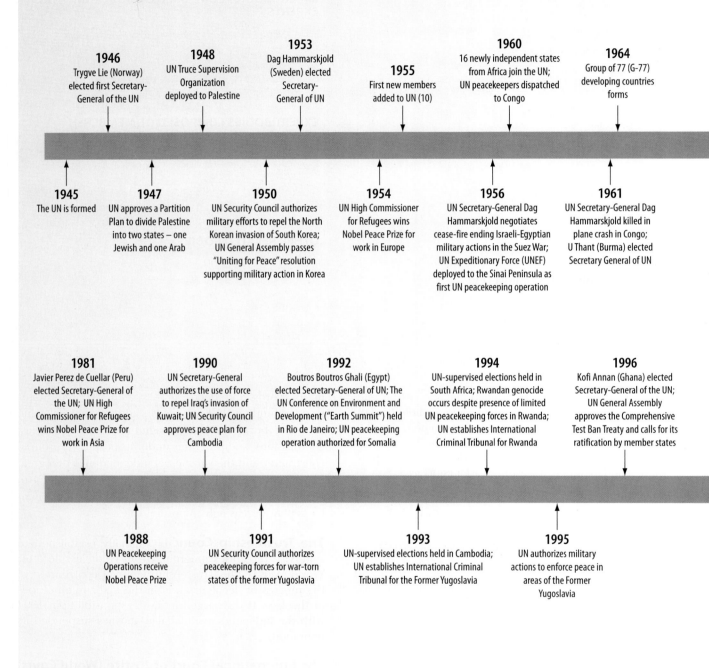

FIGURE 7-5   A TIMELINE OF KEY UN EVENTS, 1946–2014

1946
Trygve Lie (Norway) elected first Secretary-General of the UN

1948
UN Truce Supervision Organization deployed to Palestine

1953
Dag Hammarskjold (Sweden) elected Secretary-General of UN

1955
First new members added to UN (10)

1960
16 newly independent states from Africa join the UN; UN peacekeepers dispatched to Congo

1964
Group of 77 (G-77) developing countries forms

1945
The UN is formed

1947
UN approves a Partition Plan to divide Palestine into two states – one Jewish and one Arab

1950
UN Security Council authorizes military efforts to repel the North Korean invasion of South Korea; UN General Assembly passes "Uniting for Peace" resolution supporting military action in Korea

1954
UN High Commissioner for Refugees wins Nobel Peace Prize for work in Europe

1956
UN Secretary-General Dag Hammarskjold negotiates cease-fire ending Israeli-Egyptian military actions in the Suez War; UN Expeditionary Force (UNEF) deployed to the Sinai Peninsula as first UN peacekeeping operation

1961
UN Secretary-General Dag Hammarskjold killed in plane crash in Congo; U Thant (Burma) elected Secretary General of UN

1981
Javier Perez de Cuellar (Peru) elected Secretary-General of the UN; UN High Commissioner for Refugees wins Nobel Peace Prize for work in Asia

1990
UN Secretary-General authorizes the use of force to repel Iraq's invasion of Kuwait; UN Security Council approves peace plan for Cambodia

1992
Boutros Boutros Ghali (Egypt) elected Secretary-General of UN; The UN Conference on Environment and Development ("Earth Summit") held in Rio de Janeiro; UN peacekeeping operation authorized for Somalia

1994
UN-supervised elections held in South Africa; Rwandan genocide occurs despite presence of limited UN peacekeeping forces in Rwanda; UN establishes International Criminal Tribunal for Rwanda

1996
Kofi Annan (Ghana) elected Secretary-General of the UN; UN General Assembly approves the Comprehensive Test Ban Treaty and calls for its ratification by member states

1988
UN Peacekeeping Operations receive Nobel Peace Prize

1991
UN Security Council authorizes peacekeeping forces for war-torn states of the former Yugoslavia

1993
UN-supervised elections held in Cambodia; UN establishes International Criminal Tribunal for the Former Yugoslavia

1995
UN authorizes military actions to enforce peace in areas of the Former Yugoslavia

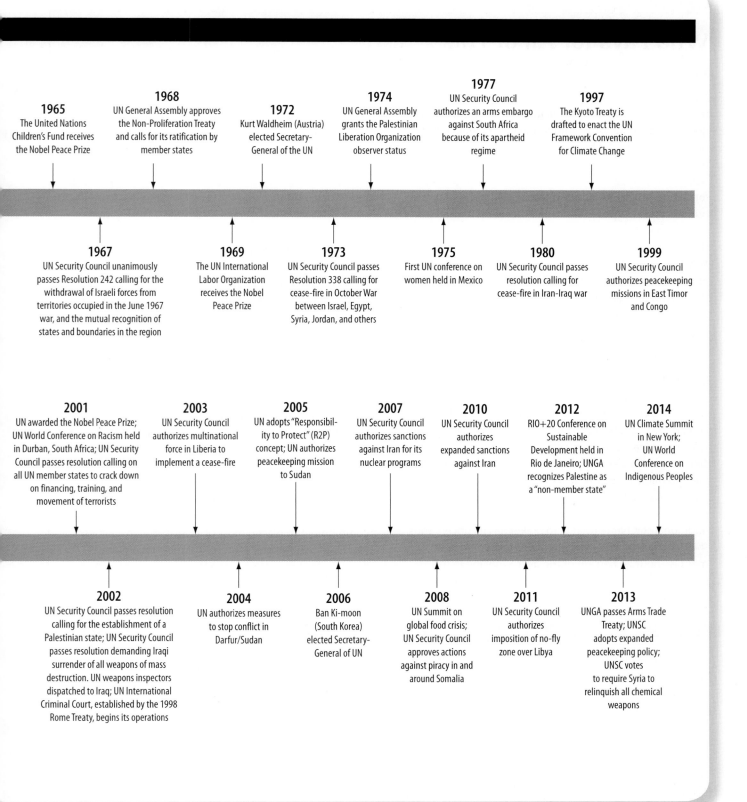

1965
The United Nations Children's Fund receives the Nobel Peace Prize

1968
UN General Assembly approves the Non-Proliferation Treaty and calls for its ratification by member states

1972
Kurt Waldheim (Austria) elected Secretary-General of the UN

1974
UN General Assembly grants the Palestinian Liberation Organization observer status

1977
UN Security Council authorizes an arms embargo against South Africa because of its apartheid regime

1997
The Kyoto Treaty is drafted to enact the UN Framework Convention for Climate Change

1967
UN Security Council unanimously passes Resolution 242 calling for the withdrawal of Israeli forces from territories occupied in the June 1967 war, and the mutual recognition of states and boundaries in the region

1969
The UN International Labor Organization receives the Nobel Peace Prize

1973
UN Security Council passes Resolution 338 calling for cease-fire in October War between Israel, Egypt, Syria, Jordan, and others

1975
First UN conference on women held in Mexico

1980
UN Security Council passes resolution calling for cease-fire in Iran-Iraq war

1999
UN Security Council authorizes peacekeeping missions in East Timor and Congo

2001
UN awarded the Nobel Peace Prize; UN World Conference on Racism held in Durban, South Africa; UN Security Council passes resolution calling on all UN member states to crack down on financing, training, and movement of terrorists

2003
UN Security Council authorizes multinational force in Liberia to implement a cease-fire

2005
UN adopts "Responsibility to Protect" (R2P) concept; UN authorizes peacekeeping mission to Sudan

2007
UN Security Council authorizes sanctions against Iran for its nuclear programs

2010
UN Security Council authorizes expanded sanctions against Iran

2012
RIO+20 Conference on Sustainable Development held in Rio de Janeiro; UNGA recognizes Palestine as a "non-member state"

2014
UN Climate Summit in New York; UN World Conference on Indigenous Peoples

2002
UN Security Council passes resolution calling for the establishment of a Palestinian state; UN Security Council passes resolution demanding Iraqi surrender of all weapons of mass destruction. UN weapons inspectors dispatched to Iraq; UN International Criminal Court, established by the 1998 Rome Treaty, begins its operations

2004
UN authorizes measures to stop conflict in Darfur/Sudan

2006
Ban Ki-moon (South Korea) elected Secretary-General of UN

2008
UN Summit on global food crisis; UN Security Council approves actions against piracy in and around Somalia

2011
UN Security Council authorizes imposition of no-fly zone over Libya

2013
UNGA passes Arms Trade Treaty; UNSC adopts expanded peacekeeping policy; UNSC votes to require Syria to relinquish all chemical weapons

Who Pays for All of This Anyway?

The most recent two-year budget for the United Nations totaled nearly $14 billion. While this might seem to be a great deal of money, remember that this includes a core budget of about $5.4 billion and extra-budgetary amounts of about $7 billion for peacekeeping and security operations, and all the activities of many of its special programs for development, social, educational, environmental, and humanitarian purposes all around the world. This is clearly a very broad global mandate, and when one remembers that the entire U.S. federal budget now approaches $4 *trillion* (or almost 30 times the budget of the UN), the limits of the UN budget are even more obvious. Still, where does the UN funding come from?

The UN's budget comes from two main sources. First, all member states are assessed dues, based on the relative size of their gross domestic product, which make up the core budget. In 2014, these dues ranged from 0.001 percent of the budget to 22 percent. The top figure used to be 25 percent but was adjusted down at the insistence of the United States in 2000 (the United States is the only state paying the top rate). In 2014, the top dues-providers were the United States at 22 percent, Japan at 10.8 percent, and Germany at 7.1 percent. Additional special assessments are also made for all UN peace and security operations based on a similar formula, but the five permanent members of the UN Security Council are also responsible for an additional surcharge (that veto power has its price!). Thus, the U.S. share of the security and peacekeeping assessment is about 26 percent of the over $7 billion in this category. Second, for the specialized programs, voluntary contributions from member states provide the budget, which means that available funds may vary considerably for these programs.

According to the UN Charter, payment of dues is obligatory. In Chapter IV, the Charter states

A Member of the United Nations which is in arrears in the payment of its financial contributions to the Organization shall have no vote in the General Assembly if the amount of its arrears equals or exceeds the amount of the contributions due from it for the preceding two full years. The General Assembly may, nevertheless, permit such a Member to vote if it is satisfied that the failure to pay is due to conditions beyond the control of the Member.

As of 2014, the UN claimed that its members were over $4 billion in arrears. Seven countries (Central African Republic, Comoros, Guinea-Bissau, Liberia, Sao Tome and Principe, Somalia, and Yemen) were in arrears then (or behind in their payments and *not* making payments to catch up), with only Yemen prohibited by the UNGA from voting in 2014.

Historically, however, the most problematic country when it came to paying dues was the United States. Beginning in 1985 under the Reagan administration, the United States began deliberately withholding a portion of its dues, a practice continued for a decade by Congress in the U.S. budgetary process. Eventually, U.S. unpaid dues to the UN amounted to over $1 billion. In the late 1990s, U.S. Senators Jesse Helms (R-NC) and Joe Biden (D-CT) worked out a deal with the Clinton administration and the UN in a highly contentious debate that lasted several years before it produced an outcome. The resolution combined a U.S. commitment to pay up most of its arrears in installments (the United States still contests a significant amount) in return for a reduction in the U.S. assessment for the regular budget from 25 percent to 22 percent. The United States now pays its annual assessed dues in full.

specialized agencies of the UN system and the contributions they make in many political, social, economic, cultural, and environmental issues (see Table 7-3 for a list). When you consider all the particular problems and issues that are addressed, the transnational cooperation and coordination and the technical expertise and resources that are pooled in these agencies, it is easy to understand the arguments offered by functionalists (see Chapter 6) and others about how IOs can foster and extend linkages among states.

Second, it is in the various elements of ECOSOC, and in the UN Secretariat as well, that the thousands of nongovernmental organizations concerned with virtually every issue imaginable are linked into IOs. We will talk about this in detail in Chapter 13, which is expressly devoted to transnational networks. Let's just say for now that these networks are fostered in part through the structures and institutions of cooperation within the UN system.

THE CONTRIBUTIONS AND LIMITS OF THE UN So how has the UN contributed to cooperation and the management of conflict? First, we can safely say that the UN's effectiveness is hampered by the same three challenges that impact every other aspect of world politics. Anarchy means that the UN ultimately depends in large part on the willingness of its members—sovereign states—to support and participate in its activities. Remember, the UN is not the "world police" and does not have the ability to enforce international law, agreements, or even the outcome of its own votes. Diversity means that the UN is hampered in part by the wide array of perspectives and preferences held by the widely diverging member states, nations, and non-governmental organizations with whom it works. Complexity means that the tasks confronting the UN are not simple, but complicated and increasingly linked. Moreover, the forces of interdependence and globalization are adding new issues to the agenda daily, and the UN's resources are not infinite.

Second, it is safe to say that the UN has fallen short of the expectations of its founders and early supporters in the area widely thought to be its primary purpose—collective security. As the quote from George H. W. Bush at the very beginning of our chapter suggested, there is consensus that the Cold War contest between the United States and the Soviet Union locked up the UN Security Council and prohibited it from addressing many issues of peace and security from 1946 to 1989. However, former President Bush's comments that the UN was poised to fulfill its lofty goals in the post–Cold War world seem awfully optimistic with the advantage of hindsight. To be sure, the UN has authorized and engaged in a great many peace operations since the end of the Cold War. But as our discussion in Chapter 6 suggested, it has struggled to contribute to the prevention, containment, and resolution of post–Cold War conflicts—especially the civil wars and non-state conflicts of the last 20 years. These struggles suggest that the machinery forged in response to the experiences of the early twentieth century to deal with conflicts *between* states faces many challenges in dealing with conflict and security issues today. The UN has made many positive contributions to peace and security in many cases, but its overall record is mixed.

Third, we should point out that the UN's most significant impact may well be in the arenas in which its roles and functions were originally deemed secondary (due to the pressing peace and security problems of the time). Indeed, when we consider the contributions of the UN to fighting disease, protecting the environment, caring for refugees, and promoting and protecting human rights on the one hand, and the far-reaching impact of the UN's specialized economic agencies in building and facilitating economic interdependence and cooperation, it is hard to resist concluding that these more technical and functional areas are the arenas of the UN's greatest accomplishments. Fortunately, it is precisely to these areas that our next chapters now turn, so we will be better positioned to make such judgments in our concluding chapter.

CONCLUSION

Former U.S. President George H. W. Bush may have been overly optimistic when he speculated that the end of the Cold War and the successful international response to Iraq's invasion of Kuwait in 1990 heralded a new era in which collective security and the rule of law prevailed in international relations. As we have seen, the problems facing the world continue to exceed the world's capacity to resolve them peacefully and effectively. However, our discussion in this chapter also indicates that cooperative approaches to those problems by states, international organizations, non-governmental organizations, and individuals play a role in managing conflict and seeking security. Even the arena of international security is not solely about military power and the use of force. As we reflect on the ideas and information we have covered in Part Two of our text, you should consider again the traditional arena of international security and the approaches that states and others have embraced in pursuit of security. Do you see an evolution or trend, or are the actors in world politics stuck in cycles in which problems and solutions are endlessly repeated? To what degree do you think military power and force will continue to take center stage in this arena? What changes do you think are most important for the future?

STUDY TOOLS 7

LOCATED AT BACK OF THE BOOK:
☐ Rip out Chapter in Review card

LOCATED ON COURSEMATE:
Use the CourseMate access card that came with this book or visit CengageBrain.com for more review materials:
☐ Review Key Terms Flash Cards (Print or Online)
☐ Download Chapter Summaries for on-the-go review
☐ Complete Practice Quizzes to prepare for the test
☐ Walk through a Simulation, Animated Learning Module, and Interactive Maps and Timelines to master concepts
☐ Complete Crossword Puzzle to review key terms
☐ Visit IR NewsWatch to learn about the latest current events as you prepare for class discussions and papers

THINK ABOUT THIS REFORMING THE UN SECURITY COUNCIL

At the end of World War II, U.S., British and Soviet leaders took the lead in establishing the United Nations Security Council as part of the new United Nations international organization. These three, with France and China, established themselves as permanent members of the UNSC, and provided themselves with the veto power in the council. More than six decades later, and despite the dramatic changes that have occurred in the world, these five states continue to hold their privileged position in the UNSC. Many proposals for reform of the UNSC have been offered in recent years, with then-UN Secretary General Kofi Annan calling for speedy action to expand the council's membership in 2005. While many suggestions for reform have been made, the most attention has been directed to changing the number of permanent members (with the veto power). After all, why should the UN's most powerful organ reflect the conditions at end of World War II? Proposals to add Brazil, Germany, India, and Japan (called the G4 in this context) to the ranks of the permanent members have been offered (Russia, France and the U.K. have indicated their support for this proposal). Africa has also argued for a permanent member from among the states of its region, and the Islamic world has argued for the same for its members. Opposition exists to every proposal: for example, Mexico and Argentina oppose Brazil; South Korea and China oppose Japan; Italy and Spain, and much of the developing world, oppose Germany; Pakistan opposes India; and so on. Significant disagreement also exists over whether any new permanent members should also have the veto power enjoyed by the existing P-5. To achieve UN Security Council reform, at least two-third of the members of the UN, and all the current permanent members of the UNSC, must agree. What do you think:

John Moore/Getty Images

The UN Security Council Chambers, 2014 | Who should be in this room now?

Leaders from the U.S., Britain, and Soviet Union discussing the UN Security Council at the 1944 Dumbarton Oaks Meeting

Keystone-France/Gamma-Keystone/ Getty Images

Is UNSC reform a good idea, and what are the most important prospects and implications, good and bad, of doing so?

REVIEW QUESTIONS

1. How do anarchy, diversity, and complexity set the stage for understanding the contributions and challenges of structures and institutions of cooperation?

2. How is international law different from domestic law?

3. What are the sources and mechanisms of enforcement for international law, and what are their consequences for its role and impact in world politics?

4. Why do states form international organizations?

5. What are the central forms and types of international organizations, and how do they affect world politics?

6. What are the main pieces and contributions of the UN?

FOR MORE INFORMATION . . .

For more on international law and international organizations, see:

Cini, Michelle, and Nieves Perez-Solorzano Borragan (eds.), *European Union Politics,* 4th ed. Oxford: Oxford University Press, 2013.

Diehl, Paul F., and Brian Frederking. *The Politics of Global Governance: International Organizations in an Interdependent World,* 4th ed. Boulder, CO: Lynne Rienner Publishers, 2010.

Morrow, James D. *Order Within Anarchy: The Laws of War as an International Institution.* New York: Cambridge University Press, 2014.

Murphy, Sean D. *Principles of International Law*, 2nd ed. Eagan, MN: West Law School, 2012.

United Nations (official English language website), www.un.org/en

Weiss, Thomas G., David P. Forsythe, Roger A. Coate, and Kelly-Kate Pease. *The United Nations and Changing World Politics,* 7th ed. Boulder, CO: Westview Press, 2014.

8 | The Pursuit of Economic Security:
Trade, Finance, and Integration

After finishing this chapter go to **PAGE 240** for **STUDY TOOLS**

OIL AS *THE* STRATEGIC RESOURCE AND THE LENGTHS STATES GO TO ATTAIN IT

A common theme in science fiction is conflict over a scarce and valuable resource. Movies like *Oblivion* (2013), books like *Dune*, and video games like *Gears of War* all portray the conflict and consequences of the struggle for resources. Just like these movies illustrate, the struggle for important resources is commonplace in human history. Let's consider one of the most important physical resources in the planet: oil.

Beyond our biological needs for fresh water and oxygen, we must have oil. Oil touches *everything* because if oil isn't a component in the product, it was used in the shipping and manufacture of the product. Imagine trying to go just one day without using products that somehow involve oil. Can you go without your car? Can you avoid all plastics? Can you throw away all your clothes that have some form of synthetic like polyester or microfiber in the fabric? Now imagine trying to secure a country without a steady supply of oil.

Because it is so important, countries have relentlessly pursued oil for decades. In 1917, the United Kingdom captured Baghdad from the Ottoman Empire (modern-day Turkey). For more than four decades the British supported leaders who were friendly to the United Kingdom, and when that didn't work they invaded Iraq to prop up leaders they wanted to keep or put in power. The modern state of Iraq was actually created by the United Kingdom to control its unobstructed access to the oil reserves. Not until the rise of Saddam Hussein did control finally slip through the United Kingdom's fingers.

Similarly, U.S. involvement in Saudi Arabia dates back to the 1930s. The United States brokered a deal that gave Standard Oil Company exclusive rights to explore and extract oil in Saudi Arabia. After oil was found, the United States built military bases to protect Saudi Arabia, train its military, and ultimately keep the pro-U.S. monarchy in power. It also tried, unsuccessfully, to gain control over all Saudi oil. Even though the terrorists who attacked the United States on September 11, 2001, were Saudi citizens, the United States maintains a military presence in Saudi Arabia and supplies it with weapons and training. To this day, Saudi Arabia is the second largest supplier of U.S. oil.

In Iran in 1953, the United States and United Kingdom overthrew a democratically elected leader to install a non-democratic leader who was favorable to their interests. The United States later sold weapons to Iraq and provided it with military intelligence before the American relationship with Saddam Hussein soured; the United States then went to war to liberate Kuwait (another oil producer) from Iraqi control in 1991 and invaded Iraq itself in 2003. Clearly, countries will go to great lengths to secure oil.

These are just three examples, but these episodes raise interesting questions:

1. What are the characteristics of economic security and how do the players in world politics achieve it?

2. What would happen to the Middle East if a cheap, sustainable substitute for oil were invented?

3. What other resources are so important that a country would use violence to gain control of the supply of those resources?

An American soldier patrolling near a burning oil well in Iraq in 2003 | To what lengths should a country go to secure energy?

Yannis behrakis/Reuters

INTRODUCTION: MONEY IS POWER

The idea that "money is power" is as old as money itself, and as states seek greater security in the world, many argue that they must therefore seek money. Machiavelli argued that good soldiers could be used to attain gold, but that gold alone would not attain good soldiers. He meant that even a wealthy and well-equipped army could have a low morale and no desire to fight, while good troops follow orders and fight more effectively. While Machiavelli was largely right in the sixteenth century, a state's wealth is a critical component to its power and security in the modern era. Modern weapons—costing trillions of dollars to develop and deploy—have been proven to sweep aside enemy forces almost effortlessly in conflicts such as the U.S.-led wars against Iraq in 1991 and 2003. There should be little doubt that money equals power in the interstate system. But how does wealth translate into power? Does more wealth always mean more security? How has the pursuit of wealth and power evolved in world politics and how has it shaped the relations between the players?

8-1 MONEY, POWER, AND SECURITY

Japan is the world's third largest economy, but its military is very small because the Japanese constitutionally limited their military spending after their defeat in World War II. Would you consider Japan a powerful state even though it has fewer than 250,000 active military personnel (the United States has almost 1.4 million)? Would you consider it secure? In 1989, the U.S. economy totaled $5.44 trillion, Japan's economy totaled $2.97 trillion, and the Soviet Union's totaled only $2.66 trillion. It is not controversial to say that the United States was the most powerful country in 1989, but which was more powerful—Japan or the Soviet Union? If money equals power, then it should be Japan, but it was the Soviet Union that had the large nuclear arsenal and standing military. Clearly, wealth can equal power, but it's not a simple equation.

There must be more to the connection between money and power than simply building a powerful military and then using the military to secure critical resources such as oil. In fact, the complex linkages between politics and economics touch every part of international relations. Wealth cannot only be used to gain power, but it can alter anarchy. That's a big feat, since we discuss anarchy throughout this book as an enduring feature of international relations. However, consider the European Coal and Steel Community, which we just discussed in Chapter 7. The ECSC started as a six-state organization in 1950 to control and coordinate the production of steel in Europe. The French developed the concept in part to ensure that Germany did not build an aggressive military—a country needs steel for its military—and threaten European stability as it did in 1914 and 1939. Thus, the ECSC was an economic organization that coordinated steel production and helped to create a type of security community for Europe. Its effect over the course of several decades was dramatic. This organization was the seed that led to the European Union, which is now a highly integrated, 28-state economic union. Thus, the *political* desire to constrain Germany after World War II led to *economic* integration. In turn, this created new order in part of the international system, effectively reducing the anarchy between the EU member states. In this case, money did not mean power, but it did create more security.

The logic linking economic integration and peace is quite intuitive. If two countries with significant political divisions, such as an historical rivalry, are joined by economic integration, they become dependent on one another. In time, their mutual dependency will not only reduce the conflict, but may lead to a true positive peace—not simply a lack of conflict, but a sharing of norms and beliefs about society. The peace through integration idea, also referred to as "peace by pieces" (see the discussion in Chapter 6 on security communities), should work both between countries and within countries. For example, if a hostile ethnic division exists within a country, conflict could be reduced by tying the two ethnic groups together so that they need each other for their survival.

Another example is the loans granted by the World Bank, an international organization that funds development projects around the world. While loans are generally given to countries in need, the World Bank often requires the recipient country to engage in free-market reforms, thereby compelling recipient states to do something they have previously resisted. Such mandated free-market reforms change local relationships, with some local economic actors benefitting and others losing the advantages they previously enjoyed. More directly,

World Bank loans have sometimes been used to coerce other states, as the United States did when it blocked loans to Chile between 1970 and 1973 in an attempt to coerce the Chilean president, Salvador Allende, to step down from power. In this example, *economic* power was used to seek a *political* goal. Similarly, donors may use **bilateral** foreign aid (loans from one state directly to another) to accomplish both economic and political goals. When donors like Japan require recipients of their foreign aid to purchase Japanese products and services, the donors are doing more than just benefitting their own economies and pleasing locally important constituencies; they are also denying the recipient of other choices in the international free market. Once again, money is power. Another "golden rule" can be inferred: *those who have the gold get to make the rules!*

8-1a Markets and Governments: A Sometimes Tense and Codependent Relationship

Fundamental to the connections between politics and economics is both the tension and symbiotic relationship between the government and the market. Governments try to maintain control of their territorial borders; Chapter 2 notes that this is a necessary component of sovereignty, but businesses see borders as slowing down their ability to sell goods and services. When governments tell local businesses they cannot sell products to certain states, such announcements cannot endear the government to those corporate entities. For example, Hughes Communications would love to sell more satellites and services to Chinese purchasers (and the Chinese would love to buy them), but U.S. regulations on the export of high-technology items limit what Hughes can sell. Similarly, U.S. agribusiness giant Archer Daniels Midland would like to sell more food on the world market, but again governmentally imposed sanctions limit (as in the case of Cuba) or prevent such sales (as in the cases of Iran and North Korea).

Governments also create and enforce property ownership laws, thereby protecting commercial investments and creating the law and order that businesses require. Governments can be the agents of businesses in prying open previously closed foreign markets, as the United States did in the 1990s when China sought U.S. support for its entry into the World Trade Organization (WTO). Entrance into the WTO meant lower and fewer restrictions on trade with China. One result of that pressure is that China purchased about 3 million General Motors vehicles and about 1 million Ford vehicles in 2013— that's more than 300,000 automobiles sold each month!

bilateral relations between two states. For example, a bilateral summit is a high-level conference between two states.

FIGURE 8-1 THE DEVELOPMENT OF THE WORLD ECONOMY

 The National Economy Era, 1648–1815

 The International Economy Era, 1815–1975

The Global Economy Era, 1975–present

© Cengage Learning®

Additionally, governments provide public goods—such as infrastructure and education—that businesses need. Smooth highways and educated workers make for more profitable business. The economy provides the government with the source of tax revenues needed to maintain power and security in the global system. Thus overall, businesses and governments need each other, but at times their individual interests diverge, if not directly clash.

While the connections between politics and money may be straightforward and ubiquitous, the question of how states acquire wealth is not. The means by which a state could gain wealth and thus security have changed dramatically since the Treaties of Westphalia. Over time, states pursued wealth by colonialism/mercantilism, capitalism/liberalism, and Marxism. While the dominant system today is a liberal (meaning "free") or capitalist market economy marked by relatively free or liberal trade, the wide acceptance of that system is only relatively recent, and the capitalist system has experienced serious difficulties over the past half-decade. To understand the pursuit of wealth and power and how the world economy has developed, let's consider different economic practices and policies that evolved through time. If we begin with the establishment of the Westphalian system in 1648, we can divide the development of the world economy into three major eras, each of which had some distinctive characteristics. Figure 8-1 shows those eras graphically.

8-2 THE NATIONAL ECONOMY ERA: COLONIALISM AND MERCANTILISM

The first major era of the world economy was the National Economy Era, which best describes the late stages of the pre-Westphalian and early part of the Westphalian eras. During this phase of the world economy, most economic activity occurred within, rather than across, the borders of states. During this period, the pursuit of wealth and security had two most important features: mercantilism and colonialism. As states engaged in economic activity and competed with each other for wealth and power, most of them embraced an economic philosophy called **mercantilism**. Mercantilism promoted the idea that the government would work directly with business leaders to promote economic growth by subsidizing the businesses and forbidding the purchase of goods and services from other countries unless absolutely necessary (a practice called **protectionism**). Governments would also use their militaries to secure resources for businesses—a process nicely illustrated in the film *Master and Commander: The Far Side of the World* (2003). By helping domestic businesses make money and protecting them from foreign competition, the government could make its economy stronger. With a stronger economy came a stronger military that could be used to gain more colonies.

As states engaged in these mercantilist strategies, they also competed for control of foreign territories to gain exclusive access to its resources. Even before the Westphalian era began, European powers such as Spain and Portugal started to seek out new territories for conquest and colonization as it became more difficult to take European territories from societies better able to protect themselves. This process, **colonialism**, was the first modern way in which states could increase their wealth. Going back centuries, states would attack and pillage each other for economic gain, but colonialism was different. The imperial state would discover new territory, claim the land, inhabitants, and wealth for itself, and create a colonial government to rule the new land, such as Spain's colonization of the Americas. As the cartoon suggests, the colonial government would extract raw materials, such as gold, silver, and agricultural products, and

mercantilism an economic policy that combines free enterprise and government. The government uses its power—including its military—to enhance private business, and private business provides revenues to the government to maintain and enhance its power.

protectionism a policy of blocking or restricting the trade from other countries in order to "protect" domestic businesses from economic competition with foreign companies.

colonialism the situation where one country takes over another country and administers it with a local bureaucracy.

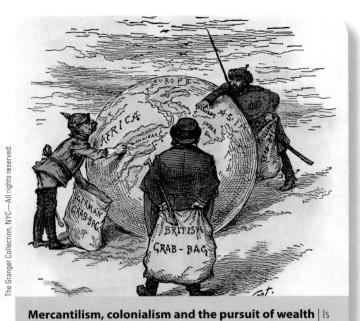

Mercantilism, colonialism and the pursuit of wealth | Is it surprising that European countries sought colonies?

send them back to the **metropole**, or mother country. It was like adding another smaller economy to the existing state, rather than simply plundering the land for a one-time gain of wealth.

Of course, once the Europeans discovered the Americas as well as the value of territories throughout Asia and Africa, serious competition for the new land began. These conflicts were imperialistic wars that aimed to gain and maintain the most valuable colonies around the globe. For example, the British and French fought over North American colonies, the British and Dutch fought over Indonesia and South Africa, the British and Portuguese fought over India, the British and Russians fought over Afghanistan, and so on. As a result of such conflicts, by the late nineteenth century one could say

metropole the "mother city" or center of an empire. The metropole of the British Empire (which included colonies on every continent except Antarctica) was London.

beggar-thy-neighbor an economic policy that stresses trade protectionism and causes other countries to bear the costs of efforts at securing prosperity at home.

absolute advantage when a country is more efficient at producing a single good than another country.

comparative advantage being more efficient at producing a good or service relative to another good or service. Even if one country has an absolute advantage over another in all products, both countries benefit by specializing in the products they each produce most efficiently (their comparative advantage) and trading for the others.

that "the sun never sets on the British Empire" because it in fact did not. It was always daylight somewhere in the British Empire. As these examples demonstrate, the British were not the only European imperialists, but they were arguably the most successful imperialists in history.

The problem with mercantilism is that if all states follow this **beggar-thy-neighbor** philosophy and forbid most trade with other countries, then there would be almost no international trade. Consequently, states would not be able to increase their wealth except through the acquisition of more colonies. As you can imagine, this led to a very competitive and conflict-oriented world economy.

8-3 THE INTERNATIONAL ECONOMY ERA: FREE TRADE, LIBERALISM, AND MARXISM

In the second era, trade between states grew to much greater levels and played an increasingly important role in world politics. Two factors more than any others arose in the latter part of the National Economy Era and led to the International Economy Era. In the late eighteenth century, economists Adam Smith and David Ricardo advanced powerful arguments for the idea of free trade rather than mercantilism as the optimal approach for the pursuit of wealth and power. In his path-breaking work *The Wealth of Nations*, Adam Smith argued that efficient, competitive nations should specialize their economies to be more effective at creating wealth, focusing their activities on the product or products they produced better than other countries, and trading with other states for the rest. This idea became known as **absolute advantage**.

David Ricardo then added to Smith's ideas and argued that through free trade, all countries—even inefficient ones—would develop and could become wealthy by focusing on producing the products they themselves did better than other products—even if they did not produce these things better than another country. This concept—the basis of modern trade theory—is known as **comparative advantage**. (See the box Theory in Action: Should Countries Pursue Free Trade? for a discussion of these ideas and the advantages of free trade.) What is important for us to understand here is how this idea emerged and influenced key leaders—especially in Britain—to engage in different approaches to economic security.

Smith's and Ricardo's ideas—and the policies to which they led—are referred to generally as "liberal economic policy." Before we go any further, it is important to understand what we mean by *liberal*. It is not the U.S.

domestic political meaning, for example, a "liberal Democrat," nor are we discussing the international relations theory called "liberalism." Instead, liberal economic policy simply means economic policy that is driven by supply and demand in a free market rather than controlled or regulated by government.

The second factor is mostly technological—the rise of the **Industrial Revolution**. At about the same time that free trade was being advanced, a major transformation of economic activity also began. The Industrial Revolution fundamentally involved the development of new manufacturing processes that shifted economic activity from hand production to processes involving increasingly advanced machines that enabled large-scale production on the farm, in businesses, and in factories. Manufactured products—first textiles and then other goods—became the core of economic growth in more and more countries as the Industrial Revolution proceeded in the nineteenth and twentieth centuries.

The combination of these two factors—free trade and the Industrial Revolution—led to the International Economy Era. As we said, in this era, trade *between* countries became more important—you have to be able to get the raw materials needed for manufacturing and then be able to sell all those products somewhere! This era was not without its ups and downs, of course, and both mercantilism and colonialism also persisted as major practices. By the 1800s, as the Industrial Revolution was well underway, the competition for foreign trade and colonies was fierce. In the mid-1800s, Great Britain began to rise in economic and military power and gained the status of hegemon, or dominant world power. For the next seven decades, the leaders in London pushed the world to engage in less protectionism and greater free trade. During this period, the amount of trade worldwide increased significantly, and states increased their overall wealth

> **Industrial Revolution** the transition of many of the world's states from an agricultural economic system to one that was based on industry. During this period, factories replaced farms as the biggest producer in many countries.

THEORY IN ACTION

Should Countries Pursue Free Trade?

Why should states engage in free trade? Wouldn't it be better for a country to sell products to other countries but not buy any foreign goods so that it could make money from other countries? With some exceptions, the answer is no. Free trade benefits all states that participate, even if the two states are not equal in their abilities.

An example will help (see Table 8-1). Imagine two states, District 1 and District 12. District 1 is particularly good at producing food—it only takes its citizens one hour to produce a pizza, but it takes District 1 two hours to produce a bicycle. District 12 is better at bicycle

TABLE 8-1 BENEFIT OF SPECIALIZATION

	No Specialization or Trade			
	Hours to Produce		**Total Produced in an 8-Hour Day (splitting time evenly for both products)**	
	Pizza	Bicycle	Pizzas	Bicycles
District 1	1	2	4	2
District 12	6	3	0.67	1.33
Total Combined Production = 4.67 pizzas + 3.33 bicycles = 8 units produced				
	With Specialization and Trade			
	Hours to Produce		**Total Produced in an 8-Hour Day (specializing in one product)**	
	Pizza	Bicycle	Pizzas	Bicycles
District 1	1	2	8	
District 12	6	3		2.67
Total Combined Production = 8 pizzas + 2.67 bicycles = 10.67 units produced				

© Cengage Learning®

production compared to pizza production. It takes that country three hours to produce a bicycle but six hours to produce a pizza. If the two countries divided an eight-hour day evenly between pizza and bicycles, District 1 would produce four pizzas and two bicycles. District 12 would produce one and one-third bicycles but only two-thirds of a pizza. In total, eight units (four and two-thirds pizzas and three and one-third bicycles) would have been produced between the two countries.

If the two countries specialized in what they do best and then traded with each other, both countries would be better off. District 1 would produce eight pizzas in an eight-hour day and District 12 would produce two and two-thirds bicycles. In total, that's ten and two-thirds units produced—more than before. Thus, by specializing and trading, the two countries both have more.

In the real world, there are many goods and many countries, but the principle still applies. The United States is better at producing the designs for iPods because of the technical skill and training of its workforce. China is better at assembling those iPods because its labor costs are significantly lower. Similarly, the United States is better at producing higher education—American colleges and universities are the best in the world. Saudi Arabia is best at producing oil. This does not mean that the United States does not produce some oil and Saudi Arabia has no higher education, but that the two countries specialize more in the areas where they have a comparative advantage.

So should countries always engage in trade? If you ask economists, they would likely say yes. There are many situations, however, in which a country should not trade specific products, or perhaps even most products. First, trading military weapons could put a country at risk if the state from which it buys its weapons becomes an enemy. If a state depends on another state for its weapons, it is also dependent on that state for its security. Smaller states do not have much choice, but for larger states, there is a long history of producing many of the state's weapons domestically to avoid such vulnerabilities.

Similarly, selling weapons to a potential enemy isn't a good policy since those weapons could be turned against you. The United States is the world's largest arms seller and in several cases sold weapons to countries that later became its enemies. For example, the United States armed the mujahideen in Afghanistan with Stinger surface-to-air missiles when they were fighting the Soviets in the 1980s. Some of the mujahideen later became members of the Taliban and al-Qaeda, and not all of those Stinger missiles have been accounted for!

Quality control is another issue that could lead a state to not purchase goods from other countries. There was a large recall of toys produced in China in 2007 because lead paint—dangerous to small children who might ingest it—was used. Similarly, environmental and labor concerns could influence people to purchase only domestically produced products. Some may only purchase locally produced vegetables and fruit because transporting those products from other countries tends to pollute heavily. As we discuss later in the chapter, some universities will not sell college apparel made in countries that do not have laws protecting the workers making all of the clothes with the university's logo.

Another reason not to engage in trade is to develop an industry within your own country. For example, allowing only domestically produced farm equipment to be sold in one's country gives farm equipment producers more customers and thus profits. Those profits could be used to develop the industry. We go into a deeper discussion of this policy, called import substitution industrialization, in Chapter 10. Beyond that, some argue that certain industries are so vital for economic growth and competition (in today's world, microchips are a good example), or so strategic for security (perhaps steel, or some strategic metals) that a country should be engaged in their production if possible.

In each of these cases, an economist might tell you that specialization and trade are still better because they are more efficient (Table 8-1). It is a compelling argument, but perhaps efficiency is not the only factor to consider in this situation.

1. What other goods or services might a country not want to trade freely?

2. Could you defend that argument before an economist?

substantially. During the early and middle 1800s, British leadership—and economic power—was central to the establishment of free trade and significant economic growth. As the earliest beneficiary of the Industrial Revolution and the most powerful state of this time, the British took the lead in reducing barriers to trade to encourage others to do the same.

8-3a World (Trade) War

However, the British economy began to suffer relative to the other states in the late 1800s, particularly compared to two rising powers: Germany and the United States. Both the Germans and the Americans raised tariffs to protect their infant industries. Since neither of these countries had the tremendous industrial capacity that

Why Did the Europeans Colonize Asia, Africa, and the Americas and Not the Other Way Around?

For centuries the international system has been dominated by states in Europe, and for the past 70 years a former European colony, the United States, has been a dominant power. The world's most powerful militaries and economies are mostly European or American. The international system is based on European history, and the *lingua franca* is English. This situation is just something that most of us accept as the way things are. We may think there are both good and bad consequences to the European dominance of the world, but have you ever asked yourself why Europe has such a dominant role and not China, or Egypt, or Brazil, or some other country? For example, China was more advanced than Europe when Marco Polo visited it in the 1200s. So why didn't the Chinese colonize the world? Similarly, the Inca civilization was very advanced and powerful and yet was easily toppled by the Spanish—why?

In *Guns, Germs, and Steel*, Jared Diamond argues that Europe provided the right physical environment to domesticate plants and livestock not found in other parts of the world. These plants and animals not only provided food but were also easily transplanted into other areas. Wheat is an excellent example of a food that developed in Europe but can be grown in many climates around the world. Domesticated plants and animals gave Europeans an edge because they provided easy access to a fundamental resource—food—that they could take with them when they explored new areas. Still, why did they seek out other lands?

Although history is too complex to name a single cause, the rise of capitalism in Europe is one very powerful reason for Europe's dominance to this day. At its root, capitalism promotes the constant seeking of more wealth, and

seeking more wealth means *expansion*. European merchants and governments continually sought to expand their reach and consequently colonized and conquered much of the world. In addition to the push of capitalism, Christianity also promoted the idea that the Europeans should go out and convert the world's population to their religion. Thus, religious impulses reinforced economic ones.

Compare Europe's push for exploration to the Chinese. Despite the fact that Chinese Admiral Zheng took seven voyages to explore much of Asia and the Indian Ocean between 1405 and 1430, the successors of the Chinese emperor he served turned inward. Satisfied with their wealth and culture, they sought to isolate themselves from the rest of the world. By 1500, it was illegal in China to build an oceangoing ship. It isn't surprising, then, that the Chinese didn't colonize the world.

It is now easier to answer the question: why did the British and other Europeans states end up controlling China? Because these countries developed oceangoing vessels that not only allowed them to explore but also to project their power and conquer countries they discovered. Without having a capitalist economy, China didn't have the same internal pressures to continually increase profits, nor did China have a religion that pushed it to create missions around the globe.

Thus, the capitalist search for more wealth and power led the Europeans to seek out and control the rest of the world, and their more robust plants and animals helped pave their way to controlling much of Africa, Asia, and the Americas.

1. Had the Chinese not isolated themselves, how would the world be different, or would it?

2. Is there something else about Europe that made it the powerhouse it was for so many years?

Sources: Jared Diamond, *Guns, Germs, and Steel: The Fates of Human Societies* (New York: W.W. Norton, 1997); and Fareed Zakaria, *The Post-American World* (New York: W.W. Norton, 2009).

the United Kingdom did, they were not as dependent on trade, and in the case of the United States, its domestic economy was so large, it had plenty of customers at home. Although France was already established as an economic power, it followed suit and instituted a series of protectionist measures that restricted foreign trade. It did this in part to hurt the British and in part to protect its own economy from the trade restrictions in the United States and Germany. These actions hurt the British economy

by reducing the flow of goods and services it could sell overseas. Because the United Kingdom is an island state, it was very dependent on trade with other countries (another revenge of geography). Thus, the restrictions in trade by the United States, France, and Germany were particularly problematic for the British.

As other states gained in power relative to the British, London was no longer able to compel them to engage in free trade. Markets began to close to foreign trade, and the competition to sell goods overseas and colonize the remaining areas left unclaimed by the imperial powers contributed to World War I. In particular, the United Kingdom and France already controlled many colonies, and the United States controlled large sections of Latin America (although these were not officially colonies). Germany, on the other hand, had few colonies (chiefly in Africa), and these were not particularly valuable. The Treaty of Versailles that ended World War I placed a huge debt burden on Germany, forcing the fragile democracy to pay for costs of the war. This crushed the German economy and sent it into a state of **hyperinflation**. When an economy suffers from hyperinflation, it simply means that its money loses its value at a very fast rate. Instead of a typical rate of inflation, say 3 percent (the level targeted as healthy in the United States prior to 2007), hyperinflation can mean inflation rates in the hundreds or thousands of percent. For Germany, it meant that the cost of a loaf of bread could go up by ten times in a single day! At the worst point in its economy, the German Bundesbank actually printed a currency note worth 100 trillion marks; postage stamps were valued at 50 billion marks. In today's terms, that would mean a stamp in the United States would cost about $63 billion. Just imagine what your latte would cost! It's almost impossible to even imagine such economic problems.

By the mid-1920s, the major countries in the world decided that the best way to help their weak economies was to close off trade with other countries and resume many of the beggar-thy-neighbor approaches to wealth that were characteristic of mercantilism. Instead of helping matters, these protectionist policies caused a serious **trade war** between the major world economies, and as a consequence the level of global trade plummeted. When trade plummeted, there was less money changing hands and thus less wealth produced. Many argue that this trade war contributed to the Great Depression in the United States and around the world. This economic disaster also had major political consequences. The severe economic depression provided a perfect environment for an extremist like Adolf Hitler to rise to power in Germany, and it pushed the Japanese military to attempt to secure and put under direct Japanese control additional

resource-rich territories around the Pacific Rim. While these were not the only causes of the Second World War to be sure, they did contribute directly to it.

It is important to note that even though mercantilism was viewed as a contributing factor to World War II and roundly criticized by the leading economists in the world, it did not disappear after World War II. Several states continue to practice modern-day forms of mercantilism such as import substitution and export-led growth. In Chapter 10, we discuss these policies and the countries like Japan, South Korea, and Mexico that either have practiced them or continue to practice them to this day.

8-3b Marxism

As the ideas of Smith and Ricardo were beginning to take hold, another economic approach was born. Though embracing the Industrial Revolution, this economic system did not seek to gain wealth as much as it sought equality among all people. As we discussed in Chapter 4, Karl Marx developed the theory of communism that asserted there were five historical epochs in the history of human society. The first was primitive communism, which was essentially the simple hunter-gatherer society found throughout the world before the rise of civilizations. Second was feudalism, the agricultural system of lords and serfs that reigned during the Middle Ages and into the very early modern times in Europe and Asia. Next was capitalism, the system where goods and services (labor) were sold. Marx predicted that capitalism would end with a revolution of the workers and the creation of a new government that would take over the economy and make it equal for all people. This stage, called socialism, would end when the government "withered" away and a new utopian, communist world would exist with no government, no inequality, and no poverty.

Marx expected the socialist revolution to start in Great Britain during the Industrial Revolution. Instead, it started in Russia in 1917 and led to the rise of the Union of Soviet Socialist Republics (better known as the Soviet Union). More socialist revolutions began, most notably in China, North Korea, Vietnam, Cambodia, and Cuba. The Soviet Union also created or sponsored socialist governments throughout Eastern Europe in countries such as Poland, East Germany, Czechoslovakia, Romania, Bulgaria, and Hungary.

Sadly, these regimes became little more than autocracies seeking to control their people and the wealth of the country. Three of the world's four worst mass murderers were Marxist dictators. Joseph Stalin, the leader of the Soviet Union from the late 1920s to 1953, had

hyperinflation a situation where a currency loses its value very quickly. Regular inflation occurs at relatively low levels (3 to 5 percent per year), but hyperinflation means a currency can lose most of its value in a year, month, or even day.

trade war a situation when many or all states engage in protectionism. The states try to block imports and promote exports, but since all countries do this, very little international trade occurs.

approximately 38 million Soviet citizens murdered, nearly five times the number of people that died in the Nazi concentration camps during the Holocaust. The leader of China from 1949 to 1976, Mao Zedong, also presided over the deaths of millions of people, and Pol Pot, the dictator of Cambodia, had 20 percent of that country's population tortured and killed. Each of these three dictators all professed to follow some form of Marxism, though in reality they were no more than dictators. Marxist ideology and policy itself does not endorse mass killing or the repression of people. In fact, it aims to liberate people from unjust working conditions and the misbelief in capitalism. The philosophy created by Marx, however, has been misused regularly throughout history.

8-3c Marxism Implemented

Aside from the autocratic nature of the regimes and some homicidal leaders, most of the Marxist countries attempted to modernize their economies and provide full employment for all of their citizens. In a Marxist system, the government controls the economy entirely or almost entirely. Thus, every business, factory, and firm is owned by the state and every worker is employed by the state. The government determines what will be produced, how much it will cost, and when people are permitted to purchase goods. This is referred to as a **centrally planned** (or **command**) **economy**.

While the Soviets and Chinese were able to make some strides toward modernizing and developing their economies, ultimately, central control of the economy failed. In the case of the Soviet Union, as long as it was relatively easy to do *more* of what the Soviet economy already had the ability to do—cultivate more land, cut more lumber, make more steel, and so on—the Soviet economy grew nicely. However, once the easy limits of such additional effort were reached and the Soviet economy had to become more innovative, its growth slowed. For example, the Soviets largely missed the electronics revolution brought on by the use of transistors and then semiconductors that led to the development of personal computers in the 1980s. By the mid-1980s, the Soviet economy stopped growing altogether and began to shrink. The result was a near economic collapse and a complete collapse of the government. In China's case, the government started moving away from the centrally planned economy in the late 1970s. The free market reforms improved the economy and greatly increased the standard of living for many Chinese. To this day, there are few governments that profess a belief in Marxism as an economic policy—North Korea and Cuba being the only notable cases, and Cuba is now beginning to allow limited buying and selling of some private property. The rest of the world has embraced some form of capitalism, although as we discuss in the following chapters, some of Marx's ideas are implemented in even the most capitalist countries to this day.

It is important to note that many Marxist scholars and activists argue that the failure of Marxism was not because the theory and its prescriptions were wrong but because all of the countries that adopted Marxism were not ready. They argue that unless a state has gone through capitalism, it cannot become socialist and then finally communist. None of the countries that embraced Marxism were truly capitalist before Marxism took hold, and many were simply advanced feudal societies. According to this perspective on Marxism, they were doomed to fail from the start and Marx is still right: as it develops and spreads, capitalism will ultimately fail and give way to a socialist government. Do the consequences of globalization, including the recent Great Recession of 2008–2010, suggest that could happen?

8-3d From International to Global Economy Eras: The Liberal International Economic Order after World War II

As World War II drew to a close, American leaders reflected on what they thought had led to such a destructive conflict. The general sense of governmental leaders was that World War II was largely a consequence of the trade war and economic discrimination between nations. The trade war created greater discord between the states and drove their economies into severe crisis. The economic discrimination took the form of competition for resources and colonies—Germany wanted more and better colonial assets and Japan wanted more resources, while the entrenched imperial powers had no interest in giving up any of their wealth. Leaders in the United States, and to a lesser extent in the United Kingdom and France, began to believe that if countries could agree to trade freely—and cooperate together to do so—then countries would become wealthier and there would be a greater chance for continuing peace after the war. Looking at Figure 8-2, you can see why U.S. leaders believed trade was so important—the United States accounted for a large portion of world trade by the end of World War II.

centrally planned (or **command**) **economy** an economy that is run by the government rather than private citizens. Examples include the Soviet Union and North Korea.

INTERNATIONAL TRADE AND INTERNATIONAL PEACE Why should liberalized trade make countries better off and promote peace? First, as we noted earlier, modern theories of free trade are based on Ricardo's idea of comparative advantage (more so than Smith's idea of absolute advantage). Ricardo showed that if countries specialize in making the products at which they are most efficient (compared to what else they produce), and then trade them with other countries, they would be able to make more money than if they tried to produce all the products they need. For example, the United States can get oil more cheaply from Saudi Arabia than produce all of it in America, while the Saudis can buy apples more cheaply from the United States rather than try to grow them in the desert. There are serious consequences to free trade (see Theory in Action: Should Countries Pursue Free Trade?), but its overall economic benefits are widely accepted by the major industrial powers in the international system.

The second advantage of international trade is that countries that trade with one another tend not to fight each other on the battlefield. The idea originated with Immanuel Kant, who suggested over 200 years ago that commerce and war were not compatible. If two countries exchange many goods and services, such as the United States and China, then war between the two would be bad for business. A war between the United States and China would end the exchange between the two countries. For the United States, that would mean the production of iPods, iPhones, iPads, and other consumer electronic devices would have to be moved. That is, the factories that produce these goods would have to be built in another country. Your cell phone, laptop, or TV would cost significantly more if the company that made it had to rebuild an entire factory. Similarly, the birthday gift for your nephew or niece could cost twice as much if it wasn't produced in China. On the other hand, the Chinese would no longer receive the large payments for assembling the electronics,

toys, and other goods that the United States purchases. Many of their factories would have to shut down, unemployment would rise, and their economy would suffer. War would simply not be good for business. What would China do with all these unemployed workers—put them in the military? Could it afford to pay them?

There is another pacifying effect of trade that is less obvious than the costs to business. As two states trade with one another, they begin to learn about each other's cultures. Levi's blue jeans and the television show *Dallas* were popular in the Soviet Union in the final years of the Cold War. In 1989, Pepsi launched a commercial about how Soviet young adults were drinking Pepsi and acting just like Americans. This cultural exchange made it so Americans and Soviets realized they were not that different. Essentially, it is harder to hate someone if they like the same clothes, entertainment, and food because they are not so strange and foreign; they are a lot like you. Thus, trade can help countries better understand each other, and with understanding comes a greater willingness to talk rather than fight.

New York Times columnist Thomas Friedman once argued that countries with McDonald's franchises never go to war with each other.[1] Although this "Golden Arches theory" has been proven wrong—for example, NATO countries went to war with Serbia over Kosovo, Russia invaded the Republic of Georgia and Ukraine, and Israel invaded Lebanon—and the issue was obviously more about the economic and cultural linkages represented by McDonald's than the fast-food operation itself, the idea that commerce can lead to peace is a powerful one.

BUILDING A LIBERAL INTERNATIONAL ECONOMIC ORDER Given these reasons that trade may help keep the peace, in 1944, the United States convened a meeting in Bretton Woods, New Hampshire, to help ensure that countries would not engage in another trade war

Young Soviet citizens drinking Pepsi in Moscow in 1983 | If you didn't see the Cyrillic letters on the Pepsi sign, could you tell that these weren't Germans, or French, or Canadians? Does profit have a nationality?

like the one precipitating the Great Depression and World War II. The result was the establishment of what is often referred to as the **Liberal International Economic Order (LIEO)**, which combined commitments to the ideas of free trade and free market economics with the construction of international institutions to help countries coordinate and cooperate in their pursuit of economic security. Like the early decades of the International Economy Era, the LIEO also involved the leadership of a hegemon, with the United States drawing on its role as the most powerful country in the world to build the LIEO and help it operate.

Taking its name from the location of the talks, the meeting established what came to be known as the **Bretton Woods System**, which created the **World Bank** and the **International Monetary Fund**, or **IMF**, international organizations that we introduced and described in Chapter 7. (Chapter 10 discusses how the Bretton Woods system promotes economic development as well as other development issues.) As noted in Chapter 7, the World Bank is an IO that seeks to help countries develop their economies. The organization provides loans to countries for development projects such as building port facilities, water systems, airports, or other infrastructure. Some of these loans have been very successful and others very problematic and troubled. The successes are almost completely limited to smaller projects, such as building schools and clinics. The failures, unfortunately, tend to be big. For example in the early 1980s, the World Bank loaned Brazil funds to develop iron ore mining. When the price of steel (iron infused with carbon through smelting) dropped, Brazil turned to cutting down its rainforests to make charcoal for the

smelting so that it could pay back the loan. Thus, the World Bank contributed—unintentionally—to deforestation. Because of these big failures, the World Bank is often criticized, and its sole focus on growth for the first five decades led to many tragic mistakes such as the one described in Brazil. Since the 1990s, more attention is paid to sustainable development, and the World Bank tries more to provide advice, collect data, and report on the economic development of the world in an attempt to help developing countries be part of the plan to grow their economies in responsible ways.

The IMF, also described in Chapter 7, seeks "to foster global monetary cooperation, secure financial stability, facilitate international trade, promote high employment and sustainable economic growth, and reduce poverty around the world."[2] Originally, the IMF had two functions. First, it was a source of emergency, mostly short-term loans and financing for countries facing balance-of-payments imbalances, so its member states would work together to address these problems rather than act unilaterally and inflict harm on others (we discuss this function in Chapter 10).

Second, the IMF also sought to fix all currencies at one level and coordinate those levels so that there would be no floating or changing exchange rate. This policy also reduced beggar-thy-neighbor policies by requiring IMF members to work together to manage their currency values rather than acting alone in self-serving ways that could hurt other states. However, the IMF was too small and too underfunded to accomplish such a task. Instead, the United States took on this role until 1971 when currencies were allowed to be traded in the market and thus float. This system was called the "U.S. gold standard"

Liberal International Economic Order (LIEO) the post-World War II international economic system built on commitments to free trade and free market economies, with international institutions to help countries coordinate and cooperate.

Bretton Woods System the global economic system established by the United States and other countries after World War II to promote capitalism, free trade, and policy coordination. Nicknamed "Bretton Woods" for the location of the conference in New Hampshire, the two core institutions created were the IMF and World Bank.

World Bank a Bretton Woods organization created in 1945 that provides loans and grants to countries for long-term development. The World Bank started by helping fund the reconstruction of Europe after World War II and later focused on helping countries in the developing world grow their economies.

International Monetary Fund (IMF) one of the Bretton Woods organizations created in 1946 to help maintain a cooperative international financial system. The IMF helps countries facing balance-of-payment problems with short-term loans and also helps countries reschedule their debt.

Why Don't All States Sign Free Trade Agreements?

The work by Smith and Ricardo on free trade theory makes a tremendous amount of sense and, as this chapter lays out, much of the world accepts the fundamental idea that trade is good. Not only has world trade become freer and more extensive, there are also an increasing number of Free Trade Agreements (FTAs) among various groups of countries as well, for just this reason. FTAs normally encompass many industries and reduce or eliminate tariffs. As Smith and Ricardo postulated, FTAs spur economic growth for all the states involved. If that is the case, however, why haven't all the states in the world signed FTAs with each other?

For several decades after World War II, most of the developing world resisted the move to liberalized trade policy. In a variety of ways, countries from all regions embraced policies that involved more state management and protectionism, and tried to use their numbers in majority-rule institutions such as the UN to establish organizations and initiatives that gave them advantages. In just one example, in Chapter 10, we discuss a policy called import substitution industrialization. This is basically a mercantilist policy aimed at protecting an economy from foreign trade while it develops. During the 1960s and 1970s, many developing countries—especially in Latin America—used this policy and thus did not engage in free trade. However, starting in the 1980s, more and more countries started to open their borders to trade with others. Many developing countries sought out trade agreements with the developed world—Mexico joined with the United States and Canada to form the North American Free Trade Agreement in 1993, for example. In many regions, developing countries established trade agreements with each other to improve their standing in the global economy. Still, this process was and continues to be very slow.

To understand why states don't jump into trade agreements with each other, we must understand the importance of domestic politics. Trade with other countries creates winners and losers in each country. For example, if Japan freely allowed rice to be imported from other countries, Japanese rice producers would go out of business. Land and labor are extremely expensive in Japan, so the price of domestically grown rice

is quite high. Thus, trade would mean domestic rice farmers would lose. The Japanese consumer would win, of course, because the cost of rice would drop. For this reason, free trade is not a simple choice. Instead, it involves groups within each country that are both for and against the trade.

It is not just the domestic politics of winners and losers that lead states to either sign or reject an FTA. First, states are concerned with their security. An FTA can provide important economic growth, strategic products, and a reduced likelihood of conflict with the other member or members of the FTA. Thus, signing an FTA can enhance a state's security. Similarly, if all of the other countries in a region are signing FTAs, then *not* signing one could threaten a state's security. In essence, it is not good to be the last state left out in the cold while all the neighboring countries have joined FTAs. On the other hand, becoming vulnerable to the actions of others through increased trade may have security consequences as well. Ask Europeans if they feel more secure by being increasingly dependent on Russia for natural gas.

A recent article shows that South Korea prefers to sign FTAs not only with other countries who have signed FTAs but also with fellow democracies.[3] South Korea, like other developed democracies, has a preference for signing FTAs with other democracies because democracies are more accountable and thus less likely to cheat on an agreement.

So for as much as Smith and Ricardo were right—free trade helps all participating economies grow—we must consider the domestic politics of the states, their security interests, and how trustworthy they consider each other. Thus, a realist, liberal, or Marxist perspective can't explain fully *why* states engage in trade and particularly FTAs. We must employ a foreign policy perspective to understand international trade.

1. What factors explain the shift of much of the developing world toward free trade practices over the past several decades?

2. How might other domestic factors such as culture influence the trade relations between states?

3. How can a government overcome domestic objections to free trade?

4. Should states consider moral and ethical issues when choosing to trade with another state?

Fixed and Floating Exchange Rates

What are fixed and floating exchange rates? A fixed exchange rate sets the exchange between two currencies, such as the U.S. dollar and the Japanese yen, to always be the same; it would not change from day to day. So if one U.S. dollar was equal to 77 Japanese yen today, it would be the same tomorrow, next week, next month, and so on. However, in a floating system, which is what we have now, the exchange rate changes not just from day to day but also from minute to minute. For example, on May 21, 2014, one dollar was equal to 101.3 yen; on June 10, 2014, one dollar was worth 102.3 yen. That difference isn't much if you're only exchanging a few dollars, or even a few thousand dollars. Imagine you were exchanging $1 million. You would get 1,000,000 more yen on June 10—that's $9,772!

Because these small differences add up quickly, countries are tempted to set their exchange rates so that they favor their own economy. Americans will purchase more Japanese products when the exchange rate is 102.3 yen to the dollar simply because the Americans are getting more Japanese yen for their dollar. If a country sets the exchange rate, it can make its products cheaper and thus sell more to other countries. This is exactly what China does right now. There is an official exchange rate that makes Chinese products cheaper than if the Chinese currency (the *renminbi*, or *yuan*) floated (which simply means it is exchanged in free currency markets). The United States and European countries regularly criticize China and pressure the country to alter its exchange rate so that Chinese citizens will buy more American and European products, but China has made only a few changes to its currency, preferring to send the problem to other nations in a true beggar-thy-neighbor policy. China is pursuing its narrowly defined national interests, but do you think that the Chinese decision is a wise one?

---

because the United States fixed its currency value to gold (at $35 per ounce) and the other IMF members pegged their currency rates to the gold-backed U.S. dollar (with small ranges for adjustment as coordinated and approved by the IMF). The U.S. gold standard is often referred to as one of the four Bretton Woods institutions (see the following for the fourth), but by 1971, the United States could no longer support the system and was running out of gold to back the dollar. In 1971, President Nixon ended the U.S. gold standard and, while the emergency loan/financing function of the IMF continued, its fixed exchange rate function ended. See Spotlight On: Fixed and Floating Exchange Rates to see what happened next.

Although the IMF could not control currencies, it did take the lead in helping countries that were having difficulty paying their debt obligations. This process is similar to an individual person facing bankruptcy and rescheduling their debt. At the country level, the IMF provides large loans and guarantees loans for commercial banks to provide the country the cash to continue paying its debts. Think of an infusion of cash that allows the country to pay the minimum required on its loans. These loans and guarantees do not come unconditionally. Instead, the IMF compels the troubled country to decrease its spending; this policy is referred to as an **austerity program**. The indebted country usually must cut back all non-essential spending—as defined by the IMF—such as assistance to the poor, public health

spending, and public education. The programs "work" in that these countries regain the ability to continue making their payments, but there is a serious cost. The state placed under the austerity program cuts spending so much that its citizens often get hurt—less food, medical care, and education. Are these the costs of fixing your economy?

Both of these organizations are supported by dues paid by member states based on the wealth of the member state. Thus, the United States pays more to the two organizations than does Canada or South Korea. Control of the organizations is also based on how much the member states contribute; thus the wealthiest nations, such as the United States, Japan, and Germany, have tremendous control over the organizations. Because of their large contributions, traditionally the IMF president is from Europe while the World Bank president is from the United States. How do you think critical theorists view these organizations?

BUT WHAT ABOUT TRADE During the Bretton Woods conference, the diplomats also tried to create an organization that would govern international trade.

> **austerity program** program of severely restricted government spending, often on welfare programs, imposed when the country must balance its accounts.

Negotiations for the International Trade Organization failed, however, largely because of disagreements over how agriculture could be traded. Shortly after the failure to create a functioning trade organization, the **General Agreement on Tariffs and Trade (GATT)** was created with a more limited goal: to promote free trade in the world. The organization promoted trade liberalization through **Most-Favored Nation (MFN)** status (in the United States, MFN is now referred to as NTR, or Normal Trade Relations). Each GATT member was required to give all other members the lowest tariff rate available—this rate was considered the MFN rate. During the many rounds of negotiation, GATT encouraged that states reciprocate toward each other when making trade deals. Thus, if Canada offered Japan a lower tariff rate on imported sake, Japan should offer Canada a lower rate on its imports of maple syrup.

GATT had two big weaknesses. First, it could not enforce any of the agreements its members made. Cooperation was completely voluntary. If a member did not want to reciprocate or it wanted to cheat on a trade deal, there was nothing that GATT could do about it. Second, GATT only covered tariffs, but there are other barriers to or problems with trade. Countries can subsidize a business, using tax dollars to pay for the development of products. This is considered "unfair" because the private business is getting help from its government. Airbus, the multinational European airplane manufacturer, benefitted from significant subsidies, which the United States complained bitterly about but GATT could do nothing. The other type of trade issue is the **nontariff barrier**. These are simply arbitrary rules that make it difficult to impossible for one country to sell its products in another. For example, the Japanese claimed it was a safety requirement that all cars could hold a certain amount of air pressure when the windows were rolled up. American cars were "leaky" at the time, making it more difficult for them to be sold in Japan. Thus, the

Japanese government was able to block trade with the United States without using a tariff, and again, GATT was unable to do anything about it. Even with these limitations, GATT nudged major economies in the direction of freer trade for nearly 50 years.

8-4 THE GLOBAL ECONOMY ERA

The establishment of the LIEO after World War II contributed to the development of the current era of the world economy—the Global Economy Era. The LIEO promoted and spread free trade and encouraged market economies that worked together, and it established international institutions to tie states together and help them cooperate. The LIEO also created the foundations for non-state actors such as multinational corporations and private financial institutions to operate more freely across borders and to extend their operations to more and more countries. Consequently, the LIEO basically fostered the forces of globalization that led to the Global Economy Era. Just as technology played a key role in the transition from the National to the International era, it also was central to the transition from the International to Global eras as well. In the latter case, the dramatic revolutions of technology in the last several decades— the computer era, the radical advance of information and communication technology, and the rapid development of faster and more efficient transportation—all played critical roles in transition to and nature of the Global Economy Era. Together, these factors constitute the

dpa/Landov

Apple founders Steve Jobs and Steve Wozniak in a garage in California in 1976 | U.S. entrepreneurs produced the world's first personal computers in the 1970s. In what year did the Soviet Union produce its first homegrown, mass-marketed personal computer? Is capitalism the best system for innovation?

General Agreement on Tariffs and Trade (GATT) an organization of countries that agree to work together to reduce trade barriers and promote free trade. Other members were considered "most favored nations" and received preferential trade agreements. The GATT was replaced by the World Trade Organization in 1995.

Most-Favored Nation (MFN) the preferential trade status that members of the GATT gave to other members. MFN could also be granted to non-members if a country chose to do so. The United States granted China MFN status for years before China entered the agreement.

nontariff barrier a requirement that foreign goods or services must meet that is specifically designed to block or obstruct those goods or services from sale in that market.

core of the forces of globalization that shape the modern economy and the pursuit of economic security in it.

8-4a The Modern Economy

In the Global Economy Era, the world has gravitated toward **liberal capitalism** as the dominant economic system. Even leaders from socialist parties—such as President Dilma Rousseff of Brazil—promote liberal trade with other countries. Instead of closing their borders to other countries and enacting laws that allowed the government to take over the economy as many Latin American leaders did in the past, leaders such as Rousseff and her predecessor President Lula da Silva enacted policies to limit inflation, pay off loans to the IMF, and push for stable economic growth—policies that are very similar to those of the developed capitalist states like the United States and Germany.

In the Global Economy Era, the share of virtually every country's economy made up of exports or imports has grown dramatically. European countries such as France, Italy, Germany, and the U.K., all have well over half their economies determined by trade, and the U.S. is over one-third. Interestingly, in the early 1970s, the share of the U.S. economy determined by trade was in single digits! Both China and Russia are about half international, and most developing countries are even higher. This is one very good illustration of what the Global Economy Era means—talking about a national economy makes less and less sense when so much of economic activity crosses borders, and a good share involves the activities of foreign companies in other states.

GLOBAL TRADE, ON STEROIDS In 1995, GATT, the LIEO institution promoting free trade, was replaced by the more powerful and effective World Trade Organization (WTO). Like GATT, the WTO is essentially a trading club in which all member countries agree to keep their markets open to foreign trade from other members by limiting tariffs and other trade barriers. If one state blocks another state from selling its products, the two states can go to the Dispute Settlement Body—effectively a "trade court"—and the WTO will determine if a rule is being broken. If the trade barrier is illegal under WTO rules, then the plaintiff state is permitted to sanction the other state to regain the revenue lost by not being able to sell its goods and services. In short, the WTO has the ability to write rules, administer them, adjudicate disputes, and penalize those who break the rules—effectively enforcing the agreements GATT could only hope were accepted voluntarily.

Let's consider an example to illustrate this process. Even before the WTO was created, the EU placed a ban on hormone-fed beef—such beef could not be sold in Europe. The United States contested the ban, and in 1997, the WTO ruled in favor of the United States because there is no scientific evidence suggesting that hormone-fed beef has any health-related side effects. Preferring "traditional" to "new and improved," the EU would not lift its ban on the meat, so the United States placed tariffs, as authorized by the WTO, on certain EU products to recoup the money lost from not being able to sell beef in the EU. The dispute continues to this day.

While the United States was on the winning side in that dispute, that is not always the case. In 2002, President Bush initiated an 8 to 30 percent tariff on all steel imports—a huge increase from the previous 0 percent to 1 percent tariff. The EU, Japan, South Korea, and several other states filed suit against the United States in the WTO's Dispute Settlement Body. The WTO found against the United States, but the Bush administration would not back down. The EU threatened to sanction the United States in accordance with the WTO ruling (just as the United States sanctions the EU over its hormone-fed beef ban), and the United States lifted the steel tariffs.

Another recent example involves U.S. cars and SUVs sold in China. Following the U.S. government bailout of American automobile companies, the Chinese government applied tariffs of 8 to 22 percent on U.S. cars and SUVs. That meant that a Chevrolet Suburban would cost 22 percent more in China than in the United States. The Chinese government claimed that these tariffs were to compensate for the loans the U.S. government gave to the auto companies. The U.S. claimed the tariffs were a violation of WTO rules, essentially accusing China of cheating. After a year of deliberation, the WTO found in favor of the United States. Although China had already lifted the tariffs, the WTO said that it had violated WTO rules by imposing the tariffs with no evidence that Chinese auto producers or the Chinese people were hurt by Chrysler, Ford, and GM.

Although the case was settled easily, it does show how a trade war begins. The Chinese saw an opportunity to gain against U.S. automobile producers, and so they exploited it. These tariffs clearly hurt the U.S., especially beleaguered Detroit, Michigan. Without the WTO, might the U.S. have retaliated with tariffs against Chinese products? Could that have led to more tariffs

---

liberal capitalism a philosophy of complete or near complete free markets and no governmental regulation in the economy. There are variations to liberal capitalism, but the idea is minimal government involvement in the economy.

by China? Of course, neither happened because each country has willingly subjected itself to WTO rule, thereby limiting its sovereignty.

It is not just the trade of goods and services that tie the global economy together. The speed of communication makes things possible today that weren't even dreamed of a few decades ago. During the Iraqi invasion of Kuwait in 1989, as its capital city was evacuating, employees of the National Bank of Kuwait *faxed* bank records out of the country that enabled the bank to continue functioning even after the invasion. It took hours and hours. This was considered a modern miracle, and it was for the time. Now, however, we can transfer information almost instantaneously. The speed with which we can access and transfer financial information means that we are all a little closer together. When you travel to Scotland, for example, you can get off the airplane, walk over to an ATM, and withdraw money from your bank account denominated in pounds sterling. There is only a second or two wait, and you are on your way to getting some delicious haggis. All of the sudden, the foreign country isn't so foreign and you're not so far away from home.

NON-STATE ACTORS AND THE PURSUIT OF WEALTH Liberalism not only promotes free markets and free trade, but it also creates an environment in which non-state actors of a wide variety matter, from international and non-governmental organizations to multinational corporations to individual people. In the global economy, international organizations, such as the WTO and IMF, affect the behavior of and relations between states in many ways. NGOs are also increasingly active and can have very dramatic effects as well (see our discussion of the neo-Westphalian era in Chapter 2 and our discussion of transnational advocacy networks in Chapter 13). Multinational corporations play a very powerful role as well. According to the WTO, world foreign direct investment (FDI) increased from $200 billion in 1989 to over $1.1 trillion at the start of the current century. Moreover, the top 500 MNCs in the world controlled over 70 percent of global trade by the start of the twenty-first century. As if that isn't impressive enough, the volume of money that crosses borders *each day* now approaches $2 trillion, as businesses, banks, and investors move money around in pursuit of profit.

devalue a situation when a currency, such as the U.S. dollar, loses its value compared to other currencies. For example, the Chinese government sets the exchange rate between the U.S. dollar and the Chinese yuan, and currently, the yuan is devalued; it is worth more than the Chinese will trade it for.

In the globalizing world, individuals matter, and sometimes they matter a lot. It is certainly easier to understand how an organization such as the IMF or WTO, or a major MNC such as Nike can affect how nations pursue wealth, but do you think an individual can affect an entire country? On September 11, 2001, we witnessed a non-state actor—al-Qaeda—mobilize the world's most powerful military, but can a person or small group affect a state's economy? Surprisingly, the answer is sometimes yes.

In 1992, George Soros contributed to the severe devaluation of the British currency, the pound sterling, so much that it was said he "broke" the Bank of England. Soros is a currency speculator, meaning that he and his company buy and sell other currencies for profit. In 1992, Soros's group had purchased approximately 10 billion pounds, and on September 16, it sold them—all of them, in one day. The selling of such a large amount of pounds caused the weakened currency to **devalue**, or become worth less than just the day before, because suddenly the supply of pounds sterling on the market far outweighed the demand for them. Immediately after the devaluation, Soros bought up pounds since they were much cheaper. The process netted Soros a profit of $1.1 billion. Great Britain lost an estimated 3.3 billion pounds (almost $7.5 billion in today's market). Aside from the economic costs, the Conservative Party in Britain lost the elections following the crisis, leading to the continuing rule of the Labor Party. Thus, one man was able to shake a large country's economy to the point that there were significant economic and political repercussions. We have not since seen Bill Gates (the world's richest person) or either Carlos Slim Helu of Mexico or Warren Buffett of the United States (who are the next wealthiest) make a profit-based decision on a scale like Soros did, but in 2011 French and Swiss financial institutions were shaken when hitherto largely unknown individual employees made huge unauthorized investments that went bad.

The influence does not always have to be negative, however. It should be noted that Soros has donated billions to charity over the years. An example of individuals making an even bigger impact is the Bill and Melinda Gates Foundation. The foundation is dedicated to promoting world health, and with its $33 billion endowment and health budget of approximately $800 million, it spends as much on promoting world health as the UN's World Health Organization! To put this in some perspective, it means that Bill and Melinda Gates along with co-investor Warren Buffett matched the amount of money being spent on global health by the UN.

Bill Gates holds a child in Mozambique | The Gates Foundation takes a very practical approach to philanthropy by funding projects such as medical research in Africa that will yield big payoffs in the form of lower infant mortality. Should all grant programs seek to maximize the benefits or is there some value to funding smaller issue projects?

These stories are not commonplace, of course, but they demonstrate how, in a liberal world economy, a few individuals can have an impact on politics, economy, and the global quality of life. It is not just the big countries and organizations that matter.

LIBERALISM IN PRACTICE Although most countries in the world are capitalist and engage in foreign trade, they are not entirely liberal. Instead, all three of the economic systems discussed play a role in most countries. For example and as mentioned earlier, the governments in Great Britain, France, and Germany created a joint initiative to build commercial airplanes. The governments each gave the contracts to build different components of the planes to different companies within each of the three states. In the end, the multinational company Airbus was born and now supplies about half of the world's commercial airliners. This policy was clearly not Marxist or liberal, as the governments created a company and gave the business to private industries. This was mercantilism, or more commonly called in recent times "national industrial policy."

Those governments also allow private capitalism to operate within limits, but rely on socialist-themed programs like substantial government benefits to citizens such as fully paid maternity leave and universal health care. These services, many of which are under serious pressure from the economic crisis in Europe, are paid for by higher levels of taxes than most U.S. citizens would find acceptable. For its part, the United States also engages in at least two of these three economic approaches. While largely capitalist and liberal in its basic economic approach, the United States has a long history of regulating private industry and providing social programs to ease the impact of capitalism on such things as the environment, poverty, and inequality, the welfare of children, and, in the case of the recent health care reform bill, health insurance and access to medical care. Indeed, all developed market economies engage in such practices to one degree or another and often impose significant regulations on a private industry in the name of the greater good. At the same time, the U.S. federal government can and does direct businesses not to sell certain products to certain parties currently being sanctioned for political reasons (i.e., a mercantilist approach).

Thus, the three systems—mercantilism, capitalism, and Marxism—all contribute to how states function today, with liberal capitalism having the largest impact of the three (Table 8-2). These systems and the modern functioning of the world's economy are not perfectly smooth. There are at least two major challenges driving the way the global economy functions. Globalization and the Great Recession have both shaped how economies work and shaken the most powerful states. How the future will unfold is not entirely clear. Let's turn to these challenges now.

8-4b Globalization and the Global Economy

The first challenge is the continuing process of **globalization** itself. The term is somewhat loose and covers a very broad range of economic phenomena, but it is important that we reexamine it. As noted in Chapter 2, globalization is the global spread of technology, money, products, culture, and opinions through foreign trade, investment, transportation, and cultural exchange. Through this process, countries become integrated into a common global network whereby they know more about each other but are also tied to each other through interdependencies. This definition

globalization the increasing integration of global society through the spread of technology, foreign trade, transportation, cultural exchange, political institutions, and social connections.

TABLE 8-2	SUMMARY OF ECONOMIC APPROACHES		
	Colonialism/Mercantilism	**Liberalism**	**Marxism**
Core principles	The state works with private business to procure more wealth. Aggressively targets other states to colonize or take their money.	State and private business must be separate. Economy must be free to be efficient. Free economies are efficient so that means more wealth for everyone.	State must take over and administer the economy to create an equitable distribution of wealth.
Core critique	Tends to cause trade wars between powerful countries. The costs of colonization can be severe to weaker states.	Not all countries gain wealth at the same rate, so there are large inequalities. There are also huge fluctuations in the economy such as the Great Recession.	There are large inefficiencies in a state-run economy, and they usually fail.
Relation to security	The relationship between the state and business is to work together to make the state more secure by attaining more wealth.	Security is enhanced by economic connections and interdependencies between states.	Since the government controls the economy, it can use it at will to develop its military. Many Marxist countries had large militaries.
Relation to power	Money is power.	While money can be used to develop power, wealth has other effects.	Money is considered the root of all political strife as well as power.
Relation to anarchy	System is anarchic, which the state uses to take control of other countries.	Anarchy can be overcome or reduced by complex interconnections between countries such as the EU.	While anarchy exists only because non-Marxist states compete, considerable friction occurs between different Marxist regimes because of different interpretations of policy.

© Cengage Learning®

clearly covers a vast array of issues, so it is worthwhile to discuss a few examples. We focus mainly on trade, production, and information in this chapter and take up investment, especially foreign direct investment, in Chapter 10. In each of these examples, we try to show how globalization can challenge both the security of a state and the way anarchy functions.

IPHONES, HOLLYWOOD, AND TERRORISTS The Apple iPhone is famous and almost ubiquitous on campuses around the United States. Many know that Apple has its headquarters in California—Cupertino to be exact. The conceptual development, technical design, and manufacturing process are all centered in the headquarters in California. The actual manufacture of the iPhone is not in the United States, however. It is assembled in Longhua, China, a city nicknamed "iPod City" because of the dominant role that iPods used to play in its economy. Thus, when you open your Web browser and go to the Apple website to order an iPhone, you are gaining access to a server somewhere in the United States. Once you have ordered the iPhone, the order is ultimately transmitted to the facility in China where the iPhone is assembled, packaged, and shipped. The shipping company, UPS, will likely move the package through Hong Kong, China, where it will clear customs to come into the United States. It will then probably travel through South Korea, Alaska, and finally the local UPS facility in your region.

Your order will have traversed the Pacific Ocean for a product designed in the United States, assembled in China, and shipped through South Korea, and all of this may take place within a matter of days. Compare that to the 30 to 100 days it can take to cross the Pacific in a sailboat—the dominant mode of ocean transportation about 100 years ago.

Realize that creating the iPhone involved three countries (the United States, China, and South Korea), and had someone from Germany or Brazil ordered it, more countries would likely have been involved. What does this mean for how we think of anarchy? Clearly, and as we have said all along, anarchy is not chaos. That three or more countries can be involved in such complex and profitable business deals means that the international system has order, even though it is decentralized. Do you think it is pretty secure? When you order something like an iPhone, do you worry about it being stolen before it arrives? Apple doesn't need to ask the United States to provide military protection in China for its production facility, so that must mean Apple is not too concerned about the physical security of its investment. Do you think globalization might increase security? Let's turn to another example that tells another story.

The reach of U.S. media around the world and the effects those media have can be dramatic. American movies, typically produced in Hollywood, California (and often filmed in Canada), provide excitement and romance to viewers around the globe. They also create great offense to conservative cultures, particularly extremist religious groups. **Islamists** find the wide reach of Hollywood extremely offensive.

Islamists extreme fundamentalist Muslims.

Terrorist organizations such as al-Qaeda use the entertainment media that Hollywood creates as an example of the corrupt nature of Western civilization, particularly almost globally available U.S. television shows such as *Modern Family* and *Revenge* and movies that include revealing love scenes, semi-nude actors, or families with homosexual couples. These extremist groups view the content of this type of program as an attempt to pollute and destroy their culture and to corrupt their young. They thus feel justified in attacking the United States and are able to recruit members because they claim to be defending what is morally right (at least in their eyes). To be sure, Hollywood did not create Islamist terrorists, but the cultural exchange of popular entertainment contributes to the hatred directed at the United States. In one of the many ironies of globalization, the al-Qaeda terrorists use modern technology—such as cell phones, satellite phones, websites, and e-mail—developed by the same countries they hate and attack. In this case, globalization may have partly caused a decrease in U.S. security.

THE SPREAD OF GLOBALIZATION The means through which globalization spreads around the world is best understood through two processes: broadening and deepening. Broadening refers to new states becoming incorporated into the global economy. Today, nearly every country in the world is involved with the global economy in some significant way through trade and cultural exchange (Table 8-3). In fact, states that are not globally integrated must actively choose to stay separate from the world. For example, Bhutan, the tiny state east of the Himalayas, did not allow television or the Internet

A Bhutanese spiritual leader using a laptop | Not until 1999 did Bhutan allow the Internet to be connected, and now it is beginning to touch all parts of the society. Do you think such a small, poor country will benefit from the Internet?

TABLE 8-3	GLOBALIZATION INDEX FOR TOP AND BOTTOM THREE COUNTRIES, 1971, 1991, AND 2011	
1971	Luxemburg	71.53
	Canada	70.83
	Belgium	68.41
	Rwanda	15.23
	Nepal	13.74
	Bangladesh	12.03
1991	Netherlands	83.94
	Switzerland	83.87
	Belgium	83.81
	Burundi	19.24
	Equatorial Guinea	19.02
	Laos	17.76
2011	Ireland	92.17
	Belgium	91.61
	Netherlands	91.33
	Kiribati	26.20
	Solomon Islands	25.43
	Somalia	24.03

Source: Adapted from Swiss Federal Institute of Technology, Zurich, KoF Index of Globalization, http://globalization.kof.ethz.ch.

until 1999. Another example is North Korea, which is such a closed, autocratic society that very little trade and exchange occurs with the rest of the world. Aside from countries such as Bhutan until 1999, or North Korea to this day, most of the world is integrated to some extent into the global economy.

The second process, deepening, is how much of a state is touched by globalization and to what extent. Bhutan did not immediately and entirely enter the global economy. Instead, gradually more of its population modernized and integrated with the rest of the world. For example, by 2008, 6.5 percent of the Bhutan population was using the Internet. That may not seem like much compared to the 75 percent of Americans who use the Web every day, but a better comparison country would be India where only 4.5 percent of the population uses the Internet (data from the World Development Indicators). Thus, in a span of nine years, more and more the Bhutanese started going online and gaining access to the wide array of information on the Web to the point where a greater share of their population is online than their huge neighbor. By 2012, about 30 percent of Bhutanese had access to the Internet, mostly through wireless connections to their smartphones!

Contrasting technology in India | These pictures are both from India, but they are clearly different. Can you think of a similar situation in your country?

The deepening of globalization, while quite advanced, continues to this day. Most locales around the world are affected in some way by the global economy. There may be many small towns in countries like India that have never had an American visit them, but many people in these towns will have watched U.S. television programs (*The Big Bang Theory, Dancing with the Stars*). Similarly, in 2012, 11.1 million people visited South Korea, but in just the last half of 2012, there were more than 1 billion viewings of "Gangnam Style" on YouTube. Further, when the price of oil more than doubled between 2007 and mid-2008, the entire world was affected. Because oil is used in every product, at least for its transportation if not also its production, prices on all products increased. Because of globalization, we can all be affected by events a world away. For example, horrible floods in Thailand (as in 2011), where about 45 percent of the world's mobile computers are manufactured, mean the supply of hard drives plummeted and the costs skyrocketed, which affected governments, businesses, and consumers alike. A successful terrorist strike in another state on a port critical for shipping oil to your country would mean that you will pay more to fill up your car's gas tank or buy products made from plastic.

GLOBALIZATION'S POSITIVE IMPACT We have thus far discussed how most of the world is connected in this integrated network we call "globalization"; we now consider the effects of this integration. Globalization has both positive and negative consequences for the world. On the positive side, the more a country is open to trade and thus globalization, the less likely there will be forced labor, particularly among women. Women also benefit from less economic discrimination when their country is more globalized. These benefits result from the presence of multinational corporations that tend not to discriminate against women and do not engage in forced labor. These corporations are often concerned with their public image in large, developed states and wish to avoid the bad press that some companies (such as Nike) have experienced in the past. (See the following discussion in the section The Costs and Consequences of Globalization). The presence of these international employers can push local employers to mimic the labor practices of their competitors. Many of these MNCs also pay their workers a salary that is competitive by local standards, although as we discuss in the following pages, there are many complaints about how MNCs treat the local workers. What is particularly important to realize about the jobs created by the MNC is that they would not otherwise exist if the company did not build or operate a manufacturing plant in the country. Cannondale Bicycle Corporation, for example, has almost all of its bikes made in Taiwan, although its headquarters are in Connecticut. As mentioned earlier, Apple manufactures most of its products in China. In both of these cases, Cannondale and Apple are creating jobs in the respective countries. Thus, those workers have more opportunities for employment, and employment provides money, and, especially for women, greater independence.

Another benefit of open trade and connection to the global economy is peace, both inside countries and between states. First, greater trade openness makes genocides and ethnic cleansing less likely because if the country tends to trade with other countries, there are international businesspeople and journalists in the country. This attention from the outside world means that widespread, horrific violence like the kind that occurred in Rwanda in 1994 is less likely. In that case, there was very little trade with the outside world, and

Vacant streets in the Democratic Republic of Congo | Civil violence in a country destroys not only people and buildings but also the desire to run a business. How might a country recover from such violence when this is what is left?

as the situation in Rwanda became violent, businesses and even states withdrew their personnel. Without the presence of international diplomats, businesspeople, and journalists, the world did not fully know that genocide, perpetrated mostly with machetes, was beginning and would end only after approximately 800,000 people were murdered. It is not clear that the international community would have responded if the news camera had been everywhere, but it is also not clear that the militias would have attacked defenseless adults and children in front of the cameras. Rwanda is an extreme case, but the lesson is that a foreign presence including the media tends to limit what a government might do to its people. Look at the pressures on Egypt's economy after the Arab Spring when tourists chose to go elsewhere.

One of the main reasons for U.S. leadership in creating the IMF, World Bank, and GATT/WTO, as previously discussed, was to ensure more cooperation and trade between states with the hope that they would help limit interstate war. Further, Chapter 6 discussed the democratic peace—the concept that two democracies will not fight each other. Along with democracy, significant trade between two countries makes them much more peaceful toward each other. Thus, globalization, with all of the interstate trade and exchange that it entails, may make wars between states less likely. Consider the extremely close relationship between the United States and Canada. The two are among each other's largest trading partners with more than $1.5 billion in merchandise crossing the border each day. The thought of a militarized dispute between the two states is ridiculous but that is in part because of the close trade relationship. (For a humorous treatment, see the movie *Canadian Bacon* [1995].)

Not only do Americans and Canadians buy and sell a great deal from each other, but that relationship is indicative of the understanding the two societies have of each other. Think about this, which is more foreign to you, Canada or Russia? Which do you see as potentially more threatening to U.S. interests?

Finally, it is worth noting that exposure to other cultures is generally good. From such simple pleasures as having access to international foods and foreign films, we can learn more about our fellow humans and come to appreciate their cultures and views. While this benefit is not tangible and certainly not universally appreciated, a truly closed society does not have access to German beer, French wine, American movies, Swiss cheese, Canadian maple syrup, Vietnamese prawns, Japanese electronics, South African diamonds, and so on. Open trade and globalization bring all of these things to our doorstep.

THE COSTS AND CONSEQUENCES OF GLOBALIZATION We now turn to the drawbacks of globalization, and there are many to choose from. First, we discussed how MNCs can bring jobs to a country that result in less economic discrimination and forced labor, but not all MNCs are so benevolent and certainly not everyone agrees that MNCs benefit the people who work for them. For example, many apparel companies such as Nike and Reebok have been severely criticized for the labor conditions in the overseas factories that manufacture their products. In 1989, a Nike contractor in Thailand was accused of paying its employees a "training wage," an amount far below the legal minimum wage. Following these reports, strikes and protests hit the Nike production facilities. Through negotiations, many of these issues were addressed, but problems still persist. Nike contracted with producers in Vietnam where workers are not permitted to organize outside the official communist party. Although the workers are constrained by the government, they still initiated a strike in 2008 for higher wages, which at the time were only $59 a month.

In addition to poor wages, many of these factories or sweatshops have long hours and poor working conditions. Because the factory is only subject to the local laws and many of these countries do not have labor protection laws, 16-hour days, child labor, and few physical protections exist. In the past 20 years, the conditions have improved considerably as world public opinion turned against such inhumane practices. Organizations such as the Worker's Rights Consortium report on poor labor practices, attempting to bring them to the attention of the public and thereby put pressure on the companies. In April 2010, for example, the University of Wisconsin ended its contract with Nike because the company could

A sweatshop in Southeast Asia | These unpleasant working conditions show that there are other costs involved when making apparel. When you spend your money on jeans, shirts, and hoodies, who profits?

not adequately explain why workers at two plants in Honduras were not paid severance when the plants closed.[4] Although such actions do not usually critically wound the MNC's profits, they do put pressure on MNCs to reform so as to avoid future boycotts and lost profits. No corporation's management team likes to have a negative media spotlight shining on the company!

One way of ameliorating these low wages is an idea originated by U.S. religious groups in the 1940s. The idea, called **fair trade**, is simply to pay the original producers of a product more. Originally it applied to handcrafts sold mostly in churches. Today fair trade is big business that has moved well beyond church sales. Most fair trade products, which include coffee, chocolate, handcrafts, and so on, are certified by the Fairtrade International organization. Products with the "fair trade" designation are typically sold at a slightly higher price, with the idea that the increased price, or at least a portion of it, will go to the original producer. While the idea is a good one, it is not clear how much more profits go to the original producer. In some studies, less than 2 percent of the increased price actually went to the producer. Studies showed coffee farmers only received $0.18 more for a pound of coffee costing $5 more than a non-fair trade pound of coffee. One of the best studies of fair trade is *Brewing Justice*, in which the author (Daniel Jaffee, an economist) shows that coffee farmers did tend

to earn more for fair trade coffee and that those earnings helped increase the development of the farmer's community (because the farmer had more to spend and invest). However, the book also warns that fair trade is not the cure for the costs of globalization. It can help, but more needs to be done.

Another negative effect from globalization is that it can put tremendous pressure on states and ultimately weaken them. When countries open their economies to the global marketplace by engaging in foreign trade, they also expose themselves to considerable competition. As noted earlier, interdependencies *create* vulnerabilities. Some people within the country will benefit from the foreign trade, and some will be harmed. Imagine a country that chooses to open up its markets because it has a very profitable mining industry; however, the country's agriculture production is small and not very efficient. When exposed to the global food market, the country's farmers would likely be unable to compete. If the country does not subsidize or protect the farmers in some manner, they will lose their livelihoods. Thus, there is pressure on the country both to join the global economy so that its mines can make profits and to compensate the farmers who lose their farms and ability to support themselves.

A real-world example of this can be found in Mexico. Due to the **North American Free Trade Agreement (NAFTA)** of 1994, Mexico's previously largely closed economy was opened up to U.S. and Canadian businesses. While this was great for the Mexican workers employed assembling televisions and other electronic products in *maquiladoras* (export assembly plants near the U.S.-Mexican border) or those manufacturing U.S.-branded cars and trucks, it was catastrophic for many Mexican farmers and agricultural companies that suddenly had to compete with products from industry giants such as ConAgra and Archer Daniels Midland. When the same thing happened in Japan beginning in the 1960s, Japan's openness to trade with others meant very small Japanese rice farms suddenly had to compete with very efficient rice producers from Burma, the United States, and other states. Japan's strong economy at the time allowed the government to respond in two ways: first, with heavy subsidies to keep Japan's iconic rice farmers in business; and second, with a heavy media campaign to convince Japanese consumers that domestically produced Japanese rice was superior (in nutrition, taste, consistency, stickiness, etc.) to cheaper, imported rice.

Globalization's pressure on states is made worse because the government will want to attract MNCs to invest in the country. To attract the MNCs, the government must typically offer significant tax breaks, and these tax breaks must be competitive with other countries,

fair trade the concept that producers should be paid a fair price for their products.

North American Free Trade Agreement (NAFTA)
a free trade agreement between Canada, Mexico, and the United States. The agreement greatly reduced all barriers to trade between the three countries and resulted in a significant increase in trade of goods and services between the three.

Levels of Interdependence and Integration

Historically, states have integrated slowly and through a rather regular process. Here we describe the different levels of integration that occurred through the past 200 years.

Level I (nineteenth and twentieth centuries). States trade goods and some services with each other. Trading is somewhat limited early in this period because of the cost and limitations of transportation. In the twentieth century, transportation improved so that more than high-cost goods could be shipped at a profit.

Level II (mid-twentieth century). Businesses begin to locate production facilities in other states, thus creating MNCs. Trade between states increased with the ability to fly goods from one country to another instead of using surface transportation and the development of standardized container ships that allowed even bulk cargoes to be carried across oceans at a lower cost. Services such as banking, insurance, and investment begin to be traded across state borders.

Level III (late twentieth century). Businesses, governments, and individual people begin to invest and own businesses in other countries. For example, the American automobile manufacturer Chrysler (originally one of Detroit's "Big Three" automobile businesses) was purchased by a German firm, Daimler AG, and then by Italian automobile manufacturer FIAT. Thus, what was once a huge American firm is now owned by an Italian firm. Individuals and groups of investors also regularly buy and hold stocks and other stakes in companies from other countries. For example, anyone with investments in mutual funds or a pension program typically has their wealth tied to the economic success of companies around the world, not just their from their own country.

Level IV (late twentieth century). Many European states integrate into a **Eurozone** to create **supranational organization**. Not only did many of European countries create a free trade zone and customs union, they merged their currencies into the euro. As a result, these countries must coordinate how much debt their governments can accrue and how much currency can remain in circulation. Imagine the United States coordinating with Canada and Mexico on how much money the United States could print and spend. This level is the highest integration attained in the modern era.

---

otherwise the MNC has less reason to invest in the country. The consequence of the tax breaks is that the government may attract MNCs, but it has less tax revenue to pay for the displaced farmers. Furthermore, MNC profits normally go back to their home state; they generally do not get reinvested in the host country that produced the wealth. Thus the "multiplier effect" that economists stress from private direct investment is limited for the host society. In the end, the country may benefit from globalization, but the government has less money to help out those citizens who are hurt by open trade policies.

Russia faces a slightly different problem due to globalization. When the Soviet Union controlled the economy, people had to buy domestic products—only those made within the Soviet Union and some other government-approved products. As it opened its markets to foreign products, many Russians lost their jobs. Simply put, they worked at factories that produced products so poor in quality or performance that no one would buy them if they had a choice. Once European-, Japanese-, Chinese-, and U.S.-made products were available, why buy inferior, Russian-made ones? While some companies attempted to increase the quality of their goods, this process takes a long time. This problem is worse in Russia than in many other states because many Russian cities are built around a single, massive factory, with the factory being the primary employer and reason for the city to exist in the first place. In such ultimate company towns, when the factory closes, no other significant options for employment exist. In the face of such economic uncertainties, parents living in such areas are choosing to have fewer—or in many cases, no—children. The result is Russia's population is decreasing. To try to reverse this trend, Russia has created a program of cash incentives to parents for each child born and has created a new holiday for the purpose of procreation—in short, a day of conception!

Finally, globalization tends to be non-democratic, at least in states where governments attempt to represent the public. This may seem counterintuitive,

Eurozone the portion of the European Union that uses the euro currency rather than a national currency. These countries include: Austria, Belgium, Cyprus, Finland, France, Germany, Greece, Ireland, Italy, Luxembourg, Malta, the Netherlands, Portugal, Slovakia, Slovenia, and Spain.

supranational organization an institution, organization, or law that is over other states. For example, the EU is a supranational organization because it has authority over many European states.

but consider the following logical sequence. Part of the globalization process involves states joining international organizations, particularly trade organizations such as the WTO. In many cases, such as the WTO, the states agree to the rules of the organization. For example, the WTO does not permit steel tariffs like the ones the United States initiated nor does the organization allow a state to ban a good without proof that the good in question is dangerous. Thus, the EU ban on hormone-fed beef was ruled illegal. By joining the WTO, countries give up a part of their sovereignty. Essentially, the rules of the WTO supersede the domestic laws of the member states. Banning hormone-fed beef, for example, is a domestic decision, albeit one with international consequences. The EU ban does not say that foreign beef cannot have been fed hormones; it says that any beef, domestic or foreign, cannot be sold in the EU if the cattle were fed hormones. Thus, the WTO ruling violates the idea of Westphalian sovereignty. The EU wanted non-hormone-fed beef, but the WTO overruled its sovereignty by ruling that it could not ban such beef. Of course, the EU still bans hormone-fed beef, but it pays a penalty to do so—sort of like paying a penalty to exercise your sovereignty!

Another example of how the WTO can circumvent democratic rule concerns the gasoline shipped to the United States from Venezuelan refineries. In 1993 the U.S. Environmental Protection Agency ruled that all gasoline sold in the United States must meet certain standards for minimal contaminants. Venezuela challenged the rule, saying that it treated foreign refineries differently from domestic refineries. The WTO agreed, and after an unsuccessful appeal, President Clinton changed the rule so that Venezuela and other foreign refineries did not have to comply with the U.S. Clean Air Act. Realize that the Clean Air Act was enacted by a democratically elected body—the U.S. Congress—but it was effectively overturned by an international organization that has no responsibility to the American public.

The hormone-fed beef and Clean Air Act are good examples of how governmental preferences for the domestic population (i.e., sovereignty) are no longer sacrosanct. To be sure, the United States and the states in the EU chose freely to join the WTO. The process to join was very democratic. However, by agreeing to the rules, all countries give up a bit of their right to rule themselves.

Yet another example of sovereignty slipping away concerns the EU. While not directly part of globalization, the economic and political integration in Europe is connected to and facilitates greater globalization with the European states. Countries joining the EU transfer significant authority to the EU from the individual government. In many European states, such as Sweden and Germany, parents are restricted to what they may name their child. In Sweden's case, the child may not have a double surname (i.e., two last names). In Spain, however, having both parents' names is traditional. A case arose when a married couple—the wife was Spanish and the husband Swedish—had a child in Sweden. The Swedish government would not permit the parents to give their son a double surname. The parent appealed the decision, and the EU overruled Sweden. Thus, Swedish law and tradition were overturned by the supranational EU.

CAN STATES "OPT OUT" OF GLOBALIZATION

One might suggest that if the member states do not like the rules or decisions of the organizations to which they belong, they could simply leave the organization. However, the costs of leaving the WTO, the EU, or most large international organizations are very high. If a country resigned its membership from the WTO, it would have to negotiate new trade arrangements with each of its trade partners. Thus, if the United States left because of the gasoline dispute with Venezuela, it would have to negotiate with well over a hundred countries to strike a deal on what could be traded and what tariffs should be—on all traded goods and services, not just gasoline.

Further, if a state decided to leave one or more organizations and withdraw itself even partially from the global economy, other states would likely not trust the departing state very much. Could one rely on a country that decided to pick up its marbles and not play just because it didn't like a specific ruling? One would certainly be right to be concerned whether a state that quit once might not do so again. Thus, one's reputation for trustworthiness or credibility is involved in such arrangements, and while intangible, these are meaningful factors that will be considered by policymakers.

While some states could bear the cost of leaving the global economy, for all it would be difficult and for most it would be crippling. As a result, leaving is not really an option that countries entertain. They may resist the pressures as the EU did with hormone-fed beef by simply paying the cost of the sanctions. Alternatively, states may create education programs for workers displaced by globalization, and in some cases countries will choose not to join organizations. Other countries simply go along with globalization as best they can. Regardless of the tactic that a state follows, the world is becoming more and more globalized.

8-4c The 2008–2010 Great Recession and Its Aftermath

Between the end of the Cold War in 1989 and 2008, more and more states democratized and embraced liberalism and the global economy. As Figure 8-3 shows, both the level of trade and democracy rose rapidly in the last two decades. To be sure, many states sought to improve their standards of living with policies that helped overcome some of the detrimental effects of globalization. For example, Brazil instituted a countrywide program that paid families a stipend if their children attended school and were vaccinated. The program sought to alleviate poverty at least temporarily and, more importantly, increase the education level of the average Brazilian, making them more competitive in the globalized economy. At the same time, Brazil fulfilled its obligations to the IMF by gaining a government budget surplus and continuing to work out trade agreements with different countries. Thus, it was able to balance the benefits and costs of globalization.

The 1997–1998 Asian Financial Crisis showed that all countries are not so fortunate in their policy decisions. Thailand's inability to keep its currency (the baht) tied to the dollar and to dampen international speculation regarding the strength of its economy kicked off a crisis that reverberated through the Asian region and then the world. Similarly when a global real estate bubble began to burst in 2006, a **liquidity crisis** was sparked that brought many banks and even countries to their knees. Leading up to 2006, real estate values in developed countries such as the United States, Ireland, Greece, and Great Britain were rising at a rapid pace. The increase in prices was the result, in part, of policies in the United States and Europe that allowed banks to give home loans more easily, often to people who might not be able to afford them; these were referred to as **subprime loans**. As more people sought to buy houses, the value of existing houses increased and building dramatically increased.

THE SKY BEGINS TO FALL When people were unable to pay their mortgages, building stopped, banks lost immense sums of money, and people lost their jobs. As unemployment rose, more people couldn't pay their mortgages, and the cycle continued and accelerated. Banks and investment firms began to lose vast sums of money because the loans they gave out during the housing bubble were no longer being paid back and the homes which they took ownership of in foreclosure were no longer worth but a fraction of their original value. Unsure of the worth of their assets, many banks basically

Failed investments and haunted houses | This subdivision was meant to be full of homes, but after the crisis, all work and development was stopped. The houses became haunted even before they became occupied. What will become of these buildings? In a struggling economy, isn't such waste really inefficient?

stopped loaning money, and a credit crisis ensued. Further, global stock markets plunged in value. For example, the Dow Jones Industrial Average—the gold standard for how stock markets perform—reached a high in October 2007 of 14,164. A mere 17 months later on March 2009, it had lost 54 percent of its value, closing at 6,547. A grim interpretation of these numbers suggests that the value of people's investment and indeed a good portion of the global economy had lost more than half of its value! Think of what that did to families' college or retirement funds.

The now infamous case of Greece provides a good, if not frightening, example. The Greek economy grew at the fastest rate in the Eurozone between 2000 and 2007, and this rapid growth attracted many foreign investors, which subsequently allowed the Greek government to engage in heavy spending that exceeded its tax revenues. Greece began to run up significant debts—much like individuals who spend more than they earn and run up huge credit card debts. To cover their bad policies, Greek government officials lied about their borrowing, downplaying the true size of their debt. While the deception lasted for just a short time, it ended with a crisis for the Greeks and the European states in the Eurozone.

liquidity crisis a situation when a government runs out of cash and is unable to make minimum payments on its debt.

subprime loans loans given by banks to private citizens that would be considered to have a high likelihood of default. These loans were made to promote home ownership, but drove up prices and ultimately created an unsustainable economy that collapsed and caused the Great Recession.

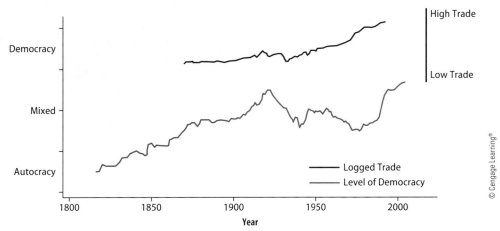

See how trade and democracy go together? Do you think democracy causes trade or does trade cause democracy?

If the Greek economy collapsed and the government went bankrupt, it could drag many other European states down with it.

If this seems hard to follow, imagine a group of four roommates who pool their money to pay for rent and food. Without all four contributing, they could not afford the rent or food where they were currently living. Then imagine if one of them lost a job and ran such credit card debt that that person had to declare bankruptcy. Two middle-income roommates would be unable to pay for rent or food and would be left homeless and in legal trouble since they defaulted on their lease, although the third roommate who earned more money could afford to live elsewhere. This is essentially the situation with Greece and the other EU members (with the wealthiest roommate being a country like Germany or France).

Violent protest in Greece | Even in a normally tranquil country like Greece, an economic meltdown can reduce the country to violence. Could this happen in your country?

After several months of negotiations between the Greek government and other EU states and IMF, a bailout loan was finally reached. The Greeks would have to make severe cuts to their spending and raise taxes to balance the government's budget and begin paying off the debt. In return for making deep spending cuts and raising taxes—policies that are referred to as an "austerity program"—the Greeks would receive billions in loans from the EU and the IMF.[5] As we said in Chapter 2, the austerity program angered the Greek population because their benefits and pensions were being cut; workers took to the streets and protested. While their plight is certainly understandable, there were no other acceptable options available, and external lenders were even able to force the Greek prime minister to resign. The global economy determined what the Greek government could and could not do. Once again, sovereignty is not absolute.

SUNNIER DAYS For several years, the strongest economies in the world have sought to recover from the Great Recession. The unemployment rate in the United States fluctuates. It reached a high of 10 percent in 2009 and, in 2013, it still averaged 7.4 percent. By October 2014 it had fallen to 5.9 percent. Though the largest economy in the world is no longer in a recession, it is not thriving even though the government continues policies that should increase growth and lower unemployment. Europe is not so lucky. The unemployment rate in the European Union was under 7 percent when the economic crisis began, and it has risen pretty steadily ever since. It reached 10.4 percent in 2013 and continued to rise to 11.9 percent in April 2014. So, on June 5, 2014, the European Central Bank began charging a **negative interest rate**. That means that the government charges banks for holding too much money in reserve—they are not permitted to save, so to speak. The policy is aimed at getting banks to make more loans to businesses, which should in turn help the economy grow. Only time will tell how effective this will be.

CONCLUSION

Think back to Figure 8-1 that showed the national, international, and global economic systems. Those three eras capture much of the history of the world's economy over the centuries. These were big changes, but even within each era, there were constant changes. In 1992, Francis Fukuyama wrote a book titled *The End of History and the Last Man*. His basic thesis was that democracy and capitalism had not only won the day, but had become the final stage of human history. He suggested that there would be no new economic or political systems. Many would have probably agreed with him in 2008, before the start of the Great Recession. Capitalism seemed to be a juggernaut; it seemed unstoppable, inevitable. That is now longer so clear. Instead, governments have had to intervene in the private market to keep it from collapsing—a policy more akin to mercantilism than capitalism.

The Globalization Index has increased 55 percent over the past 40 years, so clearly the world economy is becoming more and more interconnected. Does that mean that the Great Recession was just a bump in the road? Is capitalism slowly chugging forward? Are mercantilism and communism dead?

Perhaps Fukuyama was right, and that our economic history is over. Perhaps, however, Einstein's assertion that the only constant is change should be applied to the global economy. Though the world has shifted to a global economy, it still seems possible that the future is not yet written. It seems reasonable to conclude that states will try anything to attain wealth, power, and security from their economies. If that is true, in which type of country would you be happiest? Why? Now that the world's economy is so much more global and interconnected, how does that affect the role and practices of states as they try to gain economic security? Given the need for countries to secure resources and wealth to maintain their physical security, which economic system—mercantilism, capitalism, communism, or some combination—is best suited to create wealth and transfer it into security for its people, especially in the current global economy? Which type of state will likely be the most peaceful? These are hard questions to answer, but they are the questions that will face the world in the coming years.

negative interest rate a government policy of charging banks for holding too much of their currency in reserve. The policy is meant to make loans more available and spur economic growth.

THINK ABOUT THIS IS GLOBALIZATION GOOD, BAD, OR UGLY?

Well-known economist Dani Rodrik's book, *Has Globalization Gone Too Far?*, asks whether the wide and rapid spread of trade, technology, and culture that is globalization is costing people in developing countries too much. As developing countries compete for trade opportunities, they lower the conditions in which their citizens must work. Lower pay, fewer benefits, longer hours all lead to greater human costs. To stay competitive, governments cannot easily raise taxes to alleviate these costs. So globalization can end up extracting large human costs from countries. It can also bring wealth and better human rights. Globalization is good, bad, and at times, ugly. Consider this complicated issue: What are the major pros and cons of globalization? How might states make globalization sustainable or "good"? Are the human costs of globalization simply the cost of development and progress? Now, think about this:

On balance, is globalization a positive or negative force in world politics?

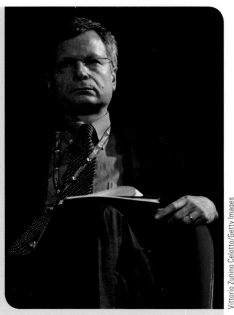

Vittorio Zunino Celotto/Getty Images

Dani Rodrik

STUDY TOOLS 8

LOCATED AT BACK OF THE BOOK:
☐ Rip out Chapter in Review card

LOCATED ON COURSEMATE:
Use the CourseMate access card that came with this book or visit CengageBrain.com for more review materials:

☐ Review Key Terms Flash Cards (Print or Online)

☐ Download Chapter Summaries for on-the-go review

☐ Complete Practice Quizzes to prepare for the test

☐ Walk through a Simulation, Animated Learning Module, and Interactive Maps and Timelines to master concepts

☐ Complete "Crossword Puzzle" to review key terms

☐ Watch the videos for real-world application of this chapter's content

☐ Visit IR NewsWatch to learn about the latest current events as you prepare for class discussions and papers

REVIEW QUESTIONS

1. How have countries historically sought wealth?

2. How does the historical pursuit of money differ from the current pursuit?

3. Is communism dead, or do aspects of it influence states to this day?

4. Why has capitalism had such a big impact on the world and will it continue to have a powerful impact in the future?

FOR MORE INFORMATION . . .

For more on:

Global economics: Gilpin, Robert with Jean M. Gilpin. *Global Political Economy*. Princeton, NJ: Princeton University Press, 2001.

Globalization: Bagwati, Jagdish. *In Defense of Globalization*. Oxford: Oxford University Press, 2004.

Rodrick, Dani. *Has Globalization Gone Too Far?* Washington, DC: Institute for international Economics, 1997.

Mercantilism: Rogowski, Ronald. *Commerce and Coalitions*. Princeton, NJ: Princeton University Press, 1990.

9 | Economic Statecraft:
Sanctions, Aid, and Their Consequences

LEARNING OBJECTIVES

After studying this chapter, you will be able to …

9-1 Outline the history and identify the many ways in which wealth can be used to influence other countries.

9-2 Trace the complex nature of economic sanctions, why they are used, and what consequences they have.

9-3 Identify the potential benefits and consequences of foreign aid.

After finishing this chapter go to **PAGE 270** for **STUDY TOOLS**

CERTIFIED IN THE WAR ON DRUGS OR JUST CERTIFIABLE? U.S. AID TO MEXICO AND COLOMBIA

In 1986, the U.S. Congress passed a resolution that required the president to "certify" annually that countries involved in drug production and trafficking were working with the United States in good faith to stem the flow of illegal drugs. If a country was "decertified," it would not be permitted to receive aid from the United States, a serious penalty for developing states. In 1997, the Clinton administration released its list of certified and decertified countries. Included in the decertified list was Colombia because, according to U.S. officials, "corruption remains rampant at the highest levels of the Colombian government."[1] That decision, while devastating to Colombia, did not attract much attention. What did attract attention, however, was the certification of Mexico. In the months preceding Clinton's decision, several high-level Mexican law enforcement officials were arrested on charges of corruption. Just weeks before the report, Mexico's highest-level anti-drug official, its "drug czar," was arrested for taking money from drug lords to protect them from the law. Even with this serious evidence of "corruption at the highest levels" in Mexico, the White House certified Mexico. Why?

While White House officials claimed that Mexico had been working in good faith, the contrast between the two countries drew attention from the news media and Congress. Many elected officials, both Democrats and Republicans, were outraged and sought to overturn the certification. However, the House and Senate failed to reconcile their positions, and nothing was done. Still, the question remains, why did Mexico get certified?

The answer lies in the political consequence of decertification. Had the United States chosen not to certify Mexico, it would have ended all aid and likely jeopardized the trade relationship with Mexico. Given that the two countries share a border and a long history, cutting off the supply of aid and trade would certainly result in a serious souring of the relationship. Mexican officials would have been furious and could have reacted by cutting their sale of oil to the United States as a punishment; they could also consider shutting down the factories in Mexico owned by Ford and General Motors, threatening a devastating shock to the car companies' manufacturing process and supply chain. It is also possible that Mexico would have reduced its efforts to stop drugs from traveling to the United States.

Unfortunately for Colombia, the United States was not as concerned about decertifying it compared to Mexico. In fact, it had been decertified the previous year, as well. It is possible that the United States could have formed a closer relationship with Colombia if it had given it aid, but the two countries are more than 2,000 miles apart, and that distance reduces the critical nature of the relationship.

Thus, even though U.S. law stipulates that aid can only be given to countries working in good faith to combat illegal drugs, this case shows how complicated politics can be. Most importantly, we see that the official reason or rule for a policy is not always followed. Instead, countries often act in ways that are politically expedient or "easy" rather than "right."

This episode raises some interesting questions:

1. Should Mexico have been decertified or was the White House correct in considering other *political factors* in the decision?

2. What other reasons might lead a country to go against the official purpose of aid?

3. What is more important in these situations, following the law or addressing political concerns?

4. Do any of our theories seem to cover such situations?

U.S. Air and Naval Forces Intercept a Russian Tanker Bound for Iraq in 2000 | How hard must it be to control the flow of money, goods, and people while imposing sanctions on a country?

United States Navy, Department of Defense defense.gov

INTRODUCTION: USING WEALTH TO INFLUENCE OTHER COUNTRIES

As we discussed in the previous chapter, there are many reasons for states to seek wealth and even more ways for them to attain it. In addition to the military power and prestige that wealth brings to an individual state, it also endows the state with a tool that can be used to influence or coerce other states. Both the power and the potential to coerce can mean greater security. In fact, a famous political economist, Albert Hirschman, argued that countries should structure their trade to make other states dependent on them because that would increase their influence and security. In the simplest of terms, one state can *give* money or it can *take away* money (and thus business opportunities) from other states. By attaching conditions or demands to the *giving* or *taking* of money, one state can influence another state and pursue economic security for itself. For example, the primary purpose of U.S. anti-drug aid is reducing the flow of illegal drugs into the United States, subsequently lowering crime and making the United States more secure. The process of giving and taking money for political purposes is called **economic statecraft**: the use of economic means (money) to secure political ends (or goals).

 ECONOMIC STATECRAFT

What are we getting at when we say "giving or taking" money or economic opportunity? The concept is actually quite simple, although the ways in which states can give and take money are many. For example, Russia might give money in the form of grants or low-interest rate loans to Kazakhstan so that the Kazakh government treats ethnic Russians living there fairly. Russia might also expect that Kazakhstan will allow the Russian military to keep bases in the country in return for the grants and low-interest rate loans, and they might expect Kazakhstan to ratify the proposed Eurasian Economic Union treaty that they signed with Russia and Belarus. Thus, Russia provides funds and economic opportunity to Kazakhstan to increase Russia's own economic (and international) security, as well as the security of Russians living abroad. Another example appears at the opening of the chapter—the U.S. aid given to combat illegal drug trade in Mexico and Colombia. Clearly, the United States expects countries receiving this aid to cooperate with American authorities and maintain a legitimate effort in combating illegal drug production and trafficking.

economic statecraft　the use of economic means to secure political ends.

DEA, FBI, and Coast Guard agents make a huge cocaine bust | With drugs like these slipping through state borders, what does it take to stop them? Was this bust lucky? Do governments need to use their economic power to stop this problem?

Another less obvious example is for one country to give another a special trade deal. If a country like Japan normally charges a 10 percent **tariff** on beef but it offers Australia a 5 percent tariff, then it has made it cheaper and easier for Australian ranchers to sell their beef to Japan. That is effectively the same as giving the Australians money. This trade deal could be offered in return for a similar deal for the Japanese—for example, a lower tariff on Japanese televisions and Playstation game consoles sold in Australia.

Each of these examples is about "giving" money in return for some economic or political benefit. What about "taking" money or economic opportunity? A good example of taking wealth or money is the **economic sanctions** imposed by the UN against Iran for its development of nuclear weapons. The UN, led by European countries and the United States, cut off trade with Iran because the country is developing the **fissile material** needed to make a nuclear weapon. The intention of the policy is to coerce the Iranian government to give up its nuclear weapons program so that it can trade again with the countries that participate in the sanctions. Recently,

the Iranians have begun negotiating to limit their nuclear program in return for a lifting of the sanctions. Do you think this will work?

The United States also maintains comprehensive sanctions against Cuba. Soon after Fidel Castro took over Cuba in 1959, the U.S. began sanctioning the Caribbean island with hopes that Castro would step down. As a communist, Castro was seen as a security threat to the United States, since Cuba is only 90 miles from the U.S. coast and the island would provide an opportune base of operations for the Soviet Union. This threat became especially obvious during the 1962 Cuban missile crisis when the Soviet Union placed medium- and intermediate-range nuclear missiles in Cuba. Though originally Castro had no intention of breaking ties with the United States, American leaders saw the situation as dangerous and attempted to coerce the new leader. First, the White House only put a quota on sugar imports, but those sanctions rapidly grew into a complete embargo on all goods and services. For more than five decades now, U.S. citizens have been prevented from buying Cuban products (including the famous Cuban cigars), directly traveling to Cuba, or selling the island-state almost anything. There is also a limit on how much money family members in the United States can send their relatives in Cuba. In the 1990s, in an attempt to coerce Castro even further, the United States threatened to sanction *other countries* doing business with Cuba. Originally, the U.S. government tried to topple the Castro regime through an economic embargo, and now it continues to try to use its vast economic power to coerce Cuba to allow democratic reform in the country.

Another example is the recent Russian military and covert actions in Ukraine. When President Putin

A Russian pipeline transporting gas to Europe | The ability to turn this switch and cut off fuel to Europe is tremendously powerful. What would happen to the EU if Russia cut off its supply of heating fuel this winter?

tariff a tax on products imported into one country from other countries.

economic sanction the cessation of some or all economic exchange between two countries.

fissile material nuclear material used to make atomic weapons.

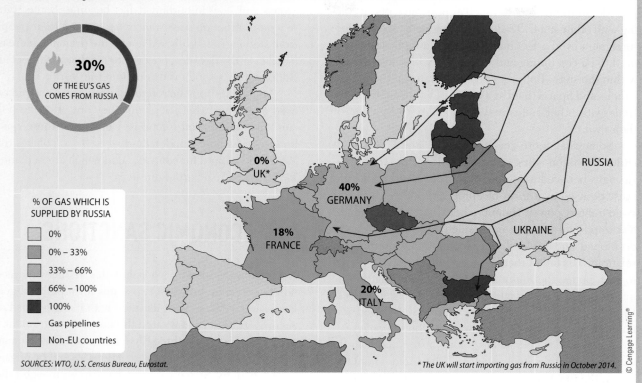

Map 9-1

The European Union's Reliance on Natural Gas from Russia

30% OF THE EU'S GAS COMES FROM RUSSIA

0% UK*

40% GERMANY

18% FRANCE

20% ITALY

RUSSIA

UKRAINE

% OF GAS WHICH IS SUPPLIED BY RUSSIA

- 0%
- 0% – 33%
- 33% – 66%
- 66% – 100%
- 100%
- — Gas pipelines
- Non-EU countries

SOURCES: WTO, U.S. Census Bureau, Eurostat.

* The UK will start importing gas from Russia in October 2014.

© Cengage Learning®

Source: I. Chapple and I. Kottasova, "West Threatens Russia with More Sanctions, but Trade Relations Complex," *CNN,* http://edition.cnn.com/2014/03/07/business/russia-sanctions-why-the-u-s-and-europe-are-not-quite-in-step/.

moved his troops into the southern Ukrainian province of Crimea, the U.S. and EU leaders began placing sanctions on Russian high-level officials and firms. The economic pressure is meant to stop the Russians from taking more provinces in Ukraine and push them out of the Crimea. So far, the sanctions have had no effect—Russia has annexed Crimea and continues to put pressure on Ukraine over territory in the eastern part of the country where many of the people are Russian-speaking and of Russian ethnicity. Europeans are also concerned that Russia carry out its threat to cut the flow of natural gas. In the winter of 2009, Russia cut off the flow of natural gas, Europe's second largest energy source (see Map 9-1), because it claimed Ukraine was siphoning off gas from the pipeline that passes through its country without paying for it; clearly, Russia and Ukraine have a troubled history. The embargo immediately led to downstream shortages throughout Europe and consequently more expensive energy for the Europeans for the rest of the 2009 winter.

These examples illustrate that "taking money" to coerce another country can be accomplished simply by cutting off an important resource, and that countries can retaliate for being sanctioned in the first place.

Now that we understand that wealth by itself can be used to influence other states and increase security, we need to explore briefly the long history economic statecraft has in international relations. Then we will turn to the many different ways in which economics are used for political purposes.

9-1a The Long History of Economic Statecraft: Money as a Carrot and a Stick

References to economic statecraft date back to approximately 500 BCE when the famous Chinese general Sun Tzu spoke of defeating one's enemies without resorting to military conflict and how important the economy was to leaders and their armies. A few hundred years later in ancient Greece, both Plato and Aristotle feared the power economic statecraft could have on a state. Between 400 and 300 BCE, they argued that states should be as self-sufficient as possible. That is, states should be able to provide for themselves as much as possible without trading with other states. Trade with foreigners (even if those foreigners lived a few hundred miles away) was considered to be corrupting and would likely lead to weakness within the state. Both the great city-states of the period, Athens and Sparta, held as a badge of honor their limited trade with other states and their ability to function on their own.

Somewhat more recently in the late 1700s, Alexander Hamilton—first secretary of the U.S. Treasury—strongly believed that the state's economy could and must be used as a form of influence, not just a way to build military power. Hamilton held that a strong military was important but that economic power should also be developed and wielded when conducting international relations. His belief that commerce itself was a coercive foreign policy tool influenced George Washington during his presidency and when writing his farewell address. From the time of its birth, the United States used economic statecraft as a crucial part of its foreign policy.[2]

Economic statecraft has a long history, both in the writings of intellectuals such as Plato and Hamilton, and in the practice of international relations. One of the major reasons Japan decided in 1941 to bomb the U.S. naval fleet at Pearl Harbor was an embargo that Australia, Great Britain, the Netherlands East Indies (the colony that later became Indonesia), and the United States placed on Japan. In an effort to keep the Japanese from expanding their empire in Asia and the Pacific, the four Western powers stopped selling the Japanese empire iron, steel, and oil. All three of these goods were critical to the Japanese plans for continued expansion. This move by the Western powers seriously threatened Japan's industrial strength and military power. Japanese officials believed that if they did not strike back at the United States and other countries promptly, they would be quickly weakened to the point that they would be unable to attack at all. Thus, the economic pressure hastened Japanese aggression, their eventual attack on Pearl Harbor, and the U.S. entrance into World War II.

The history of granting aid to other countries is more difficult to follow until the last five decades because states and international organizations did not carefully track aid. Further, most transfers of money were based on colonial ties and mostly flowed from the colonies back to the imperial power. However, in the last five decades, aid has become an important part of international relations. In 1960, approximately $37 billion (in 2008 constant dollars) of development aid was given globally. By 2011, that number had risen to more than $133.5 billion. In that time, world population has doubled, while aid has more than tripled. It is notable how much aid has grown and how important it has become. Some states rely on international assistance just to keep their people from starving, and sadly, even with the dramatic increase in aid over the decades, poverty and malnourishment are still pervasive problems throughout the world.

Many questions surround how sanctions and aid are used as well as whether or not they are effective policies. In the following sections, we explore these questions to get a better understanding of these policies that have been around for centuries and which are becoming more and more a part of our lives.

9-2 ECONOMIC SANCTIONS

An economic sanction is a policy that reduces the economic exchange between two states for a political goal. For example, Russia cut its trade with its neighbor Latvia in 1992 because it wanted the Latvian government to protect the rights of ethnic Russians better. However, not all economic reductions or restrictions should be considered sanctions. States regularly bargain with each other over trade, and this bargaining does not constitute a sanction because it involves economic issues rather than political issues. For example, in 1992 the United States believed that the Europeans were flooding the market with oilseeds (used to make vegetable oil) and threatened to impose a tariff on all European white wine that would have tripled its price in the United States. The Europeans agreed to reduce oilseed production, and the tariffs were never imposed. While this may sound like a small disagreement, European and American leaders both feared a possible trade war if negotiations failed. However, the threat to raise tariffs was aimed at an economic issue and was part of a trade negotiation. This is fundamentally different than sanctioning Iran to end its nuclear weapons program. Because these kinds of negotiations are so common, it is better for us not to think of them as sanctions. Instead, we need to focus on those economic means that are aimed at political ends.

9-2a The Different Types of Economic Sanctions

One state can impose an economic sanction on another state in four basic ways. These are often, but not always, combined into one set of sanctions. The most common type of sanction is a trade sanction that cuts the exchange of goods between the two countries. The second type is exemplified at the opening of the chapter—cutting foreign aid. Sanctions that cut aid to another country were used more during the Cold War and, although not uncommon, are used less today. Another very common type is a financial sanction that freezes the movement of assets (e.g., bank accounts) for the sanctioned country. Finally, third-party sanctions actually threaten a third country that is doing business with the main target of the sanctions. This type of sanction is relatively new and far more complicated than the other forms of economic coercion. Let's explore each of these more carefully.

IMPORT AND EXPORT SANCTIONS Trade sanctions are the most common and easy to understand, whether they are import or export sanctions. In both types of sanctions, the sanctioning state (referred to as the sender) reduces or cuts off completely either (1) goods and services coming from the sanctioned country (referred to as the target)—these are import sanctions (boycotts) or (2) goods and services being sold to the sanctioned country—export sanctions (embargoes). When we think of sanctions, **import and export sanctions** are most often what come to mind, and with good reason: 69 percent of all sanctions include import or export restrictions.[3]

Together, these types of sanctions can be referred to as trade sanctions, but such trade sanctions do have distinct differences. Import sanctions hurt businesses in the target country by not allowing them to sell their goods in the sender country—such as not letting Cuban sugar or cigars be sold in the United States. This can cause those businesses in the target country to go bankrupt or at least lose significant profits.

Sanctions affect the sender country, as well. Import sanctions also often cause the prices of goods made by the target country to rise in the sender country. Since the supply of the good is limited due to the sanction, prices may go up. Thus, if Japan decides not to buy Burmese rice to punish the repressive former military government in Burma, Japanese consumers might have to pay more for rice, and Japanese rice farmers will earn more for their crops. There are also businesses in the sender country that imported and then sold the sanctioned goods. They lose business as well, as did the U.S. sugar companies that used to import raw cane sugar from Cuba, refine it, and then sell it on the U.S. market. Some of those businesses were so closely tied to Cuban suppliers that they went bankrupt after import sanctions were imposed on Cuba (and the CEO of one of those firms committed suicide!).

Imagine if the United Kingdom decided to sanction all of the countries in the Persian Gulf for human

Ali Haider/epa/Corbis

Oil fields in Saudi Arabia | Though it may not look like it, oil is power. Can you think of another commodity that gives a country so much influence … if the country can control it?

rights violations by not buying any oil from them. The United Kingdom would have to rely on its oil from the North Sea, which could not match the production from Saudi Arabia and the other Gulf states. As a consequence, oil prices in the United Kingdom would skyrocket. This would hurt the British citizens who have to pay more for gasoline, but it would help oil firms like British Petroleum because BP could sell its products for much more than it could before the sanctions. While this hypothetical example is extreme—no country would stop buying oil from the entire Persian Gulf region—it illustrates how the sanctions can have different effects in the sender country.

Export sanctions tend to cause prices to rise in the target country because there are fewer products being sold. This type of sanction can also cause serious production problems in the target. For example, the United States began restricting the sale of replacement truck parts to Chile in the early 1970s as part of a set of economic sanctions. The U.S. government didn't like

import and export sanctions when one country reduces or stops buying or selling products from/to another country.

Salvador Allende, the new, democratically elected Chilean president, who was accused of ties to socialism and the Soviet Union. Without the truck parts, it became very difficult for Chile to keep its truck fleet on the road. While the parts may not have had much monetary value, their importance to transporting goods within Chile was dramatic. Due to tactics such as this, the Chilean economy was destabilized and Allende was later overthrown by his military.

Export sanctions do not normally cause prices to rise in the sender country because they restrict the sender's domestic businesses from selling to the target. For example, China might restrict the sale of rare metals to the EU if it did not like the EU policy toward the Chinese province Tibet. This would not cause prices to rise in China, but it would make it more difficult for EU countries to manufacture certain electronics requiring those metals and thus cause the price of those products to increase in Europe. Russian natural gas export sanctions on countries like Ukraine would not cause natural gas prices in Russia to increase; they would just cause Gazprom to lose some expected revenue.

AID SANCTIONS In addition to cutting off the trade with another country, the sanctioning state can also reduce or eliminate the monetary aid it gives, which is called an **aid sanction**. Of course, this assumes that the sender gives aid—whether it is military, development, or humanitarian—to the target country before the sanctions are initiated. The example about the anti-drug aid that the United States gives to Mexico and Colombia is a great example of this type of aid conditionality. The United States provides these funds but each year must determine if the country receiving the aid is fulfilling its obligations. While the example of Colombia and Mexico shows how the decision can be very politicized, it is still true that the U.S. State Department must certify each country receiving aid.

In the case of anti-drug aid, the U.S. State Department must certify that the country receiving the aid is doing its part in battling the production and trafficking of illegal drugs. If it is determined that the country is failing to combat drugs, then the aid is cut off. While this may seem like a simple transaction—stop paying the country when it fails to do its part, it is very much a sanction.

Think of it this way: the United States is sanctioning the target for allowing drugs to be produced or trafficked by reducing or ceasing to provide aid. The country is being punished for not following through on the policy the United States wants.

This process of certification extends beyond anti-drug aid. In 1974, the U.S. Congress passed the Jackson-Vanik Amendment that required the State Department to certify that all countries receiving any type of aid not engage in human rights violations. Originally, the amendment was aimed at the Soviet Union, which at the time was not allowing Soviet Jews to emigrate to other countries, but it soon became a way for the United States to sanction other countries that violated human rights. This practice was not evenly applied—for many years countries that were allied with the United States were permitted to violate human rights, but the law required closer inspection of the aid-granting process.

A similar strategy was adopted in 1976, when the U.S. Congress began requiring that all countries receiving aid not be involved in supporting terrorist groups. This list of terrorist supporters is relatively short, but the consequences of being on it are severe: the United States cannot provide aid or conduct trade with any listed country. Since the United States is the largest economy in the world, this can be a severe penalty. Being denied access to U.S. consumers is very costly for foreign providers of goods and services. As such, several countries on the list have worked to change their policies. The best example of this—ironically given recent events—is Libya. Realizing that he needed trade and support from the United States to boost his economy, former Libyan leader Muammar Gaddafi took steps to formally end his support of Islamic terrorists and normalize relations with the United States in 2006. Clearly, that more positive relationship with the United States ended once Gaddafi ordered his troops to fire on the Libyan people during the civil war that led to his downfall in 2011.

FINANCIAL SANCTIONS The third type of sanction is a **financial sanction**. The most common version of this kind of sanction is when the sanctioning country freezes the bank accounts of the target country, its government officials, or other members of the elite hierarchy of the society. For example, when Iranian students stormed the U.S. embassy and took hostages in 1979, President Carter froze all of the Iranian bank accounts in the United States. There were approximately $12 billion in money, gold, and other assets held by U.S. banks. Once the accounts were frozen, the Iranian government did not have access to any of the funds. This placed a serious burden on the Iranians, especially once the Iran-Iraq

aid sanction cutting off aid to a country in order to get it to change its behavior.

financial sanction the freezing of a country's financial assets held in another country.

war started in 1980 and they needed the money to support their war effort. More recently, the Arab League made headlines in late 2011 when its member countries imposed financial sanctions against Syria, such as freezing assets and cutting off transactions with the Syrian central bank for the Assad regime's violent crackdown against Arab Spring dissenters. Western countries also froze the bank accounts of Syrian business leaders with close ties to Syrian President Bashar al-Assad as a way to put pressure on the regime. The U.S. and EU sanctions on a set of specific Russian leaders with close ties to President Vladimir Putin are hoped to have the same effect. By freezing the assets of these particular individuals—and only them—held in U.S. and EU banks and limiting their use of those banks for international transactions, the United States and European Union have made their lives less profitable. The hope is that they will pressure Putin to stand down in Ukraine.

While this type of sanction was very effective in punishing the Iranians during the late 1970s, such sanctions have become more difficult to impose because of the proliferation of offshore banks. As major banks took hold in places such as Bermuda, Antigua, Barbuda, the Cayman Islands, and elsewhere, governments and leaders began keeping their funds in more than one country. Thus, if Japan wanted to freeze the assets of China, it could only freeze China's money that was kept in Japanese banks. If funds were held in other countries, Japan would have to get the cooperation of each country and bank to freeze the funds. Given that those offshore banks are successful because they typically do not permit such political meddling, financial sanctions have become less effective with time.

One significant exception is worth noting. In 2007, the U.S. Treasury requested that Banco Delta Asia in Macao freeze the assets of Kim Jong-il, the late North Korean dictator who died in 2011. Kim had been laundering money from the sale of drugs and illegal weapons through this and other banks in order to support his oppressive regime. Normally, such a request would be ignored. However, the United States told the banks that if they did not comply, it would be illegal for U.S. banks and firms to do business with them. Although Banco Delta Asia did not comply, many other banks in Macao did stop doing business with North Korea because they valued business with the United States more than their business with North Korea. Further, Macao officials tightened money-laundering laws and enforcement.

THIRD-PARTY SANCTIONS The most recent type of sanction gained notoriety in 1996 when the U.S. Congress passed the Helms-Burton Act (also known as

Cuba is full of vintage cars because Cubans were unable to purchase new U.S. cars after 1958 | These cars are certainly an odd side-effect of the sanctions against Cuba. What do you think will happen to them and the rest of Cuba once the sanctions are ended?

Joe Sohm Visions of America/Newscom

the Libertad Act). Senator Jesse Helms and Representative Dan Burton believed that the sanctions against Cuba were not working. Since 1960, the United States had severed all economic interactions with the Caribbean island-state, making the sanctions against Cuba some of the most comprehensive in the world. Yet after 36 years and eight U.S. presidents, the leader of Cuba—Fidel Castro—was still in power. Helms and Burton proposed a new way to put pressure on Cuba. Since the United States did not have any economic interactions directly with Cuba, there was no direct way to apply more economic pressure. The United States simply could not trade less with Cuba because it did not trade with Cuba at all. Instead, the Helms-Burton Act directed the United States to sanction other countries doing business with Cuba.[4] For example, if a Canadian hotel corporation planned to invest in building a resort in Cuba, the United States could sanction Canada to stop the investment, limit the ability of that Canadian company to do business in the United States, or even arrest its CEO if that person happened to enter the United States. This is considered a **third-party sanction** because a third country (Canada, in this example) is the target of the sanctions.

third-party sanction a sanction levied against a third-party state to keep that state from doing business with the primary target of the sanctions.

The Helms-Burton Act drew considerable criticism from both within the United States and—not surprisingly—other countries such as Canada and Spain, both states that did considerable business with Cuba. For several years, however, the sanction did put much greater pressure on Cuba because fewer countries wanted to invest for fear that they would be sanctioned by the United States.

These third-party sanctions are particularly important when the sanctioning state does not trade or invest in the target state. For example, the U.S. sanctions against banks laundering North Korean funds were third-party sanctions. The United States did not sanction North Korea (since it has no economic relationship with the totalitarian state), but it did threaten sanctions on a third party—in this case, offshore banks in Southeast Asia.

The downside to third-party sanctions is that the sanctioning country may end up sanctioning its own allies. Certainly, the United States and Canada have a close, friendly relationship. The Helms-Burton sanction put significant stress on the diplomatic ties between the two states. While the strong relationship survived intact, states must be careful when employing this kind of sanction.

9-2b Total Sanctions

It is worthwhile to note that all of the previously described types of sanctions are not exclusive. Countries can deploy multiple types of sanctions, including total or comprehensive sanctions, or the cutoff of all economic connections to the target. While these are not common, they do exist. The U.S. sanctions against Cuba, North Korea, and Iran are good examples. There is some minor economic activity between these countries and the United States, but it is ultimately trivial compared to what it would be like if there were no sanctions.

Two other examples are the sanctions against South Africa and Rhodesia (now called Zimbabwe) during their apartheid regimes. In both cases, a white minority ruled the country, and when called on to open the political system to all citizens of the state, both refused. The UN mandated comprehensive sanctions against each country, and slowly almost all other countries began to follow the UN mandate. In Rhodesia, a long civil war broke out, which ultimately ended white minority rule. South Africa's transition away from apartheid was somewhat more peaceful. The tremendous pressure from around the world—including sanctions by most countries and divestment by huge multinational corporations—led the white minority regime in South Africa to negotiate an end to apartheid, which paved the way for the election of Nelson Mandela, South Africa's first black president.

These total or comprehensive sanctions are not the norm, but they do occur and extract a huge cost on the targeted country. Many policymakers and activists argue that military action might actually be more humane than a total embargo of a state. That may sound far-fetched, but when you consider that sanctions—when applied severely—can cut a state's economy in half, one can certainly understand why sanctions are not necessarily considered the most humane option available when trying to coerce another state.

9-2c A Cornucopia of Goals: The Many Purposes of Sanctions

We have discussed thus far the different ways in which one state can sanction another, but what might the sanctioning country seek from the sanctions? The list of different sanction goals is long and includes some rather specific and even obscure goals. For example, in 1978, China sanctioned Albania for making anti-Chinese comments. In this case, the sanctions were used simply as a way to signal to the Albanians and the world that China was upset about the critical comments. That may sound a little childish, but signaling other countries is an important part of international relations because it informs countries about each other's preferences. For most sanctions, however, their goals can be divided into five types.

First, one of the goals sought by a sanctioning country is to weaken the target state's military and economy. This goal harkens back to the writing by Sun Tzu and is often considered "economic warfare" because it is so closely tied to military conflict. The basic idea is that the sanctioning country wants to weaken the target before attacking (or being attacked). Thus, the sanctions have a distinct security objective and are often used as a prelude to war. While such sanctions were rather common in the first half of the twentieth century, they have become very uncommon because sanctioning other countries as a way to soften them up before an invasion violates international norms of conflict resolution. Today, countries are expected to try to work out their differences before going to war rather than slowly bleeding their opponent's military before attacking them. Obviously, things have changed over the last 100 years or so!

Second, sanctions are also commonly used to destabilize a government, often in hopes of changing the leadership or type of government. The sanctions against Cuba fit this description, as do the U.S. sanctions against the regimes in Cuba, Nicaragua, Panama, and Yugoslavia. These sanctions not only sent a signal to the world that the United States opposed the regimes in these countries, but that the U.S. also meant to make it difficult if not impossible for these regimes to function. By causing unemployment, inflation, and supply shortages, the sanctions were supposed to lead to disruptions in the economy and public life. Such efforts worked well in some places—Panama and Yugoslavia come to mind—but not in others (Cuba, for example).

Third, in another security-related purpose, states often use sanctions in an effort to limit the proliferation of nuclear weapons. Canada has taken the lead several times, starting in the 1970s when it sanctioned India and Pakistan for proliferation and the EU (known as the European Community at the time) and Japan for a failure to maintain nuclear safeguards. Other states such as Australia and the United States have also used sanctions as a means to stop countries from developing nuclear weapons. The **International Atomic Energy Agency (IAEA)** can also have a profound effect on anti-proliferation sanctions. The agency is authorized to determine if a country is proliferating or maintaining adequate nuclear safeguards. When the IAEA reports that a state like Iraq is developing nuclear weapons, it often triggers many countries to impose sanctions. The current sanctions by the United States and European Union against Iran are a prime example of these efforts. Since 2006, the UN has authorized sanctions against Iran because it continues to reject international inspections of its nuclear program. Leading the sanctioning effort, Europe and the United States have cut off trade and investment with Iran. It is not clear yet whether Iran will end its nuclear weapons program, but there have been some progress in the negotiations that suggests there may be hope.

The final two goals have also become the most popular in recent decades. Since 1990, more than half of all sanctions were aimed at human security goals such as promoting better human rights, democracy, or both. With the end of the Cold War, democracy, as a form of governance, developed into an international norm, and as discussed in Chapter 11, a minimal level of human rights has also largely become a norm of accepted behavior. With these changes to the international norms, developed democratic states embraced the norms and the idea that they should promote democracy and human rights. It was, so to speak, "time to put your money where your mouth was." If the democratic countries in the world believed in spreading democracy and human rights, then they needed to support it.

The West African country of Guinea offers a prime example. A former French colony, Guinea gained independence in 1958 and has since had a series of autocratic rulers. In an attempt at democratization, the country held elections in 2002, but there was widespread fraud by the then dictator, President Lansana Conté. The EU

sanctioned Guinea—one of the poorest countries in the world—by cutting off all aid. In 2004, the EU and Guinean leaders met to address the problems identified by the EU. At first the negotiations worked, and Conté allowed for some freedom of the press by licensing several private radio stations in 2006. The EU started sending aid to Guinea again, but within months, Conté's police began shooting protestors. A year later, President Conté declared martial law. The Guinean people continued to fight for democracy, and, after the death of President Conté and a subsequent military coup, in November 2010 they elected a new leader.

Although this case is certainly not a successful example of sanctioning, it is very typical. Sanctions aimed at promoting democracy usually fail. Sadly, most dictators do not care if the European Union, the United States, or some other democratic country cuts their aid or trade. The leaders are primarily interested in staying in power, so they ignore the sanctions and—as we discuss in detail in the following section—shift the harm caused by the sanctions onto the public. Even with the poor record of performance, however, economic sanctions have become one of the primary means by which countries try to compel and coerce autocratic leaders into democratic reforms.

Sanctions are also often used to promote human rights reforms. Sometimes, the sanctions are as simple as an attempt to bring a civil war to an end. In 2003, the UN imposed an **arms embargo** and a subsequent asset freeze on the Democratic Republic of Congo because of the tribal fighting and civil war. In just five years, the violence killed an estimated 2.5 million people. Once again, the sanctions did not succeed in significantly limiting the fighting, but it was the international community's attempt to stop the violence and subsequent massive human rights violations.

Most human rights sanctions are more direct than the 2003 sanctions against the Congo. Usually, they are responses to poor treatment of people by a government rather than a civil war. The sanctions imposed by the Arab League against Syria in late 2011 are an example of this objective, but there are many others. In 1989, for instance, the United States sanctioned the People's Republic of China following the Tiananmen

International Atomic Energy Agency (IAEA)
an independent intergovernmental organization that reports to the UN and UNSC concerning the peaceful use of atomic energy, nuclear proliferation, and nuclear safeguards.

arms embargo   not selling weapons to a country.

Square massacre. When pro-democracy protestors filled Tiananmen Square in the spring of 1989 and refused to leave, the Chinese government called in the army to disperse the protestors. There is not an accurate death count, but hundreds and maybe thousands of protestors were killed. President George H. W. Bush suspended all arms sales to China, but within months he began lifting the sanctions. For six more years, the United States and China argued over the connection between trade and human rights, as the United States pushed China to improve its treatment of the Chinese people. In 1995, President Clinton ended these sanctions and threats by "delinking" China's human rights policies and U.S. trade policies. There still has not been a significant change in human rights in China.

9-2d The Failure of Economic Sanctions

As you may have noticed from the many examples of sanctions previously discussed, they do not often attain their goals. Estimates of economic sanction success assert that only between 5 and 33 percent of economic sanctions meet their goals even modestly. Most sanctions fail because the economic costs they impose on the target country are limited and usually lower than the cost of compliance. That is, the sanctions may cause the economy to lose 3 percent of its annual growth (the average for all sanctions)—to put that in relative terms, that's about 7 million jobs lost in the United States—but the cost to the leaders of the sanctioned country to comply with the sender's demands is often very high. We should not be surprised, for example, that Fidel Castro did not give in to the U.S. sanctions. If he had, he would not have been able to remain the leader of Cuba. The choice between trading with the United States, on the one hand, and being the leader of Cuba, on the other, is not exactly a difficult one for a dictator. Similarly, the Chinese might have lost billions of dollars if the United States had fully sanctioned them after Tiananmen Square, but they believed that giving into demands for better human rights would be the beginning of the end of the Chinese Communist Party's rule of the People's Republic of China—again, not a difficult choice to make.

Another reason sanctions often fail is related directly to anarchy. First, sanctions impose costs on the target, but there is nothing that can make the target comply. Because there is no central authority in the international system, one state can sanction another, but there is no authority that can resolve the dispute conclusively. Thus, the target can ignore the sanctioning state and only pay the cost of the sanctions. Second, other countries can trade with the sanctioned state—busting the sanctions, so to speak. Because there is no central authority, there is nothing to keep other countries from busting the sanctions except fear of the sanctioning state. For example, the French could sanction Angola, but there is nothing to keep the United States from trading with Angola. In this way, anarchy has a profound way of weakening a country's ability to use its economy to influence other states.

So, if sanctions fail so often, why do leaders continue to use them? Let's try to answer that question next.

THE PARADOX OF ECONOMIC SANCTIONS: WHY DO STATES USE THEM IF THEY FAIL SO OFTEN

For many years, scholars thought that sanctions were used not to influence the target but to help out domestic producers. For example, Germany might sanction the importation of Japanese cars to help out domestic car manufacturers like Volkswagen. However, more recent research shows that sanctions tend not to be used to protect domestic producers. Instead, most sanctions are initiated in reaction to something the target country did. For example, poor human rights and ethnic cleansing by the Sudanese government in Darfur led to sanctions by the UN. Thus, most sanctions are used to influence the target country.

That still does not answer the question of why sanctions are used when they fail so often. We cannot assume that the leaders of countries that use sanctions are stupid and do not know that sanctions usually fail. We must instead assume that leaders fully understand that sanctions rarely work. So again, why do they continue to use them?

The answer lies in the message the sanctions send to the target country and to the rest of the world. Even though the sanctions themselves may not coerce the target state into changing their human rights, for example, it does send the message that the sanctioning countries disapprove. The United States and UN both levied sanctions against Sudan because of the ethnic cleansing of non-Arab Muslims and others in Darfur. More than actually expecting the conflict in Darfur to end, the United States and UN needed to send a message to the Sudanese government that it strongly disapproved of the treatment of its non-Arab inhabitants. Sanctions are a way for the sender to show the target how much it disapproves, disagrees, or is angry about some actions the target country has taken.

In addition to sending a message to the target country, sanctions also send a signal to other nations. The UN sanctions against Sudan showed the world that the UN would not ignore ethnic cleansing, that it would respond

Smart Sanctions?

The frequency of economic sanctions increased with the end of the Cold War, with some scholars referring to the 1990s as "The Sanctions Decade" in a book with that title.[5] While more and more sanctions were being initiated, the most striking case the world has ever seen is the sanction regime against Iraq. For more than a decade, the world ceased trading with the Iraqis, causing their economy to shrink by almost half. To put this in perspective, the 45 percent drop in the Iraqi economy is almost twice as bad as the Great Depression in the United States. As a direct result of the sanctions, infant mortality increased, unemployment went through the roof, and women's rights fell dramatically.[6]

To compensate for the dramatic effects the sanctions had on the Iraqi people, the UN authorized the "Oil for Food Programme," which set up a system for Iraq to sell specific amounts of oil to make money that could only be used to purchase food and medical supplies for the Iraqi people. President Clinton proposed the program in 1995 in response to the devastating effect the sanctions were having on the average Iraqi. Unfortunately, the program was riddled with corruption. Profits from Iraqi oil went to an escrow account managed by UN officials. The lead official of the program was accused of siphoning money for his staff and taking considerable bribes from companies that wanted to sell food to Iraq and allegedly taking $3.5 million from the Iraqis themselves. Iraqi officials also worked to steal the profits for their own use, rather than providing food and medicine to the Iraqi people. They would give contacts to companies that would overcharge the UN program for the food and then give the excess funds to the Iraqi government. One investigation reported that much of the food purchased by the program was not fit for human consumption, while another investigation concluded that the Iraqi government resisted the program simply to increase the suffering of the people of Iraq, thereby making the UN look like a villain.

The second response to the Iraq sanctions was a concern among analysts and policymakers that sanctions must be designed to be "smart," that is, to only affect the leaders of the country and not the common citizen. For this reason, they are also called "targeted sanctions." If a sanction could target a leader such as Saddam Hussein but not hurt his people, it seemed possible that sanctions could be effective without causing any unintended consequences. From this concern, the idea of "smart sanctions" was born.

In the following years, states have attempted to target their sanctions directly at opposing leaders. For example, following a 1991 **coup d'état** in Haiti, the United States denied travel to both the leaders of the coup and to their family members, in addition to other sanctions. While a travel ban may not seem like much, the leaders' families liked to go shopping in Miami's boutiques. By denying access, the United States made the lives of the dictators far less affluent and perhaps may have forced those dictators into some very uncomfortable conversations with unhappy family members.

Another "smart sanction" case is one we already discussed: the sanctions against the banks in Macao doing business with North Korea. Not only were these third-party sanctions, but they are also considered "smart" or targeted sanctions. Former dictator Kim Jong-il was using the laundered funds from these banks to pay off his supporters to keep them happy and supportive of his autocratic rule. By reducing his ability to get those funds, the sanctions hurt him and other North Korean elites, but they did not hurt the North Korean people. Most recently, U.S. and EU sanctions against the assets and financial dealings of specific Russian leaders close to Putin illustrate smart sanctions as well.

Although UN diplomats were especially attracted to smart sanctions, there is no evidence that they are more effective than normal sanctions. Further, leaders of sanctioned countries usually have considerable resources available to them. While his people suffered in Iraq, Saddam and his family lived in opulent wealth. It is hard to imagine that smart sanctions could have put more pressure on him, but perhaps they could.

Another very unpleasant perspective on this issue is that perhaps the best way to make a country comply with a demand is to cause serious suffering in its population. Would it be a good policy to impose crushing sanctions like the kind levied against North Korea to avoid a war? Since 2011, how has the Syrian government survived an increasing cascade of international sanctions? Who is being hurt there?

coup d'état literally translated as a "strike against the state"; when there is a forceful change in government that overthrows the current leadership.

Considering the desire for limiting the suffering caused by sanctions, think about these questions:

1. Most sanctions are not nearly as devastating as those in Iraq. What can we learn from such extreme examples like Iraq, and how should that influence policy?

2. How would our different theories view the use of sanctions?

3. If sanctions cause so much suffering, is targeted military intervention better?

4. What other ways might exist to make sanctions "smart"?

with economic measures. Thus, other political regimes that may be considering violating their people's human rights can look at the Sudan case and realize that if they do "ethnically cleanse" a portion of their population, there will be consequences.

Thus, sanctions are most often used to send a message to the target country and the rest of the world. Canada has made it clear to the world, for example, that it strongly opposes nuclear proliferation because it has sanctioned several countries in the past for not taking enough care in the production of nuclear material used in bomb making. To be sure, sanctions can sometimes compel the target to change its policies, but more often they are a form of strong political communication between countries. At the very least, economic sanctions satisfy the sender's domestic political need to *do something* regarding the problem posed by the recipient state. Such domestic pressures often help to explain the sender's actions.

9-2e The Costly Consequences of Sanctions

Even though sanctions do not succeed very often and are thus often used as a way to send a message, they still can have powerful effects on the targeted state. In the most extreme cases, such as Iraq between 1990 and 2003, the sanctions caused the economy to shrink by nearly half—a devastating effect. As noted earlier, on average a sanctioned country loses 3 percent of its annual economic growth. For example, if it is growing at a healthy rate of 3.5 percent before the sanctions, the sanctions will cause the growth rate to fall to 0.5 percent. While not necessarily devastating, that loss of 3 percent in growth is a serious recession in most countries, especially if it persists over several years. Thus, sanctions may not achieve their goals, but they do considerable damage to the sanctioned country's economy. Unfortunately, as TV ads often say: "That's not all!"

Sanctions also have a detrimental effect on human rights, level of democracy, and respect for women. When a country is sanctioned, the leaders are being threatened by another country. They often react to the sanctions by tightening their hold on power, often by repressing their public to quash any possible dissent against their rule.

For example, in the mid-1980s, Manuel Noriega, the leader of Panama, became increasingly involved in drug smuggling and took a more hostile stance toward the United States. Seeing this as a threat to U.S. security, President Reagan sanctioned Panama. Shortly after Reagan announced the sanctions, Noriega created paramilitary forces called "dignity battalions" to intimidate and repress his political opponents. Until the American-led invasion removed him in late 1989, Noriega became more and more autocratic and removed all democratic rights from Panama. The sanctions—meant to influence Panama's foreign policy toward the Soviets—actually led the country into autocracy.

Another example is the arms embargo in the early 1990s on Bosnia. The idea was to limit the number of weapons in the hands of the Bosnian Serbs and the Bosnian Muslims—the two sides that were embroiled in a civil conflict. Unfortunately, the embargo only made things worse. Neighboring Serbia supported their ethnic brethren in Bosnia, and so the Bosnian Serbs were well armed. This left the Bosnian Muslims under-armed and very vulnerable. After the situation deteriorated significantly, the United States secretly encouraged Iran to give weapons to the Bosnian Muslims to even the fighting and hopefully limit the bloodshed. Only after a massive NATO intervention and occupation did the ethnic cleansing end.

So what are leaders to do if they want to coerce or at least send a message to another state? This is just one of the unfortunate trade-offs that leaders must make when considering any kind of coercive action. Military intervention is certainly more drastic, but economic sanctions have significant costs, as well.

Why Haven't European Countries Placed Severe Sanctions on Russia?

In late 2013, protests in Ukraine against the pro-Russian president, Viktor Yanukovych began to escalate. By February 2014, deadly violence erupted between the protestors and Yanukovych's forces, ultimately forcing Yanukovych to flee to Russia. An interim government was created, but that was not the end of the story. Seventeen percent of the Ukrainian population is ethnically Russian, and there are close ties between the Southern and Eastern regions of Ukraine and its neighbor, Russia. Further complicating matters, the Russian Black Sea Fleet is stationed in Crimea (in southern Ukraine) and there are significant Russian investments in eastern Ukraine. Within days of Yanukovych's departure, Russian forces moved into Crimea, securing the region in the name of ethnic Russians. Russian forces continued their invasion into eastern Ukraine.

Given this clear violation of Ukrainian sovereignty, the United States and European states condemned the invasion and called for Russian President Vladimir Putin to remove his troops. A series of moderate sanctions were levied against the Russians, but U.S. trade with Russia is minimal, limiting the ability of the Americans to coerce Moscow. As you can see from Figure 9-1 below, Europe has considerable trade with Russia and could, thus, apply severe sanctions in an effort to help the Ukrainian people regain their territory. Although the EU applied some sanctions and Germany made strong threats against further Russian incursions, no severe sanctions materialized. Why would Europe seemingly abandon its democratic neighbor?

We have to remember that trade flows in both directions, so if the EU countries sanctioned Russia, Putin could retaliate with sanctions against the EU. Both sides are vulnerable. Further, Europe gets a large portion of its natural gas and oil from Russia (recall Map 9-1). If that supply was cutoff or even reduced, there would be severe consequences for the people

FIGURE 9-1 RUSSIA'S TRADE FLOWS

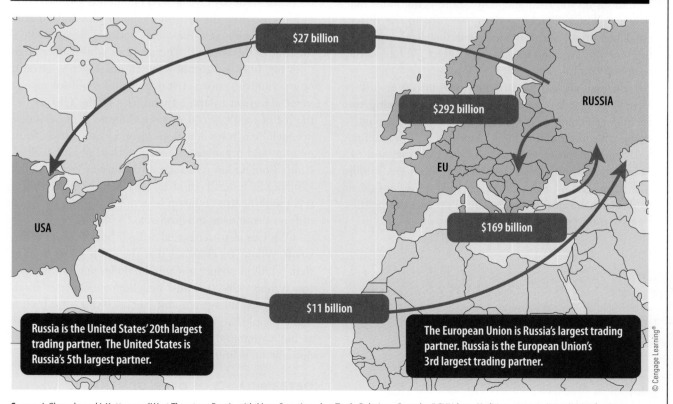

$27 billion

$292 billion

RUSSIA

EU

$169 billion

USA

$11 billion

Russia is the United States' 20th largest trading partner. The United States is Russia's 5th largest partner.

The European Union is Russia's largest trading partner. Russia is the European Union's 3rd largest trading partner.

© Cengage Learning®

Source: I. Chapple and I. Kottasova, "West Threatens Russia with More Sanctions, but Trade Relations Complex," *CNN*, http://edition.cnn.com/2014/03/07/business /russia-sanctions-why-the-u-s-and-europe-are-not-quite-in-step/.

living throughout Europe. Heating, cooking, and transportation would cost much more, endangering the health of the EU economy and making it significantly more difficult to deal with the economic troubles in Greece, Spain, Ireland, Italy, and Portugal.

While average Europeans may feel very badly for the people in Ukraine, do you think they would be willing to pay significantly more to heat their home, cook their food, or drive their car? What about losing their job to try and help Ukraine? The leaders in Europe recognize this situation and therefore are walking a fine line in trying to pressure Putin to limit his military takeover and not escalating what could become a full-blown economic sanction "war" with one of their bigger and certainly more important trading partners.

1. Would you support sanctioning Russia if you had to pay more for the energy you use? How much more for a gallon of gas would you pay to support the people of Ukraine?

2. Should the EU leaders ignore the costs that their citizens would have to pay and sanction Russia anyway?

3. What does the reluctance of the EU to put real pressure on Moscow say about its support for democracy or even sovereignty?

9-3 FOREIGN AID

We now have discussed the ways in which one state can influence or coerce another by taking money from the other state and thereby causing economic pain. In addition to an economic "stick," countries can also use economic "carrots" to entice, coax, or simply pay off another state. While most **foreign aid** does not officially impose conditions on the recipient state, there is no doubt that it is a politicized process. Next, we turn to the different kinds of aid and the conditions that lead countries to grant aid. We then turn to what effect aid has on the recipient country.

Foreign aid can be broken down into four different types: (1) development aid aimed at helping the recipient's economy, (2) military aid aimed at strengthening the recipient state's security, (3) democracy aid aimed at promoting democratic reforms, and (4) humanitarian aid aimed at providing immediate help in an emergency or disaster. Let's turn to each of these to discuss what the aid is meant to do and the politics that surround it.

foreign aid money given by one country (the donor) to another country (the recipient) for health, economic development, or poverty relief.

development aid aid given to a country to help develop its economy.

Organization for Economic Cooperation and Development (OECD) organization of 34 member states that promotes liberal economic and political reforms.

9-3a Development Aid

What we usually think about when we are thinking of aid is **development aid**—aid that is given to countries that are poor and struggling to develop their economies. Not only is development aid what we commonly think of, it is also the most plentiful type of aid. According to the Development Assistance Committee of the **Organization for Economic Cooperation and Development (OECD)**, $133.5 billion was given to states to help promote the growth of their economies in 2011 (the most recent year for which statistics are available at the time of this writing). This number, while rather large, does not fully capture how much assistance is given to other countries. Instead, it only includes official government aid given by the 34 countries in the OECD (see the list of member countries in Chapter 2). It also does not include private donations given by individuals, foundations, and organizations such as the Bill and Melinda Gates Foundation, Oxfam, and Lutheran World Relief. Why not include all countries and donors? Quite simply, it is too difficult to tally up how much is given by all the different countries and groups in the world.

We can also make that $133.5 billion seem rather small. When you consider that the aid is given to more than 5 billion people, the annual dollar amount per person is only $26.70. Thus, developing countries themselves receive a large amount, but once you consider how many people live in those states, the amount isn't nearly as big. Compared to the extent of human needs, development aid is literally like a drop in the ocean.

DETERMINANTS OF DEVELOPMENT AID Why give this aid? In the simplest of terms, aid should reduce poverty. As spelled out more specifically by the United

Women and Economic Sanctions

Previously, we discussed how sanctions often have negative and counterproductive consequences. In addition to generally hurting the population and driving down human rights and democracy, sanctions also have a particularly negative effect on women (Figure 9-2). Several case studies show how women suffer in countries that are targeted by sanctions.

The case of Iraq is particularly disturbing. Prior to 1990, Iraqi women enjoyed considerable freedoms and relative equality for a Middle Eastern country. Many of them worked outside the home because it was safe for them to travel and the state provided childcare. That changed radically after the UN imposed sanctions: women disproportionately lost their jobs and had to turn to the informal labor market, including sewing, cleaning, and too often prostitution.[7] One Iraqi physician, a woman, commented: "During the sanctions period, all of the ministries encouraged women to resign or retire early." Childcare ended, leaving women to care for their children and making it increasingly difficult for them to work. "Domestic violence, as well as street violence targeting women, increased particularly during the embargo."[8] Marriage became entirely about financial security; a husband who could provide food and a home developed into a necessity as women tried to survive.

Iraq is a very extreme case because the sanctions were so comprehensive and crushing. However, similar stories exist when less severe sanctions are used. When Burma's exports were banned, the textile businesses there were crushed. Women dominated this industry, and when it shrunk, they were left without jobs. Many turned to prostitution to feed their families.

Unfortunately, a recent study shows that these examples are not uncommon.[9] When a country is sanctioned, the women there face much greater economic discrimination by either taking pay cuts, being demoted, or losing their jobs altogether. They also face greater social discrimination. In poor countries, which tend

not to have great respect for women in the first place, sanctions almost make it a certainty that they will lose basic rights, such as deciding whom to marry, where and when they can travel, and other basic reproductive rights.

These findings raise more questions about the use of economic statecraft. While bombing and armed invasion are more extreme than an economic sanction, it

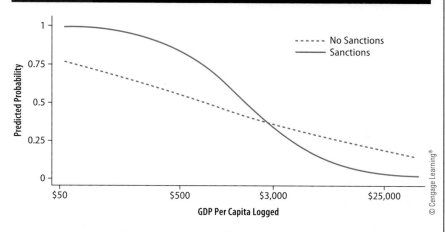

FIGURE 9-2 PROBABILITY THAT WOMEN'S ECONOMIC RIGHTS WILL BE VIOLATED

Notice how much more likely women are to suffer when sanctions (the solid line) are applied to a poor country.

Source: A. Cooper Drury and Dursun Peksen, "Women and Economic Statecraft: The Negative Impact Economic Sanctions Visit on Women" *European Journal of International Relations*, 2014.

is important to realize that these economic tools are not without costs. When a large country cuts off trade with another, it threatens the security of that country. Women are often the most vulnerable group within a country because their rights are not widely respected. However, women are not the only vulnerable group. Although research has not yet focused on children, there is good reason to suspect that they suffer more when their country is sanctioned. Clearly, sanctions can reduce both women and children's situation to one of fear.

1. Is there some way to protect women when sanctioning another state?

2. If the European Union and United States want to stop Iran or North Korea from developing or deploying nuclear weapons, are the costs involved with sanctions worth it?

3. If sanctions cause such problems and military action is an even more dangerous option for countries trying to coerce another state, what options are available?

U.S. Development Aid in Perspective

There is considerable criticism around the world about how much development aid the United States provides. Most non-Americans argue that the United States does not give enough. In fact, global public opinion almost uniformly criticizes the United States for the small portion of aid given relative to the size of its economy. So how much aid does the United States give? While there is an answer to this question, it is not a simple one—like the rest of international relations, it is complex.

Before we look at the actual numbers of U.S. aid, it is first worth considering what the average American thinks. When asked what portion of the U.S. federal budget was devoted to international aid, the median American response was 25 percent. When asked how much should be spent, the median American response was 10 percent. In reality, less than 1 percent of the budget goes to foreign aid. If one considers only discretionary spending (e.g., not interest payments on the debt or other mandated entitlement programs), then 2.6 percent of the budget is spent on aid. Thus, depending on which number you use, the average American overestimates how much the United States spends on aid by 10 to 25 times!

So what are the "real" numbers? First, let's consider the total aid in dollars. In this measure, the United States does very well. It contributed $30.69 billion in 2012. That accounts for 24 percent of all aid according to the OECD. The next largest donor is the United Kingdom, which gave $13.89 billion or 11 percent of the total. Thus, by this accounting, the United States gives approximately twice as much aid as the second biggest donor. That certainly seems generous—so why do people criticize the United States?

The second "real" number is what portion of a country's economy is devoted to aid (Table 9-1). It is certainly easier for the United States to give more than a smaller, less wealthy state. For example, a country like the United States can give a lot more aid than a country like Spain simply because America's economy is bigger and therefore has more money that it could give. Thus, it is important to consider how much aid is given compared to the size of the donor's economy. When considering the percent of GNP (gross national product, or the total size of the economy) given in aid, the United States does not stack up very well. U.S. aid only totals 0.19 percent of its economy. The United Kingdom's aid, on the other hand, totals 0.56 percent, two

and a half times the level of U.S. aid, and the United Kingdom doesn't do that well compared to other donors! The biggest aid donor, once the size of the economy is taken into account, is Norway. Norwegians give .93 percent of their economy in aid—more than five times as much as

TABLE 9-1	TOP AID DONORS BY ACTUAL AMOUNT AND AS A PERCENT OF GDP	
	2012 OFFICIAL DEVELOPMENT AID	
	AMOUNT OF AID IN MILLIONS OF CURRENT U.S. DOLLARS	AID AS A PERCENTAGE OF GDP (%)
Australia	5,403	0.36
Austria	1,106	0.28
Belgium	2,315	0.47
Canada	5,650	0.32
Czech Republic	220	0.12
Denmark	2,693	0.83
Finland	1,320	0.53
France	12,028	0.45
Germany	12,939	0.37
Greece	327	0.13
Iceland	26	0.22
Ireland	808	0.47
Italy	2,737	0.14
Japan	10,605	0.17
Korea	1,597	0.14
Luxembourg	399	1.00
Netherlands	5,523	0.71
New Zealand	449	0.28
Norway	4,753	0.93
Poland	421	0.09
Portugal	581	0.28
Slovak Republic	80	0.09
Spain	2,037	0.16
Sweden	5,240	0.97
Switzerland	3,045	0.47
United Kingdom	13,892	0.56
United States	30,687	0.19
Total Aid	**126,881**	**0.29**
Average Country Effort		0.40
OECD Targeted Effort		0.70

Source: OECD data at http://www.oecd.org/dac/stats/data.htm, Organization for Economic Cooperation and Development, 2014.

the United States. Look at Table 9-1 to see how the OECD countries stack up. The United States does great in the first column but is well below average in the second column. When you consider those numbers, one can understand why there is such global criticism.

Others are not free from criticism either. For example, when the Canadian government wanted to help farmers in the mountainous, remote regions of Lesotho, they built roads so that the farmers could get their grain to market. However, the roads had the opposite effect. Instead of taking grain out of the region, they were used to bring grain into the region—cheaper grain that was imported from South Africa. As a direct consequence of the aid project, many farmers lost their livelihoods. This was certainly not the effect the Canadians were trying to achieve, but in the end, the aid actually hurt the local economy.

Nations **Millennium Development Goals**, "Eradicate extreme poverty and hunger" by the year 2015. Under this program, states were to work together to cut in half the number of people living on less than $1 a day and the number of people suffering from hunger. Part of this goal was for wealthy states to donate 0.7 percent of their GDP as development aid. Therefore, aid should first and foremost help eliminate poverty. The funds—which may be aimed at lessening human suffering—are designed to help countries develop their economies so that they can provide for at least the basic needs of the population. In addition to alleviating suffering, aid should indirectly reduce political instability in the target. Countries whose citizens can meet their basic needs have less reason to revolt and are associated with less violence, instability, and insecurity.

Following these goals, aid-granting states officially give aid on the basis of need. Poorer, less developed countries are the only states that qualify and are officially given aid based on their need. Once a country's economy develops and rises out of poverty, and it no longer needs assistance, donor states could be expected to stop providing aid. However, the largest portions of aid do not always go to the poorest countries. In 2009 for example, Afghanistan received the most development aid of any country in the world—over $6 billion. However, there are many larger states that are much poorer. Zimbabwe, Liberia, and the Democratic Republic of Congo all have a GDP per capita of less than $400; Afghanistan has a GDP per capita of just slightly less than $1,000. Why does Afghanistan get so much aid? The answer is the United States and several of its allies are trying to develop a stable government in Afghanistan.

As this example illustrates, there is a lot more to the granting of aid than simply a desire to alleviate poverty. Political scientists and economists have studied the question of what leads countries to give aid. In addition to the level of poverty, four factors stand out as important in the allocation of development aid.

First, as the Afghanistan example illustrates, a military or strategic interest in the recipient country may lead the donor to give significantly more aid. Specifically, political scientists have shown that a military presence—troops—in a country makes it much more likely that aid will be given in large quantities. The recipient state has to be relatively poor—the United States does not give aid to Germany even though American troops are stationed in Germany. However, if the country is poor and the donor state has troops stationed there, the level of aid will be higher.

Historically, the importance of a military/strategic interest was much greater during the Cold War. When the United States and NATO were confronted by the Soviet Union and Warsaw Pact, the United States in particular gave copious amounts of money to any developing country that swore to be anti-Soviet. The Soviets did the same thing by giving aid to states that professed a dislike of the United States and Western Europe. In many cases, these small, poor states would play the two sides off against each other in an attempt to gain more aid.

A good example is Cuba. Though communist, Cuba did not originally want to sever ties with the United States. Instead, the Cuban leader, Fidel Castro, hoped to trade with and get aid from both the United States and Soviet Union. Shortly after the revolution, however, Washington began to break off all economic ties after Cuba began nationalizing private property. This led the Soviets to pour vast amounts of aid and investment into Cuba. With the end of the Cold War, Cuba's economy went into a recession simply because the Soviet Union no longer existed, and Russia was not interested in providing so much aid.

Millennium Development Goals eight goals established by the UN in 2000 to foster development in a sustainable and equal manner.

Celebration as the Berlin Wall was torn down | Can you imagine cutting your city in half and becoming enemies with the other side overnight? Years later, how would you feel about these people, some of whom were your relatives and best friends?

The last two factors that may lead a state to get more aid are (1) whether it is democratic, and (2) if it trades openly with other countries. Free-trading democracies tend to get more aid than non-democratic states or those that limit the amount of trade with other countries. Most donor countries are democratic and have large international economies that engage in a lot of foreign trade. As donors, these democratic, free-trading countries prefer to give aid to similar countries. Thus, there is a bias toward those states that lean toward democracy and are willing to "do business" with the donors.

These effects often lead to criticisms of development aid. Some countries claim that countries such as France, Japan, and the United States only give aid with strings attached, namely that if you receive aid, you must then engage in free trade and perhaps democratic reforms. While these claims are not illogical, development aid is officially "free" of such strings. In reality, the association between free-trading democracies and aid is more likely caused by the preferences of the donor states than explicit strings. However, trading relationships still matter. For example, Japan gives more development aid to states that import a lot of Japanese products than to those that do not. In short, some of that Japanese aid might be going toward the purchase of Sony personal computers, Toyota trucks, or Komatsu backhoes by the recipient regime.

IS DEVELOPMENT AID EFFECTIVE Thus far we have discussed how much aid is given worldwide and both the official and unofficial political reasons why countries tend to give development aid, but we haven't answered the question of whether the aid is effective. Does aid actually help the recipient country develop its economy and become less poor?

The answer is not particularly encouraging. Some scholars and policymakers claim that aid can effectively increase the wealth of an economy in some cases. One influential study showed that if the recipient country has good policies—namely those that promote economic growth—then aid will make a positive difference in the economy.[10] This study was extremely influential because donor organizations such as the World Bank and UN used it as a guide for their aid policies. Similarly in 2002, President Bush increased U.S. foreign aid and specified that it should be given on the condition that the recipient governments follow good policies. On the other hand, some policymakers suggested that aid should not be given to corrupt governments, regardless of their level of need, because they would likely misuse or waste the funds.

Another good example comes from Egypt during the regime of Gamal Abdel Nasser (1952–1970). President Nasser needed development assistance to build a dam across the Nile River, and both the Soviets and Americans promised aid packages. Realizing that it was being lured into a bidding war, the U.S. government withdrew its aid offer and Nasser was left with only the Soviet offer. As a result, the Egyptians found themselves locked into an increasingly close relationship with the Soviet Union, which Nasser's successor President Anwar Sadat had to sever two years into his presidency.

A second factor affecting aid donations is the colonial history of the donor and recipient. If the recipient country used to be a colony of the donor state, there is likely to be more aid given. The United States gives more aid to the Caribbean island-states that it used to control, while the British give more to the states that it used to control as colonies. Similarly, more French aid flows to French-speaking countries (former colonies) than to English-speaking countries.

Did the Berlin Wall Fall on Africa?

The fall of the Berlin Wall in November 1989 is heralded as a great moment in human history, and it should be. It marked an end to 50 years of totalitarian oppression in East Germany, and more broadly to the beginning of democratic rule throughout Eastern Europe. Given the thousands of people who were killed by the repressive, autocratic regimes in Eastern Europe, there is

little surprise that the German people were jubilant on November 9.

There were, however, negative side effects following the positive and historical end to autocratic rule in many European states. Many Eastern European countries maintained aid programs throughout Africa during the Cold War. Once those autocratic governments fell and the new democratic governments had to deal with fixing their own crumbling economies, many of their aid programs in Africa ended. States such as Romania and East Germany could not afford to continue providing development

MAP 9-2

Political Map of Africa

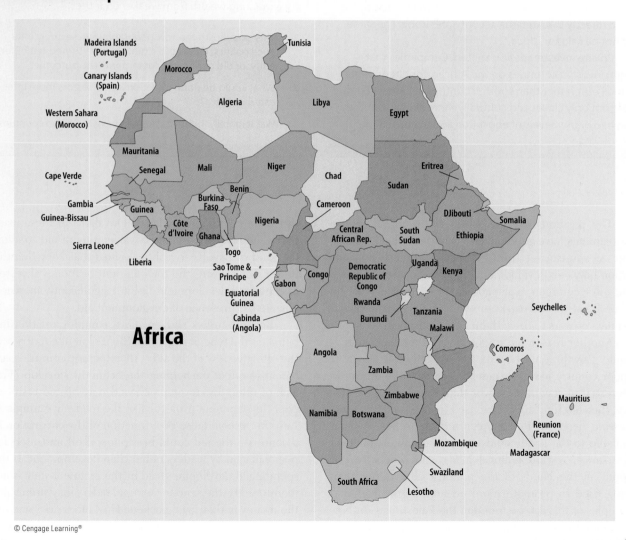

funds, loans, and investment. Without the Soviet Union to purchase their products and help fund their economies, Eastern European countries struggled to keep their own economies from collapsing completely. In this situation, it was unrealistic to think that they could continue to invest in African countries.

Additionally, West Germany began to redirect its aid to East Germany, whose economy was in shambles. After reunification, Germany had to continue to transfer funds to the former East Germany to rebuild its economy, factories, and power plants, and to clean up serious environmental disasters left behind by the autocratic government. Germany, the largest economy in Europe, was not alone in its new interest in Eastern Europe. Other Western European states began to redirect their aid away from other countries, most of them on the African continent, toward Eastern Europe. It was more important for the states in Western Europe to help secure the economies of states in Eastern Europe than those in Africa. If Romania, East Germany, or some other European state collapsed, it could directly threaten the security of Europe. The same cannot be said for Africa.

Private investment also shifted. Companies that might invest in countries on the African continent began to look east rather than south. Countries in Eastern Europe were not only closer and culturally more similar, but they also had higher levels of education and a more stable,

developed infrastructure. Ultimately, they were a safer and more profitable investment than many countries in Africa. As a result, less private investment was made in Africa.

Thus, the end of the Cold War meant freedom and development aid for millions of Eastern Europeans but less development aid and investment for millions in Africa. What could the leaders in Africa do? Sadly, there was no policy or diplomatic solution for the African leaders. This situation was a true revenge of geography—simply by being in another part of the world meant that there would be less help from wealthy countries for a full decade.

In another complex twist of fate, the lack of aid and investment from Europe in the 1990s made Africa one of the last regions open for new investment. Recently, China has begun investing significant resources into different African countries in an attempt to gain access and control of the petroleum, diamond, and other mineral resources. Only time will tell if the Chinese investments will be a benefit for the region or another example of a powerful country extracting wealth from weaker countries.

1. This case illustrates how geography can severely influence politics. Could this situation have turned out differently, or did geography "determine" the outcome?

2. What could be done to get private investors more interested in Africa?

3. Was it morally "right" that less aid went to African countries?

The position that aid "works" in countries whose governments have good policies is hotly contested, however. As you can see from Figure 9-3, there is no association between development aid and economic growth. The most common explanations are corrupt use of the aid and that the aid can compete with local farmers and business owners to drive them out of business.

Another reason aid might have little effect on economic growth could be due to a substitution effect. If a poor country has governmental leaders who are more interested in staying in power than in the people's welfare, then aid funds might be used to meet only the most pressing needs of the people, and any other revenue available to the state could be used to pay off political adversaries, reward political allies, and otherwise put money in the hands of the political elite rather than being used to promote more economic growth. Good examples of this can be found in the Palestinian Authority under the leadership of Yasser Arafat, Afghanistan under the leadership of Hamid Karzai, or Haiti under

the leadership of Jean-Claude Duvalier. All these leaders relied on the presence of development aid to allow the kind of payoffs to political elites that kept them in power. In this way, the total amount of money invested in economic development did not significantly increase, despite the presence of development aid.

Recent studies show a more complex relationship between the type of regime in the recipient country and the effectiveness of the aid.[11] In autocratic countries, aid has little effect on helping the economy develop. This lack of effect by development aid may be the result of poor development projects, like the roadway example in Lesotho. It could also be a function of the corruption in a country—the aid could be siphoned off and used for personal gain by leaders rather than development. If the spending of development aid by the recipient state is not monitored by the sender, corrupt leaders may simply put the money in their own pockets. How often does one see leaders of third world countries being forced from power only to flee to some pretty fancy homes? Haiti's Duvalier

Toyota advertisement in Vietnam | Should the aid that Japan gives to countries like Vietnam be conditional on Toyota's right to sell cars there? Do you think that the person on the bike even notices or thinks about owning a Camry?

HOANG DINH NAM/AFP/GETTY IMAGES/Newscom

isolated from the people and can act to provide only for the select few in the government. Democracies cannot ignore their people because if they do, they will be voted out of office. As a result, democratic governments tend to allocate more money toward public services. These include not only services such as education and infrastructure—both of which tend to enhance economic growth—but also services that subsidize fuel and food. The latter certainly tend to help the poor working class, but they are not engines of economic growth. Both Venezuela and Iran use their oil wealth to subsidize the cost of fuel and food, and both their economies suffer from sluggish growth.

When democracies receive aid, they often divert more funds to subsidies and other public projects. Some of these expenditures may enhance growth, but many do not. Even if the aid is targeted toward public works projects such as building a new road or airport, the democratic government can then spend more of its own funds on subsidies. Thus, the aid can often directly or indirectly subsidize public consumption of goods such as food and fuel. The end result is a negative effect of aid in democracies—less growth rather than more. The presence of such aid might even allow the recipient regime to postpone making necessary but hard choices about how it invests its scarce economic resources.

fled to his chateau in the south of France; Joseph Mobutu of Zaire fled first to his yacht on the Congo River and then headed for his home in Morocco and his villa on the French Riviera; Ferdinand Marcos fled the Philippines to his two homes in Hawaii; and some members of the Pahlavi royal family in Iran fled to their mansions in Beverly Hills. Whether due to poorly conceived projects, substitution effects, or siphoning off through corruption, the aid has little or no effect on growing economies in autocratic states.

In democratic countries, however, aid is actually associated with *negative* growth (or a decrease) in the size of the economy. Why would aid actually do damage to a democratic economy? The answer probably lies in the close tie a democracy forms between the government and the people. In autocracies, the government is not beholden to the people. While a good government should provide for its people, autocratic regimes are

FIGURE 9-3 AID AND GROWTH IN AFRICA (10-YEAR MOVING AVERAGES)

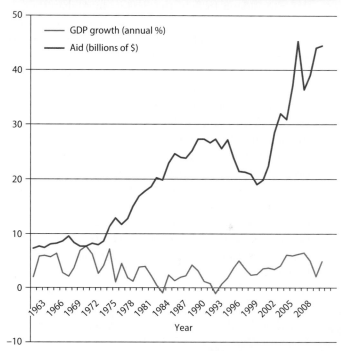

- GDP growth (annual %)
- Aid (billions of $)

Source: World Development indicators online. World Bank, 2012.

Mobutu's French villa | With most of the country he ruled—Zaire, now the Democratic Republic of the Congo—on the verge of starvation, President Mobutu lived in opulent wealth. How different is that from the French Revolution and Marie Antoinette's infamous line about cake? Why haven't humans learned about inequality?

9-3b Military Aid

Another common type of foreign assistance is **military aid**. Often more controversial than development aid, military aid is given to allies in the form of funds to purchase military equipment or training; it can also be the simple gift of military equipment. Imagine Santa Claus delivering 1,000 Stinger surface-to-air missiles to the mujahideen to fight the Soviets in Afghanistan! In the case of the Stinger missiles that the United States gave to the mujahideen, the aid was actually covert. The United States hid the gift of the missiles—even the mujahideen didn't know for certain from where they came—so as not to challenge the Soviets overtly. Military aid is often more complicated since the donor state gives the money to be used to purchase weapons or training from the donor state. When given in this manner, the aid serves two functions. First, it supplies the recipient state with weapons. Second, it generates business for the arms producers in the donor country. For example, in 2014 Russia provided military aid to Iraq so it could operate Su-25 attack jets purchased from Russia's United Aircraft Corporation. The Iraqi government got the jets it needed quickly, and the Russian corporation made more sales.

military aid aid given to a country that directly enhances its military capability.

Another less common use for military aid is money that is given to expand the number of troops in the recipient state. For example, the United States gave money to Colombia to expand and upgrade its military to better combat the drug producers and traffickers there. In this case, the aid was used for recruiting and training more troops. It is important to realize, however, that the outcome was the same regardless of the form the aid takes: a better-armed, more powerful ally.

While other countries provide military aid, the United States is the biggest arms seller in the world and consequently, the biggest provider of military aid. Aid is most often given to states for them to purchase U.S.-made military equipment. The actual aid can come in the form of grants, low-interest loans, or other financial instruments. Of this type of military aid, Israel is the largest recipient. Since 2000, the United States has provided Israel an average of $1.7 billion each year. The aid certainly provides a high level of support for Israel, but it also tends to keep relations between the United States and the other Middle Eastern states more tense since so many of them are opposed to or even enemies of Israel.

The aid is not entirely one-sided in the Middle East. The United States has supported controversial sales of weapons to Saudi Arabia, Egypt, and Jordan, just to name a few examples. In the 1980s, the United States provided Airborne Warning and Control aircraft (AWACs) and later sold the F-15S fighters to Saudi Arabia. Neither of those U.S. sales was well received by the Israeli government.

U.S.-made M1A1 tanks owned by Kuwait | What are the consequences for the United States when foreigners see U.S. military hardware on their streets? What are the consequences for the rest of the world?

In the Egyptian case, the United States historically provided approximately $1.3 billion in military aid annually. The aid supported weapons purchases but also enhanced the professionalism of the military. The International Military Education and Training program (IMET) seeks to increase foreign militaries' cooperation with the United States and to promote democratic control of the military. This training was an important factor in the 2011 overthrow of Egypt's dictator Mubarak. The army refused to shoot on unarmed civilians partly because there is a closer relationship between the army and the people and partly because the Egyptian military has a higher level of professionalism than many of its neighbors.

In the case of the Egyptian military's professionalism, U.S. military aid ended up helping make the transition from Mubarak's autocratic rule more peaceful. However, this view is a bit like wearing rose-colored glasses. It is true that the IMET increased the military's professionalism, but U.S. military aid to Egypt and other Middle Eastern states such as Saudi Arabia almost certainly helped to keep those authoritarian leaders in power for many years. Prior to Mubarak's overthrow, he was able to maintain his power largely because he had a military made powerful by U.S. weapons and training. Saudi Arabia is similarly dependent on the United States for weapons. Without that military aid, the House of Saud, the ruling family of the country, could go the way of Egypt and Libya, except those taking over might easily be radical Islamists.

Another form of U.S. military aid is peacekeeping operations outside of the UN. The goal of this type of aid is to increase the involvement of regional organizations such as the **Organization of American States (OAS)** and the **African Union (AU)** to deal with regional security problems such as in Haiti and Sudan, respectively. The aid is also used to gather more multilateral support, such as the UN, for peacekeeping operations around the world.

It is important to note that military aid can often come back to hurt the donor country. The United States funded the mujahideen's fight against the Soviets in Afghanistan for years. Fighting as part of the mujahideen was Osama bin Laden! Similarly, the United States gave aid to Saddam Hussein in the 1980s during his war with Iran. The U.S. military also gave support to Ho Chi Minh's fight against the Japanese in Vietnam during World War II. In each of these cases and many others, what was once a convenient ally later became an enemy.

DETERMINANTS OF MILITARY AID Unfortunately, most academic studies of military aid concentrate on the United States so we do not have a good understanding

Mujahideen with Stinger missile | While they started out as U.S. allies, the mujahideen became the Taliban and an enemy of the United States. What other countries are friendly with the United States now but could soon become opponents?

of the factors that other countries consider when giving military aid. In the United States, three components are critical to the decision. The first is the strategic value of the recipient country. During the Cold War, for example, the United States gave more military aid to those countries that were anti-communist and those that shared a border with a communist bloc state. The Cold War concern with Soviet expansion led the United States to provide vast quantities of aid to those "frontline" countries and to those pledging loyalty to the United States and Western Europe. A good example is South Korea, which received significant levels of aid because of its proximity to China and North Korea as well as its staunch anti-communist stand during the Cold War.

After the Cold War, strategic value was more loosely defined. Middle Eastern countries receive more aid, as do Latin American countries. The United States has provided billions of dollars, for example, to Colombia in an effort to combat the production and trafficking of cocaine. This type of security concern was less common during the Cold War, but in the past two decades has become more common.

Organization of American States (OAS) international organization composed of states in the North and South American continents.

African Union (AU) organization in Africa devoted to representing the interests of African states.

The second factor influencing military aid is human rights. To some degree, the United States is less likely to provide military aid to countries violating human rights, especially after the end of the Cold War. There are many notable exceptions, especially during the Cold War. Many Latin American dictatorships—such as Honduras and Guatemala—received significant aid because they professed anti-communism and loyalty to the United States. In the Middle East, many countries benefitting from U.S. aid have poor human rights records (e.g., Egypt and Saudi Arabia). On average, however, countries violating human rights are less likely to receive aid, and this effect has apparently become more pronounced since the end of the Cold War.

Finally, the regime type of the recipient countries matters—democratic countries are somewhat more likely to receive more aid. This democratic effect is also a more recent phenomenon starting in the 1990s, after the end of the Cold War. Once the United States was no longer concerned with the Soviet Union, it began to consider the value of democracy when providing military aid.

9-3c Aid for Democracy

Another form of aid is targeted directly at promoting democracy. This support, **democracy aid**, is relatively new to the world, having really only started in the 1980s. The idea behind the aid is to help a country become more democratic or to help keep the country from slipping back into autocratic rule after a democratic transition. Like humanitarian aid, support for democracy is selectively targeted to specific countries.

Developed democratic countries like the United States and others have increasingly provided democracy assistance to try to spread democracy more widely throughout the international system. According to one study of the foreign policies of 40 developed countries between 1992 and 2002, there were substantial, although widely varying, commitments and efforts toward this end.[12] Figure 9-4 shows the proportion of U.S. foreign aid devoted to democracy assistance between 1975 and 2010—you can clearly see that such aid for democracy became a much higher priority after the end of the Cold War. Naturally, the kinds of aid vary widely across donors, but in general, democracy

democracy aid aid given to a country to enhance and consolidate its transition to democracy.

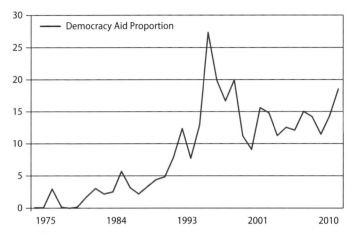

FIGURE 9-4 U.S. DEMOCRACY AID AS A PROPORTION OF FOREIGN AID

Source: Adapted from James M. Scott and Ralph G. Carter, "From Cold War to Arab Spring: Mapping the Effects of Paradigm Shifts on the Nature and Dynamics of U.S. Democracy Assistance to the Middle East and North Africa," *Democratization*, March 2014, DOI: 10.1080/13510347.2013.877893

aid from the developed world shares a number of characteristics.

First, the assistance is typically directed to one or more of a common cluster of targets. Aid may be directed toward the establishment and functioning of elections and other constitutional arrangements to build the foundations of democratic rule (including actually monitoring elections to ensure fairness). Aid may also be directed toward helping to build and empower the institutions of democratic government, including legislatures, independent judiciaries, and competent and accountable bureaucracies. Increasingly, democracy aid from the developed world has been directed to non-governmental organizations—or civil society actors such as women's rights, labor, and other public advocacy groups—to empower them to participate in democracy and hold governments accountable.

Second, democracy aid tends to come in smaller, more nimble packages. These packages are usually more carefully targeted to specific recipients and generally bypass the formal aid channels so that they actually reach the agents and purposes that are intended. For the United States, for instance, democracy aid generally constitutes only about 10–20 percent of U.S. foreign aid, and the average aid package is considerably smaller than traditional developmental aid. This is not hard to imagine: the cost of a copying machine and a few computers to a women's rights group in east Africa is obviously *much*

Egyptians gather in protest against their regime in June 2013. Could aid from other countries have helped Egypt democratize? | In what other undemocratic countries might aid contribute to such a peaceful transition?

smaller than the cost of building and maintaining a dam in the same country! And yet, such small packages may have payoffs far exceeding their size.

Finally, democracy assistance is most definitely a state *and* non-state phenomenon. An elaborate network of international organizations, official state aid agencies, quasi-state foundations, and private organizations from all over the globe collaborate to provide aid, advice, and support for democracy. As an example of this complicated network, the U.S. Agency for International Development channels some of its efforts through the semi-private U.S. National Endowment for Democracy, which, in turn, provides grants to civil society organizations in support of democratization in many countries.

The effectiveness of democracy assistance of these kinds is still an open question. Some studies have found that the combination of democracy aid and incentives generated by international organizations like the EU has been pretty effective in promoting and supporting democratization, and some assessments of state-provided democracy assistance have concluded that recipients tend to make more progress toward democracy than non-recipients as you can see in Figure 9-5.[13] Others, however, express concerns that such aid programs can be problematic because they too often ignore the perspectives and unique characteristics of the recipients and instead force an ill-fitting template of democracy that reflects donor interpretations, concerns, and values. For example, Russian leaders have long accused Western groups like the National Endowment for

FIGURE 9-5 CHANGE IN DEMOCRACY FOR DEMOCRACY AID RECIPIENTS AND NON-RECIPIENTS

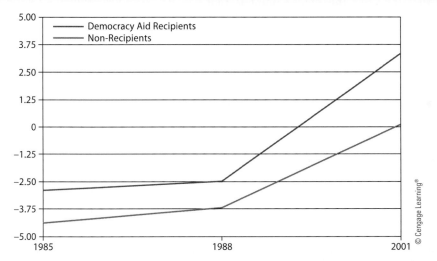

Source: James M. Scott, "Funding Freedom? The United States and US Democracy Aid in the Developing World, 1988-2001," Figure 2.3. From *Liberal Interventionism and Democracy Promotion*, Dursun Peksen, Editor. Lexington Books, 2012.

Democracy as being havens for spies and provocateurs who want to overthrow the Russian regime. Other countries such as Mexico and China have also objected to the National Endowment for Democracy operating within their borders. However, given the embrace of democracy by the developed world, such aid is not likely to disappear.

9-3d Humanitarian Aid

So far we have discussed development aid, military aid, and democracy aid. Each of these is quite different, although development and democracy aid are clearly both meant to directly improve the recipient state. The last form of aid we will consider is or is meant to be the most directly positive in their intention. In its most benign form, states can give money to other states to help them recover from disasters such as earthquakes, floods, and famines. This type of grant is considered **humanitarian aid**. It is specific to the event and meant to help the country overcome the trauma caused by the disaster.

The 2011 earthquake, tsunami, and subsequent nuclear power plant accident in Japan offers a poignant example. Even though Japan is one of the wealthiest countries in the world, countries from around the globe offered their assistance in dealing with the devastation. It would be difficult to not feel bad for the Japanese and want to offer them help. Yet had the earthquake not occurred, there would be no need for assistance. Japan has the third largest economy in the world, and its GDP per capita is $46,731, just $5,018 less than the United States at $51,749.

This may seem like a silly point—of course one would only give disaster aid to a country that was struck with a disaster—but the bigger point is that unlike other forms of aid (development, military, and democracy), humanitarian assistance is a direct response to an emergency. As such, policymakers like to think that this type of aid is less politicized. In fact, people working in the disaster and humanitarian aid divisions of government (e.g., the U.S. Office for Foreign Disaster Assistance) pride themselves in being apolitical (i.e., non-political).

What disasters trigger the giving of humanitarian aid? For the United States to disperse aid, the highest-ranking U.S. official in the country struck by the disaster (usually the ambassador) must determine that the

A modern-day ghost town in Japan | A discarded bicycle in the exclusion zone around the Fukushima nuclear plant after the tsunami-caused melt-down in 2011. Do wealthy countries like Japan still need help after a disaster?

Jeremy Sutton-Hibbert/Getty Images

disaster is so big that the country requires assistance. That official must then contact the U.S. State Department and request aid. Officials at the State Department then decide whether or not to send aid and how much is needed based in part on the ambassador's report.

The United States is by no means the only country that provides humanitarian assistance. However, all of the developed countries that do provide aid coordinate with each other to ensure that each disaster is responded to properly. For example, it would make little sense for every country to give huge amounts of aid to Peru for its recent earthquake thinking that no other countries were going to donate aid, and then to give no aid to Japan after its earthquake thinking that other countries would give aid. Because humanitarian aid is, at least officially, based on need, there must be some coordination between donor countries.

In fact, this coordination is very thorough. Donor states work together to transmit the needed aid to the affected country. Donors coordinate not only actual dollar amounts and types of aid (e.g., food, temporary shelters, and medical supplies) but also the transportation of those supplies. For example, the U.S. military has the ability to transport huge quantities of goods via air in its C-130 Hercules and C-5 Galaxy transports. Countries such as Canada do not have that kind of transport capability, so the Canadians may provide the humanitarian supplies and the Americans could supply the transportation.

The success of humanitarian aid varies considerably. In the most successful cases, there are stories from relief

humanitarian aid aid given to a country to help mitigate the effects from a disaster or other humanitarian emergency.

Humanitarian workers delivering supplies in the Sudan | Can you imagine depending on supplies like these to stay alive? Do you think countries should donate more food, especially when so many in wealthy countries are overweight?

workers that in a mere week after a catastrophic earthquake, the assistance was so successful that the previous homeless and starving people began to ask if there was anything better to eat besides the military Meal, Ready-to-Eat (MREs). That's pretty successful.

In other cases, the affected country is so corrupt that a considerable amount of the aid is stolen. Humanitarian aid is also rendered ineffective when the emergency itself involves a civil conflict. To get humanitarian aid to the starving people of Somalia in the early 1990s, the United States—backed by the UN—sent thousands of troops to protect the aid workers and the food that was being delivered to those in need. At first the effort was successful but then degraded into urban warfare, culminating in the two-day Battle of Mogadishu in which 19 Americans and between 1,000–3,000 Somalis were killed. The case is portrayed in the movie *Blackhawk Down* and is hard to consider a humanitarian success.

Finally, it is worth asking whether humanitarian assistance is purely humanitarian or also political. For the most part, disasters themselves drive the aid process. That is, more severe events get more aid, usually. Politics does enter into the decision, however. If a hurricane had hit both Cuba and the Bahamas in 1985, only the Bahamas would have received U.S. aid. Why? Because the Bahamas was a friend and Cuba was an opponent of the United States and would not have been provided humanitarian support.

Aside from obvious political issues such as this, other political issues have been shown to affect humanitarian

aid. Scholars estimate that for each story in the *New York Times* (or other international and renowned media source), an additional half million dollars in aid is given. To put this in grim perspective, it means that each story is worth approximately 1,500 fatalities.[14] Why are news stories so important? Because government officials use them to determine what is important to the public. One could interpret this to suggest that the government is being responsive to its citizens, but that would be cold comfort for disaster victims who don't get media coverage.

CONCLUSION

Thus wealth buys military power, prestige, and, as this chapter has hopefully demonstrated, the ability to use that wealth to influence other states. Whether the biblical assertion that "the love of money is the root of all evil" is true or not, it certainly seems to be the case that money is the root of all power and potential influence.

Economic statecraft is a far more complex form of power than the military. While the military can shield, threaten, and destroy, economic power can be used to buy loyalties and give altruistically; it can be taken away to weaken other states or simply punish them. In the neo-Westphalian era, it seems that economic power rivals military power as a source of a state's relative standing in the international system. Perhaps economic power even exceeds military power at times.

It is often said that money is the most **fungible** form of power. We have shown here that money can be used for a huge variety of different goals and in a huge variety of different ways. It really seems that money can be used for anything, although as this chapter has also demonstrated, it does not always work: sanctions fail and development aid can hurt growth.

In the next chapter, we focus specifically on the development of those countries without much wealth and their relationship with the developed, wealthy states. You will see that each of the chapters in this section on international economics fits together in one big system. The way states trade with one another, try to influence one another, and try to develop their economies are all tied together in the web of the world political economy.

---

fungible   the ability to use one type of power for multiple purposes.

THINK ABOUT THIS GUNS OR MONEY?

Realists maintain that power defined in military terms is the most important instrument in international politics. However, world systems theorists and Marxist analysts would argue that wealth gives rich countries far more dominance in the international system—on a daily basis—than does military might alone. Some liberal, constructivist, and feminist theorists would also argue that economic statecraft is more usable and likely to be more effective in the current world than military force. Given what's going on in world politics and what you've learned up to this point, which position do you think is correct? Does might make right or do those with the gold make the rules?

Under what conditions are the tools of economics likely to be most effective, and when are they likely to be least effective?

STUDY TOOLS 9

LOCATED AT BACK OF THE BOOK:
☐ Rip out Chapter in Review card

LOCATED ON COURSEMATE:
Use the CourseMate access card that came with this book or visit CengageBrain.com for more review materials:

☐ Review Key Terms Flash Cards (Print or Online)
☐ Download Chapter Summaries for on-the-go review
☐ Complete Practice Quizzes to prepare for the test

☐ Walk through a Simulation, Animated Learning Module, and Interactive Maps and Timelines to master concepts
☐ Complete Crossword Puzzle to review key terms
☐ Watch the videos for real-world application of this chapter's content
☐ Visit IR NewsWatch to learn about the latest current events as you prepare for class discussions and papers

REVIEW QUESTIONS

1. In what ways can one state influence another state without using its military?

2. Are sanctions successful, failures, counterproductive, or some combination of these?

3. Why is aid given, and what effects does it have?

FOR MORE INFORMATION . . .

For more on:

Economic sanctions, Peterson Institute for International Economics, "Economic Sanctions," *International Trade/and Investment*, http://www.iie.com/research/researcharea.cfm?ResearchtopiciD=31&ParentTopicID=6#sanctions.

Democracy promotion, Dursun Peksen, *Liberal Interventionism and Democracy Promotion* (New York: Lexington Books/Rowman and Littlefield, 2012).

Aid, OECD, Aid Statistics, http://www.oecd.org/development/stats/.

Aid and economic growth, Kamiljon T. Akramov, *Foreign Aid Allocation, Governance, and Economic Growth* (Philadelphia: University of Pennsylvania Press, 2012); Jonathan Krieckhaus, *Dictating Development* (Pittsburgh: University of Pittsburgh Press, 2006).

10 | International Development:
Relations between the Haves and Have-Nots

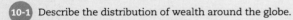

A TALE OF TWO ECONOMIES

In 1980, both Ecuador and South Korea were at similar levels of development. Both had a GDP per capita of slightly more than $5,500. South Korea had a slightly longer life expectancy (2.8 years longer than Ecuador), and the population got a little more education in South Korea (1.9 years more). Several factors seemed to be working against South Korea's prospects for development. Unlike Ecuador, it did not have significant oil reserves and so could not draw income from that precious resource. Further, South Korea suffered the effects of a vicious war in the early 1950s.

Just three decades later, the similarities were gone . . . and it was not South Korea with its costly war and lack of oil that had fallen behind. Instead, South Korea now has an average income per capita of over $30,000 and has evolved into a wealthy, developed country with less than 15 percent of its people living below the poverty line. Ecuador, on the other hand, has an average per capita income of less than $8,000, and about one-third of its population lives below the poverty line. That's an income difference of almost four times and a poverty difference of more than two times! What happened? Could two years more of education and three years of life allow you to increase your income by almost five times in just three decades? Shouldn't oil help a country build its economy? It certainly seems like having something so valuable should help, but clearly it did not.

Probably the best explanation for the difference lies in the policies that South Korea followed. Sometimes acting like a drill sergeant, its government promoted exporting manufactured goods to other countries. This policy meant that to be successful, you had to be involved directly in industry. Businesses that made goods that could be sold to countries in North America and Europe were valued above other companies, and the population sacrificed what could be considered basic luxuries such as televisions and cars so that the economy could grow rapidly.

Ecuador, alternatively, did not promote exports. Instead, it protected many of its own companies and subsidized necessities for its people. Further, the country did not industrialize the way that South Korea did. Instead, most of its income came from natural resources such as oil, seafood, and other agricultural goods, rather than manufactured products.

Certainly other factors played a role. South Korea benefited from being an important military ally of the United States during the Cold War. Because of its proximity to the Soviet Union, North Korea, and China, South Koreans were given some preferential treatment when it came to their trade policies. As a result, they were able to sell more goods in the United States while purchasing less from their ally. Ecuador, while an ally of the United States, was not as strategically important and thus tended not to receive the same preferential treatment as South Korea. South Korea also has a larger population than Ecuador. In the end, however, the stark fact remains that South Korea is now a wealthy state and Ecuador is not, even though they both started out poor.

This comparison raises some interesting questions:

1. How was South Korea able to become so wealthy?

2. What failures did Ecuador experience that caused its economy to stagnate?

3. Could other countries have helped Ecuador?

The lives of the rich and the poor | What does the disparity between these two photos suggest about the problems between the wealthy and poor? If the people in these photos traded places, could they even understand their new surroundings?

INTRODUCTION: THE DIFFERENCES BETWEEN THE RICH AND POOR

Just as the tale of two economies at the beginning of this chapter illustrates how two countries can follow different policies and reach very different levels of development, levels of development throughout the world differ radically. Many scholars and policymakers categorize the differences between the rich and poor as the North and South, sometimes referred to as the north–south divide. This refers to the general tendency for wealthy countries to be in the Northern Hemisphere, while the poorer countries tend to be in the Southern Hemisphere. Of course, this does not work perfectly. For example, Australia is a wealthy, developed country clearly in the south, and the Republic of Georgia is a poor, developing country in the north. A more accurate description of these two types of countries is as either a **developed country** or a **less-developed country (LDC)**. Like rich and poor, have and have-not, these terms provide a better and more accurate view of the world, so let's use those terms to understand the complexity of which countries are and which are not wealthy.

10-1 THE WEALTH GAP

Whether you call a country North, developed, rich, or wealthy, the amount of money it has relative to the size of its population is critical to the survival and well-being of its people. It is important to realize that when we say "rich" or "wealthy" in this chapter, we do not mean to imply these countries and their populations are able to afford every luxury and take vacations in exotic locales. Instead, the terms "rich" or "developed" mean that a country's economy can clearly support more than the basic necessities of life. "Poor" or "less developed" or "have-not," on the other hand, means that the country's

> **developed country** a wealthy country with an economy that tends to produce manufactured goods and services for export.
>
> **less-developed country (LDC)** a country that is poor or has an economy that is less able to support its population. These countries typically export raw materials and agricultural products.

economy may not be strong enough for its population to get the minimum 1,400 calories a day as recommended by the **World Health Organization**.

It is also important to realize that a lack of development, or being a poor country in this sense, is the cause of far more deaths than all the international and civil wars discussed in Chapter 5 combined. While we all know about the horrors of war—and wars are horrible—many more people die each day because they cannot get enough food or clean drinking water. Just think: that means more people die from malnutrition and water- and food-borne parasites than from bullets and machetes. Perhaps we should ask ourselves why the world spends more on weapons than on development, when the lack of development is a bigger killer and thus a bigger threat to human security for more people than any war has ever been. What do you think?

As we noted in Chapter 8, money means power, which in turn often means security. Wealthy states have more **autonomy** because they are more secure thanks to their stronger economies. For example, Canada can disagree with China more easily than Bangladesh can because Canada is less vulnerable to economic coercion. Canada's citizens are also more secure because they have ample access to nutrition and medical services, unlike Bangladesh. Development means not only that a country's people can meet the minimum daily caloric intake but also that the country has a stronger, more secure position in the international system. Do you think that is why countries spend so much on weapons—because they want more security? Could a strong, developed economy alone give a country security? That is, could a wealthy country still be secure without a military because it claimed neutrality? It would be a big risk to take; both Sweden and Switzerland are rich, neutral powers, but both still spend money on their militaries. Japan, on the other hand, is wealthy and spends less than 1 percent of its governmental budget on the military. Is it secure? If so, is its human security derived from its economy and its international security derived from its island status and its military alliance with the United States?

World Health Organization (WHO) the UN organization that deals with health issues around the world. It is responsible for the eradication of smallpox.

autonomy state of independence from another country, the ability to act by oneself.

GDP per capita the measure of a country's development. It is the total size of a country's economy divided by the population.

Clearly, the consequences of between being born in a rich or a poor country are dramatic. For that reason, scholars and policymakers exert significant effort trying to figure out why countries are poor and how they can develop their economies. Also, the gap between rich and poor states exerts a powerful effect on the international relations between states in each group. We will address these issues in the following, but first let's turn back to exploring the differences between the haves and have-nots.

10-1a Our Understanding of the Rich and Poor

As we have discussed throughout this book, complexity is a true theme in international relations, and its role in the distribution of wealth is no different. Not only is wealth distributed differently, but people's perception of rich and poor countries also tends to differ radically. For instance, most Americans viewed Japan's economy in the 1980s as much stronger and more vibrant than that of the United States. Many Americans thought that the Japanese economy was bigger and that the Japanese **GDP per capita** (the nation's wealth divided by the population, or wealth per person) was higher. As you can see from Figure 10-1, that perception was simply wrong. Today, many Americans tend to think that the Chinese economy is larger and more powerful than it really is, particularly when measured by GDP per capita. These misperceptions are unfortunately not uncommon.

It wasn't just the average American who thought that the Japanese were in the process of rising above the United States. In a famous book published in 1987, *The Rise and Fall of the Great Powers*, historian Paul Kennedy argued that powerful nations rise and fall largely based on their economies, and he predicted that Japan's time had come to take its place at the top of the world. Nothing illustrated his thesis better than the cover art for the book: a Japanese businessman climbing to the top of the world pedestal while the Uncle Sam character steps down. But that prediction couldn't have been more wrong. Beginning in 1991, Japan entered a long recession from which it still hasn't fully recovered. Originally referred to as the "lost decade," it is now called the "lost decades" because it spans 20 years and counting. Further, in 2010 China's economy passed Japan's to become the second largest in the world and will probably surpass the U.S. economy around 2020 to become the largest.

Because of these complexities, we cannot easily answer the questions of why some countries are wealthy and some are poor, how those countries relate, and what the future looks like. Instead, we must first have a good picture of how wealth is distributed around the world.

FIGURE 10-1   GRAPH OF SELECTED GDP FROM 1980–2012

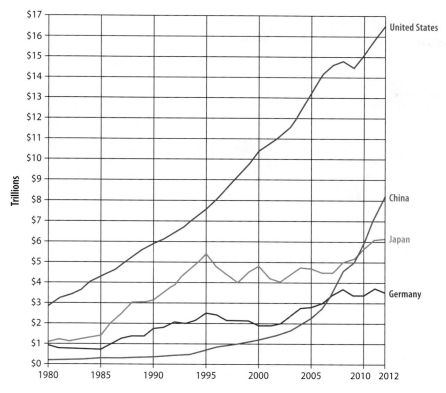

Source: World Bank *World Development Indicators,* 2012.

In the next two sections, we discuss the details of how wealth is distributed across countries and then within countries. Once we have an understanding of where the money and economic productivity is, we can turn to understanding how it was made and what consequences that has for international relations.

10-1b The Countries That Have Wealth and the Countries That Don't

In 2012, the average GDP per capita in the world was $10,291, according to World Bank data. That number—while low—may not sound too horrible at first. Many college students live on not much more than that amount in the United States, but think about the fact that the *average* per capita income in the world is $1,379 *lower* than the U.S. poverty line! However, that number does not give the best picture of the world. It is an average and does not show how much difference there is between the rich and the poor. For example, the average GDP per capita in China and India was only $7,594. That means that almost 2.5 billion people—about 37 percent of the world's population—lived at only 74 percent of the world's average GDP per capita.

Compare that to the United States where the GDP per capita was over $51,000, the ninth highest in the world. Alternatively, the top two countries, Luxemburg and Norway, had GDP per capita exceeding $100,000, while the lowest two countries, Burundi and the Malawi, each had a GDP per capita below $400. In fact, all of the ten poorest countries had a GDP per capita below $550. To emphasize this point, that meant that in the ten poorest countries, the average person lived on less than $1.50 a day. That's less than the cost of a cup of coffee at Starbucks! For a striking contrast, take a look at the following maps, which depict the countries of the world by their population and by their wealth.

The UN uses another measure for extreme poverty: the percentage of people living on less than $2 a day. As Map 10-3 shows, there are many countries where only a small fraction of the population lives on so little money. Unfortunately, there are many countries in which the majority of the population lives on less than $2 a day.

Thus, although it's overly simplistic, the world can be divided into these two groups: developed countries and developing countries. In the simplest of terms, these are the rich and the poor, the haves and have-nots of the world. To be sure, there is a middle ground—countries

Map 10-1

The Countries of the World, Sized by Population

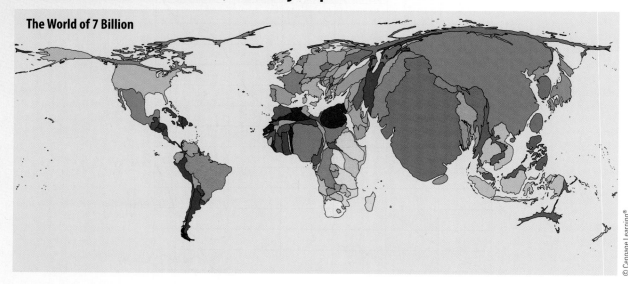

The World of 7 Billion

© Cengage Learning®

Source: Views of the World, http://www.viewsoftheworld.net/?p=1660.

Map 10-2

The Countries of the World, Sized by GDP per Capita

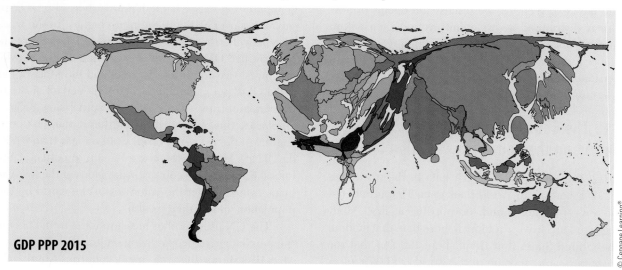

GDP PPP 2015

© Cengage Learning®

What does the contrast between these two maps suggest about economic security and world politics?

Source: Views of the World, http://www.viewsoftheworld.net/wp-content/uploads/2010/11/gdpppp2015.jpg.

Map 10-3

Percent of Population Living on $2 a Day or Less

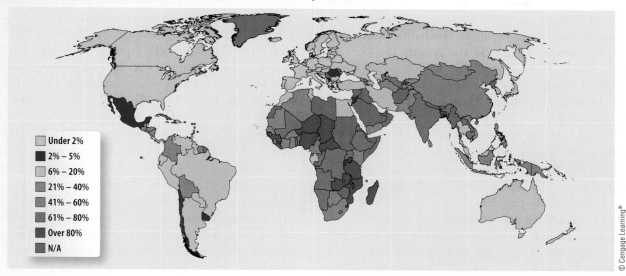

Under 2%
2% – 5%
6% – 20%
21% – 40%
41% – 60%
61% – 80%
Over 80%
N/A

© Cengage Learning®

Could you live on $2 a day? What's the absolute minimum that you could live on?

Source: The World Bank: "Poverty headcount ratio at $2 a day (PPP) (% of population)," World Development Indicators, 2012.

that are moderately developed such that their economies can support the basic needs of the people plus a little more. However, it is striking how easily we can place the world into two categories.

Let's compare what might be considered "middle class" around the world. To make this comparison across countries, we need to understand what a dollar will purchase in different countries. To do this, economists have developed a measure called **purchasing power parity (PPP)**, a tool that lets us compare the value of currencies across countries. PPP converts a currency to a common value so that it can be compared to other countries. For example, it is much cheaper to live in Mexico than it is in Norway (the state with one of the highest costs of living). Perhaps the simplest way to understand PPP is the **Big Mac Index**, a measure created by the magazine *The Economist* to explain different costs of living and values of currency. The Big Mac Index surveys the cost of the famous hamburger around the world and compares it to the average cost of a Big Mac in the United States. For example, a Big Mac costs (on average) $4.62 in the United States. In Mexico, it costs $2.78 (in U.S. dollars), but in Norway, it costs a whopping $7.80!

Purchasing power parity allows us to adjust the currencies of countries so that we can compare them in a meaningful way. To create the PPP measure, economists

compare a "basket of goods," that is, a group of basic products that every country uses. This is the same idea as the Big Mac Index—the basket is a group of common products that can be compared. Creating this basket can be quite difficult. While Big Macs are sold in many countries, there are few products that are common to all countries. Peanut butter, jelly, and bread may be the foundation for many college students' diets, but that isn't the case in China or even Germany. Thus, economists must consider similar products like bread and rice.

Now that we can compare the value of different countries' economies, let's see how many people in the world have enough money to fit into the middle-class category (or higher). Generally speaking, the minimum amount of money needed for an individual to be considered middle class in the United States is approximately

purchasing power parity (PPP) a measure that compares two currencies and adjusts them so that they can be compared in a meaningful way. PPP allows us to compare the purchasing power of the yen in Japan with the peso in Mexico, for example.

Big Mac Index a measure created by *The Economist* magazine that compares the value of currencies by comparing the cost of a Big Mac hamburger in different countries. The United States is used as the baseline cost for the index.

$20,000. Using purchasing power parity, 38 countries fit into this category, and that a total of 1.3 billion people in the world are on average *at least* middle class. That's only 18 percent of the world's population.[1]

Now let's consider the poverty line as defined in the United States. In 2014, the poverty line is $11,670 for one person. Again using the purchasing power parity, 100 countries fall below the poverty line according to the U.S. standards. That includes more than 4.8 billion people—notice that's almost 5 billion people; 66.7 percent of the world's population lives below the U.S. poverty line.

As you can see, there is a great deal of inequality in the world. Realize also that we defined middle class as being the absolute minimum in U.S. standards, just $20,000 a year. That number includes only the top 18 percent of the world's population. Just think: if you lived in the United States and earned enough money to be in the top 18 percent, you would be earning over $100,000. This means that even people in the middle class of the world (by U.S. minimum standards) are the very wealthy by global standards. The poor, on the other hand, make up the vast majority of the world's population.

10-1c The Distribution of Wealth and Development within Countries

So far we have shown how there is tremendous diversity and unevenness in the distribution of wealth across countries. That may seem like enough inequality to cause problems and be a serious cause for concern. However, that's not the end of the story. There is also a great deal of inequality *within* countries. When we discussed the level of wealth across countries, we were using averages. For example in 2012, the GDP per capita in Canada was $51,206 and the GDP per capita in Pakistan was $1,257. That does not mean that everyone in those two countries each earned $51,206 and $1,257, respectively. Some people earned a lot more and some a lot less. For this reason, we must look inside countries to see what kind of inequality lives there.

One way to measure inequality within countries is through a statistic called the **Gini coefficient**.

Gini coefficient a measure of the distribution of income in a country ranging from 0 to 1 where 0 means perfect equality and 1 means perfect inequality.

Human Development Index (HDI) a measure of the level of human development in a country. It includes GDP per capita, life expectancy, and education levels.

This measure ranges from 0 to 1, with 0 meaning that a country's income is shared equally by everyone. That would mean, for example, that everyone in the United States would have earned $51,748 in 2012, even real-life billionaires like Bill Gates and Warren Buffett. A Gini coefficient equaling 1 would mean that all of the wealth in a country is owned by one person. In reality, there is no country that is perfectly equal or perfectly unequal. As you can see from the map of worldwide Gini coefficients (Map 10-4), there are considerable differences between countries. The most equal states tend to be in Europe, while the greatest inequalities appear in Africa and South America. The most equal country is Norway with a score of 0.25. Norway's extensive social welfare and tax system helps explain why it is the most evenly distributed of all countries. The most unequal country is South Africa in which the Gini coefficient is 0.65.[2] Just to give some comparison, the United States falls almost exactly in the middle of these two countries. That means that the wealthiest 10 percent of the population has just slightly less than half of the country's income, leaving the rest of the wealth to the remaining 90 percent. The distribution of income in the United States doesn't sound very equal in those terms, does it?

Another way to look at inequality within states is to compare the average GDP per capita with the other two measures used to create the **Human Development Index (HDI)**. The HDI is a measure created by the UN to determine how developed a country is in terms of its people, and later in the chapter we'll talk about how important that is for an economy. The index combines the wealth, life expectancy, and education of the population. If the income in a country is reasonably distributed, then life expectancy and education level should be commensurate with income. What do we mean here? Well, in a wealthy, developed country like Canada, the GDP per capita is $51,206, the life expectancy is 81 years, and the average adult has 16 years of education. In Qatar, the GDP per capita is $93,825, but the life expectancy is only 78 years, and the average adult only gets 12 years of education. You might say that isn't that big a difference, but when you consider that Qatar's GDP per capita is so high, those differences become striking.

Let's take a look at two other countries. In Nigeria, a poor state but one with oil, the GDP per capita is $1,555, the life expectancy is 52 years, and the average length of education is 9 years. In Costa Rica, a developing country without oil, the GDP per capita is $9,386, the life expectancy is 79.7 years, and the length of education on average is 12 years. Note that Costa Rica does better than Nigeria *and* Qatar in life expectancy and education.

Map 10-4

CIA World Factbook of Worldwide Gini Coefficients

Gini Coefficient

- < 0.25
- 0.25 – 0.29
- 0.30 – 0.34
- 0.35 – 0.39
- 0.40 – 0.44
- 0.45 – 0.49
- 0.50 – 0.54
- 0.55 – 0.59
- > 0.60
- No Data

© Cengage Learning®

The Western Hemisphere is the most unequal part of the world when it comes to Gini coefficients. What do you think this means?

Source: Data from The World Factbook, United States Central Intelligence Agency.

Why? Because Costa Rica has a much higher level of equality than either of the other two states. Take a look at Table 10-1 and compare the different HDI indicators. You may find some more startling differences.

Unfortunately, it is much more difficult to get a good picture of how equal or unequal income is within countries than it is between countries. Notice that there are many countries that are missing Gini coefficients in the map. That is because calculating the measure is very difficult. To accurately measure equality, researchers must complete a sample of household surveys in each country. While that would be easy—though expensive—in the United States, can you imagine completing a household survey in war-torn Afghanistan or Somalia? Thus, our understanding of how equally wealth is distributed within countries is just an estimate. What we can conclude is that there is a great deal of difference between the rich and poor in many countries, as well as between countries, and that those differences have important consequences for world politics.

TABLE 10-1 HDI, GDP PER CAPITA, LIFE EXPECTANCY, AND EDUCATION				
Country	**HDI**	**GDP per Capita**	**Life Expectancy**	**Expected Years of Education**
United States	0.937	$51,749	78.7	16
Canada	0.911	$51,206	81.1	16
Qatar	0.834	$93,825	78.5	12
Mexico	0.775	$9,749	77.1	13.9
Costa Rica	0.773	$9,386	79.4	11.7
China	0.699	$6,091	73.7	11.6
Nigeria	0.471	$1,555	52.3	8.9

© Cengage Learning®

Source: The World Bank, *World Development Indicators*, 2012.

10-2 WHY ARE SOME COUNTRIES RICH AND OTHERS POOR?

Now that we have explored the striking differences between the wealth and development of countries around the globe, we need to examine how they got that way and how some have been able to improve over the past several decades and others have not. There is not, of course, an easy answer to these questions.

Before we turn to the different policies that countries use to develop, we need to look at some of the **structural factors** that can either increase or decrease a country's level of development. These factors include natural resources and the colonial history of a country. We refer to these as structural because they cannot change, or at least it is difficult to conceive of how they would change. Thus, they are the structure or foundation with which a country must work as it develops.

10-2a Natural Resources

The first and probably most obvious factor to consider is the natural resources a country has. Just like the unequal distribution of income, the world's resources vary tremendously by country. For example, the United States is fortunate to have an abundance of land and good climate for agriculture, and it is rather rich with natural resources such as oil and coal. Looking at the history of the United States, much of its initial power came from these natural resources, especially its agriculture.

structural factors historical and environmental factors that influence how a country can develop its economy.

The relative ease with which the United States could grow food meant that it could export products and expend less effort feeding its population and focus more on industrialization. Given all those natural resources, it would be hard for the United States not to become a powerful and wealthy state.

Conversely, Afghanistan has few natural resources, a very inhospitable climate, and poor land for crops. The difficulty in growing food meant that Afghanis had to expend a huge effort just to feed themselves. Spending all of that time and effort on food production left little time for industrialization or the education that it requires. Given the lack of resources, how could it grow and develop into even a moderately developed state?

While these two examples leave out a great deal of detail in how the different countries developed, the point is what resources a country starts with will have a big effect on how wealthy the country becomes. But is it that simple? Do countries with resources always develop? To answer that question, we only need to look at a country such as Nigeria. The country has significant oil and natural gas reserves and is considered "oil rich" by the CIA World Factbook. Having resources as valuable as oil and natural gas should make one rich, right? When gasoline sells for over $3 a gallon in the United States, having a bunch of oil should mean you could develop your economy into a wealthy state. That's not always the case. Nigeria's GDP per capita is only $1,555. Even if you control for the cost of living with purchasing power parity, it is still only $2,295 and, in fact, has changed very little since 1970. In Iran, another country rich with oil, the GDP per capita (using purchasing power parity) is just below the current U.S. poverty line at $10,754, but that's well below what Americans consider middle class.

Afghanistan and the United States | Given these pictures, is it surprising that the United States is wealthy and Afghanistan is destitute?

Former Venezuelan Oil Minister Pérez Alfonzo once called oil "the devil's excrement," and he didn't call it that because it's messy and dark.[3] Instead, he meant that while oil may seem like a great gift, it is really a curse, specifically, what economists refer to as the **resource curse**.[4] As it turns out, having a wealth of natural resources that are non-renewable (such as oil and minerals) does not make a country wealthy—it makes it poor.

The reason for this peculiar relationship between resources and economic development is threefold. First, oil and other high-profit minerals tend to drive up the costs in an economy. Since oil is so valuable, companies are willing to pay workers more to extract the oil. This means that the cost of labor increases in a country. That's fine if you work in the oil industry, but if you don't, you can't compete with other countries. For example, if oil workers earn $30 a day, then other jobs will have to pay a similar amount to attract workers. However, many companies cannot afford to pay their workers that much or even close to that amount. Thus, those companies fail, and without them, the country's only source of economic growth will be oil.

Second, oil and minerals are commodities, and their prices can shift radically over short periods of time. For example, the inflation-adjusted price of a barrel of crude oil in 1980 was $102.26, in 1990 it was $39.80, in 2000 it was $35.76, in 2010 it was $73.44, and it is now $107. Such fluctuations make economic growth difficult, to say the least. In one decade, a country could be making large sums of money from exporting oil, and in the next, the price has almost been cut by two-thirds! Because it is difficult to develop other industries when a country is oil or mineral rich, these fluctuations mean the entire economy goes up and down based on the world price for their natural resource. For example, in 2008 Russia had to slash its government spending because the Great Recession caused oil revenues to fall to about half of what had been expected. Imagine your yearly income or student loans being reduced by half or even two-thirds. Would you still be able to afford college?

The third cause of the resource curse is not economic—it's political. In many oil- and mineral-rich countries, the governments tend to be very corrupt and inefficient. The wealth that these resources can produce is simply too tempting, and unfortunately, that temptation is too often not resisted. Often, leaders will extract wealth from the state to pay off their supporters—a tactic called **patronage politics**—while ignoring the needs of their people. In cases like Nigeria, the profits from oil have been squandered through extremely high levels of corruption and generally poor governance, and the Nigerian people have paid for it with poverty and

The rich and poor live in close proximity in Mumbai, India | Do you think these stark differences just across the street from each other make for a stable society?

frequently recurring civil conflict. In cases like Saudi Arabia and Kuwait, the gap between the rich and poor is estimated to be huge.[5] Many live in abject poverty, while a few enjoy opulent wealth that is hard to imagine. Oil did not bring these societies security; for most of their citizens it brought *insecurity*.

The great income gap within these countries means that the elite in control of the resources—those in government—do not spend those resources on building the country's infrastructure and improving the common good. Instead of using the oil money to build schools and roads and to invest in manufacturing, the money is often used to build palaces. Unfortunately, palaces do not help a country develop its economy.

It's important to remember that resources don't just mean oil and minerals. At the beginning of this section, we mentioned the value of fertile land. The United States could not have risen up to the superpower that it has become without the abundance of its agriculture. Cheap food means that citizens and the government can spend more money investing in the economy, particularly investing in industrialization.

Of course, the United States is just one case and perhaps not the best example because of its large size and the protection from the rest of the world that the Atlantic and Pacific Oceans provide. Geographer Jared Diamond shows that one reason European states were

resource curse the curious negative effect for a country's economy when the country has a valuable resource such as oil.

patronage politics using state funds to pay off private or semi-private political supporters.

Does Being in the South Make You Poor?

While the terms North and South may be inaccurate, they were created for a reason. Countries in the Northern Hemisphere tend to be more developed than those in the Southern Hemisphere. Again, that is a gross over-simplification and one that does not help us understand what is going on in the development of different countries. But is there something to being in the south?

It is not "south" that matters, but whether or not the country is in the tropics. Countries that are in the tropics tend to develop only to the level that the size of their economy can support. That may sound obvious, but economies in temperate climates tend to develop into wealthy states—regardless of their size. Look at the small countries such as the United Kingdom. It's relatively small, but it has a very large, developed economy. In the tropics, small states do not develop into large economies. Why?

Certainly, it's unpleasant to work outside when it's very hot. It can even be dangerous when the heat and humidity are both high. Although some scholars argue that the growth of bureaucracy in the United States is connected to the development of air conditioning, that doesn't seem like enough to make a difference since humans adapt extremely well to their environment. Humans live in frozen tundras, swampy jungles, and arid deserts. What other animal can do that?

Scholars think that in temperate climates frost tends to kill off parasites and other organisms that compete for food grown in agriculture.[6] This also includes the ability to store food once it has been harvested. Hot, wet conditions make storing grain very difficult. This is the main reason that spicy food often comes from countries that have a hotter climate—the spices were originally used to preserve the food and cover the taste of food that was beginning to go bad.

In the temperate climates, agriculture was far more viable and thus made a better investment. It also produced more food that could be stored, which produced more wealth that, in turn, allowed the countries to grow more rapidly. As we have discussed before, agriculture helps create a foundation for a country to industrialize. Tropical climates simply do not have that same foundation.

Is the story that easy? Does heat limit growth? Of course, the answer is "no"; there are many factors that influence economic development. Factors such as a country's regime type (discussed in the following pages) and whether or not it suffers from the resource curse are also critically important to development—more than the distance from the equator. However, it is important to realize that a factor as simple as the temperature can influence development. When countries face difficulties in growing and storing food, they must invent ways to overcome those difficulties. That means it is harder and more costly just to survive. Clearly, that means it is more difficult to build up profits, invest them, and develop into a modernized, developed economy.

1. What other factors could make hot weather impede economic growth?

2. What can countries in the tropics do to improve their economies?

3. If the climate is getting warmer, will that make it more difficult for all countries or has technology made that irrelevant?

so successful in colonizing the world—and not the other way around—was that they were fortunate to develop domesticated plants and animals that could live in many regions in Europe. That allowed their civilizations to grow and develop into powerful states that then searched and conquered much of the less-developed world.[7] While food was not the sole source of their power, it did provide them with a strong base on which to develop. Similarly, modern Europe provides another example of the importance of agriculture. Compare the northern European states with southern European states. Northern Europe is wealthier and more developed. Why? Northern Europe had more fertile ground and thus needed less land to support its population and fewer farmers to produce the food. That meant more wealth and consequently greater industrialization, which led to more development. The same was not true for southern Europe. Farm productivity was lower, more resources were needed just to produce enough food, and so there was less wealth and less subsequent industrialization—both conditions that continue today. Agriculture may not be the powerful development engine that industry usually is, but without it, it's hard to have industry.

As you can see, a country's natural resources can be an important factor in its development but not always in the way one would expect. Particularly valuable resources like oil, natural gas, and diamonds tend to make development more difficult, while basic resources such as food and building materials can be powerful engines of development. Natural resources aren't the only structural factor that influences whether a country is rich or poor, but those resources are tied to the next structural factor we'll discuss—a country's colonial history.

10-2b Colonial History

The original settlements by Europeans in Australia, Canada, New Zealand, and the United States created great benefits for both the colonial powers and their former colonies. These countries inherited from Europe two important factors that led to their economic success. First, John Locke's idea of property rights created an important rule of law that is required for successful capitalist growth. Second, the settlers brought with them a tradition of education—the only way a country can improve its workforce. Both of these traditions were adopted by the governments in these emerging countries (originally colonies), and as a result their levels of development came to equal or even rival those in Europe.[8] These original European—almost completely British—settlements or colonies fared relatively well and some can now be considered among the best and most secure countries in the world in which to live. Of course, the true costs to the indigenous populations in these states were very high, but here we are only considering the development of the modern economy.

Unfortunately, elsewhere colonization by European powers did not have such a beneficial impact—quite the opposite, in fact. For example, countries colonized by European powers in the later 1800s tend to be poor, underdeveloped, and far less secure. While some countries such as Japan and China were able to ward off the imperial powers and stay largely independent, many countries—especially those with valuable natural resources—fell prey to the European and American desire for profits and raw materials. Instead of bringing traditions of property rights and education, the imperial powers tended to force their colonies to produce raw materials for use back home in the **metropole**. Many of these states were new imperial powers in Europe—such as Belgium and Germany—and sought colonies for short-term gains to their own economy and ability to build a more powerful military rather than the longer term-investments that the United Kingdom created with its colonies. Needless to say, extracting raw materials was not a recipe for growth and development.

This is where there is a connection to the resource curse. Powerful countries like the United States, United Kingdom, and France sought valuable natural resources in places such as Saudi Arabia, Iran, and Nigeria. While not always successful in attaining control and extraction of the oil, these powerful states often exacerbated the problem of bad governance common to these particularly resource-rich states. When trying to control the resources, the powerful countries found it useful to pay off the leaders of the resource-rich state or to provide them other benefits they desired. While this policy would not help the people within the state, it did make the leaders loyal to the powerful, pseudo-imperial country. It also tended to make the leader dependent on the political and military support of the powerful country since much of his population saw the payoffs for what they were: corruption. The benefit of this policy—for the powerful country—was that even if the resource-rich state gained its independence, it was still tied closely to the powerful state, which could maintain control or at least influence over the resources—a process known as **neocolonialism**. As a result, the great powers often contributed to the corruption and bad governance of the country. However, this was certainly not always the case, and the temptation of easy money was often enough to lead to corruption and bad government policies without any outside help.

10-3 DEVELOPMENT THEORIES AND POLICIES

As the second half of the twentieth century wore on, colonialism gasped out its last few breaths. That meant that most countries were independent and thus able to determine their own economic policies. To be sure, the great powers and former colonizers still had a great deal of influence in their former colonies, or in the case of the United States, its zone of influence. Still, countries around the world, both great and small, started developing theories and policies that would help the poor countries develop into modern, wealthy states. Of course, we already know the end of the story because so many people in the world continue to live in poverty. A handful of these policies worked, and sadly, most failed

metropole the capital city of the empire; for example, London was the metropole of the British Empire.

neocolonialism the practice of maintaining control over smaller, developing countries by keeping strong, dependent links to their governments and/or dominating their economies. This allows a powerful state to control a smaller state without colonizing it.

completely or at least mostly failed to attain their goal of development. Let's turn now to the different ways in which countries pursued development.

10-3a Modernization

Beginning in the 1950s, economists and policymakers set out to duplicate the massive success of the European and U.S. economies. While there certainly were problems with the modern economies in these countries, overall they had generated tremendous wealth and lifted several of those states to great power status. Clearly, they had done something right, hadn't they? If poorer countries simply followed the path laid out by the developed countries, then they too should develop. From this logic was born **modernization theory**.

The theory is pretty simple. Countries simply need to follow the path that the already wealthy states followed, and they too will become rich. This process entailed transforming a country's traditional society and economy into a modern one. What exactly was "modern" in the 1950s? Basically, it meant embracing Western ideas about the functioning of a society and its economy. Specifically, an emphasis on individualism was important. Following the ideas of liberalism (see Chapter 8), if individuals follow their own desires, the country as a whole will prosper. That means that individuals succeeding in an economy should be rewarded with profits, and those who do not succeed should get no such reward or profit. Consequently, there will be some winners, who should subsequently continue to do well and contribute to the economy, and there will be some losers, who do not.

While this may seem very logical or at least familiar for those of us raised in Western society—some businesses succeed and some fail—it was a significant change from some traditional societies that emphasized the group (family, tribe, clan, etc.) over the individual. Imagine growing up in a society where everyone in a family works for the success of the family as a whole and then being told that you should only work for your own success. That would be quite a shock.

This emphasis on individual economic rewards was supposed to spur economic growth. Successful entrepreneurs would reinvest in the economy, building more and more wealth. In the end, the country as a whole would benefit, just as it had in Europe and the United States.

modernization theory theory in the 1950s and 1960s that suggested all countries should be able to develop by following the practices of wealthy states in Europe and North America.

The other aspects of modernization theory argued that countries should industrialize as much as possible and move away from agricultural production. This meant that there should be emigration into the cities as the country urbanized. Clearly, this theory was developed well before the ideas of environmental responsibility and organic-anything had appeared. The more processed and urban a country was—the better.

There were significant problems with modernization theory, and perhaps the best way to explain them is with a metaphor. Imagine that you had the idea of starting a fast-food restaurant in 1940. You could serve burgers, fries, and soft drinks. Given that no such restaurants existed at that time, you could easily begin to dominate the market. Just think, you could be the first restaurant to spread out along the new interstate freeway system in the United States. The idea that people could enjoy the same food as they traveled across the country would be worth billions. We know this for a fact because McDonald's was founded in 1940 and is now a multi-billion dollar corporation.

Now imagine trying to start a new fast-food restaurant in 2014. You would have to compete with all of the current restaurants from McDonald's to Taco Bell to Subway, and all the others! It would be hard to think of a way to compete with these giants and actually make a profit, yet that is essentially what modernization theory suggested. Undeveloped countries should just do what the rich countries did, but when the rich countries developed, they didn't have any competition except for themselves. This doesn't mean that it couldn't be done. It simply means that it would be difficult and thus rather unlikely that countries would succeed. At a minimum, it meant that states wanting to modernize needed to develop strategies that worked in the current world environment rather than one in which there were no modern super-powered economies.

Another problem with modernization theory is the idea that the path taken by Europe and the United States was an easy one. The Industrial Revolution may have been an exciting, dynamic period in history, but it was also plagued with horrible working conditions, little or no protection for workers, heavy pollution from coal, and so on. To think that the rest of the world should modernize in the same manner would mean that the global environment would suffer (as noted later in Chapter 12) and the people in each of those developing countries would also suffer. It certainly seems like there should be a better alternative, don't you think?

10-3b Dependency Theory

The first alternative to modernization theory was driven partly by theory and partly by a desire for social change. Scholars and policymakers focused

Multinational Corporations and Foreign Direct Investment

Foreign direct investment, the way MNCs are created, is a very political issue. FDI means that a company from one country is investing and taking ownership of a company in another country. Imagine if another country purchased your favorite sports team and renamed it. Would fans of the Denver Broncos like it if their mascot became the camels, the llamas, or the giraffes? Certainly not! This example is a silly one, but it illustrates one of the issues in FDI: when "foreigners" own property in your country. Now imagine that the United States is the foreign country. How do you think French or Japanese people feel about McDonald's? Although it's a successful business and convenient food source, McDonald's and many other fast-food chains are gathering more and more critics in the United States for being unhealthy. How do you think other countries feel about the United States exporting an unhealthy food source?

Putting aside the reaction citizens may have, realist thinkers and policymakers have an ambivalent take on FDI. For their own country, they do not like the idea of FDI because they interpret it as foreign control over the economy. However, if the FDI is invested in another country than the realists' country, then they consider it a good thing since it means their country has control over another. Liberals do not make this distinction and uniformly see FDI as a mutually beneficial activity. Marxists see it as uniformly bad because it signals the extending control of the rich countries over the poor countries.

While no country fits a realist, liberal, or Marxist perspective completely, almost all of them place restrictions on FDI. The most obvious restrictions concern security. Allowing any country to invest enough to control your defense industry, military, police forces, and so on makes little sense to anyone. Most governments go further and restrict investments in media by foreign firms because they are concerned with a foreign power controlling their news media, something that could give that foreign power tremendous influence. Another way governments restrict FDI is to maintain a "golden share." That is, they keep one share of a company that allows them to buy the entire company back at any time—without the permission of the foreign owners of the company. This isn't expropriation because they are paying for the company and have a legal claim because of the "golden share."

If the host government permits it, then FDI can take two basic forms. It can be an investment in which the MNC builds a company in another country from the ground up. For example, when McDonald's builds restaurants in another country, this is *greenfield investment*. The other form—perhaps best named acquisitions and mergers—is to purchase or merge with another company already in the host country. In this case, McDonald's would purchase another fast-food chain and repurpose it into McDonald's restaurants.

Both of these examples are of horizontal integration, when an MNC gains a presence in another country to sell more of its products—like McDonald's, Coca-Cola, InBev, or Unilever. The other form is vertical integration. In this case, the company is using the companies it owns in other countries to maintain a supply of parts and raw materials. For example, General Motors owns factories in Mexico to take advantage of the cheaper labor. Those factories supply the main assembly plants in the United States with the parts used in their vehicles. That is vertical rather than horizontal integration.

1. Should foreign companies be permitted to own property and companies in your country?

2. What types of goods and services shouldn't be sold to foreign companies?

on the critique that modernization theory would not work because the less-developed states would have to compete with the huge Western economies. They began to argue that it wasn't just the competition from the large economies that was stifling growth in developing countries. Instead, they argued that large corporations in Europe and the United States created a system of dependency when they invested in poorer countries and that dependency made it so the poor countries would never be able to grow.

First, let's explore the background on multinational corporations (MNCs). When a company from one country invests enough money in a company in another country to control that company or it creates a new subsidiary company in another country, it is considered foreign direct investment (FDI). Normally, any investments of 20 percent or more of a company's stock give control and are considered FDI. During the early 1900s, more and more corporations from wealthy countries invested heavily in the developing countries. For example, United Fruit Company (now Chiquita Brands International and based in Ohio) owned fruit plantations throughout Latin America and virtually controlled those exports. Similarly, International Telephone and Telegraph Corporation (based in New York) held a stake in Chilean copper mines and owned and controlled the telecom industry in Chile and elsewhere in South America. Once a company controls companies in other countries, it is considered a multinational corporation. Current-day examples of MNCs are McDonald's, which has restaurants all around the world, Anheuser-Busch InBev, the Belgian brewing company that purchased Anheuser-Busch in 2009, and Unilever, which began as Lever Brothers in the 1890s by selling soap in Britain and now sells consumer goods in 180 countries.

Foreign direct investment can be a good thing because it indicates that there is value in the **host country**. However, these MNCs often tended to extract raw materials (bananas, copper, etc.) for use or consumption in their **home country** and keep the profits from the sale of those raw materials in the home country. This was particularly true through the 1970s.

An example should highlight how this worked and how it could be detrimental to the host country: United Fruit grew bananas in Guatemala and sold them in the United States and around the world. The profit from the bananas did not stay in Guatemala; it went to the United States, where United Fruit was headquartered. The workers on the banana plantations were paid, but rather poorly, and United Fruit had to build some infrastructure to ship the bananas (it owned the only railroad in Guatemala), but all of the profits from bananas grown in Guatemala left the country.

foreign direct investment (FDI) when a company in one country invests in a company in another country that leads the investor to have control over the new company.

host country the country in which a multinational corporation owns other companies.

home country the term used to describe where the headquarters of a multinational corporation is based.

expropriation the taking—or nationalization—of property owned by a foreign company with or without compensation.

nationalization when a government takes ownership of private property—land, a company, or an asset.

As a consequence of this process, Guatemala (or any developing country with MNCs) could not develop because it didn't have any capital to invest—all of the capital was owned by foreign corporations and profits generated were taken out of the country. This new idea was called dependency theory, and its proponents argued that because large multinational corporations kept the profits, the poor countries would always stay poor. Dependency theorists noted that even though the large multinational corporations paid local workers and built infrastructure such as roads and ports needed to export the raw materials, these benefits did not provide the developing country with much and certainly not enough to begin to develop an economy independent of the large corporation.

At the beginning of this section, we pointed out that dependency theory was part theory and part call for social change. Thus far, we have explained the theory part; what about social change? As you probably noticed, the theory rests on logic very similar to Marxism. Although Marxism emphasizes economic class above all else, that logic is simply applied to countries (rather than people) by the dependency theorists. So instead of a focus on the capitalist owner extracting profits from the worker, the theory argues that rich states, such as Belgium, extract profits from the poor states, such as the Congo. Thus, the social change aspect of dependency theory came from Marxist ideas.

Proponents of dependency theory argued that developing states needed to revolt against the corporations and take their property, whether that was a copper mine, a fruit plantation, or a factory. This process of taking foreign-held property is called **expropriation**. One example of this is Cuba, where Fidel Castro, after overthrowing the Batista government, in 1960 confiscated all property in Cuba (including plantations, resorts, etc.) in the name of the Cuban people. (For another example, see the box Spotlight On: ITT Corporation, the CIA, and Chile). He then proceeded to redistribute the profits to the Cuban people with varying degrees of success. To this day, there are Cubans who fled Castro's revolution who claim they still own property in Cuba and will someday take it back.

Once the new socialist governments had taken the property from the corporations and nationalized it, they could begin developing their economy. With **nationalization**, the profits from those holdings would provide money for investment and allow the government to engage in socialist policies rather than capitalist policies. A good example is Egypt. In the 1950s, Egypt's new socialist government nationalized major enterprises with the stated intent of reinvesting this new capital in the Egyptian economy. By the time President Hosni Mubarak was overthrown in 2011, Mubarak himself was

ITT Corporation, the CIA, and Chile

In 1970, Salvador Allende took first place by a very close margin in Chile's three-way presidential race. After a month of debating in the legislature and the assassination of the head of Chile's military by anti-Allende plotters, Allende became the first socialist president elected in Latin America. Democratic or not, Allende was deemed dangerous for U.S. political interests because of his socialist and Marxist leanings. President Richard Nixon feared that Chile would become an ally of the Soviets and give the U.S. nemesis a stronghold in South America. U.S. businesses also feared Allende because they correctly predicted that he would expropriate their property in Chile. ITT Corporation in particular had significant investments in Chile—copper mines and the Chilean telephone company. These fears were strong enough to prompt a covert intervention that led to the death of Allende and the rise of a right-wing dictator in Chile.

Following the election and confirmation of Allende as president, the United States initiated a series of economic sanctions to "make the economy scream" and thereby make President Allende's rule difficult and short. Part of this effort involved ITT Corporation helping fund the CIA effort to destabilize the Chilean economy and, through a Chilean newspaper, print anti-Allende propaganda. Funds were also funneled to the military to foster a group of officers who would plan and execute a coup d'état against Allende.

On what has become a truly infamous day in world history—September 11, 1973—the Chilean military led by Augusto Pinochet overthrew the Allende government and installed Pinochet as a dictator. Allende refused to leave the presidential palace and committed suicide before being taken by the military.[9] In the three years that Allende held office, the CIA and a U.S. multinational corporation spent millions to overthrow a democratically elected leader. They may have kept the Soviets out of Chile, and they definitely recovered their lost property. But, Chile suffered under the repressive rule of Pinochet for 17 years, only transitioning back to democracy in 1990. Chile's economic growth rate increased after that 1990 transition.

What does this example suggest about the paths to development for countries such as Chile?

---

thought to be a billionaire, but the Egyptian economy was stagnant and most Egyptians were poor, living on less than $2,300 a year.

Thus, the end result was not often beneficial to the developing country. Of course, expropriation was met with great resistance by large corporations and their home countries. The home governments did not want their MNCs to lose their property in the host countries and their ability to make so much money. Even though expropriation was taking privately held property, states often saw it as a threat to their security because it threatened their economic well-being. As a consequence, they often funded covert activities against socialist movements and supported dictators who guaranteed that they would get to keep their property. As you can see from the box Spotlight On: ITT Corporation, the CIA, and Chile, governments would also get involved in these disputes and try to keep the property from being taken.

The socialist policies often did not work for the same reason Marxism tended to fail around the world. In theory, an economy that strives for equality makes sense, but in reality, it is often too inefficient to succeed. Cuba might be the most successful example because it is still truly socialist and has a rather high level of equality and human development compared with its level of wealth. Of course, at least some of Cuba's success can be attributed to the support it received from the Soviet Union for 30 years. When it received aid from Moscow, Cuba did well, but with the collapse of the Soviet Union and end of the Cold War, that aid dried up. Now its level of development is far behind many other Latin American countries. It is also beginning to allow private ownership, perhaps a sign that it is moving toward a non-socialist, semi-liberal economy.

In addition to the failure of many of the policies advocated by dependency theorists, later studies showed that there was little evidence to support the idea of dependency. Most studies found that investments by multinational corporations—FDI—tended to benefit countries rather than hurt them. While profits and raw materials were often extracted from countries, significant capital was left behind along with a developing infrastructure to support the multinational corporation. Thus, few people today espouse dependency theory, at least under that name.

Dependency theory did fail in practice, and FDI was shown to have a number of beneficial effects in the host countries, but the theory was not simply a flash in the pan or an unfortunate fad. Not all of the scholars working with dependency theory espoused radical social change. Instead, they pointed to the inequalities of the exchange common to the relationship between poor and rich countries (and their corporations). With time, many less-developed countries took a stronger stance toward the corporate investment and made sure that there were clear benefits for their people. While there are certainly many cases of poor working conditions and poor treatment by large corporations in developing countries (see Chapter 8 for examples), those conditions have improved greatly over the past decades—perhaps partly due to the work of dependency theorists.

10-3c World Systems Theory

The failure of dependency theory did not mark the end of socialist approaches to development. World systems theory (WST), which developed concurrently with dependency theory, is a Marxist-inspired theory we described in Chapter 4 that argues the political-economic world is divided into different levels or zones of power.[10] That power structure determines each individual state's ability to develop its economy; it also constrains its foreign policy, but we will focus on the economy here. Notice that WST suggests there is a hierarchy of power in the world, but the world system is still based on a lack of a world governing authority. Wealthy states are able to develop their economies better than poor states because the system is anarchic.

According to WST, the world is divided into three economic zones: the core, the semi-periphery, and the periphery (see Map 10-5). These zones divide up the world's production similar to a division of labor with each zone producing specific types of products. There is a hierarchy to these zones and to the products they produce, so let's turn to that next.

The core states are the wealthy, capitalist countries like most European states, Australia, Canada, Japan, and the United States. These states tend to make first-generation products that provide the highest level of profits. First-generation products right now would include iPhones and iPads, financial instruments (stocks, bonds, etc.), pharmaceuticals, and advanced military weapons. All these products are cutting-edge technologies that have been developed in core states. Sometimes referred to as secondary goods because they require

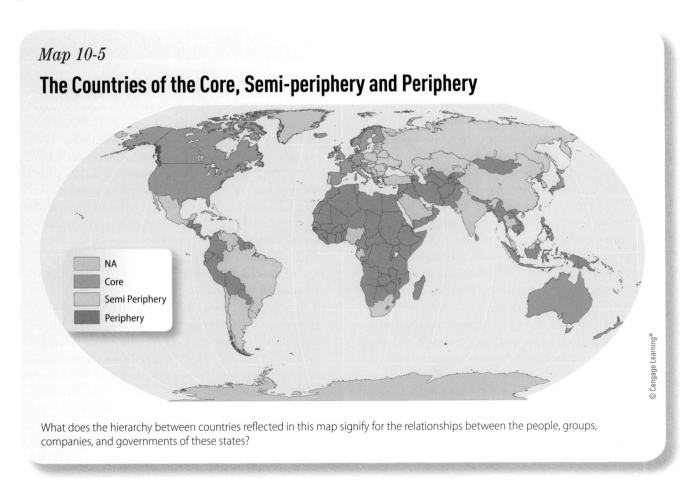

Map 10-5

The Countries of the Core, Semi-periphery and Periphery

NA
Core
Semi Periphery
Periphery

© Cengage Learning®

What does the hierarchy between countries reflected in this map signify for the relationships between the people, groups, companies, and governments of these states?

some processing or building, they all have value added by the labor that is used to make them. They also provide the biggest profit margins to the core states. Core states promote free trade of these goods, arguing that tariffs are bad for development.

The semi-periphery and the periphery are the middle and poor states, respectively. Peripheral states tend not to produce manufactures but instead export raw materials—sometimes called *primary goods*—to the core and, to a lesser extent, the semi-periphery. The core tends to place tariffs or other trade barriers on these products. The effect of this policy is to reduce the profits for the peripheral country and to protect workers in the core who might be engaged in producing raw materials such as food, lumber, and so on.

Examples of peripheral states include Honduras, Kenya, Iraq, and Vietnam. These states all produce raw materials or cheap labor that benefits the rest of the world but provides little profit to the producing state. According to WST, the core and semi-periphery states exploit the periphery countries by extracting value from them. Put simply, the rich and middle states force the poor states to sell their products more cheaply, and thus the poor countries have an extremely difficult time developing their economies.

It is worth noting that many of the oil-producing states are often considered to be in the periphery. While they make a high profit off of the oil they sell, their economy is completely dependent on oil—they have nothing (or almost nothing) else. This puts them in a very vulnerable position, and it means their economy is not very dynamic. It cannot grow without an increase in oil prices. Just think what would happen to states in the Middle East if we discovered a cheap, clean, and widely available form of fuel that replaced gas. Would the world still be concerned about Middle East peace? Would the region become like Africa—poor and relatively ignored by the rest of the world?

Semi-peripheral states act as the middle ground between the core and the periphery. They tend to make second-generation products that are profitable but not as much so as products made in the core. Examples of these products are automobiles and components for electronics. Just a decade ago, computers would have been on the list of first-generation products, and while many computers are still high technology products, states such as China have begun producing and selling these on the world market. Computers are not as profitable as they once were. In 1990, an entry-level desktop computer was around $2,400; today it costs less than $400. Clearly, they aren't as profitable as they once were. Notice that many of these products are still made in the core.

The important thing to realize is that things like automobiles are also made in the semi-periphery and are not the high-profit products they once were decades ago.

Examples of countries in the semi-periphery include China, India, Mexico, and Brazil. Each of these countries sells both raw materials or cheap labor and manufactured goods. They make more profit from their production than the periphery states but not nearly as much as core states.

The relationship between these states is exploitive, according to WST. The core exploits the semi-periphery and periphery by demanding lower prices for imports and selling its goods at higher prices. The semi-periphery does the same to the periphery, which in the end is at the bottom of the ladder and simply gets exploited. This exploitation and hierarchy is economic but also concerns security. Core states tend to be the most secure, their citizens have the longest life spans, and there is less internal and external conflict. Peripheral states have much less security, are more often involved in violent internal or external conflict, and have fewer human rights and a lower life expectancy. Remember, for example, from Chapter 5 that military conflict since World War II has almost exclusively been located outside the core states. Semi-peripheral states fall in between these two. States can move up and down zones, although movement tends to be upward and uncommon. For example, China was in the periphery in 1973 when it began to open up to foreign trade. Today, with its rapid economic growth and developments such as taking over the ThinkPad laptop line from IBM (by Chinese-based Lenovo), it is solidly in the semi-periphery. The United States, Canada, and Australia were all originally periphery states but became core states 100 to 200 years ago.

WST has much to offer in its explanation of the world economic structure, and it has generally eclipsed dependency theory. The description of what products the three zones produce, what profits they make, and how WST affects their development is quite accurate. It also nicely describes the differing levels of security each zone enjoys because of the close connection between economic development and physical security.

The theory does, however, have limitations. First, it places so much emphasis on structure that there is no way to explain how different states can develop out of one zone and into a higher one. If everything is structural, for example, then why do some economic policies work and some fail?

The second issue is that the theory is only partly scientific; it is also based in the Marxist ideology that ultimately advocates social change. While there is nothing wrong with social change or taking an ideological position on an issue such as development, it is important to remember that part of the theory is ideology and only part a social scientific approach to the world economy.

10-3d Import Substitution Industrialization

Another approach to development that was very popular throughout the developing world—especially Latin America—and inspired by dependency theory and WST is **import substitution industrialization (ISI)**. Sometimes used in conjunction with expropriation policies, the main purpose of ISI is to enable the poor country to develop independently a manufacturing sector of its economy that will be the growth engine for its development.

ISI policy was supposed to help countries develop by first protecting their domestic industry. The government of the developing state would limit or even stop imports of manufactured goods with tariffs, quotas, and so on. This policy would force those goods to be produced domestically since they were either too expensive or unavailable for import. As domestic manufacturing firms started up, they could more easily succeed because they would not have to compete with the big companies in the wealthy countries. As these domestic companies got better at producing their products, they could begin to export them and compete on the world market. Once they had developed enough to compete with the wealthy states, the government could begin to allow imports again.

It sounds like a very good plan. Provide protection to new, infant industries so that they can become profitable, improve their products, and become truly competitive. However, these best laid plans unfortunately failed to bring about development for the poor countries that adopted them.

The key to the ISI policy was first that the domestic producers would work to become more profitable and efficient. Only by doing that could they ever compete on the world market. Second, the government could only give protection for a short period, enough time for the domestic producer to become competitive. If the producer could not be effective on the world market, the government would have to let it fail. If the government did that, then the domestic producers would all work toward increasing their competitiveness.

import substitution industrialization (ISI) a development policy that promotes cutting off international trade and substituting it with domestic production.

At first, ISI worked well. The first products that were "substituted" for imports were nondurable items such as clothes. In all of these countries, there was a large domestic market for these items. Domestic producers were able to meet the continuous demand and grow their production capabilities.

ISI was working so well initially that countries began emphasizing industry over agriculture, a step prescribed by ISI policy. Thus, more people began to work in industry and less food was being produced. Slowly, many countries that never imported food before had to start. This was not a problem originally because the industrialization helped pay for the food imports. So for a time, everything seemed to be working according to plan.

The next step in the process proved problematic, however. Domestic producers needed to produce durable goods such as cars and appliances. None of the countries attempting ISI had large enough populations to support a large domestic demand. Paraguay, for example, needs a steady supply of clothes but it only needs so many refrigerators. Because there was less of a market for these durable goods, it was more difficult to make them profitable and therefore competitive with other countries.

Domestic producers quickly learned that they had a pretty sweet deal. Since the government limited imports from other countries, they could produce cheap products and charge relatively high prices, thus making huge profits. Instead of investing these high profits back into the manufacturing and thereby making it more efficient and competitive, they kept them. As a result, the people were left with high-priced, inferior products—so much for "durable" goods.

To ensure that the government would not pull the plug on their protection from foreign goods, the companies would often bribe government officials. Using their excess profits, they could pay off bureaucrats, legislators, and presidents. Once paid off, the government would continue the protection so that the companies could stay in business and keep making all that money.

To make matters worse for these countries, there was a global food shortage in the 1970s. Demand from the Soviet Union and crop-destroying weather drove food prices up. Since these countries had emphasized industrialism more than agriculture and were importing food, they had to pay even more for the food just to survive. Consequently, the ISI policies intended to develop their economies ended up hurting them.

10-3e Export-Led Growth

Not all countries fell into this ISI trap, however. South Korea, Taiwan, Hong Kong, and Singapore all started ISI policies in the 1950s, but by 1960 they realized

TABLE 10-2	GDP PER CAPITA IN SOUTH KOREA AND BRAZIL IN CONSTANT (2000) DOLLARS	
	South Korea	**Brazil**
1960	$1,109	$1,448
1970	$1,994	$1,990
1980	$3,358	$3,538
1990	$6,895	$3,354
2000	$11,346	$3,701
2010	$16,373	$4,699

Source: The World Bank, *World Development Indicators.*

that the policies weren't working and switched to the model that Japan used to rise from its post–World War II ruin. Instead of emphasizing the production of goods for domestic consumption—"substitutes" for imports—these countries began pushing their industries to produce goods for export.

This policy, called **export-led growth**, worked less by protecting domestic industry and more by promoting exports. To be sure, domestic industries were protected from foreign competition just like the ISI policies, but generally they were protected only if they focused on developing exports. The governments of these countries gave tax breaks and other **subsidies** to domestic businesses that would create products for export. The governments also lifted minimum wage requirements and made sure that unions could not demand too much of their employers. This provided cheap labor, low taxes, and other valuable monetary incentives to export goods. As such, the producers in these countries became very good at competing on the world market.

Export-led growth was a fantastic success in these four countries. In fact, they were called the "Asian Tigers" because they were so successful and their economies had become so dynamic and competitive. Let's compare South Korea, which followed export-led growth, with Brazil, which followed ISI. As you can see from Table 10-2, South Korea started with a lower GDP per capita. In the first decade of export-led growth, it tied Brazil. In the following decades, it clearly sped ahead of Brazil. By 2010, it had a GDP per capita 3.5 times as large.

Other Asian countries began to follow the Asian Tigers by adopting export-led growth policies. Indonesia, Malaysia, and Thailand did not have the same fantastic success as illustrated by South Korea but grew fivefold in the period between 1960 and 2010—significantly more than the ISI countries such as Brazil.

So why haven't all countries followed export-led growth? One reason is that, as the world's economy

has evolved to its current form—the global economy, as we described in Chapter 8—the ways of production have changed as well, and it is harder to compete in the global economy now than before. Globalization has also changed the way production occurs, so that companies are able to spread components and subsidiaries all over the world, and contract with others, in ways they didn't used to do. That has made it more challenging for countries to establish export-led sectors in the same way they used to.

Another major component of the answer is that it's one thing to understand a policy and another to implement it. The successful Asian countries all had very strong, effective governments that were willing to place significant burdens on the population. The workers in these countries had low pay and few rights for many years. Consequently, the businesses could make even more profits and then reinvest them to become more efficient and successful. Many of the Latin American and African governments that adopted ISI policies were not nearly as strong or effective. They were more likely to take bribes and payoffs from industrial leaders. Many of them also tried to be populist in nature by providing benefits to the public and so did not want to squeeze their populations in the same way the Asian governments did. While the earlier years of export-led growth were often very difficult for the average citizen in these countries, their sacrifices helped create a developed, wealthier country for their children.

10-3f The Washington Consensus

By the late 1970s, global economic policy began to shift toward economic liberalism. Many of the attempts at socialism had failed to produce great gains in development, and the nationalist ISI policies had also led many countries into worse situations than they had previously experienced. From these failures, policymakers began to embrace more **orthodox liberal** ideas. In particular, Prime Minister Margaret Thatcher (United Kingdom) and President Ronald Reagan (United States) pushed

export-led growth the idea that to develop a country's economy, the government should push for companies to focus on products that can be exported to other countries. The policy was most successful in the Asian countries such as South Korea and Singapore.

subsidies funds given to companies by a government to help them grow.

orthodox liberal an approach to economics that favors an extreme free-market approach where government is very limited and most of a country is composed of private enterprise.

Ronald Reagan and Margaret Thatcher | These two people had a tremendous impact on global economic policy that lasts to this day. Do you think they were right?

the idea that economic growth would not come from government involvement in the economy but from a liberal economy and policy. This **neoliberal** approach was called the **Washington Consensus** because of the powerful push from the White House and from the Washington-based IMF and World Bank to adopt a package of economic and political reforms.

So what specifically did the Washington Consensus prescribe for the world's many economies? Let's begin with the political part of the consensus. Thatcher, Reagan, and the other proponents pushed the idea that the best way for a country to develop was through democratic governance. In a democracy, those with a strong desire to succeed should be free to be more productive. That productivity should be a driving force for the development of a country.

Second, not only should the polity be free, but the market should as well. Countries should adopt policies that promote a free market domestically—that is, a market that is relatively unimpeded by government regulation and taxes. That free market should also be extended to international trade, where the country should promote and certainly not limit trade with other countries. Finally, the Washington Consensus pushed the idea that the private sector—not the government—was the best engine for economic growth and development.

neoliberal a return to liberal or free-market economics.

Washington Consensus an orthodox liberal approach to development that took hold in the 1980s and was used to try to promote economic growth in poor countries. It had very limited success.

The socialist and ISI policies in the earlier decades relied heavily on government involvement in the economy; this policy, according to the consensus, must be rejected.

Whether through direct ownership of companies and resources or comprehensive interventions in the market, governments in developing countries had taken a very hands-on approach to economic growth. The Washington Consensus sought to change all of that and pushed its view through the policies of many of the large states (such as the United Kingdom and the United States) and through international organizations like the World Bank and the IMF.

The problem with the Washington Consensus was twofold. First, it was very much a top-down approach. That meant that policymakers in rich countries and in international organizations dictated to the poorer countries what economic policies they must follow. They were able to have this much power because many of the developing states needed loans to keep their economies from collapsing. The two big international organizations, the World Bank and the IMF, made loans conditional on the recipient government engaging in the liberal reforms named in the consensus. Thus, many of these developing countries had no choice but to adopt the liberal reforms. You might think that sometimes people have to be forced to do what is best for them, and sometimes that can be true. However, the problem with this top-down approach was that it was a "silver bullet" approach: one solution was to fit all problems. The liberal reforms required would cause massive economic and social change in many countries. Not only can such dramatic change be difficult to implement and truly follow, but it can also create such a shock that the society simply rejects it after a short period of time.

The second problem with the Washington Consensus was that it placed all of its emphasis on economic growth through efficiency and ignored the human costs of those efficiencies. Just as the export-led growth policies in the Asian Tigers tended to be hard on the population, so too were the liberal reforms being advocated by the consensus. A free market creates many winners—businesses that thrive and produce wealth for their owners. Free markets also create many losers—failed businesses and fluctuating unemployment that leaves many without the ability to earn a living.

Beginning in the late 1980s, policymakers began to question some aspects of the Washington Consensus. They did not abandon it but responded to criticisms that it ignored poverty in the name of economic efficiency. Thus, the consensus was moderated, and while liberal markets and policies were still considered the best way to develop, social welfare policies were no longer seen as bad government policy but as the choice of the country to provide a social safety net for its population.

In 2002, many of the changes to the Washington Consensus were laid out in a UN conference on development in Monterrey, Mexico. The result was the **Monterrey Consensus**—a new policy that officially promoted the idea that liberal market reforms were the best way for countries to develop their economies but that growth must be made sustainable, humane, gender-sensitive, and it must be aimed at the reduction of poverty. It would take good governance to meet these latter goals, something often lacking in many developing states.

What is interesting about the report is that it unequivocally states that FDI is good for developing countries and that international trade is required for economic development. That alone is not surprising or interesting—much of the developed world has been advocating that for years. What makes the report different is that it also emphasizes human security—the need to promote human rights, gender equality, and protection of the environment. These last three points create a mixture of free-market economics and social welfare. Do you think this may be a way for countries to develop without putting undue burdens on their people?

10-3g The Aftermath of the Great Recession

How has the recent Great Recession (2008–2010) changed international development? That's a good question, and one the world is still trying to figure out. As developed countries cope with the significant loss to their economies, their governments have less revenue from taxes, and, therefore, their budgets are getting squeezed. Whenever governments have to cut spending, one of the first items considered is foreign aid. As discussed in Chapter 9, it is questionable whether aid actually enhances growth, but it does reduce the suffering of the poor, even if only temporarily. Thus, one consequence is the likelihood that governments will cut their donations to the poorest countries.

Another factor might be captured in the saying, "Charity begins in the home." Just as the fall of the Soviet empire and the Berlin Wall led many European states to shift their aid giving from Africa to Eastern Europe, so too might the problems in Greece, Ireland, and the other hard-hit European states. The EU may have to make a choice to give support to its neighbors (those at "home") or to give support to the rest of the developing world. While it is not a black-or-white choice, the reduced budgets mean that some hard choices may have to be made.

It may be hard to imagine European states continuing to need aid after the initial crisis, but several do. Bankers often use the terms PIGS or PIIGS when referring to the poorest European countries: Portugal, Italy, Ireland, Greece, and Spain. In worst shape is Greece. The economy is still struggling after bailouts and debt rescheduling from the EU and other international organizations, and a large majority of the population disagrees with the government cuts to social spending and has little confidence in the government's ability to repair the current situation. What happens in a democracy when the people don't like the government's solution to a problem but that solution may be the only option?

The developed world hasn't started raising trade barriers like it did right before the Great Depression, and it seems unlikely that the wealthy states would or even could abandon international trade. However, the suffering economies in places like the United States, United Kingdom, and Japan have led to a reduced demand for imports. Recall that the Monterrey Consensus notes that international trade is critical for growth. The reduced demand for imports means that many developing countries cannot sell as much of their products to the wealthy states, and that means it will be harder for them to grow their economies. Literally millions of Chinese factory workers were laid off during and shortly after the Great Recession because the wealthy countries spent less money on imported goods.

The crisis of the Great Recession may or may not be over, but the economic downturn continues to drag down the wealthy states. As a consequence, many poor states are also being held down, making their economic development problematic and more difficult.

10-4 THE ROLE OF DEMOCRACY IN DEVELOPMENT

We have discussed several different policy approaches to development, all of which focus on economic policy. This makes a lot of sense since we are concerned with economic development. The Washington Consensus was the only policy to explicitly link democracy and economic development. The idea was a free market and a free

Monterrey Consensus a 2002 framework for global development in which the developed and developing countries agree to take joint actions for poverty reduction, with emphasis on free trade, sustainable growth and development, and increased financial aid.

polity naturally went together—like the old commercial for Reese's candy about chocolate and peanut butter.

There is good reason to think these two have more than a coincidental link. All truly functioning democracies are at least minimally developed. Now think of the oldest democracies: the United States, United Kingdom, France, and more recently Japan and Germany. In addition to being solidly democratic, what else characterizes those countries? They are five of the top six largest economies. Only China, the second largest economy, is not democratic. It seems like, given these simple facts, democracy must be good for economic growth, right? That should mean that democratization should solve the developing world's poverty problem, maybe? Let's explore that possibility next.

10-4a Is Democracy Good or Bad for an Economy?

The idea that democracy—a free and open government—should help growth not only has some compelling evidence but there is also a logical story that goes along with it. People in a democratic society have adopted the ideals of freedom of thinking, individual responsibility, and choice. This should mean that the population is more dynamic and innovative. They should be more likely to try new ideas in the marketplace and thus create innovative new products. Even more importantly, a democratic government should be one that does not interfere in the economy. Because it is a government of, by, and for the people, it should only regulate those portions of the market that need to be regulated to protect people (e.g., child labor laws). Less government involvement in the economy should mean a more dynamic economy.

While it is true that most democracies are well developed, it is not the case that those democracies have high, dynamic growth rates. The fastest growing economies are not democratic—just look at China. It managed to maintain a double-digit growth rate for years, and it is an authoritarian government that gives few freedoms to the people. Conversely, the United States and United Kingdom, the world's oldest democracies, have had growth rates only between 2 and 3 percent for years. If your country is developing, wouldn't you rather grow at a rate of 10 percent rather than 3 percent? Is state capitalism the answer to sluggish growth?

So what about the story that democratic governance is good for economic development? Scholars agree that there are characteristics of democracy that are good for economic growth, in particular, the non-involvement in the economy. However, democracy has a characteristic that can be very detrimental to economic growth: it

can be populist. When poorer states democratize, there is often a strong desire by the government to do something for the poor. For example, the government could raise taxes to pay for subsidized food or fuel prices. Lower prices would clearly help the poor, and because democracies are more representative of all people, they would be more likely to aid the poor. Higher taxes are generally bad for economic growth, and so the attempt by the democratic government to help its people hurts the economy.

Another example that comes from this populist characteristic is the nationalization of private industry. Recall the story about Allende in Chile described previously. He expropriated the copper mines (and threatened the telecom industry) so that the Chilean people could gain from the wealth of their own country. That, of course, hurt the MNCs, making them rather angry and hostile. Moreover, threats of nationalization (through expropriation) scare international investors away from newly democratic countries, and fewer investors in a country are certainly bad for business.

ANTONIO SILVA/epa/Corbis

Luiz Inácio Lula da Silva, former president of Brazil | President Lula was pro-labor and pro-poor, but he accomplished both economic growth through liberalization and managed to help the poor. Could you think of how to design policies that worked to grow the economy but also benefited the poor in your country?

For example, in 2002, Luiz Inácio Lula da Silva was elected to the presidency of Brazil. Lula was from a socialist workers party, and international investors were deeply concerned that he would radically change the business environment in Brazil; there were concerns that he might nationalize some industries. As a consequence, investors pulled out of Brazil, leaving significantly less capital in the country by the time Lula took office in 2003. However, the new president did not change the business environment. He turned out to be very pro-business and international trade, while also promoting social programs to alleviate poverty. When he ran for his second term as president, the international investors didn't get nervous because they knew Lula wouldn't change Brazilian policy against business.

There are two stories, then, of how democracy might affect growth: one where it helps and the other where it hurts. Still, democracy has so many benefits—its citizens live longer, happier, healthier lives—it's hard to believe that it doesn't also have positive effects for an economy. After all, isn't it common sense that happier, healthier people who live long lives are more productive?

10-4b The Many Side Benefits of Democratic Governance

Reluctant to give up on the idea that democracy should have some benefit for an economy, scholars continue to search for a connection. There are two interesting answers that show how liberal government leads to a stronger economy, but both of these effects are indirect.

The first study shows that democracies provide more public health and education services than autocracies. Because democratic leaders are responsible to the entire public, they tend to make policies that help everyone compared to autocratic leaders who are only responsible to a few elites. That is why citizens of a democracy tend to be healthier and better educated.[11] Does that matter for an economy? Yes, it does.

In poorer countries, democracy increases the life expectancy considerably when compared to poor authoritarian countries. A population that lives longer can also work longer. That means it is more productive and that productivity can help the economy develop. In poor autocracies, people live shorter lives and consequently cannot contribute to the economy for as long.[12]

Democratic countries also tend to have much higher levels of primary and secondary education. More educated people tend to be better workers. They are more efficient, reliable, and better at solving problems. These abilities make the labor force more effective and productive. Thus, citizens of democratic countries tend to live longer and are better educated. That makes for a much more effective and long-lasting workforce. So democracy itself doesn't make an economy develop more quickly or better, but it does increase other factors that can dramatically aid the development of a country's economy.[13]

Democracy has been shown to have one more indirect, positive effect on a country's economy—it tends to make the growth-sapping effects of corruption go away. A corrupt government is not only frustrating and morally reprehensible, but it also puts the brakes on economic growth. Imagine you wanted to start a business selling coffee in a little shop right next to your campus. If you lived in a country like Canada, one of the least corrupt countries in the world according to Transparency International, you would probably have to get a business license and pay some registration fees. However, if you lived in Uzbekistan (one of the most corrupt countries in the world), you would not only have to get licenses and pay registration fees but also pay bribes to officials to get those licenses. Every office you went into would have officials who demanded to be paid off. That would make it more difficult to open a business and much less profitable because you would be paying all of those bribes.

So how might democracy fix that problem? Corruption in democratic countries tends to be different. In an autocratic country, the leaders only have to worry about keeping their supporters happy. That generally means a few business elites and the military. Thus, a dictator can allow and engage in corruption just so long as it doesn't hurt those supporters (the Mubarak regime in Egypt comes again to mind). Democratic leaders must keep their supporters happy, too, but they need to keep a lot more people happy—it's not just elites and the military, it's the voters and you need a lot of happy voters to stay in office. The best way to keep voters happy is "peace and prosperity." Although wars can boost a leader's popularity, it's generally true that staying out of a war and having a healthy economy is the best way to be reelected. Thus, democratic governments can be corrupt as long as the corruption doesn't hurt the economy. Authoritarian leaders can be corrupt in any way that doesn't hurt their elite supporters. Consequently, the economies in corrupt democracies grow as fast as non-corrupt states, while the economies in corrupt authoritarian countries tend to be stagnant.[14]

What can we conclude from these contradictory findings about democracy and economic growth? First, democracy does not directly help or hurt economic growth because it has characteristics that can be both positive and negative for economic development. Second, democracy does have several indirect benefits for an economy. Longer, healthy life, more education, and a way to wash away the negative effects corruption has on an economy can all be attributed to the liberal form of government.

10-5 INTERNATIONAL ORGANIZATIONS AND DEVELOPMENT

So far we have discussed how countries can use policies to influence how they develop their economies and how other states—through MNCs—can also affect a country's development. As we know from Chapter 8, there are other actors in the international system who play a key role in the economies of both developed and developing states. Let's now turn to a discussion of these different organizations and how they affect the developing world. While many organizations play a role in international development, we will discuss the four most important here.

10-5a The International Monetary Fund and the World Bank

The first two organizations to discuss are part of the Bretton Woods system and are sometimes called **Bretton Woods organizations**. As we explained in Chapter 8, the International Monetary Fund or IMF was created to monitor the system of **pegged exchange rates** (in which other countries' currencies were pegged to the value of the U.S. dollar, which was fixed at $35 per ounce of gold) and to provide countries with short-term loans to help with **balance-of-payments** problems. Because the United States ended the pegged exchange rate system in 1971, the IMF's primary role now is to deal with this second issue: balance-of-payments problems. This role makes

Bretton Woods organizations the organizations created at the Bretton Woods conference. They include the World Bank, IMF, and later the GATT.

pegged exchange rates foreign currency exchange rates that are fixed or "pegged" by government officials against another currency or standard (e.g., gold) rather than freely traded in a market setting.

balance-of-payments a country's balance between exports, imports, and debt. If exports are too low and cannot support the country's debt, there is an economic crisis.

the IMF the main international organization responsible for finance and debt. Balance-of-payments problems are created when a country cannot pay its external debt held by other countries or banks in other countries. This would be very similar to when people cannot pay their minimum payments on their credit cards and other loans. For an individual, bankruptcy is often the option, but not for sovereign countries.

When a state cannot make payments on its debt, the IMF can step in and provide a short-term loan to help the country restructure its debt and budget. Referred to as structural adjustment loans, the loans are conditional on specific policies that the country must adopt, often including reducing its spending. Typically, spending cuts involve social spending and food and fuel subsidies. That is, the IMF requires that the government cut back spending on public education, health services, and support for the poor (including food and fuel subsidies). As a result of these policies, the IMF is not terribly popular in developing countries when it has to step in to keep their government from going bankrupt. While Greece is not a developing country, its economic problems have been so severe that both the IMF and the EU have provided loans to keep it from going bankrupt. The Greek government has also raised taxes and imposed many cuts to its budget, leading to an extreme backlash from the population—including demonstrations and a few riots. In such cases, it is an international organization that is causing great turmoil within another country. What does that mean for a country's security? Imagine you are the leader of a small, developing country, and you are forced to make severe cuts to your budget—including those that affect the provision of basic services such as law enforcement, education, and other social services. How would you react?

The success of the IMF is mixed. Some countries are able to pull out of their debt crisis and go on to build their economies. However, some countries cannot break the cycle of debt crises, and as a result, they and their people suffer. Often called HIPCs (pronounced HIP-see for Highly Indebted Poor Countries), these states do not have a strong enough economy to pay back their loans, and so they continue to cycle back and forth from spending cuts and new loans from either private banks or the IMF. Over the past decade, a movement has developed to provide debt forgiveness for these particular countries in order to break this cycle and give them a better chance toward progress.

The other major component of the Bretton Woods system relevant here is the World Bank. The World Bank is actually a group of five organizations that provide loans to countries for the purpose of

Women in International Development

One of the issues long ignored by policymakers concerned with development was the status of women and the effect development had on them. Even though women comprise approximately 50 percent of the world's population, they do not have equal status in most countries, and in undeveloped countries, their status and rights in society typically range from bad to abysmal.

According to all the theories of economic growth we have discussed, a growing, developing society should benefit men and women. In fact, there is nothing in ISI, socialism, export-led growth, or the Washington Consensus that would suggest that men should benefit more from development compared to women. If these theories are correct in the way they treat men and women equally, then why aren't women doing better in developing countries?

Women tend to work in either unpaid jobs or in the informal sector of the economy. In poorer countries, women are almost completely responsible for the work of raising children and feeding the family. This work is unpaid and thus women would not benefit from a growing economy unless the man of the house was to benefit from the economy. Further, development policies that follow the Washington Consensus or export-led growth tend to cut government spending, and the first items to be cut are social spending, which hurts women even if the economy benefits. For example, if the government spends less on supplying drinkable water, then it falls on women to walk farther to get the water.

When women work outside the home in poorer countries, it is often in jobs such as food service, cleaning, and prostitution. The value of these jobs does not rise at the same rate as male-dominated jobs in agricultural exports and especially industry. Women working as maids, cooks, and prostitutes are not part of a growing economy.

A cruel and ironic problem is that when women do well, so does the economy. States that ignore the status of women actually hurt their own economies. Thus, it is best

for an economy if development policies pay special attention to making women part of the workforce.

One particularly successful way this goal has been accomplished is through microcredit. In its modern form, Muhammad Yunus, a Bangladeshi economist, developed microcredit as a way to alleviate rural poverty in his country. The idea behind microcredit is simple—give small, often short-term loans to poor entrepreneurs so that they can start their own business. Using his own money at first, Yunus quickly found that the recipients of microloans not only lifted themselves out of poverty but they also paid the loans back at a very high rate. What does this have to do with women? Approximately three-quarters of all microloans today go to women, largely because they are more successful and more likely to pay the loans back.

Overall, microcredit has been very successful, so much so that larger banks are getting involved in an effort to capitalize on the success of the loans. There are some pitfalls, however, to this increasingly popular form of development aid. Some studies show that larger loans to women are sometimes taken by their male relatives, thereby perpetuating the subservient role of women in these developing countries. Additionally, microcredit is based on capitalist values, which can maintain and extend inequality in developing countries. The loans help some, but not all. As such, only a few are raised up out of poverty, while many others are left behind.

Even with these drawbacks, microcredit continues to be an effective way to enhance the lives and security of women as well as help their economy develop, so long as the purpose of the loans are carefully considered in each case and high-profit margins are not the primary motivation of the lender.

1. What other policies might be helpful in lifting women up to an equal status in developing countries?

2. Should development policies focus on women or simply wait until the country has developed to try to equalize their status?

3. As countries elect more women leaders, will more attention be paid to this important part of the economy?

development projects. Originally called the **International Bank for Reconstruction and Development** because it was aimed at providing loans to Europe and Asia for reconstruction after World War II, the World Bank now aims at providing loans to poorer

International Bank for Reconstruction and Development the original organization of the World Bank designed to promote reconstruction, especially in Europe after World War II.

countries for economic development. These loans fund projects such as port facilities to increase the shipping capacity of a country, hydroelectric dams to provide electricity to cities in developing countries, and so on.

Like the IMF, the World Bank has had varying levels of success in its development grants. Too often, the development projects do not match the needs of the country or simply try to bring a very undeveloped economy into the modern world economy without considering the possible negative side effects. In one perverse case, the World Bank helped Brazil develop steel smelting capacity. When the price of steel fell and that of coal (used in the process) rose, however, the Brazilians couldn't profitably produce steel and pay back the World Bank. So they began cutting down their rain forests to make charcoal for the smelting process. Thus, the World Bank indirectly contributed to deforestation. Certainly not all of the bank's policies have gone awry, but because it focuses so strongly on liberal reforms, it historically has made some mistakes that hurt both the environment and people.

Both the IMF and World Bank get their funding from dues paid by member states. The largest and wealthiest countries pay the most, but they also have the most control in the organization. As we discussed in Chapter 7, both organizations have weighted voting, which means that the countries that contribute the greatest amount of loan capital to these institutions also have the most votes in the organizations. For years if the United States opposed a loan, it had enough weighted votes by itself to stop the loan from going forward. While that is less true now, it still means that several very wealthy states can veto loan proposals if they choose to do so. Finally, the IMF president has traditionally been from Europe and the World Bank president from the United States. Thus, the developed world maintains a great deal of influence in—if not control over—the organizations.

The World Bank, International Monetary Fund, and World Trade Organization | These three groups are very powerful actors in the world economy, but they don't answer to the people. Is this "democratic deficit" a problem? Can you imagine how you would react if one of their policies affected you and your country and you couldn't do anything about it?

Debt Forgiveness

One of the defining characteristics of the modern world economy is the accumulation of debt by many states. Indeed, there are many states that struggle with extremely high debt loads. Officially, this means the debt is in excess of 200 percent of their exports. To put that in the perspective of personal finance, it would mean that your debt is 200 percent greater than your income. While some mortgages can exceed this amount, imagine having a monthly credit card bill debt that is three times as high as your monthly income! In many of the poorest countries of the world, this is the reality. In fact, in some, it is even worse: the interest on their accumulated debt alone exceeds their government revenues. Imagine if the *minimum* monthly payment on your credit card was greater than your monthly income! In poor countries, such a high debt load is considered unsustainable and perpetuates the extreme poverty in the country. As a result, one solution to this problem that has really emerged in the last decade or two is debt relief.

Although debt relief has a long history dating back to **war reparations** in World War I, more recent policies aimed toward alleviating the seemingly never-ending cycle of extreme poverty developed in the 1990s. Starting with religious organizations around the world as well as several NGOs, the movement was called Jubilee 2000, after the Catholic Church's celebration of the year 2000. The truly grass roots movement gathered activists from many different countries and walks of life and aimed to eliminate $90 billion in debt for the poorest countries in the world. This initiative eventually became known as the "Highly Indebted Poor Countries (HIPCs) initiative."

In 1998, large, peaceful protests were held in Birmingham, UK during the G8 Summit. British Prime Minister Tony Blair took particular note, and began pushing the issue of the HIPCs in the UK and with the other G8 countries. Around the same time, the World Bank and IMF launched an initiative to provide aid to the HIPCs. The aid was aimed at reducing the debt load so that the countries could begin to develop and subsequently service the remaining debt. Table 10-3 shows the most current list of HIPC countries that are funded by the World Bank and those under consideration. It is worthy to note that most of the countries in the list are in Sub-Saharan Africa.

The efforts to attain complete debt relief failed, not surprisingly since that would mean many wealthy

TABLE 10-3	HIPC DEBT RELIEF BY THE WORLD BANK
Funded	
Afghanistan	Madagascar
Benin	Malawi
Burkina Faso	Mali
Burundi	Mauritania
Cameroon	Mozambique
Central African Republic	Nicaragua
Chad	Níger
Comoros	Plurinational State of Bolivia
Côte d'Ivoire	Republic of Congo
Democratic Republic of Congo	Rwanda
Ethiopia	São Tomé Príncipe
Ghana	Senegal
Guinea	Sierra Leone
Guinea-Bissau	Tanzania
Guyana	The Gambia
Haiti	Togo
Honduras	Uganda
Liberia	Zambia
Under Consideration	
Eritrea	Sudan
Somalia	

Source: World Bank, "Heavily Indebted Poor Countries," *Economic Policy and Debt,* 2012, http://web.worldbank.org/WBSITE/EXTERNAL/TOPICS/EXTDEBTDEPT/0,,contentMDK: 20260049~menuPK:64166739~pagePK:64166689~piPK:64166646~theSitePK:469043,00 .html.

countries and commercial banks would lose a tremendous amount of money. Jubilee 2000 slowly disappeared, as did its spin-off organizations. However, the activists successfully brought the issue to the table and were able to influence the foreign policy of G8 countries and the largest international financial organizations in the world.

There are, of course, critics of debt relief, and not just from the banks that hold the debt. Some argue that the relief will not reach the poor and ultimately not lead to poverty reduction. These critics argue, money should be spent directly on the poor rather than the elites in government. Another criticism is that by waiving a country's debt, there is no reason for the HIPC not to

war reparations payments from one country—usually the loser of a conflict—to compensate the victor's cost in money, lives, and property.

take out more loans in the future and spend unwisely. Further, debt relief programs create an incentive for developing countries to manage their debt poorly because, if they do, they may be given debt relief. These criticisms are not without merit, but that still leaves the question of what to do with countries that cannot pay off their debt, ever.

1. Who do you think is right: the HIPC relief advocates or their critics?

2. How might we best help both the indebted governments and the poor people in those countries?

3. Are there other movements like Jubilee 2000 that you can think of that made a big impact in the way governments and organizations work?

10-5b The World Trade Organization

We already discussed the World Trade Organization (WTO) in some detail in Chapters 7 and 8, but it is important to mention again here because of the role it plays in promoting free trade and the links between trade and development. Recall that the Asian Tigers were successful because they promoted exports, making their economies reliant on trade for development. Figure 10-2 shows how dependent some countries are on trade. Notice how the United States is not particularly dependent, even though it's the biggest trader in the world. Countries like South Korea, however, are very dependent. Because the WTO is the main governing body for international trade, it can have a powerful effect on a country's development.

The voting structure in the WTO is one-country-one-vote, just like the UN General Assembly and dramatically different from the World Bank or IMF. However, the developed states still have control of the WTO's agenda. Thus, the issues that come up for discussion and vote are determined by the wealthiest countries. As a result, the rich states maintain significant control over the policies that the WTO adopts.

10-5c The United Nations

The last organization to discuss is probably the most well known, though not necessarily because of its role in development. The United Nations has many functions and acts as an umbrella organization in many ways. It is actually not as involved directly

FIGURE 10-2 TRADE AS A PERCENTAGE OF GDP RATIO FROM 10 COUNTRIES FOR 2012

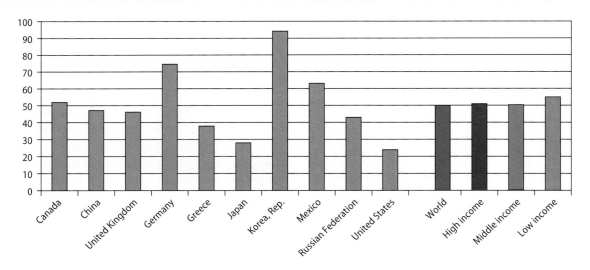

Source: Data from World Bank.

with development and takes a backseat to many of these other organizations. Probably the most important role the UN plays in development is as a forum for all nations to discuss and build solutions to development issues. Because the UN represents all nations, it provides an open forum in which the poor countries can bring their issues to the table and discuss them with the wealthier states. That clearly is difficult if not impossible in the World Bank, IMF, and even the WTO. While these issues can also be addressed in the other organizations, the UN is more open to the developing states. That does limit its power, as developed states tend to put most of their efforts and funds into the IMF and World Bank because they have greater control of those organizations. However, the UN's broad mandate allows it to build a larger consensus.

The best example of this was the negotiations that led to the Millennium Development Goals (MDG). The MDG are eight goals that address human security broadly through an effort to reduce poverty, discrimination, and disease, and boost education and environmental sustainability. The MDG set 2015 as the year to attain these goals. The progress toward them is very uneven, with some countries moving forward with development and others far less so. What the MDG has accomplished is to place these issues on the agenda of all countries so that even when 2015 arrives and the goals have not been achieved, the world is working toward providing a minimal and sustainable life for all people.

The second area where the UN influences development is indirect but extremely important: health. The World Health Organization (WHO), a specialized agency of the UN, is responsible for responding to world health problems. Perhaps no problem was more horrible and deadly as smallpox. The disease killed between 200 and 300 million people in the twentieth century.[15] By 1979, the WHO had exterminated the virus causing smallpox through a long campaign of vaccinations around the world. Significant improvements have been made in reducing the death tolls of HIV/AIDS, as well. While not always so successful, WHO responds to epidemics and outbreaks, limiting their impact and spread around the world or even within a country. Successes such as this reduce the strain diseases place on a country and thus its economy.

CONCLUSION

We said toward the beginning of this chapter that there was no surefire way to develop an economy, and as you can see from the many failures and few successes, it's true. As the Great Recession has shown, even rich countries have trouble understanding how to put people to work in the short term. National economies are very complex layers of local, regional, national, and international interactions. Today's rich countries got rich through centuries of trial-and-error approaches, but the poor countries of today don't want to wait centuries to improve their people's lives and their own security. When it comes to improving human security, there is need for haste. Thus, many different means of improving the economies of poor countries have been tried and many others surely will be tried in the years to come.

STUDY TOOLS 10

LOCATED AT BACK OF THE BOOK:
☐ Rip out Chapter in Review card

LOCATED ON COURSEMATE:
Use the CourseMate access card that came with this book or visit CengageBrain.com for more review materials:
☐ Review Key Terms Flash Cards (Print or Online)
☐ Download Chapter Summaries for on-the-go review

☐ Complete Practice Quizzes to prepare for the test
☐ Walk through a Simulation, Animated Learning Module, and Interactive Maps and Timelines to master concepts
☐ Complete Crossword Puzzle to review key terms
☐ Watch the videos for real-world application of this chapter's content
☐ Visit IR NewsWatch to learn about the latest current events as you prepare for class discussions and papers.

THINK ABOUT THIS CLOSING THE GAP BETWEEN RICH AND POOR

The gap between the haves and the have-nots in world politics is large and growing, and it impacts almost every aspect of economic security, as well as important features of international and human security. But achieving development—improving conditions and closing the gap between rich and poor—has been elusive for the players in world politics. Some observers, including economics professor William Easterly in his 2006 book *The White Man's Burden: Why the West's Efforts to Aid the Rest Have Done So Much Harm and So Little Good*, have argued that aid from the developed world has been ineffective at best, and part of the problem at worst. Others, such as economist Jeffrey Sachs, whose work includes *The End of Poverty* (2005), argue that assistance from the developed "is needed and can be highly successful." What do you think?

William Easterly

Bloomberg/Getty Images

TED ALJIBE/AFP/Getty Images

Jeffrey Sachs

Is aid from the developed world the answer to poverty in the developing world?

REVIEW QUESTIONS

1. What structural factors lead a country to be rich or poor?

2. How unequal is the development in the world— both between countries and within countries?

3. What strategies do countries follow to develop their economies?

4. How do international organizations affect development?

5. If democracy doesn't have a direct effect on an economy, does it play any role at all?

FOR MORE INFORMATION . . .

For more on:

The Big Mac Index, "The Big Mac Index," *The Economist*, http://www.economist.com/blogs/dailychart/2011/07/big-mac-index.

Microcredit and Muhammad Yunus, *Grameen Bank: Bank for the Poor*, http://www.grameen-info.org.

Colonies and development, Acemoglu, Daron and James A. Robinson. *Why Nations Fail: The Origins of Power, Prosperity, and Poverty*. New York: Crown Business, 2012.

Collier, Paul. *The Bottom Billion: Why the Poorest Countries Are Failing and What Can Be Done About It*. New York: Oxford University Press, 2008.

Krieckhaus, Jonathan. *Dictating Development*. Pittsburgh: Pittsburgh University Press, 2006.

World development data, The World Bank, *World Development Indicators*, http://www.google.com/publicdata/explore?ds=d5bncppjof8f9_.

11 | Human Rights:
Protecting the Most Basic Security

HUMAN RIGHTS IN NIGERIA: WHO PROTECTS THE PEOPLE?

With 177 million people, Nigeria is the largest country in Africa and the seventh largest in the world. Economically, the country has a lot going for it. According to the *CIA World Factbook*, its 2013 estimated gross domestic product (GDP) of $478 billion places it thirty-first in the world, and its annual economic growth rate is substantially larger than the annual growth rate of its population (6.2 percent versus 2.47 percent, respectively). The largest single component of its economy is oil and gas production, its crude oil exports rank fifth in the world, and overall the country's economy is nicely balanced between industry, agriculture, and services. One would think that the future looks good for Nigerians.

Yet appearances deceive. The military junta that ruled until 1999 allowed corruption to flourish to the point where it is now systemic in nature. Enterprises controlled by the regime dominated the industries that brought in the most income, and thus over time state revenues increasingly flowed into private pockets. For example, of $30 billion in oil income specifically earmarked for the desperately poor Niger River delta region, $22 billion disappeared and cannot be accounted for.[1] In short, the rich got richer and the poor got poorer. The advent of civilian rule did not produce many improvements for rank-and-file Nigerians. By 2010, 70 percent of the population lived below the poverty line. By 2010, the largest country in Africa ranked sixty-eighth in the world in electricity generated. At this writing, Nigerians ranked number 212 in the world in life expectancy (at only 53 years)! In 2012, Nigerians led the world in HIV/AIDS-related deaths and suffered from other preventable diseases as well (see more on Nigeria in chapter 10 on development and world politics).

Not only have Nigerians been unable to depend on the government to make meaningful progress in terms of the staggering poverty and dire medical threats they face, but neither can they expect the regime to protect them from violence. Over 250 different ethnic groups are found in Nigeria, and many find reasons to prey on each other. These domestic conflicts are based on many things: economic disputes (pitting Nigerians against foreign oil corporations or each other), tribal rivalries that date back over time, and increasing religious tensions (massacres between the 50 percent of the population that is Muslim and the 40 percent that is Christian). When such violence erupts, citizens who call upon the government for protection are almost as likely to be attacked by the military or imprisoned by the police as they are to be protected from their erstwhile attackers. The result is that domestic violence and repression by government security forces have resulted in the deaths of thousands of civilians in Nigeria in recent years. For all these reasons, Nigeria is quietly becoming one of the most dangerous places to live in the world.

This case raises interesting questions, such as:

1. Given its means, why hasn't Nigeria's government provided its citizens better economic, medical, and physical security?

2. Will civilian governments in the future fare any better in this regard than the repressive, military-based governments of the past?

3. Is Nigeria a unique case, or is it representative of the poor quality of life many routinely experience around the world?

Security forces gather at the scene of a bombing in the Nigerian capital of Abuja | Why can't the Nigerian government protect its citizens from violence?

INTRODUCTION: REDEFINING SOVEREIGNTY FROM PROTECTING BORDERS TO PROTECTING PEOPLE

The idea that the people have rights that deserve protection is not new. Ancient Greeks and Hebrews established a tradition of moral philosophy, and this emphasis on the rights of individuals was then well reflected in later Christian thought and actions of the early current era. Due to the moral norms established in Europe by the Catholic Church and writers such as Saint Augustine, it was possible in 1215 for King John of England to be forced by his noblemen to sign the **Magna Carta**, which specified a series of rights due to freemen. Most notably, the document included the idea that a person could not be imprisoned without cause sanctioned by law or the judgment of one's peers. Since that time, the rights people deserve—just because they are human beings—have evolved and grown in both number and type.

 11-1 # THE EVOLUTION OF HUMAN RIGHTS

Over time, three major types of human rights have evolved due to changing events and political circumstances. These include individual rights, societal rights, and group rights. Let's discuss each in turn.

11-1a Individual Rights

As indicated previously, human rights began as an insistence that monarchs could not do whatever they wished, whenever they wished. By the time of the English Enlightenment, writers like John Locke had extended the basic argument made by religious writers such as Saint Thomas Aquinas—that people had some rights that could not be

> **Magna Carta** the "Great Charter" signed by King John of England in 1215 (and reaffirmed in 1297 by King Edward I), which noted that freemen had certain rights that the monarch could not take away, including the right not to be imprisoned without legal justification or a judgment by one's peers.

JULIA:
**VIOLENT PIMP
NO FREEDOM
30 MEN A DAY
INDEBTED
ENSLAVED**

250,000 Slaves exist in North America,
27 Million worldwide.

THE SALVATION ARMY

thetruthisntsexy.ca

Laurent Hamels/PhotoAlto Agency RF Collections/Getty Images

The effort to stop criminal assaults | Why do some argue that prostitution is a victimless crime?

taken away by the government—to make the broader point that governments existed based only on the consent of the governed. By the late eighteenth century, many in Europe and North America had embraced the ideas that government should be limited to the powers granted to it by its citizens and that the citizens possessed natural rights. Such ideas shaped the justifications of both the American and French Revolutions and were incorporated into the U.S. Declaration of Independence (1776), the French Declaration of the Rights of Man (1789), and the U.S. Constitution's Bill of Rights (1791). Because they led the way, these individual rights are now referred to as **first-generation human rights**.

These first-generation individual rights emphasized political and civil rights. As such, they prescribe the rights to freedom of speech, freedom of assembly, freedom of religion, freedom of the press, the right to due process of law, and so on. They also often included the economic right to property, but what that actually meant varied by who was asked. For most people, it initially meant tangible things like real estate. Remember, however, that the Magna Carta specified the rights due to "freemen." Obviously, not all people

were equal under the law. Some were not free, as slavery existed almost everywhere in the world. Slaves were considered property to be bought and sold against their will, and those willing to be indentured servants could sell their services for an agreed-upon period of time. However, attitudes changed over time, particularly as Christianity expanded in the Western world and Christian culture precluded Christians from owning other Christians. Slavery began to be outlawed by various Western states and principalities across the eighteenth and nineteenth centuries.

Although now outlawed virtually everywhere, slavery continues to exist informally in many places, often in the form of indentured immigrants or servants or those held captive by the sex trade. For example, as the photo indicates, sexual slavery traps millions of people around the world. Girls, boys, women, and men can be the victims, and regions such as Southeast Asia, Eastern Europe, Central America, and the Middle East are particularly notorious for human trafficking rings. Films such as *Taken* (2008), *The Whistleblower* (2010), and *Not My Life* (2011) provide graphic depictions of this practice.

As the term "freemen" also suggests, political rights generally did not apply to women as much as to men, as men initially held most of the political rights in society. Still, the idea of "women's rights" is not new. The Quran articulated the idea that women had specific rights, medieval women had some rights to own property and

first-generation human rights (individual rights)
rights that individuals have simply because they are human beings and which are not to be violated by governments.

participate in municipal government in parts of Europe, and feminists like Abigail Adams and Mary Wollstonecraft advocated for women's rights during the time of the American and French Revolutions. However, women generally did not achieve full political rights in most developed countries until the early twentieth century. In many developing countries, they still lack equal rights in society and under the law. We discuss this more later in the chapter.

11-1b Societal Rights

The emphasis on individual rights came under significant attack by intellectuals speaking on behalf of the working class in nineteenth-century Europe. While the industrial revolution produced a large working class, capitalism practiced without any societal protections often transformed the working class into what would now be called the working poor. In Britain, Karl Marx wrote that these impoverished working classes should rise up in revolution against their oppressors, while democratic socialists embraced the desire for political change through nonviolent means to empower the working class—thus giving rise to the British Labour Party. These critics and reformers were united by the idea that "the people" deserved certain material and economic rights, not just individual civil and political rights. These so-called **second-generation human rights** included societal rights such as the rights to shelter, employment, education, and health care.

More attention was placed on these rights in the early to mid-twentieth century. The establishment of a communist regime in Russia in 1917 gave birth to the new Soviet Union, and it proclaimed itself to be a "worker's paradise." Everyone was guaranteed food, shelter, and employment. When the Great Depression of the 1930s arrived, those guarantees made communism look pretty attractive compared to capitalism in other countries. The socialist initiatives seen in Europe became more widespread, and the U.S. government also undertook large-scale public employment and social security programs to meet growing societal needs. Thus, as suggested in Chapter 4, initiatives in the United States such as Social Security, Medicare, and Medicaid that were once decried as "radical" or "the first steps on the slippery slope to socialism" now are widely accepted and embraced programs.

However, such societal or "material" human rights—whether guarantees of minimum levels of nutrition, shelter, health care, education, or employment—cost a significant amount of money. Such costs pose challenges, even for developed countries. In recent years Greece required massive bailouts by wealthier members of the EU to avoid falling into bankruptcy, in part because the Greek economy could not support the costs of existing social programs promised by the government to its citizens. It was as if Greece was living on its credit cards and could no longer make the minimum monthly payments. If these costs are challenging for some members of the EU such as Greece (or Portugal or Ireland or Italy or Spain), think how difficult it must be for extremely poor countries like Haiti, Democratic Congo, Nepal, or Zimbabwe to guarantee any minimal levels of societal human rights to their citizens! In most of these countries, expectations for basic second-generation human rights cannot be met or even dreamed about.

Furthermore, the Arab Spring of 2011–2012 shows what can happen when expected levels of societal human rights are not met for most people while elites seem to live very well. In both Tunisia and Egypt, there was widespread unemployment even among college graduates, yet the families of leaders such as Ben Ali of Tunisia, Mubarak of Egypt, and Gaddafi of Libya were amassing considerable personal wealth. Corruption by governmental elites may be harder for the public to accept when basic societal rights have not been met. As we noted in Chapter 5, revolutions often start over such societal disparities! Beyond the problem of meeting societal needs, some in society face additional challenges. We turn to group rights next.

11-1c Group Rights

The third major development in the evolution of human rights was sparked by the events of the Holocaust in World War II. Persecution of unpopular minority groups within society was nothing new, but the genocide conducted against Jews, Roma (or Gypsy) peoples, and homosexuals by the Nazi regime in Germany shocked many around the world once the truth was learned. Quickly the notion arose that regimes should not be free to persecute oppressed or unpopular groups simply because the actions happened within their national borders. Thus **third-generation human rights** sought to protect unpopular or minority groups from the oppression of the majority in society.

second-generation human rights (societal rights) material and economic rights that apply society-wide, such as the rights to education, employment, shelter, health care, and so on.

third-generation human rights (group rights) rights needed to protect unpopular or minority groups from the oppression of the majority.

Given the events of World War II, the initial concern was to protect those facing oppression based on race, ethnicity, or religion. That effort led to struggles for equal rights by a number of racial minority groups in the United States and many other countries. An important threshold was surpassed in the early 1990s when arguably the most overtly racist regime, the Afrikaner regime in the Republic of South Africa, abolished apartheid, its official policy of apportioning political, economic, and civil rights based on one's skin color.

However, oppression based on ethnicity or religion is harder to eradicate. Such oppression continues in many states and involves many groups. Ethnic struggles have beset Europe in recent years, whether between Serbs, Kosovars, Croats, and Bosnians in the former Yugoslavia, France's deportations of Roma peoples back to Romania and Bulgaria, or the request by pro-Russian separatists in eastern Ukraine for local Jews to "register" as such. Religious intolerance is also fairly widespread in the international system. Violence is often directed at minority religious or spiritual groups; depending on the location they could be Christians, Muslims (Sunni or Shi'a), Baha'i, Hindus, Falun Gong, or others.

Other groups are the victims of discrimination and violence, as well. In most societies in the world, women's rights are more limited and poorly protected than those of men. For example, even in developed countries such as those in Europe and North America, women do not enjoy the same economic opportunities as men and face a variety of forms of subtle and not-so-subtle discrimination. Worse still, in many locales in the Middle East and southwest Asia, women face restrictions that most reading this book would find appalling. They are often the subject of arranged marriages; in practice they often have limited legal rights compared to men; in some cases they cannot travel outside the home without a male relative accompanying them; restrictions are often placed on their ability to be in the company of men not part of their immediate family unit; and so on. In Saudi Arabia, it's even illegal for them to drive cars! These restrictions are based on religious interpretations, traditional customs, or both.

For example, Islam calls upon its followers to dress modestly. However, for women that can range from wearing scarves (called *hijabs*) that cover their hair in more liberal Islamic societies (such as Morocco or Kuwait) to *burkas* or *chadris* in more conservative societies (like Afghanistan) that cover their entire body head-to-toe and leave only a mesh through which to see. Violation of these rules can result in punishments up to and including public execution, which happened in Iran during the 1980s.

These clothing issues are not limited to the Middle East and southwest Asia. In 2011, a new law went into

A French woman arrested for wearing a veil in public | Should group identity outweigh individual and religious liberties? How would you feel if your government said you couldn't wear shorts, jeans, or simple t-shirts?

Ian Langsdon/EPA/Landov

force in France that banned the wearing of any scarves or veils that cover the face. Thus, Islamic women who wear the *niqab*—a veil covering the face below the eyes—or the burka can be fined, as can their husbands if their husbands mandated such attire. The official justification of the new law is public safety related; government-issued photo IDs mean nothing if the face cannot be seen. Of course, some Islamic women prefer to dress in this way, as the woman in the accompanying photo shows.

Harm against women is also widespread. Sometimes it is culturally reinforced. In many traditional societies, women are often denied access to education, as schooling is seen as unnecessary to women's roles as wives, mothers, and homemakers. Where women are expected to move into the home of their husband, they may face abuse from their mothers-in-law. In places such as India, wives sometimes face such physical and emotional abuse from their husband's family that they commit suicide, even to the extreme of setting themselves on fire with cooking oil. In some societies, women who stray from socially accepted sexual roles face being murdered by their husbands, fathers, or brothers in what are called honor-killings, and the perpetrators are typically not punished. Finally, an estimated 70 million girls and women from Africa and southwest Asia have experienced **female genital mutilation** (sometimes referred to as *female circumcision*) as a societal ritual marking one's transition to womanhood. The UN has condemned this practice as a form of child abuse.

Women are also the targets of even more violent behaviors, as well. Women worldwide face being sold as indentured servants, workers in the sex trades, or sexual slaves by brokers or their own family members, and violence is routinely used to keep them in line. In many locales, unaccompanied women are targets for sexual predators. For example, in 2011, former U.S. Peace Corps volunteers testified before Congress that the Peace Corps tried to cover up the frequency with which its female volunteers have been raped while on duty abroad, and that same year female journalists began more openly talking about the number of times they faced sexual assaults while reporting from other countries.

However, the worst violence against women may come during civil wars, insurgencies, or other instances of intrastate wars. In such circumstances, out-of-control troops rape and kill women either because they can, as part of a deliberate strategy to punish or shame one's enemies, or as a means to bond conscripted soldiers to their unit or militia.[2] For example, during the civil war in Bosnia, Muslim women were captured, raped, and sent back to their homes only to be ostracized or worse by their own families because of the rape. For a graphic, compelling story about these "rape camps," check out the 1998 movie *The Savior*. Even when women and girls escape the immediate violence of civil war, they are not necessarily safe, though. Often, in refugee camps set up to provide care for people fleeing violence, women face similar abuse. For example, in 2014 numerous reports indicated that women and children in refugee camps set up to care for those fleeing civil war in Syria faced horrible abuse as men from neighboring states used the camps for sexual exploitation and sex trafficking.

Not surprisingly, in recent years, women have become the focus of considerable human rights activity in the global arena. The United Nations has historically included a focus on the needs of women, both in terms of eliminating overt discrimination and identifying ways to empower women in their local societies. Likewise, the needs of children, particularly those who are in circumstances where they are powerless to help themselves, have historically been an important and highly visible focus of the UN. Children face exploitation as well when they are denied access to education, are forced to work

long hours for little or no pay, are conscripted into militias and are forced to kill or be killed, or are bought and sold like commodities. We will have more to say later in the chapter about UN efforts on behalf of the needs of women and children.

A third-generation human rights example that has not yet been as well addressed by the global community concerns the rights of lesbians, gays, bisexuals, and transgendered individuals. Generally, more developed states tend to be more tolerant regarding one's sexual orientation, but in numerous places in Africa, Asia, and the Middle East, homosexuality is not just frowned upon, it is illegal. In some Islamic societies, homosexuality is punishable by death! Even where homosexuality is not illegal, most societies still discriminate against same-sex couples having marriage rights or legal rights as families—such as rights to adopt children or to be considered "next-of-kin" during health crises. In fact, only 13 countries legally recognize gay marriage while some others permit civil unions of some sort. That's less than 20 percent of the countries in the world. To the extent that societies often become generally more liberal over time, we can expect more tensions between the lesbian, gay, bisexual, and transgendered community and more conservative elements within those societies.

As you might guess, efforts to enumerate and enforce such group rights are controversial. Some in developing countries argue that minority group rights are counter to their own cultural values that prioritize the rights of the majority. Thus, they raise the issue of **cultural relativism**; are third-generation rights really universal or are they an expression of Western values that are imposed on non-Western societies? A number of Asian leaders, particularly those in Malaysia and Singapore, have raised this issue over time, arguing essentially that societal harmony and order are higher priorities in Asian culture than the

---

honor-killings the murders of girls or women by their husbands, fathers, brothers, etc., when they are thought to have violated socially acceptable sexually based roles. By killing the offender, the males in the family seek to restore the family's honor and are typically not prosecuted for their crimes.

female genital mutilation the cutting away of part of the external genitalia, based on the belief that, by reducing sexual pleasure, women will remain chaste until married and faithful to their husbands thereafter. Some societies also believe this is a religious requirement for women to behave modestly or may increase fertility.

cultural relativism the idea that human rights are not truly universal and that different cultures have different systems of rights. This term particularly comes into play when non-Western societies argue that international human rights standards have a Western bias and do not reflect non-Western values.

Argentinian President Cristina Fernandez (center) celebrates Argentina becoming the first Latin American state to legalize gay marriage | Should majoritarian religious beliefs outweigh the civil rights of same-sex couples? What about other minority groups?

rights of individuals or minority groups. What do you think? Are human rights universal, or do they vary from culture to culture?

However, it would be difficult to argue that the worst-case example of third-generation human rights is not a universal concern, and that is the problem of genocide—the killing of an entire group of people because of who they are. While the Treaties of Westphalia included an expectation that sovereigns would respect the religious rights of their citizens, the Holocaust showed that unpopular minorities still faced the threat of extinction from their own governments. Thus, Raphael Lemkin, a Jewish legal expert who fled Poland after the Germans invaded in 1939, created a new word in his 1944 book *Axis Rule in Occupied Europe* by combining the Greek word "genos" (for race or tribe) and the Latin word "cide" (for killing). After the war, Lemkin successfully pressed to get the term "genocide" accepted in international law, which it was in the 1948 Convention on Genocide. He spent the rest of his life pressing states to accept the Convention on Genocide, thereby helping to create the precedent that such horrific crimes could not be ignored simply because they were done by the state within its own borders.

responsibility to protect (R2P) the norm that states have a responsibility to protect their citizens from avoidable harm, and if they cannot or will not do so, the international community has a responsibility to intervene to do so.

While the term may be of relatively recent origin, the practice of genocide may be as old as humanity. Although use of the term is highly controversial, a number of governmental or societal campaigns in the last century have been considered by many to be genocidal in nature, and unfortunately the list is long. Candidates for the genocide label over just the past 100 years are listed in Table 11-1. The total number of dead over the last 100 years from such genocidal campaigns has been estimated in excess of at least 100 million people.

Such complex interactions of national and tribal groups in just one area are illustrated in Revenge of Geography: Turmoil in the African Great Lakes Region.

Both the recurrence of genocides and long-term conflicts such as the one between Hutus and Tutsis demonstrate that in the late twentieth and early twenty-first centuries, unpopular groups inside a state were increasingly likely to be the targets of violence, either by other groups within the state or by the state itself. Based on this new security challenge, an international norm arose that stressed that states had "a responsibility to protect their own citizens from avoidable catastrophe, but that when they are unwilling or unable to do so, that responsibility must be borne by the broader community of states."[3] At first this **responsibility to protect (R2P)** was directed at threats of physical violence, based on the belief that all groups within a state had the right to survive. In 2005, the UN General Assembly's World Summit formally embraced the responsibility to protect its citizens from such violence as a responsibility of each state. However, this notion evolved quickly into a broader norm that all groups within a society have a right to a reasonable, and sustainable, quality of life. Getting to this point took a circuitous path. We turn to it next.

11-2 THE HUMAN RIGHTS REGIME: FROM NORMS TO RULES

After World War I, the overriding concern of the international community was the prevention of another "great war," and so the new League of Nations sought to deter the outbreak of war through collective security as noted in Chapter 6. Then, following the horrific events of World War II, an important concern of the new United Nations was to acknowledge and protect human rights. Two very important early

TABLE 11-1 GENOCIDAL CAMPAIGNS OVER THE PAST CENTURY

DATES	AGGRESSORS	VICTIMS	ESTIMATED DEATH TOLL
1915–1923	Ottoman Empire/Turkey	Armenians, Assyrians, Greeks	1.75 million or more
1919–1920	Soviet Union	Don Cossacks	300,000–500,000
1930–1932	Kuomintang Chinese regime	Tibetans	thousands
1932–1933	Soviet Union	Ukrainians, Chechens	8 million
1937	Dominican Republic	Haitians	20,000–30,000
1939–1945	German Nazi regime	Jews, Slavs, Roma, mentally ill, homosexuals	8 million
1941–1945	Croatian Ustashe regime	Jews, Serbs, Roma	300,000–350,000
1947	India and Pakistan	Muslims (India) and Hindus and Sikhs (Pakistan)	500,000–1 million
1959	China	Tibetans	92,000
1963–2005	Indonesia	West Papuans	100,000 or more
1964	Zanzibar	Arabs	2,000–4,000
1966–1969	Nigeria	Ibos	600,000–1 million
1968–1979	Equatorial Guinea	Bubis	80,000
1968–1996	Guatemala	Maya	150,000 or more
1969–1979	Idi Amin regime in Uganda	Various tribal groups	300,000
1971	Pakistan	Bangladeshis	1.5 million or more
1972	Tutsi regime of Burundi	Hutus	80,000–210,000
1974–1999	Indonesia	East Timorese	100,000–150,000
1975–1979	Khmer Rouge regime in Cambodia	Various ethnic and professional minorities	1.7 million
1977–1979	Ethiopia	Ethiopian People's Revolutionary Party	150,000–500,000
1982	Maronite Christian regime in Lebanon	Palestinians	700–3,500
Mid 1980s–2006	Sudan	Darfuris	400,000–500,000
1988	Iraq	Kurds	3,200–5,000
1992–1995	Bosnian Serbs	Bosnian Muslims	97,000–200,000
1993	Hutu majority in Burundi	Tutsis	25,000
1994	Hutu majority in Rwanda	Tutsis	800,000
1998–2003	Both sides in Congo civil war	Twa (Pygmies)	unknown

© Cengage Learning®

Source: R. J. Rummel, *Death By Government* (Piscataway, NJ: Transaction Publishers, 1997); "Genocide in the 20th Century," *The History Place,* available online at: http://www.historyplace.com /worldhistory/genocide/html; and others.

actions by the UN were the passage of the Convention on Genocide and the Universal Declaration of Human Rights.

The 1948 Convention on the Prevention and Punishment of the Crime of Genocide, better known as the **Convention on Genocide**, was a treaty that both defined genocide and made it a crime, whether it occurred in peacetime or in wartime. Genocide was defined as "acts committed with intent to destroy, in whole or in part, a national, ethnical, racial, or religious group," and those acts included killing or causing physical or mental harm to group members, putting the group in conditions that would destroy its members, preventing the group from having children or taking the group's children away by force.[4] As of April 2014, 145 states were parties to the treaty.[5]

In a 48 to 0 General Assembly vote, the UN also approved the **Universal Declaration of Human Rights (UDHR)** in 1948. Based in part on the longstanding ideas of natural law and the more recent fears of fascism, the UDHR was a remarkable document for its time. It provided a comprehensive listing of natural rights people should be able to expect, and the list was long.

Convention on Genocide a 1948 UN treaty that both defined genocide and made it a crime whether it occurred in peacetime or in wartime.

Universal Declaration of Human Rights (UDHR) a 1948 UN resolution, which provided a comprehensive listing of the rights of all people.

Turmoil in the African Great Lakes Region

Geography, politics, and clashing collective identities can combine to create a potent stew, and that has certainly been the case in the Great Lakes region of Africa. Comprised of Uganda, Rwanda, Burundi, the western part of Tanzania, and the eastern portion of the Democratic Republic of the Congo, this area has been the site of considerable suffering in recent years.

The East African Rift Valley forms a string of rivers and lakes that provide the headwaters of the Nile and are considered by many to be the birthplace of humankind. Long before Europeans "discovered" the region in the 1860s, the mountains, valleys, rain forests, and abundant water supply combined to draw many Africans into relatively close proximity, thus promoting the development of indigenous kingdoms. When the British, Belgians, and Germans arrived as colonial rulers, they drew borders that made sense to them with little regard for the natural borders of existing communities.

These colonial powers also sought to rule by co-opting local elites where possible and by pitting different ethnic and tribal groups against each other in a "divide

Map 11-1

The Great Lakes Region of Africa

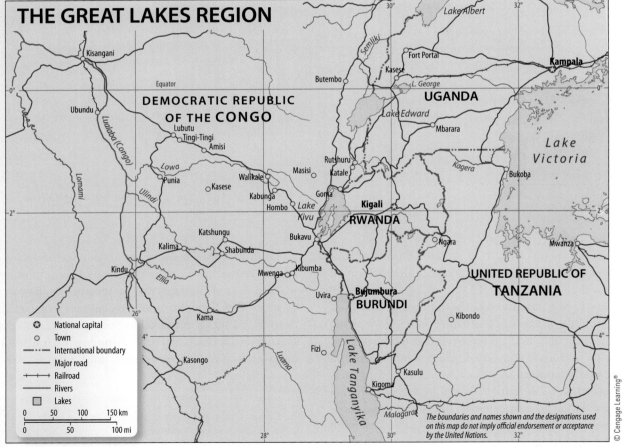

Map No. 4004.1 UNITED NATIONS
January 2004

Department of Peacekeeping Operations
Cartographic Section

© Cengage Learning®

Source: United Nations Peacekeeping Operations © United Nations, 2012.

Map 11-2

Tribal Groups of the Great Lakes Region of Africa

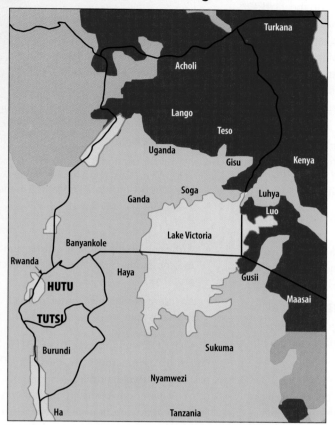

Notice how historical tribal boundaries fail to conform to the political boundaries!

and conquer" approach. In line with the Social Darwinist themes of the times, Europeans also attributed characteristics to groups based on their physical appearance. Since the minority Tutsis often appeared to be taller and slimmer than the majority Hutus, the Belgians decided that the Tutsis were the superior of the two groups and allocated power on that basis. Given that Hutus comprised around 85 percent of the population in the region, they were destined to be dissatisfied with this arrangement, and some Tutsis added insult to injury by mistreating Hutus. Three years before Belgium granted Rwanda its independence in 1962, local riots broke out there between Hutus and Tutsis. At least 20,000 Tutsis were killed, and many more fled to nearby Burundi, Uganda, and Tanzania. After independence, Rwandan Hutus used their numerical majority to control the government, and they often made Tutsis the scapegoats for their problems. Thus over time tensions between the two groups escalated and remained high. In the early 1990s, Tutsi exiles along with some

moderate Hutus in Uganda formed the Rwandan Patriotic Front (the RPF) to overthrow the existing Hutu regime, and a campaign of violence between the Rwandan government and the RPF began.[6]

The flashpoint came in April 1994 when someone shot down an airplane carrying the presidents of Rwanda and Burundi, both of whom were Hutu. Tutsis were immediately blamed, and the Rwandan military, Rwandan militias, and many in the Rwandan public turned on the Tutsis. By the time the killing largely ended 100 days later, approximately 800,000 Tutsis and moderate Hutus—or about one of every ten Rwandans—had died. The Tutsi-dominated RPF responded by driving the Rwandan government from power. With Tutsis back in charge in Rwanda, 2 million Hutus fled across the border into the eastern Congo.[7]

Not surprisingly, the Hutus and Tutsis in eastern Congo soon formed militias for their own self-protection and went to war against each other. The Tutsi-led government in Rwanda invaded Congo twice to fight Hutu rebel forces there, and Tutsi forces from Uganda intervened in eastern Congo as well. The result of all this violence has been a *death toll estimated at 5 million* in the Democratic Republic of the Congo alone. A force of nearly 20,000 UN peacekeepers proved to be far too few to stop the violence, and at times some of its members have preyed on the local population, becoming killers and rapists as well. In a violent area where there is little rule of law or personal accountability and where women are often seen as a commodity rather than as individuals with rights, the inclusion of some "peacekeepers" *from the nearby region itself* may have been a very bad idea!

Tensions continue in Rwanda, as well. Critics maintain that stringent laws passed to stop the genocide are now being used to silence the political opponents of the Tutsi-led regime. Two Hutu candidates who ran for office in 2010, as well as two journalists, were convicted of crimes and imprisoned, although it appears their offenses may have been nothing more than criticizing the regime's policies. Thus it seems the region's inhabitants cannot escape these conflicts.

1. What do you think could be done to dampen the violence of this region?

2. Is it possible to separate them physically until their passions cool and mutual fears of each other subside? Would more peacekeepers help?

3. Has the inclusion of African peacekeepers actually made things worse, and if so, would non-African peacekeepers be a better choice, or would they just reinforce memories of imperialism in the region?

4. Would educational opportunities that integrated young Hutus and Tutsis be a long-term answer, or do society's lessons override what is learned in the classroom?

The UDHR declared that all people have equal rights, regardless of race, gender, religion, language, culture, birth status, national origin, or opinion. Everyone had the rights to:

- Life, liberty, and security, and not be tortured or enslaved

- Be equal before the law with access to courts; be protected from arbitrary arrest or detention; be presumed innocent until proven guilty

- Privacy and to protection of one's reputation

- Leave one's home country and to come back, as well as seek asylum in other countries, and have a nationality that can be changed if desired but not arbitrarily denied

- Marriage upon consent, and to divorce

- Own property

- Freedom of thought, religion, speech, opinion, and assembly

- Participate in governance through free elections and public service

- Social security and employment at a compensation sufficient for a life of dignity, health, and well-being, with special attention given to the needs of mothers and children, and with provisions for rest, leisure, and holidays from work with pay

- A free education at least through elementary school, with parents being able to choose the type of education for their children

- Participate in the cultural, artistic, and scientific life of the community and have their intellectual property protected

- An international social order in which all of these rights were possible

The UN's adoption of the UDHR set in motion what ended up as an almost two-decades' effort to flesh out its principles. Two landmark documents were adopted by the UN General Assembly in 1966 and came into force in 1976 that, in their own way, were products of the Cold War. The **International Covenant on Civil and Political Rights** was an agreement strongly supported by the United States and other Western states. It again enumerated the first-generation civil, political, and legal rights identified in the UDHR, coupled them with the idea that all peoples should have the right of self-determination, and set out procedures for the UN to monitor these rights. However, communist-governed states led by the Soviet Union wanted to emphasize second-generation collective rights, such as societal rights to adequate food, shelter, jobs, and so on. These collective rights became enumerated in the UN's **International Covenant on Economic, Social, and Cultural Rights**. This treaty did the same thing for those types of rights, again specifying that all peoples should have the right of self-determination and setting out procedures for the UN to monitor these rights. In the eyes of the UN, these agreements along with the UDHR comprise an International Bill of Human Rights.

The effort to transform such international norms into rules has continued over time through the creation of ten core UN human rights treaties. In addition to the International Covenants on Civil and Political Rights

International Covenant on Civil and Political Rights a 1966 UN treaty identifying the civil, political, and legal rights of all humans and establishing procedures for the UN to monitor these rights.

International Covenant on Economic, Social, and Cultural Rights a 1966 UN treaty identifying the economic, social, and cultural rights of all humans and establishing procedures for the UN to monitor these rights.

and on Economic, Social, and Cultural Rights, the other eight and the years they entered into force are:

1. International Convention on the Elimination of All Forms of Racial Discrimination (1969)

2. Convention on the Elimination of All Forms of Discrimination against Women (1981)

3. Convention against Torture and Other Cruel, Inhuman, or Degrading Treatment or Punishment (1987)

4. Convention on the Rights of the Child (1990)

5. Optional Protocol to the Convention against Torture and Other Cruel, Inhuman or Degrading Treatment or Punishment (2002)

6. International Convention on the Protection of the Rights of All Migrant Workers and Members of Their Families (2003)

7. Convention on the Rights of Persons with Disabilities (2008)

8. International Convention for the Protection of All Persons from Enforced Disappearance (2010)

These treaties demonstrate that the idea of what constitutes human rights has expanded considerably over the last 350 years. Most recently in the early twenty-first century, a number of experts have been discussing the possibility of an international convention specifying the right to development. To date, these discussions have primarily revolved around the legal and political difficulties that addressing this right would raise. Can you think of what some of those would be?

While the UN has been very active in human rights matters, it has not been the only IO dealing with such rights. Regional IOs have acted in the human rights sphere, as well. In 1953, the **European Convention on Human Rights** went into effect. Created by the Council of Europe, it listed a wide array of human rights, one of which is the abolishment of capital punishment. The European convention is the strongest of the regional efforts on human rights, and it also created the **European Commission on Human Rights** to investigate allegations of human rights abuses and to monitor situations involving potential human rights violations. If it finds that human rights abuses may have occurred, it can refer them to the European Court of Human Rights, which we will discuss in more detail later.

In 1978, a somewhat similar **American Convention on Human Rights** went into effect. Created by the Organization of American States, the convention listed rights and created both an Inter-American Commission on Human Rights to investigate possible human rights violations and an Inter-American Court of Human Rights to issue rulings in such matters. One difference

from the European version is that capital punishment was frowned on but not abolished.

In 1986, the **African Charter on Human and Peoples' Rights** came into force and was a product of the Organization of African States and its successor organization, the African Union. Like the other regional efforts, it created an African Commission on Human and Peoples' Rights and an African Court of Human and Peoples' Rights. The most interesting aspect of the African effort is the "peoples' rights" component. Not only did the charter list individual human rights, but it also listed social responsibilities that people were to meet. These included duties to enhance family and community security and to recognize that individual rights existed in the context of collective and communal rights. Thus like the "Asian values" mentioned earlier, these "African values" raise the issue of cultural relativism—to what extent are values universal or culturally defined.

By the late twentieth century, human rights concerns began to coalesce around the broader idea of **human security**—an emphasis on the security of individuals and groups of people, not on the security of territory. People needed certain things to live and needed more to live in dignity. For millennia, families, local communities, religious groups, and others we would now call **civil society groups**, addressed human security

---

European Convention on Human Rights the Council of Europe treaty that went into force in 1953, which listed individual rights and created the European Commission on Human Rights and the later European Court of Human Rights.

European Commission on Human Rights created by the European Convention on Human Rights, a very active body monitoring human rights situations in Europe. Individuals who believe their rights have been abused can appeal to the commission, which may, after investigation, refer the case to the European Court of Human Rights.

American Convention on Human Rights the Organization of American States treaty that went into force in 1978. It created an Inter-American Commission on Human Rights and an Inter-American Court of Human Rights.

African Charter on Human and Peoples' Rights the treaty by the Organization for African Unity (later the African Union) that went into force in 1986 and listed individual rights and the responsibilities of individuals in a communal context. It also created the African Commission of Human and Peoples' Rights and the African Court of Human and Peoples' Rights.

human security an emphasis on the security of people, not territory, first set out by the UN Development Program in 1994. It includes economic, food, health, environmental, personal, community, and political security for people.

civil society groups NGOs that promote democracy and human rights on a global basis.

at the local level, if it was addressed at all. In the neo-Westphalian era, however, the international community endorsed the right to human security. First set out by the UN Development Programme in 1994, human security involved meeting a variety of needs if local governments and communities did not do so. These needs included economic security (meeting minimum needs to provide for oneself and family), food security (meeting minimum nutritional standards for all, particularly women and children), health security (assuring meaningful access to medical care sufficient to maintain reasonable health and avoid preventable diseases and deaths), environmental security (ensuring that the physical surroundings of peoples' lives did not harm them, and vice versa), personal security (ensuring minimum safety from violence or physical threats), community security (ensuring that social and communal groups were protected from violence or other threats), and political security (ensuring that people had meaningful opportunities to participate in a form of governance that they saw as legitimate). One can easily see how the human security principle blended easily with the responsibility to protect principle mentioned previously.

Moving such norms into rules meant most governments would have to take on far more tasks than ever before. The principle of human security thus quickly became mired in controversy. For some critics, the first question was whether it was even appropriate for governments to take on these responsibilities or whether they should be left in private hands—in short, the question of exactly where the private sector ended and the public sector began. If governments were the appropriate entities to guarantee human security, the second concern was how much would such programs cost and how would the needed funds be raised. Who pays for a reasonable quality of life for everyone? These questions have long bedeviled U.S. foreign policymakers, as shown in Foreign Policy in Perspective: The United States and Human Rights.

11-3 THE CHALLENGE OF IMPLEMENTATION AND ENFORCEMENT

In an international system marked by anarchy, the problem is not just identifying which human rights matter most. The problem is also determining who will implement and, when necessary, enforce human rights standards. Without authoritative institutions to govern, enforcement of any rules and norms—human rights included—is especially challenging. In general, the global political system relies mainly on decentralized efforts that depend on the players themselves to implement and enforce human rights rules and norms. Not only does this ensure that diversity of values and perspectives complicates such efforts, but it also means that capabilities and interests affect decisions to try to enforce the standards. In this context, actions to promote and enforce human rights rules and norms can come from many quarters. States, international organizations, and nongovernmental organizations have all played such roles.

11-3a State-Based Initiatives

When they so desire, state governments or their people can contribute to progress in the human rights arena in several ways. They can engage in direct actions to implement or encourage human rights at home and abroad, they can provide incentives for others to do so or impose punishments for those who will not abide by global human rights norms, or they can enforce human rights standards through their own judicial systems via claims of universal jurisdiction.

AP Images

Retired Colombian General Jaime Uscategui was sentenced to 40 years in prison for allowing Colombian death squads to use his military base | Does looking the other way become passive support for human rights violations?

The United States and Human Rights

If asked, most U.S. citizens would probably say that the United States has always been strongly associated with the promotion of human rights. In that conversation, the Constitution's Bill of Rights would probably be mentioned, and some might remember that in the 1970s both Presidents Gerald Ford and Jimmy Carter elevated human rights concerns to be a central focus of their foreign policy agendas. Yet others in the international arena might well argue that the overall record of the United States regarding international human rights is at best uneven, if not poor. The political culture of the United States champions some human rights but not others, and the consideration of human rights issues gets complicated by the interaction with other political concerns in the United States. There is a long history to such concerns.

The 13 original colonies that made up the United States were populated by those (and their descendants) who left Europe looking for freedoms and opportunities not available in their old country. They sought limitations on government to protect their civil and political rights. Beyond those rights, the other elements of what we now call human security were thought to be largely individual responsibilities. Providing for the broader needs of others might be taken on as tasks of charitable individuals or organizations, but it was not generally seen as the responsibility of the government.

Beyond such philosophical concerns, other concerns complicated U.S. public support for international human rights, as well. For example, like others most Americans were shocked by the events of the Holocaust in World War II. The UN responded with the Convention on Genocide in 1948, which President Harry Truman signed and sent to the Senate in 1949. However, the Senate did not approve the treaty until 1986, 35 years after the treaty had gone into force in 1951! Over those many years at least three different arguments were raised against the treaty in the U.S. Senate. First, in its initial consideration early in the Cold War, some critics wanted "political groups" added to the list of national, ethnic, racial, or religious groups protected by the treaty. If political groups were added to the list of those protected, the Soviet Union's extermination of internal dissidents could be seen as acts of genocide under the treaty. A second argument came from those senators

who feared that the United States would be charged with genocide for its past and present policies toward Native Americans or African Americans. A third objection came from others who feared that approving the treaty would mean international law could override U.S. state and federal laws. In essence, they feared a loss of Westphalian sovereignty. These sovereignty concerns were ultimately allayed by the strong support of President Ronald Reagan and legal reservations (or qualifying conditions) inserted by the Senate that noted that the United States could exempt itself from any compulsory jurisdiction of the World Court in a genocide case and that nothing in the genocide convention overrode the U.S. Constitution.

This concern over the loss of U.S. sovereignty was nothing new. It had arisen after World War II when the Senate considered approving U.S. membership in the new United Nations. Some feared the UN Charter could override the U.S. Constitution. U.S. approval of the UN Charter was facilitated when Senator Tom Connally (D-TX) attached a reservation noting that, when it came to the jurisdiction of the World Court, the determination of what was a domestic matter—and thus beyond the court's jurisdiction—would be up to the United States, not the UN or the World Court.

The fear of international law overriding domestic law has surfaced at other times since then. The Covenant on Civil and Political Rights went into force in 1976. The United States did not ratify it until 1992, and Senate approval came with multiple reservations and understandings, the most important of which was that it in no way contravened domestic U.S. law. The United States has also not adopted an optional protocol to the covenant that abolished capital punishment. In 1989, the UN General Assembly passed the Convention on the Rights of the Child. The convention entered into force in 1990 and now has been ratified by all states except the United States and Somalia! U.S. critics of the convention generally worry that it provides more legal protections to children than to their parents, while some fear it will override the laws of the 22 U.S. states that allow the execution of juveniles for capital crimes. In the 1990s, the U.S. Clinton administration initially supported the creation of the International Criminal Court (ICC), which prosecutes individuals for **war crimes**,

war crimes excessive brutality in war, in violation of international treaties or conventions.

crimes against humanity, genocide, and aggression. Clinton's support was conditioned on the premise that the court's prosecutions would be subject to the approval of the UN Security Council—as one of the five permanent members the United States had a veto with which to protect itself. However that provision made it appear that prosecutions of British, Chinese, French, Russian, or U.S. military personnel would be highly unlikely, and so other states insisted it be deleted. Without the provision, some U.S. critics, including President Clinton, feared that U.S. military personnel might become the targets of capricious or politically motivated prosecutions. Other U.S. critics had consistently opposed the court as an infringement on U.S. sovereignty. Not only did the Senate refuse to approve the treaty creating the court, the U.S. Congress passed a law authorizing the U.S. government to go "rescue" any U.S. military personnel from prosecution by the ICC!

More recently, a proposed UN convention to ban the illicit sales of small arms and light weapons—which kill more people in the world than weapons of mass destruction—was initially derailed by U.S. opposition during the George W. Bush administration. Conservative critics of the UN convention feared that it would override the U.S. Constitution's Second Amendment, which allows citizens to keep and bear arms. Despite the active opposition of the National Rifle Association, the Obama administration signed the treaty in 2013 but as of this writing, it had not been sent to the Senate for ratification.

Beyond these concerns, other international human rights issues founder because they run counter to widely held U.S. beliefs. As previously noted, the framers of the U.S. Constitution were motivated by the need to restrict the power of government and to provide as much individual liberty to the people as possible. Many U.S. citizens still feel that the responsibility for providing broadly defined human security falls upon the shoulders of individuals, who are free to succeed or fail based on their own merits. These citizens are less comfortable with the idea of the government taking greater responsibility for ensuring a minimum standard of economic well-being, as well as minimum levels of health, food, environmental, and community security. Perhaps as a result of these cultural biases, the United States ranked only sixteenth in the Social Progress Index for 2014 (New Zealand is first!).[8] Contemporary debates about issues such as health care reform, immigration reform, the imposition of new environmental standards, and the like often illustrate these tensions over where to draw the dividing line between the public and private sectors.

So let's bring these issues back to you.

1. Where do you think the government's responsibilities to promote human security end and yours begin?

2. What does the U.S. record of support for universal human rights suggest about the factors that affect this issue of human security?

3. When it comes to the international promotion and protection of human rights, should the United States lead, follow, or get out of the way?

Source: See the Social Progress Index website, http://www.socialprogressimperative.org/data/spi.

> **crimes against humanity** acts of war against a civilian population; these can include, among others, the crimes of murder; enslavement; deportation or forcible transfer; imprisonment; torture; rape, sexual slavery or any other form of enforced sexual violence; persecution on political, racial, national, ethnic, cultural, religious, gender, or other such grounds; enforced disappearance; apartheid; and other inhumane acts that create great suffering or serious mental or physical injury.
>
> **aggression** the unjustified use of force against another state.

DIRECT ACTIONS In most societies, the protection of human rights happens at the local level. While local groups often find ways to protect the rights of members of their communities, sometimes state regimes get involved by modifying their own behavior to promote human rights within their borders. In recent years, Burma released democracy activist and Nobel Peace Prize winner Daw Aung San Suu Kyi from house arrest, a Colombian court sentenced two leaders of right-wing death squads to jail for their massacres of civilians, Argentina and Uruguay became the first two Latin American countries to legalize gay marriage, and the United States Supreme Court ruled that all states must recognize gay marriages performed in the states where such marriages are legal. Serbia and other parts of the former Yugoslavian state have cooperated in turning over some suspected war criminals for international prosecutions. Burundi lifted restrictions on the activities of a number of civil society groups. Angola reduced the number of extrajudicial killings and held a legislative election that external observers found to be a credible representation of the public's will. Each of these represents direct actions taken by states to deal with their own human rights issues. If such direct actions are not taken to protect human rights by state authorities, states may try other approaches.

One such approach may be to conduct public campaigns to confront past human rights violations in the search for **restorative justice**. The basic idea of restorative justice can be found in its name: a justice that seeks to restore to victims what was lost through human rights abuses. While it may not be possible to repair all the damage done to victims, a series of steps can promote societal healing:

1. Publicly recognizing and acknowledging the hurt and damage done to victims

2. Allowing the victims to publicly confront their abusers so the abusers must hear what harm they've caused

3. Encouraging the abusers to acknowledge their actions and to take responsibility for them (and under ideal circumstances to apologize for the harm they've caused)

4. Allowing the victims a voice in the resolution of their grievances, and then where possible, reintegrating both victims and the offenders into a more just society

For example, South Africa sponsored a **Truth and Reconciliation Commission** to deal with the injuries caused by apartheid, in which the victims got to be heard and the perpetrators were offered amnesty if they fully and publicly confessed to their crimes. Brazil created a Truth Commission as well to identify the human rights abuses of past military regimes, with blanket amnesty for any government or military officials accused of such wrongdoing. Australia's prime minister apologized for crimes against aboriginal peoples, including the kidnapping of children from their parents so they could be raised in foster homes. Canada created a new province where native peoples could govern themselves—Nunavut, or "our land" in the Inuit language. South Korea acknowledged that fears of communist subversion drove some of its military units to massacre civilians in the confusing days shortly after the North Korean invasion in 1950. Cambodia allowed the radio and television broadcast of its trial of former Khmer Rouge officials for crimes against humanity, torture, and murder during the 1970s. In such ways, some regimes have tried to come to grips with the ghosts of their pasts.

Sometimes regimes that repeatedly fail to meet human rights standards will be successfully challenged by their own people. Such **populist revolutions** have become increasingly common in the late Westphalian and neo-Westphalian eras, and successful ones are typically directed against authoritarian regimes that do not allow sufficient freedom of speech, freedom of assembly, and elections seen as free and fair. A short list of popular revolts against authoritarian rulers would include at least the following:

- The 1979 Iranian overthrow of the Shah's regime

- The 1986 Filipino overthrow of the Marcos regime

AP Images/Yair Klein

Former Israeli army Lieutenant Colonel Yair Klein, convicted for training Colombian death squad members | What responsibility does a state have for its citizens who commit human rights violations elsewhere?

- The 1989 overthrow of the communist Husak regime in Czechoslovakia

- The 2003 overthrow of the Shevardnadze regime in Georgia

- The 2004 overthrow of the Yanukovich regime in Ukraine (returned to power in 2010)

- The 2005 revolt against the Syrian military occupation of Lebanon

restorative justice a justice that seeks to repair the damage done to victims, allow the victims a voice in the resolution of their grievances, and where possible to reintegrate both victims and the offenders into a more just society.

Truth and Reconciliation Commission the entity created by the new South African government following the abolition of apartheid. Victims of apartheid were encouraged to tell their stories for the record and for the psychological benefit of being heard while the aggressors were offered amnesty for their crimes in return for full and public disclosure of those crimes.

populist revolutions grassroots revolts typically against repressive governments, dominated by mass turnouts of the people.

The South African Truth and Reconciliation Commission meets to investigate the murder of 26-year-old Stanford graduate student Amy Biehl | Can reconciliation heal the wounds of systematic human rights violations? Would it make you feel better if your family had been murdered?

- The 2010 overthrow of the Ben Ali regime in Tunisia
- The 2011 overthrow of the Mubarak regime in Egypt
- The 2011 overthrow of the Gaddafi regime in Libya
- The 2014 overthrow of the Yanukovich regime in Ukraine

In such instances, the public's unwillingness to continue to tolerate abusive regimes reaches a critical mass and, given the right stimulus, topples regimes that previously appeared to be very stable.

Still, human rights challenges remain. In 2010, China prevented imprisoned democracy rights activist Liu Xiaobo or any of his family from attending the ceremony where he was to be awarded the Nobel Peace Prize. This same year, France shocked many in the European Union by deporting over a thousand Roma back to Romania and Bulgaria. Rape continues to be a weapon against one's enemies in Eastern Congo.

Other examples may be less dramatic but are still quietly evident. Women's rights to education, to employment outside the home, to the protection of law, and so on are still woefully inadequate in many parts of the world. Human trafficking—primarily of women and children—still occurs, and 2.5 million is considered a low estimate of the number of its victims.[9] Past estimates of the number of homeless people in the United States ranged as high as 2.5 million, and that number was almost certainly increased by the Great Recession of 2008 to 2010.[10] Recently, the president of Peru refused to approve a law giving indigenous peoples the right to stop oil drilling and mining operations on their own land, and Uganda made homosexuality a crime punishable by death. In 2012, a couple was stoned to death by Taliban

forces for the crime of adultery in Afghanistan. As discussed earlier, genocide can still occur. Examples like these lead many states to seek to change the behaviors of others, and such state efforts fall into two broad categories: incentives and punishments.

INCENTIVES States concerned with promoting and protecting human rights in other countries often choose to reward those who improve their human rights record and work with other states and societies to facilitate improvements in human rights. A common method is through foreign assistance used as incentives.

Considerable activity has been generated in recent years in efforts to enhance democratization, by encouraging nondemocratic states to embrace democratic reform or by helping regimes that have started down the democratic path to become even more democratic in practice. Such democratization efforts may be politically based. As such, they direct foreign aid to help fund and promote the work of civil society groups and political parties and to make free and fair elections the norm. A good example of the political approach is the work done by the U.S. government directly (typically by the State Department) or by the non-governmental organizations that the government funds. These include groups such as the National Endowment for Democracy, the National Democratic Institute, and the International Republican Institute, which operate on a global basis. In Europe, both the European Union and its individual member states direct foreign assistance for similar purposes. In fact, many political parties in Europe have government-supported foundations that promote democracy abroad. Examples include the Konrad Adenauer Institute in Germany, the Jean-Jaures Foundation in France, and the Westminster Foundation in the United Kingdom. As we described in Chapter 9, often smaller amounts of targeted democracy aid—such as support for free elections, aid to create or empower democratic institutions, and support for civil society organizations—produce more democratic reform and better human rights practices than do larger amounts of conventional foreign economic aid alone.

Still, more effort goes into foreign aid programs that are developmentally based than those that are politically based. These include efforts to improve the quality of life, improve delivery of basic community services, and promote the greater good. European states generally favor these approaches, as does the U.S. Agency for International Development. Examples of such development programs include providing the loan capital so farmers and small business owners can borrow what they need to prosper; arranging the logistical support so local businesses can export their goods or services; helping to build infrastructure such as roads, bridges, railroad lines, and airports; digging wells or building irrigation and water systems for local communities; constructing hospitals and medical clinics; building schools; and training needed professionals such as teachers, engineers, and medical personnel. The basic idea is that improvements in the overall quality of life directly address second-generation human rights and may also produce a citizenry that demands the right to play a greater role in their own governance (first-generation rights). States that lead the way in developmental assistance as a percentage of their GDP include countries like Norway, Sweden, Luxembourg, Netherlands, and Denmark.

Sometimes external incentives are provided to acknowledge past wrongs. In 2011, the head of France's national railway company apologized to victims of the Holocaust for the railway's complicity in delivering thousands of European Jews to Nazi Germany for persecution. The incentive to make such an apology was the possibility of bidding on future contracts to build high-speed rail networks linking Orlando and Tampa, Florida, and San Francisco and Los Angeles, California. Members of Congress had France's national railway company in mind when they introduced a bill in the U.S. House of Representatives in 2010 that required all bidders for such contracts to disclose any role they may have played in shipping Holocaust victims during World War II.

PUNISHMENTS States also take actions to punish those who abuse human rights. The mildest form of these involves public admonishments that embarrass a regime. For example, the United States routinely chastises China for its human rights record, which includes the repression of Tibetans and Uighurs in the western part of the country, the persecution of a variety of religious faiths and spiritual groups, the lack of political freedoms, and so on. China in turn publicly criticizes the United States for its problems of homelessness, treatment of Native Americans, and the treatment of detainees in the war on terror, as well as restrictions on personal freedoms due to the war on terror.

However, other penalties can carry more significance. As noted previously, most Western states enacted an array of economic sanctions against the white minority regime in the country of South Africa in response to its harsh apartheid policy that kept black South Africans—the majority of the population—separate and denied them economic, political, civil, and even the most basic rights to physical integrity. Although these sanctions were unevenly applied and their impact is hard to measure precisely, they contributed to the pressure at home and from abroad that eventually helped lead to the end of the repressive regime. However, these sanctions also generated serious hardships on the very people they were intended to help.

Belarus provides another interesting example. In 1994, Aleksandr Lukashenko was elected president of this former Soviet republic. After the election, he steadily increased his power, diminished the ability of others to oppose him politically, and changed the constitution to remove limits on presidential terms. Prior to the 2010 presidential election, the European Union offered Belarus investment opportunities and nearly $4 billion in economic aid in return for an election that could be certified as "free and fair." Shortly after winning an election widely derided as fraudulent, Lukashenko had 600 dissidents arrested, including seven of the nine other candidates who ran against him for the presidency! The United States and the EU countries imposed a variety of targeted sanctions against a total of 157 Belarusian officials, including Lukashenko and two of his adult sons. The identified individuals were banned from entering the United States or EU countries, any assets they had in the United States or EU were frozen, and additional U.S. sanctions were imposed on a large Belarusian government-owned company. Perhaps not surprisingly, Lukashenko dismissed these actions as part of a Western plot to dethrone him and as unwarranted interference in the domestic affairs of Belarus.

The efforts to identify specific individuals who can be held accountable for their regime's human rights abuses and to find ways to target them are a relatively recent trend in international politics. As discussed in Chapter 9, **smart sanctions** seek to punish those individuals actually responsible for a regime's bad behavior—and who are in a position to initiate changes in such behavior—rather than punishing the state's population as a whole. In large part, smart sanctions are a response to the impacts of comprehensive sanctions on Iraq by the international community following the 1991 Persian Gulf War. To punish the Saddam Hussein regime for its invasion of Kuwait in 1990 and to push it to stop human rights abuses at home against Shi'a and Kurdish separatists, these sanctions basically banned most economic transactions with Iraq. Most products would not be sold to Iraq, and Iraqi oil would not be purchased by others.

The human consequences of these sanctions were counterproductive, if not horrific. Saddam Hussein's

smart sanctions sanctions that target specific individuals thought to be responsible for a regime's human rights abuses rather than targeting a state's entire population.

family became even wealthier, as family members profited from their control of the illegal smuggling of luxury goods into Iraq. The quality of life for Saddam Hussein and the top officials of his regime thus did not suffer, and the regime did not change its bad behavior. Those who suffered were the citizens of Iraq. By the late 1990s, children died at the rate of 4,000–5,000 per month due to a lack of medicines and medical supplies, poor nutrition, and poor sanitation. Families were disrupted as skilled professionals left the country, economic stresses resulted in more divorces and instances of domestic violence, and couples wishing to wed often could not afford to do so. Crime and prostitution flourished as well, and many young people came of age with a profound sense of victimization at the hands of the international community. After the regime was overthrown, outsiders were shocked at the deterioration in Iraq's basic infrastructure over the 12 years that the sanctions had been in force. The electric grid barely functioned, poor maintenance had taken its toll on the production and shipping of oil and natural gas, and basic sanitation and clean water systems were lacking in many areas of the country. In short, it was clear that heavy-handed sanctions could produce as much or more harm as the human rights abuses that justified the sanctions. Thus the idea behind smart sanctions was born. Led by Switzerland, Germany, and Sweden in the latter-1990s, the European Commission and the UN began studying ways to target sanctions at those actually making the decisions that led to human rights violations.

UNIVERSAL JURISDICTION Another way states can enforce human rights standards is through claims of universal jurisdiction, which we introduced in Chapter 7. Long applied to crimes such as piracy on the high seas, universal jurisdiction regarding human rights holds that states have a right and a duty to enforce international law when it comes to the most serious human rights abuses—such as genocide, crimes against humanity, torture, war crimes, extrajudicial killings, and forced disappearances—*regardless of where these offenses may occur*. Australia, Austria, Belgium, Canada, Denmark, Finland, France, Germany, Netherlands, Norway, Senegal, Spain, the United Kingdom, and the United States have all exercised some form of universal jurisdiction over these serious human rights violations in the post-World War II period, subjecting the accused to trials before regular or specialized courts. According to an Amnesty International study, more than 125 states have claimed universal jurisdiction over at least one of these crimes. Some other human rights treaties—such as the Convention on Genocide and the Convention against Torture—require the states approving the treaties to accept the principle of universal jurisdiction to ensure that the rights get enforced!

A good example of this behavior comes from Spain. In recent years, Spanish courts have issued arrest warrants for former Chilean General Augusto Pinochet for the civilian deaths and disappearances that occurred during his rule, for Osama bin Laden for his promotion of terrorist attacks, for former Guatemalan military strongmen Efrain Rios Montt and Oscar Humberto Mejia for their actions during the Guatemalan Civil War, and for an Argentine naval officer accused of genocide and terrorism during Argentina's military rule. Spanish courts also launched investigations regarding the torture of detainees at the U.S. base at Guantanamo Bay, suspected crimes by the Colombian rebel group FARC (the Revolutionary Armed Forces of Colombia), genocide authorized by Chinese officials in Tibet, and alleged crimes against humanity authorized by Israeli officials in the Gaza Strip. Such actions send the important message that human rights violators may not escape prosecution elsewhere. However states are not the only enforcers of human rights standards. International organizations are deeply involved in these enforcement efforts.

Perhaps the most significant development in universal jurisdiction is the creation of a permanent international court where individuals accused of genocide, war crimes, crimes against humanity, and aggression can be tried. That permanent court is the **International Criminal Court (ICC)**, located in The Hague, Netherlands. The treaty proposing the court was signed in Rome in 1998, and the court was officially established in 2002. By April 2014, 122 countries had ratified the treaty, and 17 others had signed but not ratified the agreement (but not the United States for reasons discussed previously in this chapter). The ICC has undertaken cases arising from a variety of African conflicts, a number of which include the forcible use of child soldiers. While child soldiers are used throughout much of the world, about a third of them are found in African conflicts.

Yet, while situations have been investigated in Afghanistan, Chad, Colombia, Georgia, Guinea, Honduras, Iraq, Nigeria, the Palestinian territories, South Korea, and Venezuela, for the ICC the most significant issue to date is the fact that all the *cases* involve Africa. Do you think Africa is the only region in the world that experiences war crimes, crimes against humanity, genocide,

International Criminal Court (ICC) the ICC is an international court in the Netherlands that tries individuals accused of war crimes, crimes against humanity, genocide, and aggression.

TABLE 11-2 SUMMARY OF CASES AND CHARGES BEFORE THE ICC AS OF 2014

SITUATIONS BY INITIATION DATE	CHARGES
2004 Democratic Republic of the Congo	Warlord leader convicted of war crimes involving the use of child soldiers; two other warlords charged with war crimes and crimes against humanity for murder, rape, sexual slavery, and use of child soldiers against civilians; one of these warlords was found not guilty in 2012.
2004 Northern Uganda	Five senior leaders of Lord's Resistance Army charged with crimes against humanity (murder, abduction, and sexual enslavement) and war crimes (use of child soldiers).
2004 Central African Republic	Central African Republic warlord (who was formerly a vice president of Democratic Republic of the Congo) charged with war crimes (rape, murder, and pillaging) and crimes against humanity (rape and murder).
2005 Darfur	Sudanese president charged with crimes against humanity (rape, murder, pillaging), war crimes (attacks on peacekeepers), and genocide against the Fur, Masalit, and Zaghawa ethnic groups; three others charged with war crimes (attacks on peacekeepers).
2010 Kenya	Six suspects from two political parties that are part of the governing coalition investigated for crimes against humanity in post-election violence directed at civilians in 2007–2008. A Kenyan prosecution may preclude an ICC prosecution.
2011–2013 Libya	Arrest warrants issued for former leader Muammar Gaddafi (prior to his death), his son Saif, and the former intelligence chief of his regime. The current Libyan government has yet to decide whether it will turn over to the Court the latter two.
2011 Cote d'Ivoire	Arrest warrant issued for former warlord for war crimes and crimes against humanity following presidential election there, and a decision is pending on his trial before the Court.
2011 Kenya	Arrest warrant issued for Kenyan president for crimes against humanity including murder, rape, and deportation.

Source: Coalition for the International Criminal Court, *Cases and Situations*, http://iccnow.org/?mod=home; and International Criminal Court, *Republic of Kenya*, http://www.icc-cpi.int/en_menus/icc /situations%20and%20cases/situations/situation%20icc%200109/related%20cases/icc01090211/Pages/icc01090111.aspx.

© Cengage Learning®

or aggression? If not, you agree with the African Union! In October 2013, the AU held a special summit meeting to discuss a mass withdrawal from the court over its seeming targeting of Africa and African leaders such as Sudanese President Omar al-Bashir and Kenyan President Uhuru Kenyatta. While no mass withdrawals have yet occurred, the ICC is on notice that some perceive it to be unfair in its operations. Do you think it is unfairly targeting weak states in Africa or is this region just where the worst human rights violations occur? Table 11-2 summarizes the current cases before the ICC.

The idea of a new international court that would hold individuals accountable for their actions in such horrific situations was a major step in human rights protection. What accounts for such a landmark move? There are multiple explanations for the creation of the ICC, and many of them are theoretically driven, as shown in Theory in Action: Creating the ICC.

Though not a part of the UN, the ICC works closely with the UN and its Security Council. That raises the issue of how international organizations address human rights matters. Let's turn to that topic now.

11-3b International Organization-Based Initiatives

Not only have international organizations set global standards for human rights, they have also set up enforcement mechanisms, as well. Sometimes they use "soft power" to try to create and enforce human rights standards, and at other times they use the "hard power" approaches available to them.

SOFT POWER As noted in Chapter 3, soft power involves the ability to get others to share your values, to get others to want what you want, to persuade, to embarrass, to cajole, to lead by example, and so on. International organizations have long done that in the arena of human rights. For example, one of the six original main organs of the United Nations was the Economic and Social Council, which has functional commissions that deal directly with our broader notion of human security in the arenas of sustainable economic development,

Dang Ngo/ZUMA Press/Newscom

A child soldier from a Burmese insurgent militia | What age is too young for military service?

Creating the ICC

One of the most significant developments regarding human rights since the end of World War II is the creation of the International Criminal Court, or the ICC. How do we account for its creation and the reactions it generated in the international community? Our various theories provide a good starting point. Many state actors and groups pushed for the creation of the ICC, while some opposed it. Let's work through these theoretical lenses.[11]

Liberalism

According to liberalism, states are important actors, but their behavior and interactions are shaped by the individuals, groups, organizations, and institutions that make up their society and government and by non-state actors in the international system. Power is multifaceted and wielded in a variety of ways. Liberalism stresses democracy and individual rights, social rights, and the idea that the government's role is to serve the people. Neoliberalism further stresses the voluntary creation of international institutions designed to foster cooperation.

The ICC fits nicely here. For liberals and neoliberals, the creation of the ICC was a no-brainer. The genesis of the idea for such a court came from 16 Caribbean and Latin American nations that wanted such a court for dealing with the crimes committed by narco-traffickers, and the idea was picked up and expanded by the International Law Commission and supported by the United Nations General Assembly. For liberals and neoliberals, enhancing the rule of law and holding individuals responsible for their war crimes, crimes against humanity, genocide, and aggression seemed to be in the best interest of the international community and all its members. There would now be a venue where victims could seek the punishment of the guilty, and the fact that such an international court existed might deter some human rights abuses from happening in the future. State and non-state actors could cooperate in bringing the worst offenders in humankind before the bar of justice. How could this be a bad thing?

Constructivism

According to constructivism, collective identities can be powerful motivators of behavior, and reality is socially constructed through discourse. The combination of both of these is evident in the creation of the ICC.

As noted, some Latin American states were involved in pushing the idea for such an international court. There has long been a strong belief in Latin America regarding the importance of international law, and at least to some degree this reality was socially constructed over time as a response to the power of the United States in the region. International law was seen as a way for weaker states to restrain more powerful ones. Other important early backers of such a court included Canada and most Western European states. For Canada and Western Europe, a collective identity emphasizing shared values and cooperation had existed since the creation of NATO in 1950. For the Western Europeans themselves, this collective identity of international cooperation and shared values was reinforced through the many iterations that began with the European Coal and Steel Community and resulted in the present European Union.

One of these states—France—at first worried about politically motivated prosecutions of its citizens. However after the principle of complementarity was accepted in the Rome Statute creating the ICC, France removed its objections. Complementarity meant that the ICC would *not* take on such a case if the accused's state prosecuted the case itself through its own national courts. That principle satisfied the French.

Political Realism

The main thrust of realism is that states pursue their national interests primarily defined in power terms, and coercive—or military—power is the ultimate tool of the state. The United States, China, Israel, Iraq, Libya, Qatar, and Yemen arguably saw the creation of the ICC through this theoretical lens, and they were the only states to vote against its creation.

U.S. rejection of the court was based on the perception that U.S. troops were deployed all around the world, both keeping and enforcing the peace. In so doing, occasionally mistakes got made and innocent people were hurt or killed. U.S. officials feared that a politically motivated ICC prosecutor would target U.S. troops to harm or embarrass the U.S. government. That seemed patently unfair to U.S. officials and to U.S. military officers who lobbied against the treaty. From this perspective, the United States was simply protecting its troops from unwarranted judicial harm in the future and thereby pursuing its national interest. Like the United States, Israel had reasons to oppose the new court. Israel relied heavily on its military to ensure its protection. When they seemed called for, Israeli leaders authorized both preemptive military strikes and punitive raids on its enemies. Yet this effort to protect Israeli citizens often resulted in Palestinian civilians and others being killed. So Israel did not want to expose its troops to such prosecutions. For their parts, China, Iraq,

Libya, Qatar, and Yemen all suffered from poor human rights records and occasional excessive uses of force. They too wanted no part of this court.

Other Critical Theories

Two other critical theories we have examined include world systems theory and feminism. Each can be applied to the creation of the ICC, but one may fit the facts here better than the other.

World systems theory (WST) explains international phenomena through the lens of classes of states grouped by wealth. As noted earlier, the core is composed of the wealthy states who exercise much power in international politics, the periphery is composed of poor states who are often pawns of the rich, and the semi-periphery is composed of those states in between the core and the periphery who have evolved beyond an economy primarily based on the export of commodities but are not yet as well-developed economically as the core states.

From this perspective, the creation of the ICC is a bit confusing. All the core states except the United States and Israel supported the creation of the court. Why would core states support the creation of a court that could punish their citizens? Core support for the court seems odd from the point of view that the rich typically rig the rules of the game to favor themselves. However, as Table 11-2 shows, the court's cases so far have come from Africa. Could core support be based on the idea that the ICC would provide a socially acceptable means to punish bad behavior in parts of the world where such punishments, if doled out by the core states, would be resented as imperialist intrusions into other countries' domestic affairs?

On the other hand, there seems little doubt why feminists would support the creation of the court. Earlier in this chapter, we noted that women are far too often the victims of human rights abuses—particularly in wartime. The creation of a court to try cases involving war crimes and crimes against humanity when many such victims are women should be something that most feminists could easily and readily endorse.

1. So which explanation works best for you?

2. Which theory do you think best explains the creation of the court and reactions to it?

---

social development, women's rights, population control, crime prevention, and the applications of science and technology for development. Getting others to share an increasingly global set of values is arguably more effective in addressing such human rights issues than is the ability to coerce others to do so. All 15 specialized agencies of the UN illustrated in Chapter 7 address some component of human security—from economic regulation to food and nutrition issues to travel to cultural preservation—and they do so via the process of shared norms and values, negotiated agreements and standards, and so on. All of these are usages of soft power.

Two particular human rights emphases of the UN have long been addressed through soft power means. One involves the needs of children, which became readily apparent after World War II. This need prompted the creation of the United Nations Children's Fund in 1946, better known as **UNICEF** from the agency's original name, United Nations International Children's Emergency Fund. It became a permanent part of the UN organization in 1953. Since then it has proven to be one of the most popular UN entities, and it received the Nobel Peace Prize in 1965 for its good works. In 1981, UNICEF sponsored the Child Survival and Development Revolution, an intensive effort to promote children's health through four readily available means: monitoring rates of growth; preventing avoidable deaths through oral rehydration therapy for children with dysentery; promoting breastfeeding to give children the best chance of good health during infancy; and expanding the availability of immunization against routine childhood diseases. In 1989, the UN General Assembly adopted the Convention on the Rights of the Child and in 1990 held a World Summit for Children to set global goals for their protection. In 2002, a special session of the UN General Assembly was held to assess global progress toward these goals for children and for the first time children were seated as delegates at the UN. All of these diplomatic efforts emphasized the establishment of shared values and thus can be considered soft power initiatives.

Another major UN soft power emphasis has addressed the needs of women. Although a variety of women's rights were listed in the Universal Declaration of Human Rights, the global women's movement of the 1970s put increased emphasis on women's rights. The UN declared 1975 as the International Women's Year to put a spotlight on global women's issues. It declared 1976 to 1985 as the UN Decade for Women, and in 1979

UNICEF the United Nations Children's Fund; created in 1946 and recipient of the Nobel Peace Prize in 1965.

Thirteen-year-old Gabriela Azurduy Arrieta of Bolivia addresses the UN's Special Session on Children, May 2002 | What might world leaders learn from children?

Beyond seeking to empower women more generally in areas of economic and social development, the UN Security Council has also used soft power approaches in addressing the impact of violence on women. In 2000, the Security Council urged member states to include more women's representation in the areas of conflict prevention, conflict management, and conflict resolution. The next year an International Conference on Women and Conflict Management in Africa stressed that wars no longer sought just to defeat enemies; aggressors further relied on the use of rape, forced pregnancies, and sexual slavery to break down societies by inflicting pain and humiliation on their victims. In resolutions passed in 2008 and 2009, the Security Council called upon all parties in conflicts to protect women and girls from gender-based violence. Because the targeting of women and girls for mass rapes and other forms of gender-based violence has become so pronounced, in 2010 UN Secretary General Ban Ki-moon appointed his first Special Representative on Sexual Violence in Conflict, Sweden's Margot Wallstrom. Perhaps even more significant, given the challenges facing women in Africa, was the 2012 election of Nkosazana Dlamini-Zuma as the new chairperson of the African Union Commission. Formerly the South African minister of home affairs, Dlamini-Zuma became the first woman to lead the AU.

The rest of the UN family of organizations has also been active in pressing for women's rights through soft power means. In 1993, the UN General Assembly passed the Declaration on the Elimination of Violence against Women. Other such efforts followed, including the UN Secretary-General's 2008 global campaign "UNiTE to End Violence Against Women." More recently, the UN has taken on an institutionalized form of violence—the practice of female genital mutilation. Not only is this practice very painful and often dangerous to young women and girls, it can cause later health problems like recurring infections and problems with childbirth. Due to the UN's efforts to educate local communities about the harm caused by this practice, thousands of African communities have pledged to end female genital mutilation but the practice continues in 29 countries in Africa and the Middle East. So far, 125 million women and girls have suffered such cutting, and 86 million more will be by 2030 if trends continue. Thus, it is not surprising that the UN designated February 6, 2014 as the International Day of Zero Tolerance for Female Genital Mutilation.[12]

However, the most significant change regarding protecting the rights of women has been the 2010 creation of a new organization—the United Nations Entity for Gender Equality and the Empowerment of Women, or

the **Convention on the Elimination of All Forms of Discrimination against Women (CEDAW)** was adopted by the General Assembly. Four UN World Conferences on Women have been held: in Mexico City in 1975, in Copenhagen in 1980, in Nairobi in 1985, and in Beijing in 1995. In 2000, women's rights were included in the UN's Millennium Development Goals. Again, diplomatic efforts such as these are soft power initiatives. They seek to develop shared values regarding women's rights around the world. To get an idea of the challenges facing women in many societies, take a look at the box Spotlight On: Women's Rights in Guatemala.

CEDAW the Convention on the Elimination of All Forms of Discrimination Against Women, approved by the UN General Assembly in 1979.

Women's Rights in Guatemala

Member states to CEDAW (the Convention on the Elimination of All Forms of Discrimination against Women) are required to make periodic reports regarding the situations facing women in their country. In 2006, Guatemala reported that one of its biggest challenges was to bring national laws into harmony with international norms regarding women. To understand how far Guatemala must go in this regard, we can note some findings from the *Initial Report of Guatemala Submitted to the CEDAW Committee, 2 April 1991.*

The *Initial Report* indicated the following about gender roles:

- Guatemala is a patriarchal system where "the man is expected to be the breadwinner, the legal representative, the repository of authority; the one who must 'correct' the children, while the mother is relegated to their care and upbringing, to household tasks, and to 'waiting on' or looking after her husband or partner."

- Boys are guided to "masculine" work and girls to "feminine" work.

- Women are responsible for all matters regarding the family's health and hygiene.

- If the male head of household's income does not meet the family's needs, it is the woman's responsibility to augment it; if the male head of household is irresponsible in this regard, all the responsibility falls on her.

- Women generally have lower levels of education than men, so their paid employment generates less income.

Regarding rights and responsibilities in marriage, the *Initial Report* stated:

- A woman may be employed outside the home, "where she is able to do so without endangering the interests and the care of her children, or other needs of her household."

- Men, not women, are responsible under law for representing the marriage and administering its assets.

- Parental authority goes solely to the man unless he is imprisoned or otherwise legally barred.

- Judicial decisions on paternity in cases of rape depend on the behavior of the woman.

- Rape is an offense "against honor," rather than an offense "against personal integrity."

- Domestic violence is not considered an offense against the person but is rather included in the category of other domestic injuries or threats.

These points raise the following questions:

1. What rights do Guatemalan women have as individuals?
2. Where do women fit in Guatemalan society?
3. Are the gender situations in most other countries generally similar to or different from that of Guatemala?

Source: United Nations Convention on the Elimination of All Forms of Discrimination against Women, *CEDAW 35th Session, 15 May to 2 June 2006,* http://www.un.org/womenwatch/daw/cedaw/35sess.htm; and *Initial Report of Guatemala Submitted to the CEDAW Committee, 2 April 1991,* CEDAW/C/Gua/1-2.

---

simply **UN Women** as it is called. UN Women represents the merger of four components of the UN that worked for gender equality and the empowerment of women:

- The Division for the Advancement of Women (DAW)
- The International Research and Training Institute for the Advancement of Women (INSTRAW)
- The Office of the Special Adviser on Gender Issues and Advancement of Women (OSAGI)
- The United Nations Development Fund for Women (UNIFEM)

Initially led by former Chilean President Michelle Bachelet and now by former South African Deputy President Phumzile Mlambo-Ngcuka, UN Women works directly with specific member states to implement international agreements regarding gender equity and women's empowerment. This emphasis means working more closely to match country-specific programming to local needs than has been the case in the past, as well as getting multiple governments to work together for such purposes. UN Women also coordinates UN efforts so the organization speaks with one voice on women's rights issues, and it also serves as a broker and clearinghouse for information and knowledge about women's issues.

UN Women the United Nations entity for gender equality and the empowerment of Women, created in 2010 with the merger of the Division for the Advancement of Women (DAW), the International Research and Training Institute for the Advancement of Women (INSTRAW), the Office of the Special Adviser on Gender Issues and Advancement of Women (OSAGI), and the United Nations Development Fund for Women (UNIFEM).

Nkosazana Dlamini-Zuma, the first female chairperson of the African Union Commission | What does the election of the first woman to head the African Union suggest about the evolution of African attitudes and actions toward women?

More broadly, the UN's Human Rights Commission was meant to be one of the leading international institutions dealing with human rights issues. This commission was instrumental in drafting the Universal Declaration of Human Rights and issuing recommendations regarding human rights issues—again, employing soft power approaches by articulating a statement of shared values. However, since its members were elected by the UN Economic and Social Council in open session on the basis of geographic representation rather than on the basis of their own human rights record, over time its membership and actions became more controversial. Not only were states with poor human rights records often elected as members, they could also be elected to leadership positions (such as Libya, which was elected to chair the commission in 2003!). The Human Rights Commission also appeared to make politicized decisions, like taking a particularly hard line toward the human rights violations of certain states (like South Africa or Israel) while ignoring the human rights situations in others where the bulk of its members were located (such as the rest of Africa, the Middle East, and Asia). Based on these shortcomings, the UN replaced the Human Rights Commission with a new body in 2006, the **UN Human Rights Council**.

UN Human Rights Council the body created by the UN General Assembly in 2006 to replace the UN Human Rights Commission in making recommendations regarding human rights issues.

The UN Human Rights Council was meant to be an improvement over the Human Rights Commission in the sense that its members would be elected by secret ballot of the entire UN membership, and voters could take into consideration the candidate state's contributions to the promotion of human rights! Once elected, member states could be suspended from the Human Rights Council by a two-thirds vote of the General Assembly if their own human rights records merited such action. Unfortunately, so far the Human Rights Council has failed to produce any significant changes. Since states were still elected to the Human Rights Council on the basis of regional geographic representation, the frequency of states with the worst human rights records being elected to the council decreased only slightly (Libya was still elected to the council), the council issued fewer resolutions critical of the human rights situations in specific states than did the Human Rights Commission, and the number of resolutions critical of Israel actually increased.[13] Only time will tell if the majority of UN members continue to be most comfortable with a human rights entity that is not overly aggressive in pursuing its role.

As this discussion demonstrates, not everyone will embrace a new set of values just because others do so. Some will resist the power of example or persuasion to change their human rights behavior. In those cases, hard power approaches may be needed to punish bad behavior or reward good behavior. Let's talk about those next.

HARD POWER The spread of shared values, persuasion, the power of example, and other forms of soft power are not the only ways for international organizations to promote human rights. As we referenced in Chapter 3, hard power—the ability to coerce or reward—can be employed at times as well, even by international organizations. Humanitarian interventions are one example of the use of such hard power. In just the post-Cold War era, the Economic Community of West African States (ECOWAS) intervened to stop civil wars in Liberia and Sierra Leone; the UN authorized humanitarian interventions to stop violence and protect civilians in Bosnia, Somalia, Rwanda, Haiti, Sierra Leone, and East Timor; and NATO intervened in Kosovo.

If and when peace can be largely established, international organizations will often authorize and provide armed peacekeepers to ensure the safety of civilians in areas of potential conflict. UN peacekeepers can be found in Africa (in the Democratic Republic of the Congo, Sudan, Cote d'Ivoire, Liberia, and Western Sahara), and the UN Security Council authorized other peacekeepers to be sent to the Central African Republic in 2014. As UN Secretary-General Ban Ki Moon noted: "There is a hole in the heart of Africa."[14] UN peacekeepers can also be found in Asia (in East Timor, along the India-Pakistan border, and in Afghanistan), in Europe (in Cyprus and Kosovo), in the Middle East (in Egypt, Lebanon, and other countries along the Israeli border), and in Haiti. The African Union has peacekeeping troops in the Democratic Republic of the Congo, Somalia, and Sudan, while NATO has peacekeeping troops stationed in Afghanistan, Bosnia, and Kosovo. In the past, the Organization of American States has engaged in peacekeeping missions in the Dominican Republic, Panama, and Haiti, and it has intervened to settle maritime conflicts between Colombia and Venezuela and between Trinidad and Venezuela. Finally, both NATO and the European Union have multinational naval fleets patrolling the waters off the Somalia coast to protect against piracy.

Hard power approaches involve other punishments, as well. For example, in 2011 Syria engaged in widely condemned violence by its government against dissenters. While the Arab League voted to suspend Syria's membership and impose sanctions, the UN's Human Rights Council authorized an Independent International Commission of Inquiry to undertake an investigation that concluded that the Syrian regime was engaged in crimes against humanity. The UN High Commissioner for Human Rights (Navanethem Pillay, a South African woman) estimated that at least 4,000 Syrians had been murdered by regime forces in 2011, leading the Human Rights Council to vote 37 to 4 to condemn the Syrian regime for the violence and transmit the report to the UN Secretary General and other UN institutions (including the UN Security Council) for further consideration and action. Stymied by Chinese and Russian opposition in the UN Security Council, continued violence in Syria, including a number of massacres, led the United States and EU to impose economic sanctions on Syrian elites to try to bring hard power to bear on those responsible for the violence against civilians.

The case of Libyan human rights and the UN also took an interesting turn in 2011. Colonel Muammar

A Libyan and his son survey the damage from NATO bombs in September 2011 | At what point does flouting international norms justify violent responses by IOs such as NATO?

Gaddafi's regime turned the military and other security forces loose against civilians protesting the authoritarian regime's rule, resulting in hundreds or possibly thousands of deaths. The UN Security Council responded in multiple ways to what morphed into a civil war in Libya. First, it imposed smart sanctions against the regime. Gaddafi, his four sons and a daughter, and ten other top intelligence and defense officials of the regime were banned from international travel and their foreign financial assets were frozen. An arms embargo against the regime was also imposed, and mercenaries were banned from international travel to or from Libya. Second, the Security Council referred the Libyan use of deadly force against civilians to the International Criminal Court (which we discussed previously) for investigation of possible war crimes. These actions came one day after the United States imposed a freeze on Libyan governmental assets in the United States as well as on the assets of top Libyan leaders. Not surprisingly, the Human Rights Council voted to recommend to the UN General Assembly that Libya's membership on the council be suspended. Third, the Security Council authorized the imposition of a no-fly zone against Libyan military aircraft and called on members to protect the Libyan people. With that UN Security Council authorization in hand, NATO members began attacking Libyan military airfields, command-and-control centers and networks, and governmental troops and compounds. Clearly, the UN and NATO had moved from soft to hard power.

Another form of hard power involves trials and the threat of imprisonment for individuals who commit human rights abuses. International organizations have pursued these judicial efforts through the creation of temporary tribunals as well as through regularly established courts.

Due to the presence of ethnic cleansing, indiscriminate attacks on civilians, and the use of rape as a weapon, the UN moved to create a special tribunal for the conflicts within the former state of Yugoslavia in the mid-1990s. As of 2014, this special court in the Netherlands had indicted 161 individuals, including heads of state, heads of government, senior military and police commanders, interior ministry officials, and lower-level security and political officials. Seventy-four were convicted of their crimes, and 20 cases were still ongoing. The genocide in Rwanda also prompted the creation of another such special tribunal. As of 2014, this special court in Tanzania had convicted 63 individuals and acquitted twelve.

A similar set of trials is currently ongoing in what may be seen as hybrid national and international efforts. One set of trials regards the crimes committed against the Cambodian people by the Cambodian Khmer Rouge government of the late 1970s. That temporary tribunal is a special court of the Cambodian government, but it features a mix of Cambodian judges and international judges nominated by the UN Secretary-General. In 2010, Kaing Guek Eav (known as "Comrade Duch") was convicted by the court of multiple war crimes and crimes against humanity and received a 30-year prison sentence. Upon appeal in 2012, his sentence was increased to life in prison for the killing of 15,000 people, and his conviction as a senior member of the Khmer Rouge government is the most prominent conviction to date by the Cambodian tribunal.

Another hybrid court is the Special Court for Sierra Leone, which is a joint effort by the government of Sierra Leone and the UN. So far, nine people have been convicted and sentenced to prison terms ranging from 15 to 52 years. Its highest profile case involved former Liberian President Charles Taylor who was convicted of crimes committed by the rebel forces he led while they were massing next door in Sierra Leone. Those crimes included both war crimes and crimes against humanity, including the murder and rape of civilians, hacking off the hands of civilians, the use of slave labor in diamond mines, and reports of cannibalism. Sixty-four year old Taylor was sentenced to 50 years in prison in 2012.

Beyond the ICC and these special tribunals, there are other regional human rights courts, the most active of which is the **European Court of Human Rights (ECHR)**. Initially created in 1959 by the Council of Europe, the court's current operation is based on the European Convention of Human Rights, which went into force in 1953. Unlike many other international courts that are based in The Hague, Netherlands, the ECHR is located in Strasbourg, France. It has judges from all Council of Europe members, and it hears a wide array of types of human rights cases. These include:

- Clarifying criminal rights (including the rights of the accused, the rights of prisoners and those being detained, the rights of states and citizens regarding terrorism, and opposition to the death penalty)

- Protecting endangered or discriminated groups (women, children, homosexuals, transsexuals, the mentally ill, those seeking asylum or trying to avoid expulsion or

European Court of Human Rights (ECHR) a court created in 1959 by the Council of Europe; one of the most active courts involved in human rights cases.

extradition, conscientious objectors, racial minorities, Roma [Gypsies] and Travelers [Irish nomadic peoples], those pressed into forced labor or victims of trafficking, and so on)

- Protecting professional and personal rights (such as protecting journalistic sources, rights to join trade unions, data protection, Internet-based and online rights, and the like)

- Protecting the environment

- Providing for social welfare

If the court finds against a government, the most typical judgments are instructions to change the offending policies or actions and, as needed, to pay monetary damages to the person or persons victimized.

The ECHR is particularly noteworthy because of how many cases it handles. In 2008, the ECHR issued its ten-thousandth judgment, in which Russia was found guilty of violations of the right to life and inhuman or degrading treatment in the case of disappearances of Chechen nationals at the hands of Russian military personnel. In fact, the Russian government has been a very popular target before the court. Since its first judgment involving the Russian Federation in 2002, through 2010 the ECHR has found Russia in violation of human rights standards in 815 of 862 cases heard, and there are over 33,000 other cases pending that involve Russia![14] It will take some time to work through these cases, as the ECHR has only been able to process about 1,500 cases each year. Recently, the number of judgments against Turkey has risen, rivaling those against Russia in 2013. Luckily, other options exist to press for the promotion of human rights. We turn to the roles played by NGOs next.

11-3c NGO-Based Initiatives

Non-governmental organizations also get heavily involved in the implementation and enforcement of human rights standards using both soft and at times hard power approaches, as this arena is an important focus of the emerging **international civil society**—an international system based on norms promoting democracy and human rights. Many human rights NGOs exist and work toward the improvement of human rights conditions around the world. Consisting of organizations such as Amnesty International, Human Rights Watch, the Red Cross, and hundreds of other organizations, small and large, local and international, such groups engage in a variety of activities to help strengthen human rights practices. First, they monitor and publicize human rights

ALBERTO PIZZOLI/Getty Images

An Amnesty International rally to stop the use of the death penalty | How can protest demonstrations in one country stop human rights abuses in other countries?

violations through both regular and special reporting. Amnesty International, for example, publishes an annual review of human rights practices around the world, and periodic special reports on critical problems as they arise. Second, these groups engage in "shaming" violators of human rights standards through reporting and other publicity to try to persuade violators to end abuses. Third, they recommend courses of action to try to bring pressure on the violators of human rights through avenues such as those we have discussed. Finally, these groups try to support and empower local groups and victims of human rights abuses. As a result, their actions are important but not always appreciated by more powerful actors.

There are literally hundreds of such groups, and ten of the more notable ones are listed in Table 11-3. A good example of such groups is Human Rights Watch (www.hrw.org). It began during the Cold War as Helsinki Watch in 1978, which was formed from a coalition of NGOs dedicated to monitoring the human rights practices of the Soviet Union in Eastern Europe.

Helsinki Watch embraced the concept of "naming and shaming," both in the press and in direct contacts, regimes that abused human rights—particularly civil and political rights. It found that even very repressive regimes would change their

---

international civil society an international system based on the norms of democracy and human rights. This emerging system is marked by civil society organizations, NGOs that promote these values on a global basis.

TABLE 11-3 TEN SELECTED HUMAN RIGHTS NGOS, THEIR MISSIONS, AND LINKS TO THEIR WEBSITES

NGO	MISSION	LINK
Aga Khan Development Network	Promote education and economic growth through grants, microfinance, and rural development	www.akdn.org/default.asp
Amnesty International	Protect prisoners of conscience and promote all areas of human rights under the Universal Declaration of Human Rights	www.amnesty.org
Bill and Melinda Gates Foundation	Reduce inequities around the world so all lives have an equal value	www.gatesfoundation.org
CARE International	Address the underlying causes of poverty and provide disaster assistance	www.careinternational.org
Carter Center	Alleviate suffering, resolve conflicts, and promote democracy	www.cartercenter.org
Committee to Protect Journalists	Promote freedom of the press through the protection of journalists from reprisals	www.cpj.org
Doctors Without Borders	Provide emergency medical aid in areas of conflict, epidemics, or natural disasters	www.doctorswithoutborders.org
Empowerment and Rights Institute	Promote human rights for ordinary people and disadvantaged groups in China	www.erichina.org
Freedom House	Promote democracy, free markets, and the rule of law	www.freedomhouse.org
International Committee of the Red Cross	Protect victims of war and violence, provide humanitarian relief in emergencies, and support the rule of law	www.icrc.org/eng/

Source: Duke University Libraries, "NGO Database," *NGO Research Guide*, http://library.duke.edu/research/subject/guides/ngo_guide/ngo_database.html.

behavior to get such a media spotlight off of them and directed elsewhere. The success of Helsinki Watch led to the creation of Americas Watch in 1981, which had among its initial concerns war crimes and the abuse of civilians in the various civil wars sweeping Central America at the time. Asia Watch (1985), Africa Watch (1988), and Middle East Watch (1989) quickly followed, and in 1988 Human Rights Watch was chosen as the umbrella name for all these NGOs.

The new Human Rights Watch quickly responded to the challenges of the times, focusing on helping to bring those accused of genocide and ethnic cleansing to justice. It soon added the challenges of terrorism and of counterterrorism campaigns and began to focus on the continuing problems of endangered groups such as women and children, gays and lesbians, and the victims of human trafficking. It lent its support to the creation of the ICC and the passage of the treaty banning land mines (the 1997 Mine Ban Treaty). Human Rights Watch also now deals with long-term problems like homelessness and poor access to education. Whereas many national governments push these issues as well, NGOs such as Human Rights Watch can do so with a single-mindedness of purpose without other cross-cutting national interests entering the policy equation. In short, these NGOs try to make headway on a wide variety of fronts to advance human security.

Human Rights Watch is certainly not alone in advancing human security. A number of NGOs have been instrumental in advancing the causes of human rights, especially when one focuses on particular human rights issues. A good example was provided in South Africa by the struggle to end apartheid, which was considered a crime against humanity.

After a steady upswing in the number and severity of strikes and demonstrations against apartheid inside South Africa in the 1970s, the regime relaxed some of its restrictions on political and economic activity, and, as a result of this opening, local black civil society organizations—such as trade unions and other societal groups—began to operate. By the mid-1980s, external NGOs and national governments funneled large sums of money directly into the hands of these internal, anti-apartheid groups to support their activities. Moreover, these external NGOs put pressures on their own governments to distance themselves from South Africa, which was increasingly depicted as a racist regime. A very significant development came when foreign corporations became pressured by stockholders to break their economic ties with South Africa. Fearing stockholder revolts, those corporations began to sell off their South African operations or assets and to take their money out of the country. Due to these external and internal pressures in which NGOs played a prominent role, the South African government abandoned apartheid. Since the end of apartheid, anti-apartheid NGOs inside South Africa have continued to monitor the actions of the government and of other, more conservative groups, to ensure that elements of apartheid do not reappear.

Another good example comes from meeting the needs of women. Besides UN Women, a number of NGOs address women's needs, as well. For example,

A Red Cross ambulance becomes a target in war-torn Lebanon | When first responders are targets, is anyone safe?

the International Association for Maternal and Neonatal Health seeks to reduce the mortality rates for mothers and newborns in developing countries. Pathfinder International seeks to provide a number of programs to promote women's reproductive health, broadly defined. Besides maternal and neonatal care, these needs include family planning services, HIV and AIDS-related programs, community-based health care programs, and so on. The Coalition Against Trafficking in Women has regional offices in Africa, Asia, Europe, and Latin America and the Caribbean. Women for Women International seeks to meet the many needs of women who are war survivors. The Central Asia Institute seeks to provide education primarily for girls in remote areas of Pakistan and Afghanistan. Many such organizations now exist to promote the rights of women and to respond to their needs.

The examples could go on and on, but the point is clear. Many NGOs exist to promote

human rights in the international community. They raise funds, raise awareness, step in to provide services that national governments cannot or will not provide, and monitor the actions of national governments, as well. They are vital players in the promotion of global human rights and human security, just as are states and international organizations.

CONCLUSION: THE EVOLVING HUMAN RIGHTS REGIME

As this chapter has demonstrated, human rights have come a long way from limited concerns about preventing a monarch from imprisoning enemies without just cause. Human rights began with limiting what governments can do and promoting the idea that humans possess some natural rights simply by existing, but they have evolved into a set of norms, rules, and international agreements regarding the responsibility to protect the people—both entire societies and endangered groups—from preventable harm. These norms, rules, and agreements are monitored and enforced by states, international organizations, and NGOs alike, and the combination of all three makes it difficult for egregious violators of human rights to continue their actions without some international repercussions. Since the end of World War II and escalating in the neo-Westphalian international system, the idea that states can do whatever they want within their own borders is an idea whose time has passed.

Yet past cases reveal a mixed picture. In some instances, the people of a state—often with the help of NGOs and international organizations—can reverse a pattern of human rights abuses themselves or even overthrow an abusive regime. In other cases, the victims of human rights abuses are relatively powerless to act on their own in the face of brutality, and soft or hard power interventions by state actors or other international organizations become necessary to protect human rights. Do you think human rights are becoming sufficiently recognized at the international level so that abusive behavior by regimes can be changed by the spotlight of negative publicity, or will outside interventions still be necessary in the future to curb the behavior of abusive regimes that are willing to use any means to stay in power?

College of Saint Benedict

According to scholars such as Thomas Risse and Kathryn Sikkink, there are some elemental rights of the person that are truly universal. Certainly the UN's Universal Declaration of Human Rights is predicated on the premise that we all share a common set of rights. However, that declaration was written and passed in 1948 when the UN had only 58 members, the vast majority of which were from Europe and the Americas. Since the Americas had been colonized by European powers, this overlap in what these actors saw as universal human rights is not particularly surprising, as all these states reflected a Western/European heritage.

Kathryn Sikkink

Now the UN has 193 members, with the vast majority of the new members coming from Asia and Africa. We noted earlier that some Asian and African leaders prioritized collective rights over individual ones. So what do you think?

Are human rights universal, or are they culturally based?

STUDY TOOLS 11

LOCATED AT BACK OF THE BOOK:
☐ Rip out Chapter in Review card

LOCATED ON COURSEMATE:
Use the CourseMate access card that came with this book or visit CengageBrain.com for more review materials.
☐ Review Key Terms Flash Cards (Print or Online)
☐ Download Chapter Summaries for on-the-go review

☐ Complete Practice Quizzes to prepare for the test
☐ Walk through a Simulation, Animated Learning Module, and Interactive Maps and Timelines to master concepts
☐ Complete Crossword Puzzle to review key terms
☐ Watch the videos for real-world application of this chapter's content
☐ Visit IR NewsWatch to learn about the latest current events as you prepare for class discussions and papers

REVIEW QUESTIONS

1. What are human rights, and what are the three major types (or generations) of human rights?

2. How did human rights evolve into a system of international norms, and what are the major international human rights agreements?

3. What different types of things can states do to promote and protect human rights?

4. What different types of things can international organizations do to promote and protect human rights?

5. What different types of things can non-governmental organizations do to promote and protect human rights?

6. How do the major international relations theories apply to the protection and promotion of human rights?

FOR MORE INFORMATION . . .

For more on:

The United States and human rights, see David P. Forsythe, *The United States and Human Rights: Looking Inward and Outward* (Lincoln, NE: University of Nebraska Press, 2008); and the U.S. Department of State, *Human Rights*, http://www.state.gov/g/drl/hr/.

Enforcement, see Emilie M. Hafner-Burton. *Making Human Rights a Reality* (Princeton, NJ: Princeton University Press, 2013).

The UN's efforts, see United Nations, *Human Rights*, http://www.un.org/en/rights/.

International human rights, see Henry J. Steiner, Philip Alston, and Ryan Goodman. *International Human Rights in Context: Law, Politics, Morals*, 3rd ed. (New York: Oxford University Press, 2007).

12 | Managing the Environment:
Sharing the World or Dividing the World?

LEARNING OBJECTIVES

After studying this chapter, you will be able to . . .

 12-1 Identify the "tragedy of the commons," collective goods, and the environmental challenges facing humankind.

 12-2 Describe the evolving environmental regime and the roles of states, IOs, and NGOs in that regime.

 12-3 Explain the concept of sustainable development and steps toward that goal.

After finishing this chapter go to **PAGE 361** for **STUDY TOOLS**

CAN WE BE PROTECTED FROM OURSELVES?

During one horrific night in Bhopal, India, over half a million people were exposed to deadly gases and thousands died. In 1984, the local chemical plant owned by Union Carbide suffered a catastrophic leak in a tank holding 42 tons of methyl isocyanate—a key component of the commonly used pesticide Sevin. Deadly gases drifted over the city while townspeople slept. The initial death toll exceeded 2,000 victims. Over time, estimates of the deaths from the leak ranged from 5,000 to 25,000 and the Indian government reported that over 500,000 suffered injuries from exposure to methyl isocyanate.

Accidents happen, but could this have been averted? It's hard to know, but a variety of factors were involved. First, the tank holding the methyl isocyanate was quite large and filled beyond recommended levels. Second, multiple safety systems failed to prevent the disaster; some failed due to faulty maintenance over time, and others were apparently shut down to save money. Third, a reliance on manual operation by inadequately skilled employees and inadequate evacuation plans may have contributed to the death tolls, which were made worse by the presence of densely populated slums near the factory. Local indignation was later fueled by the realization that the factory had been plagued by previous leaks and Union Carbide had moved Sevin production out of the United States because it was deemed to be too dangerous.

After the leak, the factory was closed and the premises abandoned, with toxic chemicals still stored there in deteriorating containers. Soil and water samples from the site are still toxic. Following a lawsuit by India against Union Carbide, in 1989 a settlement was reached in which the company paid India $470 million, funded the construction of a hospital, and agreed to pay for free health care for the next eight years for the survivors of the accident; in return Union Carbide got a full release from any further *corporate* civil or criminal liability. However, in 2010, seven former employees were *individually* convicted in India of negligent homicide and sentenced to the maximum punishment available—two years imprisonment and a fine of nearly $2,000. In the United States, civil and criminal cases are pending in New York against Union Carbide and multiple employees.

Again, accidents happen, but:

1. Could this accident have been avoided, and if so, at what cost?

2. To what degree do our own actions contribute to environmental dangers?

3. What steps should be taken to make toxic chemicals safer to manufacture?

4. Do Western corporations place a lower value on the lives of people in developing countries than they do on the lives of Westerners? To what extent are governments like India's also to blame?

DIBYANGSHU SARKAR/AFP/Getty Images

BHOPAL
23,000 DEAD
AND COUNTING...

Protesters demonstrate on the 25th Anniversary of Union Carbide's leak of deadly chemicals in Bhopal, India | Where does the responsibility for environmental disasters lie?

INTRODUCTION: ENVIRONMENTAL CHALLENGES AND THE CONSEQUENCES OF HUMAN ACTIONS

When an environmental disaster occurs within a state, Westphalian sovereignty suggests that the state involved is ultimately responsible for what happens within its borders. Its leaders may ask for international assistance, but the responsibility to ensure economic and human security is theirs. However, who is responsible when the radiation from Japan's 2011 Fukushima nuclear meltdown pollutes the Pacific Ocean or blows toward North America on the winds of the jet stream? Who is responsible for taking care of what is beyond the borders of any particular state or common to all humankind, such as air, sea, and space?

12-1 THE "TRAGEDY OF THE COMMONS"

According to Westphalian sovereignty, *no one is responsible*, and thus our planet's health could be imperiled. This problem is captured by the concept known as the **tragedy of the commons**: the idea that when no one actor owns a resource—like air or water—then no one takes responsibility for its protection. Individual actors rationally seek their own individual gain, and the common resource is depleted or degraded as a consequence of their individual use and misuse. So-called public, or **collective goods**—things that benefit everyone whether or not one pays for their cost or maintenance—are not the responsibility of any one state actor, and thus their care typically falls through the cracks of Westphalian sovereignty. Yet do you want to breathe toxic air or drink toxic water? Where does the neo-Westphalian "responsibility to protect" enter this picture?

tragedy of the commons the idea that no one state is held responsible for things held in common—so-called collective goods—like the air and water, and so their protection often goes unaddressed.

collective goods things that benefit all concerned—whether they participate in their protection and maintenance—and are not owned by any one state actor.

12-1a The Collective Goods Problem Illustrated

When considering environmental politics, illustrations of the collective goods problem are easy to find. Some of these issues cascade into others to produce even more collective goods problems.

POLLUTION Pollution of our air, ground, and water provides clear examples of the collective goods problem. In the course of everyday human economic activity, we create tremendous amounts of waste—much of which is toxic or at least not easily biodegradable—that the planet has to cleanse. Our automobiles, factories, power plants, and machines generate enormous amounts of pollution in many forms, and post-consumer waste literally piles up all around the globe. While the smoke from a fireplace or a barbecue pit may smell great, when entire societies cook their food and heat their homes with wood-burning fires or rely on **slash-and-burn agriculture** every year, tremendous amounts of carbon dioxide (CO_2) and particulates are released into the air.

However, when coal is burned to fuel stoves, provide heat, power industry, or generate electricity, carbon dioxide and particulates are not the only things released. According to the Union of Concerned Scientists, here is what is released by a typical coal-fired power plant each year (note that this does not include the pollution caused by mining the coal):

- 3.7 million tons of carbon dioxide, equivalent to cutting down 161 million trees
- 10,200 tons of nitrogen oxide, which causes ozone and smog
- 10,000 tons of sulfur dioxide that causes acid rain
- 720 tons of carbon monoxide, a deadly gas
- 500 tons of particulates that get trapped in lungs and contribute to respiratory illness
- 220 tons of hydrocarbons that contribute to ozone and smog formation
- 225 pounds of arsenic, a toxic chemical
- 170 pounds of mercury, a toxic chemical
- 114 pounds of lead, a toxic chemical
- 4 pounds of cadmium, along with other toxic heavy metal compounds[1]

slash-and-burn agriculture the practice of clearing fields by cutting down and burning existing plant growth to prepare land for new agricultural use each season, common in many developing countries.

These compounds imperil our human security because they not only get into the air we breathe, they also fall to the earth and poison the ground and groundwater, run off into the oceans, and eventually find their way into the food that we eat. In children, the effects of such pollutants include cancers of the lung, bladder, kidney, and liver; they contribute to birth defects, mental disability, and learning disorders; and they can produce convulsions, comas, and ultimately death. Respiratory diseases are more likely for all who breathe these compounds. In just the United States alone, coal-fired power plants produce 30,000 premature deaths each year. Overall, air pollution shortens lives—by as much as two years on average in heavily polluted areas.

There is obvious economic impact, as well as consequences for our health. For years, the U.S. steel industry relied on coal power to fuel its plants in the Midwest. Due to prevailing southerly and southwesterly winds for much of the year, the emissions from these plants drifted north to Canada where they fell back to earth in the form of acid rain. The acid rain killed off huge tracts of forest, thereby both hurting the timber industry (an important component of the Canadian economy) and reducing the number of trees that could be absorbing such toxic wastes from the atmosphere. No wonder the Canadians were mad at the United States—their economic security was being harmed.

At least these actions were relatively inadvertent, in the sense that relying on coal for industrial use began long before most people understood the negative consequences of what was released in the emissions. For years, however, the Soviet Union secretly disposed of some of its nuclear waste by dumping it in the Sea of Japan. The Soviets knew this radioactive waste was toxic, but they got rid of it the fastest, easiest way they could. Do the Japanese eat seafood? Do they fish the Sea of Japan? Are you surprised Japan's relationship with Russia deteriorated when these revelations made the news? While the health damage done to the Japanese as a result of this dumping of nuclear waste is unknown, the Japanese had reason to be concerned. They had previously experienced major episodes of health-related disasters due to pollution's effects. Previous Japanese victims of cadmium poisoning (from industrial wastes discharged into the sea) suffered from degenerative kidney disease, brittle bones, and extremely painful back and joint disabilities. Japanese who consumed mercury-poisoned fish had excessive degeneration of their central nervous systems. So it's not hard to understand that, while much of the Sea of Japan is legally considered international waters, the Japanese did not appreciate this threat to their health and livelihood.

Aerial view of the Haiti/Dominican Republic border | On which side of the border would you prefer to live?

Finally, nuclear waste is not the only thing that gets tossed into the ocean. All kinds of trash can be found in the world's oceans, particularly plastic, which does not biodegrade quickly at all. At least two large floating trash dumps have recently been found. Estimates of their sizes vary, from twice the size of Texas (or over 500,000 square miles) to 1 percent of the size of Texas (about 269 square miles) if the trash was compacted and all the water was squeezed out.[2] One is in the Pacific about 1,000 miles west of California. Another one is also in the Pacific closer to Asia.

Ocean currents sweep the trash into increasingly large clumps to create these floating garbage patches. We don't yet know how much damage such floating trash piles do to marine life or how, given their size, they may change surface ocean currents. They move with ocean currents and continue to collect more trash over time. The sad fact is that, since they are in the area of the global commons, they—like many other examples of pollution—potentially affect everyone, but they are no one's specific responsibility to clean up.

DEFORESTATION As mentioned previously, pollution can kill off forests; just ask the Canadians. However, the bigger threat to forests is the intentional cutting down of trees. While the timber industry in many countries does plant new trees to replace those cut down, that is not the case for those who cut down trees simply because they need wood to fuel their cooking or heating fires. Thus, the forests of Haiti are now almost completely gone, while the forests of the next-door Dominican Republic are still largely present, as the photo shows. Haiti is the brown country on the left. Unfortunately, Haiti is not alone, and significant **deforestation**—the destruction

of forests faster than they can be replenished—has occurred in many developing countries. As we will see, such deforestation endangers both human and economic security.

While cutting down trees for firewood for cooking and heating is a serious problem, an even graver threat to the world's forests is cutting down trees to clear land for alternative usage. The Brazilian rain forest provides a good example. According to official records kept by the Brazilian government since 1988, the average amount of deforestation in Brazil each year is approximately 6,400 square miles.[3] That is an area larger than the state of Connecticut and almost three-fourths the size of New Jersey! The primary reason the rain forest is being cut down is to clear land to raise cattle, a more profitable use of the land by private landowners.

So what difference does this make? First, trees are among the most productive generators of oxygen. Like other plants, trees breathe in carbon dioxide, convert it to food, use it and store it, and then breathe out oxygen as a waste product. As the oxygen mixes with hydrogen in the atmosphere, water forms and rain occurs. So fewer rain forests mean less oxygen and ultimately less rain! Second, trees reduce the most prominent of **greenhouse gases**—carbon dioxide— by using it as food and storing it. As we will see in the section on global climate change, greenhouse gases contribute to such climate change, which is another serious problem. Third, by increasing the number of cattle being raised, landowners contribute to the generation of methane gas, a natural gas produced in part by bovine waste (that was carefully phrased). While carbon dioxide gets a lot of attention as the leading greenhouse gas, methane is the second leading greenhouse gas. So deforestation in the Brazilian Amazon reduces the ability of the planet to clean its air of pollutants, reduces the amount of oxygen and water available to support life, and adds to the amount of greenhouse gases in the atmosphere. The only good news here is that the rate of deforestation in Brazil is generally slowing down. With the exception of two years in which it rose (2008 and 2013), it has declined each year since 2004. These improvements are due to the Brazilian government's decision to assign more police personnel to protect the rain forest from illegal tree cutting, active roles being

deforestation the destruction of forests at a rate faster than they can be replaced or replenished.

greenhouse gases those gases that trap the sun's heat and hold it close to the earth's surface; they include carbon dioxide, methane, nitrous oxide, and water vapor.

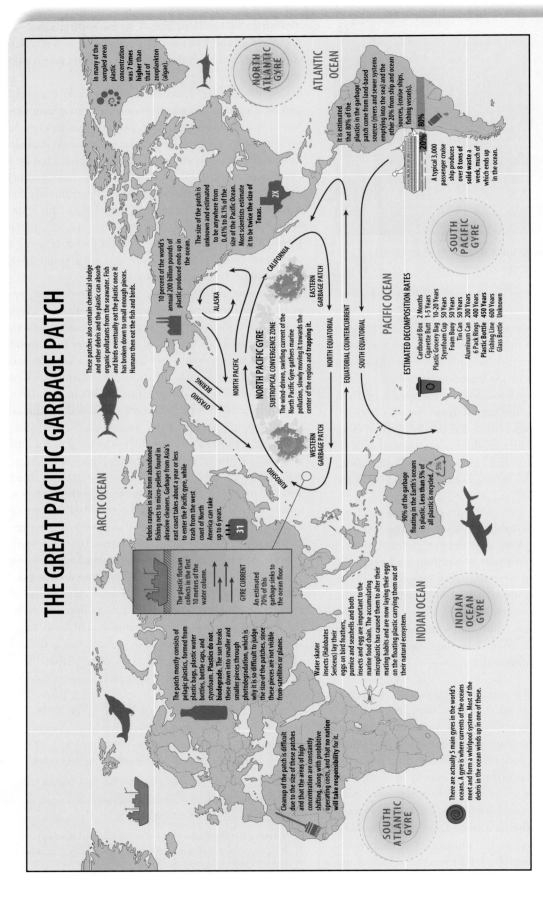

The Great Pacific Garbage Patch near Hawaii | What impacts might such pollution have on marine life?

Sources: Scripps Research Institute Wikipedia.org (Great Pacific Garbage Patch) NOAA (National Oceanic and Atmospheric Administration) SEAPLEX (Scripps Environmental Accumulation of Plastic Expedition)

© Cengage Learning®

played by NGOs there, and educational campaigns to show the effects of deforestation.

On a global basis, the news regarding deforestation is still bad but is slowly improving. A 2010 report by the UN Food and Agriculture Organization indicated that over the prior decade, 32 million acres of forest per year were lost globally to deforestation. At 50,000 square miles, that's an area slightly larger than the state of New York. However, that figure is somewhat lower than for the ten years prior to that when 39 million acres were lost annually to deforestation. That's an area of almost 61,000 square miles, thus larger than the states of New York, New Jersey, and Connecticut combined! Despite these relatively modest improvements in the rate of depletion, we are still diminishing the planet's ability to produce oxygen, generate water, and absorb carbon dioxide.

Beyond the impact on air quality, deforestation also carries other negative effects. Removing the forests also means removing most of the plant and animal species that live there. We return to this issue in the subsection Biodiversity Challenges, but one intriguing potential consequence is the impact this could have on future pharmaceutical drugs. As you probably know from the illustration of moldy bread leading to the discovery of penicillin, most pharmaceutical drugs come from organic compounds found originally in nature. Thus, as unknown chemical compounds and bacteria get destroyed through deforestation, who knows if the loss involves chemical combinations that could form the basis for the life-saving drugs of the future?

Another major negative impact of deforestation is an increased risk of floods and mudslides. Forests help mitigate the force of rain hitting the ground, and the tree roots help hold the soil together, thereby preventing soil erosion. Rain hits the upper canopy of leaves, filters through the leaves and branches, and then drops to the ground, there to be absorbed into the soil. Without the leaf canopy to filter the rain and the tree roots to hold the soil, rain hits the ground harder and a larger portion of that water runs off before it can soak in, thereby creating more flooding and mudslides nearby. Thus overall, fewer trees mean less rain, less rain means harder ground and more runoff when rain does fall as well as more heat reflected back into the atmosphere at other times, and more heat means the creation of larger deserts, to which we turn next.

DESERTIFICATION Desertification is another threat to economic and human security. The term literally means the ongoing creation and expansion of deserts. More and more land each year is lost to desertification. The process is fairly straightforward. As trees get cut down, less rain is generated. With less rainfall (and often aided by overgrazing of livestock), groundcovers become sparser, and the ground becomes harder. Thus, when rain does fall, it soaks in less and runs off faster, leaving the soil drier and reflecting more heat back into the air. At some point, there is insufficient moisture in the ground to support plant life, and new desert areas are formed or existing deserts get bigger.

China provides a good illustration. Almost a quarter of China is desert, and that desert is growing by about 1,300 square miles each year—or about the size of Rhode Island! As many as 400 million Chinese have lost the productive use of their land due to desertification, often having to move to cities for work, thereby putting even more stress on each city's resources. As more and more water gets drained from the soil, underground aquifers also dry up. As a result, the city of Shanghai has sunk about six feet in the last 20 years. According to the Chinese government, a total of 660,000 square miles overall have been lost to desertification—an area two-and-one-half times the size of Texas or about the size of Alaska. Fortunately, the rate of desertification has slowed in recent years through aggressive governmental actions to reclaim the land. While the Chinese believe about a third of this lost land can be reclaimed from the desert, they estimate it will take *300 years* to do so![4]

The problem of desertification is not just a Chinese problem, it is a global one. The UN estimates that by 2025, two-thirds of the arable land—land suitable for agricultural cultivation—in Africa will be lost to desertification, while one-third of the arable land in Asia and one-fifth of South America's arable land will be lost. As more of the earth's surface becomes desert, more heat from the sun is reflected into the atmosphere, which contributes in part to global climate change, to which we now turn.

GLOBAL CLIMATE CHANGE Many of the problems discussed previously contribute to the broader phenomenon known as global climate change, which also threatens economic and human security. To be sure, the earth has undergone warming and cooling cycles over time. There have been ice ages and then most of that ice melted for reasons we don't fully understand.

---

desertification the creation of new, or enlargement of existing, deserts.

arable land land capable of sustaining agriculture.

global climate change marked changes in the warming and cooling of the planet's temperatures, thought to be accelerated by human activity such as industrialization and fossil fuel emissions, which produce greenhouse gases.

Is Global Climate Change Real?

In spite of the mounting evidence and broad scientific consensus on the matter, not everyone accepts the idea that global climate change is real. Some question whether the earth's climate is changing in any significant way or believe that humans have not caused it if it is. In 2009, e-mails leaked to the press from the University of East Anglia appeared to raise concerns over the scientific data and the ways scientists have studied it. Also, a study published by the Oregon Institute of Science and Medicine pointed out a number of potential flaws in the global climate change hypothesis:

1. While global temperatures have gone up and down over the last 3,000 years, the average earth temperature trend line over that time has not changed. Thus, the increase in global temperature that has occurred since the last Little Ice Age in the early 1800s is part of a normal earth cycle.

2. The increase in shrinkage of glaciers began prior to the sharp rise in carbon dioxide emissions (around 1950), and the trend line in that shrinkage has remained unchanged.

3. The number of tornadoes in the United States has decreased over the last 50 years.

4. The average number of hurricanes making landfall in the United States has remained unchanged over the last 100 years.

5. The trend line for the intensity of Atlantic hurricanes (in terms of wind speeds) has remained unchanged over the last 50 years.

6. The slope of the trend line for average increases in sea levels has remained unchanged since 1850.

7. The trend line of the average increase in temperatures in 49 California counties has remained unchanged from 1940 to 1996, regardless of the increase in population of those counties.

The study concludes by arguing that "There are no experimental data to support the hypothesis that increases in human hydrocarbon use or in atmospheric carbon dioxide and other greenhouse gases are causing or can be expected to cause unfavorable changes in global temperatures, weather, or landscape."

Others agree, as over 30,000 scientists since 1998 have signed an online petition stating that there is no scientific evidence that human activity is driving global climate change and that proposed limits on greenhouse gas emissions could harm the environment, hinder science, and damage human health and welfare.

Yet these critics have critics. These and other arguments advanced by climate change skeptics have drawn responses of their own. Those opposing note that:

1. The evidence of global warming starting around 1800 is not contradictory but rather is consistent with the premise that the increased release in global hydrocarbons coincides with the arrival of the industrial revolution.

2. Of the more than 30,000 signatures on the petition questioning the science underlying the contention that humans are amplifying the global climate change phenomenon, just about 150—only 0.5 percent (or 0.005) of the signatories—have degrees in climatology or atmospheric science.

3. The Oregon Institute of Science and Medicine is a small think tank with six employees listed as faculty members, and it has no classrooms and no students.

4. The study produced by the Oregon Institute of Science and Medicine has not been published in peer-reviewed scientific journals but is instead self-published on the Internet.

5. Several organizations, including the Science and Technology Committee of the British House of Commons, investigated the allegations of academic misdeeds at the University of East Anglia and found that the Climate Center there did not distort the data or misrepresent the science behind the idea of global climate change.

So like most ideas, there are two sides to the theory of global climate change. Which do you think is most compelling?

Sources: Associated Press, "British Panel Says Climate Center Did Not Distort Data." *New York Times*, March 31, 2010, A11; Kevin Grandia, "The 30,000 Global Warming Petition Is Easily-Debunked Propaganda," *The Huffington Post Green*, July 22, 2009, http://www.huffingtonpost.com/kevin-grandia/the-30000 -global-warming_b_243092.html; *Oregon Institute of Science and Medicine*, http://www.oism.org/; The Center for Media and Democracy, "Oregon Institute of Science and Medicine," *Source Watch*, http://www.sourcewatch.org/index .php?title=Oregon_Institute_of_Science_and_Medicine; Arthur B., Robinson, Noah E. Robinson, and Willie Soon, *Global Warming Petition Project*, http://www .petitionproject.org/gw_article/Review_Article_HTML.php.

As a result, some believe that our planet heats and cools in cycles independent of human activity. These skeptics thus question the fundamental premise that global climate change is occurring or that human activity is responsible for it. See the box Spotlight On: Is Global Climate Change Real? for a look at that debate.

Despite the views of some critics, there is widespread global agreement on the phenomenon we call global climate change. We have known since the nineteenth century that the earth's atmosphere traps the sun's heat and that the major contributors—so-called "greenhouse gases"—include carbon dioxide, methane,

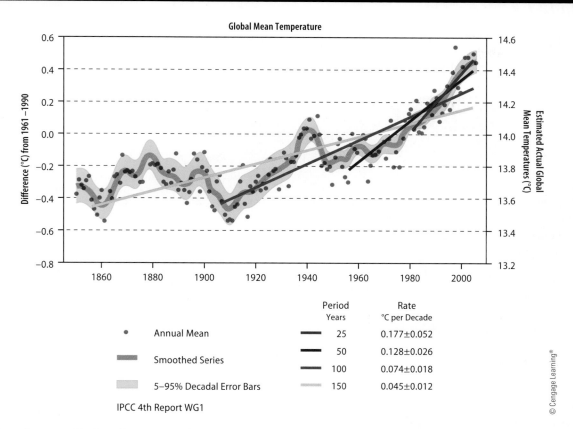

		Period	Rate
		Years	°C per Decade
•	Annual Mean	25	0.177±0.052
	Smoothed Series	50	0.128±0.026
	5–95% Decadal Error Bars	100	0.074±0.018
		150	0.045±0.012

IPCC 4th Report WG1

© Cengage Learning®

Source: *Climate Change 2007: The Physical Science Basis, Working Group I Contribution to the Fourth Assessment Report of the Intergovernmental Panel on Climate Change,* Figure TS.6 (bottom). Cambridge University Press, 2007.

nitrous oxide, and water vapor. What we have witnessed in recent years is a relatively rapid increase in the average temperatures on the planet, as shown in Figure 12-1.

As Figure 12-1 shows, the earth seems to have experienced significant warming patterns over time, and the increasingly steep trajectories of the colored lines show that the rate of change appears to be accelerating quite significantly. Indeed, the 13 hottest years ever recorded have occurred in the first 14 years of the twenty-first century, and each of the last three decades was hotter than the preceding one![5]

In recent years, scientists have theorized that human activity—particularly the burning of fossil fuels, which release greenhouse gases, and the use of aerosols—has made the current cycle more extreme. Former U.S. Vice President Al Gore drew attention to this conclusion in his well-publicized book and documentary film *An Inconvenient Truth*, but it is also the conclusion of the thousands of scientists from 195 countries who form the **Intergovernmental Panel on Climate Change (IPCC)**, a scientific body created by the UN's Environment Programme and the World Meteorological Organization.

According to the IPCC, the scientific evidence is conclusive; human activity has contributed to making the current cycle of climate change more extreme than would be the case otherwise. Indeed, in the spring of 2014 the IPCC released its most recent report, concluding with 95 percent confidence that climate change is underway and a consequence of human activity. Moreover, a study of more than 12,000 peer-reviewed scientific papers on the subject of climate change published from 1991–2011 found that over 97 percent of those who took a position agreed on the human causes of global warming.[6] Virtually every major national science academy around the world agrees, and none dissents.

Although overall average global temperatures are increasing, as shown on Map 12-1, as parts of each continent warm up, other parts cool down. Hence the

Intergovernmental Panel on Climate Change (IPCC)
a scientific body with 195 member states, created by the UN's Environment Programme and the World Meteorological Organization in 1988.

Map 12-1

Increases in Annual Temperatures for a Recent Five-Year Period, Relative to 1951–1980

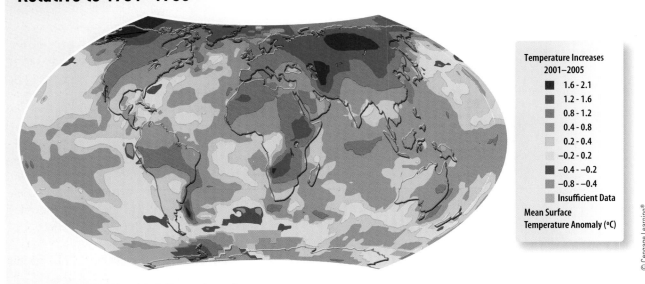

**Temperature Increases
2001–2005**

- 1.6 - 2.1
- 1.2 - 1.6
- 0.8 - 1.2
- 0.4 - 0.8
- 0.2 - 0.4
- −0.2 - 0.2
- −0.4 - −0.2
- −0.8 - −0.4
- **Insufficient Data**

**Mean Surface
Temperature Anomaly (°C)**

© Cengage Learning®

Who is most affected by global climate change?

Source: Data from Hugo Ahlenius, "Increases in annual temperatures for a recent five-year period, relative to 1951-1980," GRID-Arendal, http://www.grida.no/graphicslib/detail /increases-in-annual-temperatures-for-a-recent-five-year-period-relative-to-1951-1980_d666.

preferred scientific term for this phenomenon is global climate change rather than simply global warming. Graphic changes can be seen as a result of this average warming of the planet's land and water surfaces. Polar ice caps are melting at an unprecedented rate, threatening species such as polar bears and some seals with a loss of habitat and spawning massive new icebergs that break off from polar ice caps and threaten some shipping lanes. In 2010, an iceberg four times the size of Manhattan broke off from Greenland! Mountain glaciers are melting at an increasing rate as well, with some nearly disappearing from view. For example, the ice on Tanzania's Mount Kilimanjaro has decreased by 86 percent since 1912 and by 26 percent since just 2000.

The result of fresh water ice melt is a rise in global sea levels. Initial estimates suggest that sea levels could rise as much as three feet over the twenty-first century. If so, 13 of the world's 15 largest cities—cities such as New York City, London, and Tokyo—would face serious flooding problems. In the United States alone, 40 million people living in coastal cities would be affected by such rising sea levels. Particularly hard-hit would be the densely populated Northeast portion of the United States, where Massachusetts already

loses 65 acres a year to the ocean. Sea levels have already risen a foot over the last 100 years, and those living in flat coastal plains rely on old, deteriorating seawalls to protect them from the ocean. Low-lying countries like the Netherlands and Bangladesh could face even more devastating consequences, and entire islands or island nations—such as the Maldives in the Indian Ocean—could be entirely under water by the end of this century. Two studies reported in 2014 even worse news. The West Antarctica ice shelf is becoming destabilized as multiple glaciers that feed it are rapidly melting, passing the point of no return for the ice shelf. The results would most likely be seen after the twenty-first century, but they are highly alarming. The release of this much fresh water could result in ocean levels rising an additional four to 12 feet.[7]

If that isn't bad enough, releasing this much cold, fresh water into the warming salt waters of the world's oceans could have another impact. Ocean currents could change! While surface ocean currents can be directed by winds, deep ocean currents are products of differences in temperatures and salinity levels in water. Do you ever wonder why northern Europe has a relatively temperate climate despite being about as far north as Alaska?

FIGURE 12-2   NOAA GFDL CM2.1 MODEL SIMULATION

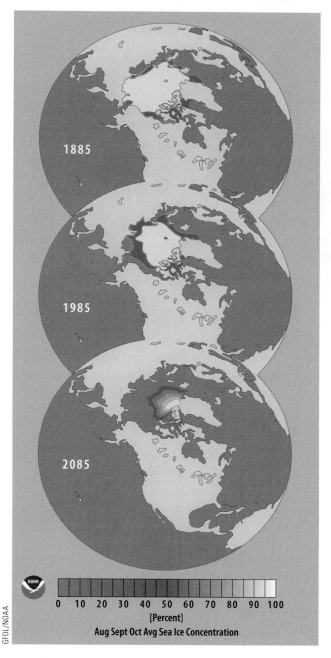

1885

1985

2085

GFDL/NOAA

0   10   20   30   40   50   60   70   80   90   100
[Percent]
Aug Sept Oct Avg Sea Ice Concentration

Image from National Oceanic and Atmospheric Administration (NOAA) of the shrinking arctic ice cap. What might be the consequences of no ice cap in the Arctic?

Source: GFDL/NOAA, http://www.gfdl.noaa.gov/the-shrinking-arctic-ice-cap-ar4

The answer is the Gulf Stream, which circles through the warm waters of the Gulf of Mexico and then carries that warmth across the Atlantic Ocean toward Europe. If melting ice caps caused salinity and temperature levels to change enough in the Atlantic that the Gulf Stream

changed directions, Europe might enter a deep freeze. While movies such as *The Day After Tomorrow* (2004) sensationalize the phenomenon and timeframe, a new ice age is not entirely out of the question for the future.

Whether or not ocean currents change directions, the waters of the earth's oceans are warming overall, and meteorologists agree that warmer waters produce more storms that are sufficiently intense to rise to the level of being "named" (and perhaps more frequent ones as well, but there is less scientific agreement on that). In recent years, there have been more "named" storms than normal. More tropical depressions are intensifying to become named tropical storms, and more of these named tropical storms continue to strengthen until they become hurricanes (also called cyclones and typhoons). As the accompanying infrared photo shows, hot winds from the Sahara blow across the mid-Atlantic, heating the water and spawning tropical storms that increasingly often become hurricanes. Finally, more of the hurricanes that develop become more powerful ones, routinely reaching Category 3 or 4 status in recent years. The result is considerable destruction and often many deaths, as Hurricane Katrina in the United States and Hurricane Ike in Cuba demonstrated in the past decade. There is also scientific speculation—but not definitive proof yet—that global warming patterns increase the amount of moisture in the atmosphere, which can lead to more intense and frequent tornadoes (and maybe other extreme weather too). This might help explain why the U.S. recorded more than 600 tornadoes in the month of April 2011 alone.

BIODIVERSITY CHALLENGES Human activity is not just harming the planet; it reduces the diversity of species found here, as well. This reduction in the diversity of life on our planet occurs in two primary ways. First, as forests are diminished, the many species that live in those forests are often killed off as well. Plant and animal life is thus threatened. As noted in the previous deforestation discussion, many pharmaceutical drugs are derived from chemical compounds found in nature. We have no idea how many undiscovered forms of life exist within the tropical rain forests of the world, but as they are destroyed, we may be killing off potential cures for deadly or other dread diseases in the process. The 1992 movie *Medicine Man* (starring Sean Connery and Lorraine Bracco) illustrated this dynamic well. In the film, developers cut roads through the Amazon rain forest in order to exploit the area's natural resources. In the process of destroying the trees, they unknowingly destroy the habitat that gives shelter to a species of insects that had developed a natural cure for cancer! While the film was fictional entertainment, the premise on which it was

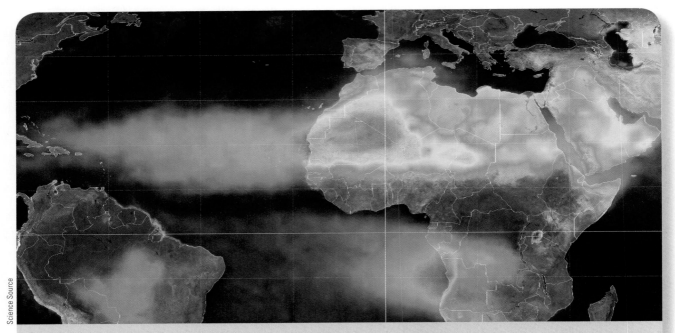

Thermal images of African heat and dust storms sweeping over the Mid-Atlantic Ocean where hurricanes begin | How interconnected are long-term global climate patterns?

based is frighteningly real. We could be missing out on unknown medical or other benefits by wiping out entire species of living things that exist only in unique micro-climates or microenvironments. We could be killing the goose that laid the golden egg and not even know it!

Two other aspects of protecting species deserve mention. First, we know that different species affect each other in different ways. An easy example is the fact that we depend on bees to pollinate many food crops. If the bee population died off like this, it would imperil overall food production. However, we should be wise enough to know that we don't understand all of these connections. So wiping out species could come back to haunt humans in ways we cannot foresee at this time. Second, there is an ethical argument to be made here. What gives humans the right to eradicate other species? We may assume we are superior to other species, but how accurate is that assumption? We are only beginning to understand how intelligent sea mammals such as whales and dolphins are, that some trees and plants can communicate with others of their species in ways we cannot see, and so on. There is more to other species than many humans realize, and killing them off—even accidentally—may be a

more profound act than most of us comprehend. If we are superior, shouldn't we realize these complexities and know better than to wipe out entire species?

Again, at least these consequences are largely acci-dental. What is not accidental is the creation of plant seeds whose prominence in the agricultural markets reduces the diversity found among species. These are gener-ally referred to as **genetically modified organisms (GMOs)**: organisms whose genetic makeup is inten-tionally altered to produce some advantageous result. Roundup Ready cotton provides a good example of a GMO. In 1997, the U.S.-based multinational agricultural corporation Monsanto patented a process that would introduce a gene not normally found in cotton that made the cotton resistant to Monsanto's widely sold herbicide, Roundup. As Monsanto noted, the promise was entic-ing. Farmers could plant the cotton and then spray their fields with Roundup, eliminating the time-consuming and expensive process of manually removing the weeds that steal nutrients and moisture from the cotton. The result would be greater yields of cotton, more income for farm-ers, the potential use of otherwise marginal agricultural land in the developing world, and possibly a reduction in apparel costs due to increased cotton supplies. Who wouldn't like spending less for denim? This is great, right?

Unfortunately, the process can also have negative consequences. First, as farmers in an area begin to use Roundup Ready cotton, other cotton farmers in the area

genetically modified organisms (GMOs) those organisms whose genetic makeup is intentionally altered to produce some advantage.

face pressures to switch to this cotton as well. Again, fewer weeds mean potentially bigger cotton yields and thus more income. Also, if their neighbors are using Roundup Ready cotton and they are not, the Roundup sprayed on neighboring fields could drift over to fields of conventional cotton, killing the cotton plants in the adjoining fields. Second, there are unanticipated side effects. The gene introduced to make Roundup Ready cotton is a protein that has to be fed, and it takes nutrients from the rest of the plant. Thus, yields from individual plants can fall from levels they otherwise could reach. Finally, one must keep in mind that nature is dynamic. As the world's cotton production becomes dominated by Roundup Ready cotton, any disease or insect hazard that successfully targets that species of cotton could imperil most of the cotton production in the world.

If the impact of this last point is relative scarcity and thus higher cotton prices, most people would simply notice the higher prices. While more expensive clothing is not a welcome development, what if this same dynamic hit a food crop? Then the consequence would be less food for the planet. This is not a mere hypothetical concern. Just as Monsanto has developed Roundup Ready cotton, it has also developed many genetically modified seed strains for foodstuffs that offer obvious benefits to farmers—higher yields, crops more resistant to disease or insect pests, crops needing less water, and so on. These benefits could dramatically improve the human security of farming families in developing countries, so long as the costs of buying new seeds each year is not too expensive. You see, unlike natural seeds many genetically modified seeds are sterile, so the traditional practice of holding some of the harvest back to use as seeds for the next year won't work and farmers have to buy new seeds each year. Furthermore, some of the seed companies will not allow farmers to reuse seeds, even if the seeds are not sterile; this practice ensures the seed company profits each year.

Yet as more and more farmers choose to switch to those seeds, food harvests increasingly involve only one species of the plant concerned. If a disease or bug develops in nature that can attack that species, there are not as many alternative species of such plants that might offer other opportunities for food production. Should such diversity be lost in the various species of cereal grains that feed large parts of the world—like corn or wheat—the effects on the global food supply could be devastating.

The more diversity there is among plant and animal life, the less threatened those species are by disease, and their reproductive yields are greater as well. Thus, we all benefit from greater levels of biodiversity. The diversity of life on our planet took more than 3 billion years to develop. Yet due in large part to human activity, the current rate of species extinction is 1,000 times higher than the rate of extinction found in the fossil record, and the projected rate of species extinction in the future is expected to be ten times higher than the present rate. Like the other environmental issues discussed previously, biodiversity challenges also threaten economic and human security.

Whether considering pollution, deforestation, desertification, global climate change, or reductions in the earth's biodiversity, our current practices damage where we live and often destroy the habitats of other species, as well. Not only is our economic and human security endangered, international security could be as well—to the extent that future conflicts may be waged over control of food supplies, clean water, and other vital resources. Gold could even be one of those resources. Illegal gold mining has now become a global problem. In countries such as Peru, Colombia, Ecuador, Brazil, and Bolivia, illegal gold mining has resulted in both deforestation and mercury poisoning (mercury is used to help separate the gold from other minerals) of both the workers and of the Amazon Basin. Peru has resorted to sending in the army to try to shut down such illegal mining operations, but with profits of $1,000 per ounce, the miners reappear as soon as the troops leave! In Africa, mercury poisoning is increasingly commonplace in Ghana, where local gold miners have operated—often illegally—for decades. A quick Google search indicates similar illegal gold-mining operations with similar dangerous consequences for the environment and miners' health in places such as the Democratic Republic of the Congo, Mongolia, Nigeria, South Africa, and Venezuela.

Thus, humans have learned how to wring more and more economic benefit from the earth and its resources. The irony is that our actions are creating long-term threats to the quality of life for humanity, and perhaps its future existence, as well. Yet steps can be taken to produce more beneficial changes, and we turn to those next.

12-2 THE EVOLVING ENVIRONMENTAL REGIME

Many different types of actors are expending considerable effort to arrest and change the damaging actions noted previously. Given the impact of anarchy on phenomena that occur in the global commons, states, international organizations, and NGOs all become involved in the effort to protect the earth's environment.

12-2a State Actions

States have tried any number of steps to address the environmental challenges they face, obviously with varying levels of success. Yet try as they might, individual state actions can only do so much. Environmental problems are global in scope, and not all states are able or willing to engage in significant efforts to do what they can to clean up their part of the environment. Existing state efforts can be seen primarily in battling pollution, deforestation, desertification, and global climate change within their borders.

POLLUTION Unlike some environmental challenges, pollution can often be seen and is thus not easily ignored. Relatively affluent states may have the advantage in this regard, possessing the resources to devote to cleaning up obvious pollution problems. European countries have done quite well in this regard. Due to its concentration of heavy industries, Germany can still have some regional pollution problems at times, but most European states have experienced considerable success in cleaning up air pollution. Take a look at how clean the air is in this picture of Athens, a very large and congested urban area in Greece—one of the poorer countries of Europe.

When it comes to clean air, the other end of the spectrum may be China, which has some of the dirtiest and deadliest air in the world, as shown in the daytime photo of Tiananmen Square in Beijing.

The Chinese have tried periodically to clean the air (particularly before the Beijing Olympic Games in 2008) by closing dirty factories, making auto emission standards more stringent, and reducing the use of coal for heating homes. They have also begun prosecuting officials responsible for egregious pollution incidents. For the first time in 2009, a Chinese court allowed a lawsuit filed against the government by a Chinese environmental group to proceed. In that court case, the complaint was resolved when the government quickly pledged to fix the problem. So the Chinese government is beginning to take steps to clean up pollution, but when environmental concerns conflict with the commitment to rapid industrialization and economic expansion, economic security in China still typically gets prioritized over environmental or human security. In 2016, new tougher air standards for ozone and particulate matter are scheduled to go into effect in China, yet in March 2012, the Chinese vice minister of environmental protection noted that two-thirds of China's cities will fail to meet those new standards.

Some pollution cannot be seen yet can still be deadly. Japan has been unable to fully stop the leakage of radioactive water into the Pacific Ocean from the damaged Fukushima nuclear reactor complex. For their part, French firms are currently building a 32,000-ton steel arch to cover the entire Chernobyl nuclear reactor complex in Ukraine, in an attempt to stop the leakage of radiation into the atmosphere from the 1986 explosion and fire there. The G7 states and nearly two dozen other countries share the costs of the project—estimated at around $1.5 billion. Once the arch is in place in 2017, it is not known how much it will cost to remove and store the radioactive debris it covers or if Ukraine will have to bear that cost alone.[8] Capping the facility may limit the genetic mutations and increases in cancer rates caused by long-term exposure to radiation.

DEFORESTATION Many countries have engaged in significant efforts to increase tree planting to slow down the deforestation trend. The U.S. Agency for International

A sunny day in Athens, capital of one of the poorer countries in Europe | How can relatively poor Western states still have clean air?

Air pollution in Beijing's Tiananmen Square | What is the impact of Beijing's pollution on its residents?

The French-built Steel Arch over the former Chernobyl Nuclear Reactor Complex | Will building caps over nuclear disaster sites like this one in Chernobyl, Ukraine, protect us?

Development contributed millions of dollars over time to such efforts in Africa, Asia, and Latin America. Some countries, such as like Costa Rica, prohibited logging in certain forestlands in return for forgiveness of portions of their foreign debt. By 2004, Kenya had sponsored the planting of 25 million trees in Africa. In 2009, Brazil announced it was doubling the number of agents assigned to combating illegal logging during the Amazon's dry season, local prosecutors were going after meatpackers who could not certify that the cattle they purchased were not produced in illegally deforested areas, and some local supermarkets were refusing to purchase beef unless it was certified to have been raised in line with environmental standards. In 2007, Norway announced a $500 million annual initiative to help developing countries combat deforestation. In 2010, Norway and Indonesia announced a new anti-deforestation partnership. Norway would provide Indonesia with a $1 billion grant, to be paid out in stages based upon demonstrable progress in saving forests. Indonesia's president pledged that he would personally oversee the project and announced a two-year moratorium on new logging permits.

Despite such efforts, the commercial appeal of cutting down forests—to clear land for agriculture, for livestock, for mining, or simply for the income the timber industry provides—can be overwhelming. Even in countries held up as success stories like Costa Rica, the damage has already been done. Only about half of Costa Rica's original rain forest remains, and only about half of the remainder is federally protected. For many people, the tangible benefits of income in hand far outweigh the less obvious or often intangible aspects of cleaner air, less soil erosion, or the protection of forest species. What do

you think is more important, development (often out of poverty) for the people of a country or the protection of the environment? In most cases, private goods trump collective goods.

DESERTIFICATION Halting the spread of the earth's deserts is a challenging task, as ways have to be found to retain the little moisture available in those regions so new plantings can survive and barren ground can be covered. As noted earlier, China faces a considerable challenge in this regard, and so in 1978 the Chinese began a project to create a "Great Green Wall" of forested lands 2,700 miles long to contain the spread of the desert. The project was expected to take 73 years to complete. So far, the program has only had mixed success, as trees were planted in areas with insufficient rainfall to support robust tree life and not all the trees were drought-resistant varieties. About a quarter of the trees planted so far have died, and the rest have not reached their normal growth due to the lack of available water. According to local experts, the government would be more successful by simply fencing the land so it cannot be used by others. In as little as two years, fenced lands have returned to grassland naturally, and such ground cover can help keep the desert from spreading.

In contrast, India has tried a multimodal effort to combat the spread of deserts: Irrigation projects replenish local water supplies, rooftop systems catch and store rainwater, and wells channel rainfall runoff back into underground aquifers to augment the available groundwater supply. Planting drought-resistant vegetation barriers has helped to retain the soil and prevent water runoff. Drought-resistant tree species also help and have been used to reduce the spread of sand dunes. Keeping livestock off the endangered lands has also been a key to helping the land recover from desertification.

Similar multimodal efforts have shown some success in reclaiming land from the Sahara Desert in Burkina Faso. In pilot projects there, small barriers are built and large depressions are dug, both of which slow down rainfall runoff so it has time to soak into the ground. Hedges of shrubs or trees are planted around the depressions to help serve as windbreaks. Then the bare ground is covered with straw during the dry season to help retain the moisture. These techniques, relatively easily done at the local level, have shown some promise in reclaiming land from the Sahara.

GLOBAL CLIMATE CHANGE While skeptics might argue that global climate change is beyond the ability of any one state to influence, some are trying. Since 1990, Germany reduced its fossil fuel emissions by 21 percent (while those of the United States went up by approximately 16 percent). Germany managed this reduction by raising taxes on the use of petroleum, requiring recycling and reductions in solid waste, and using biomass technologies to capture methane gas and recycle it into the natural gas distribution system. Some large public buildings are constructed to utilize natural light as much as possible, and some also store cold and warm air underground to use in summer and winter, respectively. German laws provide subsidies to homeowners to use renewable energy sources (like solar or wind) to generate their own electricity, and homeowners can sell any surplus energy they generate back to the state. As an added benefit, nearly a quarter of a million jobs have been created in the renewable energy industry in Germany! Not all is well in this regard, however. After the 2011 Japanese Fukushima nuclear accident, Germany began shutting down its nuclear power reactors and building more coal-fired power plants—which again increase the fossil fuel emissions.

Another European leader in this regard is the United Kingdom. Between 1990 and 2003, the British cut their greenhouse gas emissions by approximately 13 percent. They did so by cutting emissions in the energy, forestry, and agricultural sectors and by making large cuts in the industrial solvents and waste management sectors. Another means chosen by the British was an Emissions Trading Scheme, in which companies that found it hard to reduce emissions could purchase emissions credits from those companies that could reduce emissions more readily. The result was lower emissions overall and more resources to those that could reduce emissions further and faster.

Other states have undertaken initiatives to reduce fossil fuel emissions, as well. The United States recently increased CAFE standards (the Corporate Average Fuel Economy) for the domestic auto industry. By 2016, the overall fuel economy figures for automobiles and light trucks must average 35.5 miles per gallon, up from the prior average of 27.5 miles per gallon. By 2025, the CAFE standard for cars and light trucks increases to 54.5 miles per gallon. Further, the United States leads the world in wind-generated energy, Germany is in second place, and Spain comes in third.[9] The Netherlands has begun planning a system that captures the power of the tides and converts that kinetic energy into electricity. Brazil produces 85 percent of its energy from renewable

resources, which include hydroelectric power, wind energy, solar energy, and biomass technology.

In conclusion, multiple states are trying a wide variety of means to improve their environments. Some are clearly doing better than others, and one would reasonably expect that affluent states are outdoing less wealthy ones. In even numbered years, Yale University's Environmental Performance Index measures progress by states on **ecosystem** vitality (with indicators for agriculture, air effects on the ecosystem, biodiversity and habitat, climate change, fisheries, forestry, and water effects on the ecosystem) and environmental health (air pollution effects on humans, environmental burden of disease, and water effects on humans). Those countries near the bottom of the rankings are among the poorest in the world. In 2014, the bottom ten countries of the 178 ranked are unquestionably poor (Bangladesh, Democratic Republic of the Congo, Sudan, Liberia, Sierra Leone, Afghanistan, Lesotho, Haiti, Mali, and Somalia). On the other hand, eight of the top-ten-ranked countries are in Europe. The ranking, in descending order, is Switzerland, Luxembourg, Australia, Singapore, Czech Republic, Germany, Spain, Austria, Sweden, Norway, and the Netherlands. The richest country in the world, the United States, comes in thirty-third in the rankings, just ahead of Malta but just behind Belarus! Rankings for other countries we have discussed in the previous pages include the United Kingdom (12), Greece (23), Indonesia (112), China (118), Burkina Faso (126), Kenya (140), and India (155).[10] So wealth helps provide the resources to address environmental challenges, but it also takes political will—and that does not always require great affluence.

Regardless of their commitment to the environment, there is only so much individual states can do within their own borders to address the greater environmental threats found in the global commons. For these threats, multilateral efforts are required, and like anything else, the questions of "who pays" and "how much" quickly arise. See the Foreign Policy in Perspective box for a rundown of recent actions on one such issue. Oftentimes, actions must begin at the grassroots level and work up from there. We turn to such multilateral initiatives next.

12-2b Public and Non-Governmental Organization Actions

Steps by ordinary citizens (better known as grassroots action) and NGOs help stimulate awareness of environmental challenges facing the planet. These recognitions of the dangers resulting from certain human activities are

ecosystem the interaction of living things and the material world around them.

Who Pays for Better Air?

We all benefit from clean air and a reduction in greenhouse gases. Yet whose responsibility is it to reduce emissions and clean up the air? Is it those with the most money, or those who contribute the most to the problem? Again, the "tragedy of the commons" suggests that when something benefits everyone yet isn't anyone's particular responsibility—like clean air—fixing problems can get complicated. Poor countries generally want rich countries to provide the funding to improve their air quality as well, while rich countries often think poor countries should clean up their own pollution. How have states done? How important is this issue on their foreign policy agendas? The answers vary.

At the 2009 International Climate Change Conference in Copenhagen, an informal agreement was reached between Brazil, China, India, South Africa and the United States. It set as a goal reaching a funding level of $100 billion per year by 2020. Those funds would go to developing countries to help them reduce their emissions. One hundred billion dollars per year is an impressive goal, but it is only a goal. No binding commitments were made in Copenhagen regarding each one's contribution to that funding level.

At the 2013 International Climate Change Conference in Warsaw, Norway, the United Kingdom, and the United States combined to pledge $280 million toward helping developing countries reduce the emissions caused by deforestation and the degradation of forests. Further, over $100 million was pledged—by Austria, Belgium, Finland, France, Germany, Norway, Sweden, and Switzerland—to the Adaptation Fund, designed to help the poorest 48 countries cope with global climate change.

So some of the wealthiest countries have pledged about $380 million, but that's only 0.38 percent of the $100 billion that was pledged! Where will the other $99.62 billion *per year* come from?

1. How high a foreign policy priority is this?

2. What other foreign policy priorities should G20 states deemphasize in order to prioritize this goal? Or should they?

---

nothing new. While humans have always had an impact on the environment, the industrial revolution sped up the release of toxic materials into the environment. By the nineteenth century, urban reformers were beginning to call for water sanitation systems, proper waste disposal, and in the United States, the Sierra Club was formed to protect wilderness areas from being spoiled by extensive human development.

In the early twentieth century, wars and depression generally overshadowed efforts by reformers to protect coasts from pollution and people from the dangers of leaded gasoline. However, by the 1950s, deadly smog epidemics had helped promote more research into air quality, and the 1962 publication of *Silent Spring* by Rachel Carson helped launch the modern environmental movement. The fact that Cleveland's Cuyahoga River was so heavily polluted that it caught fire in 1969 further dramatized the problem. Also that year, SCOPE—the Scientific Committee on Problems of the Environment—was formed as an international NGO to coordinate science-based knowledge of environmental issues. The following year at the prompting of U.S. Senator Gaylord Nelson and aided by the organizational resources of Common Cause, the first Earth Day was held on April 22, 1970.

Over time, many NGOs took on the task of educating the public about the need to conserve resources and protect the environment. For example, Friends of the Earth International started in 1969, and it now acts as an umbrella organization for 74 national environmental groups with a total membership of over 2 million people. Based in Amsterdam, Netherlands, it focuses on promoting environmentally sustainable practices around the globe. Founded in 1974, Worldwatch Institute was created to be a totally independent research entity promoting sustainable development and has partner organizations in 24 countries. NGOs like these pool resources, create human networks, publish research, create programs at the grassroots level, and promote actions by states and international organizations. For example, for Earth Days 2014 and 2015, the Earth Day Network sponsored the Green Cities Campaign. Since over half the world's population now lives in urban areas, the campaign focuses on improvements in energy use, building construction, and transportation systems to reduce the carbon footprint of our urban areas.[11]

However, for some people and organizations, such efforts are not enough. Some activists want to get out there and save the planet themselves! A few will put themselves in harm's way to stop actions that they oppose.

During the Cold War, for example, Greenpeace tried to stop French nuclear weapons tests in the Pacific by sailing its ship—the *Rainbow Warrior*—into the area of the nuclear tests. The crew was literally daring France to conduct the tests, knowing that people surely would die in the process. The tactic worked, but needless to say, it irritated the French government considerably. In 1985, the French dispatched a covert operations team that sunk the *Rainbow Warrior* in a New Zealand harbor, but one of the ship's crew was killed in the process and two French operatives were captured before they could leave the country. The UN Secretary-General arbitrated the resulting dispute between New Zealand and France, and a deal was struck. The French were required to acknowledge that they had broken international law, to formally apologize, to compensate the victim's family and Greenpeace, and to compensate New Zealand. In return, the two French operatives were ordered to serve three-year prison terms at a French naval base in the Pacific, but the French allowed them to return to France after less than two years! A new *Rainbow Warrior II* now sails the seas on behalf of Greenpeace's mission to promote sustainable use of the planet's resources. Yet for some, Greenpeace hasn't done nearly enough, as discussed in the box Spotlight On: Sea Shepherd Conservation Society.

12-2c International Organization Actions

Given the global nature of environmental challenges, coordinating the actions of states and NGOs is essential. IOs can perform such tasks, as well as actively address the many environmental challenges found in the global commons. The United Nations has been at the forefront in this regard. While the UN's environmental efforts are literally too numerous to discuss in their entirety, we can examine what the UN has done through focusing on one important policy issue—the problems associated with global climate change—as well as other environmental priorities.

UN AND GLOBAL CLIMATE CHANGE As we suggested earlier, global climate change is a problem that has been taken seriously for decades by the international community. The magnitude of the problem and its global scope—whether located within the territorial boundaries of sovereign states or in the areas known as the global commons—make it the focus of concerted efforts at international cooperation. In 1972, the UN Conference on the Human Environment met in Stockholm, Sweden, and among its recommendations was the establishment of a new UN entity for the environment. That entity was the **UN Environment Programme (UNEP)**, which made addressing global climate change one of its priorities. By the mid-1980s, there was a growing awareness of the apparent impacts of global climate change, and in 1988, the previously mentioned Intergovernmental Panel on Climate Change was formed. This group of hundreds of scientists was aided by hundreds of economists, diplomats, and other public officials in its efforts to document the impacts of global climate change, determine its causes, and seek strategies to offset its effects. A series of environmental conferences resulted in the drafting of the **UN Framework Convention on Climate Change (FCCC)**, which was approved at the UN's Earth Summit in Rio de Janeiro, Brazil, in 1992. The convention recommended that fossil fuel emissions be reduced to 1990 levels by the year 2000, and it created a **Global Environmental Facility** to collect and distribute the resources needed to enact such reductions on a worldwide basis. While many environmentalists had pressed for making such fossil fuel emission reductions mandatory rather than merely voluntary, the United States refused to support mandatory restrictions. As the world's largest fossil fuel emitter at that time, the United States had leverage. Without some form of U.S. participation in the FCCC, the convention would have little meaning.

The effort to convert voluntary reductions in fossil fuel emissions to mandatory ones began almost immediately after the Rio Summit, and it was led (not surprisingly) by the leaders of small island states who feared rising seawaters. By 1997, the effort had produced the **Kyoto Protocol** to the FCCC. At this conference in Kyoto, Japan, the delegates approved a plan mandating that 37 developed states and the European Community (the predecessor to the EU) reduce their fossil fuel emissions by an average of 5 percent from the levels recorded in 1990. As the leading emitter of greenhouse gases, the United States was required to reduce its emissions by 7 percent. On the other hand, developing countries

UN Environment Programme (UNEP) the UN agency dedicated to environmental protection, created in 1972.

UN Framework Convention on Climate Change (FCCC) a 1992 treaty calling for the reduction of fossil fuel emissions to 1990 levels by 2000.

Global Environmental Facility the UN entity created by the UN Framework Convention on Climate Change to collect and distribute the financial resources needed to combat global climate change.

Kyoto Protocol an addendum to the UN Framework Convention on Climate Change, which was negotiated in 1997 and entered into force in 2005, which imposed mandatory reductions in fossil fuel emissions for 37 developed countries and the European Community.

Sea Shepherd Conservation Society

Canadian Paul Watson, one of the original cofounders of Greenpeace, left that organization to form the Sea Shepherd Conservation Society in 1977 because he felt Greenpeace had become too timid. He wanted sea mammals aggressively protected, and state actors weren't doing enough to help. In the past, Sea Shepherd Conservation Society members physically placed themselves between baby Arctic seals and the hunters trying to kill them for their pelts. Given that the seal hunters used clubs, getting between them and their "harvests" was at times a risky proposition.

More famously, society members also tried to sabotage whaling ships at sea and even placed themselves between whaling ships and the whales being hunted for their meat and oil. Members attacked the whaling ships and their crews with water cannons and stink bombs; at times they tried to foul the propellers or rudders of whaling ships with chains and ropes. In 2007, Watson claimed that his group had sunk ten whaling ships while the ships were in port. While that claim is unverified, at least two sinkings of whaling craft have been confirmed. However, the whalers struck back. In January 2010, a larger Japanese whaling ship collided with the Sea Shepherd's *Ady Gil*, a speedboat valued by the group at $2 million, destroying the smaller boat. Both sides blamed the other for the incident. Just a month later, the Sea Shepherd ship *Bob Barker* collided with the Japanese whaler *Yushin Maru 3* in the waters of Antarctica. Both ships reported only minor damage from the collision.

The group's activities have been captured on the reality television program *Whale Wars*, which airs on the cable network Animal Planet. With the resulting publicity, celebrities like Darryl Hannah, Mick Jagger, and Sean Penn have endorsed Sea Shepherd's activities, and Bob Barker, the former host of TV's *The Price Is Right*, donated the $5 million needed to buy the ship renamed after him in 2009.

However, mainstream environmental groups have routinely criticized Sea Shepherd's aggressive tactics, noting

HO/Corbis Wire/Corbis

A Sea Shepherd vessel challenges a Japanese whaling vessel in 2008 | Is violent confrontation necessary to stop the extermination of some species? Would such violence be justified?

that by attacking others, Sea Shepherd is committing crimes against people or property. In the case of the baby seals, these hunts are sanctioned by Canadian law during specified periods in the year and are thus fully legal. Sea Shepherd members counter with the argument that the Canadian laws are morally wrong and provisions of international whaling treaties that allow the limited "harvesting" of whales for scientific purposes are intentionally exploited by countries like Japan simply to get whale meat, which the Japanese consider a luxury. In short, in an anarchic international system, if states won't protect animals at risk, members of the Sea Shepherds will. They will do so by enforcing international norms when no one else seems willing to do so, and they are willing to enforce some laws, as well. For example, in 2011 Sea Shepherd signed an agreement with the Republic of Palau to jointly patrol a newly established shark sanctuary in Palau's waters.[12] One wonders what will happen if violators in Palau are discovered by Sea Shepherd members.

What do you think? Are Sea Shepherds environmental heroes or well-intentioned criminals? Is it appropriate for NGOs to go beyond monitoring international activity to enforcing international norms and laws through direct, and at times violent, action, and if so, how far should they be willing to go?

were encouraged, but not required, to reduce their emissions. As developing country delegates argued, not only did poor countries not have the financial resources to impose such fossil fuel emission reductions on their

economies, a question of fairness was involved, as well. In their view, why should developing countries be denied the same right to industrialize their economies using whatever cheap energy supplies were available to them, just as currently rich countries had done in their own past?

As you may imagine, exempting developing countries from the mandatory reductions imposed on developed countries was controversial. Some developing countries in the global semi-periphery—such as China, India, Mexico, and others—produced considerable fossil fuel emissions on their own by burning coal, wood, and petroleum products for heat or energy. Those emissions contributed to the amount of greenhouse gases in the atmosphere just as those from developed countries did. Further, reducing emissions at the turn of the twenty-first century, *from the levels found in 1990*, was going to mean economic hardships. Many Americans feared that businesses would have to cut back on their operations to meet their emissions reduction targets, some businesses might be forced to close down, and some workers would face reduced wages or lost jobs as a result. Thus, it was not entirely surprising that the U.S. Senate voted 95 to zero in 1997 to oppose the Kyoto Protocol as it was written. Although President Bill Clinton signed the treaty so the United States could be an "insider" to the process and continue to try to negotiate its text, the protocol was never sent to the Senate for formal ratification.

Given the economic changes that would ensue from approving the treaty, it took until late 2004 before the requisite number of states ratified it. This delay was significant because the protocol was meant to be only a first step in offsetting the buildup of greenhouse gases, and thus, an expiration date of 2012 had been written into it. In 1997, the delegates in Kyoto had expected that by 2012 an international consensus would exist to take more aggressive actions to limit greenhouse gases. A follow-up conference was thus scheduled for late 2009 in Copenhagen, Denmark, to set the new fossil fuel reduction figures. As that date drew closer, it became clear that *no fundamental basis for a new agreement existed*. Rich countries wanted developing countries to accept mandatory commitments to do more to limit their fossil fuel emissions. A number of developing countries resisted any kind of mandatory restrictions being placed on them, and they wanted rich countries to provide the monies required to fund developing world efforts to restrict emissions. As a result of such differing perspectives, the only agreement that arose out of the Copenhagen meeting was the voluntary call by Brazil, China, India, South Africa, and the United States noted earlier to do whatever necessary, not to cut future emission levels, but to limit future *increases* in global warming to no more than 2 degrees Celsius (or nearly 4 degrees Fahrenheit) and to call on all to provide $100 billion annually by 2020 to help developing countries limit their emissions.

A subsequent meeting in Durban, South Africa, in 2011 produced an agreement *to negotiate a binding, universal agreement by 2015* to cut fossil fuel emissions after 2020. By 2014, no such agreement had yet been reached!

So while the UN has been an active leader on the issue of global climate change, a breakthrough is needed to get past the current situation where the only agreement possible is to try to limit future increases in the planet's average temperatures. The global community is looking at an environmental situation in which everyone seems to agree on the big picture goals but cannot agree on the actionable steps needed to accomplish them. Given the anarchy in the international system, can more than talking be done? The answer may depend on your theoretical orientation as suggested in the box Theory in Action: Can Carbon Dioxide Levels Be Reduced?

UN AND OTHER GLOBAL PRIORITIES For all the talk about it, global climate change is only one of UNEP's priority areas. Beyond global climate change, UNEP's five other priority areas deal with disasters and conflicts, ecosystem management, environmental governance, harmful substances, and resource efficiency.

Disasters and conflicts present a variety of challenges. In the past, UNEP has responded to disasters like the 2004 tsunami that impacted Indonesia, Maldives, Seychelles, Somalia, Sri Lanka, Thailand, and Yemen. UNEP coordinated international responses and worked at reviving coastal ecosystems, getting the salt out of the soil and groundwater, and provided training to deal with future disasters. It also engaged in environmental relief efforts following the Haiti earthquake of 2010 and sent a team of international experts to assess damages following the Japan earthquake/tsunami/Fukushima nuclear reactor disaster of 2011. UNEP also assisted in dealing with oil spills in Ukraine, long-term oil contamination in Nigeria, and hazardous waste management in Cote d'Ivoire.

Like accidental or natural disasters, wars also create environmental dilemmas. The destruction caused by wars releases toxic substances into the environment, damages the ecosystem, and typically leads to the breakdown of local infrastructures that deal with environmental issues. UNEP has been called in to deal with the environmental consequences of wars in or near Afghanistan, Albania, Democratic Republic of Congo, Iraq, Lebanon, Liberia, Macedonia, the occupied territories of Palestine, Rwanda, Serbia, and Sudan.

Ecosystem management is another priority for UNEP. Preserving fragile or endangered ecosystems first requires a focus on developing the tools to manage ecosystems. These tools include building the scientific

Can Carbon Dioxide Levels Be Reduced?

The single biggest culprit for the rise in global temperatures is the growing levels of carbon dioxide in the atmosphere, as it is the most common of the so-called greenhouse gases. Lowering carbon dioxide levels in the air would help more heat escape into space. So what explains the global response to this problem? Can global carbon dioxide levels be reduced? The answers lie in our theoretical approaches to world politics. Liberals and constructivists see this as a solvable problem, while realists, world systems theorists, and Marxists are much more pessimistic that meaningful global responses to this problem can be found. The reasoning of each group is pretty straightforward based on their basic orientations to international politics.

Liberals see international cooperation as both necessary and possible, and neoliberals stress the creation of institutions that promote cooperation. So liberals and neoliberals argue that the Kyoto Protocol was a good first step at reducing fossil fuel emissions—a large source of the carbon dioxide in the atmosphere. They would probably say that the global community just needs to do a better job of educating everyone that we're all in this together and must cooperate to solve this shared problem.

Constructivists contribute the idea that the socially constructed reality many share on this matter has dramatically changed in recent years. Many people once questioned the basic premise of global climate change. Now many, if not most in the developed world, accept the idea that lowering fossil fuel emissions is good for all concerned. Consequently, it is now commonplace for many of us to talk about ways to lower our **carbon footprints**—the amount of carbon dioxide we generate through our daily activity. Looking for ways to use less energy and thus emit less carbon dioxide has become the "new normal" for many people.

What actions resulted from this new socially constructed reality? What cooperation was achieved? A variety of actions stand out. Since 1990, EU countries decreased their overall greenhouse gas emissions by more than 15 percent. Germany led the way by reducing its emissions by more than 21 percent, with France second at 11 percent.[13] Multiple countries invested in new, carbon-friendly technologies. European countries, China, and the United States either have land or sea-based wind farms to generate electricity in place or in the planning stages.

China invested heavily in manufacturing solar electric-generating panels and now leads the world in their production. Japanese and U.S. automakers spent huge sums on developing hybrid or totally electric cars, while European carmakers have increasingly reduced the emissions of diesel engines. The International Chamber of Shipping, which represents about 80 percent of the world's maritime trade, called for a carbon tax on shipping vessels as a way to curb their use of heavy fuel oils. The European Union has imposed a carbon tax on international airlines flying in European airspace—which the Chinese said they won't pay! In 2011, the U.S. Bipartisan Policy Center endorsed efforts to aggressively reduce global temperatures through means such as reflecting more sunlight back into space before it hit the earth's surface. Finally, a 2011 study by the Climate Policy Initiative showed that at least $97 billion a year was going from developed countries to developing ones to help poor countries improve their environmental practices, with most of the money coming from private lenders!

On the other hand, realists argue that our first priority is to maintain, if not increase, our power. At this point in human history, having a larger or more capable military as well as a stronger economy requires a considerable amount of carbon dioxide–producing fossil fuel. Thus, realists would say that if reducing one's carbon footprint lowers one's ability to project power in world politics, then it should not be done. From the realist perspective, in a world marked by anarchy, a state cannot afford to be environmentally friendly if that weakens its ability to protect itself and its interests.

The best recent example of such realist theory in action came from Russia. There, highly inefficient and heavily polluting oil and natural gas exploration continued, because increased oil and gas sales brought in the new revenues needed to modernize the Russian military and to pay for new weapons systems and training missions. In the case of the United States, airpower is a major way the United States can project power on a global basis. However, military aircraft are heavy consumers of jet fuel, and only in new "fifth-generation" aircraft like the F-22 Raptor and F-35 Lightening II has fuel economy become an issue. When these airplanes are fully deployed, they will only comprise a small share of total U.S. military aircraft, and their development was the product of concerns over fuel costs, not environmental concerns.

carbon footprint the amount of carbon dioxide we generate through our daily activities.

Finally, both world systems theorists and Marxists would argue that convincing the rich countries that make up the core of the international system to voluntarily slow down their economies—and to pay the costs of poor countries on the global periphery lowering their fossil fuel emissions—is simply impossible. Both these groups of thinkers would say that it is contrary to human nature for the rich and powerful to willingly give up significant portions of their wealth or relative power over others.

What actions resulted from these perspectives? Neither realists nor alternative theorists were surprised when the United States reopened oil drilling in the Gulf of Mexico after only a very short suspension following the huge BP Gulf oil spill or when the Obama administration chose not to impose new air cleanliness standards that would have reduced, at least in the short term, economic output. Singapore continued its dredging of river sands in order to build up new land masses, even though the dredging created pollution that destroyed the fisheries on which multiple Cambodian and Vietnamese villages depended. China continued its headlong economic development even though it contributed to worsening air pollution over the Chinese industrial heartland. At the 2009 Copenhagen, 2011 Durban, and 2013 Warsaw conferences to extend the Kyoto Protocol, no binding agreements were reached as poor countries continued to insist that their fossil fuel reductions be paid for by rich countries and rich countries insisted that poor countries also accept any mandatory emissions restrictions imposed on the rich.

1. Which of these theoretical perspectives makes the most sense?

2. Is this problem solvable?

---

knowledge base required to understand how the material environment and living organisms interact and then learning how best to share such knowledge with relevant officials and other stakeholders in the area. Then these methods need to be put into use in locales where such tools are underdeveloped or missing. To date, UNEP has undertaken ecosystem management initiatives involving the broader regions of Africa's Congo River Basin and Central Asia's Himalayan mountain range, as well as more specific programs in Kenya, Mali, and Uganda.

UNEP's environmental governance goals include helping to create and support international decision-making processes dealing with environmental governance matters; promoting the implementation of such agreed-upon norms and goals; helping environmental governing institutions at the regional, subregional, and national levels; and promoting sustainable development at the national level. In Africa and Europe, UNEP has supported ministerial conferences focusing on environmental issues. In Asia, it has focused its efforts on the problem of brown haze in the atmosphere and worked with the World Health Organization to address health issues in East and Southeast Asia. In West Asia, UNEP is helping to collect the information needed to create geographic information system (GIS) databases for use in dealing with current and future environmental challenges in the Arab world. In North America, UNEP works with television's Discovery Network as an official partner of its Planet Green channel, building knowledge networks among the viewers. Efforts to combat the effects of harmful substances are another priority for UNEP. There is a convention on the shipment and disposal of hazardous wastes and a policy framework for dealing with hazardous chemicals. UNEP has studied the issue of persistent organic pollutants like polychlorinated biphenyls (or PCBs) and others, and there is a convention on controlling these substances, which are toxic and often carcinogenic. UNEP has also worked to reduce the pollution caused by toxic, heavy metals such as cadmium, lead, and mercury, as well as commonplace pesticides.

The final priority area for UNEP is resource efficiency, which in many ways is another term for **sustainable development**. The idea is to find ways to promote economic growth that do not degrade the environment or deplete non-renewable resources, and that is a major challenge for the global community. Sustainable development is arguably the twenty-first century's greatest environmental challenge, so let's devote some special attention to it.

12-3 THE CHALLENGE OF FOSTERING SUSTAINABLE DEVELOPMENT

As we suggested earlier, developed countries—the rich countries of today—got rich by exploiting the resources available to them. For most of human history, people

sustainable development promoting economic growth without degrading the environment or depleting its non-renewable resources.

exploited local resources with little concern about the possibility that the resources could become endangered or literally run out. Now in the words of UN Secretary-General Ban Ki-moon, we have reached a point at which such possibilities must be considered, both in developed and developing countries. While there are many such challenges, three of the most fundamental ones involve water, food, and energy issues. We discuss each of these in turn.

12-3a Sustainable Water Supplies

We need fresh water to survive and *clean*, fresh water to safeguard our health. Yet as humans put economic demands on their environment, water issues often arise. Some are more readily visible than others.

A very visible example can be found in Central Asia. The Aral Sea used to be the fourth largest lake in the world. Situated between Uzbekistan and Kazakhstan, it was part of the old Soviet Union. In the 1960s, Soviet leaders chose to divert the waters from the two main rivers feeding the lake in order to irrigate nearby desert areas; by doing so these leaders sought to increase both cotton and rice production. Yet without the water from those rivers, the Aral Sea began to shrink. Unfortunately, the exposed lake bottom was heavily polluted with salt and toxic chemicals. As the lake bottom dried out, the winds picked up those salts and chemicals and blew them into the neighboring farming areas. The results included decreased agricultural productivity, devastation of the Aral Sea's fishing industry, high cancer and respiratory ailment rates nearby, and both hotter summers and colder winters without the moderating effects of the lake's waters. The Aral Sea is now less than 10 percent of its former size and was described in 2010 by UN

The salty lakebed of the Aral Sea | What did the agricultural policies of the old Soviet Union cost Kazakhstan and Uzbekistan?

Secretary-General Ban Ki-moon as one of the world's most shocking disasters.

Unfortunately, the Aral Sea is not the only example of such an environmental disaster. In California, the inland Salton Sea was created by massive flooding of the Colorado River in 1905 that took engineers two years to contain. The new "sea" collected at one of the earth's lowest points on land. At first a tourist attraction, the Salton Sea later became an environmental waste dump as salt and agricultural chemicals accumulated in the waters—with predictable consequences. The YouTube video "The Accidental Sea" provides a stark view of the Salton Sea area now, and the State of California is currently trying to find the money and means to clean up the area. As the discussed in the box Revenge of Geography: Controlling the Nile or Controlled by It?, such environmental problems can happen on an even more massive scale.

Yet the greatest challenge of all is for people to have access to clean, fresh water, and that concern raises the basic population issue. With over 7 billion people on the planet, we are stressing the earth's resources—at least in certain locations and perhaps on a global basis, as well. According to the UN, each of us requires 20 to 50 liters (or roughly 5 to 13 gallons) of clean, fresh water a day to meet our basic needs for drinking, cooking, and cleaning. Unfortunately, nearly one in every seven people on the planet—1.1 billion—falls short of that amount. Ninety-two percent of these people live in Asia and Africa. Those without access to clean, fresh water are at great risk of disease. Up to 2 million people per year die from diarrheal diseases brought on by lack of clean, fresh water; 90 percent of these deaths are children under five. Over a million die each year from malaria. About 2.6 billion suffer from lack of adequate sanitation. These are problems that can be readily fixed, if the money is locally available.[14]

Even in developed states, the rise in population levels stresses water supplies. For instance, the American West has experienced a sharp population increase in recent decades, and the stress that places on local water supplies has been extreme. For years, many states and local municipalities have recycled wastewater for use in watering parks, athletic fields, and other public green spaces. However, most communities resisted reusing treated wastewater for human consumption, even though scientific studies showed it was safe. However, prolonged droughts and population pressures have led Australia, Namibia, Singapore, and some communities in the United States to use purified wastewater for human consumption.[15]

Making measurable progress on both the linked water and sanitation issues has been significantly aided in developing states by including those issues as part of the UN's

Controlling the Nile or Being Controlled by It?

For millennia, Egyptians depended on the fresh water provided by the Nile River to survive. Long ago they learned to dig ditches to divert some of the water into adjacent fields where food could be grown. Thus Egyptian society developed, never straying far from the waters of the Nile. In the 1950s, Egypt's government faced a problem. More food was needed to feed its burgeoning population, much of the country lacked electricity, and the country needed more income. The government's response was to build a dam across the Nile, creating a huge lake. Lake Nasser provided the reserve water supply to expand irrigation further out into the desert. Irrigating the desert allowed more food to be grown, and it also increased the land available for cotton production—Egypt's main source of revenue at that time. Hydroelectric turbines built into the dam's gates generated electricity. Thus the Aswan High Dam seemed to be a godsend—one project met all three of these developmental needs.

Yet as time went by, problems arose. The dam stopped the flooding of the Nile, an annual process that had historically deposited nutrient-rich soils on the farmers' lands along the river and into the nutrient-poor Mediterranean Sea. Without those added nutrients in the sea, fishery stocks decreased at a catastrophic rate for at least the first decade following the dam's completion, hurting all the surrounding states that traditionally fished those waters. Lake Nasser backed up into Sudan, and the plant life in the lake provided a breeding ground for the snails that carry the disease schistosomiasis. In both Sudan and Egypt, children in particular faced additional exposure to this chronic illness that damages internal organs and impairs cognitive development. Also without that soil replenishment, the Egyptian lands being cultivated began to degrade and soon required chemical fertilizers to restore their ability

Time & Life Pictures/Getty Images

Egypt's Lake Nasser formed behind the Aswan High Dam | Can rivers like the Nile be controlled by humankind, and if so, at what cost?

to produce robust harvests. Unfortunately, the financial cost of those fertilizers ate into the country's new revenues, as this was an expense Egypt's agricultural sector had not previously faced. The increased use of such fertilizers caused chemical runoff into the Nile downstream from the dam, thereby hurting downstream fisheries with the chemical pollution. Also, without the flushing actions of the annual floods, the salt content in the land gradually increased, decreasing its harvests. In short, the dam has been a mixed blessing.

1. Did the Egyptians control the Nile, or did the Nile have its revenge on Egypt?

2. Do you think this enormous expense is worth it for a poor country?

Source: Matt Rosenberg, "Aswan High Dam," *Geography, About.com,* March 2, 2011, http://geography.about.com/od/specificplacesofinterest/a/nile.htm.

Millennium Development Goals. IOs and NGOs have begun to work on these issues. The UN, the World Health Organization, and both the African and Asian Development Banks have banded together to create partnerships between water system operators to share and promote the best practices to solve these problems. By 2008, improvements over the UN's baseline year of 1990 were seen in the percentages of rural populations with access to an improved water source, but problems remain, particularly in Sub-Saharan Africa and the island states of the Pacific. In 2010, the UN declared clean, fresh water to be a fundamental human right and called for all member states to do more to solve this global challenge, so the problems caused by a lack of clean, fresh water remain on the global agenda. But we need more than just clean, fresh water to survive, so we turn to food issues next.

12-3b Sustainable Food Supplies

After clean, fresh water, the second thing we must have to survive is food. Early hunter-gatherers had little impact on the earth itself, but as soon as humans began cultivating crops and domesticating livestock, they began to change their physical environment. Land was cleared for agriculture and the raising of livestock, food crops pulled nutrients from the soil that needed to be replaced, and overgrazing reduced arable land to desert. As humans stressed their arable lands, their population continued to grow. At the dawn of the nineteenth century, Thomas Robert Malthus wrote that population growth would exceed the growth of food supplies. This **Malthusian dilemma** was thought to be largely over after World War II when new, high-yield strains of cereal grains developed in the so-called green revolution promised to feed the world.

The euphoria over solving the world's food problem proved short-lived, however. While the global population continued to grow, the effects of pollution, poor farming and livestock practices, global warming and cooling, and natural disasters like droughts, floods, and hurricanes combined to prevent food production from becoming sufficient among the global poor. A fungal disease known as wheat rust that dramatically reduces wheat harvests was once thought eradicated by agriculture's green revolution; it is currently on the rebound. The disease has spread from Africa to India in recent years.

Despite these concerns, some argue that the problem is fundamentally one of food distribution and not of food production; the idea is that there's enough food to go around if some of us would just eat a bit less and make sure the rest gets shipped to those in real nutritional need. Whatever the reason, the results are hard to ignore. At least 1 billion people worldwide are chronically malnourished or starving. That's an even more striking figure when compared to the fact that over 50 percent of Americans are considered overweight according to the standards of the Centers for Disease Control.

Moreover, conflicts can easily arise over food issues. Currently, conflicts in Sudan and Kenya pit nomadic groups who raise livestock for their livelihood against farmers. As desertification cut into their normal grazing grounds (in part due to their own overgrazing), nomads began running off the farmers so they could graze their herds and flocks on the farmers' land. Thus part of this fight is over food production—and survival for the two groups.

Another global issue is the rising cost of food itself. Many developing countries have to import food, and the costs are trending upward. In 2011, the UN's Food and Agriculture Organization reported that its food price index had reached an all-time high. According to the World Bank, global food prices rose an average of 6.5 percent each year from 2000 to 2012.[16] Since many poor countries subsidize food prices, they get squeezed when prices sharply rise. If they raise the prices of subsidized foodstuffs, the people are immediately hurt, since buying food often takes as much as 70 percent of the family income in poor countries. Compare that with the 13 percent of family income spent by U.S. families on food! In 2010, rising food prices caused the government of Mozambique to increase the price of bread 30 percent; the resulting riots caused the deaths of ten people.

Several reasons help explain rising prices of food items. Some are natural. Severe weather in Australia, China, and Russia decimated the wheat harvests in each country in 2011, causing them to bid up the price of wheat on the world market. Floods in places such as Pakistan destroyed local food harvests, again forcing the governments to purchase more food on the global markets. Civil wars and other conflicts caused harvests to decrease in numerous places. Then there's the fact that an increasing amount of land is being devoted to cultivation of foodstuffs *to be turned into fuel*. Countries like Brazil, China, Thailand, and the United States are turning to biofuels to help solve their energy needs (discussed more in the following section). An increasing share of the world's corn crop now goes to the production of ethanol (nearly 40 percent in the United States), and other global crops like cassava, cane sugar, and palm oil are being diverted to create biofuels. While that diversion might help address the energy problem, it takes food out of people's mouths, as farmers get better prices for selling their foodstuffs to biofuel manufacturers than to local consumers as food. As food prices climb, groups such as the UN's World Food Programme can buy less food to meet the needs of the hungry. To combat this, in May 2011, the Food and Agriculture Organization adopted a new strategy, placing more emphasis on increasing greater food-producing capacity in developing countries on a case-by-case basis. Mindful of the fact that there is no "one solution" for the food problem worldwide, the idea was to empower local populations to find ways to produce more food at the local level so high-priced food does not have to be imported.

One example of doing what is possible at the local level comes from Brazil. In 2011, the Botanical Research

> **Malthusian dilemma** named for its author, Thomas Robert Malthus, the notion that population growth outstrips the growth of the food supply.

Americans now use more corn for fuel than for food | What does this mean for global hunger?

Institute of Texas gave its International Award of Excellence in Conservation to John Cain Carter. An American expatriate living in Brazil's Mato Grosso region, Carter was brought there by his Brazilian wife Kika, whom he met when they were both students in Texas Christian University's Ranch Management Program. In Brazil, he became alarmed when fires used to clear the rain forest from his neighbor's land, to increase pastureland for cattle production, caught their land on fire as well. After learning how much rain forest was being lost to such burning for cattle operations, he formed an NGO, Aliança da Terra (Land Alliance), which uses market-based incentives to encourage cattle producers to reforest parts of their lands and to certify their cattle as being raised by environmentally friendly means. Now members of Aliança da Terra control 350 properties comprising 5.5 million acres of land, of which over half—3 million acres—is left to native vegetation! They are profiting by producing food in an environmentally friendly manner.

While the hungry still need help, there seem—hopefully—to be sustainable ways to increase food production without undue damage to the environment. It takes education, coordination of effort, and creative thinking to break out of the "we've always done things this way" pattern that led to environmental degradation. However, nothing can be done without access to energy, and we turn to that subject now.

12-3c Sustainable Energy

While early energy sources placed little demand on the planet—they depended on the ability of humans and animals to push, pull, lift, and carry, as well as the reliance on energy supplied by wind and water mills—the advent of the steam engine opened the door to the widespread use of fossil fuels. Burning wood to generate steam, which could be harnessed to turn wheels, soon gave way to the burning of coal and petroleum products. Thus, the modern industrial age was born in the eighteenth century, and as countries industrialized, their economic productivity jumped. Industrial mechanization seemed to be the key to generating wealth!

However, the single-minded pursuit of economic output came at an environmental cost. The need for wood for steam engines caused large portions of forests to be cut down without replacement trees being planted. Coal was mined with little concern about the health of the miners, the toxic waste produced, or the huge scars left on the land by open-pit mines. Then the coal was burned with little or no concern about the toxic chemicals being released or their impact on the environment (refer to the previous discussion of hazardous chemicals released in the burning of coal). By the mid-nineteenth century, the petroleum age began with the drilling of the first commercial oil wells. Oil and natural gas production also polluted the ground and air with toxic chemicals and greenhouse gases. Now many developing countries are making some of the same choices to use whatever energy supply is readily available, regardless of the environmental consequences, just as Europeans and North Americans did in previous centuries. So the global challenge is clear: how can we find energy sources that allow economic development to be pursued in such a way that it can be sustained over the long term with minimal damage to our environment? How do we get the golden eggs without harming the goose?

Many people are involved in developing alternative energy sources. For vehicles, some advocates stress the burning of natural gas because it generates fewer pollutants than burning gasoline or diesel fuels. While this statement is true as far as burning the natural gas in the vehicle goes, critics argue that many toxic chemicals are released into the air and ground during the production and distribution phases of the natural gas industry, and those emissions make natural gas far less attractive overall as an alternative than it first appears. Others propose stretching the use of fossil fuels by developing hybrid engines that run on a combination of battery and gasoline power, as an increasing number of Japanese and U.S.-made automobiles now do. Many, particularly in Europe, simply say we need to further refine diesel engine technology to squeeze as many miles per gallon out of those relatively efficient engines. Others put their hopes in biofuels or combining gasoline with ethanol to stretch existing petroleum supplies. Some put their hopes in all-electric vehicles—automakers such as Nissan, Chevrolet, Tesla, BMW, Volkswagen, Mercedes Benz, Cadillac, and Kia all have electric cars either in or near production—though the electricity must come from somewhere, increasing the need for nuclear or coal-fired power plants. Some see hydrogen fuel cells as the long-term answer for vehicles, as they would produce no harmful emissions but would require an all-new hydrogen distribution network. Thus, there are many different avenues being pursued to power vehicles.

When it comes to generating electricity, a lot of alternatives are on the drawing board and many have been implemented. The Netherlands and France have explored tidal power as a way to generate electricity. A relatively cheap form of alternate energy is wind power. Wind farms—concentrations of turbines powered by huge windmills—are sprouting up in places such as the United States, Germany, Spain, Italy, the United Kingdom, and Morocco, but some critics question the impact of these wind farms on bird and insect populations as well as the amount of energy produced. Some—like Brazil and France—still have heavy investments in nuclear power to generate electricity, although the 2011 Japanese Fukushima nuclear disaster casts a shadow on that technology. Countries such as Denmark burn trash to generate electricity, and the Swedish city of Kristianstad relies on the generation of biogas—a methane-like gas captured from degrading biological waste—for all of its heat and electricity needs.

Despite these efforts, as noted earlier there are still some who will pursue their energy needs via the cheapest possible route, with little or no concern for the environment. China is the world's largest producer of fossil fuel emissions, largely because it is the world's largest user of coal. Despite its rhetoric to improve its environmental record, China is also quickly becoming one of the world's largest purchasers of imported coal. Thus, when it comes to choosing between protecting the environment or making money, making money still generally wins out. Economic security (and profits) apparently trumps human security. In short, the challenges facing the global environment are many and the need for international cooperation seems obvious. Unfortunately, state actors often lack the will or the means to invest in methods designed to reduce the impact of human activity on the planet or to clean up our collective messes.

CONCLUSION: FACING THE ENVIRONMENTAL CHALLENGE

As our knowledge about how human actions impact the environment grows, efforts to protect the environment increase, as well. Since the first Earth Day in 1970, considerable progress has been made, in both rich countries and some poorer ones. However, the tradeoff between economic growth and protecting the environment is a difficult one for many to accept. Environmentalists are beset by the **time horizon problem**—the fact that the worst effects of the problem have not yet been seen, but to avoid them one needs to act (and spend money or make sacrifices) now. Getting people to sacrifice now for a problem they don't yet see, have not yet experienced, or may never experience personally (though their children probably will) is a tough sell. But as environmental awareness grows, taking steps to protect the environment becomes the "new normal" for many, and that's the good news. We may be able to save the planet from ourselves; our economic, human, and even international security might hang in the balance.

STUDY TOOLS 12

LOCATED AT BACK OF THE BOOK:
☐ Rip out Chapter in Review card

LOCATED ON COURSEMATE:
Use the CourseMate access card that came with this book or visit CengageBrain.com for more review materials:

☐ Review Key Terms Flash Cards (Print or Online)

☐ Download Chapter Summaries for on-the-go review

☐ Complete Practice Quizzes to prepare for the test

☐ Walk through a Simulation, Animated Learning Module, and Interactive Maps and Timelines to master concepts

☐ Complete "Crossword Puzzle" to review key terms

☐ Watch the videos for real-world application of this chapter's content

☐ Visit IR NewsWatch to learn about the latest current events as you prepare for class discussions and papers

time horizon problem the fact that the worst effects of environmental problems have not yet been seen, but to avoid them one needs to act (and spend money or make sacrifices) now.

THINK ABOUT THIS RAPID URBANIZATION AND ENVIRONMENTAL SUSTAINABILITY

According to a 2013 UN report, by 2050, 70 percent of the world's population will live in urban areas, but 80 percent of that global urban population will be located in developing countries.[17] Recent statistics bear out these locations. In 2012, the top ten largest urban population centers (with their populations) were Tokyo-Yokohama, Japan (37 million), Jakarta, Indonesia (26 million), Seoul-Incheon, South Korea (22.5 million), Delhi, India (22.2 million), Manila, Philippines (22 million), Shanghai, China (21 million), New York tri-state area, United States (20.4 million), Sao Paulo, Brazil (20.1 million), Mexico City, Mexico (19 million), and Cairo, Egypt (18 million).[18] Think about the different types of environmental challenges created by this continuing urban population growth.

Given those challenges, who should bear the "responsibility to protect" the environmental sustainability for those living in these developing world megacities and how might that be done?

REVIEW QUESTIONS

1. What is the "tragedy of the commons"?

2. What do terms such as pollution, deforestation, desertification, global climate change, and biodiversity challenges mean?

3. How have states, IOs, and NGOs dealt with environmental problems?

4. What is sustainable development, and why is it a desirable goal?

FOR MORE INFORMATION . . .

For more on global environmental issues:

Books:

Easton, Thomas A., ed. *Taking Sides: Clashing Views on Environmental Issues*. New York: McGraw-Hill, 2012.

Gore, Al. *An Inconvenient Truth: The Planetary Emergency of Global Warming and What We Can Do About It*. Emmaus, PA: Rodale Books, 2006.

O'Neill, Kate. *The Environment and International Relations*. New York: Cambridge University Press, 2009.

Sen, Amartya. *Development as Freedom*. New York: Anchor Books, 1999.

Movies:

An Inconvenient Truth (2006)

The Cove (2009)

The Day After Tomorrow (2004)

Erin Brockovich (2000)

Medicine Man (1992)

Websites:

Carbon Footprint Calculator, http://www.carbonfootprint.com/calculator.aspx.

About My Planet, https://www.facebook.com/pages/AboutMyPlanetcom/18684128159?sk=info.

Alternative Energy, http://www.alternative-energy-news.info/.

Live Science, http://www.livescience.com/.

National Geographic, *Environment,* http://environment.nationalgeographic.com/environment/.

Pure Energy Systems Wiki, http://peswiki.com/index.php/Main_Page.

On food sustainability and the planet: Mark Bittman, "What's Wrong with What We Eat," *TED Talks,* http://www.ted.com/talks/lang/eng/mark_bittman_on_what_s_wrong_with_what_we_eat.html; and Michal Pollan, "A Plant's-eye View," *TED Talks,* http://www.ted.com/talks/michael_pollan_gives_a_plant_s_eye_view.html.

The Salton Sea, an example of environmental degradation in the United States: *The Accidental Sea,* http://www.youtube.com/watch?v=otIU6Py4K_A.

13 | Transnational Advocacy Networks:
Changing the World?

LEARNING OBJECTIVES

After studying this chapter, you will be able to . . .

13-1 Explain the concept of transnational advocacy networks (TANs) and how they differ from other international actors.

13-2 Identify how TANs affect human security.

13-3 Describe the two major types of TANs and the kinds of actions in which they engage.

After finishing
this chapter go
to **PAGE 387**
for **STUDY TOOLS**

WHY DO PEOPLE STILL GET POLIO?

Poliomyelitis, more commonly known as polio, is a highly contagious viral infection that attacks the central nervous system and causes paralysis that can range from mild to acute. *There is no cure.* In the 1950s, it was common to see worst-case polio victims totally enclosed from their necks down in metal cylinders called "iron lungs" that assisted their breathing. However, the introduction of newly developed vaccines in the 1960s immunized the body so the virus could not survive. Without human hosts for the virus, it died out.

Or did it? While the virus virtually disappeared from wealthy and developed nations that could afford mass inoculation campaigns, it never died out in other places. In 2014, the World Health Organization declared a global health emergency regarding polio and specifically recommended immunizations for those traveling to Israel, Syria, Iraq, Afghanistan, Pakistan, Nigeria, Cameroon, and Equatorial Guinea.[1]

Because polio never fully disappeared, in 2010 the Global Polio Eradication Initiative (GPEI) was started. This initiative is a network of international organizations (IOs), non-governmental organizations (NGOs), state actors, and private individuals that promotes the efforts to combat polio and coordinates actions for the greatest impact. According to its records, the total amounts of funds contributed or pledged to combat polio for the 1985–2018 period is nearly $12 billion. The largest share (43 percent) comes from G8 countries and the European Commission, and the next largest share (26 percent) comes from NGOs (such as the Bill and Melinda Gates Foundation and Rotary International) and private individuals (like Abu Dhabi's Crown Prince Mohammed bin Zayed al Nahyan). Developing countries with polio outbreaks contribute 14 percent, about the same amount as IOs. The remaining funding comes from other donor countries.[2]

GPEI's efforts to eradicate polio and to prevent its return are certainly in the interest of the greater good. This highly contagious disease can be spread easily by an infected person boarding an airplane, and within 12 to 24 hours that person could arrive anywhere in the world and could have infected all the plane's passengers (if they haven't been immunized). Yet the need for such a network of international actors is troubling and raises questions such as:

1. Why wasn't the polio problem addressed sooner in developing countries?

2. What do you make of the fact that the second largest share of GPEI's funding comes from the private sector?

3. What other global problems might best be handled by such international networks of actors?

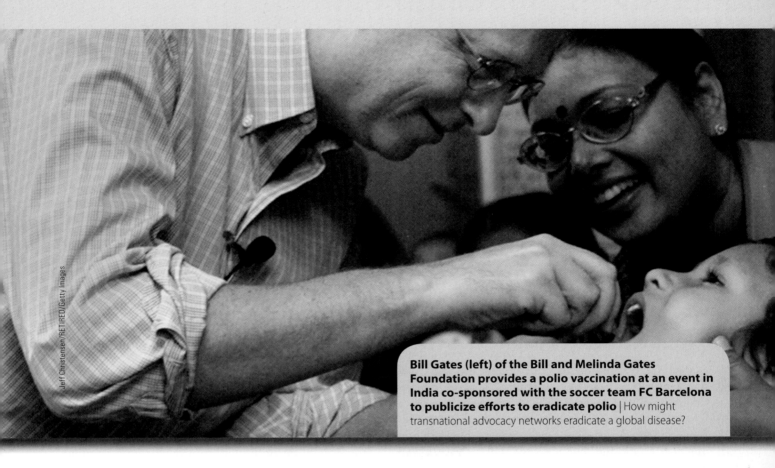

Bill Gates (left) of the Bill and Melinda Gates Foundation provides a polio vaccination at an event in India co-sponsored with the soccer team FC Barcelona to publicize efforts to eradicate polio | How might transnational advocacy networks eradicate a global disease?

INTRODUCTION: A NEW FORM OF INTERNATIONAL ACTOR?

As we noted in Chapter 2, NGOs have been around for a long time. The Catholic Church has long been an influential NGO—in the pre-Westphalian era it often had great influence over otherwise independent rulers! Beginning in the early nineteenth century, civil society organizations, as a type of NGO, were at the heart of the anti-slavery and women's suffrage movements. In the modern neo-Westphalian system, however, NGOs increasingly work together to achieve common aims, and they often work with other types of actors such as states, IOs, individuals, and social movements. Like some other scholars, we think that *when these networks become recurring entities in their own right*—in which the new network is greater than the sum of its individual parts—a new type of international actor has been formed. Thus, our focus in this chapter is on transnational advocacy networks— what they are, what they do, how they affect human security, and what impact they may have in the future.

WHAT ARE TRANSNATIONAL ADVOCACY NETWORKS?

When we talk about **transnational advocacy networks (TANs)**, the operative word is "networks." In Chapter 2, we discussed states, international organizations, non-governmental organizations, and even individuals as types of actors in international politics. TANs are formed when these types of actors come together from multiple countries in coalitions to form broader recurring networks. Thus TANs are networks defined by reciprocal, voluntary actions across national borders by IOs and states, domestic and international non-governmental actors, social movements, and individuals from around the world.

> **transnational advocacy networks (TANs)** networks defined by reciprocal, voluntary actions across national borders that (1) must include non-state actors (such as individuals acting alone, social movements, or non-governmental organizations), (2) may include states or international organizations as well, (3) represent a recurring, cooperative partnership with (4) differentiated roles among the component parts.

While some scholars specifically exclude governments from membership in TANs, we take a broader view. We share the idea that any definition of TANs *must* include NGOs, social movements, or individuals because a network comprised solely of governmental actors would be an IO, an international regime, or perhaps some form of alliance structure. Thus the presence of non-governmental actors is the key to identifying TANs. That said, other national and international governmental actors may often act as network members when they contribute to the network by providing it funding and other forms of sponsorship or by actively promoting its goals, as shown in the chapter opening vignette.[3] So, our working definition of a TAN is a multinational network that (1) must include non-state actors (like individuals acting alone, social movements, or NGOs); (2) may include states or IOs as well; (3) is a recurring, cooperative partnership; with (4) differentiated roles among the component parts.

Some skeptics might argue that TANs are nothing more than groups of NGOs and thus are not distinct actors. We respectfully disagree: When the impact of the network is greater than the sum of its parts, then we should treat it as a new actor in its own right. Perhaps a historical example will help to illustrate our point. Following their unsuccessful revolt against Roman rule in the year 70 CE, the Jewish people did not have a land they could claim as their own. Jews became a minority group in numerous countries. Fast-forward to 1894. In that year, French Army Captain Alfred Dreyfus was convicted of treason. The evidence against him was not compelling, but he was convicted anyway. According to most observers, the main reason he was convicted was because he was Jewish and thus an outlier in a Roman Catholic country.

One of those observers was Theodor Herzl, an Austrian journalist covering the trial who happened to be Jewish. He became convinced that Jews would never be safe from harm as long as they were a minority group in someone else's country. Herzl was moved to write a book (*The Jewish State*), in which he called for Jews to move back to their ancient home in Palestine and form a state of their own where they could be the majority. He called his movement Zionism and created the Zionist Organization (now called the World Zionist Organization) to promote the movement of Jews to Palestine. For its part, the Zionist Organization created national Zionist Organizations in multiple European countries. Those national Zionist Organizations helped promote the idea

of Zionism and recruit new members who would be willing to move.

However, money was needed to facilitate the movement of Jews to Palestine. An important early benefactor of the Zionist Organization was Baron Edmond de Rothschild, a French Jew who was part of a multinational European banking conglomerate. He contributed millions of dollars to help European Jews move to Palestine. Also helping were other organizations such as the Jewish Colonial Trust, which handled the Zionist Organization's finances, and the Jewish National Fund, which actually purchased the land in Palestine. Upon arriving, these new immigrants needed homes, jobs, schools for their children, and so on. Another organization was waiting there to meet those needs: the Jewish Agency for Palestine. Its representatives met the new immigrants and got them settled into their new lives. When Zionism triumphed with the declaration of a new Jewish state called Israel in 1948, its first prime minister was the leader of the Jewish Agency for Palestine—David Ben-Gurion.

What we see in this historical example is an early version of a TAN—a transnational network dedicated to creating a Jewish homeland in Palestine. It took actions by key individuals (Herzl to popularize the notion, de Rothschild to provide key early funding) and multiple NGOs (the Zionist Organization, its subsidiary national Zionist Organizations, the Jewish Colonial Trust, the Jewish National Fund, and the Jewish Agency for Palestine) working cooperatively over time and across countries with defined roles to organize the effort globally, in Europe, and in Palestine in order to realize Zionism's ultimate goal of a Jewish homeland. The network also succeeded despite the fact that local Arabs were not disposed to accept a new state carved out of their midst! (The UN tried to satisfy both parties by calling for two new states to be created in Palestine: one Jewish and one Arab, but that didn't happen.) None of these actors could have accomplished this goal alone. It took all of them working together for 53 years to create a new state where Jews would be the majority of the population.

A more recent illustration of a TAN is Islamic Relief Worldwide. Created in the United Kingdom in 1984, it has 13 independent and distinct affiliate organizations—in Australia, Canada, Germany, Italy, Malaysia, Mauritius, Netherlands, South Africa, Sweden, Switzerland, United States, United Kingdom and a regional one for the Middle East. Beyond the programs Islamic Relief Worldwide runs in specific affiliate countries, it has field programs in 22 other countries, it partners with the International Red Cross and Red Crescent Movements,

---

Zionism the movement to create a Jewish homeland in Palestine.

and it has consultative status with the UN's Economic and Social Council. Many of its affiliates are themselves members of humanitarian networks. For example, Islamic Relief USA is networked with the Alliance to End Hunger, the Center for Interfaith Action on Global Poverty, InterAction, InsideNGO, National Voluntary Organizations Active in Disaster, and the Society for International Development. The six main areas of emphasis for Islamic Relief Worldwide are sustainable livelihoods, health and nutrition, water and sanitation, education, orphans and child welfare, and emergency relief and disaster preparedness. As these examples show, such networks arise and are maintained on the basis of shared values and differentiated roles. Network members advocate and act upon shared ideas, positions, or goals, and they make choices to protect, defend, and advance those shared notions. So while the component

parts that make up TANs are unique actors in their own right, when they join into such networks to pursue shared goals in a cooperative enterprise, they create a new entity entirely.

These networks are not entirely new; they probably arose as soon as people began to cross national borders regularly. For instance, during the era of the Crusades, such a network linked European governments, the Roman Catholic Church, wealthy (and pious) individuals, and the Poor Fellow-Soldiers of Christ and of the Temple of Solomon—better known as the Knights Templar. The values these actors shared included securing Jerusalem and the surrounding area as bastions of Christianity and safeguarding the ability of Christian pilgrims to travel to and from the Holy Land safely. Later this network evolved into one of the first international banking systems, as the Knights Templar created a monetary transfer process that freed travelers from having to carry large amounts of cash and from which the Knights Templar profited handsomely!

While TANs might not be new, the accelerating globalization of the last 50 years or so has greatly facilitated their creation and operation. As noted in Chapter 2, globalization refers to the increasing integration of global society through economic, technological, political, and cultural means. If you are passionate about a subject, you could potentially create a TAN by searching the Internet by topic area or keyword to find other people or organizations that share your values; creating a Facebook page and encouraging others to sign up; or by creating a blog or website regarding the subject at hand. Then those identified as sharing your values could be linked, either online or perhaps in person, and the network would be formed. For much of the world, e-mail and social media outlets can be the communications link between network members, and for those areas with limited computer availability, cell phones (and particularly smart phones) can serve this role. What TAN might you want to create? Would it contribute to human security?

The Knights Templar joined the Catholic church in an effort to protect European pilgrims traveling to Jerusalem | How have transnational advocacy networks changed over time? What similarities still exist?

13-2 HOW DO TANS AFFECT HUMAN SECURITY?

TANs are innovators. They seek to create or change norms—or unwritten standards of acceptable and unacceptable behavior—which help to reduce the consequences of anarchy in the international system that realists tend to emphasize. If successful, their efforts in this regard tend to follow a **norms life cycle**.[4] The first phase of the cycle involves *creating new norms*. The individuals who are passionately committed to the issue, often called **policy entrepreneurs**, do everything they can to get others to share their vision and commitment. In essence, they define or frame the issue in ways designed to persuade others to accept that the values or goals they are pressing are legitimate ones for the public arena. For example, these goals could include the idea that it is unacceptable to ignore the victims of conflicts or that access to adequate nutrition or health care is a human right. The second phase is a *norms cascade*, in which the number of people sharing these values increases until there are enough people pressing the issue that it reaches the agendas of governments, which are held accountable for their actions or inactions on the matter. Examples could include rich countries now routinely budgeting money each year to meet the needs of refugees or being held accountable for their environmental records. Finally, the third phase is *norm internalization*, where so many international actors share the norm that following it becomes virtually automatic. In such instances, the only time the issue becomes contentious is when the norm is not followed. A good example would be the international shock and outrage directed at the United States for its treatment of detainees in the War on Terror that followed the September 11, 2001, attacks on New York City's World Trade Center and the Pentagon building across the river from Washington, DC, as this violated long-standing Geneva Conventions regarding the treatment of prisoners of war.

In their efforts to create and enforce norms, TANs play at least three important roles in international politics. They popularize ideas, influence states, and encourage and enable cooperation. Let's discuss each of these important roles. Keep in mind that what is most important here is not memorizing the names of actual TANs. Instead our focus should be on what these examples illustrate in terms of the kinds of ways TANs affect world politics.

---

norms life cycle the idea that TANs are successful when they can create new norms, create a norms cascade forcing governments to act on those norms, and get norms internalized to the point that following them becomes routine and largely unquestioned.

policy entrepreneurs individuals committed to innovative policy change and who voluntarily work to achieve such changes.

13-2a Popularizing Ideas

As we noted in Chapter 4, constructivists argue that reality is socially constructed on the basis of shared ideas. People agree on how things are and then act on that basis. The power of TANs to influence human security comes from this starting point. What does security mean in society? For much of human history, security meant protection from violent harm, and states developed military forces to meet this need. However, in the modern period, other aspects of security have arisen as concerns.

What about the consequences of wars? As more and more wars are internal (or intrastate), the fighting takes place in the midst of civilian populations. What do many civilians do in such a situation? They leave! The problem is that these refugees have pressing needs; in the short term they require water, food, shelter, and medical care, and in the long term they require assistance to go back home to resume their lives or to set up new homes and lives elsewhere. Who calls attention to their needs?

One such group is the Toronto-based Refugee Research Network. Its office is at York University, and its management committee is made up of individuals based in Canada, Colombia, India, Iran, and the United Kingdom. As Figure 13-1 shows, this TAN—like many others—is actually a network of networks. It brings together a Refugee Scholars Research Network to study the problems refugees face, a New Scholars Network to ensure that research continues into the future, NGO/Grassroots Refugee Networks that publicize the issues and provide both fund-raising and volunteer support, a Refugee Policy Network (composed primarily of national governments and IOs) to coordinate policy responses, and a variety of other international and

Princess Diana of Wales walks along a carefully marked path through an Angolan minefield | Would you want to take this walk?

FIGURE 13-1 THE CANADIAN-BASED REFUGEE RESEARCH NETWORK FLOWCHART

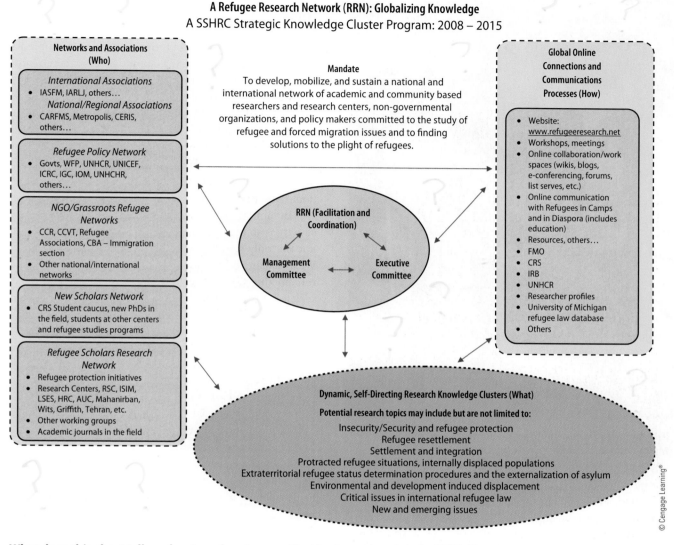

A Refugee Research Network (RRN): Globalizing Knowledge
A SSHRC Strategic Knowledge Cluster Program: 2008 – 2015

Networks and Associations (Who)

International Associations
- IASFM, IARLJ, others...

National/Regional Associations
- CARFMS, Metropolis, CERIS, others...

Refugee Policy Network
- Govts, WFP, UNHCR, UNICEF, ICRC, IGC, IOM, UNHCHR, others...

NGO/Grassroots Refugee Networks
- CCR, CCVT, Refugee Associations, CBA – Immigration section
- Other national/international networks

New Scholars Network
- CRS Student caucus, new PhDs in the field, students at other centers and refugee studies programs

Refugee Scholars Research Network
- Refugee protection initiatives
- Research Centers, RSC, ISIM, LSES, HRC, AUC, Mahanirban, Wits, Griffith, Tehran, etc.
- Other working groups
- Academic journals in the field

Mandate
To develop, mobilize, and sustain a national and international network of academic and community based researchers and research centers, non-governmental organizations, and policy makers committed to the study of refugee and forced migration issues and to finding solutions to the plight of refugees.

RRN (Facilitation and Coordination)

Management Committee

Executive Committee

Global Online Connections and Communications Processes (How)
- Website: www.refugeeresearch.net
- Workshops, meetings
- Online collaboration/work spaces (wikis, blogs, e-conferencing, forums, list serves, etc.)
- Online communication with Refugees in Camps and in Diaspora (includes education)
- Resources, others...
- FMO
- CRS
- IRB
- UNHCR
- Researcher profiles
- University of Michigan refugee law database
- Others

Dynamic, Self-Directing Research Knowledge Clusters (What)

Potential research topics may include but are not limited to:
Insecurity/Security and refugee protection
Refugee resettlement
Settlement and integration
Protracted refugee situations, internally displaced populations
Extraterritorial refugee status determination procedures and the externalization of asylum
Environmental and development induced displacement
Critical issues in international refugee law
New and emerging issues

© Cengage Learning®

What does this chart tell us about modern transnational advocacy networks (TANs)?

Source: Centre for Refugee Studies, 2012. Copyright © 2012 by Centre for Refugee Studies.

regional associations. Through these other networks, the Refugee Research Network promotes research, issues press releases, sponsors events, and seeks to mobilize others to get the word out about refugees and their needs.[5]

Another consequence of war is the weapons left behind that can still injure or kill. Landmines and cluster munitions are good examples. These cheap and effective weapons are easy to deploy. Unfortunately, very few combatants make the effort to remove them after a conflict. The result is that they cause injury and deaths for local civilians for years after a conflict has ended. Just imagine knowing that you couldn't walk through an area on your way to school because it might be filled with mines.

The International Campaign to Ban Landmines is a global network of more than 1,400 different groups active in over 90 countries that brought media attention to these pressing issues. This TAN was formed in 1992 by American aid worker Jody Williams and groups such as Handicap International, Human Rights Watch, Medico International, the Mines Advisory Group, Physicians for Human Rights, and the Vietnam Veterans of America Foundation. When Princess Diana of Wales championed the effort, media attention to this cause increased dramatically, and winning the Nobel Peace Prize in 1997 further bolstered the group's efforts to popularize the need to deal with the problem of landmines and cluster

Prince Harry meeting victims of landmines in Mozambique | How has the personal involvement of royals affected this effort?

munitions. Following her death, Diana's son Prince Harry continued her work with this effort.

TANs popularize other aspects of human security, as well. As noted in Chapter 12, over a billion people are chronically malnourished. One network seeking to bring publicity to that issue, as well as addressing it more directly, is the Global FoodBanking Network. This TAN was created in 2006 by national food bank associations in Argentina, Brazil, Canada, Mexico, and the United States. Its component parts include Founding Partners (including The Harry and Jeanette Weinberg Foundation and Cargill Incorporated), Leadership Partners (such as

---

boomerang model internal groups repressed by their own states can turn to TANs to put pressure on other states and those states then put pressure on the repressive state from the outside. In short, repression against internal groups can boomerang back and cause new external pressure on the repressive state.

---

the General Mills Foundation and Kellogg's Corporate Citizenship Fund), Supporting Partners (ranging from Bank of America Charitable Foundation to Share Our Strength), Associated Partners (like MAZON: A Jewish Response to Hunger and Taste of NFL-Hunger Related Events), Mission Partners (ranging from Campbell's Soup to Walmart), and Collaborative Partner Organizations (including Catholic Relief Services, the UN's Food and Agricultural Organization, and Lion's Clubs International).[6]

An interesting question is whether the values and norms popularized by these TANs are universal or reflective of just a certain region or culture. This issue is discussed in the box Revenge of Geography: Do Transnational Advocacy Networks Reflect Their Home Cultures?

In almost all cases, the ultimate target of TAN activity is states. As noted in Chapter 2, while states are not the only significant international actors in the neo-Westphalian international system, in many ways states remain the most powerful actors in the system. TANs seek to influence their behaviors, and we turn to that next.

13-2b Influencing States

The essential goal of most TANS is to get sovereign states to act on the values embraced by the TAN. Like many of the NGOs that often comprise them, a common way most TANs do this is through the practice of "naming and shaming." As a child, you may have been told "sticks and stones may break my bones, but words can never hurt me." That's true, if you have a very thick skin and a healthy dose of self-esteem! Still, no one likes to be publicly called out for bad behavior—that includes the leaders, elites, and people of a state. For states, their reputations are prized possessions, and states will often change behavior that others find objectionable to get the international spotlight off them and shifted elsewhere.

The way this often happens has been called the **boomerang model** as shown in Figure 13-2. If NGOs within a state are unsuccessful in changing the state's actions that they oppose (which is quite often the case in authoritarian states), they can use TANs to mobilize individual opinion leaders, NGOs, other states, and IOs, which can then pressure the state from outside. State regimes that might be unwilling to change as a result of domestic pressures will often change their behavior when it becomes clear that their behavior has hurt them internationally.

One very good example of the boomerang model in operation is the anti-apartheid network that helped to bring an end to the discriminatory white minority

Do Transnational Advocacy Networks Reflect Their Home Cultures?

It's ironic that advocacy networks expressly designed to transcend national borders have become objects of criticism by those who see them as missionaries of a foreign culture. In essence, some see TANs as instruments of a form of cultural imperialism that has clear geographic roots.

The most common expression of this idea begins with the fact that many TANs are headquartered in developed countries, overwhelmingly in North America and Europe. Thus, the norms they are popularizing are basically *Western* norms. For example, TANs emphasizing the spread of democracy focus on the presidential or parliamentary forms of democracy practiced in Europe and North America. Critics would say that the result is an overemphasis on a particular *form* of democracy—with a resulting obsession by Westerners with elections and civil society organizations—and a lack of appreciation for non-Western modes of public input. Is relying on a council of elders to make important decisions a legitimate form of representation more in line with local customs in a place like Afghanistan? When Afghanistan's president wants to reach out to the Afghan people, he hosts a *loya jirga*—a grand council of elders. Local assemblies of elders, called simply *jirgas*, often deal with community concerns in both Afghanistan and parts of Pakistan, as well. Is this also representation?

Women's rights organizations provide another example. Is the idea that women and men should have the same rights a universal value, or just a Western perspective? For example, most in North America and Europe would consider gender equality rights a universal value, as does the UN's Universal Declaration of Human Rights. However, some women in non-Western societies might disagree, and certainly it seems some of the men do. To take a more extreme example discussed in Chapter 11, a set of surgical practices performed in some traditional societies may be thought of there as "female circumcision," which has an almost-clinical connotation. Yet in most Western societies these practices are increasingly called "female genital mutilation," which sounds awful! Do you think this is a case of Western TANs imposing their cultural values on traditional societies, or is it a violation of values that should be considered universal?

Here's a different type of example. Many groups and individuals affiliated with the terrorist TANs known as jihadist networks have expressed the desire to create a "new Caliphate." That is, they want to impose Islamic rule over as much of the world as possible, thereby merging the secular and religious sectors. Is this another instance of groups and individuals from one region or culture using transnational networks to impose their values on others? So what do you think?

1. Are TANs reflections of the geography from which they are based?

2. Can TANs ever escape the cultures of the regions from which they arose?

3. Are there universal values that trump regional or cultural ones and, if so, who decides which ones are universal?

---

regime in South Africa about 25 years ago. Through most of the latter half of the twentieth century, neither violent nor nonviolent protest directed at the Republic of South Africa from within could force the white Afrikaner regime to end its policy of apartheid—the assigning of legal and societal rights based on skin color. However, literally hundreds of groups in Europe, Australia, the United States, and elsewhere, along with thousands of individuals who formed an anti-apartheid social movement, were able to create a network coordinating their actions with states and other IOs to bring pressure on the Afrikaner regime. This "naming and shaming" campaign had important effects. As noted in Chapter 9, corporations felt the pressures of this movement, as well. Their shareholders demanded that the corporations stop doing "business as usual" with the Afrikaner regime. South Africa found itself a pariah state in international politics. Most others in the international system felt South Africa's policies were morally wrong, almost no one wanted to cooperate with a state with such policies—particularly one that had been "called out" for its actions. Consequently, businesses and money fled the country. The anti-apartheid TAN increased the outside pressures on the regime until the costs—moral, political, and economic—were more than the regime was willing to pay. So South Africa changed the apartheid policy that had been in force since 1948, allowing full multiracial elections in 1994.

A different example of the boomerang model came in 2014 as states reacted to the kidnapping of hundreds

FIGURE 13-2 THE BOOMERANG MODEL OF TAN ACTIVITY

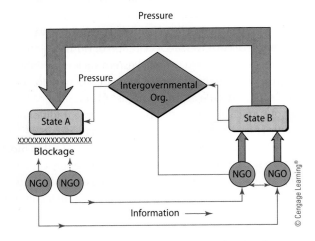

How vital are TANs to citizens facing authoritarian regimes?

Based on *Activists Beyond Borders: Advocacy Networks in International Politics*, by Margaret E. Keck and Kathryn Sikkink. Cornell University Press.

of Nigerian schoolgirls, illustrated in Foreign Policy in Perspective: The Case of the Nigerian Schoolgirls.

A different example of a TAN influencing a state involves a criminal network. The Russian Mafia fits our definition of a TAN since it is a network marked by reciprocal, voluntary actions across national borders by domestic and international non-governmental actors and individuals who fulfill differentiated roles in pursuit of shared values. The values these TAN members advocate are acquiring wealth, via illegal as well as legal means. An example of this TAN's ability to influence states came in 1999. When NATO launched a bombing campaign against Yugoslavia for its repression of the residents of its Kosovo region, a number of the properties being bombed were owned or controlled by elements associated with the Russian Mafia. Several members of the Russian State Duma (the lower body of Russia's national legislature) introduced a prominent Yugoslavian businessman, Dragomir Karic, to a visiting delegation of members of the U.S. House of Representatives at a meeting in Vienna. According to the congressional leader of the trip, Karic had been previously identified to him by the CIA as the leading representative of the Russian Mafia in Yugoslavia. Karic told the members of the congressional delegation that NATO was destroying his property and, if they could tell him what the government of Yugoslavia had to agree to in order for the bombing to stop, he could get Yugoslavian President Slobodan

Milosevic to accept those terms. When asked how he could be sure Milosevic would agree, Karic replied that he "owned" Milosevic. Despite the fact that Milosevic had previously said he would never allow NATO peacekeepers in Kosovo, such peacekeepers were a crucial component of the agreed-upon terms. When Karic faxed those terms to Milosevic, Milosevic reversed his previous position (perhaps mindful of the fact that telling the Russian Mafia "no" was often extraordinarily bad for one's health). One week later former Russian Prime Minister Viktor Chernomyrdin formally proposed those terms to NATO and Yugoslavia, both NATO and President Milosevic accepted them, the Kosovo War ended, and this TAN's membership had to be pleased that their assets in Yugoslavia were no longer being bombed!

13-2c Encouraging and Enabling Cooperation

While the Russian Mafia illustration may be an extreme case, the fact remains that TANs routinely facilitate international cooperation. A more typical example is provided by the International Red Cross and Red Crescent Movement. Comprised of nearly 100 million individual members, the International Committee of the Red Cross, the International Federation of Red Cross and Red Crescent Societies, and 189 national Red Cross or Red Crescent societies, the movement is the world's largest humanitarian network. Its four major areas of emphasis include promoting humanitarian values, providing responses to disasters, helping others prepare for disasters, and providing health and community care where needed. In just 2010 alone, the network coordinated international efforts to respond to the victims of floods and cyclones in Australia, the earthquake in Haiti, and a tsunami in Japan. It also coordinated the provision of clean drinking water to Sudanese refugees, the fight against a polio epidemic in Congo, and the international response to 25 natural disasters in Europe. Due to its neutrality, the network was able to coordinate relief efforts to 12,000 victims displaced by violence in Côte d'Ivoire, and it coordinated the efforts of Libyan, Tunisian, and Egyptian Red Crescent societies to get humanitarian relief and medical supplies to the victims of Libya's growing civil war.

Another way TANs promote and encourage international cooperation is by endorsing international agreements. When widely-respected TANs endorse a new treaty or agreement, that endorsement may sway the minds of undecided legislators who must cast a vote on the agreement or provide the political cover for those who have already decided to cast what they feel could be a controversial vote for the agreement.

The Case of the Nigerian Schoolgirls

Boko Haram, an Islamist militant group operating in northern Nigeria, received seed money from Osama bin Laden in 2002 to help it create an Islamic state ruled by Sharia law in northern Nigeria, where most of Nigeria's 50 percent Muslim population live. Due to this and its links to al-Qaeda in the Islamic Maghreb, Boko Haram was designated by the U.S. Department of State as a foreign terrorist organization in November 2013.

Inside Nigeria, the group remained a deadly, but largely local, threat. However, the global notoriety of Boko Haram shot off the charts in April 2014 when it kidnapped nearly 300 largely Christian Nigerian schoolgirls, forced them to convert to Islam, and threatened to sell them (to places such as Chad and Cameroon) unless hundreds of Boko Haram militants jailed in Nigeria, Niger, and Cameroon were released. When the Nigerian government failed to launch an operation to find the kidnapped girls, the girls' mothers—and other Nigerian mothers—began a social movement: "Bring Back Our Girls!" With the help of Twitter, the movement went global at #BringBackOurGirls, with both Pope Francis and U.S. First Lady Michelle Obama responding to the call.

U.S., British, and French offers to send military advisers to assist the Nigerian government in locating the girls were initially rebuffed. Yet after two weeks of international shaming in the mainstream press and social media and by both Nigerian and global civil society organizations, the Nigerian government accepted the external offers of assistance to help find them. Nearly a month after the girls' abduction, Nigerian President and Commander in Chief Goodluck Jonathan declared that a military offensive would be undertaken to return the girls and evict Boko Haram from northern Nigeria.

That military offensive never occurred, as Nigerian military leaders apparently don't think they have the capability to defeat Boko Haram on its "own" turf. As of

KarenBleier/Getty Images

How can a network like #BringBackOurGirls force a state to act?

October 2014, the families of the kidnapped girls were urging the Nigerian government to negotiate a prisoner swap for their release. What do you think about this episode?

1. How would the Nigerian government have responded without the pressure from this quickly formed, transnational network of individual activists, groups, and state actors?

2. Does this mean the boomerang model did or didn't work?

Sources: U.S. Department of State, "Background Briefing on Designation of Boko Haram and Ansaru as Foreign Terrorist Organizations and as Specially Designated Global Terrorists," November 13, 2013, http://www.state.gov/r/pa/prs/ps/2013/11/217532.htm; Paul Cruickshank and Tim Lister, "Boko Haram Has Kidnapped Before – Successfully," *CNN*, May 12, 2014, http://www.cnn.com/2014/05/12/world/boko-haram-previous-abductions/index.html; Eli Lake, "Boko Haram's Bin Laden Connection," *The Daily Beast*, May 11, 2014, http://news.yahoo.com/boko-harams-bin-laden-connection-041508136--politics.html; Vivienne Walt, "Nigerians Critical of Government's Slow Kidnappings Response," *Time*, May 11, 2014, http://time.com/95558/nigeria-kidnappings-government/; Hannah Strange, "Bring Back Our Girls? The Nigerian Government Is Focusing More on Its PR Strategy and Silencing Criticism," *The Telegraph*, July 2, 2014, http://www.telegraph.co.uk/women/womens-life/10940077/Bring-back-our-girls-The-Nigerian-government-is-focusing-more-on-its-PR-strategy-and-silencing-criticism.html.

For example, the International Criminal Court (or ICC) provides a service many in the international system see as absolutely necessary: holding individuals to account for crimes against humanity, war crimes, genocide, or aggression when their home states will not prosecute them for such crimes. However, when facing a vote to ratify the Rome Statute that created

the ICC, some legislators might worry about the political costs involved. Their critics may charge that those legislators are supporting a supranational organization that threatens their state's sovereignty. However, the Coalition for the International Criminal Court could help legislators who support the ICC. This TAN—composed of 2,500 civil society organizations in over

150 different countries—provides expert opinions showing how the ICC's principle of complementarity allows national courts to retain their full sovereignty over such cases—thus preventing the ICC from ever hearing the cases—if those national courts are willing to prosecute the cases themselves. Thus, the coalition can provide political cover and protection for those who want to vote to approve membership in the ICC by giving them arguments that counter the "protect our sovereignty at all costs" challenge.

TANs also monitor the actions of states to ensure effective cooperation with established norms. A network of human rights organizations regularly reports on the human rights records of states with member organizations like Freedom House, which releases an annual listing of freedom scores for each country, and Human Rights Watch, which also issues country reports each year. A group called UN Watch does the same thing for the UN. Similar networks exist to ensure compliance with environmental agreements and norms. One such network is the Millennium Ecosystem Assessment. This network of networks was created in 2001 at the recommendation of UN Secretary-General Kofi Annan to assess how human activity was affecting ecosystems and how those ecosystems worked to enhance human security. The Millennium Ecosystem Assessment relies on the work of over 1,300 experts worldwide and is governed by a diverse board of directors. The board includes representatives from IOs, including the UN, the World Health Organization, the World Bank, the Caribbean Development Bank, and the Global Environmental Facility; NGOs such as the Consultative Group on International Agricultural Research, the United Nations Foundation, the International Council for Science, the World Conservation Union, and others; and individuals from the business, scientific, development, and educational sectors in the Americas (Brazil, Canada, Costa Rica, Trinidad and Tobago, and the United States), Europe (Italy, the Netherlands, Norway, Russia, Slovenia, Spain, Sweden, Switzerland, and the United Kingdom), Africa (Egypt, Kenya, South Africa, and Tanzania), and Asia (Bangladesh, China, India, and Malaysia).

As we suggested, however, not all TANs are alike. Let's take a look at different types of TANs and what they do.

self-oriented TANs TANs that advocate values that primarily benefit the network members.

THE DIVERSE WORLD OF TRANSNATIONAL ADVOCACY NETWORKS

As noted at the beginning of the chapter, transnational advocacy networks *must* include non-governmental actors—usually NGOs but at times social movements, individuals, or some combination thereof. They may *also* include governments and governmental bodies such as IOs. When you think about it, this range of membership means TANs can be quite diverse in their interests and actions. We categorize TANs by their basic orientation—self-oriented or other-oriented—and then introduce some specific examples and their actions. Again, keep in mind that the types of TANs being illustrated are more important than trying to remember the specific examples used.

13-3a Self-Oriented TANs and What They Do

Some TANs advocate values that benefit themselves and their members, rather than non-network members. These can be thought of as **self-oriented TANs** because they exist *primarily* to pursue private goods. You could say these are actors rationally pursuing their own self-interests. While many such self-oriented TANs exist, three types that come immediately to mind include business TANs, organized crime TANs, and terrorist TANs. We'll consider each of these in turn.

BUSINESS TANS One example could be a network comprised of businesses and the people and groups that benefit from their activity. Here we are talking about something more than just multinational corporations, which as institutional actors are networks of corporations tied together through common ownership and responsive to common management. Business TANs exist when individuals and groups join with business entities to create a network that cooperatively exists over time and across national boundaries. A good illustration occurs when a business from abroad comes into a new country. For example, when Toyota chose to build a truck assembly plant in San Antonio, Texas, a TAN was created that included Toyota Motor Corporation and a new entity called Toyota Motor Manufacturing, Texas, Inc. It also included groups in Texas that wanted to bring the business there. Those included the Economic

Development and Tourism division of the Office of the Governor of Texas, the Texas Workforce Commission, the Greater San Antonio Chamber of Commerce, and the City of San Antonio. Even though the plant's subsequent manufacturing employees would be non-union employees, a variety of labor unions were included in the TAN, as union contractors got the opportunity to bid for construction contracts for the plant.

The result of this TAN was the development of a pickup truck assembly plant that directly employed 2,800 workers and on-site suppliers of component parts of the trucks who employed an additional 2,700 workers.[7] Conservative estimates suggest at least 1,000 other jobs in the area were created by the economic stimulus the Toyota plant generated. Other members of the TAN included those other businesses in Japan and Mexico that manufactured the component parts for trucks assembled in San Antonio. All these TAN members shared an interest in seeing Tundra and Tacoma pickups rolling out of the San Antonio plant because they all benefited in some way. As long as the TAN members helped each other, they all were winners.

However, not all self-oriented TANs produce such win-win scenarios. Some pursue their own private interests at the expense of others; a good example would be transnational organized crime groups.

Texas Governor Rick Perry welcomes Toyota Motor Corporation President Fujio Cho to San Antonio, the site of a new Toyota Tundra factory | Are Tundra pickups American or Japanese vehicles? Do you care?

ORGANIZED CRIME TANS Many organized crime networks fit our definition of TANs, at least to the degree they involve networks of people and groups engaged in ongoing *transnational* activity with defined roles. In some instances, participants in these criminal networks may even include government officials, either as active participants or as more passive participants who simply choose to look the other way.

Members of the Russian Mafia and Japanese Yakuza Undergo Extensive Tattooing | Once a member, can one later choose to leave these criminal TANs?

There are many prominent transnational criminal networks. A common pattern for their international networking with other groups begins with narcotics trafficking—getting the drugs from areas of cultivation, to processing facilities, and then to final shipments to markets. Once involved in such international networks, other markets are seen, such as human trafficking for the sex trade or for slave labor. As their activities and revenues increase, network members need to hide their profits from law enforcement and taxing agencies, which leads them into global money laundering networks. As these cooperative activities increase and become routine, the members of such networks may engage in reciprocal services—such as murder-for-hire schemes. Examples of such global criminal TANs include the Russian Mafia, the Italian-American Mafia, an Italian-based network called the *Camorra*, the Japanese-based *Yakuza*, Chinese-based networks like the *Fuk Ching* and the Triads, the *Heiji* network based in Taiwan, Thailand-based networks with names such as *Jao Pho* and *Red Wa*, and Mexican-based cartels like *Los Zetas*. Some criminal TANs have been alleged to promote what has been called a modern-day form of cannibalism. See Spotlight On: Trafficking in Human Organs, which focuses on trafficking in human organs.

As globalization made it easier to travel, communicate, and transfer funds on a worldwide basis, transnational organized crime increased. As a result, the UN General Assembly passed the **UN Convention against Transnational Organized Crime** in 2000 and it went into force in 2003. The convention seeks to promote awareness on the part of signatories to the transnational aspects of organized crime, encourage the passage of new national laws against such crimes, and facilitate cooperation in the arrest and extradition of such criminals. It also has specific protocols that emphasize efforts to stop the trafficking in people, smuggling of migrants, and illegally manufacturing or trafficking in firearms. Over 175 states are members of the convention. There is also a **UN Convention against Illicit Traffic in Narcotic Drugs and Psychotropic Substances**, passed by the UN General Assembly, which entered into force in 1990. It has over 180 members. This treaty expanded a previous one from 1961 that dealt only with narcotic drugs. In these ways, the UN has sought to promote international cooperation in opposing the actions of criminal TANs.

However, transnational criminal networks predated the creation of the UN, and since 1923 the International Criminal Police Organization, better known as **INTERPOL**, has been promoting international cooperation in pursuing criminals across national borders. Based in Lyon, France, INTERPOL has 190 member countries, and it seeks to enforce national criminal laws and enforce the spirit of the Universal Declaration of Human Rights (see Chapter 11). At the present time, INTERPOL is placing particular focus on combating criminal networks operating in Europe and Asia, those specializing in serial murder and rape offenses, and those engaged in maritime piracy.

What's really frightening is the possibility that transnational organized crime networks might get involved with another type of self-oriented TAN—terrorist networks. We turn to these next.

TERRORIST TANS As noted in Chapter 5, terrorism involves indiscriminate violence aimed at noncombatants to influence a wider audience. Terrorist groups have been around since ancient times, but they were usually active just within their own home political territory. Transnational terrorist networks did not become a notable factor in international politics until the rise of loosely associated anarchist networks in the late nineteenth and early twentieth centuries. As terrorists form networks to use violence to impose their values on others, they fit our definition of self-oriented TANs.

But what values are they trying to impose? In Chapter 5, we differentiated terrorists into four groups. The first is criminal terrorists, which we just discussed. The second is nihilist terrorists who simply want to destroy the existing order without an agenda of replacement. The anarchists previously mentioned would fit this definition. So too would Germany's Red Army Faction (also known as the Baader-Meinhof Gang). This 1970s network included German Marxists trying to bring down what they saw as a fascist-leaning, German state and groups like the Palestine Liberation Organization, which provided weapons training, and the Popular Front for the Liberation of Palestine, which provided ideological support.

The third type of terrorist group is nationalist terrorists. A variety of Palestinian groups would fit this definition, to the extent that they cooperated as networks. Although many in the Arab world considered

UN Convention against Transnational Organized Crime a treaty promoting international cooperation to deal with transnational organized crime, which went into force in 2003.

UN Convention against Illicit Traffic in Narcotic Drugs and Psychotropic Substances a treaty promoting international cooperation to stop the transnational trafficking in illegal drugs, which went into force in 1990.

INTERPOL the International Criminal Police Organization created in 1923 and based in Lyon, France.

Trafficking in Human Organs

Human organ *donation* is a long-established practice, but there are not enough donors to meet the global need. Not surprisingly then, some with the requisite financial means who cannot get a transplant through legal channels will turn to the black market of illegal organ sales, and criminal organizations have sprung up to meet this need. According to a Council of Europe study, during the 1999 Kosovo War some members of the Kosovo Liberation Army executed Serbian prisoners and then sold their transplantable organs on the black market. Hashim Thaci was the political leader of the Kosovo Liberation Army at the time, and he is now the prime minister of Kosovo. According to the Council of Europe study, he also heads the Drenica Group, an organized crime network based in Kosovo and Albania involved in the sale of human organs. Others alleged to be part of the ring include doctors in Kosovo, Albania, Turkey, and Israel who harvested the organs from poor people who were willing to sell them for as much as $20,000—money which some of them claimed they never received. These organs were then transplanted into wealthy recipients from Canada, Germany, Israel, and Poland who were willing to pay up to $200,000 for the transplants. Talk about a profit margin! Seven individuals associated with this group have been criminally charged to date. Further, this network may also be linked with another one based in South Africa that enticed poor Brazilians and Romanians to sell their kidneys, which were then sold to wealthy Israelis.

Yet these are not the only such criminal networks engaging in these practices. The sale of healthy kidneys may be most pronounced in India. Beginning in the 1980s, many from the Middle East traveled to India to purchase kidneys from living donors. The practice was outlawed in India in 1994, but it continues on the black market, often controlled by crime rings that began as drug traffickers. According to many news reports, China has also been a

Victims of human organ trafficking display their scars | Can the international community take effective action to end this practice?

market for black market human organs, harvesting healthy organs from executed prisoners for sale in China, Taiwan, and elsewhere. One study claims imprisoned members of the Falun Gong—a spiritual movement outlawed in China—have been specifically targeted as unwilling organ donors by the Chinese government. According to that study, over 40,000 transplants occurred in China between 2000 and 2005 in which the source of the transplanted organ cannot be identified.

In most countries, the sale of human organs is illegal, and it is considered unethical by the World Health Organization. Yet criminal rings seeking profits exist to meet the needs of what has been come to be called "transplant tourism." Should this practice be decriminalized? Is "informed consent" to donate their organs really possible when the donors are very poor? What do you think about this?

Sources: Dan Bilefsky, "Seven Charged in International Organ-Trafficking Ring Based in Kosovo," *New York Times*, November 16, 2010, A4; Doreen Carvajal and Marlise Simons, "Report Names Kosovo Leader as Crime Boss," *New York Times*, December 16, 2010, A19; Gregory M. Lamb, "China Faces Suspicions about Organ Harvesting," *Christian Science Monitor*, August 3, 2006, http://www.csmonitor.com/2006/0803/p16s01-lire.html; Nancy Scheper-Hughes, "The Global Traffic in Human Organs," *Current Anthropology* 41 (2000): 191–224.

them freedom fighters, an umbrella group such as the Palestine Liberation Organization (PLO) sought to create an independent Palestinian state through the use of indiscriminate violence against noncombatants. The PLO included many different groups located in different countries, the largest of which ultimately was Fatah—the group led by Yasser Arafat.

The fourth type of terrorist group is revolutionary terrorists, those seeking to overthrow the social and political order and replace it with something more to their liking. Groups such as the Revolutionary Armed Forces of Colombia (or FARC) and Peru's Shining Path fit this description. In the twenty-first century, the better-known examples of revolutionary terrorist networks would include those hoping to overthrow the existing secular order and replace it with a regional or global Islamic regime. One such example would be Hezbollah. While Hezbollah is based in Lebanon, it qualifies as a terrorist network since it has cells in Africa, Europe, and both North and South America; it relies heavily on the material support it receives from Iran and Syria; it has provided support to Hamas in the Gaza Strip; and it has conducted operations in Lebanon, Israel, Argentina, and Egypt. Its goal is to create Islamic regimes in Lebanon and Palestine and potentially elsewhere in the Arab world. So it fits here. However, the best contemporary example of a revolutionary terrorist self-oriented TAN would be al-Qaeda, and we devote an entire box to it: Spotlight On: Al-Qaeda.

Regardless of the type of terrorist network involved, the international community has sought to confront it. In the 1970s and 1980s, the key concern was coordinating police efforts to protect airliners from being hijacked. By the 1990s, the focus had turned to confronting violent attacks by more revolutionary terrorist groups. After 9/11, state actors like the United States, United Kingdom, Canada, and others went to war with the Taliban regime in Afghanistan over its support of al-Qaeda, aided by the local anti-Taliban Northern Alliance—a group made up of several minority ethnic groups in Afghanistan, including Tajiks, Hazaras, Uzbeks, and Turkmen. Once that war was largely over, an International Security Assistance Force authorized by the UN Security Council took responsibility for Afghanistan, and then NATO forces took control of the effort to occupy and rebuild a stable, relatively peaceful, and hopefully democratic Afghanistan. NATO forces were scheduled to leave Afghanistan by the end of 2014 but a limited number of U.S. forces are to stay there to help train Afghan troops; history will determine whether this international effort to help the Afghans was successful.

In 2006, the UN General Assembly passed a **Global Counter-Terrorism Strategy** to address the root causes of terrorism, to promote international cooperation in dealing with terrorist threats, to build the capacity of both states and the UN to combat terrorism, and to make sure that the global fight against terrorism did not violate standards of the rule of law or human rights. By stressing that terrorism represented criminal acts *regardless of its motivation*, the UN was trying to get beyond the political debate that previously deadlocked over the notion that "one person's terrorist is another's freedom fighter." Such definitional dilemmas caused the UN to be largely hamstrung in dealing with terrorism before the events of 9/11.

However, as we noted earlier, self-oriented TANs are not the only ones out there. Other TANs advocate values that are primarily oriented at helping others. Let's change our focus and take a look at them.

13-3b Other-Oriented TANs and What They Do

When we talk about **other-oriented TANs**, it is hard to escape our emphasis on broader aspects of human security, as that theme seems to connect such groups who generally seek to promote collective goods. There are many possible examples of such networks. Let's talk about networks focusing on personal, economic, health, and environmental security.

PERSONAL SECURITY–ORIENTED TANS These TANs emphasize the needs of people to be safe from physical harm. At one extreme is the threat of nuclear war. While there is the Nuclear Non–Proliferation Regime we discussed in Chapters 2 and 6, it is composed solely of state actors and IOs. However, a number of NGOs form a transnational network to assist in this effort to prevent the use of nuclear weapons. One such actor is the U.S.-based Nuclear Threat Initiative. In 2008 it created the World Institute for Nuclear Security in Vienna, which joins together NGO and national officials from Australia, Finland, Norway, the United Kingdom, and the United States, along with representatives of the International Atomic Energy Agency, in a cooperative effort to strengthen the protection of existing nuclear materials from theft or misuse.

A well-known example of a human security–oriented network is the International Campaign to Ban Landmines mentioned earlier in this chapter. Less well-known examples would be other human rights–related networks that seek to protect people's right to personal security. One such network is the Universal Human Rights Network (UNIRIGHTS), which emphasizes the resolution of internal conflicts, demobilization of armed groups, reintegration of insurgents into society, civilian peacekeeping, and other human rights issues related to protection from violence. Its partner organizations include NGOs concerned with better peacekeeping,

Global Counter-Terrorism Strategy a 2006 UN General Assembly document that seeks to prevent terrorism by addressing its root causes, to promote international cooperation in dealing with terrorist threats, to build the capacity of both states and the UN to combat terrorism, and to make sure that the global fight against terrorism does not violate standards of the rule of law or human rights.

other-oriented TANs TANs that advocate a set of values that primarily benefit others besides themselves.

Al-Qaeda: One Part of a Global Jihadist Network

In 1988, a 31-year-old Saudi named Osama bin Laden took a step that still reverberates today. He created what would become a major Islamic terrorist network dedicated to conducting **jihad**—or a holy war—against Western nonbelievers. That network has now outlived him, as he was killed by U.S. Special Forces in 2011 at his hideout in Abbottabad, Pakistan.

To begin, bin Laden was the 17th of 52 (or possibly 54) children of Muhammad bin Laden (who had more than 20 wives over his lifetime). Muhammad bin Laden was a Yemeni who worked his way up to become the wealthiest construction contractor in Saudi Arabia. Shortly after the Soviet Union invaded Afghanistan in 1979, young Osama bin Laden left Saudi Arabia to go fight on behalf of his Muslim brethren there. With a college degree, construction expertise, and a personal inheritance of approximately $250 million, he was able to help support the Afghan mujahideen in its armed resistance to Soviet rule. As the fighting was winding down in 1988, bin Laden created an organization called al-Qaeda, Arabic for "The Base." If Islamic forces could defeat a superpower such as the Soviet Union, bin Laden thought anything might be possible in the name of Allah, including purging Islamic areas of Western corruption and reinvigorating Islam everywhere.

Like other TANs, al-Qaeda advocated its own values (using violence to expel nonbelievers from the Islamic world and expand Islamic rule around the globe) and sought to influence the actions of states to achieve those goals. To do so, al-Qaeda established camps in Afghanistan where volunteers from multiple Islamic countries were trained in the use of weapons and explosives and screened for their skills, potential to move freely in Western societies, and willingness to become martyrs as needed. Al-Qaeda also engaged in some coordination with groups like Lebanon's Hezbollah and Nigeria's Boko Haram.

While al-Qaeda's most dedicated operatives may at any time have only numbered several hundred, security officials have broken up al-Qaeda cells in Albania, France, Germany, Italy, Uganda, United Kingdom, and the United States. Al-Qaeda furnished these cells with training materials, often with arms and explosives, and initially with funding, as well. The following are among the operations now widely attributed to al-Qaeda or its affiliated groups:

- **1992:** the bombing of a Yemen hotel where U.S. troops were thought to be staying.

REUTERS/Hamid Mir/Editor/Ausaf/Newspaper for Daily Dawn /LANDOV Photographers/Source: HO/Reuters/Landov

Osama bin Laden (left) and Ayman al Zawahiri (right) | Who would have predicted the impact that these two men would have on world politics?

- **1993:** the bombing of the underground garage of New York City's World Trade Center, the thwarted bombing of multiple sites in and around New York City, the deaths of U.S. troops in Somalia in what is largely known now as the Blackhawk Down incident, and unsuccessful attempts to assassinate former Pakistani Prime Minister Benazir Bhutto and Crown Prince Abdullah of Jordan.

- **1994:** an unsuccessful effort to bomb the Israeli Embassy in Bangkok, a meeting in Sudan between bin Laden and the military leader of Hezbollah who advised bin Laden on how the 1983 bombing of the U.S. Marine barracks in Beirut helped drive the United States out of Lebanon, the bombing of a Shi'ite shrine in Iran, an unsuccessful attempt to assassinate Pope (and now Saint) John Paul II during a visit to the Philippines.

- **1995:** in cooperation with Egyptian Islamic Jihad, an unsuccessful attempt to assassinate Egyptian President Hosni Mubarak during a visit to Ethiopia, a bombing of a Saudi military communications station killing 5 U.S. troops and 2 Indian police officers.

- **1996:** the bombing of the Khobar Towers apartment complex in Saudi Arabia, killing 19 U.S. troops and injuring 400.

- **1998:** the bombing of U.S. Embassies in Kenya and Tanzania, killing 12 Americans and over 200 others—mostly Kenyans.

- **1999 to 2000:** thwarted attempts to kill American tourists in Jordan and to bomb Los Angeles International Airport, the bombing of the *USS Cole* in Yemen resulting in the deaths of 17 sailors.

- **2001:** the use of hijacked airliners as weapons in the attacks on New York City's World Trade Center—killing

jihad "holy war" in Arabic. To some Muslims it means the daily struggle within oneself to overcome evil; to others it means conducting war against non-Muslims.

nearly 3,000—and on the Pentagon—killing over 180 people, the attempted "shoe-bombing" of a Paris–Miami flight.

- **2002:** multiple bombings and attacks throughout the year, with over 200 killed in a nightclub bombing in Bali, Indonesia; other targets included a Protestant church in Islamabad, Pakistan, the U.S. Embassy in Peru, a synagogue in Tunisia, multiple locations in Karachi, Pakistan, a French tanker ship in Yemen, U.S. Marines in Kuwait, a U.S. aid worker in Jordan, Israeli tourists in Kenya.

- **2003:** multiple attacks targeting Saudi security officials or foreign residents in Riyadh, Saudi Arabia; tourists in Casablanca, Morocco; German peacekeepers in Afghanistan; Westerners at the Marriott Hotel in Jakarta, Indonesia; two synagogues, a British bank, and the British Consulate in Istanbul, Turkey; multiple attempts on the life of Pakistani leader Pervez Musharraf.

- **2004:** a bombing of the Moscow Metro; the bombing of a Philippine ferry boat; nearly 200 killed in bombings at the Madrid, Spain, central train station; multiple attacks on Saudi security forces, foreign oil workers, and non-U.S. employees of a U.S. Consulate in Saudi Arabia; the bombing of Christian areas in the Philippines.

- **2005:** bombings of the London Underground and buses, killing 56 in one attack and none in another; bombings in Sharm el-Sheik, Egypt, killing 63 tourists and Egyptians.

- **2007:** the assassination of former Pakistani President Benazir Bhutto.

- **2008:** bombing the Danish Embassy in Pakistan, killing 6; bombing the Marriott Hotel in Pakistan, killing 54.

- **2009:** the attempted bombing of Northwest Airlines Flight 253 by "underwear bomber" Umar Farouk Abdulmutallab; the suicide bombing at Camp Chapman in Afghanistan, killing 8.

- **2010:** the bombing of a German bakery in India, killing 17; the attempted bombing of multiple cargo planes traveling from Yemen to the United States.

- **2013:** taking more than 800 people hostage at a natural gas facility in Algeria, resulting in 39 hostages killed.

- **2014:** attack on a Pakistani warship in the port of Karachi, resulting in 3 militants killed.

Preventing such attacks became an obvious goal of Western or pro-Western governments. Public buildings were hardened, more security personnel were employed, and so on. However, interdicting al-Qaeda's ability to transfer funds internationally was an early emphasis of U.S. officials, and it was quite successful. With the aid of a previously negotiated **International Convention for the Suppression of the Financing of Terrorism**,

International Convention for the Suppression of the Financing of Terrorism a treaty that went into force in 2002, making it easier to get international cooperation to trace and shut down terrorist financing networks.

Anwar al-Awlaki, the English-speaking voice of al-Qaeda in the Arabian Peninsula | Who will become the Internet face of al-Qaeda now that U.S.–Yemeni cleric Anwar al-Awlaki has been killed?

which went into effect in early 2002, the financial assets of groups associated with al-Qaeda were frozen, and banks doing business with "terrorists" were threatened with both public exposure and legal action. As a result, it became harder for al-Qaeda to transfer funds electronically from one country to another. Forced to rely on informal *hawala* systems of money transfer (traditional money broker–based systems found in the Middle East, North Africa, and South Asia) or on the use of couriers actually carrying suitcases filled with cash, large-scale transnational terrorist operations became more difficult to finance and thus have largely ground to a halt.

Still, al-Qaeda has connections to, cooperates with, or serves as an inspiration to many other grassroots jihadist groups and networks, and they often have the ability to conduct operations in their local areas. These networks and groups can be found in Afghanistan (the Taliban), Algeria (al-Qaeda in the Islamic Maghreb and the Armed Islamic Group), Egypt (Egyptian Islamic Jihad), Iraq (al-Qaeda in Iraq and Jama'at al-Tawhid wal Jihad), Lebanon (Hezbollah), Libya (Libyan Islamic Fighting Group), Pakistan and India (al-Qaeda in the Indian Subcontinent, the Haqqani Network, Lashkar-e-Taiba, Jaish-e-Muhammad, and the Pakistani Taliban), the Philippines (Abu Sayyaf), Somalia (Al-Shabaab), Southeast Asia (Jemaah Islamiya), Uzbekistan (the Islamic Movement of Uzbekistan), and Yemen (al-Qaeda in the Arabian Peninsula and the Islamic Army of Aden).

While he was alive, bin Laden seemed to embody the network. In 1996 and 1998, he issued *fatwas*—or religious edicts—with the first calling on devout Muslims to drive the U.S. military out of the holiest land in Islam (Saudi Arabia) and the second calling upon them to kill Christians and Jews wherever possible—including women and children. Yet even before bin Laden's death, American-born Yemeni Anwar al-Awlaki was becoming the new "public face" of the network. As a member of al-Qaeda in the Arabian Peninsula, he hid in Yemen for years, posting his English-language sermons on the Internet, calling for Muslims to rise up and attack the United States. However, he was identified, located, and killed in a U.S. missile strike in 2011.

What do you think the deaths of bin Laden and al-Awlaki will ultimately mean for this network? Will it continue with leaders such as Ayman al Zawahiri—who was announced as al-Qaeda's leader after bin Laden's death? Did the Arab protest movements of spring 2011—which went forward with virtually no input from jihadist leaders—suggest that the jihadist network's time on the global stage is passing? Or will it continue with local, small-scale attacks carried out on an opportunistic basis?

the needs of displaced people, and promoting democracy, civil society, and the rule of law internationally. UNIRIGHTS has affiliated groups in Côte D'Ivoire, Egypt, Ghana, India, and Nepal.

Finally, another example of a network seeking to ensure personal security deals with human trafficking, a crime that often imperils women and children as sex slaves and men, women, and children as involuntary workers. The website HumanTrafficking.org provides a virtual hub for a network of NGOs and states that coordinate actions to combat human trafficking. It focuses on preventing such trafficking; rescuing the victims and getting them back home and reintegrated into society; prosecuting the criminals involved in these actions; coordinating national, regional, and international efforts; raising awareness of the problem on a global scale; and supporting research to deal with all aspects of the scourge of human trafficking. While the network was initially created to focus on the trafficking of women and children in the East Asia and Pacific region, it now has gone global by providing contacts with network actors in Europe and Eurasia, South and Central Asia, North America and the Caribbean, Central and South America, the Middle East and North Africa, and Sub-Saharan Africa.

Once people's security from physical harm has been addressed, they need to provide a living for themselves and their families. That brings up economic security–oriented TANs.

ECONOMIC SECURITY–ORIENTED TANS In the twenty-first century, those seeking to ensure the economic security of others generally begin with an emphasis on some form of sustainable economic development, as we mentioned in Chapter 12. The foundations of sustainable economic development involve food and energy security.

It's no surprise that having sufficient food supplies is a huge challenge in many poor countries, and having food supplies that are sustainable is a further challenge. Afrique Verte International (Green Africa International)

is a French-based NGO that creates networks to deal with food issues in West Africa. It has ongoing affiliate groups in Burkina Faso, Mali, and Niger, and it creates temporary networks with other actors on a project-to-project basis. For example, in a study of market prices for the primary cereal grains these states consume and produce for export (rice, corn, millet, and sorghum), Afrique Verte International worked with various governmental agencies and NGOs in France, Burkina Faso, Mali, and Niger. The study highlighted ways these states were improving their abilities to handle food crises through better planning, organization, and timely access to information for their farmers. By focusing on the "best practices" that work, Afrique Verte International provides guidance and assistance for many beyond these three countries.

The International Food Security Network provides another such example. Co-funded by the NGO Action-Aid and the European Commission, this network was formed in 2009 to address the hunger problems on a global basis. It links 30 national or regional food networks with 1,400 smaller groups active in North America and the Caribbean, Central America, South America, Africa, and Asia. It works to ensure that families have the ability to produce enough food to meet their own nutritional needs and to have access to food markets as both buyers and sellers. It also works to prevent farmers and livestock operators from losing the land they have (either to natural forces or predatory market forces), increasing the land to which they have access, and finding ways for them to offset the rising price of food purchased. With ActionAid, the International Food Security Network also seeks to address the specific needs of women farmers, as shown in the box Spotlight On: The World of Women Farmers.

Beyond ensuring that people have enough to eat, another foundational step for sustainable development is getting people sustainable sources of energy. Nearly a third of the people on the planet—2.4 billion—rely on traditional biofuels like wood, straw, and dried dung to cook their food and heat their homes. Not only are these

The World of Women Farmers

Although they constitute half of the global population, women often find themselves marginalized in society. That is as true in agricultural societies as it is anywhere else. On the one hand, women farmers play an extraordinarily important role in global agriculture, as they constitute 43 percent of the agricultural labor force in developing countries, produce 60 to 80 percent of the food in poor countries, and produce half of the world's total food supply. Yet women farmers face gender-based challenges that men do not. While both men and women work in food production, women typically tend to be malnourished as they eat less so the men and children in the family can eat more. They also do other tasks after the day's farming work is done, like hauling water, gathering firewood, and cooking for the family. They rarely get to own the land they work and find it much harder than men to get credit to support their agricultural efforts, receiving less than 10 percent of the loan credit available.

Thus it is not surprising that networks such as the International Food Security Network put a particular

Women working in rice fields in India | Would you want this job? What if it was your only choice?

emphasis on assisting women farmers, both in terms of increasing their food production but also in aiding them to know and pursue their legal or societal rights. The aid provided to women farmers produces significant societal benefits in the developing world. What else could be done on a global basis to help women farmers meet the needs of themselves and their families?

Source: "Women Farmers," *International Food Security Network*, http://www.actionaid.org/international-food-security-network.

---

inefficient heat sources, the smoke and emissions they produce—often in homes without chimneys or other ventilation—are dangerous when inhaled and contribute to greenhouse gases. The International Network for Sustainable Energy (or INFORSE) is a Danish-based network of 140 NGOs working in 60 different countries in Europe, Africa, North and South America, and Asia. It has regional coordinators in Argentina, Brazil, Denmark, India, Japan, Senegal, Slovakia, South Africa, and Uganda. Created at the Earth Summit in Rio de Janeiro in 1992, it has observer status at the UN's Economic and Social Council and has participated in the environmental conferences that followed the 1992 Earth Summit. Another Denmark-based network is more oriented to problem solving at the local level. The Global Network on Energy for Sustainable Development seeks to enable poor countries to develop more energy sources that are cleaner, more efficient, and sustainable over the long term. So far, the network has had some success promoting small-scale biogas operations, solar cookers, solar water heaters, and both rural and urban electrification.

Sustainable energy is not just the concern of developing countries and their Danish partners. As noted in Chapter 12, many developed countries are also seeking to find ways to exploit renewable and sustainable energy sources. The solar-powered photovoltaic (or solar PV) electric industry has a European-based advocacy network. Its members include the European Photovoltaic Industry Association headquartered in Belgium, national solar PV associations in Europe, private and governmental electric companies in Europe, and the European Commission. The network's goal is a very pragmatic one—enabling solar-powered electricity to be incorporated into national and regional electricity grids in Europe, particularly in times of peak demand.

One of the global leaders in solar power generation is China. Its China Clean Energy Network links suppliers of clean and renewable energy sources, such as solar, wind, biomass, and geothermal energy. These providers include both Chinese and foreign private corporations, and other network members are national government agencies, industry associations, and academic research centers. This transnational advocacy network focuses on ways to improve China's access to energy sources that will not add to China's horrific air pollution problem.

With food and energy needs met, the foundations of economic security have been addressed. Once economic and physical security is assured, we often then begin to address our health security. Here, too, the transnational advocacy networks are involved in health-related areas—the topic of the next section.

HEALTH SECURITY–ORIENTED TANS There are many ways to improve one's health security. Let's start at birth, since networks exist that seek to ensure the health of mothers and their newborns. Two that differ in their approaches are the International Planned Parenthood Foundation and Human Life International.

The International Planned Parenthood Foundation is a TAN that provides a variety of health-related services to women. Headquartered in London, it has affiliated organizations in 172 different countries and over 65,000 health care facilities. The services provided include help with family planning decisions, reproductive health, HIV-related care, maternal and child care, and contraception and abortion-related services. On the other hand, U.S.-based Human Life International seeks to ensure maternal and child health while outlawing abortion-related services wherever possible. Affiliated with the Catholic Church, it also links anti-abortion groups and activists outside the church, raises awareness of the

Liba Taylor/Encyclopedia/Corbis

Solar panels power a water pump in Kenya | How far does the reach of TANs such as The Global Network on Energy for Sustainable Development extend?

need to stop abortion and artificial means of contraception, and provides maternal and health care services in 160 countries. Not surprisingly, members of these two TANs typically see each other as rivals.

Beyond "beginning of life" questions, other TANs seek to promote better health for diseases that are difficult to treat. A good example is HIV/AIDS. Lots of attention is placed on Sub-Saharan Africa in this regard, as there are more cases of HIV/AIDS there than anywhere else. In 2012, 25 million Sub-Saharan Africans were living with HIV/AIDS—that's about 5 percent of the entire adult population! Table 13-1 shows those African states meeting or exceeding that

TABLE 13-1 SUB-SAHARAN STATES WITH 5 PERCENT OR MORE OF ADULTS WITH HIV/AIDS (2011)

COUNTRY	PEOPLE LIVING WITH HIV/AIDS	ADULT (15–49) PREVALENCE PERCENT	WOMEN WITH HIV/AIDS	CHILDREN WITH HIV/AIDS	AIDS DEATHS	ORPHANS DUE TO AIDS
Botswana	300,000	23.4	160,000	34,000	12,000	140,000
Gabon	46,000	5.0	24,000	3,100	2,500	21,000
Kenya	1,600,000	6.2	800,000	220,000	62,000	1,100,000
Lesotho	320,000	23.3	170,000	41,000	14,000	140,000
Malawi	910,000	10.0	430,000	170,000	44,000	610,000
Mozambique	1,400,000	11.3	750,000	200,000	74,000	800,000
Namibia	190,000	13.4	100,000	20,000	5,200	75,000
South Africa	5,600,000	17.3	2,900,000	460,000	270,000	2,100,000
Swaziland	190,000	26.0	100,000	17,000	6,800	75,000
Uganda	1,400,000	7.2	670,000	190,000	62,000	1,100,000
Tanzania	1,600,000	5.8	760,000	230,000	84,000	1,300,000
Zambia	970,000	12.5	460,000	170,000	31,000	680,000
Zimbabwe	1,200,000	14.9	600,000	200,000	8,000	1,000,000

© Cengage Learning®

Source: "Africa HIV and AIDS Statistics," *AVERT*, http://www.avert.org/africa-hiv-aids-statistics.htm.

Map 13-1

HIV Prevalence throughout the World

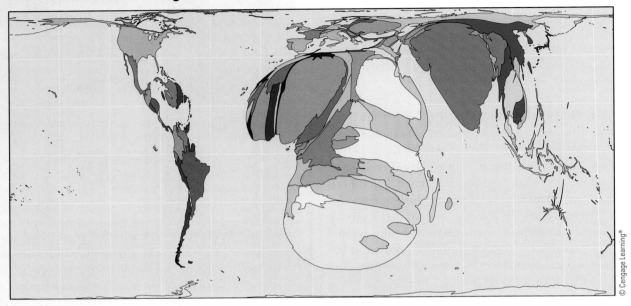

© Cengage Learning®

What does this map of the geographic concentrations of the HIV/AIDS epidemic suggest about its consequences and the challenges for addressing the problem?

5 percent figure in 2011, the latest year for which comprehensive data is available. Have a look at Map 13-1 which shows what the world would look like if countries were sized according to the proportion of their populations (18–49) infected with HIV. What do you think the implications of this *very* uneven distribution of the disease might be? There are TANs dedicated to treating these patients. Examples of such networks include ones such as the Network of African People Living with HIV/AIDS, the Eastern African National Networks of HIV/AIDS Service Organisations, the Canada-Africa Prevention Trials Network, and the African-European HIV Vaccine Development Network.

However, we'd be wrong to conclude that such networks only target HIV/AIDS in Africa. Let's consider some of the other, less obvious examples, too. One such network links AIDS clinics and medical care providers in Mexico City with counterparts in the international foundation sector, national and international governmental entities, and NGOs. Another such network is TREAT Asia (Therapeutics Research, Education, and AIDS Training in Asia). This network seeks to provide health care to the almost 5 million people

living with HIV/AIDS in the Asia/Pacific region. It connects the research of amFAR (the Foundation for AIDS Research) and corporate funding sources with participating medical clinics and research centers throughout Asia.

Finally, some TANs deal with a variety of health concerns that involve underserved communities. A good example is the Global Health Council. Its membership is made up of over 400 entities, including universities, hospitals, NGOs, private corporations, and think tanks. Its board of directors draws individuals from major pharmaceutical companies and a host of other NGOs. It brings medical care to women and children; to those facing HIV/AIDS, malaria, and tuberculosis; and it promotes the development of health care systems more broadly. It and its members conduct programs and projects in North America, the Caribbean, South America, Africa, the Middle East, the Caucasus region of Eurasia, South Asia, and Southeast Asia.

As mentioned previously, the activities of some of these health security TANs intersect with environmental issues. There are environmental security–oriented TANs, too, so let's take a quick look at them.

Evaluating TANs in the International System

Like numerous other examples we've used in this book, evaluating TANs typically depends on your theoretical orientation. Realists and neorealists argue that in an international system marked by anarchy, states are the most important actors, and nothing matters to them as much as the ability to protect their national interests through military means. From that perspective, TANs are relatively unimportant, as they are too weak to force states to change their behavior if states choose to hold firm. Realists would see TANs as important only to the extent they can be mobilized to help reach a state's goals. Otherwise, they are unimportant or perhaps even a nuisance. Take Russian elections, for example. NGOs such as the National Endowment for Democracy, the National Democratic Institute, the International Republican Institute, and the International Foundation for Electoral Systems worked for years to promote democratic values, viable and functioning political parties and other civil society organizations, and respect for free and fair elections in Russia. Since promoting democracy in Russia has been a goal of all post–Cold War U.S. administrations, the United States thinks this democracy promotion network is doing good work! However, since the network's activities hamper the Russian government's ability to do what it wants in the ways that it prefers and its statements and activities at times embarrass Russian officials, you can be sure that the Russian government thinks it is more than a nuisance; it thinks that members of the network are actually Western—if not U.S.—covert agents seeking the overthrow of the Russian regime!

Liberals and neoliberals see states, IOs, NGOs, and a host of subnational actors as part of a very complex and diverse international system, and TANs fit right into that mix. More to the point, TANs promote and enable cooperation among the various component actors in the system, thereby serving the needs of those who might otherwise be left out or marginalized. With the exception of criminal or terrorist TANs, liberals and neoliberals would typically view TANs as forces for good in the international system. Thus, TANs promoting the rights of women and children, enhanced global health, environmental protection, democratic values, and so on are seen as the leading edge of a new, more cooperative international system, one that is becoming an international civil society.

Since they emphasize the social construction of reality and the importance of identity politics, constructivists see TANs as important facilitators in the evolving narrative that defines international politics. For example, if enough TANs say apartheid is wrong (i.e., it is not a matter of internal sovereignty for South Africa but instead is an affront to global human rights norms), then this new reality says apartheid is wrong and steps must be taken to abolish it. Further, TANs can help groups develop and express their collective identities (for example, seeing fundamentalist Muslims as victims of Western oppression or workers in San Antonio seeing themselves as part of a larger Toyota-based family). Thus constructivists would see TANs as an essential component of an international system based more on shared ideas than on physical realities.

More critical theorists would offer a different view depending on their theoretical orientation and the nature of the TAN involved. In his work, Karl Marx emphasized the need for the international working class to revolt against the bosses and owners. Thus Marxists might well see revolutionary TANs as a way to work outside the state system to achieve a more just world. Certainly, early anarchist TANs did so.

World system theorists would probably interpret TAN importance by the type of TAN, as well. Other-oriented TANs often rely on either network members from the core region of the international system or core states for funding. Thus world system theorists might see core-dominated TANs as agents of core interests. In other words, they might see TANs as a disguised means for core states and elite classes to manipulate poor states located on the periphery of the international system in directions the core wants them to go. On the other hand, world system theorists might see at least some self-oriented TANs as agents of change in the core-defined international system. Thus while they might not approve of the methods of terrorist TANs, for example, they might appreciate how the actions of terrorist TANs can get a new set of concerns included on national or global agendas. Arise, oppressed minorities!

Finally, feminist theorists probably share world system theorists' appreciation of TANs as a means by which new issues can get on the global agenda. Through TAN activities, women's rights, women's needs, women's concerns, and women's roles in national and international affairs have been the focus of new attention over the last 40 years in ways that would have seemed unprecedented in earlier periods of the international system.

So what do you think?

1. How important are TANs in international affairs?

2. Do they do things states won't do?

3. Do they merely represent the efforts of the weak to challenge more powerful state interests?

4. Are they a vehicle for states to accomplish their purposes through other means?

ENVIRONMENTAL SECURITY–ORIENTED TANS

Like the other TANs, environmental security–oriented TANs seek to popularize ideas, to influence states by helping to set their agendas and subsequent actions, and to enable cooperation. An example of one such network that links environmental and health security is the International Society of Doctors for the Environment. This TAN links doctors whose focus is on environmentally caused health problems—such as pollution's linkage to disease and early death. It educates doctors, the public, corporations, and governments on such issues and links up with a variety of other international networks to do so. Another example of such an environmental security TAN is the one put together by the Transnational Institute. It links a number of resource-based networks in Africa, Europe, and the Western Hemisphere to ensure that local people have access to and control over clean water supplies and to protect environmental resources such as water supplies and forests from ownership by corporations. Much of the network's activities lie in the areas of grassroots organizing and seeking to set national government agendas.

Both of these TANS are global in scope, but there are regional ones, as well. Climate Action Network Europe (CAN-E) is pretty much what the name suggests. It focuses on climate change, emissions, and sustainable energy issues in Europe. This network links together over 120 member organizations in more than 25 European states. Among its major priorities is the careful monitoring of the EU's Emission Trading System—a carbon trading mechanism designed to use market forces to reduce Europe's carbon footprint. While CAN-E is a regional TAN, it also is a component of a global one. The broader Climate Action Network has similar regional networks in North America, Latin America, Asia, and Africa.

13-3c Evaluating TANs

Other-oriented TANs seek to make the world a better place for all; that's why they are often associated with the phrase "the greater good." In an increasingly globalized world system, both self-oriented and other-oriented transnational advocacy networks play important roles and can have surprisingly significant consequences for international politics. Whether or not you think these are positive roles and impacts probably depends on your theoretical orientation and perhaps even the network under consideration, as pointed out in Theory in Action: Evaluating TANs in the International System.

As you can see, TANs can be evaluated from a variety of different viewpoints, and these evaluations vary dramatically. Regardless of how they're evaluated, TANs are an increasingly prevalent phenomenon in international politics and seem likely to become even more prevalent in the twenty-first century.

CONCLUSION: TANS AND THE GLOBAL FUTURE

TANs are far more than just NGOs and their friends. When these transnational networks form, they become distinctly different entities that have an effect that is more than just the sum of their parts. TANs are not just an increasingly prevalent phenomenon in the neo-Westphalian system; they are increasingly significant actors in their own right. As the examples in this chapter show, TANs can change the structure of the playing field of international politics by introducing new issues and opening up that playing field to newer or weaker players, redefining the rules of the game of international politics to make it less state-centric by allowing non-state actors increasingly visible or important roles in world politics, threatening the security of even the largest states, and allying with other international actors—states, IOs, NGOs, social movements, and individuals—to create new issue alliances and foster counter-alliances among those actors that do not share their values.

How they do these things varies, of course, and the variance seems to depend on the type of TAN involved. Self-oriented TANs such as economic, criminal, or terrorist groups usually engage in direct actions to achieve their goals. Such actions may involve working with states, around states, or against states. Other-oriented TANs seeking to improve the greater good often rely on more indirect means, such as using their control of information to redefine issues and get them on governmental agendas, relying on symbolic politics to persuade other actors that their behaviors need to change (such as linking what they do to some unpleasant or negative symbol), working with state actors to accomplish their goals, and serving as monitoring agencies to hold governments publicly accountable for their actions.

Given these trends, TANS are forcing a space for themselves on the main stage of international politics in the twenty-first century. For good or ill, they address global needs that are either underemphasized or go unmet. They don't rival states in power, but highly successful TANs can create and change parameters of acceptable behavior regarding specific issues that leaders of states and IOs increasingly choose not to violate.

THINK ABOUT THIS TANS, STATES, AND THE FUTURE OF WORLD POLITICS

As the international system becomes more globalized, TANs increasingly connect a wide array of actors around their shared interests. Scholars representing the "English School" of international relations theory (people like Hedley Bull, Barry Buzan, Martin Wight, Robert H. Jackson, and others) have long talked about an emerging "global society," a real community with norms and shared values. Could TANs be the glue that helps hold such a society together?

Hedley Bull

Hedley Bull

Barry Buzan

Barry Buzan

Do you think TANs will replace states as the most significant actors in a more "human-friendly" international system at some point, or will states remain preeminent with TANs seeking to influence state behavior whenever possible?

STUDY TOOLS 13

LOCATED AT BACK OF THE BOOK:
☐ Rip out Chapter in Review Card

LOCATED ON COURSEMATE:

Use the CourseMate access card that came with this book or visit CengageBrain.com for more review materials:

☐ Review Key Terms Flash Cards (Print or Online)

☐ Download Chapter Summaries for on-the-go review
☐ Complete Practice Quizzes to prepare for the test
☐ Walk through a Simulation, Animated Learning Module, and Interactive Maps and Timelines to master concepts
☐ Complete Crossword Puzzle to review key terms
☐ Watch the videos for real-world application of this chapter's content
☐ Visit IR NewsWatch to learn about the latest current events as you prepare for class discussions and papers

REVIEW QUESTIONS

1. What are transnational advocacy networks (TANs)?

2. How do TANs differ from other international actors already studied?

3. How do TANs influence human security broadly defined?

4. What are the two major types of TANs, and how do they differ?

5. What do such TANs do?

6. How might the importance of TANs be evaluated?

FOR MORE INFORMATION . . .

For more on transnational advocacy networks, see:

Keck, Margaret E., and Kathryn Sikkink. *Activists beyond Borders*. Ithaca, NY: Cornell University Press, 1998.

Morselli, Carlo. *Inside Criminal Networks*. New York City: Springer, 2009.

Sageman, Marc. *Leaderless Jihad: Terror Networks in the Twenty-First Century*. Philadelphia: University of Pennsylvania Press, 2008.

Slaughter, Anne-Marie. *A New World Order*. Princeton, NJ: Princeton University Press, 2004.

Smith, Jackie. "Exploring Connections Between Global Integration and Political Mobilization." *Journal of World-Systems Research* 10 (2004): 255–285.

14 | International, Economic, and Human Security in the Balance:
Future Directions and Challenges

LEARNING OBJECTIVES
After studying this chapter, you will be able to . . .

14-1 Identify the ways anarchy, diversity, and complexity shape world politics.

14-2 Describe the continuity and change in the meaning and role of security in world politics.

14-3 Explain the trends and emerging areas of concern for future world politics.

14-4 Assess the different ways in which theory, geography, and foreign policy perspectives will change and shape the future of the world.

After finishing this chapter go to **PAGE 403** for **STUDY TOOLS**

WHO OWNS THE ARCTIC?

In 2007, Russia shocked its neighbors by claiming a large section of the Arctic Ocean and its seabed as part of its national territory. Russia became the first state to plant a national flag on the ocean floor at the North Pole, thereby staking its claim just as explorers have done for hundreds of years. The Russians also base their claim on the fact that the undersea Lomonosov Ridge runs over 1,000 miles from Russia under the Arctic Ocean and past the North Pole. The Russians say that the ridge makes the waters around it part of *Russia's* undersea continental shelf, an area in which coastal states have long claimed special rights.

The Russian claim creates a new zone of international competition. In the past, extreme weather conditions and a solid ice pack prevented any state from claiming the Arctic Ocean or the seabed beneath it. However, global climate change has caused melting in the once-solid ice pack. The fishing stocks that live under the ice are now more accessible to commercial harvesting. Moreover, the newly accessible water routes have opened many opportunities for commercial wealth in the areas of oil, mineral, and natural gases, with predictable consequences for competition over them. Modern deep-sea mining technologies have also improved, so oil exploration firms now have the ability to tap the vast deposits of oil and natural gas thought to be under the Arctic waters. Such competition is not new: Arctic usage rights have been a bone of contention since the 1950s. However, now whoever controls this area stands to benefit dramatically. Consequently, what has ensued is an almost "Cold War–like scramble reminiscent of the United States–Russia moon landing rivalry," as one account put it.[1]

More than just resources are at stake here. Russia has stressed its security concerns over the region, with Russian President Vladimir Putin claiming the need to seek and maintain a strong foothold in the area because of the presence and activities of the United States. Furthermore, as the ice pack melts, more and more waters open up for transit. The Northwest Passage through the Arctic is now ice-free for long portions of the year, giving commercial shipping—or armed vessels of national navies for that matter—a way to quickly move between the Atlantic and Pacific Oceans. Canada claims that the Northwest Passage lies within its territorial waters as marked by its continental shelf. Others, such as the United States, disagree and call the Northwest Passage part of the high seas, open to all international shipping traffic. As a result of these issues, the governments of Canada, Denmark, Norway, Russia, and the United States—as well as the UN—are trying to sort out these overlapping claims. The UN's Law of the Sea Convention covers such contentious issues, but not surprisingly these rival states interpret its provisions differently and with an eye toward their own national interests. On a positive note, in 2010 Russia and Norway signed a treaty demarking their Arctic Ocean borders, but the other parties' issues remain unresolved.

Some interesting questions arise from this dispute, such as:

1. How does this case illustrate the challenges of anarchy, complexity, and diversity?

2. Is this the future of international relations—as changes occur and technologies develop, and as new areas of national competition, rivalry, and perhaps conflict arise?

3. Should these disputes be settled via diplomacy and international law or by power politics?

© Natalia Klenova/Shutterstock.com

INTRODUCTION: INTERPRETING HOW THE WORLD WORKS

Throughout the last 13 chapters, we discussed the problems, patterns, and complexities of international relations. We emphasized how the search for security influences the ways states and non-state actors behave in the international system, and how issues such as the powerful role of the United States and the continuing importance of geography helped illustrate these key concepts. To bring our survey of world politics to a close, rather than simply reviewing what we have already covered, let's step back and ask ourselves the fundamental question: *how does the world work?*

In our opening chapter, we suggested that making sense of world politics was often a daunting task, in part because of the many actors and the seemingly endless stream of events and activities—sometimes appearing to have no rhyme or reason to them—that constitute international relations. Now, after working together through the preceding chapters of this text, we saw many examples of the range of these issues and events. We looked at problems from conflict to cooperation and from traditional security issues to quality-of-life

concerns to identify the patterns and forces at work in the world and to try to understand their causes, connections, and consequences. We saw how states, nations, international institutions, non-governmental organizations, transnational corporations, individuals, and transnational networks contributed to the dynamics of world politics. We also worked together to organize and interpret these issues by looking at them through various theoretical lenses, and by thinking about them in the context of the challenges that anarchy, diversity, and complexity present.

So we are in a better position now to address this question: "how does the world work?" Throughout our text, we discussed how different theoretical lenses take up this question of the underlying factors or forces driving world politics. These different theoretical perspectives give us useful tools to draw our own conclusions and offer our own explanations of international relations. We certainly don't (and shouldn't) need to restrict ourselves to how realists, liberals, constructivists, foreign policy theorists, Marxists, feminists, or other theoretical approaches think the world works. Those perspectives are important and helpful, but we already covered that! Instead, each of us should look at the many parts of world politics, consider and draw from the different explanations these lenses offer us, and ask ourselves: how

FIGURE 14-1 THE FUNDAMENTAL CHALLENGES OF WORLD POLITICS

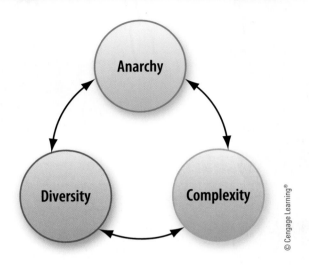

© Cengage Learning®

do these puzzle pieces fit together into a coherent picture of international relations?

By now, it should be very clear that there are a lot of moving pieces in international relations and it is hard to keep track of all of the facts. Remember what we suggested in Chapter 13 when we said it is more important to remember the types of TANs and the concepts than recalling specific examples? That same rule applies here when trying to figure out how the world works. Instead of starting to think about the role and behavior of specific states and organizations, first ask yourself what is the basic nature and behavior of humans. Are they cooperative or conflictual? What leads them to violence and what leads them to peace? Now ask yourself the same questions about the nature and behavior of large collections of people into nations and states. Does that change anything? Are people more conflict-prone or cooperative when they share a collective identity? Do states behave the way they do in world politics because of the nature of the individuals that comprise them?

The international system is—as our themes highlight—anarchic (decentralized, without an authoritative central government, but not chaotic), diverse (with actors of many types, perspectives, interests, and values), and complex (many issues, problems, actors, abilities, and goals all increasingly linked together). Remember, however, that the building blocks of all of this "stuff" are humans. War is the result of choices made by human beings; terrorism is an act in which humans engage; trade is a human activity; transnational networks are forged by human beings to address problems of global scale, and so on. So keep that in mind as you pull together all of the

different moving parts into your own view of the world. Whatever your answer to the question—"how does the world work?"—it must be based on the relationships among people.

Now, to help us answer the question "how does the world work?" let's first return to the anarchy, diversity, and complexity themes we have highlighted throughout these pages. Then we consider the concept of security, reflecting not only on its centrality to world politics, but also to the way its meaning and nature have changed over time. Once we have done that, we can feel more confident about some final thoughts about future challenges and dilemmas.

14-1 ANARCHY, DIVERSITY, AND COMPLEXITY IN WORLD POLITICS

At the beginning of our exploration, we argued that three fundamental challenges—anarchy, diversity, and complexity—condition the behavior, interactions, and processes of world politics (see Figure 14-1). We saw the impact of each of these challenges throughout our text: the anarchic structure of the international system—its lack of authoritative, central governing institutions—is a foundational element for understanding and managing conflict and war, and it conditions global economic interactions, the pursuit of wealth, the prospects for an effective regime that protects human rights, and environmental cooperation. The diversity of actors, identities, values, and cultures is a critical issue for human rights and human security, while also greatly affecting conflict and economic relations. The complexity of the global political system makes global economic interactions and coordination challenging and makes the pursuit of international security and human security difficult.

Based on what we considered in the preceding chapters, at least four main observations might be made that can provide some insights as we consider how the world works.

14-1a These Challenges Are Pervasive

By now it is clear that virtually everything that happens in world politics is shaped in one way or another by one or more of these challenges. It is often said of domestic politics that "everything affects everything," and that seems just as true for international relations. Anarchy pushes

Canadian and American vessels on patrol in the Arctic | Will the Arctic be the location of increased naval activity, including military operations, as competition for its resources heats up?

international actors to try to achieve their goals through their own efforts—what we've referred to as "self-help." Some actors, often but not exclusively international organizations and non-governmental organizations, reduce the anarchy in the system by forging connections over and across state boundaries. Their efforts help to integrate actors and their activities and change the system's norms to make both cooperation and following international norms more routine. However, their impact is influenced by the diversity of the other actors involved: states (whether rich or poor, strong or weak, large or small), international organizations, non-governmental organizations, transnational advocacy networks, and influential individuals. The wide range of differences among these actors, from types of governments, cultures, levels of wealth and development, priorities and purposes, and many more, all affect the problems that arise, which ones different actors elect to focus on, how they are defined and interpreted, and the ways in which the players interact over them. All of these actors have their own interests to pursue, and their interests often diverge or conflict with each other.

Then the complexity of the issues comes into play. States often address the security dilemma by purchasing more arms, thereby creating potential arms races at the regional or global level. The money spent on arms then reduces the amount of money available for investment to meet other security needs such as economic development, assuring a reasonable quality of life, protecting human rights and the environment, and so on. In fact, overspending in any of these areas can reduce a society's ability to meet other important needs. So finding the balance point—which provides a sustainable economy and a sustainable quality of life while at the same time protecting one's physical security from threats of harm—is a huge challenge for virtually all international actors.

Repeatedly we saw that issues are connected, and it is very rare that one can be treated in isolation. It is also increasingly challenging for the actors of world politics to determine which actions to take to address problems because of these linkages among them.

Think of the opening vignette in this chapter. What should Canadians do about the Northwest Passage? Their physical security could be in jeopardy if they do not contend for control of the polar sea, but how do they contend for it? Physical security itself is probably a less significant concern on this issue than economic security, but what is the best way to secure those resources when much more powerful states are also trying to get their hands on them? What if grabbing too hard alienates Canada's biggest trading partner, the United States? What if the United States does the same and alienates Canada? What of Russia's claims and increasing presence? If Moscow is willing to militarily intervene in Ukraine, why not in the nearby Arctic? How might the various military and economic interests—including the concerns of transnational corporations—enter into this dilemma? And what about non-governmental organizations with concerns about the environment and other issues? There are no easy answers here.

Look across the North Pole from Canada and consider Russia's dilemmas in world politics for a moment. In terms of international security, at first glance Russia seems reasonably well off, with a relatively modern military and a large inventory of nuclear weapons. Yet it lies between Europe—which is far richer, more advanced economically, and contains many NATO members—and China, which is growing far more rapidly than Russia and has recently become more assertive in pressing its national security interests against its neighbors. In terms of economic security, Russia is a developed country, at least in a number of ways. It ranks in the top ten states in the size of its gross domestic product, its people are highly literate, and so on.

However, its economy is somewhat fragile, as it is largely based on the sale of oil and gas, and those prices are highly sensitive to what other global oil and gas exporters do. Outside of its weapons sector, many of its industries produce goods that have difficulty competing in a global marketplace due to either quality control or performance issues. Again, the gross domestic products of both the EU to Russia's west and China to Russia's east are far larger than Russia's. Finally in terms of human security, alcoholism is rampant countrywide and health care is generally poor outside of the largest cities. The agricultural sector cannot provide adequate nutritional levels to maintain optimal health for most Russians, and the cost of imported food is going up globally. Crime and violence also affect human security, whether through the actions of the Russian mafia or extremist violence from groups based in Russia's Caucasus region.

As a result of these issues, the life expectancy of its citizens has actually decreased over the last two decades. Because the population is actually shrinking, the government is trying both cash subsidies and paid holidays to get couples to have children! Concerns such as these led Russia to form the new Eurasian Union we discussed in the Foreign Policy in Perspective box in Chapter 3. But think even more broadly here: when considering these interacting international, economic, and human security factors, what should Russian leaders do? Where do they focus their efforts first? How do they address these challenges? And, of course, what are the likely consequences for other states, which will surely be watching and reacting?

The pervasiveness of these three challenges across all the issue areas of world politics is obvious in another way as well. Keep in mind how often anarchy, diversity, and complexity were issues in the previous chapters. As you look at international relations now and into the future, which issues will be most affected by anarchy? What issues will be most challenged by the diversity found in world politics or the complexities involved?

14-1b These Challenges Are Changing

Anarchy, diversity, and complexity are persistent issues, but that does not mean that the challenges they pose are the same today as they were in the nineteenth century (or earlier!). Each of our preceding chapters reveals important changes in the nature and effects of these challenges. As constructivists might say, "anarchy is what

international actors make of it." Following the creation of the Westphalian international system in 1648, state sovereignty trumped everything else within a country's borders. Only in the twentieth century did meaningful cracks appear in that idea. Now in the neo-Westphalian system, national leaders cannot mistreat their own citizens within their own borders and expect members of the international system to stand idly by. The concerns of the international community over Syria's violent crackdown on its own people in 2011 and 2012—and especially its alleged use of chemical weapons and chlorine gas in 2013 and 2014—illustrate the heightened attention such states now receive. In some cases, the international reaction will be in the form of soft power—from public denunciations and criticism to economic sanctions. In some cases (such as Kosovo in 1999 and Libya in 2011), the international system will respond with force—hard power—to try to protect a country's population from a regime that has abandoned its "responsibility to protect" its own.

Even as these challenges change, they are still affected by anarchy and the diversity and complexity involved. For example, when the Libyan government essentially went to war against its own people in 2011, NATO responded with air strikes to protect Libyans opposed to the regime. While Libya exports oil and thus could potentially retaliate by withholding sales and deliveries of oil, the only NATO member heavily reliant on Libyan oil was Italy, and Italy was bearing the economic and political costs of dealing with the flood of Libyan refugees trying to escape the fighting by reaching the closest European state—in this case, Italy! So NATO felt free to use force. On the other hand, the Russian government has waged war against Chechen separatists in the southern part of the country since the 1990s, labeling virtually all who seek independence for Chechnya as "Islamic terrorists." The human rights abuses in Chechnya are at least as bad, if not worse, as those in Libya, but NATO has not reacted to Russia's anti-Chechen campaigns. When Russia forcefully annexed Crimea in 2014, thus taking a slice out of Ukraine, and supported separatists in other areas in the eastern regions of that country, it raised much furor that resulted in some economic sanctions but little other coercive response from either the European Union or the United States. Even when the Russian-backed separatists shot down a Malaysian airliner, killing almost 300 civilians in July 2014, there was no strong coercive reaction against Moscow. Russia provides between 30 and 40 percent of Europe's imports of natural gas. Without that gas, many European countries would have less heat in the winter and less electricity year-round. Russia has proven willing in the

An armed Ukrainian separatist guarding the crash site of Malaysian Airlines Flight MH-17, shot down over eastern Ukraine on July 17, 2014 | What challenges for the U.S., Europe, and the UN does Russian support for Ukrainian separatists pose?

past to cut off the flow of natural gas to Europeans, so no hard power or even any real soft power responses to these situations are arising within Europe. So despite the many challenges noted earlier facing Russia, at least in the short run Russia can push back against EU or NATO pressures (and that's not even considering Russia's large military and nuclear arsenal).

Furthermore, in today's world, a much more complex array of international institutions, transnational networks, and economic and social linkages between societies make the decentralized (anarchic) system of world politics very different from that of several centuries ago—or even just a half-century ago! As we have seen, interdependence, the spread of democracy, the development of international regimes for integration and coordination, and even the consequences of nuclear arms have altered the meaning and the effects of anarchy and the self-help it tends to produce. These institutions and connections do not centralize the international system like a strong national government might, but they do reduce the fragmentation and decentralization considerably. For example, the growing economic connections

between countries fostered by globalization links people and states and their economic activities and welfare in ways never before seen, or even imagined. The diffusion of democracy has changed the ways that governments interact with each other and the ways they relate to their own people.

The complexities and diversities continue. The world's insatiable need for more and more energy resources has generated conflict, as well as efforts to find ways to cooperate to meet those needs and address their many consequences. As states try to ensure their energy needs, they affect others. They damage the environment with their mining and drilling operations, and energy use affects our water, air, and even our global climate. Nuclear accidents like the one in Japan in 2011 give pause to those who thought nuclear power would be their ticket to energy sustainability and independence. Farmers grow more corn and sugar cane for ethanol production, but that diminishes the amount of food available in regional markets. With less food available, prices increase in the face of greater demand. As poor people scrounge for even the minimum daily calories (around 1,200—the average American gets more than twice that amount), the burdens fall most heavily on women and children. Thus, these complex linkages just go on and on.

We could continue, but again, our intent is not to restate things we already considered in the preceding chapters. The idea is to prompt you to take up this thread. What do you think are the most important ways anarchy, diversity, and complexity have evolved over time? Is the world less anarchic than it was 100 years ago? What about 1,000 years ago? What about just ten years ago? Is there more diversity, or are we simply more aware of each other's differences and different points of view? It's hard to imagine that the world isn't more complex now, but in what ways is that complexity important for the functioning of world politics and how does that affect your life?

14-1c These Challenges Are Connected

Over and over throughout our text, we have seen that these challenges do not operate in isolation. In fact, they are interrelated and their combination creates its own effects. For example, anarchy and diversity interact. Diverse actors (whether states, IOs, NGOs, TANs, or people) have widely varying needs. International anarchy means states are essentially on their own to protect their own interests because anarchy means the international system lacks central authority. This situation can easily lead to distrust and self-regarding actions. Actors do what they feel they must to protect themselves, which reinforces the anarchy of the system. In such a setting, any advances in national/international security, economic security, or human security are at best partial and incomplete. One actor's benefits may often come at another actor's expense. Think about our discussions of conflict and cooperation in Part Two, economic interactions in Part Three, and transnational issues such as human rights and the environment in Part Four. What kinds of factors, developments, and issues can help to reduce distrust and uncooperative behavior? Let's take a particularly important current issue as an example: terrorism. How do anarchy and diversity combine to make this problem even more significant, and what can be done to address it in light of these challenges?

Consider the connections between diversity and anarchy in the other direction, as well. Human rights offer a good example: while there is a Universal Declaration of Human Rights and many international treaties and conventions on specific rights, different countries (not unlike people) have different opinions or interpretations of those human rights. During the Cold War, the

Soviet Union pointed out that the capitalist countries in the West always had at least some unemployment. To the Soviets, that was a violation of the human right to work. In China, labor unions are forbidden because the Chinese Communist Party claims to represent all workers. Many in the United States would consider that a violation of a basic right shared by all people—the right to associate with others freely. Also consider the way your classmates are dressed. In more conservative countries, some of the attire you see around you would be considered inappropriate, highly offensive, or even worse! When Britney Spears first performed in China, her managers initially had to negotiate whether her midriff would show during the concert—the Chinese government did not think that was appropriate.

So what do all those diverse examples have to do with anarchy? You already know the answer. In anarchy, there is no authority to resolve these differences. How states manage the diversity between them is determined in part by the fact that there is no central lawmaking body to create the rules and no enforcement mechanism for a World Court decision saying one country is right and the other wrong when they come into conflict. They must use diplomacy or force to work out these differences.

Diversity and complexity also interact. Diverse actors have very different needs and preferences. Thus, complex issues become difficult to resolve, as actors perceive and react to different faces of those issues. The global economy provides a good example. China's emphasis on export-led growth dramatically enriched China but did so at the expense of Chinese workers whose low pay left them very poor but allowed Chinese exports to undercut their competitors' prices. Rather than improve the lives of millions of their citizens, the Chinese government chose to invest their profits in the safest possible place—the U.S. economy. As Chinese capital flowed into the U.S. treasury, the federal government could borrow and spend more money. The flow of Chinese capital was one of the factors that led U.S. banks to try to make more loans (to generate income to pay interest on Chinese and other accounts). This dynamic contributed in part to the speculative housing bubble of the early twenty-first century, one of the key causes of the global Great Recession of 2008–2010, and the hardships it has generated for people everywhere.

Complexity and anarchy also interact. Even when international actors agree, coordinating action on issues and devising effective responses are difficult in an anarchic system. For example, everyone seems to be in favor of cleaning up the environment for the good of all. However, rich countries expect poor countries to change their behavior by polluting less, and many poor countries expect the costs of their antipollution efforts to be paid for by rich countries. Some developing countries also expect to be allowed to pollute freely until their material needs are largely met and they have the wealth to take on antipollution efforts themselves. Since there is no actor that can compel some to "give in" to the other side, there's been no agreement bridging this fundamental gap between rich and poor states.

Enough prompts from us. Think back on the preceding chapters: how do you think the interrelationships between anarchy, diversity, and complexity affect international security, economic security, and human security? Are any of these factors more important, or do they affect one type of security more than the others?

14-1d These Challenges Are Not Insurmountable

The forces of anarchy, diversity, and complexity present persistent challenges for world politics and often stymie even the best efforts to address problems constructively, while generating their own problems, as well. However, we have seen in the preceding chapters that the players of world politics have been able to overcome them in many instances.

Anarchy exists—the international system lacks an authoritative central government—but international institutions *are* built, problems *are* addressed through them, and progress *is* made because of them. The UN and a host of related organizations foster cooperation in many different arenas: economic (the International Monetary Fund, the World Bank and its regional development banks, the World Trade Organization, etc.), humanitarian (the World Health Organization, UNICEF, the Food and Agriculture Organization, the UN University, the UN Commissioner for Human Rights, etc.), and legal (the World Court, the International Criminal Court, special tribunals for regional conflicts, etc.) just to name a few. Yet what factors mitigate such cooperation and progress? Can we say more progress has been made in addressing economic and human security than in national/international security? If so, why do you think this would be the case? Since the early 1960s, the members of the international system have sought to limit the spread of nuclear weapons through a series of landmark treaties and, at least according to the principles of the Non-Proliferation Treaty, to reduce existing arsenals as well. How has that worked out? How far does trust go? Can the spread of nuclear weapons really be prevented and could nuclear weapons ever be eliminated entirely? Remember the case that the Marshall Islands brought to the World Court against the world's nuclear powers in 2014 (see Chapter 7)?

As we saw in the last chapter, diversity can divide, but consensus can be built. Key roles are played by not just states, IOs, or NGOs, but by TANs linking all these actors together. Such transnational advocacy networks increasingly serve a key function of linking all those who care about solving a problem and maintaining a communications link between those actors for coordinated action. The actions by such TANs may be to monitor nuclear proliferation, link medical care to the chronically underserved communities around the globe, promote education (particularly of women), help save refugees from the ravages of intrastate wars, and foster more sustainable and environmentally friendly energy development and use. Sadly, other TANs can work to impose one set of values on others. These include terrorist or criminal networks that can bedevil the efforts of states, IOs, and NGOs to combat them.

Complexity makes effective action hard, but not impossible. In fact, the increasingly complex linkages among issues can provide opportunities as well as challenges, as we have seen. States can bargain across many of these linked issues, giving and taking across them in ways that help create some gains for each, when focusing on just one issue might have resulted in an impasse. The involvement of non-state actors such as international institutions and non-governmental organizations may complicate the playing field, but it may also introduce new forums for cooperation, and new ways of solving problems collectively. Think about the examples found throughout our text in which these things occurred: when does the complex arena of actors produce the most progress?

Again, there are not many issues more complex than trusting rivals who possess nuclear weapons. Think of all those movies about the American West where two rivals squared off against each other on a dusty street—trust was not the first thing on their minds; shooting straight and fast was! Yet arms control treaties have created a sophisticated set of rules and norms that regulate the biggest nuclear weapons powers in the system. The exceptions (such as India, Iran, Israel, North Korea, or Pakistan) have relatively few weapons and should not blind us to the larger fact that most nuclear weapons are governed by strong international norms. Another example is the global effort to control the spread of HIV/AIDS. This virus and its consequences involve a complicated mix of standards of medical care, sexual practices, cultural and societal norms, the role of women in society, human trafficking, and so on. Yet the UN and other leading state actors have united behind the Millennium Development Goals project to make a major dent in this

FIGURE 14-2   THE PURSUIT OF SECURITY IN THREE ARENAS

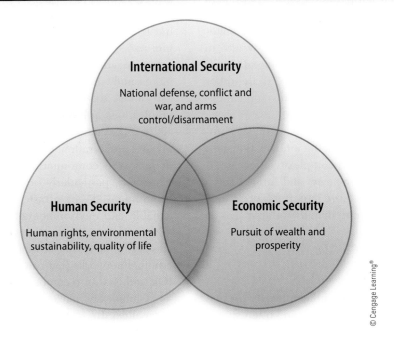

© Cengage Learning®

global health scourge. We can hope that, like smallpox, HIV/AIDS will be eliminated in the future.

Again, our most important concern at this point is not to advance what we think, and not to summarize what has been covered, but to encourage you to consider what *you* think now that you worked through the material in the text. What actions and conditions do you think are most likely to allow the players of world politics to overcome the challenges posed by anarchy, diversity, and complexity? How do theoretical lenses like realism, liberalism, constructivism, Marxism, world systems theory, or feminism help us sort through such questions? What do these lenses tell us is likely, or at least possible?

14-2 SEEKING SECURITY

We have centered our exploration of world politics on the idea that the search for security is the central motivating force in the international arena. But as we indicated in our opening chapter and throughout the ensuing pages, we think security is a broad term that encompasses much more than simply military issues. One way to interpret the chapters we just finished working through is to understand that a central aspect of world politics involves its players grappling with multiple dilemmas in the search for security.

Figure 14-2 shows the three dimensions of security that make up our conception of the matter. These dilemmas include efforts to be secure in the traditional sense of political and territorial independence, which is linked to the concerns about military power, conflict, and war. But they also involve efforts to be secure economically—to experience economic growth and development, gain or maintain access to resources and markets, and achieve good and improving standards of living for the societies and communities that the actors serve and represent. Furthermore, we argued that these dilemmas also involve a host of concerns—some old and some new—about the ability of individuals to live well and safely in their communities and environments. These human security issues have grown increasingly important as the world has grown smaller through the forces of globalization and interdependence. Attention to matters of human rights, the environment, disease and health, nutrition, and a great variety of others are of much greater importance today than at the beginning of the Westphalian system some 350 years ago.

We should also note that these dimensions of security are not separate from each other either, and they probably never have been, so, unlike the figure we started with in Chapter 1, Figure 14-2 shows their intersections and connections. As we saw, concerns about economic wealth and development have led to issues of traditional military security in a great many instances, from World War II to recent conflicts in the Middle East involving oil. Economic and human security issues are also directly linked, as well. Without adequate levels of wealth, a country cannot provide for the basic needs of its population. After World War II, South Korea worked hard to ensure economic prosperity for its future citizens, and it was successful. Elites within the Nigerian government, conversely, could not resist the temptation to steal the vast profits from oil drilling from the people. Partly because of the corruption, Nigerians have poor education and health services and, as a result, have low life expectancy. Their lack of economic security led to a lack of human security, namely early death.

It is also increasingly clear that human security concerns about things like human rights, environmental degradation, and the like have connections to the traditional security issues, as well. Consider that many of the military actions of the past two decades—wars in the former Yugoslavia, military actions in Libya, the Russian intervention in Ukraine, the recent violence between Israeli Defense Forces and Palestinians in Gaza, and the military actions by the U.S. and others in the Middle East against the Islamic State in Iraq and Syria (ISIS) for example—have human rights at their core, while many observers have recently emphasized the links between environmental factors and conflict.[2] In the 1990s, the U.S. Central Intelligence Agency even devoted intelligence gathering and analysis resources to tracking and studying environmental degradation in Africa as a means to help predict and prevent the eruption of violent conflict there!

As we think about the quest for security in this light, we can offer a few observations synthesized from across the preceding chapters. These observations reflect both the centrality and the evolving aspects of security and are just a few that might be considered.

14-2a Traditional Military Security Concerns Continue But Are Evolving

We saw throughout our text that concerns for survival and safety, linked to power and military security, are persistent problems in world politics. However, it also seems clear that the nature of those problems has evolved considerably over time, from the increasingly destructive wars between states for power and territorial control that marked the Westphalian era through World War II, to the civil wars, identity-based and asymmetric conflicts of the neo-Westphalian period. We saw what were once the most warlike and conflict-prone members of the international system— great powers—basically end violent conflict with

each other. In their place, sadly, civil conflict—mostly outside the developed world—has become the most common type of war. For instance, in Spring 2014, violence erupted again in Iraq as Sunni insurgents unleashed a series of attacks in the country, prompting violent responses by Shi'ite the population and the government. Now over ten years old, this conflict continues to exact a toll in lives and resources and presents a continuing challenge to the world. So does conflict between Israel and Palestinian forces, which escalated into serious military action in the summer of 2014.

While millions may not die in each of these conflicts like they did in World War II, these wars are still very bloody and so common that their collective death tolls more than compensate for their smaller individual scope. At the same time, transnational terror networks have posed additional challenges for security. As we discussed in Chapters 6 and 13, such challenges to international security are not easily met through traditional security policies. The members of the international system will continue to face the consequences generated by this form of conflict, as well as those caused by applying traditional security measures (such as the application of military force) to problems that don't necessarily match up.

Can the world put an end to these conflicts? They are often fought with simple weapons—assault rifles and even machetes—so it isn't a simple matter of taking away powerful weapons. While the bigger, wealthy countries can intervene to stop these conflicts, such interventions are not easy and often are "no-win" situations. Beginning in March 2011, months of bombings and other efforts to support the insurgents in Libya did not produce an easy or swift regime change, but contributed to the eventual end of the Gaddafi regime in October 2011. However, the nature of the post-Gaddafi regime in Libya is still evolving, and warring militias fight over control different areas of the country. Will Libya be a more tribal society, and what happens if the tribes cannot resolve their many differences? Will more conflict there be the result? If so, what will it take to end it? Will an Islamist party take over and convert the country to an extreme theocracy? Will Western diplomats continue to be targeted for attack as they were in 2012? Does the international community have the determination to do what it takes to end such conflicts? The U.S. Congress proved reluctant to support the Libya operation, and other NATO allies have proven unsupportive of military operations in other cases. It's also important to note that the great powers aren't great enough to stop every civil conflict.

Militants from the al-Qaida-inspired Islamic State of Iraq and Syria (ISIS) preparing to execute government soldiers in Northern Iraq in June 2014 | What challenges does renewed civil war in Iraq pose?

While millions were spent on Libya, much less effort was made to help the refugees in Darfur or the people of Syria.

14-2b Economic Security Concerns Gain Importance and Are Shaped by Globalization and Interdependence

We saw the evolution of economic security from an era of national economies at the beginning of the Westphalian system to an era in which an international economy with increasing trade and other economic transactions connected states, and finally to the development of the current global economy, which has made it increasingly difficult to separate and identify national economies at all. The pursuit of economic security has been transformed from the dominant mercantilist practices of the seventeenth and eighteenth centuries to those conditioned by interdependence, globalization, and the deepening network of international institutions affecting economic activities and interactions.

During the twentieth century, an ideological competition between capitalism and communism raged, sometimes violently. In 1989, one scholar went so far as to argue that history had ended. By that, Francis Fukuyama meant that democracy and capitalism had won the day and were the ultimate forms of government and economy that humans would ever produce. There would be no more communisms or fascisms. It seemed hard to refute his argument then, but in 2008, the world saw a near economic collapse largely because of unconstrained or under-regulated capitalism. Does that mean that we haven't ended our search for a better economic system? Even if the market corrects the mistakes made leading up to 2008, does that mean it's the best system? Poverty is rampant—remember that more than three-quarters of the world's population live below the U.S. poverty line. Is our globalized system a good one? Is it the best one we can manage? How will the players of world politics contend with the emerging problem agenda of the present, which includes energy security, food security, water security, and security from intrastate conflict?

14-2c Human Security Issues Are Increasingly Central and Connected to Both Economic and Military Security

The arena of world politics—and those issues that are now considered as international or transnational concerns—has broadened considerably. For example, 100 years ago, a few diplomats may have discussed concerns for public health briefly, but such concerns were very low on any agenda—if they appeared at all. Instead, world leaders concerned themselves with military security and using their militaries to secure colonial possessions.

Now, public health concerns are regularly on the agenda because they could affect everyone on the planet. In 2014, the Ebola virus spread in the worst Ebola epidemic in history. By late fall of 2014, international health officials were estimating approximately 10,000 cases per week in West Africa, while American and European policy-makers and citizens struggled to respond to the spread of the disease to their countries, a first for this particular transnational challenge.

Colonies are no longer acceptable and military force is no longer considered a legitimate way to secure wealth, but the competition for profits has only increased as more countries strive to pull themselves out of poverty. States no longer struggle to secure their colonies with occupation and physical force, but now they must secure their economies from foreign competition, the outsourcing of jobs, capital flight, and many other dynamics of a global economy because maintaining jobs for their people is essential. This, of course, means increased attention to the skills and education of the workforce and many other issues that relate to economic competition.

One interesting window into this transformation of security and the international issue agenda can be seen simply by taking a brief look at the kinds of international or global conferences that have occurred over the past century or so. From conferences dominated by great powers trying to place limits on the initiation and practices of warfare (e.g., the Geneva Conventions), control arms races (e.g., the Washington Naval Conference), and respond to the aggression of one state against another in the first three decades of the twentieth century, the last two decades have seen major international and global conferences on global climate change, women's rights, population and debt, development, and coping with economic crises. These conferences have also involved a broad array of states, international organizations, non-governmental organizations, epistemic communities, and individuals, sometimes acting independently, and often linked in transnational networks.

14-2d All Security Issues Have Heightened Impact on Women and Children

The transformations of security, and especially the increasing importance of human security, mean that the roles of women and children, and the effects of world politics on them, have become increasingly central to international relations. There is no issue or dimension of world politics that does not include these concerns in some way, as the many discussions throughout the last 13 chapters showed.

Think about how pervasive these issues are. In conflict, for example, the effects of war and violence on women are stark. Women continue to be horribly underrepresented in the highest levels of government, international organizations, management levels of corporations, and so on. Their absence may have a significant impact on the nature of decisions that are made by these players. If more women were leaders, would they choose violence less often? Violence directed specifically at women and children—including rape, sexual slavery, and murder—has been an instrument of warfare for as long as people have been fighting. Specific instruments of military security and warfare such as the use of land mines and cluster munitions have had devastating effects on the women and children of the societies in which their use is common. What percentage of the millions of refugees who flee violence and economic hardship each year do you think are women? And, as we saw, the struggle for subsistence and prosperity around the world disproportionately affects women and children.

There is simply no society in the world in which women enjoy the same freedom, rights, protections, and opportunities as men, and virtually every society grapples with these issues, inequities, and inequalities in one way or another. Why else would the world be working on plans to hold its fifth global conference on women even as we write this? The security issues facing women and children are an important focus of the current neo-Westphalian era, as some states and many international and non-governmental organizations increasingly turn their attention to these issues.

Think of the preceding points as you consider the search for security in world politics, its dynamics, and its implications. What trends and developments do you think are most important? How have these trends and developments contributed to both continuity and change in the nature of world politics? How have they affected the focus on and salience of different issues in world politics? And going back to the three challenges we have emphasized, how do anarchy, diversity, and complexity affect the search for security across these three dimensions?

14-3 THE ROAD AHEAD

Given the centrality of security—as we broadly defined it—the persistent challenges posed by anarchy, diversity, and complexity, and the elements of continuity and change we have discussed to this point, let's consider some future directions and challenges likely to be important as the patterns of world politics continue to unfold.

14-3a From State-Centric to Multi-Centric System

Let's begin with a basic change that will affect many aspects of international relations: future world politics are likely to be shaped by a different set of players than those dominating most of the period since the Treaties of Westphalia. Since Westphalia, states have been the primary and dominant players, and the realist theoretical lens continues to afford them pride of place. However, as we saw, especially over the last half-century, non-state actors have become more important to international relations.

There are consequences for the future of world politics, many of which we have introduced and discussed in the preceding chapters. Traditional international security is likely to prove a very different issue as non-state national groups such as Palestinians, Chechens, and Kurds, as well as terrorist organizations and other militant non-state actors, continue to rely on the use of force. Traditional mechanisms of securing oneself are not as obviously applicable in an environment in which such players are active. Just to take one example, it is much easier to deter a state like the old Soviet Union, or maybe even contemporary Iran, from attacking with weapons of mass destruction than to accomplish the same goal with non-state nations or terrorist groups such as al-Qaeda who do not have return addresses like states! What other ways is a multi-centric world of state and non-state actors likely to shape and affect international security?

Economic security has been and will continue to be shaped by this new array of players, as well. Multinational corporations have crossed state lines so much that many of them have subsidiaries all around the world. McDonald's doesn't export burgers to France because it has its own corporation and restaurants in France. For decades, international organizations worked to promote trade and economic stability, but with the creation of the WTO, the world created an organization that could enforce trade agreements. No longer are states sovereign in the way they were under the Westphalian system. Now, they must abide by rules created by international organizations or suffer serious consequences. What other ways is a multi-centric world of state and non-state actors likely to shape and affect economic security?

Human security is no different. As we have seen, transnational networks are active and important across an increasing array of issues that affect the physical safety, economic well-being, and quality of life of individuals around the world. That is likely to continue in the future, with significant consequences for world politics. On the negative side, terrorist organizations have made the most powerful states the world has ever seen feel insecure. To take a relatively minor and simple example, the now-standard practice of having to take your shoes off to pass through airport security in even the smallest airports in the United States and elsewhere is annoying. However, it is because of terrorist threats and actions that we must all walk through security in our socks or in some cases be electronically strip-searched. What other ways is a multi-centric world of state and non-state actors likely to shape and affect human security?

14-3b Emerging Challenges and Dilemmas

As we have illustrated throughout our text, multiple factors combine to create new issues that create challenges and dilemmas for humankind. The physical security of more people is arguably threatened more now by intrastate conflict and terrorism than more traditional national/international security threats. Globalization causes more societies to come in contact with each other, complicating physical and economic security as we all compete for the means of prosperity, while increasing the impact of basic identity concerns at the same time. Cooperation in sustainable development may be the path out of this particular economic dilemma, but promoting such development normally requires additional monetary or human resources. Finally, the planet's population is continually growing, creating additional competition for needed resources and services—like food, water, petroleum, other energy sources, education, health care, and so on. As noted, this squeeze on humankind hits women and children hardest. The failure to meet all these human security needs can in turn imperil economic development and create the foundations for new conflict.

These conflicts will also play out on a broader scale than before. As our opening vignette for this chapter shows, the race is on for control of the North Pole and surrounding territories. Only an international treaty limiting Antarctica to research purposes prevents a similar race to control it, and no one really knows if that treaty will be honored over the long term if something highly valuable is discovered there. As our Arctic example shows, technology and ingenuity are combining to open up new areas of the global commons—the polar regions, the deep seas and seabeds, and outer space—to national and even corporate competition. Not only are new areas opening for such competition, but more people—and the international actors that represent them—are vying for control of those areas and the possibilities that lie within them. Where once core states like the U.S. and Russia dominated "the race for space," now space vehicles are launched by semi-peripheral states (such as China and India) and even private corporations (like SpaceX and, possibly in the future, Virgin Galactic).

Thus, emerging trends suggest less frequent great wars, more frequent small or intrastate conflicts, more terrorism, and more competition for wealth and the things that contribute to its growth, with potential scarcity and relative deprivation conflicts emerging as a result. And these trends suggest that the locations and participants in the organized violence that has so often characterized international relations have shifted from the so-called great powers competing with each other to the less developed world.

That's the bad news. The good news is that there is an international architecture in place to promote global cooperation and problem solving. That architecture is composed of thousands of international organizations, non-governmental organizations, transnational advocacy networks, international conferences on shared problems, and the norms that all these actors and efforts create. So at the end of this course, how do you see it? Is our global glass half empty, or half full?

14-4 THEORY IN ACTION, GEOGRAPHY, AND FOREIGN POLICY IN PERSPECTIVE

We devoted considerable time in the text to discussing the connection between Theory in Action, the Revenge of Geography, and Foreign Policy in Perspective. In each chapter, we introduced some questions and scenarios, and showed how these different concepts had big implications for our understanding of international relations. As we conclude our exploration of world politics, let's return to these issues one last time to try to integrate what we learned so far, and to think about what they mean for the future. We are, of course, speculating about the future—no one has a crystal ball—and you may very well have different ideas than we do. That is good, however, because it means that you have thought about the world in which we live and have a new and more complete understanding of it. Let's begin considering these three concepts.

14-4a Theory in Action

All throughout the past 13 chapters, we gave examples of how theory informs the practice of international relations. We discussed issues ranging from how the democratic peace prompted the United States to increase its promotion of democracy, to how countries should—or perhaps should not—engage in free trade, to how different theories might help us build a policy to reduce carbon dioxide emissions. The questions that we must now consider are: what will the theories we have discussed prescribe for the coming years and decades, and which ones will lead to the best policies?

To answer this question, we must again think about how the world works. The different theoretical approaches told very different stories. Realism sees the world as very competitive and conflict-ridden. It clearly would suggest policies that promote the strength of the state and neglect the ideas of cooperation with other countries, equality, and environmental sustainability. Could realist policies create a world where strong states are safe, but weak states are poor and lack human security, and the global environment is significantly degraded? Liberal policies might promote cooperation and development while paying less attention to national security. Could that lead to a world where trade flourishes, countries develop, and the environment is protected until a large-scale war breaks out because state security concerns were neglected? Constructivists stress the powerful role of ideas, norms, and identities in shaping what people and states want: are the central ideas and norms of world politics changing for the better or the worse?

Marxist and world systems theory could suggest revolts by poorer states or simply more attention paid to development and equality. In the case of conflict between the rich and poor, violence could erupt into a large scale with the deaths of millions. If economic development were the only focus, what would happen to the environment? Feminist theory is too diverse to suggest a single policy, but to be sure, there would be greater attention paid to equalizing the treatment of women. Given the great diversity of cultures in the world—and their corresponding political and social institutions and practices—what consequences might that incur?

We purposely paint an extreme picture here. Not only must we consider *how* we think the world of international relations works, but also what consequences the answer to that "how" question will cause. If you think Marx was right about the world being driven by economic class, what does that mean for the future? What policies do you think would make the world a better place? Are those policies feasible? Consider all of the Theory in Action boxes—what have you learned from those and what do you conclude from them?

14-4b Revenge of Geography

Thomas Friedman argued that "the world is flat" in a book with that title. He simply meant that the world is becoming smaller, more interconnected, and more interdependent. Throughout this book, we showed how geographic factors can still have a powerful impact on politics. Perhaps the most gruesome example is the Great Lakes region in Africa that helped spawn the terrible genocide in Rwanda along with several civil conflicts. Another example was the Nile River in Egypt that creates tremendous benefits but also tremendous costs. We also showed how a country's neighbors, or lack thereof, could increase or decrease its power. The United States, United Kingdom, and Japan have all benefitted from being islands or virtual islands. Germany, Israel, and Poland all suffer from having many neighbors, and in some cases, powerful, aggressive ones.

Considering how the geographic setting can affect international relations, how will the increasingly "small" or "flat" world affect the future? There are more people, fewer resources, and a changing environment. The world will be a radically different place in 2050 than it was in 1950. What revenge will geography take next?

Perhaps it is best to think about specific changes in our environment, broadly speaking. For example, there is a theory called peak oil that suggests humans have tapped all of the big oil reserves and that our supply is going to begin dwindling, perhaps rather rapidly. Putting aside the question of when we might begin to run low on crude oil, ask yourself the question: what will happen when we do? Conflict over an increasingly scarce resource is certainly likely. Will that help or hurt oil-rich states? Will the "devil's excrement" become even more foul for humanity?

A less pessimistic view of an oil shortage might suggest that technology will develop a sustainable energy source eliminating the need for oil-based fuel. If that happens, oil-rich states in the Middle East would lose almost all of their value. That would create quite a geographic revenge—from poorhouse to penthouse and back again. The developed world does not currently spend much effort or funds helping countries in Africa; would the Middle East end up the same way?

Similarly, what effect might global climate change have? Whether the world heats up, cools down, or simply fluctuates more, agriculture will be dramatically affected. While wealthy countries like the United States and the EU states will likely be able to develop means to continue effective food production, less developed states may not. Any changes to the climate can result in temporary or even permanent loss of crops, which could result in famine. Sadly, famine often results in civil conflict. These may be apocalyptic predictions, but they are worth considering. More important, consider what geographic changes will affect the future of international relations.

14-4c Foreign Policy in Perspective

Finally, we should consider the foreign policy behavior of the states and other actors who occupy the game board of world politics. As we discussed throughout the preceding chapters, key states such as the United States play a major role in the world. The United States, for example, has the biggest economy, the most powerful military, and what appears to be a very attractive culture that has spread around the world in the form of entertainment, restaurant chains, and fashion. However, the U.S. is certainly not the only state in the world! Other states such as Russia and China, and groups of states such as the European Union also have their own interests and ideas. And, of course, the U.S. will not remain the sole superpower forever.

What about the other players and their policies? What do middle-sized, developed, and very small states want in the world? What motivates them, and how do those things differ from the things that shape the concerns and behavior of major powers? And what about those non-state actors pursuing their agendas? In what ways are they changing the nature of world politics and shaping or influencing the behavior of major states such as the U.S., China, Russia, Japan, the members of the European Union and others?

Most states face significant challenges in the global economy, for example, with debt mounting and volatility on the rise. For the U.S., even all these years after the Great Recession of 2008–2010, its economy continues to grow slowly and its financial debt is high, to say the least. A significant portion of that debt is held by other countries, and one in particular—China—is a rising power. What will that mean for the future? Will China begin to play a more powerful and assertive role? Will it tell the United States what to do in the coming decades?

The U.S. economy is not the only one suffering, and in fact, it is healthy relative to the immediate problems in Europe. Slow growth and banking problems, possibly severe ones, put the EU in a tenuous position. A severe recession in Europe could have major repercussions worldwide, and its economic weakness makes wielding the tools of economic statecraft in situations such as the 2014 Ukraine crisis difficult. Economically, a faltering European economy would hurt the United States and quite possibly send it into another recession. In international security terms, Europe could destabilize. While that may not seem likely, history shows that military conflict is often preceded by economic problems.

With constraints and challenges such as these and many others facing the major players in world politics, what courses of action might they take to address the current and emerging problems of world politics? What courses should they take? Think about the different theories we discussed and how they explain to us how the world works. Which one of those perspectives makes the most sense to you as you think about how states and others act to achieve their goals? What do you think that suggests about the nature and role of the most powerful players in the system in general?

CONCLUSION

We began this chapter with a story about the dispute over who controls and owns the Arctic. It is hard to imagine an issue and a place further from most of us both in distance and in relevance to our daily lives. Of all the issues in the world, the sea surrounding the North Pole is distant, inhospitable, and even obscure. Or is it? We also began this chapter with a suggestion that before we think of all the different facts discussed in this book, we ask ourselves what is the basic nature of humans. Are we cooperative or conflictual? How do we connect these two—human nature and the Arctic?

The answer lies in the fact that the dispute over the Arctic is a dispute among people, human beings. It may be physically distant, but the Russians who initially placed a flag on the ocean floor were humans, just like you. Thus, what might seem like the most obscure policy issue involves people and affects people. Understanding the basic nature of humans will help us understand how those people

will behave. If you see people generally as cautious cooperators, then you would expect that the dispute over the Arctic would end in a compromise, probably one that leads to declaring much of the area as international waters that can be freely traveled by people from all countries. If you tend to think that humans are less cooperative and more self-interested, then you would expect that the United States, perhaps in cooperation with Canada, would dominate the dispute because the United States has so much power. If you think wealth is the biggest factor in human behavior, then the Arctic would not be about free travel but gaining access to and controlling the resources at the bottom of the ocean and the trade routes over that ocean.

So the Arctic isn't so obscure or complicated after all. It is the same as any other dispute that people must navigate either through cooperative diplomacy, violent conflict, or some in-between option. That is why it is so important to have a view of the world and explanation for the question "how does the world work?" Because once you have an answer to that question, *you can understand any aspect of international relations.*

STUDY TOOLS 14

LOCATED AT BACK OF THE BOOK:
☐ Rip out Chapter in Review card

LOCATED ON COURSEMATE:
Use the CourseMate access card that came with this book or visit CengageBrain.com for more review materials:

☐ Review Key Terms Flash Cards (Print or Online)

☐ Download Audio or Visual Summaries for on-the-go review

☐ Complete Practice Quizzes to prepare for the test

☐ Walk through a Simulation, Animated Learning Module, and Interactive Maps and Timelines to master concepts

☐ Complete Crossword Puzzle to review key terms

☐ Watch the videos for real-world application of this chapter's content

☐ Visit IR NewsWatch to learn about the latest current events as you prepare for class discussions and papers

THINK ABOUT THIS THE CHALLENGE OF COOPERATION REVISITED

Return now to that very basic puzzle we posed at the beginning of the book. In our first chapter, before we had the benefit of the information, insights, and interpretations from Chapters 2 through 13, we noted that despite all of the apparent benefits, cooperation is often very difficult in world politics. This time, as you think about this puzzle, draw on your worldview, your understanding of how the world works. Realize that all of the theoretical lenses we covered can help you understand how humans—like you and your friends—interact, and how states and non-state actors interact. We have seen many instances of productive cooperation in the world, and the intervening pages have also shown that conflict, war, poverty, and a lack of respect for humankind continue to be pervasive problems. There is little doubt that countries would benefit from agreement and collaboration to control the costly acquisition or dangerous spread of weapons, but they frequently do not do so. Mutually beneficial collaboration to promote economic growth and development is less common than we might expect given the benefits it provides. The establishment of institutions, norms, and rules to shape behavior on human rights and environmental sustainability in mutually beneficial and predictable ways is incomplete and episodic. Transnational advocacy networks are increasingly active across many issues in world politics, facilitating the emergence of norms and patterns of cooperation, but they are challenged by the anarchic structure and diversity of interests of the world. So now that we have completed our trek through the landscape of world politics and you have thought systematically about the pursuit of all forms of security amid the challenges of anarchy, diversity, and complexity, let's ask once again:

Why is international cooperation so hard, and what factors and conditions inhibit and promote it?

REVIEW QUESTIONS

1. What are the central challenges posed by anarchy, diversity, and complexity for the pursuit of security in international relations?

2. What does it mean to be secure in international relations?

3. What are the key trends and challenges likely to shape the future of world politics?

FOR MORE INFORMATION . . .

For more on making sense of current and future world politics, see:

Acemoglu, Daron, and James A. Robinson. *Why Nations Fail: The Origins of Power, Prosperity, and Poverty.* New York: Crown Business/Random House, 2012.

Drezner, Daniel. *Theories of International Politics and Zombies.* Princeton, NJ: Princeton University Press, 2011.

Kaplan, Robert D. *The Revenge of Geography: What the Map Tells Us About Coming Conflicts and the Battle Against Fate.* New York: Random House, 2013.

Nye, Joseph S., Jr. *The Future of Power.* New York: Public Affairs Press, 2011.

Patrick, Stewart. *Weak Links: Fragile State, Global Threats and International Security.* New York: Oxford University Press, 2011.

Reveron, Derek, and Kathleen Mahoney-Norris. *Human Security in a Borderless World.* Boulder, CO: Westview, 2011.

Political World Map

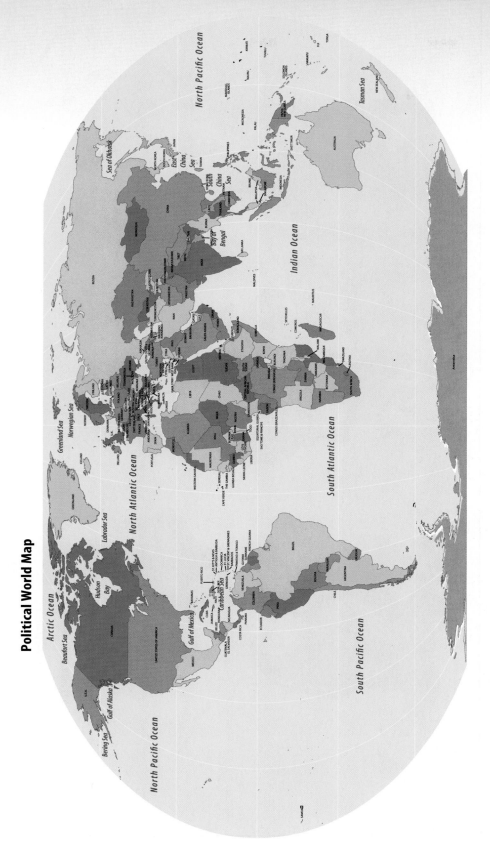

Current Ethnic Diversity of States

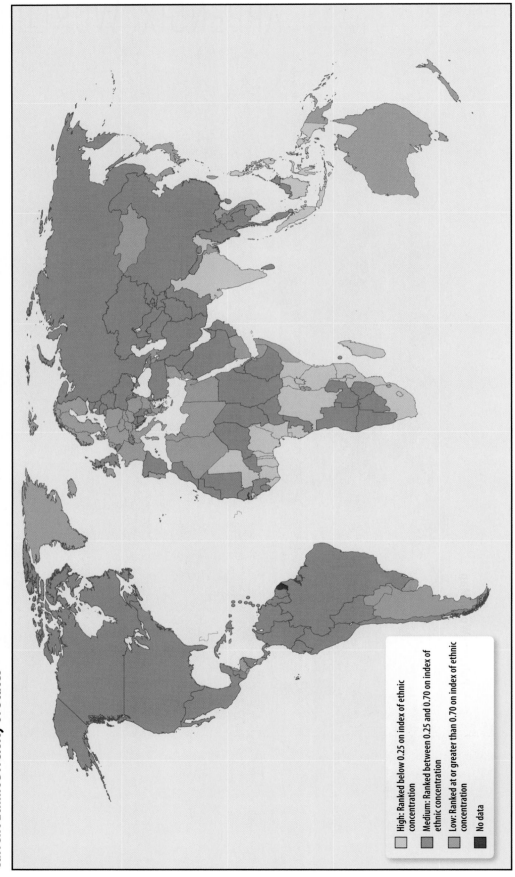

High: Ranked below 0.25 on index of ethnic concentration

Medium: Ranked between 0.25 and 0.70 on index of ethnic concentration

Low: Ranked at or greater than 0.70 on index of ethnic concentration

No data

Political Map of Europe

Political Map of the Middle East

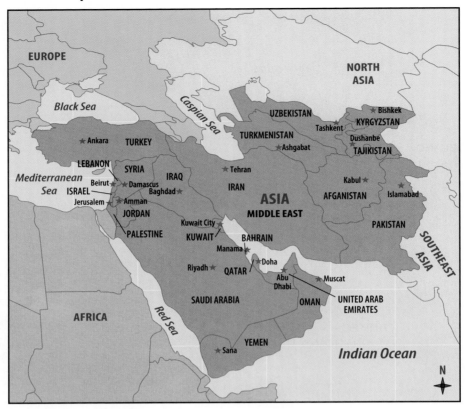

Political Map of North America

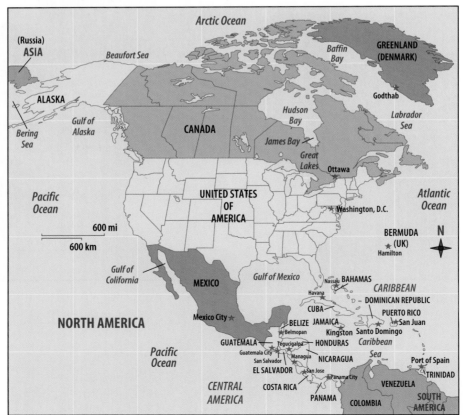

Political Map of Central and South America

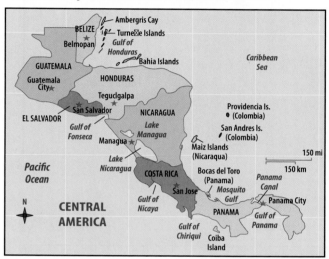

Ambergris Cay
BELIZE
Turneffe Islands
Belmopan
Gulf of Honduras
Bahia Islands
Caribbean Sea
GUATEMALA
HONDURAS
Guatemala City
Tegucigalpa
San Salvador
EL SALVADOR
NICARAGUA
Providencia Is. (Colombia)
Gulf of Fonseca
Lake Managua
San Andres Is. (Colombia)
Managua
Maiz Islands (Nicaraqua)
Lake Nicaragua
Pacific Ocean
COSTA RICA
Bocas del Toro (Panama)
Panama Canal
San Jose
Mosquito Gulf
N
Gulf of Nicaya
Panama City
CENTRAL AMERICA
PANAMA
Gulf of Panama
Gulf of Chiriqui
Coiba Island
150 mi
150 km

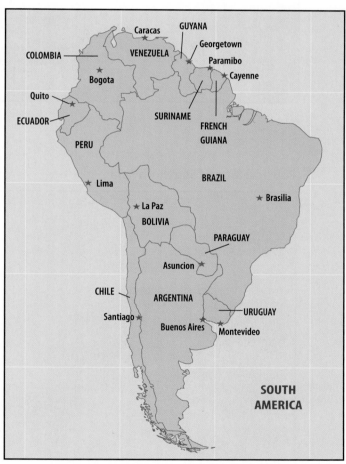

Caracas
GUYANA
COLOMBIA
VENEZUELA
Georgetown
Paramibo
Bogota
Cayenne
Quito
SURINAME
ECUADOR
FRENCH GUIANA
PERU
BRAZIL
Lima
La Paz
Brasilia
BOLIVIA
PARAGUAY
Asuncion
CHILE
ARGENTINA
URUGUAY
Santiago
Buenos Aires
Montevideo
SOUTH AMERICA

Political Map of Northern Asia

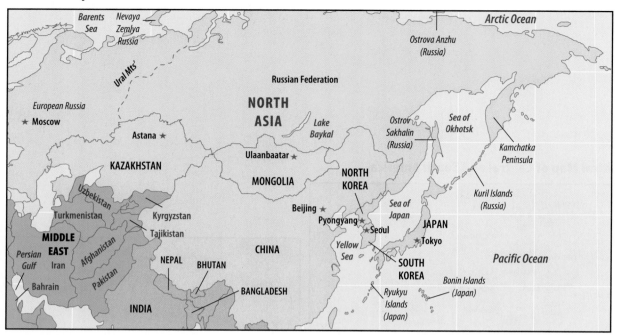

Political Map of Southern Asia

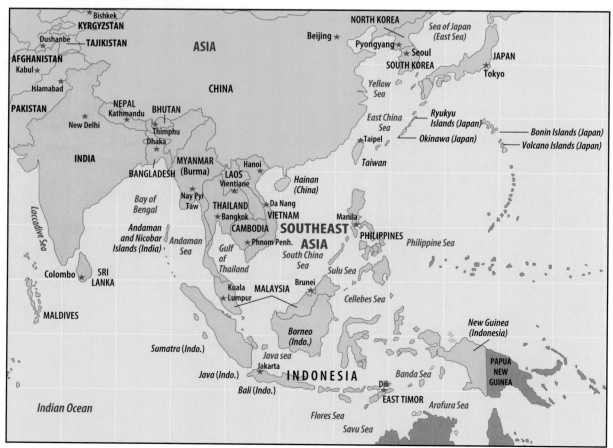

Political Map of Africa

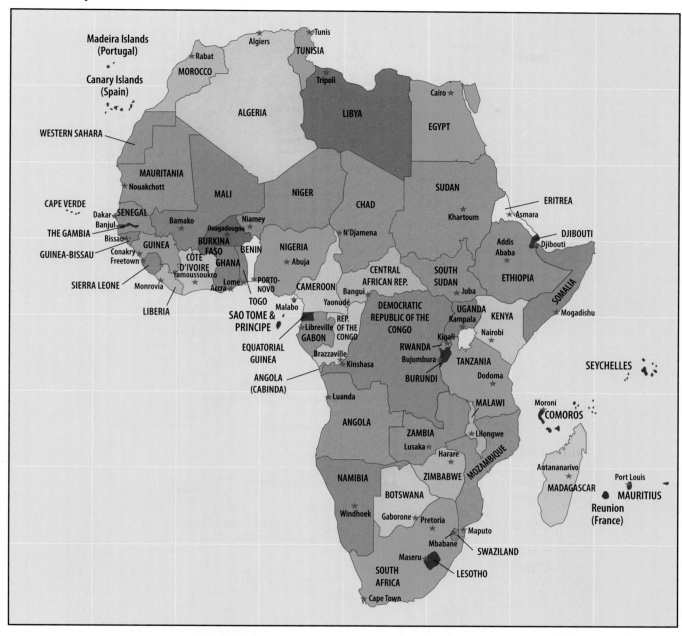

Political Map of Australia

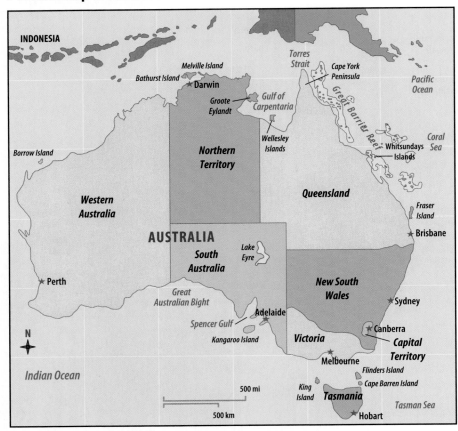

Political Map of Pacific Ocean Islands

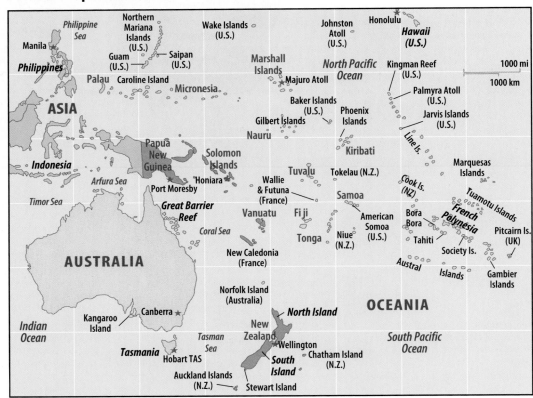

ENDNOTES

1

1. The Correlates of War data project (www .correlatesofwar.org) includes estimates of war-related casualties by combatant from 1816–2007. In 1974, Francis A. Beer estimated that war had inflicted over 1 billion casualties since 3000 BC. Beer, *How Much War in History: Definitions, Estimates, Extrapolations, and Trends* (Beverly Hills, CA: Sage Publications, 1974).

2. Barry Buzan, *People, States and Fear: An Agenda for International Security Studies in the Post-Cold War Era* (Boulder, CO: Lynne Rienner, 1991), 18.

3. Buzan, 18–19.

4. This document and related supporting material may be found at www.gwu.edu/~nsarchiv /nukevault/ebb245/index.htm.

5. See, for example, Joseph Nye, *Soft Power: The Means to Success in World Politics* (New York: PublicAffairs Books, 2004), who applies the multi-level chessboard analogy to military, economic, and transnational boards linked together in a complex fashion.

2

1. Dominic Evans, "Death Toll in Syria's Civil War Above 150,000: Monitor," Reuters, April 1, 2014, http://www.reuters.com/article/2014/04/01 /us-syria-crisis-toll-idUSBREA300YX20140401; Ben Hubbard, "Lebanon Hosts Over a Million Who Fled Syria, U.N. Reports," *New York Times*, April 4, 2014, A4.

2. Robert F. Trager, "Diplomatic Calculus in Anarchy: How Communication Matters," *American Political Science Review* 104 (2010): 347–68.

3. Samuel Noah Kramer, *History Begins at Sumer: Thirty-Nine Firsts in Recorded History*, 3rd ed. (Philadelphia: University of Pennsylvania Press, 1988).

4. Jared Diamond, *Guns, Germs, and Steel: The Fates of Human Societies* (New York: W.W. Norton, 1999).

5. Larry Neumeister and Matthew Lee, "Strip-Searched Diplomat Indicted on Fraud Charge," *Associated Press*, January 9, 2014, http://www .usatoday.com/story/news/nation/2014/01/09 /indian-diplomat-indicted-leaves-us/4394643/.

6. See Jerel A. Rosati and James M. Scott, *The Politics of U.S. Foreign Policy*, 6th ed. (New York: Cengage/Wadsworth, 2014), chap. 5.

7. Fred Ikle, quoted in Paul Gordon Lauren, Gordon A. Craig and Alexander George, *Force and Statecraft: Diplomatic Challenges of Our Time*, 4th ed. (New York: Oxford University Press, 2007), 154.

8. For more on this case, see Ralph G. Carter and James M. Scott, "Hitting the Reset Button: Changing the Direction of U.S.-Russian Relations?" in *Contemporary Cases in U.S. Foreign Policy: From Terrorism to Trade*, ed. Ralph G. Carter, 4th ed. (Washington, DC: CQ Press, 2011).

9. Manfred B. Steger, *The Rise of the Global Imaginary: Political Ideologies from the French Revolution to the Global War on Terror* (New York: Oxford University Press, 2008).

10. "McDonald's: Background," *Entrepreneur*, 2010, www.entrepreneur.com/franchises /mcdonalds/282570-0.html.

11. William Mellor, "McDonald's No Match for KFC in China as Colonel Rules Fast Food," *Bloomberg News*, January 26, 2011, www .bloomberg.com/news/2011-01-26/mcdonald-s-no-match-for-kfc-in-china-where-colonel-sanders-rules-fast-food.html.

12. Sarah Pierce, "Top 10 Fast Food Franchises," *Entrepreneur*, May 22, 2008, www.entrepreneur .com/franchises/toptenlists/article194050.html.

13. Joshua Pramis, "Number of Mobile Phones to Exceed World Population by 2014," *Digital Trends*, February 28, 2013, http://www.digitaltrends.com /mobile/mobile-phone-world-population-2014/.

14. Kirsten Acuna, "The Fifteen Highest Grossing Movies of 2013," *Business Insider*, December 24, 2013, http://www.businessinsider.com/highest-grossing-movies-2013-2013-12?op=1.

15. *Box Office Mojo*, http://boxofficemojo.com /alltime/world/, accessed January 19, 2014.

16. Internet Usage Statistics, *Internet World Stats*, June 30, 2012, http://www.internetworldstats.com /stats.htm.

17. "Globalization," Global Policy Forum, 2010, http://globalpolicy.org/globalization.

18. Walter Gibbs, "Oil Company Near Settling Over Contract in Kurdistan," *New York Times*, January 25, 2010, www.nytimes.com/2010/01/26 /world/middleeast/26galbraith.html.

19. Edward Wong, "Iraqi Court Charges Hussein with Genocide of Kurds, "*New York Times*, April 4, 2006, www.ictj.org/en/news/coverage/article/905 .html and "Timeline: Saddam's Violent Road to Execution," National Public Radio, December 29, 2006, www.npr.org/templates/story/story .php?storyId=4961744.

20. Marijke Verpoorten, "The Death Toll of the Rwandan Genocide: A Detailed Analysis for Gikongoro Province," *Population-E* 60 (2005): 331–46.

21. Francis M. Deng, "Frontiers of Sovereignty: A Framework of Protection, Assistance, and Development for the Internally Displaced," *Leiden Journal of International Law* 8 (1995): 249–86.

22. "Summit Outcome," United Nations General Assembly, A/60/L.1, September 20, 2005.

23. Bruce Jones, Carlos Pascual, and Stephen John Stedman, *Power and Responsibility: Building International Order in an Era of International Threats* (Washington, DC: Brookings Institution Press, 2009).

24. "Treaty on the Non-Proliferation of Nuclear Weapons (NPT)," United Nations Office for Disarmament Affairs, 2010, www.un.org /disarmament/WMD/Nuclear/NPT.shtml.

25. World Trade Organization homepage, 2010, www.wto.org/index.htm.

26. Europa: Gateway to the European Union, 2010, http://europa.eu/index_en.htm.

3

1. William G. Howell and Jon C. Pevehouse, *While Dangers Gather: Congressional Checks on Presidential War Powers* (Princeton, NJ: Princeton University Press, 2007).

2. Bruce Russett and Jon Oneal, *Triangulating Peace: Democracy, Interdependence, and International Organizations* (New York: W.W. Norton, 2001).

3. R.G. Herman and T.S. Piccone (eds.), *Defending Democracy: A Global Survey of Foreign Policy Trends, 1992–2002* (Washington, DC: Democracy Coalition Project, 2002) (electronic version available at http://www.demcoalition.org/html /global_survey.html).

4. Hans J. Morgenthau, *Politics Among Nations: The Struggle for Power and Peace*, 7th ed. (New York: McGraw Hill, 2005), 4.

5. John Mearsheimer, *The Tragedy of Great Power Politics* (New York: W.W. Norton, 2001), 34–35.

6. Michael Doyle, "Liberalism and World Politics," *American Political Science Review* 80 (1986): 1151–69: Bruce Russett and Jon Oneal, *Triangulating Peace: Democracy, Interdependence, and International Organizations* (New York: W.W.Norton, 2001).

7. Robert Keohane and Joseph Nye, Power and Interdependence, 4th ed. (New York: Longman, 2011).

8. Joseph Nye, *Soft Power: The Means to Success in World Politics* (New York: Public Affairs Press, 2004). Joseph Nye, *The Paradox of American Power: Why America Cannot Go It Alone* (New York: Oxford University Press, 2003).

9. Leon Neyfakh, Putin's long game? Meet the Eurasian Union. *Boston Globe*, March 9, 2014.

10. Vladimir Putin, "A new integration project for Eurasia: The future in the making," *Izvestia*, October 3, 2011, http://www.russianmission.eu/en/news /article-prime-minister-vladimir-putin-new-integration-project-eurasia-future-making-izvestia-3-.

11. Alexander Wendt (1992), "Anarchy is What States Make of It. International Organization 46:395.

12. Jean-Pierre Chrétien, *The Great Lakes of Africa: Two Thousand Years of History* (Cambridge, MA: MIT Press, 2003).

4

1. Karl Marx and Freidrich Engels. The Communist Manifesto. Unpublished Manuscript, 1848 (at Project Gutenberg, http://www.gutenberg.org /ebooks/61).

2. For instance, see Nancy E. McGlen and Meredith Reid Sarkees, *Women in Foreign Policy: The Insiders* (New York: Routledge, 1993); Nancy E. McGlen and Meredith Reid Sarkees. 1995. *The Status of Women in Foreign Policy*. New York: Foreign Policy Association. Meredith Reid Sarkees and Nancy E. McGlen, "Foreign Policy Decision-makers: The Impact of Albright and Rice." Paper presented at the annual meeting of the International Studies Association, Town & Country Resort and Convention Center, San Diego, California, March 22, 2006.

3. See, for example, Drude Dahlerup, "From a Small to a Large Minority: Women in Scandinavian Politics," *Scandinavian Political Studies* 11, no. 4 (1988): 275–99; Rosabeth Moss Kanter, "Some Effects of Proportions on Group Life: Skewed Sex Ratios and Responses to Token Women," *American Journal of Sociology* 82, no. 1 (1977): 965–90; Anne Phillips, *The Politics of Presence* (Oxford: Clarendon Press, 1995). See also http://www.unwomen.org for a variety of information on these topics.

4. Mary Caprioli, "Primed for Violence: The Role of Gender Inequality in Predicting Internal Conflict," *International Studies Quarterly* 49 (2005): 161–78; Caprioli, "Gender Equality and State Aggression: The Impact of Domestic Gender Equality on State First Use of Force," *International Interactions* 29 (2003): 195–214.

5. World Development Indicators.

6. The Daily Mail (Online), The Truly Inspiring Story of the Chinese Rubbish Collector Who Saved and Raised THIRTY Babies Abandoned at the Roadside. July 30, 2012. http://www.dailymail .co.uk/news/article-2181017/Lou-Xiaoying-Story-Chinese-woman-saved-30-abandoned-babies-dumped-street-trash.html#ixzz25odQEE5n.

5

1. US Department of Defense, *Dictionary of Military and Associated Terms*, Joint Publication 1-02 (Washington, DC: US Department of Defense, 2010). Electronic version available at http://www.dtic.mil/doctrine/new_pubs/jp1_02.pdf.

2. Bruce Hoffman, *Inside Terrorism* (New York: Columbia University Press, 1999), 32.

3. Walter Laqueur, *The New Terrorism: Fanaticism and the Arms of Mass Destruction* (New York: Oxford University Press, 1999), 6.

4. Peter C. Sederberg, *Terrorist Myths: Illusion, Rhetoric and Reality* (Englewood Cliffs, NJ: Prentice Hall, 1989).

5. Sederberg, *Terrorist Myths*.

6. Cindy Combs, *Terrorism in the 21st Century*, 6th ed. (Englewood Cliffs, NJ: Prentice Hall, 2010).

7. Sederberg, *Terrorist Myths*.

8. John Rollins, "Al Qaeda and Affiliates: Historical Perspective, Global Presence, and Implications for U.S. Policy." Congressional Research Service Report for Congress, #75700 (Washington, DC: US GPO, 2010), i.

9. Leah Farrell, "How Al-Qaeda Works: What the Organization's Subsidiaries Say about Its Strength," *Foreign Affairs* 90, no. 2 (March/April 2011): 1 (electronic version).

10. Jack S. Levy, *War in the Modern Great Power System, 1495–1975* (Lexington, KY: University of Kentucky Press, 1983).

11. John Mueller, *Retreat from Doomsday: The Obsolescence of Major War* (New York: Basic-Books, 1989).

12. Martin Van Creveld, *The Transformation of War* (New York: The Free Press, 1991).

13. John A. Vasquez and Marie T. Henehan, *Territory, War and Peace* (New York: Routledge, 2010).

14. Kalevi J. Holsti, *Peace and War: Armed Conflict and International Order, 1648–1989* (Cambridge: Cambridge University Press, 1991).

15. Holsti, 321.

16. John J. Mearsheimer, *The Tragedy of Great Power Politics* (New York: W.W. Norton, 2001), 32.

17. Mearsheimer, chap. 9.

18. See, for example, A.F.K. Organski, *World Politics* (New York: Knopf, 1968); Organski and

Jacek Kugler, *The War Ledger* (Chicago: University of Chicago Press, 1980).

19. See, for example, Robert Gilpin, *War and Change in World Politics* (Cambridge: Cambridge University Press, 1991); George Modelski, "The Long Cycle of Global Politics and the Nation-State," *Comparative Studies in Society and History* 20, no. 2 (1978): 214–35; William R. Thompson, *On Global War: Historical-Structural Approaches to World Politics* (Columbia, SC: University of South Carolina Press, 1988); Joshua Goldstein, *Long Cycles: Prosperity and War in the Modern Era* (New Haven, CT: Yale University Press, 1988).

20. For example, see Bruce Russett and Jon Oneal, *Triangulating Peace: Democracy, Interdependence and International Organizations* (New York: W.W. Norton, 2001); Edward Mansfield and Brian Pollins, eds. *Economic Interdependence and International Conflict: New Perspectives on an Enduring Debate* (Ann Arbor: University of Michigan Press, 2003).

21. For example, see Immanuel Wallerstein, *The Modern World System* (New York: Academic Press, 1974); *The Capitalist World Economy* (New York: Cambridge University Press, 1979).

22. J. Ann Tickner, *Gender in International Relations: Feminist Perspectives on Achieving Global Security* (New York: Columbia University Press, 1992).

23. G. John Ikenberry, "Introduction," in G. John Ikenberry, ed., *America Unrivalled: The Future of the Balance of Power* (Ithaca, NY: Cornell University Press, 2002), 1.

24. Mearsheimer, 2–3.

25. G. John Ikenberry, "The Future of the Liberal World Order: Internationalism after America," *Foreign Affairs*, May/June 2011, http://www .foreignaffairs.com/articles/67730/g-john-ikenberry /the-future-of-the-liberal-world-order.

26. Greg Cashman, *What Causes War? An Introduction to Theories of International Conflict* (Lanham, MD: Lexington Books, 1993), 125.

27. See Cashman, chap. 5, for the introduction of these five attributes, and a summary of the theories and evidence for each.

28. See, for example, Quincy Wright, *A Study of War* (Chicago: University of Chicago Press, 1965); Michael Doyle, "Liberalism and World Politics," *American Political Science Review* 80, no. 4 (1986): 1151–69; Bruce R. Russett, *Grasping the Democratic Peace* (Princeton, NJ: Princeton University Press, 1994); Russett and Oneal, *Triangulating Peace*.

29. See Norman Angell, *The Great Illusion* (New York: G.P. Putnam, 1910); Eric Gartzke, "The Capitalist Peace," *American Journal of Political Science* 51 (2007): 166–91.

30. John A. Hobson, *Imperialism: A Study* (Ann Arbor: University of Michigan Press, 1965); Vladimir Lenin, *Imperialism: The Highest Stage of Capitalism* (New York: International Publishers, 1939).

31. See, for example, Melvin Small and J. David Singer, "Patterns in International Warfare, 1816–1965," *Annals of the American Academy of Political and Social Science* 391 (1970): 145–55; Stuart Bremer, "National Capabilities and War Proneness," in J. David Singer, ed., *The Correlates of War II: Testing Some Realpolitick Models* (New York: Free Press, 1980), 57–82.

32. See, for example, Nazli Choucri and Robert North, *Nations in Conflict: National Growth and International Violence* (San Francisco: W.H. Freeman, 1975).

33. See, for example, Cashman, 142–45.

34. For a short summary, see Cashman, 147–49.

35. See, for example, Marvin Kalb and Deborah Kalb, *Haunting Legacy: Vietnam and the Presidency from Ford to Obama* (Washington, DC: Brookings Institution Press, 2011); John Mueller,

"The Iraq Syndrome," *Foreign Affairs* 84, no. 6 (2005): 44–54.

36. Mueller, *Retreat from Doomsday*.

37. See, for example, Konrad Lorenz, *On Aggression* (New York: Bantam Books, 1966); Robert Ardrey, *The Territorial Imperative* (New York: Atheneum, 1966).

38. Cashman, 75.

39. R.G. Herman and T.S. Piccone, eds., *Defending Democracy: A Global Survey of Foreign Policy Trends, 1992–2002* (Washington, DC: Democracy Coalition Project, 2002) (electronic version available at http://www.demcoalition.org/html/global_survey.html).

40. G. Allison and R. Beschel, Jr., "Can the United States Promote Democracy?" *Political Science Quarterly* 107 (1992): 81–98.

41. See Irving Janis, *Victims of Groupthink: A Psychological Study of Foreign Policy Decisions and Fiascoes* (New York: Houghton Mifflin, 1972); Jerel A. Rosati and James M. Scott, *The Politics of United States Foreign Policy*, 6th ed. (New York: Wadsworth/Cengage, 2014).

42. Ted Robert Gurr, *Why Men Rebel* (Princeton, NJ: Princeton University Press, 1970), 24.

43. See, for example, Robert D. Kaplan, *Balkan Ghosts: A Journey Through History* (New York: Vintage, 1994).

44. Thomas Homer-Dixon, *Environment, Scarcity, and Violence* (Princeton, NJ: Princeton University Press, 1999).

45. See M. Freeman, "Theories of Ethnicity, Tribalism and Nationalism," in *Ethnic Conflict, Tribal Politics: A Global Perspective*, ed. K. Christie (Richmond, UK: Curzon Press, 1998), 15–34; N. Jesse and K. Williams, *Ethnic Conflict: A Systematic Approach to Cases of Conflict* (Washington, DC: CQ Press, 2011); and D.A. Lake and D. Rothschild, *The International Spread of Ethnic Conflict* (Princeton, NJ: Princeton University Press, 1998).

46. Dara Kay Cohen, "Explaining Rape during Civil War: Cross-National Evidence (1980–2009)". *American Political Science Review* 107, no. 3 (2013): 461–477.

47. F. Stewart and V. Fitzgerald, *War and Underdevelopment: The Economic and Social Consequences of Conflict* (Oxford: Oxford University Press, 2000).

48. See, for example, G. John Ikenberry, *After Victory: Institutions, Strategic Restraint, and the Rebuilding of Order After Major Wars* (Princeton, NJ: Princeton University Press, 2000), and *Liberal Leviathan: The Origins, Crisis and Transformation of the American World Order* (Princeton, NJ: Princeton University Press, 2011).

49. See, for example, Bruce Bueno de Mesquita, Randolph M. Siverson, and Gary Woller, "War and the Fate of Regimes: A Comparative Analysis," *American Political Science Review* 86, no. 3 (1992): 638–46; Bruce Bueno de Mesquita and Randolph M. Siverson, "War and the Survival of Political Leaders: A Comparative Study of Regime Types and Political Accountability," *American Political Science Review* 89, no. 4 (1995): 841–55; H.E. Goemans, "Fighting for Survival: The Fate of Leaders and the Duration of War," *Journal of Conflict Resolution* 44, no. 5 (2000): 555–79; Alexandre Debs and H.E. Goemans, "Regime Type, the Fate of Leaders and War," *American Political Science Review* 104, no. 3 (2010): 430–45.

50. See, for example, H.E. Goemans, *War and Punishment* (Princeton, NJ: Princeton University Press, 2000).

51. See, for example, Marvin Kalb and Deborah Kalb, *Haunting Legacy: Vietnam and the Presidency from Ford to Obama* (Washington, DC: Brookings Institution Press, 2011).

6

1. Bernard Brodie, "The Absolute Weapon," in *Strategic Studies: A Reader*, eds. T. Mahnken and J. Maiolo (New York: Routledge, 2008), 205.

2. Theodor W. Galdi, *Revolution in Military Affairs? Competing Concepts, Organizational Responses, Outstanding Issues*. CRS Report 95–1170 F (Washington, DC, USGPO: 1995), 1.

3. Michael R. Gordon, "Russia Displays a New Military Prowess in Ukraine's East," *New York Times*, April 21, 2014, at http://www.nytimes.com/2014/04/22/world/europe/new-prowess-for-russians.html?_r=0.

4. Samuel P. Huntington, "Arms Races: Prerequisites and Results," in *Public Policy*, eds. C.J. Friedrich and S.E. Harris, vol. 8 (Cambridge, MA: Harvard University Press, 1958), 4.

5. Lewis F. Richardson, *Arms and Insecurity* (Pittsburgh: Boxwood Press, 1960).

6. See Greg Cashman, *What Causes War: An Introduction to Theories of International Conflict* (San Francisco: Lexington Books, 1993), 177–184 for a review of the empirical evidence on arms races and war.

7. See Quincy Wright, *A Study of War* (Chicago: University of Chicago Press, 1942) and Kenneth Waltz, *Theory of International Politics* (New York: McGraw Hill, 1979).

8. Stephen Walt, *The Origins of Alliances* (New York: Cornell University Press, 1987), 282.

9. Waltz, *Theory of International Politics*, stresses balancing against power/capabilities, while Walt, *Origins of Alliances*, stresses balancing against threat.

10. Hans J. Morgenthau, *Politics Among Nations*, 5th ed. (New York: Alfred A. Knopf, 1973), 29.

11. Kenneth Waltz quoted in Robert J. Art, "The Fungibility of Force," in *The Use of Force: Military Power and International Politics*, eds. Robert J. Art and Kenneth N. Waltz, 5th ed. (New York: Rowman & Littlefield, 1999), 5–6.

12. Daniel M. Jones, Stuart A. Bremer, and J. David Singer, "Militarized Interstate Disputes, 1816–1992: Rationale, Coding Rules, and Empirical Patterns," *Conflict Management and Peace Science* 15 (1960): 171–173.

13. See, for example, Alexander George and Richard Smoke, *Deterrence in American Foreign Policy* (New York: Columbia University Press, 1974); Richard Betts, *Nuclear Blackmail and Nuclear Balance* (Washington, DC: Brookings Institution Press, 1987).

14. Robert J. Art, "To What Ends Military Power?" *International Security* 4, no. 4 (1980): 3–35.

15. Ibid., 6.

16. Ibid.

17. See Thomas C. Schelling, *Arms and Influence* (New Haven, CT: Yale University Press, 1966).

18. Art, "To What Ends," 35.

19. Christopher Lamb, *How to Think About Arms Control, Disarmament and Defense* (Englewood Cliffs, NJ: Prentice Hall, 1988), 20.

20. Ibid., chap. 10.

21. Ibid., 181.

22. Ibid., 183.

23. Ibid., 184-185.

24. Inis L. Claude, *Power and International Relations* (New York: Random House, 1988).

25. Immanuel Kant, "Toward Perpetual Peace," in *The Cambridge Edition of the Works of Immanuel Kant: Practical Philosophy*, ed. Mary Gregor (Cambridge: Cambridge University Press, 1996), 311–51.

26. Karl W. Deutsch, et al. *Political Community and the North Atlantic Area: International Organization in the Light of Historical Experience* (Princeton, NJ: Princeton University Press, 1957).

27. See, for example, Emanuel Adler and Michael Barnett, *Security Communities* (Cambridge: Cambridge University Press, 1988).

28. See David Mitrany, *A Working Peace System* (Chicago: Quadrangle Books, 1966).

29. See, for example, James Caporaso, "Regional Integration Theory: Understanding Our Past and Anticipating Our Future," *Journal of European Public Policy* 5, no. 1 (1998): 1–16; as well as Ernst B. Haas, *The Uniting of Europe: Political, Social, and Economic Forces, 1950–1957* (Stanford, CA: Stanford University Press, 1958) and *Beyond the Nation-State: Functionalism and International Organization* (Stanford, CA: Stanford University Press, 1964).

30. See, for example, Eric Gartzke, "The Capitalist Peace," *American Journal of Political Science* 51 (2007): 166–191.

7

1. "Law of the Sea Convention," US Department of State website, http://www.state.gov/g/oes/ocns/opa/convention/.

2. Stephen Quackenbush and Jerome Venteicher, "Settlements, Outcomes, and the Recurrence of Conflict," *Journal of Peace Research* 45, no. 6 (2008): 723–42.

3. See Joshua Keating, "Why the Marshall Islands Is Suing the World's Nuclear Powers." *Slate*. April 25, 2014. http://www.slate.com/blogs/the_world_/2014/04/25/the_marshall_islands_is_suing_the_world_s_nuclear_powers_for_violating_international.html; Julian Borger, "Marshall Islands sues nine nuclear powers over failure to disarm." *The Guardian*. April 24, 2014. http://www.theguardian.com/world/2014/apr/24/marshall-islands-sues-nine-nuclear-powers-failure-disarm.

4. Hedley Bull, *The Anarchical Society* (New York: Columbia University Press, 1977), 127.

5. See, for example, G. John Ikenberry, *After Victory: Institutions, Strategic Restraint, and the Rebuilding of Order after Major Wars* (Princeton, NJ: Princeton University Press, 2000).

6. See, for example, Stephen Krasner, *Structural Conflict: The Third World Against Global Liberalism* (Berkeley, CA: University of California Press, 1985).

7. See David Mitrany, *A Working Peace System* (Chicago: Quadrangle Books, 1966).

8. Margaret P. Karns and Karen A. Mingst, *International Organizations: The Politics and Processes of Global Governance*, 2nd ed. (Boulder, CO: Lynne Rienner, 2010), 148–152.

9. Bruno Waterfield, "We want a United States of Europe says top EU official." *Daily Telegraph*, January 8, 2014, http://www.telegraph.co.uk/news/worldnews/europe/eu/10559458/We-want-a-United-States-of-Europe-says-top-EU-official.html.

10. Marta Bonucci, "Italian PM vows to push for United States of Europe during presidency." *EurActiv*, May 9, 2014, http://www.euractiv.com/sections/eu-elections-2014/italian-pm-vows-to-push-united-states-europe-during-presidency-302048.

11. http://www.un.org/en/ecosoc/about/index.shtml.

8

1. Thomas Friedman, *The Lexus and the Olive Tree: Understanding Globalization* (New York: Farrar, Straus, and Giroux, 1999).

2. From the IMF website, http://www.imf.org/external/about.htm.

3. A. Cooper Drury, Jonathan Krieckhaus, and Chika Yamamoto, "How Democracy Facilitates South Korean Interest in Free Trade Agreements," *Korea Observer* 45 (2014): 39–60.

4. *Huffington Post*, April 9, 2010.

5. Andy Dabilis, "EU Postpones Loan as Greece Runs Out of Money," *Greek Reporter*, September 17, 2011, http://greece.greekreporter.com/2011/09/17/eu-postpones-loan-as-greeceruns-out-of-money/.

9

1. CNN, "U.S. grants full drug certification to Mexico," February 28, 1997.

2. Felix Gilbert, *To the Farewell Address* (Princeton, NJ: Princeton University Press, 1961).

3. Gary Clyde Hufbauer, Jeffrey J. Schott, Kimberly Ann Elliott, and Barbara Oegg, *Economic Sanctions Reconsidered* (Washington, DC: Peterson Institute for International Economics, 2008).

4. The Helms-Burton Act provided for other pressures on Cuba such as the right for Cubans living in the United States to sue the Cuban government, but the primary importance of the act was its ability to sanction other countries doing business with Cuba.

5. David Cortright and George Lopez, *The Sanctions Decade* (Boulder, CO: Lynne Rienner Publishers, 2000).

6. A. Cooper Drury and Dursun Peksen, "Women and Economic Statecraft," Working Paper, 2011.

7. Yasmin Husein Al-Jawaheri, *Women in Iraq: The Gender Impact of International Sanctions* (London: IB Tauris, 2008).

8. Nadje Sadiq Al-Ali, *Iraqi Women: Untold Stories From 1948 to the Present*. London: Zed Books, 2007.

9. Drury and Peksen.

10. Craig Burnside and David Dollar, "Aid, Policies, and Growth," *American Economic Review* 90, no. 4 (2000): 847–68.

11. Sarah Xu, Jonathan Krieckhaus, and A. Cooper Drury, "Foreign Aid, Democracy, and Economic Growth," Working Paper, 2011.

12. R.G. Herman and T.S. Piccone (eds.), *Defending Democracy: A Global Survey of Foreign Policy Trends, 1992–2002* (Washington, DC: Democracy Coalition Project, 2002) (electronic version available at http://www.demcoalition.org/html/global_survey.html).

13. See, for example, Edward Mansfield and Jon C. Pevehouse, "Democratization and International Organizations," *International Organization* 60 (2006): 137–67; S.A. Finkel, A. Perez-Linan, and M.A. Seligson, "The Effects of U.S. Foreign Assistance on Democracy-building, 1990–2003," *World Politics* 59 (2007): 404–39; James M. Scott and Carie A. Steele, "Sponsoring Democracy: The United States and Democracy Aid to the Developing World, 1988–2001," *International Studies Quarterly* 55 (2011): 47–69.

14. A. Cooper Drury, Richard S. Olson, and Douglas A. Van Belle, "The Politics of Humanitarian Aid," *Journal of Politics* 67 (2005): 454–73.

10

1. These figures are from 2012, the most recent year for which reliable purchasing power parity is available.

2. These numbers are from the World Development Indicators 2011 (http://data.worldbank.org/data-catalog/world-development-indicators).

3. Jerry Useem, "The Devil's Excrement," *Fortune Magazine*, February 3, 2003.

4. Jeffrey Sachs and Andrew Warner, "Natural Resource Abundance and Economic Growth," NBER Working Paper, 1995.

5. Unfortunately, these countries have not released any data on their Gini coefficients.

6. William Masters and Margaret McMillan, "Climate and Scale in Economic Growth," *Journal of Economic Growth* 6 (2001): 167–86.

7. Jarad Diamond, *Guns, Germs, and Steel* (New York: W. W. Norton, 1997).

8. Jonathan Krieckhaus, *Dictating Development* (Pittsburgh: Pittsburgh University Press, 2006).

9. Some people dispute that Allende's death was a suicide, but most accounts and those familiar with the situation agree that it was suicide.

10. For example, see Immanuel Wallerstein, *The Modern World System* (New York: Academic Press, 1974); *The Capitalist World Economy* (New York: Cambridge University Press, 1979).

11. David Lake and Matthew Baum, "The Invisible Hand of Democracy," *Comparative Political Studies* 34 (2001): 578–621. Bruce Bueno de Mesquita et al., *The Logic of Political Survival* (Cambridge: MIT Press, 2004).

12. David Lake and Matthew Baum, "The Political Economy of Growth," *American Journal of Political Science* 47 (2003): 333–47.

13. Ibid.

14. A. Cooper Drury, Jonathan Krieckhaus, and Michael Lusztig, "Corruption, Democracy, and Economic Growth," *International Political Science Review* 27 (2006): 121–36.

15. David A. Koplow, Smallpox: *The Fight to Eradicate a Global Scourge* (Berkeley: University of California Press, 2003).

11

1. Adam Nossiter, "Riches Flow Into Nigeria, but Are Lost After Arrival," *New York Times*, February 9, 2011, A4.

2. Dara Kay Cohen, Explaining Rape during Civil War: Cross-National Evidence (1980–2009). *American Political Science Review* 107 (3), 461–477.

3. Jean-Pierre Chretien, *The Great Lakes of Africa: Two Thousand Years of History* (translated by Scott Straus) (Cambridge, MA: Zone Books/MIT Press, 2003).

4. Article 2, Convention on the Prevention and Punishment of the Crime of Genocide, 1948, http://www.hrweb.org/legal/genocide.html.

5. United Nations, "United Nations Treaty Collection," https://treaties.un.org/pages/ViewDetails.aspx?src=TREATY&mtdsg_no=IV-1&chapter=4&lang=en.

6. "Rwanda: How the Genocide Happened," *BBC News*, December 18, 2008, http://news.bbc.co.uk/2/hi/1288230.stm.

7. "The Responsibility to Protect," Report of the International Commission on Intervention and State Sovereignty, http://www.iciss.ca/report-en.asp.

8. See the *Social Progress Index*, http://www.socialprogressimperative.org/data/spi.

9. "How Widespread Is Human Trafficking?" UN Office of Drugs and Crime, 2012, http://www.unodc.org/unodc/en/human-trafficking/faqs.html#How_widespread_is_human_trafficking.

10. Maggie McCarty, "Homelessness: Recent Statistics, Targeted Federal Programs, and Recent Legislation," *CRS Report for Congress*, Congressional Research Service, May 31, 2005, http://www.fas.org/sgp/crs/misc/RL30442.pdf.

11. The material in this box is based on Donald W. Jackson and Ralph G. Carter, "The International Criminal Court: National Interests versus International Norms," in *Contemporary Cases in U.S. Foreign Policy: From Terrorism to Trade*, ed. Ralph G. Carter, 4th ed. (Washington, DC: CQ Press, 2011).

12. United Nations, "On International Day, UN officials urge zero tolerance for female genital mutilation," *UN News Centre*, February 6, 2014, http://www.un.org/apps/news/story.asp?NewsID=47092#.U1aG0dhOXIU.

13. Eric Cox, "State Interests and the Creation and Functioning of the United Nations Human Rights Council," *Journal of International Law and International Relations* 6 (2010): 87–119.

14. Steve Niko and Krista Larson, "U.N. Chief: 'There is a hole in the heart of Africa,'" *Associated Press/Fort Worth Star-Telegram*, April 6, 2014, 12A.

15. See the Country Fact Sheets, 1959–2009, European Court of Human Rights, http://www.echr.coe.int/NR/rdonlyres/C2E5DFA6-B53C-42D2-8512-034BD3C889B0/0/FICHEPARPAYS_ENG_MAI2010.pdf.

12

1. "Environmental Impacts of Coal Power: Air Pollution," Union of Concerned Scientists, 2012, http://www.ucsusa.org/clean_energy/coalvswind/c02c.html.

2. "Oceanic 'Garbage Patch' Not Nearly as Big as Portrayed in Media," News and Research Communications, Oregon State University, January 4, 2011, http://oregonstate.edu/ua/ncs/archives/2011/jan/oceanic-"garbage-patch"-not-nearly-big-portrayed-media.

3. Rhett A. Butler, "Deforestation in the Amazon," May 20, 2012, http://www.mongabay.com/brazil.html.

4. Associated Press, "China Says Desertification Process Has Slowed," *The Times of India*, January 4, 2011, http://cmsenvis.cmsindia.org/newsletter/enews/NewsDetails.asp?id=33631.

5. Terrell Johnson, "13 of 14 Hottest Years on Record All Occurred in 21st Century," *The Weather Channel*, March 24, 2014, http://www.weather.com/news/science/environment/13-14-hottest-years-record-occurred-21st-century-wmo-20140324.

6. John Abraham and Dana Nuccitelli, "Climate Consensus: the 97%," *The Guardian*, May 16, 2013, http://www.theguardian.com/environment/climate-consensus-97-per-cent/2013/may/16/climate-change-scienceofclimatechange.

7. Justin Gillis and Kenneth Chang, "Scientists Warn of Rising Oceans from Polar Melt," *New York Times*, May 13, 2014, A1, A8.

8. Henry Fountain, "Putting a 32,000 Ton Cap on Chernobyl," *New York Times*, April 28, 2014, A1, A10–A11.

9. "Spain Sets Wind Power Generation Record," *Alternative Energy*, March 13, 2009, http://www.alternative-energy-news.info/spain-sets-windpower-generation-record/.

10. Environmental Performance Index, *Results at-a-Glance 2014*, http://epi.yale.edu/epi.

11. Earth Day Network, "The Green Cities Campaign," *Green Cities*, http://www.earthday.org/greencities/about/.

12. "Sea Shepherd Partners with the Republic of Palau to Control Poaching," *Sea Shepherd News*, March 31, 2011, http://www.seashepherd.org/news-and-media/2011/03/31/sea-shepherd-partners-with-the-republic-of-palau-to-control-poaching-28.

13. Julio Godoy, "Following the Carbon Footprint to the 'Emissions Reduction' Fallacy," IPS, December 8, 2011, http://ipsnews.net/2011/12/climate-change-following-the-carbon-footprint-to-the-emissions-reduction-fallacy/.

14. "The UN World Water Development Report, Facts and Figures, Meeting Basic Needs," 2012, http://www.unesco.org/new/fileadmin/MULTIMEDIA/HQ/SC/pdf/WWAP_WWDR4%20Facts%20and%20Figures.pdf; also "UN Declares Clean Water a 'Fundamental Human Right,'" BBC, July 28, 2010, http://www.bbc.co.uk/news/world-us-canada-10797988?print=true.

15. Renee Cho, "From Wastewater to Drinking Water," *State of the Planet: Blogs from the Earth Institute*, Columbia University, April 4, 2011, http://blogs.ei.columbia.edu/2011/04/04/from-wastewater-to-drinking-water/.

16. Sophie Wenzlau, "Global Food Prices Continue to Rise," *Worldwatch Institute*, April 11, 2013, http://www.worldwatch.org/global-food-prices-continue-rise-0.

17. United Nations Department of Economic and Social Affairs, *Sustainable Development Challenges: World Economic and Social Survey 2013*, http://www.un.org/en/development/desa/policy/wess/wess_current/wess2013/WESS2013.pdf.

18. Wendell Cox, "World Urban Areas Population and Density: A 2012 Update," *New Geography*, May 5, 2012, http://www.newgeography.com/content/002808-world-urban-areas-population-and-density-a-2012-update.

13

1. Donald G. McNeil, Jr., "Polio's Return Prompts a Global Health Warning," *New York Times*, May 6, 2014, A1, A8.

2. Global Polio Eradication Initiative, "Contributions and Pledges to the Global Polio Eradication Initiative, 1985–2018," http://www.polioeradication.org/Portals/0/Document/Financing/HistoricalContributions.pdf.

3. Thus our definition is based on those found in Margaret E. Keck and Kathryn Sikkink, *Activists beyond Borders: Advocacy Networks in International Politics* (Ithaca, NY: Cornell University Press, 1998) and Anne-Marie Slaughter, *A New World Order* (Princeton, NJ: Princeton University Press, 2004).

4. Martha Finnemore and Kathryn Sikkink, "International Norm Dynamics and Political Change," *International Organization* 52 (Autumn 1998): 887–917.

5. Refugee Research Network website, http://www.refugeeresearch.net/taxonomy/term/1.

6. The Global FoodBanking Network, "Our Supporters," http://gfn.convio.net/site/PageServer?pagename=support_supporters.

7. David Hendricks, "Suppliers Will Increase Production Along with Toyota," *San Antonio Express-News*, May 26, 2011, http://www.mysanantonio.com/default/article/Suppliers-will-increaseproduction-along-with-1397805.php.

14

1. Rebecca Bluitt, "Cold, Cold War: Putin Talks Tough over US Arctic Rivalry," *ABC News*, December 5, 2013, http://abcnews.go.com/Blotter/cold-cold-war-putin-talks-tough-us-artic/print?id=21110178.

2. For example, see Thomas F. Homer-Dixon, *Environment, Scarcity, and Violence* (Princeton, NJ: Princeton University Press, 2000).

A

absolute advantage when a country is more efficient at producing a single good than another country.

absolute gains the total effect of a decision or situation on an actor.

advisory group the set of individuals from whom leaders seek decision-making assistance.

African Charter on Human and Peoples' Rights the treaty by the Organization for African Unity (later the African Union) that went into force in 1986 and listed individual rights and the responsibilities of individuals in a communal context. It also created the African Commission of Human and Peoples' Rights and the African Court of Human and Peoples' Rights.

African Union (AU) organization in Africa devoted to representing the interests of African states.

agent-centered approach Understanding and explaining international relations by focusing on the individuals and groups who make decisions within the state.

aggression the unjustified use of force against another state.

aid sanction cutting off aid to a country in order to get it to change its behavior.

alliance formal commitments between states to cooperate for specific purposes such as mutual defense.

al-Qaeda translated as "the base," this is an fundamentalist Islamic transnational terrorist organization. It is responsible for many attacks on Western countries and moderate Islamic countries. Most infamously, it organized, funded, and perpetrated the September 11, 2001, attacks in the United States.

American Convention on Human Rights the Organization of American States treaty that went into force in 1978. It created an Inter-American Commission on Human Rights and an Inter-American Court of Human Rights.

American Israel Public Affairs Committee (AIPAC) a pro-Israel interest group, thought to be the most influential interest group impacting U.S. foreign policy.

anarchy the absence of central government in world politics.

arable land land capable of sustaining agriculture.

arms control regulation of the amount, type, positioning, or use of weapons.

arms embargo not selling weapons to a country.

arms race peacetime competition in armaments by two or more states driven by conflict interests, fear, and suspicion.

asymmetric war armed conflict between two or more groups of very different military size or power.

austerity program program of severely restricted government spending, often on welfare programs, imposed when the country must balance its accounts.

authoritarian systems nondemocratic governments with leaders who rule via force, whose basis of power is the ability to coerce others or a submissive citizenry.

autonomy state of independence from another country, the ability to act by oneself.

B

balance of power politics patterns of shifting alliances, force, and counterforce among states as they seek power, counter the efforts of rivals, and confront security threats.

balance of power politics patterns of shifting alliances, force, and counterforce among states as they seek power, counter the efforts of rivals, and confront security threats.

balance-of-payments a country's balance between exports, imports, and debt. If exports are too low and cannot support the country's debt, there is an economic crisis.

balancing (in alliances) forming coalitions to counter the rising power and threat of a state.

bandwagoning (in alliances) siding with a rising power to gain benefits.

Baruch Plan a nuclear disarmament proposal authored by US statesman Bernard Baruch after World War II to place nuclear weapons and energy activities under the control and authority of the United Nations.

beggar-thy-neighbor an economic policy that stresses trade protectionism and causes other countries to bear the costs of efforts at securing prosperity at home.

Big Mac Index a measure created by *The Economist* magazine that compares the value of currencies by comparing the cost of a Big Mac hamburger in different countries. The United States is used as the baseline cost for the index.

bilateral relations between two states. For example, a bilateral summit is a high-level conference between two states.

bipolar a distribution of power in the international system in which there are two great powers.

boomerang model the notion that internal groups repressed by their own states can turn to TANs to put pressure on other states and those states then put pressure on the repressive state from the outside. In short, repression against internal groups can boomerang back and cause new external pressure on the repressive state.

bounded rationality the idea that leaders want to make rational or logical decisions but are limited by their lack of knowledge or other human factors.

Bretton Woods organizations the organizations created at the Bretton Woods conference. They include the World Bank, IMF, and later the GATT.

Bretton Woods System the global economic system established by the United States and other countries after World War II to promote capitalism, free trade, and policy coordination. Nicknamed "Bretton Woods" for the location of the conference in New Hampshire, the two core institutions created were the IMF and World Bank.

brinkmanship the strategy of escalating conflicts or crises to nuclear threats in order to force the other side to back down.

C

capitalism an economic system in which workers sell their labor for wages, there is no central authority over the economy, and market forces determine what is purchased and what is sold.

capitalist class or bourgeoisie the owners of businesses, factories, etc. that make profits from the work of laborers but do not work themselves.

carbon footprint the amount of carbon dioxide we generate through our daily activities.

CEDAW the Convention on the Elimination of All Forms of Discrimination against Women, approved by the UN General Assembly in 1979.

centrally planned (or command) economy an economy that is run by the government rather than private citizens. Examples include the Soviet Union and North Korea.

Chinese Communist Party the only legal political party in the People's Republic of China. It controls all aspects of the government.

civil society groups NGOs that promote democracy and human rights on a global basis.

civil society organizations NGOs that voluntarily work together to serve the greater social and political good within a society; they build the voluntary relationships that bind society and its members together.

civil war armed conflict between competing factions within a country, or between a government and a competing group within that country over control of territory and/or the government.

coercive diplomacy a strategy that combines threats and the selective use of force with negotiation in a bargaining strategy to persuade an adversary to comply with one's demand.

Cold War a period of intense rivalry and competition from 1947–1989 between the United States and its allies on the one hand, and the Soviet Union and its allies on the other.

collective action problem a condition in which the uncoordinated actions of individuals lead to less than optimal outcomes because, although many individuals would benefit from some cooperative action or actions, few incentives lead any particular individuals to assume the costs of such actions.

collective goods things that benefit all concerned—whether they participate in their protection and maintenance—and are not owned by any one state actor.

collective security states join together into an organization, ban the use of force by its members, and commit themselves to joining together to respond to any attack by one member on any other member.

colonialism the situation where one country takes over another country and administers it with a local bureaucracy.

colonies territories that are legally owned and controlled by another country, typically called the imperial power.

commitment problem countries have a hard time committing to cooperative courses of action that assure their partners that they will keep their end of the deal for mutual benefit and forego the possibility of their own short-term gains.

communism the anti-capitalist economic philosophy created by Karl Marx that under subsequent leaders promoted centralized control of a country and its economy for the equal redistribution of resources to the country's citizens.

comparative advantage being more efficient at producing a good or service relative to another good or service. Even if one country has an absolute advantage over another in all products, both countries benefit by specializing in the products they each produce most efficiently (their comparative advantage) and trading for the others.

compellence the use of military force to stop a foe from doing something it was already doing, or force it to start doing something it was not yet doing.

complexity the multidimensional issues, actors, and connections that characterize international relations.

compulsory jurisdiction in international law, the condition in which parties to a dispute must submit the case to a court.

Concert of Europe a nineteenth century multilateral organization composed of Great Britain, Russia, Austria, Prussia, and France to promote stability, cooperation, and multilateral diplomacy.

conference diplomacy large diplomatic meetings of many officials from states, international organizations, non-governmental organizations, academia, and other non-state actors.

consociational democracy a form of government that guarantees representation to the different ethnic or religious groups within the country.

constructivism a major theoretical approach to international relations emphasizing the importance of ideas, collective identities, and the social construction of reality.

constructivism (and ethnicity) emphasizes the social construction of identity and the ways that social interactions define ethnicity for groups of people.

consulates offices other than embassies where diplomatic officials facilitate commerce, travel, and cultural exchanges.

Convention on Genocide a 1948 UN treaty that both defined genocide and made it a crime whether it occurred in peacetime or in wartime.

conventional war armed conflict between two or more states in which military forces of each side are used against each other, and in which weapons of mass destruction such as nuclear, biological, or chemical weapons are not used.

core the economic zone composed of wealthy countries producing high-end products.

Council of Ministers Made up of sitting ministers of their national governments, the Council of Ministers represents member states and approves all EU legislation.

counter-force targeting an adversary's nuclear arsenals and other war-fighting abilities for nuclear strikes.

counter-value targeting an adversary's cities and industrial centers for nuclear strikes.

coup d'état literally, a "strike against the state"; when there is a forceful change in government that overthrows the current leadership.

crimes against humanity acts of war against a civilian population; these can include, among others, the crimes of murder; enslavement; deportation or forcible transfer; imprisonment; torture; rape, sexual slavery or any other form of enforced sexual violence; persecution on political, racial, national, ethnic, cultural, religious, gender, or other such grounds; enforced disappearance; apartheid; and other inhumane acts that create great suffering or serious mental or physical injury.

cultural exchange programs involving the exchange of citizens—students, teachers, scientists, artists, and others—between countries to foster cultural understanding and cooperation.

cultural relativism the idea that human rights are not truly universal and that different cultures have different systems of rights. This term particularly comes into play when non-Western societies argue that international human rights standards have a Western bias and do not reflect non-Western values.

custom the general practice of states accepted as law; a source of international law.

cyclical theories of war conflict based on the rise and relative decline of leading powers in the international system in which stability occurs as the victors in major wars assert themselves, and war occurs as a function of the subsequent and inevitable rise of challengers to those dominant powers.

defense deploying and using military force to fight off an attack.

defense burden the ratio of military spending to overall gross domestic product of a country.

deforestation the destruction of forests at a rate faster than they can be replaced or replenished.

democracy a form of governance in which the people have a meaningful choice in selecting their rulers.

democracy aid aid given to a country to enhance and consolidate its transition to democracy.

democracy promotion a cluster of activities ranging from diplomacy to aid to intervention designed to foster and support democratization in other countries.

democratic peace state-level theory of war stating that institutional and normative characteristics of democratic regimes lead them to peaceful relations with each other.

dependency theory a theory of development that argues that the dominance and exploitation of poor countries by rich countries prevents progress and development in the poor countries and makes them dependent on the wealthy countries.

desertification the creation of new, or enlargement of existing, deserts.

deterrence persuading a potential adversary to refrain from attacking through the threat of costly retaliation.

devalue a situation when a currency, such as the U.S. dollar, loses its value compared to other currencies. For example, the Chinese government sets the exchange rate between the U.S. dollar and the Chinese yuan, and currently, the yuan is devalued; it is worth more than the Chinese will trade it for.

developed country a wealthy country with an economy that tends to produce manufactured goods and services for export.

development aid aid given to a country to help develop its economy.

difference feminists the feminist perspective that argues that men and women are fundamentally different in their abilities, particularly in their approach to conflict.

diplomacy the art and practice of conducting negotiations between nations.

diplomatic immunity the principle that accredited diplomats are exempt in almost all cases from prosecution under the laws of the state where they are assigned.

diplomats individuals occupying positions in the foreign policy establishments of states or the management of other organizations who represent and negotiate on behalf of their country or employer.

direct deterrence the use of retaliatory threats to discourage attacks against the state making the deterrent threat.

disarmament the elimination of arsenals or classes or types of weapons.

distribution of power a characteristic of the international system emphasized by realists based on the number of great or major powers and how power is distributed among them in a given period of time.

diversionary theory the idea that leaders under domestic pressures will use military force more readily to distract their opponents or rally the public behind their leadership.

diversity variation in values, norms, identities, goals, and other political, economic, and cultural factors in world politics.

domain of gains situations in which decision makers seek to preserve their advantages.

domain of losses negative situations in which decision makers will engage in more risk-taking to change the status quo.

E

Economic and Social Council the component of the UN handling matters considered economic or social, broadly defined.

economic sanction the cessation of some or all economic exchange between two countries.

economic statecraft the use of economic means to secure political ends.

ecosystem the interaction of living things and the material world around them.

embassies properties that house the permanent diplomatic missions of other countries, typically located in the capital city of a state.

empirical theory theory based on real-world observations and explanations.

epistemic communities networks of experts who bring their knowledge and expertise to the political arena to help policymakers understand problems, generate possible solutions, and evaluate policy success or failure.

ethnic cleansing a form of violence in which an ethnic group purges or cleans a territory of its rival ethnic groups, by forced expulsion, violence, or death.

ethnic geography the spatial and ecological aspects of ethnicity (e.g., where groups live in relation to one another), which affect the culture, politics, and social practices of states, nations, groups, and individuals.

European Commission (EC) The executive branch of the EU. The Commission is led by a president, has budgetary powers, and includes a 28-member cabinet that oversees policy development in agriculture, trade, social policy, the environment, and many other areas.

European Commission on Human Rights created by the European Convention on Human Rights, a very active body monitoring human rights situations in Europe. Individuals who feel their rights have been abused can appeal to the commission, which may, after investigation, refer the case to the European Court of Human Rights.

European Convention on Human Rights the Council of Europe treaty that went into force in 1953, which listed individual rights and created the European Commission on Human Rights and the later European Court of Human Rights.

European Council Made up of the heads of government of the EU member states, the European Council represents the interests of their member states within the EU.

European Court of Human Rights (ECHR) a court created in 1959 by the Council of Europe; one of the most active courts involved in human rights cases.

European Court of Justice The EU's judicial branch whose rulings take precedent over even national law. It is charged with interpreting EU law and ensuring that it is applied equally across all member states.

European Parliament (EP) The EU legislative body made up of directly elected representatives, the EU Parliament amends, approves or rejects EU laws, together with the Council of Ministers.

European Union (EU) a supranational organization with 27 member states.

Eurozone the portion of the European Union that uses the euro currency rather than a national currency. These countries include: Austria, Belgium, Cyprus, Finland, France, Germany, Greece, Ireland, Italy, Luxembourg, Malta, the Netherlands, Portugal, Slovakia, Slovenia, and Spain.

export-led growth the idea that to develop a country's economy, the government should push for companies to focus on products that can be exported to other countries. The policy was most successful in the Asian countries such as South Korea and Singapore.

expropriation the taking—or nationalization—of property owned by a foreign company with or without compensation.

extended deterrence retaliatory threats to discourage attacks against allies and friends of the state making the deterrent threat.

external balancing countering the power of a rival by forming coalitions with other states.

extra-systemic or extra-state war armed conflict between a state and a non-state entity, such as colonial wars and wars with non-state national or terrorist groups.

extraterritoriality the principle that one is exempt from prosecution of the laws of the state; typically applied in the case of an embassy.

F

fair trade the concept that producers should be paid a fair price for their products.

Falkland Islands a group of islands approximately 300 miles off the coast of Argentina owned by the United Kingdom and populated by UK citizens.

fascism a political ideology that glorifies the state over the individuals who comprise it and relies on nationalism and violence to bond the citizenry to the state.

female genital mutilation the cutting away of part of the external genitalia, based on the belief that, by reducing sexual pleasure, women will remain chaste until married and faithful to their husbands thereafter. Some societies also believe this is a religious requirement for women to behave modestly or may increase fertility.

feminist international relations theory a feminist approach to understanding international relations that focuses on the role of women and gender and how historically the world has been male dominated.

feudalism a socio-economic-political system in which rulers would grant land to the local aristocracy in return for their loyalty and support, and others work the land in return for food, shelter, and protection from the local aristocracy.

financial sanction the freezing of a country's financial assets held in another country.

first-generation human rights (individual rights) rights that individuals have simply because they are human beings and which are not to be violated by governments.

fissile material nuclear material used to make atomic weapons.

foreign aid money given by one country (the donor) to another country (the recipient) for health, economic development, or poverty relief.

foreign direct investment when a company in one country invests in a company in another country that leads the investor to have control over the new company.

foreign policy analysis a theoretical approach that focuses on the process and outcomes of foreign policy decisions made by the people and groups that determine a state's actions in international relations.

frustration-aggression theory resort to violence under conditions of persistent denial of expected treatment, for example, fairness and equality.

functionalism and neo-functionalism technical cooperation on economic and social issues that build linkages and shared interests among societies and expand to more areas, leading to even greater cooperation and institutional connections.

fungible the ability to use one type of power for multiple purposes.

G

GDP per capita the measure of a country's development. It is the total size of a country's economy divided by the population.

General Agreement on Tariffs and Trade (GATT) an organization of countries that agree to work together to reduce trade barriers and promote free trade. Other members were considered "most favored nations" and received preferential trade agreements. The GATT was replaced by the World Trade Organization in 1995.

general deterrence threats to retaliate in a context of underlying politico-military competition, but when there is no active military conflict generating the need to respond.

general war armed conflict in which the participants seek to conquer and control territory of their opponents and use the full available arsenals against military targets and against the infrastructure of a country.

genetically modified organisms (GMOs) those organisms whose genetic makeup is intentionally altered to produce some advantage.

genocide the deliberate killing of a religious, ethnic, or racial group.

Gini coefficient a measure of the distribution of income in a country ranging from 0 to 1 where 0 means perfect equality and 1 means perfect inequality.

global climate change marked changes in the warming and cooling of the planet's temperatures, thought to be accelerated by human activity such as industrialization and fossil fuel emissions, which produce greenhouse gases.

Global Counter-Terrorism Strategy a 2006 UN General Assembly document that seeks to prevent terrorism by addressing its root causes, to promote international cooperation in dealing with terrorist threats, to build the capacity of both states and the UN to combat terrorism, and to make sure that the global fight against terrorism does not violate standards of the rule of law or human rights.

Global Environmental Facility the UN entity created by the UN Framework Convention on Climate Change to collect and distribute the financial resources needed to combat global climate change.

globalization the increasing integration of global society through the spread of technology, foreign trade, transportation, cultural exchange, political institutions, and social connections.

greenhouse gases those gases that trap the sun's heat and hold it close to the earth's surface; they include carbon dioxide, methane, nitrous oxide, and water vapor.

gross domestic product (GDP) the total amount of goods and services produced in a state.

groupthink characteristics of some decision groups that result in a shared viewpoint or preference that leads the group to ignore relevant information and exclude dissenters from that viewpoint in order to protect it.

H

hard power power based on coercive means such as military force.

head of government the person who is in charge of a state's government on a day-by-day basis and ensures that basic state functions and services are met.

head of state the person who symbolically represents a state and its people.

hegemon a country that is an undisputed leader within its region or the world. After World War II, the United States was considered the world hegemon.

hegemony domination of the international system by one country.

Hobbesian world a brutal, dangerous, self-help world with central authority described by the philosopher Thomas Hobbes.

home country the term used to describe where the headquarters of a multinational corporation is based.

honor-killings the murders of girls or women by their husbands, fathers, brothers, etc., when they are thought to have violated socially acceptable sexually based roles. By killing the offender, the males in the family seek to restore the family's honor and are typically not prosecuted for their crimes.

horizontal enforcement those measures that states themselves can take when a state violates an international law and other states can attempt to punish the violator themselves.

host country the country in which a multinational corporation owns other companies.

Human Development Index (HDI) a measure of the level of human development in a country. It includes GDP per capita, life expectancy, and education levels.

human nature innate characteristics of human beings, said to be a cause of war by some.

human security an emphasis on the security of people, not territory, first set out by the UN Development Program in 1994. It includes economic, food, health, environmental, personal, community, and political security for people.

humanitarian aid aid given to a country to help mitigate the effects from a disaster or other humanitarian emergency.

humanitarian interventions military or non-military interventions into a state by outside groups for the purpose of protecting endangered people and meeting the needs of the state's residents.

Hutu a socially constructed race in central Africa that was supposed to be poorer and physically shorter than its rival group, the Tutsis.

hyperinflation a situation where a currency loses its value very quickly. Regular inflation occurs at relatively low levels (3 to 5 percent per year), but hyperinflation means a currency can lose most of its value in a year, month, or even day.

I

ideational emphasizing the centrality of ideas and norms in shaping behavior and interactions.

IED (improvised explosive device) improvised explosive device– a homemade bomb, often placed on roadsides and other sites, fashioned from an explosive device and a detonator, usually triggered by remote device or "booby-trap" mechanism.

immediate deterrence the threat to retaliate against attackers who are believed to be actively considering specific military operations against the target.

imperialism control and exploitation by one state of the economy, culture, and/or territory of others, usually called colonies.

import and export sanctions when one country reduces or stops buying or selling products from/to another country.

import substitution industrialization (ISI) a development policy that promotes cutting off international trade and substituting it with domestic production.

individual level locating the causes of behavior and outcomes in the nature and characteristics of people.

Industrial Revolution the transition of many of the world's states from an agricultural economic system to one that was based on industry. During this period, factories replaced farms as the biggest producer in many countries.

institutions structures, patterns, and mechanisms for establishing norms, rules, order, and cooperation in world politics.

instrumentalism stresses the role of leaders who emphasize and exacerbate ethnic differences (and commonalities) as a means to their own ends.

interdependence mutual connections and reliance between international actors.

Intergovernmental Panel on Climate Change (IPCC) a scientific body with 195 member states, created by the UN's Environment Programme and the World Meteorological Organization in 1988.

internal balancing countering the power of a rival by increasing one's own power and military might.

international actors those who act in the international system; these actors can include states or non-state actors.

International Atomic Energy Agency (IAEA) an independent intergovernmental organization that reports to the UN and UNSC concerning the peaceful use of atomic energy, nuclear proliferation, and nuclear safeguards.

International Bank for Reconstruction and Development the original organization of the World Bank designed to promote reconstruction, especially in Europe after World War II.

international civil society an international system based on the norms of democracy and human rights. This emerging system is marked by civil society organizations, NGOs that promote these values on a global basis.

International Convention for the Suppression of the Financing of Terrorism a treaty that went into force in 2002, making it easier to get international cooperation to trace and shut down terrorist financing networks.

International Court of Justice also known as the **World Court**, this international institution was created in 1946 as part of the United Nations systems to apply international law to resolve conflicts brought voluntarily to it by states.

International Covenant on Civil and Political Rights a 1966 UN treaty identifying the civil, political, and legal rights of all humans and establishing procedures for the UN to monitor these rights.

International Covenant on Economic, Social, and Cultural Rights a 1966 UN treaty identifying the economic, social, and cultural rights of all humans and establishing procedures for the UN to monitor these rights.

International Criminal Court (ICC) the ICC is an international court in the Netherlands that tries individuals accused of war crimes, crimes against humanity, genocide, and aggression.

international governmental organizations (IOs) international organizations whose membership is restricted to states.

international law a body of rules that binds states and other agents in world politics in their relations with one another.

International Monetary Fund (IMF) one of the Bretton Woods organizations created in 1946 to help maintain a cooperative international financial system. The IMF helps countries facing balance-of-payment problems with short-term loans and also helps countries reschedule their debt.

international norms unwritten rules or expectations of behavior.

international system the constellation of international actors and the relationships between them.

INTERPOL the International Criminal Police Organization created in 1923 and based in Lyon, France.

interstate war armed conflict between two or more states.

Irish Republican Army (IRA) the militant terrorist organization in Northern Ireland that fought to remove the Protestant leaders from power and the British military from Northern Ireland.

irredentist claims (or irredentism) claims to territory in another state based on historical control or the presence of people with common ethnic identity.

Islamists extreme fundamentalist Muslims.

J

jihad "holy war" in Arabic. To some Muslims it means the daily struggle within oneself to overcome evil; to others it means conducting war against non-Muslims.

K

Kyoto Protocol an addendum to the UN Framework Convention on Climate Change, which was negotiated in 1997 and entered into force in 2005, which imposed mandatory reductions in fossil fuel emissions for thirty-seven developed countries and the European Community.

L

Law of the Sea Convention a treaty that first went into force in 1982 and then was revised in 1994; 165 states are parties to this treaty, as is the EU, which sets rules for the use and protection of the high seas and its resources.

League of Nations an international institution created after World War I for collective security and the resolution of disputes between states.

less-developed country (LDC) a country that is poor or has an economy that is less able to support its population. These countries typically export raw materials and agricultural products.

levels of analysis different perspectives from which international relations may be examined.

liberal capitalism a philosophy of complete or near complete free markets and no governmental regulation in the economy. There are variations to liberal capitalism, but the idea is minimal government involvement in the economy.

liberal feminists the feminist perspective that argues men and women can approach issues such as conflict the same way, but that it is important to have equal representation of the two genders.

liberal international economic order (LIEO) the post-World War II international economic system built on commitments to free trade and free market economies, with international institutions to help countries coordinate and cooperate.

liberalism a major theoretical approach to international relations emphasizing the role of individuals, norms, and institutions to explain patterns of cooperation and conflict in world politics.

limited war armed conflict with conventional weapons for limited goals and without use of full available arsenals.

linkage strategy in diplomacy, the strategy of connecting solutions on one issue to proposals on another to facilitate agreement.

liquidity crisis a situation when a government runs out of cash and is unable to make minimum payments on its debt.

M

Magna Carta the "Great Charter" signed by King John of England in 1215 (and reaffirmed in 1297 by King Edward I), which noted that freemen had certain rights that the monarch could not takeaway, including the right not to be imprisoned without legal justification or a judgment by one's peers.

majority rule in international organizations, a decision process that relies on voting with one vote per member, in which gaining a majority of the votes prevails.

Malthusian dilemma named for its early author Thomas Robert Malthus, the notion that population growth outstrips the growth of the food supply.

Marxism an argument developed by Marx and Engels that asserted all politics was determined by social class and that the world would progress through historical economic epochs.

massive retaliation the threat to respond to provocations with disproportionate and devastating nuclear attacks.

mercantilism an economic policy that combines free enterprise and government. The government uses its power—including its military—to enhance private business, and private business provides revenues to the government to maintain and enhance its power.

metropole the capital city of the empire; for example, London was the metropole of the British Empire.

Middle East the region of the world that encompasses countries in Northeast Africa and Southwest Asia.

military aid aid given to a country that directly enhances its military capability.

Millennium Development Goals eight goals established by the UN in 2000 to foster development in a sustainable and equal manner.

modernization theory theory in the 1950s and 1960s that suggested all countries should be able to develop by following the practices of wealthy states in Europe and North America.

Monterrey Consensus a 2002 framework for global development in which the developed and developing countries agree to take joint actions for poverty reduction, with emphasis on free trade, sustainable growth and development, and increased financial aid.

Most-Favored Nation (MFN) the preferential trade status that members of the GATT gave to other members. MFN could also be granted to non-members if a country chose to do so. The United States granted China MFN status for years before China entered the agreement.

mujahideen those who fight to liberate Muslims or traditionally Muslim lands from control by nonbelievers; the insurgency resisting the Soviet invasion of Afghanistan is the most widely known example.

multilateral diplomacy diplomacy involving three or more states at a time; typically many states are involved.

multinational corporations (MNCs) companies that have subsidiaries (other companies) in multiple countries. Also known as **transnational corporations (TNCs).**

multipolar a distribution of power in the international system in which there are more than two great powers.

mutually assured destruction (MAD) the ability of both sides to field a secure, second-strike capability of sufficient size to destroy a significant portion of the other side's society.

N

nation an identifiable group of people who share a collective identity typically formed around bonds based on factors like shared language, culture, etc.

national attributes features of states or nations such as regime type, type of economy, culture, geography, resources, and the like.

national enforcement states enforce some international law through their own national legal systems.

national missile defense the capability to protect a country from nuclear attack by shooting down incoming missiles.

nationalism the emotional connection of the mass public to their state.

nationalization when a government takes ownership of private property—land, a company, or an asset.

nation-state a state in which nearly all of the population are members of the same nation.

NATO the **North Atlantic Treaty Organization**, a military alliance structure created following the outbreak of the Korean War in 1950 and led by the United States.

negative interest rate a government policy of charging banks for holding too much of their currency in reserve. The policy is meant to make loans more available and spur economic growth.

negative peace a lack of conflict between two countries or groups.

neocolonialism the practice of maintaining control over smaller, developing countries by keeping strong, dependent links to their governments and/or dominating their economies. This allows a powerful state to control a smaller state without colonizing it.

neoliberal a return to liberal or free-market economics.

neo-Westphalian sovereignty the idea of sovereignty as a state's responsibility to protect its citizens.

nongovernmental organizations (NGOs) organizations whose membership is not restricted solely to states.

non-state actors international actors that are not states. They may include IOs, NGOs, multinational corporations, and individuals.

nontariff barrier a requirement that foreign goods or services must meet that is specifically designed to block or obstruct those goods or services from sale in that market.

non-trinitarian war armed conflict in which the roles and participation of government, militaries, and populations are blurred.

normative theory theory based on prescription and advocacy of preferred outcomes.

norms commonly held standards of acceptable and unacceptable behavior.

norms life cycle the idea that TANs are successful when they can create new norms, create a norms cascade forcing governments to act on those norms, and get norms internalized to the point that following them becomes routine and largely unquestioned.

North American Free Trade Agreement (NAFTA) a free trade agreement between Canada, Mexico, and the United States. The agreement greatly reduced all barriers to trade between the three countries and resulted in a significant increase in trade of goods and services between the three.

Nuclear Non-Proliferation Regime a formal treaty and its related rules set by the International Atomic Energy Agency regulating how states may develop, maintain, and use nuclear power and nuclear materials.

Nuclear Non-Proliferation Treaty a treaty prohibiting those with nuclear weapons from providing them to others and those without nuclear weapons from seeking them.

operational code analysis the idea that leaders have a tendency to 1) prefer either conflict or cooperation and 2) believe they are either very effective or limited in their ability to control others.

Organization for Economic Cooperation and Development (OECD) organization of thirty-four member states that promotes liberal economic and political reforms.

Organization of American States (OAS) international organization composed of states in the North and South American continents.

organizational/bureaucratic politics model foreign policy decisions are the products of large bureaucratic organizations doing what they know to do or see as in their organizational interest.

orthodox liberal an approach to economics that favors an extreme free-market approach where government is very limited and most of a country is composed of private enterprise.

other-oriented TANs TANs that advocate a set of values that primarily benefit others besides themselves.

P-5 (perm-5) the five permanent members of the UN Security Council—the United States, Britain, France, China, and Russia—each of which holds veto power.

parliamentary systems governments with a prime minister as the head of government and either a monarch or president as head of state.

parsimony the principle that simple explanations are preferable to complex explanations when other things are equal.

patronage politics using state funds to pay off private or semi-private political supporters.

peacekeeping the provision of third-party forces from the UN or other regional organizations to help keep peace by providing a buffer between parties in conflict, often along a border or an agreed-upon cease-fire line to monitor and maintain the peace.

pegged exchange rates foreign currency exchange rates that are fixed or "pegged" by government officials against another currency or standard (e.g., gold) rather than freely traded in a market setting.

periphery the economic zone composed of poor countries that primarily export raw materials.

personality traits varying characteristics of individuals, some of which may lead to more aggressive behavior and preferences.

policy entrepreneurs individuals committed to innovative policy change and who voluntarily work to achieve such changes.

poliheuristic theory the idea of decision making as a two step process, first options found unacceptable or impossible are discarded, and then the remaining options are rationally considered.

political sovereignty the principle that a state has authority and independence to rule without interference within its own borders.

populist revolutions grassroots revolts typically against repressive governments, dominated by mass turnouts of the people.

positive peace a situation between two countries that is not simply a lack of conflict, but a mutual affinity for each other.

positive sum a condition in which all parties to an issue can benefit or "win."

power the ability to get what you want.

power transition theory systemic theory holding that wars are most likely when changes in power distributions occur.

preemption the use of military force to strike first when an attack is imminent to blunt the effectiveness of the impending attack.

presidential systems governments with strong presidents as both the head of state and the head of government.

prevention the use of military force to strike first when an attack is inevitable to take advantage of more favorable balance of forces rather than wait for an adversary to gain the advantage from which to strike.

primordialism stresses the fundamental bonds of kinship and identity that establish ethnic differences that divide people and often generate ancient ethnic hatreds.

prisoner's dilemma a situation in which two prisoners must decide whether to collaborate with each other or not.

proletariat the working class that sold its labor for less than its value to the capitalists.

proportional representation a democratic system in which parties or factions get approximately the same percentage of legislative seats as votes they received in the most recent election.

prospect theory the idea that humans are rational but their rationality is situationally biased; that is, they are more risk-averse when things work in their favor and more risk-taking when things aren't going well.

protection (in alliances) an arrangement by a small state to gain help from a larger state.

protectionism a policy of blocking or restricting the trade from other countries in order to "protect" domestic businesses from economic competition with foreign companies.

psychological needs essential emotional and psychological requirements of humans, said to be hierarchical by theorists such as Maslow.

purchasing power parity (PPP) a measure that compares two currencies and adjusts them so that they can be compared in a meaningful way. PPP allows us to compare the purchasing power of the yen in Japan with the peso in Mexico, for example.

R

rational actor model as unitary actors, all states make decisions according to a rational process in which goals are ranked, options identified and evaluated, and selections made to maximize benefits according to the goals of the actor.

realism a major theoretical approach to international relations emphasizing the competitive, conflict-ridden pursuit of power and security among states in world politics.

reciprocity in international law, the principle that a state follows international law so that others will do so in return.

regime change the change of a country's government or type of government.

relative deprivation discrepancy between what people actually have and what they think they deserve based on what others actually have.

relative gains the comparative effect of a decision or situation on an actor relative to those of another actor.

resource curse the curious negative effect for a country's economy when the country has a valuable resource such as oil.

responsibility to protect (R2P) the norm that states have a responsibility to protect their citizens from avoidable harm, and if they cannot or will not do so, the international community has a responsibility to intervene to do so.

responsible sovereignty the idea of sovereignty as a state's responsibility to protect its citizens.

restorative justice a justice that seeks to repair the damage done to victims, allow the victims a voice in the resolution of their grievances, and where possible to reintegrate both victims and the offenders into a more just society.

revolution in military affairs the transformation of weapons, military organizations, and operational concepts for military force that leverages the information and communications revolutions of the latter 20th and early 21st centuries.

S

second-generation human rights (societal rights) material and economic rights that apply society-wide, like the rights to education, employment, shelter, health care, and so on.

security survival and safety, typically referring to the military, intelligence, and law enforcement arenas but also including economic and human dimensions.

security community a group of states bound by shared identities and interests and complex interactions among which security threats are virtually nonexistent.

security dilemma the steps that states take to make themselves secure often result in threats to other states, whose reactions to those threats make the first state less secure; thus, what a state does to gain security can often make it less secure.

selectorate those in a state who provide the power base for a leader.

self-help individual actors are responsible for making themselves secure and protecting their own interests.

self-oriented TANs TANs that advocate values that primarily benefit the network members.

semi-periphery the economic zone composed of middle-income countries that produce secondary products.

semi-presidential systems governments with prime ministers who are responsible for most day-to-day governing but also have presidents who have some significant policy-making roles.

settlement gap the difference between the minimal preferences of two parties to a negotiation.

Six-Day War the 1967 war between Israel, Egypt, Jordan, and Syria. Israel won the war and took control of the occupied territories (the Gaza Strip, West Bank, and Golan Heights).

slash-and-burn agriculture the practice of clearing fields by cutting down and burning existing plant growth to prepare land for new agricultural use each season, common in many developing countries.

smart sanctions sanctions that target specific individuals thought to be responsible for a regime's human rights abuses rather than targeting a state's entire population.

social construction a concept is created by the interactions and ideas within a society.

Social Darwinism the idea of the "survival of the fittest" applied to international politics.

socialism an economic-political system in which the government controls the economy and redistributes wealth to create economic equality in the country.

soft power power based on attraction and persuasion rather than coercion.

sovereign having supreme authority over territory and people.

Sovereign wealth funds investment funds owned by states.

stag hunt a situation in which hunters must decide whether to collaborate with each other or act on their own.

state a political-legal unit that: (1) has an identifiable population, (2) is located within defined borders recognized by others, and (3) has a government with sovereignty.

state of nature a hypothetical condition before the advent of government.

state or national level locating the causes of behavior and outcome in the nature and characteristics of states/nations.

state-sponsored terrorism includes covert and overt repression of and violence against civilian populations, and more extreme acts such as genocide, supported or perpetrated by the state.

stratification unequal distribution of power, influence, and/or other resources.

structural factors historical and environmental factors that influence how a country can develop its economy.

subnational actors those international actors normally seen as subparts of a state, such as individuals or local governmental entities.

subprime loans loans given by banks to private citizens that would be considered to have a high likelihood of default. These loans were made to promote home ownership, but drove up prices and ultimately created an unsustainable economy that collapsed and caused the Great Recession.

subsidies funds given to companies by a government to help them grow.

substate actors groups within a state such as political parties, insurgents, or ethnic groups.

summit meetings diplomatic meetings involving the top officials of their respective states (hence "the summit").

supranational organization an institution, organization, or law that is over other states. For example, the EU is a supranational organization because it has authority over many European states.

supranational regimes international organizations or sets of rules that can bind states even against their will.

sustainable development promoting economic growth without degrading the environment or depleting its non-renewable resources.

systemic or international level locating the causes of behavior and outcomes in the nature and characteristics of the international system.

T

tariff a tax on products imported into one country from other countries.

territorial integrity the principle that other actors should not violate the territory or boundaries of a state.

terrorism indiscriminate violence aimed at noncombatants to influence a wider audience.

theater missile defense the capability to protect a specific or limited geographic area from nuclear attack by shooting down incoming missiles.

theories tools for explaining cause-and-effect relationships among often complex phenomena.

third-generation human rights (group rights) rights needed to protect unpopular or minority groups from the oppression of the majority.

third-party diplomacy the engagement of an outside party in the negotiations between the actual parties to a dispute to facilitate a resolution of the disagreement.

third-party sanction a sanction levied against a third-party state to keep that state from doing business with the primary target of the sanctions.

Thirty Years' War (1618–1648) a series of wars that created many modern European states.

time horizon problem the fact that the worst effects of environmental problems have not yet been seen, but to avoid them one needs to act (and spend money or make sacrifices) now.

track II diplomacy the activities and involvement of private individuals, non-governmental organizations such as civil society organizations, and religious and business leaders in dialogue and negotiation to facilitate conflict resolution.

trade war a situation when many or all states engage in protectionism. The states try to block imports and promote exports, but since all countries do this, very little international trade occurs.

tragedy of the commons the idea that no one state is held responsible for things held in common—so-called collective goods—like the air and water, and so their protection often goes unaddressed.

transnational advocacy networks (TANs) networks defined by reciprocal, voluntary actions across national borders that (1) must include non-state actors (like individuals acting alone, social movements, or non-governmental organizations), (2) may include states or international organizations as well, (3) represent a recurring, cooperative partnership with (4) differentiated roles among the component parts.

Treaties of Westphalia two treaties in 1648 that ended the Thirty Years' War and created the modern international system.

treaty formal, written agreements among states.

Treaty of Versailles the treaty in 1919 that ended World War I, imposed heavy penalties on Germany, and created the League of Nations.

trinitarian war armed conflict in which the roles and participation of government, militaries, and populations are distinct.

tripolar a distribution of power in the international system in which there are three great powers.

Truman Doctrine the policy that the US would help states resisting communist expansion.

Truth and Reconciliation Commission the entity created by the new South African government following the abolition of apartheid. Victims of apartheid were encouraged to tell their stories for the record and for the psychological benefit of being heard while the aggressors were offered amnesty for their crimes in return for full and public disclosure of those crimes.

Tutsi a socially constructed race in central Africa that was supposed to be more elite, wealthier, and taller than their rival group, the Hutus.

UN Convention against Illicit Traffic in Narcotic Drugs and Psychotropic Substances a treaty promoting international cooperation to stop the transnational trafficking in illegal drugs, which went into force in 1990.

UN Convention against Transnational Organized Crime a treaty promoting international cooperation to deal with transnational organized crime, which went into force in 2003.

UN Environment Programme (UNEP) the UN agency dedicated to environmental protection, created in 1972.

UN Framework Convention on Climate Change (FCCC) a 1992 treaty calling for the reduction of fossil fuel emissions to 1990 levels by 2000.

UN General Assembly (UNGA) the plenary body of the UN in which all

UN members have a seat. Functioning on a majority rule decision process, it is the central forum for discussion of global issues.

UN Human Rights Council the body created by the UN General Assembly in 2006 to replace the UN Human Rights Commission in making recommendations regarding human rights issues.

UN Secretariat the bureaucracy and administrative arm of the UN.

UN Secretary-General the head of the UN Secretariat, the UN's administrative leader elected by the UNGA at the recommendation of the UNSC.

UN Security Council Resolution 688 a 1991 resolution authorizing UN members to intervene in the domestic affairs of Iraq.

UN Women the united nations entity for gender equality and the empowerment of Women, created in 2010 with the merger of the Division for the Advancement of Women (DAW), the International Research and Training Institute for the Advancement of Women (INSTRAW), the Office of the Special Adviser on Gender Issues and Advancement of Women (OSAGI), and the United Nations Development Fund for Women (UNIFEM).

unconventional war armed conflict in which civilian and non-military targets are emphasized, forces used include nontraditional forces outside organized militaries, and in which a wide array of weaponry including weapons of mass destruction may be employed.

UNICEF the United Nations Children's Fund; created in 1946 and recipient of the Nobel Peace Prize in 1965.

unipolar a distribution of power in the international system in which there is one great power.

unit veto in international organizations, a decision rule in which some or all members can block decisions with their votes: in a pure unit veto decision rule every member exercises a veto; in a modified unit

veto, only some members have the veto power.

unitary actor the simplified conception of a state as a single entity or actor.

United Fruit Company a U.S. company that owned and controlled vast plantations in Latin America.

United Nations (UN) an international institution established after World War II to promote peace and security, the development of friendly relations and harmony among nations, and cooperation on international problems.

United Nations General Assembly (UNGA) the plenary body of the UN in which all UN members have a seat. Functioning on a majority rule decision process, it is the central forum for discussion of global issues.

United Nations Security Council (UNSC) a 15-member council that carries the primary UN responsibilities for peace, security, and collective security operations.

Universal Declaration of Human Rights (UDHR) a 1948 UN resolution, which provided a comprehensive listing of the rights of all people.

universal jurisdiction the idea that states have a right and a duty to enforce international law when it comes to the most serious human rights abuses such as genocide, crimes against humanity, torture, war crimes, extrajudicial killings, and forced disappearances, regardless of where these offenses may occur or whether or not the alleged violator is from another country.

vertical enforcement the enforcement of international law by international institutions.

Vienna Convention on the Law of Treaties a 1969 agreement among states defining the nature and obligations regarding treaties under international law.

W

war organized, violent (i.e. military) conflict between two or more parties.

war crimes excessive brutality in war, in violation of international treaties or conventions.

war reparations payments from one country—usually the loser of a conflict—to compensate the victor's cost in money, lives, and property.

war weariness states that have most recently experienced a significant, costly war are more peaceful in the aftermath because of the impact of those costs and experiences.

Warsaw Pact the military alliance created by the Soviet Union as a response to the 1955 addition of West Germany into NATO.

Washington Consensus an orthodox liberal approach to development that took hold in the 1980s and was used to try to promote economic growth in poor countries. It had very limited success.

weapons of mass destruction (WMD) nuclear, chemical, and biological weapons.

weighted voting in international organizations, a decision rule in which member votes are weighted according to some factor related to size, power, or wealth.

Westphalian sovereignty the idea that within a state's borders there is no higher authority than the government of the state itself.

winning coalition the half of the voters you must get to win an election.

World Bank a Bretton Woods organization created in 1945 that provides loans and grants to countries for long-term development. The World Bank started by helping fund the reconstruction of Europe after World War II and later focused on helping countries in the developing world grow their economies.

World Economic Forum a forum held in Switzerland every year that brings together wealthy individuals, corporate leaders, industry leaders, and heads of government to coordinate economic policies and initiatives.

World Health Organization (WHO) the UN organization that deals with health issues around the world. It is responsible for the eradication of smallpox.

world politics political, economic, and social activities and interactions among states and a wide variety of non-state actors such as international organizations, non-state national and ethnic groups, transnational corporations, nongovernmental organizations, and individuals.

world systems theory a theory inspired by Marxism that argues the world is divided into three economic zones (by their level of development) and that these zones determine how states interact, with wealthier countries exploiting poorer countries.

World Trade Organization a supranational organization that promotes free trade between member countries, sets the rules for international trade, administers them, and authorizes penalties for states that violate them. The WTO replaced the GATT in 1995.

Z

zero sum a condition in which one party's benefit or gains requires comparable losses by another party.

Zionism the movement to create a Jewish homeland in Palestine.

INDEX

Note: Page references in **bold** refer to photographs, figures, or tables.

Domain of losses, 88
Domestic industries, import substitution industrialization, 290
Domestic violence, 109
Dominican Republic, **339**
Doyle, Michael, 142
Drugs, US war on, 242, **244**, 248
Dues, UN, 208
Dulles, Allen, 98
Dulles, John Foster, 98
Dumas, Alexandre, 167
Dumbarton Oaks Meeting, UN Security Council, 1944, **210**
Durable goods, import substitution industrialization, 290
Dust storms, Africa, **346**
Dynamic, balance of power as, **156**
Dynamics of international relations and liberalism, 72–73
and realism, 67–68

E

Earth Day, 351, 361
Easterly, William, 302
Eastern Europe, effect of fall of Berlin Wall on Africa, 261–262
ECHR (European Court of Human Rights), 330
Economic and Social Council (ECOSOC), UN
    defined, 40
    overview, 40, **205**
    responsibilities of, 204–205
Economic/commercial liberalism, 71
Economic Community of West African States (ECOWAS), 193
Economic crises. *See also* Great Recession of 2008–2010
    global effects of, 4–5
    new stresses on states, 45–46
Economic policy, 71
Economic rights, 307
Economics. *See also* development; Marxism
    approaches to, **230**
    average level of democracy and level of world trade, **238**
    causes of war, 128, 131–133
    colonialism and mercantilism, 215–216
    costs of wars, 140–141
    effect of on women, 109
    globalization, 226–239
    Great Recession of 2008–2010, 237–239
    levels of integration, 235
    liberal capitalism, 227, 229
    liberalism, 216–226
    markets and governments, relationship between, 214–215
    Marxism, 220–221
    modern economy, 226–239
    money, power and security, 213–214
    money as power, 213
    oil as strategic resource, 210
    regional, single-issue IOs, 189
    security communities, 172
Economic sanctions
    costly consequences of, 254–256
    defined, 244
    effect of on women, 109
    examples of, 244–245
    failure of, 252–254
    for human rights violations, 321
    overview, 246

paradox of, 252–254
    purposes of, 250–252
    smart sanctions, 253–254, 321–322
    total sanctions, 250
    types of, 246–250
Economic security
    concerns regarding, 398
    defined, 8, **9**
    as part of human security, 316
    responsible sovereignty, 47
Economic security-oriented TANs, 381–383
Economic statecraft
    defined, 243
    economic sanctions, 246–256
    foreign aid, 256–269
    history of, 245–246
    overview, 243–245
    US certification of Mexico, 242
Economic stresses on states, 45–46
Economic systems, 100
Economic theory, 56
Economic warfare, 250
Economic zones, in world systems theory, 99–101, **288**, 288–290
ECOSOC. *See* Economic and Social Council (ECOSOC), UN
Ecosystem, defined, 350
Ecosystem management, by UNEP, 354–356
ECOWAS (Economic Community of West African States), 193
ECSC (European Coal and Steel Community), 194–195, 214
Ecuador, development in, 272
Education
    and democracy, 295–296
    HDI, 278–279, **279**
EEC (European Economic Community), 195
Efficiencies, in Washington Consensus, 292
Egypt
    Aswan High Dam, **358**, 358
    democracy demonstration in, **267**
    foreign aid during Cold War, 260
    military aid in, 265–266
    nationalization in, 286–287
Eisenhower, Dwight, 88
Electricity, alternative sources of, 361
Embargo
    arms, 251, 254
    on Cuba, 244
Embassies, 23, 24, 25, 27
Emissions, fossil fuel, 349–350, 352–354, 355–356, 361
Emissions Trading Scheme, UK, 350
Empirical evidence, testing theory against, 58–59
Empirical theory, 57
Empowerment and Rights Institute, **332**
Empowerment of states, Westphalian system, 36–38
EMS (European Monetary System), 195
EMU (European Monetary Union), 195
The End of History and the Last Man (Fukuyama), 239
The End of Poverty (Sachs), 302
Energy, sustainable, 360–361, 381–383, **383**
Enforcement of human rights standards
    international organization-based initiatives, 323–331
    NGO-based initiatives, 331–333
    overview, 316
    state-based initiatives, 316–323

Enforcement of international law
    horizontal enforcement, 183–184
    national enforcement, 183
    overview, 182–183
    vertical enforcement, 186
Engels, Friedrich, 93–95, **94**, 99
Entrepreneurs, policy, 368
Environment Programme, UN (UNEP), 352, 354–356
Environmental challenges
    biodiversity, 345–347
    collective goods problem, 338–347
    deforestation, 339–341
    desertification, 341
    facing, 361
    fundamental challenges of world politics, 394, 395
    global climate change, 341–345
    international organization actions, 352–356
    overview, 337
    pollution, 338–339
    public and non-governmental organization actions, 350–352
    state actions, 348–350
    sustainable development, 356–361
    tragedy of commons, 337–347
Environmental costs of wars, 140
Environmental governance goals, UNEP, 356
Environmental Performance Index, Yale University, 350
Environmental regime, evolving, 347–356
Environmental security, 316
Environmental security-oriented TANs, 386
Environmental sustainability rapid urbanization and, 362
EP (European Parliament), 195–197, **199**
Epistemic communities, 28
Equilibrium, balance of power as, **156**
Ethnic cleansing
    benefits of globalization, 232–233
    in Bosnia-Herzegovina, 47
    defined, 47
Ethnic conflict, as cause of civil war, 136–137, 140
Ethnic geography
    and civil war in former Yugoslavia, **138**, 138–140, **139**
    defined, 136
Ethnic groups, Afghanistan, 31, 31–32
Ethnicity
    as cause of war, 128
    group rights, 308
Ethology, 134
EU. *See* European Union (EU)
Eurasia, terrorism in, 121
Eurasian Union, Russia and, 75
Europe. *See also* European Union (EU); *specific countries by name*
    agriculture and development of, 282
    clean air in, 348
    colonialism, 219, 283
    economics in, 227
    Great Recession of 2008–2010, 237, 293
    International Criminal Court, creation of, 324
    nationalism in, 38

natural gas supply from Russia, **244**, 245, **245**, 248, 255
    ocean currents, changes in, 339, 344–345
    in realist vs. liberalist perspectives, 72–73
    terrorism in, 121
    Thirty Years' War, 22–23
European Coal and Steel Community (ECSC), 194–195, 214
European Commission, 195, **198**
European Commission on Human Rights, 315
European Congress of Vienna (1814–1815), 27
European Convention on Human Rights, 315
European Council, 195
European Court of Human Rights (ECHR), 330
European Court of Justice, 198
European Economic Community (EEC), 195
European Environment Agency, 193
European Monetary System (EMS), 195
European Monetary Union (EMU), 195
European Parliament (EP), 195–197, **197**
European Union (EU)
    ban on hormone-fed beef, 227, 236
    contributions and challenges, 198
    defined, 48
    development of, 195
    economic sanctions by, 251
    founder of, Robert Schuman, **194**
    globalization as non-democratic, 235–236
    Great Recession of 2008–2010, 237
    hesitation to place severe sanctions on Russia, 255–256
    in liberalist perspective, 71
    major parts and functions of, **198**
    members of, **189**
    as the most powerful regional organization, 194–198
    origins and foundations of, 194–195
    in realist vs. liberalist perspectives, 72–73
    as regional, multiple-issue organization, 189
    sanctions against Belarus by, 321
    security communities, 172
    structure and operations, 195–198
    "United States of Europe", 198
    US role in economic problems of, 402
Euroskeptics, 198
Eurozone, 46, 235, 237
Evolution
    of war, 123–127
    of Westphalian system, 35–39
Exchange rates, 191, 225, 296
Expert bodies, UN, **205**
Explanation, in theory, 58
Export-led growth, 290–291
Export sanctions, 247–248
Expropriation, 286
Extended deterrence, 157
External balancing, 156
External pressures on states, 46
Extra-systemic or extra-state war, 114, **126**
Extraterritoriality, 23
Extreme poverty, 275

Offices, UN, **201**, **203**, 203–204
Offshore banks, 249–250
Oil
  alternative energy sources, 360
  burning oil wells in Iraq in 2003,
    213
  dependency theory, 98
  economic sanctions, 247–248
  peak, 402
  power of, **247**
  resource curse, 281–283
  states producing as in periphery,
    289
  as strategic resource, 210
"Oil for Food Programme," UN, 253
On War (von Clausewitz), 127
Operational code analysis, 87
Opinio juris, 181
Oppression, group rights and,
    307–308
Opting out of globalization, 236
Oregon Institute of Science and
    Medicine, 342
Organization for Economic
    Cooperation and Development
    (OECD), 256
Organization for Security and
    Cooperation in Europe, 165
Organization of African States, 315
Organization of African Unity
    (OAU), 193
Organization of American States
    (OAS), 194, 265, 315, 329
Organizational/bureaucratic politics
    model, 90
Organizational cooperation, **91**
Organized crime TANs, 375–376
Organs, trafficking in human, 377,
    377
Orthodox liberal, 291
Osirak nuclear reactor, Iraq, 159
Other-oriented TANs
  defined, 378
  economic security–oriented,
    381–383
  environmental security–oriented,
    386
  health security–oriented, 383–384
  human security-oriented, 378–381
  overview, 378
Outer Space treaty, 165
Ownership laws, 214

P

P-5, defined, 191
Pacific, terrorism in, 121
Pacta sunt servanda, 181
Pakistan, 21–22, **22**
Palestine
  competing nationalisms in, 30
  creation of Jewish home-land
    in, 366
  preemption by Israel in Six- Day
    War, **161**, 159–162
Palestine Liberation Organization
    (PLO), 377
Panama, economic sanctions in, 254
Parade, Chinese military, **64**
Parliamentary systems, 23
Parsimony, 59
Partial Test Ban Treaty, 167
Partly free states, **35**
Pashtunistan, **32**
Pashtuns, in Afghanistan, 31–32
Pathfinder International, 333
The Patriot (film), 123, **124**
Patronage politics, 281

Patterns
  of wars, 129–140
  of world politics, 12–13
PD. *See* prisoner's dilemma (PD)
Peace. *See also* cooperation;
    democratic peace
  benefits of globalization, 232–233
  capitalist, 173
  challenges to, 178–179
  diplomacy, 178–186
  in Europe after 1945, 81
  international law, 179–180
  international organizations,
    187–209
  international trade and, 222
  in liberalist perspective, 68
  negative, 78
  new world order, 176
  overview, 177–178
  by pieces, 214
  positive, 78, 214
  and wealth, **104–105**, 104–105
Peacebuilding Missions, UN, 2014,
    170, **171**
Peaceful use of force, 158
Peacekeeping
  defined, 169
  in Democratic Republic of
    Congo, 314, 329
  hard power, 329
  by UN, 169–170, **169**, **170**,
    170–171, **171**
  by US, as form of military aid, 265
Peace Research Institute of Oslo
    (PRIO), 116
Peak oil, 402
Pearl Harbor attack, 246
Pegged exchange rates, 296
Penalties for human rights violations,
    321
Peoples' rights, 315
Perceptions of rich and poor, 273–275
Periphery
  defined, 100
  states belonging to, **100**
  in world systems theory, 100, **288**,
    288–289
Permanent members, UN Security
    Council, 40, 191, **191**
Perpetual Peace (Kant), 68
Perry, Rick, **375**
Persad-Bissessar, Kamla, **106**, 109
Personal diplomacy, 27
Personal security, 316
Personal security-oriented TANs,
    378–381
Personality traits, as causes of war,
    134
Peters projection of world, **7**
Petroleum. *See* oil
Pharmaceutical drugs, and deforesta-
    tion, 341
Philosophy, political, 57
Physical attributes, as cause of war,
    133
Pinochet, Augusto, 182, **182**, 287
Pirates, Somali, **178**
Plato, 246
Platoon (film), 123
PLO (Palestine Liberation Organiza-
    tion), 377
Poland, security and geography,
    150, **151**
Polar ice caps, melting of, 344–345,
    345
Polar projection map, **7**
Policies
  and foreign aid, 260, 262
  influence of theory on, 72–73

Policy entrepreneurs, 368
Poliheuristic theory, 88
Poliomyelitis (polio), 364, **365**, 372
Political costs of wars, 140–141
Political instability as cause of war,
    133
Political liberalism, 71
Political maps of the world, 6
Political Missions, UN, 2014, **170**,
    171
Political philosophy, 57
Political pressures on states, 46
Political rights, 306–307
Political security, 316
Political sovereignty, 146
Political Survival (Bueno de
    Mesquita), 92
Politically based foreign aid, 320
Politics Among Nations
    (Morgenthau), 61
Pollution, 14, 338–339, **340**, 348
Pol Pot, 221
Poorest states, **34**
Pope Francis, 373
Pope John Paul II, **43**
Popularization of ideas by TANs,
    368–370
Population
  and access to water, 357
  countries of the world, sized by,
    276
  pressures, as cause of war, 133
Populist politics, and development,
    294
Populist revolutions, 18, 319–320
Positive peace, 78, 214
Positive-sum condition, 73, 147
Potential sources of power, 66
Poverty. *See also* development
  definitions of, 278
  example of, **273**
  reduction of as goal of develop-
    ment aid, 257–259
  and violence, **104–105**, 104–105
Poverty line, 278
Power
  application of, **66**, 66–67
  challenge of international security,
    146–147
  competing conceptions of, **72**
  defined, 64
  distribution of, 67, **130**, 130,
    146–147
  explanations for existence of
    international organizations,
    187–188
  geography and, 65
  hard, 71–72, 328–331
  in liberalist perspective, 70–72
  military, and world politics,
    64, **64**
  money, and security, 213–214
  money as, 213
  in realist perspective, 61–63,
    63–64, 65, 66–67
  soft, 71–72, 323–328
  sources of, **66**, 66
Power and Interdependence
    (Keohane and Nye), 69
Power transition theory, 130
PPP (purchasing power parity),
    277–278
Predation, as cause of war, 128
Prediction, in theory, 58
Preemption, 159–162
Prescription, in theory, 58–59
Presidential systems, 23
Prevention, realist approaches to,
    159–162

Pre-Westphalian international
    system, 22–23, **50**
Prices, food, 359–360
Prime ministers, 23
Primitive communism, 220
Primordialism, 136
Prince Harry, **370**, 370
Princess Diana, 102, **368**, 369–370
PRIO (Peace Research Institute of
    Oslo), 116
Prisoner's dilemma (PD)
  defined, 13
  implications of, 14–16
  overcoming, 15–16
  overview, 13, **14**
  security dilemma between India
    and Pakistan, 21
Private sector, in Washington
    Consensus, 292
Problem-based explanations for
    existence of international
    organizations, 187–188
Procommunist bloc, Cold War, 38
Professional diplomats, 23, 25, 27
Professionalism of Egyptian military,
    265
Programmes, UN, **202**
Proletariat, 94
Proliferation
  horizontal proliferation control,
    165–166
  limitation of as purpose of eco-
    nomic sanctions, 251
  nuclear, 160–161
Promotion of democracy. *See* democ-
    racy promotion
Property ownership laws, 214
Property rights, 306
Proportional representation, 91
Prosecution of violators of interna-
    tional law, 182, **182**
Prospect theory, 88
Protection dynamics, 154
Protectionism, 215–216
Protestants, in Northern Ireland, 78
Psychological needs, as causes of
    war, 134
Public admonishments, 321
Public goods, 215. *See also* collective
    goods
Public organization actions, environ-
    mental, 350–352
Punishments, state-based human
    rights initiatives, 321–322
Purchasing power parity (PPP),
    277–278
Pure unit veto, 190, 193
Putin, Vladimir, 11, **27**, **46**, **75**, 75,
    79, 86, 256

Q

Qatar, 278, **279**
Qualitative limitations, arms control,
    165
Quality control, and free trade, 218
Quality of life. *See* human security
Qualitative limitations, arms control,
    165
Quantitative limitations, arms
    control, 165

R

R2P (responsibility to protect), 310,
    316, 333
Race, social construction of in
    Rwanda, 78–79

GUIDE TO RESEARCH
and Writing in International Relations

Writing an excellent research paper is a challenging task. In order to communicate your research effectively, you must demonstrate an understanding of concepts relevant to your topic. Your paper also must reveal consistency within paragraphs and smooth transitions from paragraph to paragraph with clear organization. Moreover, you must be careful with grammar, spelling, and punctuation. In addition, a superior research paper contributes to the literature by advancing our knowledge on a topic. When you think of the attributes required in an excellent research paper, you might find yourself overwhelmed and confused. You might not know where to start the project or how to advance it. In this section, we will provide you smaller steps that can help you reach the goal of writing a research paper. We will break it up into two different parts: important questions and process. The "important questions" section is self-descriptive. It lists crucial questions you need to focus on at various stages of your project. The "process" section outlines smaller steps you can follow as you write your research paper. Note that these are general guidelines. Your instructor might ask you to tailor your research in a way that is different from what's suggested here. Please remember to use your instructor's guidelines for your research paper. Finally, three worksheets are provided at the end. You can use these worksheets to facilitate the writing process.

IMPORTANT QUESTIONS

The following questions highlight the common components of most research papers: a title page, an introduction with a research question, review of the literature, central hypothesis, and result(s). You might not have clear answers to all of these in the early stages of your research, and that is fine. It is always a good idea to take notes on your answers as you progress. Your tentative answers will guide you when you write your first draft. Worksheet #1, at the end of this section, aims to help you organize your answers. As you find answers of the questions, you can fill in the boxes provided in the worksheet. You don't need to wait until you have the perfect answer. Let your ideas run freely and take notes as you develop thoughts on how to answer these questions.

1. What are the components of your research paper that need to be reflected in the title?
2. What is your research question?
3. Did you identify the prominent scholarly works on your topic? What are their findings? Can you summarize the evidence presented? Where does your research stand in this literature?
4. Based on the literature you reviewed, what is your explanation to your research question? Construct your explanation as an empirically testable statement.
5. What kind of evidence and/or data sources are you planning to use? Why?
6. What kind of analysis are you planning to conduct? Why?
7. What are your results? Why should we care about your findings? (Remember, you need to assign meaning to your results. Think about the implications of your results considering the literature you reviewed.)
8. How does your paper contribute to the related literature? (Describe the overall contribution of your paper. Essentially, answer the question: What did the reader learn from your paper?)

PROCESS

Now you know you need to answer many questions as you write your research paper. However, the biggest question is: where do you start? More importantly, what are the smaller steps you need to follow in order to finish this project? There is no single path to an excellent research paper. Eventually, you will personalize the process. In this section, we outline a route that you can use as you perfect your own version. Please note that steps outlined here are not in a strict order. For instance, as you read various books and articles (step 4), you will develop your research question and your tentative hypothesis (step 5). You will have moments in which you will feel stuck. Although not mentioned in the steps, that is part of the process as well. When you have difficulties, identify the problem and ask guidance from your instructor. Sometimes letting your paper sit for a day or two and getting back to work with a fresh perspective can be helpful.

Step 1: Understand the Project and Your Responsibilities

Do not wait to learn what you need to do! A common pitfall is ignoring crucial guidelines in the early stages of the project. Read the syllabus, information sheets, and guidelines provided to you by your instructor as soon as you have them. Listen to your instructor's explanations very carefully. Ask questions! For instance, are there any specific instructions on how to cite the sources? Is there a page limit? Are there any restrictions on the topics that you can choose?

Step 2: Targeted Completion Date

Another common pitfall is assuming it is too early to plan a targeted completion date at the beginning of the semester. Remember that you will get busy soon. So one of the best things you can do is plan ahead. Insert due dates of all of your assignments into your calendar in the first week of classes. Be realistic about what you can accomplish in a day. Factor in all of your responsibilities as you work on your calendar. Give yourself a cushion, and schedule completion dates before the due dates of the project. Especially for writing assignments like research papers, target a completion date one week before the due date of the assignment. More importantly, follow through on your plan.

Step 3: Select a Topic

Your instructor might have specific guidelines regarding the topic you need to choose. Using the guidelines provided, think of topics that interest you. Make a list. You might not know the proper terminology, or you might not be able to put into words exactly what you would like to do. That is fine. Describe your topics of interests in your own words. Remember, you are writing this paper to learn more about the subject matter. So it is okay not to know everything. The key point is to select a topic that is engaging for you. Consider setting up a meeting with your instructor to share your ideas and get feedback.

Maybe this is your first IR course. Still, your past experiences can guide your research. For instance, maybe you have taken a history course before. As frequently highlighted in this book, the historical context of IR is quite crucial in understanding security concerns of states and their approach to international security. Perhaps, for example, you have studied abroad in China and when you were there you wrote a paper on China's economic growth. That experience might be priceless if your research paper is on different economic policy approaches to development. So think about your past learning experiences and how you can utilize them in your research project. These experiences are particularly helpful at this stage.

Step 4: Start Your Research

Your school library is the best starting point for your research. Set up an appointment with a librarian. Learn what kinds of resources are available for your project. It is important to have a clear idea about your research topic prior to your appointment. You will need both scholarly studies on your topic and data sources that you can utilize in your analysis. Note that some of the scholarly work might be hard to understand. Even if you think you are not following the piece, do not give up. You can still benefit from it. Also, finding right sources is crucial for your research. You might ask your instructor if she has any recommendations. You might also want to get feedback regarding the scholarly work you collected thus far. Keep in mind, a related source will guide you towards other related sources through its bibliography.

As you read various books and articles, and in some cases as you watch documentaries and films, you need to think about how you will use them. If you delay taking notes on your ideas, you might not remember them later. Organize your thoughts and ideas. One of the ways of organizing your thoughts as you do your research is developing an Excel file with two worksheets (so that you'll see two distinct tabs at the bottom of your Excel file when it's open). The first worksheet can be on literature review, and the second worksheet can be on ideas that can be utilized in different sections of the paper. When you read a piece that you can use in your literature review, note the source with full citation in the first column (labeled "Source") in your *Literature Review* worksheet, then enter how you will use that piece in the next column (labeled "Use of Source"), and finally copy information specifics such as page number to the third column (labeled "Further Information"). Sometimes a piece that you read might help you develop an idea that you can benefit from. In the second *Idea* worksheet of your Excel file, insert your ideas in detail in the first column (labeled "Ideas") as you read a piece. Remember that a very clear idea might get fuzzy very fast if you don't write it down. Take detailed notes. In the second column (labeled "Related Citations"), insert information regarding the piece that inspired you. You may also note the citations that this source relied upon as you construct your references and build a list for additional research. Remember to cite everything properly in your research paper. As you develop your Excel file, write clearly and consistently.

Also, you can develop your bibliography as you read. Your library might have online tools or applications that enable developing a bibliography as you read pieces. Ask your librarian about research tools available for you.

Step 5: Develop a Research Question and Tentative Hypothesis

Once you finalize your topic, you need to think about your research question and hypothesis. Narrowing down your research question and your hypothesis are crucial decisions. Your research question must be important and worth asking. In your paper, you need to convince the reader that your research question matters. Sharp research questions typically follow something like the following model:

Source	Use of Source	Further Information
Jerel A. Rosati and James M. Scott, *The Politics of United States Foreign Policy*, 5th ed. (New York: Wadsworth/Cengage, 2012).	Literature review, part on realist explanation of war.	On pages 23-34 there is a list of realist explanations of war. Also, check out books cited on pages 25 & 28.

◄ ► ►│ **Literature Review** ╱ Ideas ╱ ◌╮

Ideas	Related Citations
I can adopt the theoretical framework used in this piece in my research paper.	Ralph G. Carter and James M. Scott, "Hitting the Reset Button: Changing the Direction of U.S.-Russian Relations?" in *Contemporary Cases in U.S. Foreign Policy: From Terrorism to Trade*, ed. Ralph G. Carter, 4th ed. (Washington, DC: CQ Press, 2011). Also check the following, cited in Carter/Scott, for the same theoretical framework: A. Cooper Drury, Jonathan Krieckhaus, and Michael Lusztig, "Corruption, Democracy, and Economic Growth," *International Political Science Review* 27, no. 2 (2006): 121–36.

◄ ► ►│ Literature Review ╱ **Ideas** ╱ ◌╮

What is the impact of A on B?

Requirements:

1. *Clarity.* Specific enough to provide direction
2. *Testability.* Can be answered by empirical investigation
3. *Theoretical significance.* Adds to a more general understanding of patterns, concepts, and theories
4. *Practical relevance.* Has significant real-world implications
5. *Originality.* Forges new ground, a new synthesis, and/or explores a new puzzle

You will also need to develop a hypothesis that tests your explanation to your research question.

Step 6: Organize Your Research

The following are general research paper organization guidelines. Consider this section as recommendations rather than rules. As mentioned previously, make sure to follow your instructor's guidelines when you organize your paper. You can use worksheet #2 to organize your paper.

- **Introduction:** The main goal of an introduction is to provide a brief summary of your paper. In this section, you should introduce your topic and provide highlights of your paper. Make sure to include the aim of your research, your research question, your hypothesis, a brief summary of your findings, and your contribution to the literature. Remember that a goal of a research paper is not to surprise the reader. Imagine yourself searching for books and articles on a particular topic. To decide whether a particular source is helpful for you, you probably read abstracts and introductions first. The introduction you write should resemble the introductions you read in journal articles. It should be a true reflection of your research paper. So make sure your introduction is informative and brief.

- **Literature Review:** You will review scholarly research on your research topic in this part. One of the common pitfalls to avoid is providing a summary of the previous scholarly work without integrating different pieces of the literature. In this section you are expected to explain how major pieces in this literature speak to each other; think in terms of their shared themes. If you just summarize them individually, you will provide little pieces of the puzzle without explaining how they come together. Pick a title that reflects the substance of the literature you reviewed. For instance, if you are reviewing the literature that examines the relationship between democracy and economic growth, your title may be "Economic Growth and Regime Type." In this section you are expected to identify prominent scholars and previous studies that shed light on your research field. What kinds of research questions do they ask? What are their findings? Are their findings consistent with each other? What are the major debates in this literature? How has the literature evolved over the years? What are the gaps? Will your research address those gaps? If yes, how will you do that? You will also need to situate your research in this larger scholarly picture. Among the studies you have listed, where does your research stand? How will you answer your research question? How does the literature you outlined guide your explanation?

- **Hypothesis:** Your paper should have a hypothesis that states your main explanation to the research question stated. State your hypothesis very clearly. Make sure your hypothesis is empirically testable. Remember to get feedback from your instructor regarding your hypothesis.

- **Research Design, Methods, and Data:** In this section you will summarize your data sources and describe your variables and methodology. This section must read like a clear guide. For example, if another researcher would like to replicate your research, using this section he should be able to follow your footsteps in regard to your data and variable selection, as well as research methods you employed. Make sure in this section you answer the following questions: What are your data sources? Why did you decide to use these data sources? (For example, were there alternatives? If yes, why did you pick the one you used, but not the others?) What are your variables? What do they measure? Are there any issues you would like to address? What kind of analysis are you using? Why did you choose that particular method? In some cases, you might need to collect data, as well. If you have collected data, you need to explain the coding procedures and sources in this section.

- **Results:** In this section you are presenting your results. Present the information in a clear manner. Depending on the type of analysis you conducted, you might want to use tables and figures in this section. Make sure you answer the following questions in this section: What are your results? How will you display your results?

- **Analysis:** In this section you present the analysis of your findings. Provide a discussion regarding your results. Also, you need to assign meaning to your results. In light of the previous research, what do your findings indicate? In a way you need to situate your results in the larger picture. Are there any significant implications of your results? In some cases, results might not support your explanation. In that case, you should provide an explanation. Please note that it is fine to have results that fail to support your explanation.

- **Conclusion:** Your conclusion should summarize highlights of your paper. You also need to specify your contribution to the literature. Does your paper improve our understanding of the research topic you picked? You may also be expected to list your ideas about the direction of the future research on your topic. In other words, you need to answer the question: Where do we go from here?

Step 7: Write Your First Draft

Starting to write your first draft might be intimidating. Remember that first drafts are never perfect. So your goal is not producing the final version of your paper. Create titles of each section (introduction, a title reflecting your literature review, hypothesis section, etc.). Do not start writing with the introduction since your introduction will be shaped by the content of your paper. Gather all your notes, your Excel file that summarizes your research, everything you read and found helpful. Using your sources, develop paragraphs. Transitions from paragraph to paragraph might be weak at this stage. Fix the problematic parts as much as you can. You can improve the rest in the next revision. At this stage, your consistency within paragraphs is more important than transitions.

Step 8: Ask for Feedback

Have your instructor, a teaching assistant, or a friend review your first draft. You might also verbally summarize your research and ask for feedback that way. If you have a clear research design, you should be able to explain it to someone who is not familiar with the subject in just a few sentences. In order to benefit from the feedback, you need to be able to take criticism. Welcome and appreciate the feedback you receive. Follow your instructor's guidelines. Sometimes your instructor might ask you not to seek feedback from your classmates.

Step 9: Revise Your First Draft

Revision based on the feedback you receive is crucial. It is also important to be able to reread your first draft with fresh eyes. If you let your paper sit a day or two (the number of days you wait depends on your schedule), you might be able to see issues and problems better.

When you revise your paper, you need to get rid of all excess baggage by cutting unnecessary parts. Look for inconsistencies and gaps of logic. Make sure transitions from paragraph to paragraph are clear and that text flows well. After reading each paragraph, take a moment to look back to make sure you revised it properly. You should be able to read only the first sentence of each paragraph and still follow the paper. Can you do that?

At this stage, you should deal with all the problems and weaknesses of your paper.

A revision checklist is provided for you in worksheet #3.

Step 10: Final Review

As you read your paper for the last time, look for unnecessary sentences or paragraphs, eliminate redundancies, and make sure sources are cited properly. Check spelling, grammar, and punctuation. Read it out loud to pay attention to details.

GUIDE TO RESEARCH
and Writing in International Relations

WORKSHEET #1

You need to answer these questions in the process of writing your research paper. While you should develop clear answers to some of the questions prior to writing your first draft, answers to some may be gathered throughout the writing process. This worksheet aims to organize your thoughts as you develop answers.

	Your Notes/Answers
Title (What are the components of your research paper that need to be reflected in the title?)	
Research Question (What is your research question?)	
Scholarly work (Identify the prominent scholarly works on your topic and their findings. Can you summarize the evidence presented? Where does your research stand in this literature?)	
Your explanation of the research question stated (What is your explanation to your research question? Construct your explanation as an empirically testable statement.)	
Type of data (What kind of data sources are you planning to use? Why?)	
Type of analysis (What kind of analysis are you planning to conduct? Why?)	
Your results (What are your results? Provide interpretation.)	
Overall contribution (How does your paper contribute to the related literature?)	

WORKSHEET #2

You can use this worksheet as a checklist and to take notes on each section of the paper.

	Your Notes
Introduction (brief summary of your paper's highlights. Include your research question, your hypothesis, and brief summary of results)	
Literature review (review scholarly research on your topic, identify important scholars and pieces in the research area, identify gaps in the literature, situate your own work, state your explanation to your research question)	
Hypothesis (state your hypothesis)	
Research design, methods, and data (data sources, variables used, type of analysis)	
Results (write your results; consider using tables, figures, etc.)	
Analysis (assign meaning to your results, factor in results of previous research as you assign meanings, write implications of your findings)	
Conclusion (reiterate highlights of the paper, add your contribution to the literature and your ideas about future research)	

WORKSHEET #3

Revision checklist: Use this checklist to revise your paper.

- _____ Utilize the feedback you have received.
- _____ Make sure the following are clearly stated in your paper:
  - ____ topic
  - ____ research question
  - ____ hypothesis
  - ____ data sources
  - ____ type of analysis used
  - ____ results
- _____ Get rid of excess baggage. Cut redundant, unnecessary sentences and paragraphs.
- _____ Check citations and references to ensure that all references are present and that their citations are formatted consistently.
- _____ Make sure there are enough details and content.
  - ____ Reflect a clear understanding of the literature.
  - ____ Paper must flow logically. Are you consistent throughout the text? Are you providing plenty of examples, facts, and figures to make your point? Are transitions from paragraph to paragraph clear?
- _____ Check for spelling and grammar mistakes.
- _____ Check punctuation.
- _____ If your university or college has a writing center, you can use the resources of the center. Sometimes instructors might have policies on use of writing centers. Make sure to check this with your instructor.
- _____ Go over your instructor's guidelines one more time.

KEY CONCEPTS

1-1

Summarize the complex arena of world politics. The study of world politics involves more than the political relationships between the countries of the world. It also includes the activities and interactions—political, economic, and social—among states and a wide variety of non-state actors such as international organizations, non-state national and ethnic groups, transnational corporations, non-governmental organizations, and individuals. The range of issues extends across conflict to cooperation, and from basic security issues to quality of life concerns, so identifying the patterns and forces at work and explaining their causes and consequences is difficult. What happens in world politics has real-life consequences for ordinary citizens everywhere, so understanding and explaining the patterns and forces at work in world politics is increasingly important.

1-2

Identify the nature and challenges of security—international, economic, and human—in international relations. In world politics, security involves three arenas or dimensions:

- National and international security, which involves issues related to national defense, conflict and war, and arms control and disarmament;

- Economic security, which involves the pursuit of wealth and prosperity by countries, corporations, and others;

- Human security, which concerns the quality of life that people experience and includes issues such as human rights and the global environment.

As the players in world politics seek security in these three arenas, they grapple with three fundamental challenges:

- Anarchy, which is the absence of a central, authoritative government over the players of world politics, both states and non-states;

- Diversity, which is the myriad of differences among the players of world politics;

- Complexity, the multidimensional issues, players, connections, and interactions of world politics.

1-3

Define the levels of analysis in the study of international relations. Levels of analysis help us comprehend the interactions, causes, and consequences of world politics. The broadest of these levels is the systemic or international level, where attention is directed to the structural characteristics of the international system itself—including anarchy, the distribution of power, interdependence, globalization, and others—and their impact on the broad

KEY TERMS

anarchy the absence of central government in world politics.

collective action problem a condition in which the uncoordinated actions of individuals lead to less than optimal outcomes because, although many individuals would benefit from some cooperative action or actions, few incentives lead any particular individuals to assume the costs of such actions.

commitment problem countries have a hard time committing to cooperative courses of action that assure their partners that they will keep their end of the deal for mutual benefit and forego the possibility of their own short-term gains.

complexity the multidimensional issues, actors, and connections that characterize international relations.

diversity variation in values, norms, identities, goals, and other political, economic, and cultural factors in world politics.

individual level locating the causes of behavior and outcomes in the nature and characteristics of people.

levels of analysis different perspectives from which international relations may be examined.

norms commonly held standards of acceptable and unacceptable behavior.

prisoner's dilemma a situation in which two prisoners must decide whether to collaborate with each other or not.

security survival and safety, typically referring to the military, intelligence, and law enforcement arenas but also including economic and human dimensions.

stag hunt a situation in which hunters must decide whether to collaborate with each other or act on their own.

CHAPTER REVIEW 1

state or national level locating the causes of behavior and outcome in the nature and characteristics of states/nations.

systemic or international level locating the causes of behavior and outcomes in the nature and characteristics of the international system.

theories tools for explaining cause-and-effect relationships among often complex phenomena.

world politics political, economic, and social activities and interactions among states and a wide variety of non-state actors such as international organizations, non-state national and ethnic groups, transnational corporations, nongovernmental organizations, and individuals.

patterns and interactions among the players of world politics. The state or national level directs attention to the states—or units—themselves, and their attributes, such as the type and processes of government or the economy, culture, ethnic groups, or other state or national attributes, and how these factors shape the goals, behavior, and interactions of the players. The individual level directs attention to people—policymakers, business CEOs, and other influential persons—and how their personalities, perceptions, and preferences affect policy and interactions.

1-4

Describe the challenges of cooperation among the actors of international relations. It would make sense for countries to cooperate in order to control the costly acquisition or dangerous spread of weapons, but often they do not, even when cooperating would be in their mutual best interest. Attempts at mutually beneficial collaboration to promote economic growth and development and to protect the environment are frequent, but these attempts also frequently fail.

1-5

Assess the dilemmas of cooperation illustrated by the prisoner's dilemma and stag hunt scenarios. Stories of the prisoner's dilemma and the stag hunt highlight the tension between pursuing self-interest and broader collective interests. They also suggest that the conditions of the "game" provide incentives for the players to see things through the lens of self-interest rather than more broadly. In the prisoner's dilemma, it is logical for the suspects to confess, even though they each could derive greater mutual benefits for cooperation. By confessing, they give up the "best" mutual outcome, but they avoid the worst outcome—being held solely responsible and serving a long jail term. The opposite is true in the stag hunt, where it may be easier to cooperate and bring down the stag rather than grab a rabbit, but fear of betrayal by others can lead to individual pursuit of the rabbit anyway.

Table 1-1 on page 12 summarizes three levels of analysis and identifies some explanations at those levels. The last column applies some very simple explanations at each level of analysis to the case of the 2003 Iraq War. Identify another example of a world politics problem or issue. Referring to Table 1-1, give some simple explanations of this problem or issue at the system, state, and individual levels of analysis.

The Pursuit of Security in Three Arenas

International Security

National defense, conflict and war, and arms control/disarmament

Human Security

Human rights, environmental sustainability, quality of life

Economic Security

Pursuit of wealth and prosperity

© Cengage Learning®

KEY CONCEPTS

2-1

Summarize how the search for security has evolved in a changing international system. The formal anarchy of the international system means that there are no authoritative bodies above the players themselves. In such circumstances, some international actors behave as if the only law is survival of the fittest. In an anarchic system, self-help is the norm, as states must depend on themselves to provide for their own security and protect their own interests. The consequence is a security dilemma, in which the things that states do to make themselves secure often threaten—or at least appear to threaten—the security of other states. However, there are other features of the international system that help to create order and cooperation among the actors and their actions. One of these characteristics is interdependence among actors, the mutual connections that tie states and other players to each other. Others include common goals and/or values, shared norms and rules, and common problems to be solved. These features can lead to greater cooperation among the players, as well as the establishment of international organizations whose members are the sovereign states of the anarchic system. These organizations, such as the United Nations, the World Bank, the International Monetary Fund, and many others provide forums for members to work together to solve common problems.

2-2

List the major types of actors and relationships of the pre-Westphalian international system. The pre-Westphalian world was dominated by feudalism, a socio-economic and political system in which rulers would grant land to the local aristocracy in return for their loyalty and support. In return for the landowners meeting their material needs, peasants would work the land. The monarchies were weak, and thus the major actors were non-state actors—like the Catholic Church and local elites. As monarchs became stronger, the territories they could control grew larger and better integrated, becoming the basis of modern states—and modern state rivalries. The Thirty Years' War (1618–1648) marked a major transition. When the wars finally ended with the Treaties of Westphalia, a new international system emerged based on sovereign states and the principle of nonintervention into their domestic affairs. The power of the church was reduced and, within a state's borders, the religion of both the people and their ruler was its own business, not the business of outsiders. Thus, the modern state system—and the Westphalian era—was born.

KEY TERMS

- **al-Qaeda**
- **authoritarian systems**
- **civil society organizations**
- **Cold War**
- **communism**
- **conference diplomacy**
- **consulates**
- **democracy**
- **diplomacy**
- **diplomatic immunity**
- **diplomats**
- **Economic and Social Council**
- **embassies**
- **epistemic communities**
- **ethnic cleansing**
- **European Union (EU)**
- **extraterritoriality**
- **fascism**
- **feudalism**
- **genocide**
- **globalization**
- **gross domestic product (GDP)**
- **head of government**
- **head of state**
- **humanitarian interventions**
- **imperialism**
- **interdependence**
- **international actors**
- **International Court of Justice**
- **international governmental organizations (IOs)**
- **International Monetary Fund (IMF)**
- **international system**
- **League of Nations**
- **linkage strategy**

CHAPTER REVIEW 2

2-3

Differentiate the major types of actors and relationships of the Westphalian international system. States were the primary actors in the Westphalian international system. A state is a political-legal unit that meets three conditions: (1) it has an identifiable population, (2) it is located within defined territorial borders recognized by others, and (3) it has a government that possesses sovereignty. According to Westphalian sovereignty, within a state's borders there is no higher authority than the government of the state itself. States were not the only actors in the Westphalian system; non-state actors developed as well and existed alongside states. However, states were the preeminent actors in the state-centric Westphalian international system. Over the 341-year sweep of the Westphalian era, states continued to develop and gain strength. Some states got so strong that by the latter half of the twentieth century, the Cold War risked the threat of global annihilation. The end of the Cold War brought this system to a close.

2-4

Recognize the major types of actors and relationships of the neo-Westphalian international system. As the Cold War ended and the Soviet Union collapsed, new pressures emerged in the international arena. States remained the most powerful international actors, but in the neo-Westphalian system, non-state actors grew in power and influence in world politics. Wars between states (interstate wars) have become less commonplace, but internal conflicts within states (intrastate wars) and conflicts involving other non-state actors have become more frequent. Nations, groups of people who share a collective cultural and ethnic identity, clash when their territories do not correspond with state borders. The neo-Westphalian system is marked by a comparative rise in importance of non-state actors such as multinational corporations, non-governmental organizations, international organizations, and others. The phenomenon of globalization has also weakened states with new problems and pressures. A new principle of responsible sovereignty—the idea of sovereignty as a state's responsibility to protect its citizens—has emerged to challenge traditional state sovereignty.

Note to Student: Log in to the CourseMate Web site below to access **Flashcards, Glossaries, and Crossword Puzzles** which include all **Key Terms** and their definitions!

KEY CONCEPTS

3-1

Identify the nature and use of theory and describe the components of theory. Theory involves a set of concepts, specifies their interrelationships, and, most importantly, the reasons for those relationships. A theory links these concepts, relationships, and explanations with hypotheses: "if … then …" statements about particular relationships and outcomes that should be observable in reality if the explanation is useful. Theory involves description, explanation, and prediction. It usually offers a basis for prescription as well.

3-2

Explain the foundations of the realist approach in terms of its conception of: (a) the nature of the international system; (b) its relevant actors; (c) important resources; and (d) central dynamics. For realists, anarchy, the absence of a central government to establish order and wield power and authority, establishes a fundamentally Hobbesian world in which sovereign states, the main players of world politics, must rely on themselves to protect their interests and accomplish their goals. In this self-help world, power—the ability to get what you want—is both a central instrument and a primary objective to ensure survival and security. Realists assume that all states want the same things, with the only significant difference among them being how much power and capability they have to act. Because power is unequally distributed, the international system is stratified, with different levels of resources, wealth, and power possessed by different states. Realists view power as relative and hierarchical, with military power the most essential for the ability to get what one wants in world politics. Since power is relative and ultimately based on military strength, states cannot ever really have "enough" or trust others to be satisfied in an environment where conflict is the norm. The distribution of power among country affects how they act and the likelihood of conflict. Realists generally view international politics as zero-sum situations and consider conflict to be the normal dynamic in an anarchic system.

3-3

Explain the foundations of the liberal approach in terms of its conceptions of: (a) the nature of the international system; (b) its relevant actors; (c) important resources; and (d) central dynamics. Liberal theorists begin with the formal anarchy of the system, acknowledging the absence of formal, authoritative central government in world politics. But liberal theorists also recognize the importance of one or more additional features of the international system that reduce the impact of formal anarchy, such as international norms, mutual interests among states, interdependence, and institutions. Since these characteristics tie states together, Liberal theorists see more opportunities for cooperation and peace. System-level dynamics

KEY TERMS

absolute gains the total effect of a decision or situation on an actor.

balance of power politics patterns of shifting alliances, force, and counterforce among states as they seek power, counter the efforts of rivals, and confront security threats.

bipolar a distribution of power in the international system in which there are two great powers.

collective security states join together into an organization, ban the use of force by its members, and commt themselves to joining together to respond to any attack by one member on any other member.

consociational democracy a form of government that guarantees representation to the different ethnic or religious groups within the country.

constructivism a major theoretical approach to international relations emphasizing the importance of ideas, collective identities, and the social construction of reality.

democratic peace state-level theory of war stating that institutional and normative characteristics of democratic regimes lead them to peaceful relations with each other.

distribution of power a characteristic of the international system emphasized by realists based on the number of great or major powers and how power is distributed among them in a given period of time.

empirical theory theory based on real-world observations and explanations.

genocide the killing of an entire race within a country.

hard power power based on coercive means such as military force.

hegemony domination of the international system by one country.

Hobbesian world a brutal, dangerous, self-help world with central authority described by the philosopher Thomas Hobbes.

Hutu a socially constructed race in central Africa that was supposed to be poorer and physically shorter than its rival group, the Tutsis.

ideational emphasizing the centrality of ideas and norms in shaping behavior and interactions

institutions structures, patterns, and mechanisms for establishing norms, rules, order, and cooperation in world politics.

international norms unwritten rules or expectations of behavior.

Irish Republican Army (IRA) the militant terrorist organization in Northern Ireland that fought to remove the Protestant leaders from power and the British military from Northern Ireland.

liberalism a major theoretical approach to international relations emphasizing the role of individuals, norms, and institutions to explain patterns of cooperation and conflict in world politics.

multipolar a distribution of power in the international system in which there are more than two great powers.

negative peace a lack of conflict between two countries or groups.

normative theory theory based on prescription and advocacy of preferred outcomes.

parsimony the principle that simple explanations are preferable to complex explanations when other things are equal.

positive peace a situation between two countries that is not simply a lack of conflict, but a mutual affinity for each other.

positive sum a condition in which all parties to an issue can benefit or "win."

power the ability to get what you want.

realism a major theoretical approach to international relations emphasizing the competitive, conflict-ridden pursuit of power and security among states in world politics.

relative gains the comparative effect of a decision or situation on an actor relative to those of another actor.

self-help individual actors are responsible for making themselves secure and protecting their own interests.

Six-Day War the 1967 war between Israel, Egypt, Jordan, and Syria. Israel won the war and took control of the occupied territories (the Gaza Strip, West Bank, and Golan Heights).

social construction a concept is created by the interactions and ideas within a society.

soft power power based on attraction and persuasion rather than coercion.

sovereign having supreme authority over territory and people.

state of nature a hypothetical condition before the advent of government.

stratification unequal distribution of power, influence, and/or other resources.

substate actors groups within a state such as political parties, insurgents, or ethnic groups.

tripolar a distribution of power in the international system in which there are three great powers.

Tutsi a socially constructed race in central Africa that was supposed to be more elite, wealthier, and taller than their rival group, the Hutus.

unipolar a distribution of power in the international system in which there is one great power.

unitary actor the simplified conception of a state as a single entity or actor.

zero sum a condition in which one party's benefit or gains requires comparable losses by another party.

such as the security dilemma tend to be viewed more as trust and communication problems that can be reduced by norms, interdependence, common identity, and institutions rather than as unalterable consequences of anarchy. Liberal theorists also view differences in states—in type of government, and other features—as important for their behavior, and they see the importance of individuals, governmental institutions and agencies, non-state actors, and societal forces in shaping state behavior and interactions. The liberal lens stresses the multidimensional nature of power, recognizing the importance of military power but arguing that there are many sources of power and influence in world politics. Liberals differentiate between "hard" and "soft power" and tend to reject the realist emphasis on power's hierarchical nature. Instead, they tend to view power as situation specific or context dependent. In a formally anarchic world in which states and other actors share some common interests and goals and are interdependent and connected through institutions and other channels, cooperation, competition, and conflict are all possible. Conflict, however, is not the norm, and world politics is often a positive sum game. Progress and change are both possible and likely.

3-4

Explain the foundations of the constructivist approach in terms of its conceptions of: (a) the nature of the international system; (b) its relevant actors; (c) important resources; and (d) central dynamics. States do not, as suggested by realism, constantly engage in conflict or preparation for conflict. Social construction simply means that a concept is created by the identities and interactions of societies. Anarchy is the absence of central government, but what it means for state behavior varies according to the ideas and shared experiences and interactions of the players. For constructivists, states are important, but consist of people with identity and values. Other actors are also important, including international institutions, non-governmental organizations, and transnational networks. Moreover, constructivists pay close attention to cultural groups in world politics—nations or ethnic groups and their experiences, ideas, and values. To constructivists, the basis of power is not in the material power of states or institutions, but the ideas that people believe in and the shared understandings they develop. It is not that the material world and tangible resources of power do not matter, but that their meaning depends on shared ideas, norms, and interpretations. Since a central idea behind constructivism is that all social relationships are constructed by people and therefore are subject to change, it follows that the central dynamics of world politics are subject to great variation over time and among different players in world politics.

3-5

Assess the uses and applications of each approach as contending and complementary lenses for understanding international relations. Because realism, liberalism, and constructivism stress different characteristics, players, and dynamics in world politics, they offer contending, and sometime complementary, explanations of the patterns of world politics. Realism is the simplest perspective, focusing on the reasons for conflict. Its relevance to the balance-of-power patterns of the eighteenth, nineteenth, and early twentieth centuries is clear, but how well does it capture the changing patterns of behavior among great powers and others after World War II? Liberalism and constructivism are much more complex explanations that reduce the emphasis on conflict, but they may capture the forces underlying cooperation and change in world politics, especially after World War II.

CHAPTER REVIEW

Alternative Perspectives on International Relations

KEY CONCEPTS

4-1

Understand how the foreign policy perspective provides a foundation for international relations. The study of foreign policy is agent-centered, focusing on the individuals and groups who make decisions within the state in order to understand what states do and how they interact. Thus, foreign policy analysis focuses on individuals, small groups, bureaucratic organizations, legislatures, domestic/societal forces such as interest groups and public opinion, and different regime types. When the focus is on individuals, the emphasis is on how individual preferences or human characteristics affect how leaders make decisions. When the focus is on small groups or bureaucratic organizations, the emphasis is on how group dynamics, organizational perspective, and organizational processes affect preferences, decisions, and policy behavior. When the focus is on societal forces, the emphasis is on how interest groups, public opinion, and other factors affect decision-makers and their decisions. Regime type explanations focus on how different types of governments and political processes affect the foreign policy choices and behavior of states. Thus, foreign policy explanations look inside the state and explain how and why decisions are made, often down to the group and individual level.

4-2

Explain how economic class as explained by Marxist theory can be the core driving force for how nations interact with each other.
Marxist theory sees economic class as the driving world force rather than power. In its most basic form, the approach asserts that all actions by people and states are driven by economic desires rather than desires for power, security, etc. In this dynamic, class differences—between those who controlled wealth (capitalists) and those who did not (proletariat), drive behavior and, in world politics, lead to efforts to enrich the wealthy class, usually at the expense of the others. Marx and Engels theorized that, within countries, eventually the proletariat would rise up and revolt against the capitalists, overthrow them, and take control of the government. The new socialist government would take ownership of the economy for the proletariat, and it would begin to break down the old capitalist institutions. Over time, with the destruction of the old capitalist institutions, the government itself would wither away and society would become truly communist—a utopia where everyone cooperated and the human vices inspired by capitalist greed and envy had been eradicated. Chiefly an explanation of processes within countries, Marxism is relevant to world politics in at least two ways. First, unless a state was socialist, its motives were to promote the wealth of the capitalist class, which controlled the government and thus all foreign and domestic policies were made to benefit the capitalists. Marxist theory asserts that wars are not fought for territory or security but for the profit they will bring the wealthy class. Second, the theory asserted that socialism would spread worldwide.

KEY TERMS

advisory group the set of individuals from whom leaders seek decision-making assistance.

agent-centered approach Understanding and explaining international relations by focusing on the individuals and groups who make decisions within the state

American Israel Public Affairs Committee (AIPAC) a pro-Israel interest group, thought to be the most influential interest group impacting U.S. foreign policy.

bounded rationality the idea that leaders want to make rational or logical decisions but are limited by their lack of knowledge or other human factors.

capitalism an economic system in which workers sell their labor for wages, there is no central authority over the economy, and market forces determine what is purchased and what is sold.

capitalist class or bourgeoisie the owners of businesses, factories, etc. that make profits from the work of laborers but do not work themselves.

Chinese Communist Party the only legal political party in the People's Republic of China. It controls all aspects of the government.

colonies territories that are legally owned and controlled by another country, typically called the imperial power.

core the economic zone composed of wealthy countries producing high-end products.

dependency theory a theory of development that argues that the dominance and exploitation of poor countries by rich countries prevents progress and development in the poor countries and makes them dependent on the wealthy countries.

difference feminists the feminist perspective that argues that men and women are fundamentally different in their abilities, particularly in their approach to conflict.

diversionary theory the idea that leaders under domestic pressures will use military force more readily to distract their opponents or rally the public behind their leadership.

domain of gains situations in which decision makers seek to preserve their advantages.

domain of losses negative situations in which decision makers will engage in more risk-taking to change the status quo.

Falkland Islands a group of islands approximately 300 miles off the coast of Argentina owned by the United Kingdom and populated by UK citizens.

feminist international relations theory a feminist approach to understanding international relations that focuses on the role of women and gender and how historically the world has been male dominated.

foreign policy analysis a theoretical approach that focuses on the process and outcomes of foreign policy decisions made by the people and groups that determine a state's actions in international relations.

CHAPTER REVIEW 4

liberal feminists the feminist perspective that argues men and women can approach issues such as conflict the same way, but that it is important to have equal representation of the two genders.

Marxism an argument developed by Marx and Engels that asserted all politics was determined by social class and that the world would progress through historical economic epochs.

Middle East the region of the world that encompasses countries in Northeast Africa and Southwest Asia.

operational code analysis the idea that leaders have a tendency to 1) prefer either conflict or cooperation and 2) believe they are either very effective or limited in their ability to control others.

organizational/bureaucratic politics model foreign policy decisions are the products of large bureaucratic organizations doing what they know to do or see as in their organizational interest.

periphery the economic zone composed of poor countries that primarily export raw materials.

poliheuristic theory the idea of decision making as a two step process, first options found unacceptable or impossible are discarded, and then the remaining options are rationally considered.

proletariat the working class that sold its labor for less than its value to the capitalists.

proportional representation a democratic system in which parties or factions get approximately the same percentage of legislative seats as votes they received in the most recent election.

prospect theory the idea that humans are rational but their rationality is situationally biased; that is, they are more risk-averse when things work in their favor and more risk-taking when things aren't going well.

rational actor model as unitary actors, all states make decisions according to a rational process in which goals are ranked, options identified and evaluated, and selections made to maximize benefits according to the goals of the actor.

regime change the change of a country's government or type of government.

selectorate those in a state who provide the power base for a leader.

semi-periphery the economic zone composed of middle-income countries that produce secondary products.

socialism an economic-political system in which the government controls the economy and redistributes wealth to create economic equality in the country.

United Fruit Company a U.S. company that owned and controlled vast plantations in Latin America.

winning coalition the half of the voters you must get to win an election.

World Economic Forum a forum held in Switzerland every year that brings together wealthy individuals, corporate leaders, industry leaders, and heads of government to coordinate economic policies and initiatives.

world systems theory a theory inspired by Marxism that argues the world is divided into three economic zones (by their level of development) and that these zones determine how states interact, with wealthier countries exploiting poorer countries.

Marx and Engels saw the spread of communism to be an inevitable, evolutionary process, but other communist leaders such as Stalin interpreted Marx and Engels to mean that a socialist state is obligated to compel regime change in other states.

4-3

Identify the different aspects of world systems theory and how they explain international relations. World systems theory (WST) applies the ideas of Marxism and class differences to international relations. Using the concept of class, WST asserts there are three zones or types of states. Core states are the wealthiest, most industrialized, and most powerful in the world economy. Semi-peripheral states tend to produce goods and services and not rely on the export of raw materials (e.g., lumber, food, oil) for their economy. However, those goods and services are not as profitable as the core country's products. Periphery states have weak governments, tend to sell only raw materials or cheap labor, and have almost no influence in world politics. (See Table 4-2 for examples.) According to WST, each type of state has particular interests and behavior that are determined by its position in the economic system. The core dominates and extracts profits from the semi-periphery and periphery, the semi-periphery dominates and extracts profits from the periphery, and the periphery is simply left in relative poverty. WST argues that wars are fought between the different zones to enforce the world order, and within the semi-periphery and periphery over scarce resources, injustice, and other matters.

4-4

Outline the ways in which gender affects and is affected by international relations. Feminist IR theories address one or more of three main themes. One theme raises the question of whether world politics would be different if women held more, or most, leadership positions in states. Generally speaking, women do not hold equal status in countries around the world and are severely under-represented in government positions. A second theme asks whether our entire way of thinking about international relations is masculinized because most IR theorists—at least at first—were men. A third theme is more empirical and reverses the focus of the first theme, examining the impact of world politics on women. War, economic downturn, and economic sanctions, among many issues of world politics, have particularly harmful effects on women. Women are at a particular disadvantage in poor and developing countries, where they often have fewer rights and protections relative to men. Globalization, however, often means more employment opportunities for women.

The Rational Actor Model

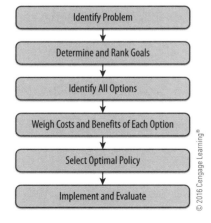

Using the above model, explain how the rational actor model influences and shapes how states interact with one another.

KEY CONCEPTS

5-1

Identify the nature and forms of armed conflict. War is a regular—though rare—and highly costly event in world politics. War occurs when the participants engage in armed struggles to gain or defend territory, resources, influence, authority, or other things of high value. The participants can involve two or more states (interstate war), two or more groups within a territory (intrastate, or civil war), or a combination of states and non-state groups (extra-systemic or extra-state war). Such armed struggles obviously range from small-scale, localized disputes to large-scale, and even global conflicts. Conventional war generally involves armed conflict between two or more states in which military forces of each side are used against each other and in which weapons of mass destruction such as nuclear, biological, or chemical weapons are generally not used. Unconventional war involves armed conflict in which: civilian and non-military targets are targeted; forces used include nontraditional forces outside organized militaries; and/or weapons of mass destruction may be employed. Civil war involves armed conflict between competing factions within a country or between an existing government and a competing group within that country over control of territory or the government. Asymmetric war pits two or more groups of very different military size or power against each other, in which the weaker participant often resorts to unconventional tactics rather than engage in traditional battlefield war. Terrorism is a form of unconventional and asymmetric war.

5-2

Describe the evolution of and trends in armed conflict. War has become increasingly destructive and deadly over time. Since 1945, wars have become more limited and increasingly have been located in the developing world. Over time, and especially since 1989, war has become increasingly internal, as civil war has become the most common form. There has been a shift from conventional to unconventional war over the last half of the twentieth century and early twenty-first century.

5-3

Assess the causes of interstate and intrastate war at the (a) system, (b) state, and (c) individual levels of analysis. War has been waged over territory; the "search for statehood" and independence; ideology; competition for economic resources, markets, or transportation; sympathy or humanitarian reasons—particularly to protect perceived religious and ethnic kin abroad; predation and survival; and to defend allies and to defend or restore the balance of power.

(a) System-level causes include anarchy, self-help, security dilemma, distribution of power, structural characteristics related to power, interdependence, male-dominated states. **(b)** State-level causes include type of government, type of

KEY TERMS

asymmetric war armed conflict between two or more groups of very different military size or power.

civil war armed conflict between competing factions within a country, or between a government and a competing group within that country over control of territory and/or the government.

constructivism (and ethnicity) emphasizes the social construction of identity and the ways that social interactions define ethnicity for groups of people.

conventional war armed conflict between two or more states in which military forces of each side are used against each other, and in which weapons of mass destruction such as nuclear, biological, or chemical weapons are not used.

cyclical theories of war conflict based on the rise and relative decline of leading powers in the international system in which stability occurs as the victors in major wars assert themselves, and war occurs as a function of the subsequent and inevitable rise of challengers to those dominant powers.

diversionary theory states suffering from poor economic conditions or internal strife are more likely to resort to force outside their borders in efforts to divert attention from those internal problems.

ethnic geography the spatial and ecological aspects of ethnicity (e.g., where groups live in relation to one another), which affect the culture, politics, and social practices of states, nations, groups, and individuals.

extra-systemic or extra-state war armed conflict between a state and a non-state entity, such as colonial wars and wars with non-state national or terrorist groups.

frustration-aggression theory resort to violence under conditions of persistent denial of expected treatment, for example, fairness and equality.

general war armed conflict in which the participants seek to conquer and control territory of their opponents and use the full available arsenals against military targets and against the infrastructure of a country.

groupthink characteristics of some decision groups that result in a shared viewpoint or preference that leads the group to ignore relevant information and exclude dissenters from that viewpoint in order to protect it.

hegemon a country that is an undisputed leader within its region or the world. After World War II, the United States was considered the world hegemon.

human nature innate characteristics of human beings, said to be a cause of war by some.

IED (improvised explosive device) a homemade bomb, often placed on roadsides and other sites, fashioned from an explosive device and a detonator, usually triggered by remote device or "booby-trap" mechanism.

instrumentalism stresses the role of leaders who emphasize and exacerbate ethnic differences (and commonalities) as a means to their own ends.

interstate war armed conflict between two or more states.

irredentist claims (or irredentism) claims to territory in another state based on historical control or the presence of people with common ethnic identity.

limited war armed conflict with conventional weapons for limited goals and without use of full available arsenals.

national attributes features of states or nations such as regime type, type of economy, culture, geography, resources, and the like.

non-trinitarian war armed conflict in which the roles and participation of government, militaries, and populations are blurred.

personality traits varying characteristics of individuals, some of which may lead to more aggressive behavior and preferences.

power transition theory systemic theory holding that wars are most likely when changes in power distributions occur.

primordialism stresses the fundamental bonds of kinship and identity that establish ethnic differences that divide people and often generate ancient ethnic hatreds.

psychological needs essential emotional and psychological requirements of humans, said to be hierarchical by theorists such as Maslow.

relative deprivation discrepancy between what people actually have and what they think they deserve based on what others actually have.

state-sponsored terrorism includes covert and overt repression of and violence against civilian populations, and more extreme acts such as genocide, supported or perpetrated by the state.

terrorism indiscriminate violence aimed at noncombatants to influence a wider audience.

trinitarian war armed conflict in which the roles and participation of government, militaries, and populations are distinct.

unconventional war armed conflict in which civilian and non-military targets are emphasized, forces used include nontraditional forces outside organized militaries, and in which a wide array of weaponry including weapons of mass destruction may be employed.

war organized, violent (i.e., military) conflict between two or more parties.

war weariness states that have most recently experienced a significant, costly war are more peaceful in the aftermath because of the impact of those costs and experiences.

weapons of mass destruction (WMD) nuclear, chemical, and biological weapons.

economy, demographic, cultural, physical, or geographic attributes, level of political instability, previous war involvement. **(c)** Individual-level causes include **human nature, psychological needs**, and personality traits.

Civil wars can arise from issues related to population, from the pressures on scarce resources (such as land) to issues related to diversity and identity. Repression and other government policies may be at the heart of civil war, prompting disaffected groups to rebel. There are "greed-based" (mostly in the **instrumentalism** and **primordialism** categories) and "grievance-based" (mostly in the primordialism and **constructivism** categories) explanations of civil war.

External factors such as the presence of conflict in neighboring countries and intervention by major regional or global powers also influence the onset and nature of civil wars.

Defining Terrorism by Means and Targets

Non-Combatants

	Murder	TERRORISM	

Discriminate Means / Indiscriminate Means

	Limited War	General War	

Combatants

© Cengage Learning®

Most Fragile and Most Stable States in the World, 2014

Most Fragile States	Most Stable States
South Sudan	Finland
Somalia	Sweden
Central African Republic	Denmark
Democratic Republic of Congo	Norway
Sudan	Switzerland
Chad	New Zealand
Afghanistan	Luxembourg
Yemen	Iceland
Haiti	Ireland
Pakistan	Australia

Source: The Fund For Peace, Fragile States Index (http://ffp.statesindex.org)
© Cengage Learning®

KEY CONCEPTS

6-1

Identify the challenges of seeking international security in world politics. The players in world politics seek security—to protect themselves from attack by other actors and guard their essential interests. The protection of political sovereignty and territorial integrity is especially important in a world without central government. The pursuit of security often results in insecurity, arms races, conflict spirals, and, sometimes, war. The absence of authoritative central institutions in world politics often makes coordination and cooperation difficult, prompting fear from the players that their interests will not be protected unless they take action themselves. The core elements of the security challenge stem from the combination of anarchy, diversity, and complexity of world politics. At the foundation of this fundamental challenge are the security dilemma and the challenge of power. Security dilemmas arise as a state takes actions it sees as defensive and non-threatening, but such actions alarm others and the result may be exactly what each is trying to avoid and produces even greater insecurities. The disparities between the "haves" and "have-nots" of power create challenges because they generate uncertainties, fears, threats, and competition.

6-2

Describe and evaluate power-based approaches to international security embraced by realists, including military might, alliances, and the uses of force. Realists stress that the dangerous world of international relations requires states to accumulate military capabilities to deter potential attackers, defend against attacks, and extend power and influence. States generally have two basic options: building their own military might and forging alliances to increase military capabilities. According to realists, states devote resources to their militaries to counter threats and to gain or maintain power to deal with the inevitable conflicts that arise in a dangerous, anarchic world. Realists also emphasize the efforts of states to forge alliances with other states to counter threats and increase strength. When there are common interests between them, such as a common enemy, states agree to cooperate militarily to meet threats. Such alliances might be driven by protection, bandwagoning, or balancing dynamics and are usually relatively temporary. Realists stress that, in a dangerous and anarchic world, force will often be used. States wishing to be secure must have power to secure themselves, and power, to realists, depends on the ability to use military force through deterrence, defense, and more proactive applications of force.

KEY TERMS

alliance formal commitments between states to cooperate for specific purposes such as mutual defense.

arms control regulation of the amount, type, positioning, or use of weapons.

arms race peacetime competition in armaments by two or more states driven by conflict interests, fear, and suspicion.

balance of power politics patterns of shifting alliances, force, and counterforce among states as they seek power, counter the efforts of rivals, and confront security threats.

balancing (in alliances) forming coalitions to counter the rising power and threat of a state.

bandwagoning (in alliances) siding with a rising power to gain benefits.

Baruch Plan a nuclear disarmament proposal authored by U.S. statesman Bernard Baruch after World War II to place nuclear weapons and energy activities under the control and authority of the United Nations.

brinkmanship the strategy of escalating conflicts or crises to nuclear threats in order to force the other side to back down.

coercive diplomacy a strategy that combines threats and the selective use of force with negotiation in a bargaining strategy to persuade an adversary to comply with one's demand.

collective security states join together into an organization, ban the use of force by its members, and commit themselves to joining together to respond to any attack by one member on any other member.

compellence the use of military force to stop a foe from doing something it was already doing, or force it to start doing something it was not yet doing.

counter-force targeting an adversary's nuclear arsenals and other war-fighting abilities for nuclear strikes.

counter-value targeting an adversary's cities and industrial centers for nuclear strikes

cultural exchange programs involving the exchange of citizens—students, teachers, scientists, artists, and others—between countries to foster cultural understanding and cooperation.

defense deploying and using military force to fight off an attack.

defense burden the ratio of military spending to overall gross domestic product of a country.

democracy promotion a cluster of activities ranging from diplomacy to aid to intervention designed to foster and support democratization in other countries.

deterrence persuading a potential adversary to refrain from attacking through the threat of costly retaliation.

direct deterrence the use of retaliatory threats to discourage attacks against the state making the deterrent threat.

disarmament the elimination of arsenals or classes or types of weapons.

extended deterrence retaliatory threats to discourage attacks against allies and friends of the state making the deterrent threat.

external balancing countering the power of a rival by forming coalitions with other states.

functionalism and neo-functionalism technical cooperation on economic and social issues that build linkages and shared interests among societies and expand to more areas, leading to even greater cooperation and institutional connections.

general deterrence threats to retaliate in a context of underlying politico-military competition, but when there is no active military conflict generating the need to respond.

immediate deterrence the threat to retaliate against attackers who are believed to be actively considering specific military operations against the target.

internal balancing countering the power of a rival by increasing one's own power and military might.

massive retaliation the threat to respond to provocations with disproportionate and devastating nuclear attacks.

mutually assured destruction (MAD) the ability of both sides to field a secure, second-strike capability of sufficient size to destroy a significant portion of the other side's society.

national missile defense the capability to protect a country from nuclear attack by shooting down incoming missiles.

peacekeeping the provision of third-party forces from the UN or other regional organizations to help keep peace by providing a buffer between parties in conflict, often along a border or an agreed-upon cease-fire line to monitor and maintain the peace.

political sovereignty the principle that a state has authority and independence to rule without interference.

preemption the use of military force to strike first when an attack is imminent to blunt the effectiveness of the impending attack.

prevention the use of military force to strike first when an attack is inevitable to take advantage of more favorable balance of forces rather than wait for an adversary to gain the advantage from which to strike.

protection (in alliances) an arrangement by a small state to gain help from a larger state.

revolution in military affairs the transformation of weapons, military organizations, and operational concepts for military force that leverages the information and communications revolutions of the latter 20th and early 21st centuries.

security community a group of states bound by shared identities and interests and complex interactions among which security threats are virtually nonexistent.

territorial integrity the principle that other actors should not violate the territory or boundaries of a state.

theater missile defense the capability to protect a specific or limited geographic area from nuclear attack by shooting down incoming missiles.

6-3

Describe and assess cooperation-based approaches to international security embraced by liberals, including arms control and disarmament, collective security, and security communities. Liberal approaches to security and conflict management emphasize cooperation and coordination. They tend to view the security dilemma as driven by uncertainty and problems with trust and understanding. Consequently, liberals stress the construction of agreements to control or eliminate weapons. Disarmament emphasizes the elimination (or the drastic reduction) of weapons, while arms control generally promotes restraint or regulation of the amount, type, positioning, or use of weapons. In part, both arms control and disarmament rest on the premise that controlling weaponry and the competition to acquire it will make states more secure and better able to manage conflict. A second major liberal approach to security and conflict is collective security, the liberal answer to balance-of-power politics. In collective security, states join together into a community and commit to respond to any attack by one member on any other member. The final liberal approach to security is the development of security communities. A security community is a group of states bound by shared identities and interests and complex interactions among whom security threats are virtually nonexistent.

U.S. Alliances

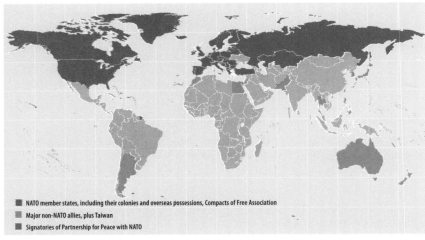

■ NATO member states, including their colonies and overseas possessions, Compacts of Free Association
■ Major non-NATO allies, plus Taiwan
■ Signatories of Partnership for Peace with NATO

© Cengage Learning®

Why does the United States have so many alliances?

Building Peace: Structures and Institutions of Cooperation

KEY CONCEPTS

7-1

Identify the underlying challenges to cooperation in pursuit of security. First, the anarchic nature of world politics complicates cooperation. The absence of a central enforcer to prevent and punish wrongdoing creates incentives for the major political players—states—to take care of themselves and their own interests instead of cooperating. Second, the diversity of states and societies in size, regime type, economic capabilities, culture, interests, and many other factors makes achieving harmony very hard. Finally, the complexity of world politics also complicates cooperation. Over time more and more players—states and non-state actors—are engaged across more and more issues that are linked together and affect them.

7-2

Describe the nature and functions of international law. International law is law in the absence of central authority, and that makes it different than domestic law. International law is also law in the absence of shared values and principles due to the great diversity in the perspectives, experiences, governments, characteristics, and cultures of the world's societies. The sources of international law are international conventions (treaties) agreed to by states; international custom or general practices of states accepted as law; "general principles of law recognized by civilized nations;" judicial decisions and the writings of eminent jurists; and the practices and decisions of international organizations such as the UN. Liberals and constructivists stress the development, application, and prospects of international law as a way to manage conflict and enhance security and trust among states. Realists tend to be very skeptical of the prospects of international law. Alternative theories often see international law as a means by the rich and powerful to structure the rules of the system for their own benefit. There are three main avenues of enforcement: national, horizontal, and vertical enforcement.

7-3

Evaluate the nature and functions of international organizations. There are power-based and problem-based explanations for the creation and maintenance of international organizations. IOs serve a range of functions, from instruments of states to influence other states, to forums for states to communicate, negotiate, and advance their interests, to influential actors contributing to problem-solving, coordination, norm and rule-creation, and enforcement. IOs may be universal or regional in membership, single-issue or multiple issue in scope, and they employ a range of voting or decision processes. The European Union is the most developed and powerful regional organization in the world, and the UN is the broadest and most universal IO.

KEY TERMS

compulsory jurisdiction in international law, the condition in which parties to a dispute must submit the case to a court.

Concert of Europe a nineteenth century multilateral organization composed of Great Britain, Russia, Austria, Prussia, and France to promote stability, cooperation, and multilateral diplomacy.

Council of Ministers Made up of sitting ministers of their national governments, the Council of Ministers represents member states and approves all EU legislation.

custom the general practice of states accepted as law; a source of international law.

European Commission (EC) The executive branch of the EU. The Commission is led by a president, has budgetary powers, and includes a 28-member cabinet that oversees policy development in agriculture, trade, social policy, the environment, and many other areas.

European Council Made up of the heads of government of the EU member states, the European Council represents the interests of their member states within the EU.

European Court of Justice The EU's judicial branch whose rulings take precedent over even national law. It is charged with interpreting EU law and ensuring that it is applied equally across all member states.

European Parliament (EP) The EU legislative body made up of directly elected representatives, the EU Parliament amends, approves or rejects EU laws, together with the Council of Ministers.

horizontal enforcement those measures that states themselves can take when a state violates an international law and other states can attempt to punish the violator themselves.

international law a body of rules that binds states and other agents in world politics in their relations with one another.

International Monetary Fund (IMF) one of the Bretton Woods organizations created in 1946 to help maintain a cooperative international financial system. The IMF helps countries facing balance-of-payment problems with short-term loans and also helps countries reschedule their debt.

Law of the Sea Convention a treaty that first went into force in 1982 and then was revised in 1994; 165 states are parties to this treaty, as is the EU, which sets rules for the use and protection of the high seas and its resources.

majority rule in international organizations, a decision process that relies on voting with one vote per member, in which gaining a majority of the votes prevails.

Most-Favored Nation (MFN) the preferential trade status that members of the GATT gave to other members. MFN could also be granted to non-members if a country chose to do so. The United States granted China MFN status for years before China entered the agreement.

national enforcement states enforce some international law through their own national legal systems.

P-5 (perm-5) the five permanent members of the UN Security Council—the United States, Britain, France, China, and Russia—each of which holds veto power.

reciprocity in international law, the principle that a state follows international law so that others will do so in return.

treaty formal, written agreements among states.

United Nations (UN) an international institution established after World War II to promote peace and security, the development of friendly relations and harmony among nations, and cooperation on international problems.

UN Secretariat the bureaucracy and administrative arm of the UN.

UN Secretary-General the head of the UN Secretariat, the UN's administrative leader elected by the UNGA at the recommendation of the UNSC.

unit veto in international organizations, a decision rule in which some or all members can block decisions with their votes: in a pure unit veto decision rule every member exercises a veto; in a modified unit veto, only some members have the veto power.

United Nations General Assembly (UNGA) the plenary body of the UN in which all UN members have a seat. Functioning on a majority rule decision process, it is the central forum for discussion of global issues.

United Nations Security Council (UNSC) a 15-member council that carries the primary UN responsibilities for peace, security, and collective security operations.

universal jurisdiction the idea that states have a right and a duty to enforce international law when it comes to the most serious human rights abuses such as genocide, crimes against humanity, torture, war crimes, extrajudicial killings, and forced disappearances, regardless of where these offenses may occur or whether or not the alleged violator is from another country.

vertical enforcement the enforcement of international law by international institutions.

Vienna Convention on the Law of Treaties a 1969 agreement among states defining the nature and obligations regarding treaties under international law.

weighted voting in international organizations, a decision rule in which member votes are weighted according to some factor related to size, power, or wealth.

World Bank a Bretton Woods organization created in 1945 that provides loans and grants to countries for long-term development. The World Bank started by helping fund the reconstruction of Europe after World War II and later focused on helping countries in the developing world grow their economies.

A Typology of International Organizations

MEMBERSHIP	SCOPE	
	SINGLE ISSUE	MULTIPLE ISSUE
GLOBAL	International Monetary Fund World Bank World Trade Organization	United Nations
REGIONAL	Andean Common Market European Environment Agency Inter-American Institute for Cooperation on Agriculture Asia-Pacific Economic Cooperation	European Union Organization of American States African Union Association of Southeast Asian Nations

© Cengage Learning®

Major Parts and Functions of the EU

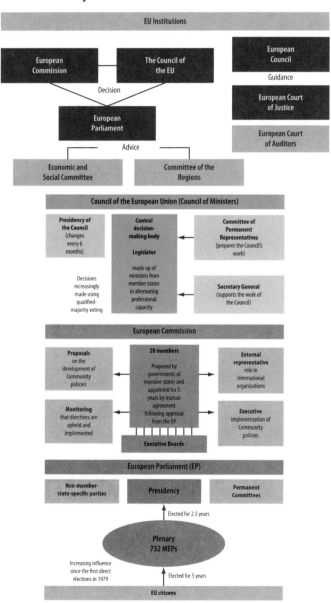

Why do states form international organizations?

The Pursuit of Money: Trade, Finance, and Integration

KEY CONCEPTS

8-1

Trace the connections between money, power, and security.
Wealth is an essential part of power and security in world politics, and there is more to the connection between money and power than building a military and using it to secure critical resources such as territory and oil. States have important interests in the pursuit of wealth and development, and politics and economics are connected. There is both tension and a symbiotic relationship between government and the market. Governments try to maintain control of their territorial borders, but businesses see borders as slowing down their ability to sell goods and services. But governments also create and enforce property ownership laws, thereby protecting commercial investments and creating the law and order businesses require. Economic interactions can also affect the consequences of anarchy, as economic interactions and interdependence can not only reduce conflict, but may lead to a true positive peace.

8-2

Identify the different historical approaches and theories that drove the world economy. The world economy has evolved through three eras since the beginning of the state system: national to international to global. In the era of the national economy, most economic exchange occurred within the borders of states. States pursued mercantilism and colonialism to help domestic businesses make money, protecting them from foreign competition, and gain wealth by controlling foreign territory. The idea of free trade developed by Adam Smith and David Ricardo and the industrial revolution led to the era of the international economy. First Britain, and then others, began to believe that if countries could agree to trade freely, then countries would become wealthier and there would be a greater chance for continuing peace after war. British power in the nineteenth century and American power after World War II helped promote liberalized trade to make countries better off and promote peace. Marxism also arose in this era as a competing idea and system, especially in the 20th century. After World War II, the U.S. led the development of the Liberal International Economic Order. The LIEO promoted and spread free trade and encouraged market economies that worked together, and it established international institutions to tie states together and help them cooperate. The LIEO also created the foundations for non-state actors such as multinational corporations and private financial institutions to operate more freely across borders and to extend their operations to more and more countries. Technological change—the computer era, advances in information and communication technology, and faster transportation—all played critical roles in the transition to and nature of the Global Economy Era, in which more and more economic transactions cross borders.

KEY TERMS

absolute advantage when a country is more efficient at producing a single good than another country.

austerity program program of severely restricted government spending, often on welfare programs, imposed when the country must balance its accounts.

beggar-thy-neighbor an economic policy that stresses trade protectionism and causes other countries to bear the costs of efforts at securing prosperity at home.

bilateral relations between two states. For example, a bilateral summit is a high-level conference between two states.

Bretton Woods System the global economic system established by the United States and other countries after World War II to promote capitalism, free trade, and policy coordination. Nicknamed "Bretton Woods" for the location of the conference in New Hampshire, the two core institutions created were the IMF and World Bank.

centrally planned (or command) economy an economy that is run by the government rather than private citizens. Examples include the Soviet Union and North Korea.

colonialism the situation where one country takes over another country and administers it with a local bureaucracy.

comparative advantage being more efficient at producing a good or service relative to another good or service. Even if one country has an absolute advantage over another in all products, both countries benefit by specializing in the products they each produce most efficiently (their comparative advantage) and trading for the others.

devalue a situation when a currency, such as the U.S. dollar, loses its value compared to other currencies. For example, the Chinese government sets the exchange rate between the U.S. dollar and the Chinese yuan, and currently, the yuan is devalued; it is worth more than the Chinese will trade it for.

Eurozone the portion of the European Union that uses the euro currency rather than a national currency. These countries include: Austria, Belgium, Cyprus, Finland, France, Germany, Greece, Ireland, Italy, Luxembourg, Malta, the Netherlands, Portugal, Slovakia, Slovenia, and Spain.

fair trade the concept that producers should be paid a fair price for their products.

General Agreement on Tariffs and Trade (GATT) an organization of countries that agree to work together to reduce trade barriers and promote free trade. Other members were considered "most favored nations" and received preferential trade agreements. The GATT was replaced by the World Trade Organization in 1995.

globalization the increasing integration of global society through the spread of technology, foreign trade, transportation, cultural exchange, political institutions, and social connections.

hyperinflation a situation where a currency loses its value very quickly. Regular inflation occurs at relatively low levels (3 to 5 percent per year), but hyperinflation means a currency can lose most of its value in a year, month, or even day.

Industrial Revolution the transition of many of the world's states from an agricultural economic system to one that was based on industry. During this period, factories replaced farms as the biggest producer in many countries.

International Monetary Fund (IMF) one of the Bretton Woods organizations created in 1946 to help maintain a cooperative international financial system. The IMF helps countries facing balance-of-payment problems with short-term loans and also helps countries reschedule their debt.

Islamists extreme fundamentalist Muslims.

liberal capitalism a philosophy of complete or near complete free markets and no governmental regulation in the economy. There are variations to liberal capitalism, but the idea is minimal government involvement in the economy.

liberal international economic order (LIEO) the post-World War II international economic system built on commitments to free trade and free market economies, with international institutions to help countries coordinate and cooperate.

liquidity crisis a situation when a government runs out of cash and is unable to make minimum payments on its debt.

mercantilism an economic policy that combines free enterprise and government. The government uses its power—including its military—to enhance private business, and private business provides revenues to the government to maintain and enhance its power.

metropole the "mother city" or center of an empire. The metropole of the British Empire (which included colonies on every continent except Antarctica) was London.

negative interest rate a government policy of charging banks for holding too

8-3

Explain the nature and implications of globalization for world politics. Globalization is the global spread of technology, money, products, culture, and opinions through foreign trade, investment, transportation, and cultural exchange. Through this process, countries become integrated into a common global network whereby they know more about each other but are also tied to each other through interdependencies. On the positive side, globalization contributes to economic growth and development. MNCs can bring jobs to a country that result in less economic discrimination and forced labor, particularly among women. There is also a greater the likelihood of peace, both inside countries and between states. There are also drawbacks of globalization. The era of the global economy has seen increasing inequality within and between states. Not all MNCs are benevolent and can exploit labor and society for their own gain. Globalization can put tremendous pressure on states by exposing them to competition in the global marketplace and ultimately weaken them. Finally, globalization tends to be non-democratic because the process involves states joining international organizations, particularly trade organizations such as the WTO, and agreeing to certain rules that are not subject to the domestic political process.

8-4

Describe the power that liberalism and globalization have in the modern economy and why there are costs to those ideas. The modern economy is driven by the power of capitalism and the forces of globalization. These forces produce increasingly broad and deep economic connections among the states and societies of the world. Over time, capitalism has produced economic growth and great wealth, and free trade and the institutions supporting the LIEO have contributed to interdependence and peace among countries. These forces have also empowered non-state actors and constrained the power of states. But these forces have also contributed to inequality and injustice, and they have made the economies of individual states far more vulnerable to global economic forces.

much of their currency in reserve. The policy is meant to make loans more available and spur economic growth.

nontariff barrier a requirement that foreign goods or services must meet that is specifically designed to block or obstruct those goods or services from sale in that market.

North American Free Trade Agreement (NAFTA) a free trade agreement between Canada, Mexico, and the United States. The agreement greatly reduced all barriers to trade between the three countries and resulted in a significant increase in trade of goods and services between the three.

protectionism a policy of blocking or restricting the trade from other countries in order to "protect" domestic businesses from economic competition with foreign companies.

subprime loans loans given by banks to private citizens that would be considered to

have a high likelihood of default. These loans were made to promote home ownership, but drove up prices and ultimately created an unsustainable economy that collapsed and caused the Great Recession.

supranational organization an institution, organization, or law that is over other states. For example, the EU is a supranational organization because it has authority over many European states.

trade war a situation when many or all states engage in protectionism. The states try to block imports and promote exports, but since all countries do this, very little international trade occurs.

World Bank a Bretton Woods organization created in 1945 that provides loans and grants to countries for long-term development. The World Bank started by helping fund the reconstruction of Europe after World War II and later focused on helping countries in the developing world grow their economies.

Economic Statecraft: Sanctions, Aid, and Their Consequences

KEY CONCEPTS

9-1

Outline the history and identify the many ways in which wealth can be used to influence other countries. The process of giving and taking money for political purposes is called economic statecraft: the use of economic means (money) to secure political ends (or goals). By attaching conditions or demands to the giving or taking of money, one state can influence another state and pursue security for itself. The ways in which states can give and take money are many, such as foreign aid of many kinds, a special trade deal, economic sanctions, or cutting off an important resource. References to economic statecraft date back to approximately 500 BCE. Over the centuries, many leaders, including Alexander Hamilton—the very first secretary of the U.S. Treasury—strongly believed that the state's economy could and must be used as a form of influence, not just a way to build military power. In the last six decades, foreign aid has also become an important part of international relations and is now carefully tracked by states and international organizations.

9-2

Trace the complex nature of economic sanctions, why they are used and what consequences they have. An economic sanction is a policy that reduces the economic exchange between two states for a political goal. Trade sanctions cut the exchange of goods between the two countries, financial sanctions freeze the movement of assets (e.g., bank accounts) for the sanctioned country, aid sanctions restrict access to foreign assistance, and third-party sanctions threaten a third country doing business with the main target of the sanctions. Comprehensive sanctions cut off all economic connections to the target, which is rarely done but can exact a huge cost on the targeted country. Senders of sanctions may seek: (1) to weaken the target state's military and economy; (2) to destabilize a government, often in hopes of changing the leadership or type of government; (3) to limit the proliferation of nuclear weapons; (4) to target human security goals, such as promoting better human rights, democracy, or both; (5) to promote human rights reforms. Estimates indicate that only 5 to 33 percent of economic sanctions meet their goals. On average a sanctioned country loses 3 percent of its annual economic growth. However, most sanctions fail because the economic costs they impose on the target country are usually lower than the cost of compliance. Sanctions have a detrimental effect on the human rights, level of democracy, and respect for women. Also, other countries can trade with the sanctioned state—busting the sanctions, so to speak.

KEY TERMS

African Union organization in Africa devoted to representing the interests of African states.

aid sanction cutting off aid to a country in order to get it to change its behavior.

arms embargo not selling weapons to a country.

coup d'état literally, a "strike against the state"; when there is a forceful change in government that overthrows the current leadership.

democracy aid aid given to a country to enhance and consolidate its transition to democracy.

development aid aid given to a country to help develop its economy.

economic sanction the cessation of some or all economic exchange between two countries.

economic statecraft the use of economic means to secure political ends.

financial sanction the freezing of a country's financial assets held in another country.

fissile material nuclear material used to make atomic weapons.

foreign aid money given by one country (the donor) to another country (the recipient) for health, economic development, or poverty relief.

fungible the ability to use one type of power for multiple purposes.

humanitarian aid aid given to a country to help mitigate the effects from a disaster or other humanitarian emergency.

import and export sanctions when one country reduces or stops buying or selling products from/to another country.

International Atomic Energy Agency (IAEA) an independent intergovernmental organization that reports to the UN and UNSC concerning the peaceful use of atomic energy, nuclear proliferation, and nuclear safeguards.

military aid aid given to a country that directly enhances its military capability.

Millennium Development Goals eight goals established by the UN in 2000 to foster development in a sustainable and equal manner.

Organization for Economic Cooperation and Development (OECD) organization of thirty-four member states that promotes liberal economic and political reforms.

Organization of American States (OAS) international organization composed of states in the North and South American continents.

tariff a tax on products imported into one country from other countries.

third-party sanction a sanction levied against a third-party state to keep that state from doing business with the primary target of the sanctions.

9-3

Identify the potential benefits and consequences of foreign aid.

Foreign aid can be broken down into four different types: (1) development aid aimed at helping the recipient's economy, (2) military aid aimed at strengthening the recipient state's security, (3) humanitarian aid aimed at providing immediate help in an emergency or disaster, and (4) democracy aid aimed at promoting democratic reforms. Factors influencing the provision of development aid include recipient poverty, a donor's military or strategic interest in the recipient country, the colonial history of the donor and recipient, and recipient regime type and trade relations. Military aid is given to allies in the form of funds to purchase military equipment or training or as straight grants of military equipment. Humanitarian aid is temporary assistance to recipients to help them recover from disasters such as earthquakes, floods, and famines. Democracy aid, which really only emerged in the 1980s, usually involves small, targeted packages of assistance designed to help a country become more democratic or to help keep the country from slipping back into autocratic rule after a democratic transition.

Russia's Trade Flows

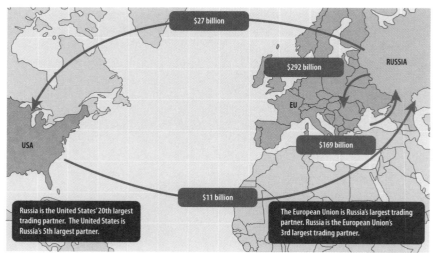

© Cengage Learning®

Source: I. Chapple and I. Kottasova, "West Threatens Russia with More Sanctions, but Trade Relations Complex," *CNN*, http://edition.cnn.com/2014/03/07/business/russia-sanctions-why-the-u-s-and-europe-are-not-quite-in-step/.

What do the trade flows between Russia, Europe, and the U.S. suggest about the possibilities for economic statecraft?

KEY CONCEPTS

10-1

Describe the distribution of wealth around the globe. In 2012, the average GDP per capita in the world was $10,291. The ten poorest countries had a GDP per capita below $550. In the U.S., the GDP per capita was over $51,000, the ninth highest in the world. The top two countries, Luxembourg and Norway, had GDP per capita exceeding $100,000, while the lowest two countries, Burundi and the Malawi, each had a GDP per capita below $400. By developed world standards, fewer than 1 billion people in the world reach "middle class" status or higher, while the remaining 6 billion are poor. There is also a great deal of inequality within countries, which can be measured through the Gini coefficient. The most equal states tend to be in Europe, while the greatest inequalities appear in Africa and South America.

10-2

Identify the reasons some countries have developed economies and some do not. Many factors affect the level of development in a country. Structural factors such as natural resources, climate and geography, and colonial history play a role. Factors such as human resources, leadership, and policy choices are also important, including the role of corruption and regime type and performance. Relations with and exploitation by foreign countries can also help or hinder development.

10-3

Compare the different strategies and policies countries have deployed to develop their economies. Modernization theory contended that countries should follow the path of wealthy states and transform their traditional societies and economies into modern ones by embracing Western ideas, industrializing, and opening themselves to foreign investment and trade. Proponents of dependency theory argued that dominance and exploitation by wealthy states would keep poor countries poor unless they worked together and separated themselves from wealthy states. Import substitution industrialization (ISI) promised to enable poor countries to develop the manufacturing sector in their economies by protecting their markets from foreign products and using government investment to develop domestic industries to produce those products instead. Export-led growth policy relies on government-industry partnerships to promote exports into the markets of wealthy countries. Neoliberal strategies stress the adoption of democratic governance, a free market, liberal trade and openness to foreign investment, and private-sector-led growth and development to achieve development.

KEY TERMS

autonomy state of independence from another country, the ability to act by oneself.

balance-of-payments a country's balance between exports, imports, and debt. If exports are too low and cannot support the country's debt, there is an economic crisis.

Big Mac Index a measure created by *The Economist* magazine that compares the value of currencies by comparing the cost of a Big Mac hamburger in different countries. The United States is used as the baseline cost for the index.

Bretton Woods organizations the organizations created at the Bretton Woods conference. They include the World Bank, IMF, and later the GATT.

developed country a wealthy country with an economy that tends to produce manufactured goods and services for export.

export-led growth the idea that to develop a country's economy, the government should push for companies to focus on products that can be exported to other countries. The policy was most successful in the Asian countries such as South Korea and Singapore.

expropriation the taking—or nationalization—of property owned by a foreign company with or without compensation.

foreign direct investment when a company in one country invests in a company in another country that leads the investor to have control over the new company.

GDP per capita the measure of a country's development. It is the total size of a country's economy divided by the population.

Gini coefficient a measure of the distribution of income in a country ranging from 0 to 1 where 0 means perfect equality and 1 means perfect inequality.

home country the term used to describe where the headquarters of a multinational corporation is based.

host country the country in which a multinational corporation owns other companies.

Human Development Index (HDI) a measure of the level of human development in a country. It includes GDP per capita, life expectancy, and education levels.

import substitution industrialization (ISI) a development policy that promotes cutting off international trade and substituting it with domestic production.

International Bank for Reconstruction and Development the original organization of the World Bank designed to promote reconstruction, especially in Europe after World War II.

less-developed country a country that is poor or has an economy that is less able to support its population. These countries typically export raw materials and agricultural products.

metropole the capital city of the empire; for example, London was the metropole of the British Empire.

modernization theory theory in the 1950s and 1960s that suggested all countries should be able to develop by following the practices of wealthy states in Europe and North America.

Monterrey Consensus a 2002 framework for global development in which the developed and developing countries agree to take joint actions for poverty reduction, with emphasis on free trade, sustainable growth and development, and increased financial aid.

nationalization when a government takes ownership of private property—land, a company, or an asset.

neocolonialism the practice of maintaining control over smaller, developing countries by keeping strong, dependent links to their governments and/or dominating their economies. This allows a powerful state to control a smaller state without colonizing it.

neoliberal a return to liberal or free-market economics.

orthodox liberal an approach to economics that favors an extreme free-market approach where government is very limited and most of a country is composed of private enterprise.

patronage politics using state funds to pay off private or semi-private political supporters.

pegged exchange rates foreign currency exchange rates that are fixed or "pegged" by government officials against another currency or standard (e.g., gold) rather than freely traded in a market setting.

purchasing power parity (PPP) a measure that compares two currencies and adjusts them so that they can be compared in a meaningful way. PPP allows us to compare the purchasing power of the yen in Japan with the peso in Mexico, for example.

resource curse the curious negative effect for a country's economy when the country has a valuable resource such as oil.

structural factors historical and environmental factors that influence how a country can develop its economy.

subsidies funds given to companies by a government to help them grow.

war reparations payments from one country—usually the loser of a conflict—to compensate the victor's cost in money, lives, and property.

Washington Consensus an orthodox liberal approach to development that took hold in the 1980s and was used to try to promote economic growth in poor countries. It had very limited success.

World Health Organization (WHO) the UN organization that deals with health issues around the world. It is responsible for the eradication of smallpox.

10-4

Trace the complex relationship between development and democracy. Most democracies are well developed, but democracies do not necessarily have high, dynamic growth rates. The fastest growing economies are not democratic. Democracy does not directly help or hurt economic growth because it has characteristics that can be both positive and negative for economic development. There are characteristics of democracy that are good for economic growth, in particular, higher levels of human resources through education and health. However, populism can be very detrimental to economic growth.

10-5

Explain the role that international organizations play in development. The IMF provides short-term loans to help countries deal with finance and debt issue problems associated with balance-of-payments (when a country cannot pay its external debt held by other countries or banks in other countries). Such loans are usually made conditional on specific policies that the country must adopt, often including reducing its spending. The World Bank is a group of five organizations that provide loans to countries for the purpose of long-term development projects. The World Trade Organization (WTO) promotes free trade and the links between trade and development. Most broadly, the role the UN plays in development is as a forum for all nations to discuss and build consensus for solutions to development issues.

The Countries of the Core, Semi-periphery and Periphery

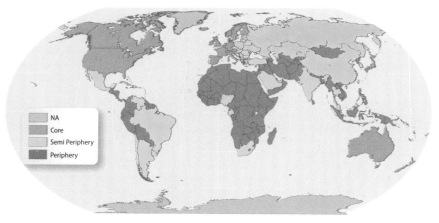

© Cengage Learning®

What does the hierarchy between countries reflected in this map signify for the relationships between the people, groups, companies, and governments of these states?

KEY CONCEPTS

11-1

Define human rights, the differences between individual, societal, and group rights, and how such rights have changed overtime. The concept of human rights means that people are entitled to certain freedoms and opportunities and governments must respect and protect those rights. First-generation rights emphasized the political and civil rights and freedoms of individuals. Obviously, not all people were equal under the law, as slavery existed almost everywhere in the world. Second-generation human rights stressed societal rights and opportunities such as the rights to shelter, employment, education, and health care. Third-generation human rights stressed group rights and sought to protect unpopular or minority groups from the oppression of the majority in society. Concerns include protections against oppression based on race, ethnicity, religion, gender, and sexual preference. The development of human rights norms since the eighteenth century has challenged the traditional notions of sovereignty and fostered attention to human security and the development of a new international norm stressing that states had "a responsibility to protect their own citizens from avoidable catastrophe, but that when they are unwilling or unable to do so, that responsibility must be borne by the broader community of states."

11-2

Describe the development of norms and codified rules regarding human rights. Right after World War II, human rights norms received significant attention from the new United Nations, which passed the Convention on Genocide and the Universal Declaration of Human Rights. About two decades later, the International Covenant on Civil and Political Rights and the International Covenant on Economic, Social, and Cultural Rights were completed. These treaties further developed the norms and ideas of the earlier documents. Since the 1960s, the effort to transform such international norms into rules has continued through the development of ten core UN human rights treaties (see p. 314), many of which sought to develop and apply the norms to particular groups. Since World War II, regional organizations in Europe, the Americas, and Africa have also developed conventions and commissions to support and protect human rights. The European convention and its supporting commission and court are the strongest of the regional efforts on human rights. By the late twentieth century, human rights concerns began to coalesce around the broader idea of human security—an emphasis on the security of individuals and groups of people, not on the security of territory—and the "responsibility to protect" norm.

11-3

Explain how states, international organizations, and non-governmental organizations attempt to implement and enforce human rights standards. State governments can contribute to progress

KEY TERMS

African Charter on Human and Peoples' Rights the treaty by the Organization for African Unity (later the African Union) that went into force in 1986 and listed individual rights and the responsibilities of individuals in a communal context. It also created the African Commission of Human and Peoples' Rights and the African Court of Human and Peoples' Rights.

aggression the unjustified use of force against another state.

American Convention on Human Rights the Organization of American States treaty that went into force in 1978. It created an Inter-American Commission on Human Rights and an Inter-American Court of Human Rights.

CEDAW the Convention on the Elimination of All Forms of Discrimination against Women, approved by the UN General Assembly in 1979.

civil society groups NGOs that promote democracy and human rights on a global basis.

Convention on Genocide a 1948 UN treaty that both defined genocide and made it a crime whether it occurred in peacetime or in wartime.

crimes against humanity acts of war against a civilian population; these can include, among others, the crimes of murder; enslavement; deportation or forcible transfer; imprisonment; torture; rape, sexual slavery or any other form of enforced sexual violence; persecution on political, racial, national, ethnic, cultural, religious, gender, or other such grounds; enforced disappearance; apartheid; and other inhumane acts that create great suffering or serious mental or physical injury.

cultural relativism the idea that human rights are not truly universal and that different cultures have different systems of rights. This term particularly comes into play when non-Western societies argue that international human rights standards have a Western bias and do not reflect non-Western values.

European Commission on Human Rights created by the European Convention on Human Rights, a very active body monitoring human rights situations in Europe. Individuals who feel their rights have been abused can appeal to the commission, which may, after investigation, refer the case to the European Court of Human Rights.

European Convention on Human Rights the Council of Europe treaty that went into force in 1953, which listed individual rights and created the European Commission on Human Rights and the later European Court of Human Rights.

European Court of Human Rights (ECHR) a court created in 1959 by the Council of Europe; one of the most active courts involved in human rights cases.

female genital mutilation the cutting away of part of the external genitalia, based on the belief that, by reducing sexual pleasure, women will remain chaste until married and faithful to their husbands thereafter. Some societies also believe this is a religious requirement for women to behave modestly or may increase fertility.

first-generation human rights (individual rights) rights that individuals have simply because they are human beings and which are not to be violated by governments.

honor-killings the murders of girls or women by their husbands, fathers, brothers, etc., when they are thought to have violated socially acceptable sexually based roles. By killing the offender, the males in the family seek to restore the family's honor and are typically not prosecuted for their crimes.

human security an emphasis on the security of people, not territory, first set out by the UN Development Program in 1994. It includes economic, food, health, environmental, personal, community, and political security for people.

international civil society an international system based on the norms of democracy and human rights. This emerging system is marked by civil society organizations, NGOs that promote these values on a global basis.

International Covenant on Civil and Political Rights a 1966 UN treaty identifying the civil, political, and legal rights of all humans and establishing procedures for the UN to monitor these rights.

International Covenant on Economic, Social, and Cultural Rights a 1966 UN treaty identifying the economic, social, and cultural rights of all humans and establishing procedures for the UN to monitor these rights.

International Criminal Court the ICC is an international court in the Netherlands that tries individuals accused of war crimes, crimes against humanity, genocide, and aggression.

Magna Carta the "Great Charter" signed by King John of England in 1215 (and reaffirmed in 1297 by King Edward I), which noted that freemen had certain rights that the monarch could not take away, including the right not to be imprisoned without legal justification or a judgment by one's peers.

populist revolutions grassroots revolts typically against repressive governments, dominated by mass turnouts of the people.

responsibility to protect (R2P) the norm that states have a responsibility to protect their citizens from avoidable harm, and if they cannot or will not do so, the international community has a responsibility to intervene to do so.

second-generation human rights (societal rights) material and economic rights that apply society-wide, like the rights to education, employment, shelter, health care, and so on.

smart sanctions sanctions that target specific individuals thought to be responsible for a regime's human rights abuses rather than targeting a state's entire population.

third-generation human rights (group rights) rights needed to protect unpopular or minority groups from the oppression of the majority.

Truth and Reconciliation Commission the entity created by the new South African government following the abolition of apartheid. Victims of apartheid were encouraged to tell their stories for the record and for the psychological benefit of being heard while the aggressors were offered amnesty for their crimes in return for full and public disclosure of these crimes.

UN Human Rights Council the body created by the UN General Assembly in 2006 to replace the UN Human Rights Commission in making recommendations regarding human rights issues.

in the human rights arena by engaging in direct actions to implement human rights at home and abroad, providing incentives for others to do so or imposing punishments for those who will not abide by global human rights norms, or enforcing human rights standards through their own judicial systems via claims of universal jurisdiction. International organizations have set global standards for human rights and both soft and hard power enforcement mechanisms. Non-governmental organizations also get heavily involved in the implementation and enforcement of human rights standards using both soft and at times hard power approaches, as this arena is an important focus of the emerging **international civil society.**

Ten Selected Human Rights NGOs, their Missions, and links to their Websites

NGO	MISSION	LINK
Aga Khan Development Network	Promote education and economic growth through grants, microfinance, and rural development	www.akdn.org/default.asp
Amnesty International	Protect prisoners of conscience and promote all areas of human rights under the Universal Declaration of Human Rights	www.amnesty.org
Bill and Melinda Gates Foundation	Reduce inequities around the world so all lives have an equal value	www.gatesfoundation.org
CARE International	Address the underlying causes of poverty and provide disaster assistance	www.careinternational.org
Carter Center	Alleviate suffering, resolve conflicts, and promote democracy	www.cartercenter.org
Committee to Protect Journalists	Promote freedom of the press through the protection of journalists from reprisals	www.cpj.org
Doctors Without Borders	Provide emergency medical aid in areas of conflict, epidemics, or natural disasters	www.doctorswithoutborders.org
Empowerment and Rights Institute	Promote human rights for ordinary people and disadvantaged groups in China	www.erichina.org
Freedom House	Promote democracy, free markets, and the rule of law	www.freedomhouse.org
International Committee of the Red Cross	Protect victims of war and violence, provide humanitarian relief in emergencies, and support the rule of law	www.icrc.org/eng/

© Cengage Learning®

Source: Duke University Libraries, "NGO Database," *NGO Research Guide*, http://library.duke.edu/research/subject/guides/ngo_guide/ngo_database.html.

How can NGOs such as these affect human rights?

UN Women the united nations entity for gender equality and the empowerment of Women, created in 2010 with the merger of the Division for the Advancement of Women (DAW), the International Research and Training Institute for the Advancement of Women (INSTRAW), the Office of the Special Adviser on Gender Issues and Advancement of Women (OSAGI), and the United Nations Development Fund for Women (UNIFEM).

UNICEF the United Nations Children's Fund; created in 1946 and recipient of the Nobel Peace Prize in 1965.

Universal Declaration of Human Rights (UDHR) a 1948 UN resolution which provided a comprehensive listing of the rights of all people.

war crimes excessive brutality in war, in violation of international treaties or conventions.

KEY CONCEPTS

12-1

Identify the "tragedy of the commons," collective goods, and the environmental challenges facing humankind. The "**tragedy of the commons**" is the idea that when a resource is shared and no one actor owns it—like air or water—then no one takes responsibility for its protection. So-called public or **collective goods**—things that benefit everyone whether or not one pays for their cost or maintenance—are not the responsibility of any one state actor, and thus their care typically falls through the cracks of Westphalian sovereignty. Transnational problems such as pollution, **deforestation**, **desertification**, **global climate change**, biodiversity challenges, and diseases are some key problems of the commons.

12-2

Describe the evolving environmental regime and the roles of states, IOs, and NGOs in that regime. In the anarchic system of world politics, states, international organizations, and NGOs are all involved in the effort to address transnational problems and protect the earth's environment. States have tried many approaches, but there is only so much individual states can do to solve problems that affect the global commons, and some states are more willing to address them than others. Non-state actors have been especially important to transnational challenges, and their actions often begin at the grassroots level and work up. Citizens and NGOs help stimulate awareness of environmental challenges facing the planet. NGOs pool resources, create human networks, publish research, create programs at the grassroots level, and promote actions by states and international organizations. IOs can set agendas as well, and they help to support and coordinate the actions of states and NGOs as well as take direct actions to preserve the global commons themselves.

12-3

Explain the concept of sustainable development and steps toward that goal. The modern industrial age gave the world dramatically increased productivity, but also generated great stress on the earth's resources. Today, the global challenge is to achieve continued economic development and progress in a way that it can be sustained over the long term with minimal damage to our environment. While developed countries—the rich countries of today—got rich by exploiting the resources available to them, the effects of development and the challenge of scarce resources demand more sustainable approaches. To meet these challenges, states, international organizations, and NGOs have all been active. Individual states increasingly embrace environmental policies to address these issues, and people and NGOs have worked together across borders to raise awareness and generate solutions. The UN's Millennium Development Goals, which

KEY TERMS

arable land land capable of sustaining agriculture.

carbon footprint the amount of carbon dioxide we generate through our daily activities.

collective goods things that benefit all concerned—whether they participate in their protection and maintenance—and are not owned by any one state actor.

deforestation the destruction of forests at a rate faster than they can be replaced or replenished.

desertification the creation of new, or enlargement of existing, deserts.

ecosystem the interaction of living things and the material world around them.

genetically modified organisms (GMOs) those organisms whose genetic makeup is intentionally altered to produce some advantage.

global climate change marked changes in the warming and cooling of the planet's temperatures, thought to be accelerated by human activity such as industrialization and fossil fuel emissions, which produce greenhouse gases.

Global Environmental Facility the UN entity created by the UN Framework Convention on Climate Change to collect and distribute the financial resources needed to combat global climate change.

greenhouse gases those gases that trap the sun's heat and hold it close to the earth's surface; they include carbon dioxide, methane, nitrous oxide, and water vapor.

Intergovernmental Panel on Climate Change (IPCC) a scientific body with 194 member states, created by the UN's Environment Programme and the World Meteorological Organization in 1988.

CHAPTER REVIEW 12

Kyoto Protocol an addendum to the UN Framework Convention on Climate Change, which was negotiated in 1997 and entered into force in 2005, which imposed mandatory reductions in fossil fuel emissions for thirty-seven developed countries and the European Community.

Malthusian dilemma the notion that population growth outstrips the growth of the food supply. Named for its early author Thomas Robert Malthus.

slash-and-burn agriculture the practice of clearing fields by cutting down and burning existing plant growth to prepare land for new agricultural use each season, common in many developing countries.

sustainable development promoting economic growth without degrading the environment or depleting its non-renewable resources.

time horizon problem the fact that the worst effects of environmental problems have not yet been seen, but to avoid them one needs to act (and spend money or make sacrifices) now.

tragedy of the commons the idea that no one state is held responsible for things held in common—so-called collective goods—like the air and water, and so their protection often goes unaddressed.

UN Environment Programme (UNEP) the UN agency dedicated to environmental protection, created in 1972.

UN Framework Convention on Climate Change (FCCC) a 1992 treaty calling for the reduction of fossil fuel emissions to 1990 levels by 2000.

include efforts to improve water use, food supply, pollution, and energy, are a good example of coordinated efforts of the actors. IOs and NGOs have begun to work on these issues. Other programs such as the **UN Environment Programme (UNEP)**—the UN agency dedicated to environmental protection, created in 1972—and the **UN Framework Convention on Climate Change (FCCC)**—a 1992 treaty calling for the reduction of fossil fuel emissions to 1990 levels by 2000—are also important examples. A key challenge is that when it comes to choosing between protecting the environment or making money, making money still generally wins out. Economic security (and profits) apparently trumps human security, as state actors often lack the will or the means to invest in methods designed to reduce the impact of human activity on the planet or to clean up our collective messes.

Increases in Annual Temperatures for a Recent Five-Year Period, Relative to 1951–1980

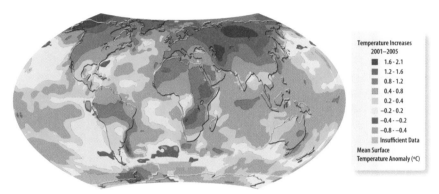

© Cengage Learning®

Who is most affected by global climate change?

Source: Data from Hugo Ahlenius, "Increases in annual temperatures for a recent five-year period, relative to 1951-1980," GRID-Arendal, http://www.grida.no/graphicslib/detail/increases-in-annual-temperatures-for-a-recent-five-year-period-relative-to-1951-1980_d666.

KEY CONCEPTS

13-1

Explain the concept of transnational advocacy networks (TANs) and how they differ from other international actors. Transnational advocacy networks or TANs are recurring networks that (1) must include non-state actors (like individuals acting alone, social movements, or NGOs), (2) may include states and/or IOs as well, (3) form a recurring, cooperative partnership with (4) differentiated roles among the component parts. Network members advocate and act upon shared ideas, positions, or goals, and they make choices—rational or otherwise—to protect, defend, and advance those shared notions. When the unique actors that make up TANs establish such networks to pursue shared goals in a cooperative enterprise, they create a new entity. The accelerating globalization of the last fifty years or so has greatly facilitated the creation and operation of TANs, which can mitigate the effects of anarchy in world politics.

13-2

Identify how TANs affect human security. Constructivists argue that reality is socially constructed on the basis of shared ideas. People agree on how things are and then act on that basis. The power of TANs to influence human security comes from this starting point: identifying problems, developing norms, and organizing and/or motivating action. For example, what does security mean in society? TANs expand the meaning and scope of security from traditional concerns about war and national security to include more emphasis on economic and human security. The essential goal of most TANs is to get sovereign states to act on the values embraced by the TAN. To achieve this, TANs engage in strategies such as "naming and shaming" in which TANs monitor the actions of states to ensure effective cooperation with established norms; mobilizing individual opinion leaders, NGOs, other states, and IOs to take action; and direct action to deliver services and solve problems. For example, TANs routinely facilitate international cooperation by helping to supply humanitarian relief and medical supplies.

13-3

Describe the two major types of TANs and the kinds of actions in which they engage. There are two major categories of TANs, distinguished by their basic orientation—self-oriented or other-oriented. Self-oriented TANs advocate values and outcomes that benefit themselves and their members, rather than general benefits that extend to non-network members. Examples of self-oriented TANs include business TANs, organized crime TANs, and terrorist TANs. Examples of other-oriented TANs include human-security-oriented TANs that emphasize the needs of people to be safe from physical harm; economic-security-oriented TANs that address food and energy security issues to alleviate poverty and promote sustainable economic development;

KEY TERMS

boomerang model the notion that internal groups repressed by their own states can turn to TANs to put pressure on other states and those states then put pressure on the repressive state from the outside. In short, repression against internal groups can boomerang back and cause new external pressure on the repressive state.

Global Counter-Terrorism Strategy a 2006 UN General Assembly document that seeks to prevent terrorism by addressing its root causes, to promote international cooperation in dealing with terrorist threats, to build the capacity of both states and the UN to combat terrorism, and to make sure that the global fight against terrorism does not violate standards of the rule of law or human rights.

International Convention for the Suppression of the Financing of Terrorism a treaty that went into force in 2002, making it easier to get international cooperation to trace and shut down terrorist financing networks.

INTERPOL the International Criminal Police Organization created in 1923 and based in Lyon, France.

jihad "holy war" in Arabic. To some Muslims it means the daily struggle within oneself to overcome evil; to others it means conducting war against non-Muslims.

norms life cycle the idea that TANs are successful when they can create new norms, create a norms cascade forcing governments to act on those norms, and get norms internalized to the point that following them becomes routine and largely unquestioned.

other-oriented TANs TANs that advocate a set of values that primarily benefit others besides themselves.

policy entrepreneurs individuals committed to innovative policy change and who voluntarily work to achieve such changes.

self-oriented TANs TANs that advocate values that primarily benefit the network members.

transnational advocacy networks (TANs) networks defined by reciprocal, voluntary actions across national borders that (1) must include non-state actors (like individuals acting alone, social movements, or non-governmental organizations), (2) may include states or international organizations as well, (3) represent a recurring, cooperative partnership with (4) differentiated roles among the component parts.

UN Convention against Illicit Traffic in Narcotic Drugs and Psychotropic Substances a treaty promoting international cooperation to stop the transnational trafficking in illegal drugs, which went into force in 1990.

UN Convention against Transnational Organized Crime a treaty promoting international cooperation to deal with transnational organized crime, which went into force in 2003.

Zionism the movement to create a Jewish homeland in Palestine.

health-security-oriented TANs that address issues such as disease control or the health of women and children; environmental-security-oriented TANs that seek to protect the environment and foster sustainable development practices. In an increasingly globalized world system, both self-oriented and other-oriented transnational advocacy networks play important roles and can have surprisingly significant consequences for international politics.

The Boomerang Model of TAN Activity

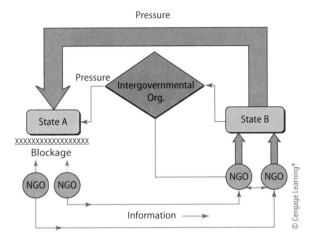

Based on *Activists Beyond Borders: Advocacy Networks in International Politics*, by Margaret E. Keck and Kathryn Sikkink. Cornell University Press.

How vital are TANs to citizens facing authoritarian regimes?

HIV Prevalence throughout the World

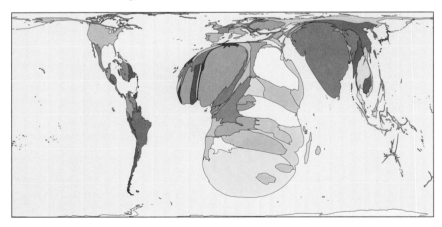

© Cengage Learning®

What does this map of the geographic concentrations of the HIV/AIDS epidemic suggest about its consequences and the challenges for addressing the problem?

International, Economic, and Human Security in the Balance: Future Directions and Challenges

KEY CONCEPTS

14-1

Identify the ways anarchy, diversity, and complexity shape world politics. The anarchic structure of the international system—its lack of authoritative, central governing institutions—is a foundational element for understanding and managing conflict and war, and it conditions global economic interactions, the pursuit of wealth, the prospects for an effective regime that protects human rights, and environmental cooperation. The diversity of actors, identity, values, and culture is a critical issue for human rights and human security, while also greatly affecting conflict and economic relations. The complexity of the global political system makes global economic interactions and coordination challenging and makes difficult the pursuit of international security and human security. Anarchy pushes international actors to try to achieve their goals through their own efforts. Some actors reduce the anarchy in the system by forging connections over and across state boundaries, integrating actors and their activities, and changing the system's norms to make both cooperation and following international norms more routine. However, their impact is influenced by the diversity of the other actors involved. The wide range of differences among these actors, from types of governments, cultures, levels of wealth and development, priorities and purposes, and many more, all affect the problems that arise, which ones different actors elect to focus on, how they are defined and interpreted, and in what ways the players interact regarding them. Then the complexity of the issues comes into play. These challenges are interrelated, and their combination creates its own effects, both challenges and opportunities.

14-2

Describe the continuity and change in the meaning and role of security in world politics. A central aspect of world politics involves its players grappling with multiple dilemmas in the search for security. These dilemmas include efforts to be secure in the traditional sense of political and territorial independence, which is linked to the concerns about military power, conflict, and war. They also involve efforts to be secure economically—to experience economic growth and development, gain or maintain access to resources and markets, and achieve good and improving standards of living for the societies and communities that the actors serve and represent. Furthermore, these dilemmas also involve a host of concerns about the ability of individuals to live well and safely in their communities and environments, human security issues that have grown in importance in the neo-Westphalian world. These dimensions of security are not separate from each other but are linked in complex ways. The nature of those problems has evolved since the pre-Westphalian era. War has shifted from the increasingly destructive wars between states for power and territorial control that mark the Westphalian era through World War II, to the civil wars, identity-based conflicts, and asymmetric conflicts of the neo-Westphalian period. Economic security issues have changed dramatically with the emergence of the global economy. Human security issues such as human rights, quality of life concerns, the environment, and the roles of women and children have risen in salience.

14-3

Explain the trends and emerging areas of concern for future world politics. Non-state actors have become more important to international relations, which affects the nature of traditional security concerns. Economic security has been and will continue to be shaped by this new array of players, as well. Multinational corporations have crossed state lines so much that many of them have subsidiaries all around the world. Transnational networks are active and important across an increasing array of issues, and that is likely to continue in the future, with important consequences for world politics. On the negative side, terrorist organizations have made the most powerful states the world has ever seen feel insecure. The physical security of more people is arguably threatened more now by intrastate conflict and terrorism than more traditional national/international security threats. Globalization causes more societies to come in contact with each other, complicating physical and economic security as we all compete for the means of prosperity, while increasing the impact of basic identity concerns at the same time. Cooperation in sustainable development may be the path out of this particular economic dilemma, but promoting

CHAPTER REVIEW 14

such development normally requires additional monetary or human resources. Finally, the planet's population is continually growing, creating additional competition for needed resources and services—like food, water, petroleum, other energy sources, education, and health care. Emerging trends suggest less frequent great wars, more frequent small or intrastate conflicts, more terrorism, and more competition for wealth and the resources that contribute to its growth. Such challenges are now confronted by an international architecture to promote global cooperation and problem solving composed of thousands of international organizations, non-governmental organizations, transnational advocacy networks, international conferences on shared problems, and the norms that all these actors and efforts create.

The Fundamental Challenges of World Politics

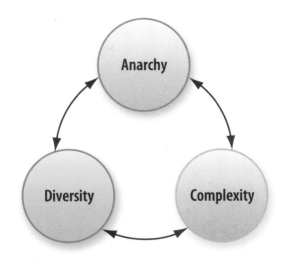

© Cengage Learning®

The Pursuit of Security in Three Arenas

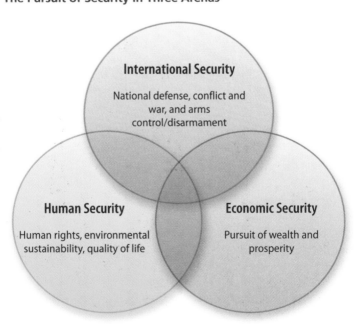

© Cengage Learning®